Palaeographical Papers

1907-1965

E. A. LOWE
From a photograph by Professor David H. Wright

E. A. LOWE

Palaeographical Papers
1907-1965

EDITED BY
LUDWIG BIELER

VOLUME I

OXFORD
AT THE CLARENDON PRESS
1972

Oxford University Press, Ely House, London W. 1

GLASGOW NEW YORK TORONTO MELBOURNE WELLINGTON
CAPE TOWN IBADAN NAIROBI DAR ES SALAAM LUSAKA ADDIS ABABA
DELHI BOMBAY CALCUTTA MADRAS KARACHI LAHORE DACCA
KUALA LUMPUR SINGAPORE HONG KONG TOKYO

PRINTED IN GREAT BRITAIN
AT THE UNIVERSITY PRESS, OXFORD
BY VIVIAN RIDLER
PRINTER TO THE UNIVERSITY

To the memory of

STANLEY MORISON

who conceived the idea of collecting
these scattered papers.
They are here dedicated in loyalty
and admiration

Contents

VOLUME ONE

List of Plates

VOLUME I (*at end*)

VOLUME II (*at end*)

Introduction

ON the eighth of August 1969 Elias Avery Lowe died at the age of eighty nine. It might appear symbolic that he should have obtained his doctor's degree from the University of Munich in that same year 1907 in which his beloved master Ludwig Traube, the pioneer of modern palaeographical studies, died. During the sixty years that have since elapsed, Dr. Lowe did more to extend our knowledge, to broaden and deepen our understanding of early Western script, than any other scholar of his generation. His books, above all the monumental *Codices Latini Antiquiores*, now happily complete, are landmarks in the study of Latin palaeography. Apart from these, however, much of Dr. Lowe's palaeographical work was scattered over numerous periodicals, not always easily accessible, and occasional publications, now mostly out of print. It has been felt that not only would a representative selection of these studies be of great benefit to students of palaeography and related subjects, but that from it there would also emerge a portrait of the author as a scholar. Dr. Lowe's scholarship was a very individual synthesis of acute observation and intuition, combined with broadness of mind, sureness of touch, and—last but not least—an inimitable charm which lightens even the most technical of details. In a letter of 15 May 1951 to Don G. De Luca, a noted literary figure in Vatican circles, a publisher of erudite works, and a friend and correspondent of Pope John XXIII, he wrote: 'My taste, my love of form, beauty of any shape and my hunting instinct—these two fundamental traits, namely, the love of form and the love of following tracks (the detective in me) made me choose palaeography as a career. I could satisfy both these primitive instincts.' These words underline how well the character of the man is suited to the subject he chose to explore.

The present selection includes all of Dr. Lowe's papers except reviews, obituaries, reports, letters to the press, the *membra disiecta* series (now absorbed in *Codices Latini Antiquiores*), and some articles the omission of which it was felt would meet with the author's approval. An exception, which hardly needs an apology, was made in the case of the obituary in memory of Ludwig Traube. It has been decided to reprint also the preface and introduction to *The Beneventan Script*, *The Palaeography of the Bobbio Missal* from Volume LXI of the Henry Bradshaw Society Publications, and the introduction to the selective facsimile of the Hatton codex of the Rule of St. Benedict;

on the other hand, it was agreed to leave out the list of half-uncial manuscripts and the new list of Beneventan manuscripts, and to reprint only the general introductions to both these papers. A complete bibliography of Dr. Lowe's published works will be found at the end of Volume II.

It is with great regret that the idea, cherished for some time, of including the palaeographical sections incorporated in the introductions to *Codices Latini Antiquiores* had finally to be abandoned. These sections, some of considerable extent, are among the most important contributions made to Latin palaeography during the last decades, and ought to be in the hands of many who cannot afford to buy, or have no easy access to, the original volumes. These sections, however, cannot simply be isolated from the plates and detailed descriptions, and an attempt at synthesis would amount to a comprehensive treatment of early Latin script.

A publication of this kind was first discussed some years ago, and consultations about it took place between Professor Bernhard Bischoff of Munich, Dr. R. W. Hunt of Oxford, and the late Mr. Stanley Morison of London. I myself am a latecomer to the enterprise. I was first approached by Dr. Lowe's son-in-law, Mr. James Fawcett of All Souls College, Oxford, in 1962 to act as editor of the collection, and to revise and bring up to date a bibliography of Dr. Lowe's publications which had been drafted twenty years ago. If my task has proved both interesting and pleasant, I have to thank the originators of the idea, who have given me every possible assistance. The bibliography would have been far less complete and accurate but for the help given me without stint by Dr. Lowe's former Assistant at Princeton, Professor James J. John, now of Cornell University, and by his successor, Dr. Braxton Ross, now of the University of Chicago; for references to reviews I am indebted also to Professor Albert Bruckner of Bâle and to Dr. Ettore Falconi of the State Archive of Parma. Dr. Ross's services to the book go far beyond his contribution to the bibliography. Not only has he been most helpful in providing photographic material for the plates; he also volunteered to read a set of proofs. Another set was read by Miss Virginia Brown, now at the Pontifical Institute of Mediaeval Studies, Toronto, who succeeded Dr. Ross at Princeton; Miss Brown also checked Dr. Lowe's hand copies of his articles for author's corrections. Professor Bischoff not only read a set of proofs but also gave most valuable advice on matters of presentation. In the final stages of my editorial work I have benefited greatly from the help of the staff of the Clarendon Press.

Dublin, Easter 1971 LUDWIG BIELER

Note on Presentation

THE original page numbers of the papers are given in the text margins, in bracketed italic figures. The original plate numbers are given similarly in bracketed italic figures, but within the text and notes, after the plate numbers (in bold type) in this volume. Page references are to the present publication.

All the plates which accompanied the papers on their first appearance have been reproduced here; while certain of them have been slightly reduced in size, others are larger than the originals.

Obvious misprints and slips in the original have been tacitly corrected.

The separate lists of manuscripts originally included in some papers have been incorporated in the general list of manuscripts at the end of Volume II.

L. B.

Acknowledgements

THANKS are due to the original editors and publishers of the papers collected in these two volumes for permission to reprint the texts and the accompanying plates. Thanks are also due to the Bodleian Library, Oxford, and the John Rylands Library, Manchester, for photographs and for permission to publish them.

Ludwig Traube (1861–1907)

IN the passing away of Ludwig Traube the University of Munich lost one of its chief ornaments and the student of medieval history and philology was deprived of a most stimulating leader. Of contemporary palaeographers he was perhaps the greatest and in his hand palaeography became vitally helpful to history and philology—an instrument at once fine, flexible, and critical. As no one before him, Traube knew how to win by means of palaeography the history of an author's tradition; knew how to make the form of a letter or of an abbreviation reveal literary relations and dependence of one culture-centre upon another. He will be remembered for his work on the *Monumenta Germaniae Historica*; for his *Perrona Scottorum*; for his *Paläographische Studien*; for the admirable *Textgeschichte der Regula S. Benedicti*; and for his *Nomina Sacra*—his master-work which is about to see light. Great as scholar he was even greater as teacher. To us who knew him he was greatest as man, as personality.

From *Bibliofilia*, IX, Sept.–Oct. 1907, p. 280.

Studia Palaeographica

A CONTRIBUTION TO THE HISTORY OF EARLY LATIN MINUSCULE AND TO THE DATING OF VISIGOTHIC MANUSCRIPTS

To the memory of
LÉOPOLD DELISLE

PREFACE

SINCE the epoch-making contention of Scipio Maffei, the illustrious Veron-
(v) ese archaeologian and palaeographer, we have come more and more to recognize with him how important a role was played by the Cursiva Romana, i.e. the notarial script of the early Middle Ages, in the formation of nearly all types or schools of early minuscule. It was the rise and rapid spread of the Caroline book-hand which proved fatal to the local manner of writing in most centres. The traditional script with its cursive letters and ligatures completely succumbed—in one place sooner, in another later—to the minuscule whose principle was simplicity and clarity. In giving thus a new direction to book-writing, the Caroline reform interrupted a development already past its first stage, and effaced the signs of relationship which united the different pre-Caroline types. Yet we can still realize the closeness of that relationship, and get, as it were, an epitome of the history of early minuscule, by concentrating attention upon one or two typical traits. And for this purpose there is perhaps nothing more interesting or instructive than a study of the usage of **i**-longa and **ti**.

In the following studies a modest attempt is made to trace the history of **i**-longa, by giving an account of its cursive origin, its entrance into calligraphic manuscripts, its rapid spread and short-lived vogue in all but two schools, and the rules which in those two schools seem to have governed its use. This account can be turned to practical use by the philologist. To the palaeographer its value lies in the light it throws on the different types of minuscule in process of formation, and in the explanation it offers for such

From *Sitzungsberichte der Königlich Bayerischen Akademie der Wissenschaften*, Philosophisch-philologische und historische Klasse, Jahrgang 1910, 12. Abhandlung. Munich, 1910.

[See Pls. 1–7]

curious phenomena as the employment of **i**-longa in early examples of schools so far removed from each other by space and tradition as the Spanish and the north Italian.

The remaining and larger part of these studies deals with the history of **ti**, and tries to show through what medium the **ti**-ligature was introduced into calligraphy; how it was used in various centres and then discarded by all but the Beneventan; how the last-named script reserved it for the specific purpose (vi)
of indicating the assibilated sound of **ti**; how the Visigothic like the Beneventan graphically distinguished the hard and soft sound of **ti**; and how this practice furnishes a *terminus a quo* for dating Visigothic manuscripts—a criterion whose application will remove some traditional errors from Spanish palaeography and prove its validity in several mooted cases. Incidentally the question of transcribing this ligature will be raised as well as that of a similar form which has been a problem in diplomatics—a form of *z* as yet unrecorded in our literature. The question of phonetics is outside the province of this investigation. If the data based upon the manuscripts which served my palaeographical purposes prove also of some value as raw material and evidence to the student of Romanic languages, it will only serve to confirm my conviction that apparently insignificant and usually neglected graphic points have their bearing upon the broader problems of history and philology.

To avoid repetition the data for **i**-longa and **ti** will be given together; their history will be treated separately.

My warmest thanks are due to Professor W. M. Lindsay. These studies have profited from his interest and advice as well as by the information which he put at my disposal with rare generosity. I am also grateful to Professor C. U. Clark for his kindness in permitting me to make use of his valuable collection of Visigothic photographs prior to their publication.

Lastly it is my pleasant duty to acknowledge my indebtedness to the American School of Classical Studies in Rome under the auspices of which I have had the privilege of continuing my studies as Research Associate of the Carnegie Institution of Washington. To the Director of the school and to the members of the committee in America I herewith express my sincere sense of obligation.

It is not to be my privilege to put this monograph into the hands of Léopold Delisle. In remembrance of his kindness in making public a portion of the results, I do myself the honour of dedicating these studies to his memory.

Rome, July 1910

(1) I. i-LONGA

i-*longa in inscriptions*. The main function of **i**-longa with which the student of Latin epigraphy is acquainted is foreign to the **i**-longa of Latin manuscripts. The **i**-longa in words like vIxit, lIberti, dIvo, prIncipi, etc., of Roman inscriptions serves the specific purpose of denoting the long quantity of the letter **i**.[1] In Latin manuscripts **i**-longa has no reference whatever to quantity. The use of **i**-longa in inscriptions is, on the whole, optional and not strictly defined. One engraver may use it, another of the same period may not. And the same engraver may use it to indicate the long vowel in one part of the inscription and not in another. It may be employed at the beginning of a line merely as a decorative element, likewise in the middle of the line as in flamIne[2] or out of a sense of reverence as in Imperatori.[3] In manuscripts on the other hand—at least in those of certain schools and certain periods—the use of **i**-longa is obligatory and subject, as we shall see, to definite rules.[4] If there are these differences, there is also one important point of similarity.

The use of **i**-longa to denote the semi-vocal sound, which in inscriptions is
(2) as old as the use of **i**-longa itself, is a constant feature of those manuscripts which regularly employ **i**-longa. Such familiar epigraphic forms as eIus, huIus, conIunx, Iunius, etc., have their exact graphic equivalent in Latin documents and manuscripts. Yet there is this difference: the engraver may make a long or a short **i** in eIus, Iunius, etc., but during many centuries the scribe of southern Italy or Spain is obliged to use the long form—as can be seen from the evidence cited below. Against the one point of similarity, then, there are several points of difference, one of which alone is so grave as to make it quite improbable that the use of **i**-longa in manuscripts is a direct inheritance from inscriptions. For, if that were the case, should we not expect to find manuscripts with **i**-longa used to indicate the long quantity? Such manuscripts, however, do not exist.

i-*longa in cursive*. Yet a point of contact between the medieval and the ancient

[1] On the subject of **i**-longa in inscriptions see Christiansen, *De apicibus et i-longis inscriptionum latinarum* (Kieler Disser., 1889), pp. 26. ff.

[2] Christiansen, loc. cit., p. 28. The *Corpus Inscr. Lat.* is full of such examples.

[3] Ibid., p. 37.

[4] See below, pp. 9 f. Excepting the brief report of my observations which was made by Léopold Delisle (*Comptes-rendus de l'Académie des Inscriptions*, 1909, pp. 775–8) and reprinted with corrections in the *Bibliothèque de l'École des Chartes*, LXXI (1910), 233–5, there exists no connected account of **i**-longa in manuscripts. The usual statement found in the descriptions of plates is that **i**-longa occurs often at the beginning of the word and occasionally in the middle.

practice respecting **i**-longa doubtless exists. It is to be sought, I believe, in the domain of cursive writing. As a matter of fact, we find **i**-longa in the Pompeian mural inscriptions in cursive used in the manner in which it is later employed in medieval documents and manuscripts, namely, at the beginning of the word regardless of quantity or the meaning of the word, and medially for the semi-vocal sound.[1] In order to see how the ancient cursive practice was taken over and introduced into calligraphy we must examine the connecting link, i.e. the medieval or 'later' cursive. Without going too far into detail the usage in the documents may be briefly sketched as follows.

The Ravenna documents on papyrus of the sixth and seventh centuries[2]—
and not a few of them have come down to us[3]—show the frequent occurrence (*3*)
of initial and medial **i**-longa: 'In', 'Interfui', 'Iterum', 'Ipsum', 'huIus', etc., etc.

Marginalia found in sixth-century semi-uncial manuscripts written in a slanting uncial-cursive of the same time also show the **i**-longa initially.[4]

North Italian documents of the Lombard regime are conspicuous for the regularity with which they use **i**-longa initially and medially. Even in words like 'illa' the long **i** is used. The usual examples are: 'Id', 'Iustitia', 'huIus', etc.[5]

The earliest south Italian documents show a similar use of **i**-longa. In the Beneventan centres the practice lasts well into the thirteenth century, and examples are known even in the fourteenth.[6]

Although no pre-Caroline documents from the papal chancery have come down to us, those of the ninth century and after may be assumed to represent an older tradition. They show the use of **i**-longa initially and medially, as do

[1] Cf. Christiansen, loc. cit., p. 36 and *C.I.L.* IV, indexes, p. 258.

[2] In fact, **i**-longa is found also in earlier documents. In Marini's facsimile (*Papiri diplomatici*, Rome, 1805), pl. 6, no. 82, a. 489 I find 'Id', 'Iubeatis'. But in the still older example of cursive on papyrus, in Strasburg (Pap. lat. Argent. 1), **i**-longa is used apparently without any system: 'domIne', 'InimItabili', 'benIvolentiae', etc. Facs. Arndt–Tangl, *Schrifttafeln*, Heft 2[4], pl. 32A; Steffens, *Lat. Pal.*[2], pl. 13.

[3] They may be studied to advantage at the Vatican library and the British Museum. Facs. *Pal. Society*, pl. 2. 28; *Arch. pal. ital.* I, pls. 1–5; Arndt—Tangl, loc. cit., Heft 1[4], pl. 1c, 2.

[4] I refer to marginalia of the type seen in Delisle, *Alb. Pal.*, pl. 7 (MS. Lyon 523). Similar cursive exists in Vatic. lat. 3375, Monte Cassino 150, Rome, Basilicanus D 182, and others.

[5] Facs. Bonelli, *Cod. pal. lombardo, passim*; Schiaparelli, *Bullet. dell'Ist. Stor. Ital.* XXX (1909), 2 plates.

[6] Facs. Russi, *Paleografia e diplomatica de' documenti delle province Napolitane* (Naples, 1883); *Codex dipl. cavensis*, vols. I–VII (1873–88); *Codice dipl. barese*, vols. I, IV, and V (Bari, 1897–1902); Morea, *Il chartularium del monastero di San Benedetto di Conversano* (Monte Cassino, 1892); Piscicelli–Taeggi, *Saggio di scrittura notarile* (Monte Cassino, 1888); Voigt, *Beiträge zur Diplomatik der langobardischen Fürsten von Benevent*, etc. (Göttingen, 1902), and *Archiv. pal. ital.*, vol. VII (1909), fasc. 31, pls. 20–6.

the Beneventan documents, for many centuries.[1] The same holds for the non-papal documents of the city of Rome and vicinity.[2]

(*4*) In the Merovingian documents, of which a considerable number exist in excellent state of preservation, the **i**-longa plays a rather inconspicuous role.[3] It is manifestly not at home there. It may be observed initially here and there. Often enough it is found in the body of a word at the end of a syllable, or at the end of a word, e.g. 'nostrI'. This use, it should be noted, is also found in some semi-uncial manuscripts and some French eighth-century minuscule manuscripts which recall semi-uncial, e.g. Épinal 68. But the Italian practice found its way across the Alps. Initial **i**-longa may be seen quite frequently in many diplomas[4] and other French and German[5] documents of the Caroline age and later, but its use is inconstant.

The Spanish notaries, as far as I can judge from the rather inadequate facsimiles of Merino and Muñoz y Rivero,[6] make constant use of **i**-longa initially and medially for **j**—precisely in the manner of the eighth-century north Italian notaries. The practice lasts as long as the Visigothic script remains in vogue.

Origin of **i**-*longa in manuscripts.* With this rapid survey before us we are more in a position to discuss the question of the origin of **i**-longa.

If we consider, on the one hand, the utter absence of **i**-longa in the oldest Latin manuscripts in uncial and semi-uncial from the fourth to the seventh century, and its gradual and tentative entrance only into uncial and semi-uncial manuscripts of the recent type, i.e. of the eighth and ninth centuries; and, on the other hand, its very frequent and continued use in cursive documents dating from the sixth to the ninth century (in many cases even much later than the ninth century), it seems reasonable to explain the presence of **i**-longa in most of the pre-Caroline manuscripts in minuscule as the result of
(*5*) direct imitation of the cursive. Nor would **i**-longa in this respect present an exceptional phenomenon. An examination of the extant examples of early minuscule of the seventh and eighth centuries shows that often enough the

[1] Facs. Pflugk-Harttung, *Specimina Selecta Chartarum Pontificum Romanorum* (Stuttgart, 1886); also Steffens, *Lat. Pal.*[2], pls. 58 and 62.

[2] Facs. Hartmann, *Ecclesiae S. Mariae in Via Lata Tabularium* (Vienna, 1895–1901); Fedele, in *Archiv. pal. ital.*, vol. VI (1909), fasc. 30, and vol. VI (1910), fasc. 34.

[3] Facs. Lauer–Samaran, *Les Diplômes originaux des Mérovingiens.*

[4] Facs. v. Sybel and Sickel, *Kaiserurkunden in Abbildungen* (Berlin, 1880–91) especially Lieferung I and III; also Schiaparelli, *Archiv. pal. ital.*, vol. IX (1910), fasc. 33, pls. 1–12.

[5] For German documents see facs. in Chroust's *Monumenta Palaeographica.*

[6] Merino, *Escuela Paleográfica*, 1780, and Muñoz y Rivero, *Paleografía visigoda* (Madrid, 1881).

calligraphic scribe of those centuries did not hesitate to appropriate from the domain of the notary many another feature beside the **i**-longa. The fact is familiar to the palaeographer. He thinks at once of the open **a**, the broken **c**, the peculiar **t**, as well as of the more striking ligatures of **fi**, **ri**, **ti**, **te**, **ta**, **tu**, etc. Moreover a comparison of the calligraphic products in minuscule of the seventh and eighth centuries with the notarial documents of the same period will convince any observer that the calligrapher borrowed freely from the notary. It is hardly necessary to demonstrate that the reverse was not the case. For the careful methods of the calligrapher were not suited to the rapid, economical, and practical methods of the notary; whereas the calligrapher, in his efforts to form a minuscule script, that is a more economical script, took over cursive ligatures and cursive forms of single letters because they were more easily traceable and thus more economical. Finally, considerable light is thrown upon the origin of **i**-longa by the fact that it flourishes in manuscripts which employ cursive elements, and that it is avoided in manuscripts in which cursive elements are few or wanting altogether. In other words, the company in which we find **i**-longa is a fair indication of its origin.[1] In view of the above considerations there can hardly be any serious doubt that **i**-longa came into manuscripts from the cursive.

Function of **i**-*longa in manuscripts*. The primary purpose which **i**-longa served in cursive writing can only be conjectured. The fact that it is most frequently found at the beginning of a word suggests that it owes its origin to the desire of facilitating the reading; the appearance of the long form of **i** indicating at once the beginning of a word. Whereas the book-hand with its *scriptura con-* (*6*)
tinua neglected such aids, partly no doubt for reasons of symmetry, in cursive, on the other hand, where symmetry played no role, where words were often abbreviated by any capricious suspension, and a short letter like **i** could be easily overlooked, the use of a long form of the letter **i** initially must have been of signal assistance to the notary who had to read or copy the document.[2] Perhaps this need of giving more body to the small letter **i** was first felt in words in which letters with short strokes followed initial **i**, as 'In',

[1] See below, pp. 12 f. In Paris 653, a north Italian manuscript of about A.D. 800, this point is clearly illustrated. On fol. 6^{v} two hands can be seen. The first used the **ti**-ligature and the **i**-longa *regularly*. The other hand used neither. Cf. Pl. 2 (*pl. 2*). This facsimile I owe to the kindness of Professor W. M. Lindsay.

[2] In this connection it is interesting to cite Zangemeister's opinion respecting the purpose of **i**-longa in the Pompeian mural inscriptions in cursive: 'Patet maxime in eis, quae cursivis litteris exaratae sunt, inscriptionibus (sc. parietariis Pompeianis) **i** saepe productam esse non alia de causa nisi ut eius litterae forma magis plana et perspicua redderetur'. *C.I.L.* IV, indexes, p. 258.

'Imperatoris',[1] etc. By analogy its use may have spread to any word, so that in the eighth-century north Italian documents 'ille' and 'ibi' are written with **i**-longa as well as 'in,' 'imperatoris', etc.

But we find **i**-longa in documents not alone at the beginning of the word, but also in the body. The reasons suggested above for using **i**-longa initially are in so far applicable to its use in the body of the word as the long form of the letter here also facilitated reading. A consideration, however, of the examples of medial **i**-longa shows that with this form of the letter went a specific pronunciation. The writing of 'huIus', 'cuIus', 'maIor', 'IeIuniis', makes it clear that the long form of **i** has reference to its semi-vocal sound.

Whatever may have been the reasons for the employment of **i**-longa in cursive, the important fact remains that in many pre-Caroline documents the long form is constantly used in these two ways: initially, and also medially for the semi-vocal sound.

(7) It is precisely this use of **i**-longa that we encounter in manuscripts.

Summary of usage in manuscripts. From data given below,[2] the course of **i**-longa in manuscripts may be sketched as follows. Unknown to the oldest types of uncial and semi-uncial, it gradually enters into their more recent types and is used there tentatively and irregularly.[3] The earliest minuscule manuscripts of Italy, France, and Spain, those manuscripts which are occasionally styled 'half-cursive' or 'minuscule-cursive' make constant use of **i**-longa. The regular use of it which is observable in eighth-century north Italian cursive documents has its exact parallel in contemporaneous north Italian manuscripts. In France the **i**-longa is a feature of those pre-Caroline minuscule types which still cling to the cursive elements, e.g. the Luxeuil type and the ⟨⟨ type. During the eighth century it already begins to lose ground in France, so that many a Corbie manuscript of the ab type either lacks it entirely or uses it sparingly. In time it is practically eliminated from French calligraphy by the Caroline reform. To the compact, orderly, and neat Caroline script such a trait as **i**-longa manifestly appeared uncalligraphic and was therefore avoided. Its employment in Italy lasts as long as Caroline influence does not interfere. When the scriptoria of northern and central Italy adopted the Caroline script, **i**-longa was given up along with the other cursive features

[1] At any rate, it is a striking fact that **i**-longa clings longest to such words as 'in', 'ita', etc., even in scripts which had given up its regular employment.

[2] See the evidence cited in the list of manuscripts, pp. 24 ff.

[3] The presence of **i**-longa in an uncial manuscript is an unfailing sign that it is of the recent type.

which formed part and parcel of the native hand. In southern Italy, however, as well as in Spain, the foreign forces never possessed sufficient energy to modify the local scripts. The old cursive practice of using **i**-longa, therefore, continued as long as the native script remained in use.

Usage in particular schools. The manner in which **i**-longa was used in manuscripts has in a general way already been indicated. But two schools demand our particular attention, for in Visigothic and Beneventan calligraphy the regular employment of **i**-longa lasted for over four centuries and died out only when the scripts went out of fashion. In the case, therefore, of these two schools it is advisable to illustrate somewhat more fully the rules which *(8)*
governed the use of **i**-longa.

In Visigothic

I. At the beginning of a word **i** has the long form.
  e.g. 'Iam', 'Ibi', 'Iccirca', 'Id', 'Iecit', 'Ignem', 'Ihs̄', 'Ille', 'Impar', 'In', 'Iovita', 'Ipse', 'Ira', 'Iste', 'Itinera', 'Ius', etc.

 Exception.
  When initial **i** is followed by a tall letter the use of **i**-longa is not obligatory.
  e.g. 'ibi', 'ihs̄', 'ille' (written with a short **i**).

II. Semi-vocal **i** requires the long form.[1]
  e.g. 'maIas', 'aIebat', 'proIciatur', 'aIt', 'gaIus', 'eIus',[2] 'IeIuniis', etc.

The Spanish scribe adhered to these rules with unusual strictness. If he wrote 'in' or 'huius' with a short **i** it happened through inattention or slavish

[1] It is interesting to note that Isidore does not speak of **i**-longa as a means of denoting semi-vocal **i**. He would perhaps have mentioned it, if scribes and notaries of his time had made such use of **i**-longa. His statement, however, is merely an excerpt from an earlier writer: '**i** litteram inter duas vocales constitutam bis scribi quidam existimabant ut Troiia, Maiia, sed hoc ratio non permittit. Nunquam enim tres vocales in una syllaba scribuntur. Sed **i** littera inter duas vocales constituta pro duplice habetur'. *Etymol.* I. 27, 11.

[2] Much light was thrown upon Visigothic palaeography by Delisle's description of the Silos manuscripts in *Mélanges de paléographie et de bibliographie*. From what he says of **i**-longa (p. 56) it appears that he failed to realize the rules governing its use: 'On trouve I capital très allongé non seulement au commencement du mot, mais encore à la fin, *surtout quand la désinence est figurée sous une forme abbréviative*: *eI*^{s} *pour ejus*' (italics are mine). The fact that the form is abbreviated is a matter of indifference. 'eius' would have the **i**-longa even if written out. When the 'us' was abbreviated the **i**-longa naturally remained. But **i**-longa at the end of a word is absolutely foreign to Spanish calligraphy. Muñoz, *Paleografía visigoda*, has nothing on the regularity of **i**-longa in Visigothic manuscripts.

copying from an original which did not use **i**-longa. In any case he was
(9) breaking a rule of the script. I have noted such irregularities in very few manuscripts.[1] The utter neglect of the rule in these cases was a proof that the scribe was labouring under foreign influences.

Here mention should be made of a type of **i**-longa peculiar to Spanish manuscripts. It is a long **i** with a forked top resembling on the whole a tall **y**. It is frequently found in the word 'ait'. Examples are cited below in the list of Spanish manuscripts.

In Beneventan

The two main rules for initial and medial **i**-longa which prevailed in Visigothic scriptoria hold for Beneventan.[2] There is, however, this difference between the Beneventan and the Spanish scribe: the former was more averse to using **i**-longa before a shafted letter. He regarded it as uncalligraphic and therefore eschewed it. It is only in very few Beneventan manuscripts—and these are all of the early period, i.e. of the eighth and ninth centuries—that we find initial **i** invariably long. The rule is to write short **i** when the following letter has an upper or lower shaft, e.g. 'ibi', 'ihs̄', 'illi', 'ipse', 'ire' (the **r** has a shaft), 'iste', etc.

Another exception to the main rule of initial **i**-longa occurs when the preposition precedes the noun which begins with **i**, e.g. 'ad imaginem', 'In italiam'. In such cases the scribe was accustomed to run the noun and the preposition together, and as he wrote them together he regarded the phrase as a unit and therefore wrote short **i**. This circumstance, it may be noted in passing, seems to confirm what has been said of the purpose of **i**-longa, namely, to call attention to the beginning of a word. On the other hand, the
(10) use of **i**-longa in 'deInde', 'exInde' is doubtless due to the inveterate habit of writing 'in' with the long form of **i**, the excuse being furnished by the composite character of the two words.

It is possible to cite not a few instances in which Beneventan scribes break the rules. But this is mainly the case during the formative and uncertain period of the script, i.e. during the eighth and ninth centuries. The careful scribe conscientiously observed them, and the best possible proof that they

[1] e.g. Paris 10876 and 10877. See below list of Spanish manuscripts.

[2] How little the rule for medial **i**-longa was recognized by Rostagno (*Praefatio*, p. ix, to the Leyden reproduction of the Tacitus manuscript, Florence Laur. 68. 2) is seen from his words: '**i** grandi, quae vocatur, usus est non nunquam librarius ineuntibus vocabulis, cum praesertim subeat **u** littera: semper, ut quidem, post **u** in vocabulo cuius; item in iniuria, obiectare, maior, coniugium, coniunctio cet.'

were rules of the script is furnished by the autograph of Leo Ostiensis (Monacensis 4623). In making the additions and corrections in his chronicle of Monte Cassino Leo was hard pressed for space. The long form of **i** is certainly not the most economical. Yet in all the pages of small and crowded writing the above rules are carefully observed.

i-*longa as a sign of relationship between the schools.* We have seen that in at least two scripts **i**-longa was a constant feature for several centuries. In this respect the Visigothic and Beneventan are different from other hands. We have also seen that the use of **i**-longa in both these schools was governed practically by the same rules (rules which already obtained in the seventh- and eighth-century documents) and that of the two the Visigothic showed stricter adherence to the rules. The question which naturally arises—and it is one of no little interest to palaeography—is this: did the Visigothic serve as a model to the Beneventan?[1]

If it were not for the fact that nearer and more likely models existed, the answer to the above question would have to be an unqualified affirmative, considering the importance and vogue of Spanish literature in the eighth century just when the Beneventan script was springing into life. But the south Italian minuscule could easily borrow the use of **i**-longa from its own notarial products; and if it went further for its models, north or central Italian documents as well as manuscripts of the seventh and eighth centuries could have supplied them. This being the case, and as no actual proof exists that the *(11)*
Beneventan took over the practice of **i**-longa or any other calligraphic feature from Spanish calligraphy, it is more reasonable to explain the matter somewhat thus: as the Beneventan has many cursive elements which are not found in Visigothic, the presence of **i**-longa must be regarded in the same light as the presence of the other cursive elements, namely as a remnant of the traditional Italian minuscule in which cursive features, adapted to calligraphic purposes, played a large role.

If it is true that the Beneventan does not depend upon the Visigothic for its use of **i**-longa, the same can be said with even greater emphasis of the north Italian schools. For if we assume for a moment for the sake of argument the direct dependence of north Italian upon Spanish manuscripts with regard to this point, we are at a loss to explain the same use of **i**-longa in contemporaneous north Italian documents. And no one would try to maintain that Italian notaries copied from the Spanish. The opposite is not only more probable,

[1] The reverse is out of the question, since the Beneventan as a script was just beginning its existence when the Visigothic had already reached maturity.

but doubtless *was* the case. The Spanish notary built upon Roman tradition; his model was the Italian notary. The knowledge of the **i**-longa which the Spanish notary had he owes to his Italian cousin. The knowledge of it possessed by the Spanish scribe is doubtless knowledge gained from the notary. And the same conditions which made the Spanish scribe turn to cursive for new material also made the north Italian scribe borrow from cursive. And that he really did so can best be illustrated by two concrete examples. It is impossible not to realize the points of similarity between the Ambrosian Josephus on papyrus of the seventh century and the Ravenna documents of about the same period. It would almost seem that the calligrapher in this case also filled the post of notary. The fact that interests us now is that the Ambrosian manuscript, whose style is little removed from a cursive document, uses the **i**-longa regularly at the beginning of a word and medially when semi-vocal, i.e. precisely in the manner of later Spanish scribes and notaries. The
(*12*) Ravenna notary certainly did not learn from the Spanish; nor was the scribe of the Ambrosianus under any obligation to a Spanish scribe; for even the existence of a Visigothic minuscule at that date can only be assumed, not demonstrated. But a more cogent example is that furnished by the eighth-century north Italian manuscript Vercelli 183 (see Pl. **1** (*plate 1*). Several other manuscripts—for instance, those from Bobbio,[1]—might also be pressed into service to illustrate my point. But I single out Vercelli 183 because its north Italian origin as well as its dependence upon notarial writing is practically demonstrable. First of all the general impression of the script bears distinct resemblance to the writing in north Italian documents of the Lombard regime, the main difference being that the manuscript is orderly and calligraphic, and manifestly the work of an expert scribe. But the scribe attempted to use a certain form of **z** (cf. Pl. **1** (*plate 1*), line 11), which is almost unique in manuscripts.[2] This form of the letter, however, is not rare in north Italian documents of the eighth century. Here we have, as it were, caught the scribe in the act of appropriating a cursive element. Now this scribe makes constant and regular use of **i**-longa initially, and medially when semi-vocal. The contemporaneous north Italian notary does precisely the same. Far from explaining this fact as due to the influence of Spanish models—and it is important to note that both the abbreviations and the orthography show no trace whatever of Visigothic influence—the above considerations force us to admit that the writer of Vercelli 183 merely took over **i**-longa, as he did the singular form of **z**, from the cursive writing practised in his region.

[1] See below the list of Italian manuscripts.

[2] See below, pp. 22 f.

The use of **i**-longa, therefore, in all the schools is due merely and entirely to the influence, mediate or immediate, of cursive upon calligraphic writing. With this in mind, we can easily understand how the Caroline reform which banished cursive elements from the book-hand, was inimical to the use of **i**-longa; also, how its use happened to remain a feature of Beneventan writing, *(13)*
which is *par excellence* the script which *calligraphicized* cursive elements; and lastly how two such distant schools as the north Italian and the Spanish used the **i**-longa in precisely the same way. Maffei's view of the common origin of the different types of minuscule is instructively borne out by the results of this little investigation of the use of **i**-longa.

i-*longa and philology*

Heretofore our considerations have been purely palaeographical; but the question has also its practical side.

(*a*) *Practical value of rules for* **i**-*longa.* Some of our important authors have come down to us through the medium of Beneventan or Visigothic transmission. When such a text depends mainly upon a single manuscript, and that manuscript is in a bad state of preservation—I need only mention the *Annales* and *Historiae* of Tacitus, Varro's *de Lingua Latina* and the fragments of Hyginus in Beneventan writing—its editor will not fail to profit from the rules formulated above (cf. pp. 9 f.). For some of the errors which creep into the text are manifestly due to ignorance of these rules. No less a philologian than Halm, in his edition of the fragments of Hyginus (Monacensis 6437) misread **i**-longa for an **l**. His unfamiliarity with another rule in Beneventan, that of the ligature **ri**, was the cause of two errors in one word. Halm gives 'malorum' where the scribe wrote 'maiori'[1] with **i**-longa as is required by the rules of his school.

In a passage in the *Historiae* of Tacitus (IV. 48, 10) editors have wavered between the readings 'ius' and 'uis'.[2] Its last editor, Andresen, gives: 'legatorum ius adoleuit'. The Beneventan manuscript upon which the text is based (Florence Laur. 68. 2) is hardly legible on that page as the ink has grown very pale. It was in fact illegible in the time of the humanists, as appears from *(14)*
the interlineal transcription of the text.[3] But the two words are impossible to

[1] Cf. Kellogg, in *Amer. Journal of Philology*, XX (1899), 411.

[2] Cf. Andresen, *In Taciti Historias studia critica et palaeographica*, II (1900), 13.

[3] The partial disappearance of the ink is noticeable in a great number of Beneventan, especially Cassinese manuscripts of the eleventh century. It was evidently due to the manner of treating the parchment then practised, for the ink has grown pale on one side of the leaf, the other, the hair-side, having retained the ink much better.

confuse in Beneventan, for 'ius' must be written with **i**-longa and 'uis' must begin with a short letter. The manuscript, even in its present state, shows plainly that the first letter was short, in which case the correct reading is 'uis' and not 'ius'—correct at least palaeographically.[1]

(*b*) *Resemblance of* **i**-*longa and* **l**. The resemblance of **i**-longa to the letter **l** could not but become a stumbling-block to ancient copyists in whose schools **i**-longa was not a rule. After the ninth century a continental scribe copying from a Beneventan or Visigothic original could easily mistake 'aiebat' for 'alebat', 'maias' for 'malas', 'obiectat' for 'oblectat', etc. Consequently editors must be mindful of this source of error, particularly if there is reason to believe that the archetype was Visigothic, Beneventan, or in early pre-Caroline minuscule.[2]

(*c*) *Interchange of* **i** *and* **g** *and vice-versa.* The fact that **i**-longa did service for semi-vocal **i** in Spanish and Beneventan calligraphy may in a measure account for the relatively frequent confusion of **i** and **g** in the manuscripts of those two schools. Owing to similarity of pronunciation this interchange is by no
(*15*) means uncommon in other schools.[3] The ancient grammarians had already treated of semi-vocal **i**.[4] And the interchange between semi-vocal **i** and **g** is evidenced by inscriptions, e.g. GEN for IAN (VARIAS) or GEIUNA for IEIUNA.[5] But in manuscripts we find not only **g** for semi-vocal **i**, but also **i**-longa, i.e. semi-vocal **i** for **g**.[6] The latter type of error seems to me less likely in a script in which the semi-vocal **i** has not a distinct graphic form. It is the presence of the graphic distinction between semi-vocal and vocal **i** which often occasions the use of **i**-longa for **g** on the part of the Visigothic and Beneventan scribes. I cite the following examples from Beneventan manuscripts:

Monte Cassino 332, saec. x, p. 13, 'diIesta' for 'digesta', p. 38 'quadraIesime';

[1] Cf. the Leyden reproduction of the manuscript in the De Vries series: *Codices Graeci et Latini photographice depicti*, tom. VII. 2, fol. 94^{v}, col. 2, line 21.

[2] Cf. Tafel, *Die Überlieferungsgeschichte von Ovids Carmina Amatoria* (Münchener Diss., 1909), pp. 27 and 36.

[3] On the confusion of **i** and **g** owing to the similarity of sound see the following works whose title in full is given on p. 15, n. 3: Corssen, *Über Aussprache*, etc., 1^{I}, 126 ff.; Schuchardt, *Vokalismus*, I. 65, see p. 70: 'Im gotischen Alphabet ist G = J; zu des Ulfilas Zeit muß also **g** vor e und **i** allgemein wie **j** gelautet haben'; Bonnet, *Le Latin de Grégoire*, etc., pp. 173 ff.; Haag, *Die Latinität Fredegars*, p. 867; Carnoy, *Le Latin d'Espagne*, etc., pp. 154–5.

[4] Cf. Keil, *Gram. lat.* I. 13; VI. 333; Isidor. *Etymol.* I. 27, 11.

[5] *C.I.L.* V. 1717; XII. 2193. 934, 3189. 649, etc. See also Pirson, *La Langue des inscriptions latines de la Gaule*, p. 75: 'l'**i**-longa ayant fini par tenir lieu du jod dans les documents de la décadence.'

[6] The use of **g** for **j** in Visigothic Verona 89 was noted by the editors of the *Nouveau Traité* (III. 449 nota).

Florence Laur. S. Marco 604, saec. XI, 'conIuIe' for 'coniuge';
Monte Cassino 289, saec. XI, 'agebat' for 'aiebat', 'progecit' for 'proiecit';
Oxford Bodl. Canon. Class. 41, 'IuIera' for 'iugera';
Monte Cassino 303, saec. XI in., 'Iesserunt' for 'gesserunt';
Florence Laur. 68. 2 (Tacitus), saec. XI, 'Iestus' for 'gestus', etc.

The confusing of semi-vocal **i** and **g** is not as familiar to editors as one might expect. An instructive case in point has been kindly brought to my attention and has since been published by the Revd. Dom De Bruyne.[1] He points out that in the important manuscript *k* of the gospels (Turin G. VII. 15) the passage Mark 15 : 11 is thus given: 'sacerdotes autem et scribae persuaserunt populo ut magis *agerent* barabban dimitte nobis'. Puzzled by the word 'agerent' some editors, as Burkitt and H. v. Soden, rejected it altogether and *(16)*
substituted 'dicerent'; another editor, W. Sanday, explained 'agerent' as used in a 'special sense'. But the original reading was manifestly 'aierent'.[2]

II. ASSIBILATION OF **ti**. THE **ti**-DISTINCTION

As there were two distinct sounds of **ti**, methods were in time adopted by both scribes and notaries of graphically marking the difference of pronunciation.[3] In some schools the distinction between soft and hard **ti** came to be represented by two different forms. Where that did not happen, **ci** often did service for assibilated **ti**. The practice of the various centres in this respect is on the whole sufficiently consistent to allow us at times to derive ideas of the provenance of a manuscript by a study of its **ti** usage. This point has here- *(17)*
tofore received less attention than it merits.[4]

[1] Cf. *Revue Bénédictine*, XXVII (1910), 498.

[2] Another instance cited by De Bruyne is that of 'agis' for 'ais', which also proved a source of worry to two editors. Cf. loc. cit., p. 498. There are other biblical passages where the confusion occurs in parts of the verb 'aio'. Cf. Wordsworth and White, *Novum Testamentum*, I. 757. Bonnet (loc. cit., p. 173) mentions similar corruption in the texts of Gregory's *Historia Francorum*.

[3] On the phonetic value of assibilated **ti** and its interchange with **ci** see Corssen, *Über Aussprache, Vokalismus und Betonung der lateinischen Sprache*, I^{1} (1858), 22 ff. (the second edition, 1868–70, I did not have at hand); Schuchardt, *Der Vokalismus des Vulgärlateins*, I (1866), 155 ff., III (1868), 317; Joret, *Du* **c** *dans les langues romanes* (Paris, 1874), pp. 66 ff.; Seelmann, *Die Aussprache des Lateins* (Heilbronn, 1885), p. 320; Bonnet, *Le Latin de Grégoire de Tours* (Paris, 1890), pp. 170 ff. and p. 751 'l'assibilation de **ci** et **ti** est un fait accompli' scil. in the time of Gregory of Tours. See also Haag, 'Die Latinität Fredegars', in *Romanische Forschungen*, X (1899), 864 ff.; Pirson, *La Langue des inscriptions latines de la Gaule* (Brussels, 1901), pp. 71 ff.: Carnoy, *Le Latin d'Espagne d'après les inscriptions* (Brussels, 1906), pp. 141 ff.; see also Meyer-Lübke in *Gröbers Grundriß der romanischen Philologie*, I (Strasbourg, 1904–6), 475.

[4] In giving the arguments against the Italian origin of the famous Missale Gallicanum from Bobbio (now Paris 13246) Traube never mentioned the fact that such spelling as 'Poncio', 'tercia', etc. was un-Italian and particularly typical of French manuscripts of that time.

As I shall often have occasion to speak of assibilated and unassibilated **ti**, it is advisable to make the points clear at the outset.

The difference in the pronunciation between assibilated and unassibilated **ti** may already be observed in Roman inscriptions of the second century.[1] The question received due attention from the grammarians. We have longer or shorter treatment of it by Consentius,[2] Pompeius,[3] Servius in his commentary of Donatus,[4] Papirius,[5] and Isidore.[6] Other anonymous grammarians of the later Middle Ages also touched upon the subject.[7] I select for quotation the passage from Papirius who wrote about A.D. 400:

(*18*) *Iustitia* cum scribitur, tertia syllaba sic sonat, quasi constet ex tribus litteris *t*, *z*, et *i*, cum habeat duos, *t* et *i*. Sed notandum quia in his syllabis iste sonus litterae *z* inmixtus inveniri tantum potest, quae constant ex *t* et *i* et eas sequitur vocalis quaelibet, ut *Tatius* et *otia iustitia* et talia. Excipiuntur quaedam nomina propria, quae peregrina sunt. Sed ab his syllabis excluditur sonus *z* litterae, quas sequitur littera *i*, ut *otii iustitii*, item non sonat *z*, cum syllabam *ti* antecedit littera *s*, ut *istius castius*.[8]

The statement of Papirius describes exactly the method of distinguishing the two sounds of **ti** which was followed by medieval scribes and notaries as far as that method can be derived from graphic distinctions. There is only this difference: in the case of **ti** followed by **i** no exception was made. The rule was simply this:

ti before any vowel has the assibilated sound. When preceded by the letter **s**, **ti** has the unassibilated sound.[9]

Cf. L. Traube, 'Paläographische Bemerkungen', in *Facsimiles of the Creeds*, edited by A. E. Burn, pp. 45 ff. In connection with the MS. Paris 13246 it should be noted that **ci** for assibilated **ti** is also frequently found in manuscripts of Rhaetian origin.

[1] Cf. Ferd. Schultz, *Orthographicarum Quaestionum Decas, Braunsberger Programm*, Paderborn, 1855; and E. Hübner, *Neue Jahrbücher* LVII. 339 ff.

[2] Keil, *Grammatici Latini*, v. 395.

[3] Keil, loc. cit. v. 104; v. 286. I quote this excerpt: 'fit hoc vitium (iotacismus), quotiens post **ti** vel **di** sequitur vocalis . . . ubi **s** littera est, ibi non possumus sibilum in ipsa **i** littera facere quoniam ipsa syllaba a litteris accepit sibilum', etc.

[4] Keil, loc. cit. IV. 445. 'iotacismi sunt, quotiens post **ti** vel **di** syllabam sequitur vocalis', etc. See also Keil, loc. cit. v. 327.

[5] Keil, loc. cit. VII. 216. For this citation I am indebted to Dr. P. Lehmann.

[6] *Etymologiae*, I, cap. 27, 28 = Migne, *Patrolog. Lat.* 82, col. 104, '**y** et **z** litteris sola Graeca nomina scribuntur. Nam cum *iustitia* **z** litterae sonum exprimat, tamen, quia Latinum est, per **t** scribendum est. Sic *militia*, *malitia*, *nequitia* et cetera similia'.

[7] Cf. Thurot, *Notices et extraits des mss.*, etc., vol. XXII, pt. 2 (1869), p. 78, who gives the following excerpt from the tenth-century MS. Paris 7505. 'Nunquam enim **T** ante duas vocales, **I** post ipsam, priore non tamen **s** precedente venire potest ut *species*, *glacies* . . . *ocium spacium* . . . *tercius* nisi sint primitiva a quibus **T** retineat, ut *scientia* a *sciente*, *sapientia* a *sapiente*, etc.' On same page '**t** ergo **s** precedente sonum non immutat, ut *molestia*, *modestia*, *ustio*, *quaestio*', etc. Cf. also pp. 144–5.

[8] See above, note 5.

[9] In his *Praefatio* (p. ix) to the Leyden reproduction of the Medicean Tacitus (Florence Laur. 68. 2) Professor Rostagno tried to formulate the rule governing the use of the two kinds of **ti**, but

As will be seen from manuscript evidence adduced below many centuries (*19*) had to pass before the phonetic distinction between the two sounds of **ti** was graphically reproduced.[1]

The ligature **ti**. *Its forms*

In rapid writing the letter **t** particularly lends itself to combination with the following letter. The cross-beam of **t**, by being drawn down, readily forms part or even the whole of the next letter. The ligatures **te**, **tu**, **tr**, and **ta** amply illustrate this tendency, but whereas they furnish examples of partial coincidence, we have in the ligature ʒ complete coincidence, since the continuation of the cross-beam constitutes the letter **i**. Cursive **t** standing by itself would look thus: ατ. By drawing down the horizontal stroke without removing the pen we get ʒ. Thus arose a form which plays an interesting part in Latin palaeography.

There are several ways of forming the ligature ʒ. It may be made in two strokes, or without removing the pen. The latter way is more usual in cursive, the former in manuscripts. An analysis of the ligature shows that the upper arc or semicircle corresponds to the cross-beam of the **t**, and that the point where the curves meet corresponds to the point where the vertical and horizontal strokes of the **t** meet. In some cases the scribe or notary begins with this point of juncture. First the lower half-curve is made, then the pen is placed at the initial point and the upper loop with its tail or continuation is formed. In other cases the pen starts at the top and forms first the two half-loops, like broken **c**, then the pen is placed at the same point and the vertical line representing the cross-beam of **t** and the letter **i** is traced. If made without removing the pen, the ligature began at the point where the two curves join, but after forming the lower curve the pen was not lifted up, but returned to (*20*)

he was not successful because he failed to realize that it was a case of graphically representing a phonetic distinction as appears from his words: 'subeunte enim vocali, *ti* litterae uno ductu (i.e. our **ti**-ligature which in Beneventan is reserved for the assibilated sound) per compendium scriptae exstant, exceptis quidem, ut par est, comparativis adjectivorum in -estus -ustus desinentium, ut *iustjor* f. 11^{r} A. XII. 40, 7, etc. Cf. *questjore* f. 9^{v}, XII. 26, 1, et ita passim.' The reason why the Beneventan scribe used the ordinary **ti** in the above examples is explained in the citations from Papirius. The scribe also wrote 'istius' and 'hostium' with the ordinary **ti** for the same reason that he thus wrote 'iustior' and 'quaestiore', i.e. for phonetic reasons, since **ti** followed by a vowel is unassibilated when an **s** precedes. The statement in Muñoz y Rivero's *Paleografía visigoda*, p. 105, is inexact and suggests that he also missed the essential point in the matter.

[1] The spelling **ci** for **ti** is much older than the conscious attempt to represent the two sounds of **ti** by two distinct forms. But **ci** for soft **ti**, instructive as it is phonetically, is after all misspelling.

the starting-point in a straight line, then continued as in the case above, thus producing a form resembling **ti**. Another form of the ligature **ti** which deserves mention occurs in the earliest cursive extant, especially in the Ravenna documents and later in Insular manuscripts. It differs from the forms already described in lacking the upper half-curve. It resembles somewhat the letter **q** with the vertical stroke extending above the loop, thus: **ti**.

Origin. The ligature of **t** and **i** is so obviously of cursive origin that no demonstration of the fact is necessary.[1] It is sufficient to remember that the ligature is found in documents as early as the fifth century when no manuscript used it, and that the first manuscripts which show the ligature are practically written in cursive.

As in the case of **i**-longa, here too a brief survey of the manner in which the notaries of the different centres used the ligature may be found instructive, for the light thrown upon the relation between cursive and calligraphic writing.

Usage in cursive. A form of the **ti**-ligature is already found in the well-known letter on papyrus (Pap. lat. Argent. 1) of Strasburg.[2] It is used regardless of the sound: 'scholas**ti**cos', 'sugges**ti**one'. It is used indifferently in a document of 489 reproduced by Marini (*Papiri diplomatici*, pl. 6, no. 82). The celebrated documents of Ravenna of the sixth and seventh centuries make very frequent use of the ligature regardless of the **ti**-distinction: 'designa**ti**s', 'mancipa**ti**oni', 'tes**ti**s', 'pre**ti**o', etc.[3]

In the peculiar uncial-cursive of the sixth century which is found in many semi-uncial manuscripts as marginalia, the ligature is found: 'uigin**ti**' in Paris 12097;[4] 'ui**ti**atis', 'u**ti**litas' in Lyon 523.[5]

(21) The ligature **ti** is a constant feature in the documents of the Lombard regime. It is used indifferently: '**ti**bi', 'uindi**ti**onis', 'por**ti**onem', 'ex**ti**ma**ti**onem', 'Ius**titi**a', etc.[6]

I found **ti** used indifferently in several eighth-century central Italian documents preserved in the Archives of Lucca.[7]

In the Merovingian documents, however, **ti** is rarely used.[8] I noted it in a document of 688: 'quolibe**ti**psa' = 'quolibet ipsa'.[9] The spelling **ci** for

[1] Not all ligatures are necessarily cursive. Combinations of **o** and **s**, **u** and **s**, **n** and **t** are peculiarities of uncial writing, just as the combination of **i** and **t** at the end of a line is typical of Spanish minuscule, but hardly of its cursive.

[2] For facs. see p. 5, n. 2.

[3] Cf. p. 5, n. 3.

[4] Facs. Delisle, *Le Cabinet des mss.*, pl. III. 3.

[5] Facs. Delisle, *Alb. pal.*, pl. 7.

[6] Bonelli, op. cit., *passim*, see p. 5, n. 5.

[7] Examples are the documents *L 75, a. 713–14, *N 100, a. 773, *B 65, a. 773, *G 46, a. 807.

[8] Facs. Lauer–Samaran, op. cit., p. 4, n. 1.

[9] Facs. Arndt–Tangl, Heft 1⁴, pl. 10.

assibilated **ti** is the rule rather than the exception in these documents. In some diplomas of Charlemagne t͡i still occurs, e.g. 'comit͡ibus', 'institut͡is' (a. 775); 'auctoritat͡is' (a. 775); 'palat͡io' (a. 775); 'prat͡is', 'tradit͡ionis' (a. 782).[1] It is only rarely to be seen in later diplomas. I noted 'trinitat͡is' in one of the year 902. The ligature t͡i is found in St. Gall documents of 752, 757, 772, and 797, used indifferently: 'agent͡is', 'prat͡is', 'donat͡ionem', etc.[2]

The reign of Charlemagne may be said to mark a turning-point in the history and function of the ligature t͡i. The influence of the Caroline reform in writing drives out the ligature. This is more noticeable in France than in Italy. The notaries of Italy, however, begin about the year 800 to reserve the ligature for the assibilated **ti**—a practice which lasts for centuries. Thus in Tuscan documents t͡i is still found in the eleventh century;[3] in southern Italy some notaries use it in the thirteenth and even in the fourteenth century, always for assibilated **ti**.[4] The same is true of the peculiar script of the papal (*22*) chancery. We find the ligature in the oldest extant documents as well as in papal bulls of the eleventh century—always for the soft sound of **ti**.[5] As soon as the characteristic script is supplanted by the papal minuscule the ligature disappears and somewhat later the **ti**-distinction.[6] The same is true of the cursive written by the notaries of the city of Rome and vicinity.[7] In a document of 1083 the **ti**-ligature still has its traditional use;[8] in documents of the early twelfth century we begin to miss both the ligature and its distinctive function.[9]

It is important to note, however, that during the eleventh century we find in documents of northern Italy and Ravenna a ligature of **ci** which is strikingly like the ligature of **ti**. That the ligature represents **ci** and not **ti** is established beyond a doubt by the circumstance that when the same word is used in the same document by a hand writing ordinary minuscule or when it is repeated by means of tachygraphic signs, **ci** is used and not **ti**.[10]

[1] Facs. v. Sybel and Sickel, *Kaiserurkunden in Abbildungen*. The five diplomas cited are reproduced respectively in Lief i. 2; Lief. iii. 3; Lief. i. 3; Lief. i. 4; and Lief. i. 13.

[2] Facs. Arndt-Tangl, Heft III^4. pl. 71 and Steffens, *Lat. Pal.*^{2}, pl. 38.

[3] Facs. *Collezione fiorentina*, pl. 36 of a document of 1013. One of the earliest instances of the ligature for soft **ti** is in a Pisan document of 780, facs. *Collez. fior.*, pl. 29.

[4] Cf. works cited p. 5, n. 6.

[5] See facs. in Pflugk-Harttung, op. cit., p. 3, n. 5. A papal bull of 1098 still has the ligature. Cf. ibid., pl. 47.

[6] For I noted that the **ti**-distinction is carefully observed in two documents of 1127 and 1138 written in ordinary or papal minuscule. Facs. Steffens. *Lat. Pal.*^{2}, pls. 80 and 81^a.

[7] Facs. Hartmann, op. cit., p. 3, n. 6, and Fedele in *Arch. pal. ital.*, vol. vi (1909), fasc. 30 and fasc. 34 (1910).

[8] Hartmann, op. cit., pl. 26.

[9] Hartmann, op. cit., pl. 27, a. 1107 and pl. 28, a. 1110.

[10] Professor L. Schiaparelli, who has kindly called my attention to this fact, furnished me with these examples: a document of Pavia of Dec. 1029, now in the Archives of Nonantola,

(23) The Beneventan notary practices the **ti**-distinction even as early as the end of the eighth century,[1] though the indifferent use of the ligature occurs during the ninth century. Later the notary shows the same care in distinguishing the two sounds of **ti** as the scribe. The practice lasts as long as the peculiar script remains in use.[2]

Spanish notaries, as far as I can judge from an examination of facsimiles, observe the **ti**-distinction. It should be noted that at first (during the eighth and ninth centuries) ꝗ serves for assibilated **ti**, and later, that is during the tenth and eleventh centuries, ɑꝗ performs that function precisely as in Visigothic manuscripts. The more recent Visigothic documents show a marked tendency toward employing **ci** for soft **ti.**[3]

So much then to give an idea of the wide use of ꝗ in documents and of its specific function in many of them since the time of Charlemagne.

Usage in manuscripts: summary

We are now ready to examine the use and function of ꝗ in manuscripts. This examination will help to bring out the closeness of relationship which existed between cursive and calligraphic writing. From the evidence given below the history of this ligature and of the **ti**-distinction in Latin manuscripts may be summarized as follows.

In the oldest manuscripts in uncial and semi-uncial we find neither ꝗ nor the **ti**-distinction. In the earliest French minuscule manuscripts of the seventh and eighth centuries ꝗ is used indifferently. It is still found in some manuscripts of the Corbie ab type, but the great majority of them do not employ it. In a number of manuscripts of the early Caroline epoch, manuscripts which
(24) still use the open **a** and the **ri**-ligature, the form ꝗ also is still to be found, but always used indifferently. With the spread of the Caroline minuscule its use gradually dies out. It is scarcely found in manuscripts written after the beginning of the ninth century. Its presence in a French manuscript is a fair hint of its date.

has 'deꝗma' (I do not attempt to give the exact forms of the ligature), 'tiꝗnense', 'faꝗas', 'sancti quiriꝗ', and the tachygraphic signs give 'queri**ci**'. In a document of Piacenza of 31 Dec. 1007, we have 'Dominiꝗ' which must be expanded by **ci**. Cf. Schiaparelli, *Tachigrafia sillabica* (Rome, 1910), p. 38. Other documents have 'pe**ci**a', 'ter**ci**a' in tachygraphic signs, and in the text 'peꝗa', 'terꝗa'. Signor Pozzi, who is working upon the later Ravenna documents, has given me numerous instances of the ligature for **ci** and not **ti** in Ravenna documents. To him and Professor Schiaparelli I here express my warm thanks.

[1] Cf. *Cod. Diplom. Cavensis*, I, pl. I.

[2] For other facsimiles see works cited p. 5, n. 6.

[3] Cf. Merino and Muñoz cited p. 6, n. 6. See also below, Part IV, where Spanish usage is discussed.

As for the **ti**-distinction in French manuscripts, the practice apparently never took root. It is only in a few manuscripts of the eighth century, and only in portions of these that the attempt to observe the distinction is noticeable.[1] Curiously enough, **ꞔ** stood for the hard sound and ordinary **ti** for the soft sound of **ti**. Of no small importance, on the other hand, is the fact—which doubtless stands in some causal relation with the absence of the **ti**-distinction—that **ci** often stood for soft **ti**.

The ligature **ꞔ** is manifestly at home in Italy. We find it already in the earliest examples of Italian minuscule where (as in contemporaneous documents) it is used indifferently for both the soft and the hard sound. At about the end of the eighth century both in north and south Italy attempts are made to observe the **ti**-distinction, reserving **ꞔ** for the assibilated sound. The ligature **ꞔ** disappears from the north Italian scriptoria during the first decades of the ninth century, owing to the influence of the Caroline reform. In south Italy, on the other hand, where the Caroline reform did not penetrate, **ꞔ** remained. Its one function was to represent assibilated **ti**.

In Spanish calligraphy **ꞔ** is in reality but a makeshift, occurring chiefly at the end of a line because space was wanting for the normal **ti**. To make the distinction between the two sounds of **ti** other means were used (see below, Part III). As in Beneventan, here too **ci** is rare. It becomes frequent as soon as the Visigothic gives way to the ordinary minuscule in which the two sounds of **ti** are not differentiated.

The absence of such spelling as 'nacio', 'leccio' in Beneventan and Visigothic manuscripts is directly and causally related to the presence of distinct (*25*)
forms for differentiating the assibilated and unassibilated **ti**.[2] Of this there can be no reasonable doubt.

Insular manuscripts do not make the **ti**-distinction. The form of the ligature used in them is probably of semi-uncial origin, and is found in manuscripts posterior even to the ninth century.

The transcription of the ligature

In view of what has been said of the ligature the question of how it should be transcribed may seem gratuitous. Yet this is not the case, for scholars are not at one on the subject. There are those who transcribe the ligature by

[1] Cf. MSS. Paris 12168; Laon 423; Laon 137; Paris 8921.

[2] This observation was already made by Mommsen in his description of the Beneventan manuscript Vatic. lat. 3342. See the preface to his edition of Solinus, p. civ, where he quotes Traube, *O Roma nobilis*, p. 13, n. 7. See also Blume in Pertz's *Archiv*, v. 259.

means of **ci**.[1] That this is incorrect is proven not alone by the origin of the ligature which is simply a combination of **t** and **i** but by the fact that for generations scribes and notaries used the ligature in words like 'satis', 'tibi', 'peccati' as well as in words like 'natio' or 'uenditio', etc. There are, to be sure, cases where notaries used a ligature like this for **ci**,[2] but in manuscripts this is hardly possible. That in Beneventan the ligature may never be transliterated by **ci** is proven by the fact that words like 'provincia', 'specie', 'Decii', 'socio', 'atrocius', etc., are written with **ci** and practically never with the ligature. We see then that the Beneventan scribe made a careful distinction be-
(*26*) tween **ci** and soft **ti**. And the fact that he (as well as the Visigothic scribe) possessed a special way of writing assibilated **ti** doubtless accounts for his rarely writing **ci** for **ti**, so that such spellings as 'nacio', 'leccio', 'pocius', which fill the pages of early French manuscripts, are a rarity in Beneventan or Visigothic.[3]

The transcription of the ligature **ȝ** in documents was some years ago the subject of lively dispute.[4] Without entering the discussion I may state that I hold with Lupi against Paoli that the ligature **ȝ** should be rendered by **ti** regardless of what its probable pronunciation may have been. When such extraordinary forms are encountered as 'acȝione', with the superfluous **i**, or 'aȝȝo' in which the ligature has plainly the value of **z** and not of soft **ti**, the editor ought to call attention to that fact.[5] The instance just mentioned of 'aȝȝo' for 'azzo' brings up an interesting question. Is it not possible that in such a case we have perhaps a reminiscence of a form of **z** which vanished in
(*27*) time, but the use of which in documents of the eighth century is fully attested?

[1] Cf. Federici's description of Rom. Casanat. 641[1] in *Archiv. paleogr. ital.* III. fasc. 22, also op. cit., vol. III. Notizie dei facsimili, p. xiii, published in 1910. I find the ligature transcribed by **ci** in the word *Translatio* occurring on fol. 31 of the Beneventan manuscript in the library of H. Y. Thompson. See *A Descriptive Catalogue of Fifty MSS. in the Collection of Henry Yates Thompson* (1898), pp. 87 f.

[2] See p. 19, n. 10.

[3] There is a form of **t** in Visigothic which strongly resembles **c**, one must therefore be sceptical of transcriptions with **ci** for soft **ti**, if the manuscript is Visigothic.

[4] Cf. C. Paoli, 'Miscellanea di paleografia e diplomatica. TI, ZI, Z' in *Archivio storico italiano*, ser. IV. vol. XVI (1885), 284 ff.; C. Lupi, 'Come si debba trascrivere il nesso TI', in *Archiv. stor. ital.*, ser. IV, vol. XX (1887), 279 ff.; ibid., Paoli's reply. Paoli transcribes the ligature regularly with **zi** when it is assibilated. Cf. *Collez. fiorent.*, pls. 21 and 29. Other Italian diplomatists transcribe the ligature by **ti**. Cf. Fedele, *Archivio della R. Società Romana di Storia Patria*, XXI (1898), 464, and Schiaparelli, *Bulletino dell'Istituto Storico Italiano*, no. 30 (1909), p. 53.

[5] The question deserves further investigation. I learn through the courtesy of Dr. F. Schneider that this strange phenomenon is to be noted in a Tuscan document of 1043. Cf. *Quellen und Forschungen*, XI (1908), 33. Curiously enough, I have found two instances of superfluous **i** after the **ti**-ligature on a single page ('uitiium', 'quotiiens') in the Beneventan MS. Paris 7530 (Monte Cassino), saec. VIII ex. This page, fol. 222, is being reproduced in part I of the *Scriptura Beneventana*.

This form of **z**, by reason of its resemblance to the usual form of the ligature **ti**, has presented considerable difficulty to editors who usually transcribe it by **ti**. The two forms are made precisely alike only that the **z** has an affix, as in capital Q, which consists of a wavy line made from left to right, thus: ꝗ. Examples of its use are to be seen in Bonelli, *Codice paleografico lombardo*. As this feature is scarcely known I give here some instances, and point out where Bonelli reads erroneously.

doc. a. 748 Bonelli, pl. 6, line 5 'pezola'; line 8 'pezola' (Bonelli petiola),
doc. a. 765 Bonelli, pl. 9, line 9 'peza',
doc. a. 769 Bonelli, pl. 12, l. 1 'zenoni' (Bonelli tzenoni), l. 2 'pezola' (Bonelli petzola),
doc. a. 774 Bonelli, pl. 16, l. 15 'florenzione' (Bonelli Florentione).

Schiaparelli (in *Bullet. dell'Istit. Stor. Ital.* 1910, no. 30) noted this curious letter in two documents, and even called attention to the difference between it and ordinary ꝗ, but he did not feel justified in transcribing it differently.

doc. a. 742, pl. 1, l. 3 'peza' (Sch. 'petia'),
doc. a. 758, pl. 2, l. 15 'pezola' (Sch. 'petiola').

A fortunate find has furnished me the evidence which establishes to a certainty that this form is to be regarded as the letter **z** and not as the ligature **ti** with a meaningless appendage. In the important MS. Vercelli 183, saec. VIII (it has $\overline{\textbf{ni}}$ = nostri, $\overline{\textbf{no}}$ = nostro, $\overline{\textbf{nm}}$ = nostrum, etc.) this form of **z** occurs many times.[1] It differs from the ligature, which also occurs continually in the manuscript, only in the matter of the affix. Examples are: fol. 99^{v} 'zelo'; fol. 104^{v} 'ezechiel', 'achaz', etc.; fol. 91^{v} 'zosimo'. The regular use of this form (28) of the letter **z** in a perfectly calligraphic book furnishes one of the clearest illustrations of the dependence of early minuscule upon cursive. The scribe of Vercelli 183 was evidently bold in employing this letter, for it appears that the form never got naturalized in calligraphy. On careful inquiry I find that Vercelli 183 is practically unique in its use of this **z**. Through the kindness of Professor Lindsay I learn that in a fairly similar form it also occurs in the north Italian eighth-century MS. Milan Ambros. C. 98 inf. This form of the letter is not mentioned in our texts on palaeography.

[1] Cf. Pl. **1** (*pl. 1*), *l. 11*.

(29)
III. THE EVIDENCE

(*a*) **ti** *in Latin manuscripts*

(*b*) **i**-*longa in Latin manuscripts*

1. To illustrate the usage of **ti** and **i**-longa I give only one or two typical examples which I noted on examining the manuscript. In some cases I have had to depend on photographs. To distinguish such evidence from that based upon a study of the whole manuscript, I prefix an asterisk (*) to manuscripts actually examined.

2. The form of ti used in the examples is the most common. No attempt could be made to reproduce the different varieties found in the manuscripts.

3. By ti *used indifferently* I mean that the ligature is not reserved exclusively either for assibilated or for unassibilated **ti**.

4. The date ascribed to a manuscript is an approximate one. To avoid ambiguity it may be stated that saec. VIII in. = first third of eighth century; saec. VIII ex. = last third of the century; saec. VIII post med. = second half of the century; saec. VIII/IX = *c*. 800.

5. The manuscripts are arranged as far as possible according to countries, in groups which present common graphic features. It is hoped that this attempt at classifying manuscripts in *early Latin minuscule* will prove helpful. Inexpensive facsimiles of these manuscripts will be made accessible to the student in an extensive collection now in press.

(30)
Uncial manuscripts

(*a*) In the oldest type the ligature ti is not found. But in the more recent type it slips in occasionally at the end of a line for lack of space, e.g. *Lucca 490 saec. VIII/IX in the uncial part: 'parentibus'.

(*b*) The **i**-longa is lacking in the oldest type of uncial. However, in manuscripts of the seventh and eighth centuries it is not infrequently used, thus showing the influence of notarial upon calligraphic writing, e.g. Paris 1732: 'In', 'IeIunio'; *Vatic. Regin. lat. 317: 'IeIunii', *passim*. **i**-longa initially, *passim* by one scribe; *Vercelli 188 initially *passim*; Paris 13246: 'In', 'IeIunauit', 'huIus', etc.; *Vatic. lat. 5007 (Naples): 'In', 'huIus', etc.

Semi-uncial manuscripts

(*a*) In the oldest kind ti does not occur. In the recent type it is occasionally found at the end of a line, e.g. *Novara 84 saec. VIII.

(*b*) **i**-longa is not used in the oldest kind. In the more recent type it occurs, e.g. Cambrai 470 initially often; *Rome Sessor. 55 (2099): 'In', 'Ioseph', 'maIore'; Ambros. S 45 sup. often initially; Lyon 523, initially *passim*; *Vatic. Regin. lat. 1024 (Spanish) often initially; Autun 27 (Spanish) often initially: 'In', 'Iudaei', 'Ipse', 'Imago', also medially: 'eIus'. In St. Gall 722 it occurs initially, but also finally after **t**: 'repletI'. In Autun 24 it is also used in other parts beside the beginning: 'ItInerIs', etc., in this respect recalling Merovingian cursive.

Early French minuscule

Paris 8913. saec. VII. The script is very cursive.

(*a*) ꝗ is rarely used: 'conꝗgeret', 'collegisꝗs'. The ordinary forms of **t** and **i** are used for both the soft and hard sounds. But **ci** occurs for assibilated **ti**: 'hospicio', 'sullercia'.
(*b*) Initially often: 'In', 'Introeat', 'Iuxta'; but 'illa', 'ibi' with short **i**.

*Paris 17655. saec. VII ex. The writing hardly differs from that of Merovin- (31)
gian diplomas.

(*a*) ꝗ used indifferently: 'monꝗum', 'alꝗtudinem'. I noted **ci** for assibilated **ti** in the uncial portion: 'commemoracione' (fol. 2).
(*b*) Initially and medially: 'In', 'cuIus', eIus'; occasionally short: 'iniurias'.

*Paris 9427. Luxeuil type. saec. VII/VIII.

Lectionarium Gallicanum.

(*a*) ꝗ used before a consonant: 'saꝗs', 'staꝗm'. Assibilated **ti** is often represented by **ci**: 'pacientiam', 'adnunciavi', 'siciantem', 'leccio', etc.
(*b*) Initially and medially: 'In', 'Ita', 'Ille', 'obIecit', etc.

*Verona XL (38).[1] Same type. saec. VII/VIII.

(*a*) ꝗ occurs for assibilated and unassibilated **ti**, but the ordinary **ti** is more usual: 'sentenꝗiam' and 'sententiam'; 'semeꝗpsam' and 'semet ipsam', 'toꝗens' and 'faꝗgat'.
(*b*) Initially and medially: 'In', 'Iob', 'Ipse', 'Iste', 'aIt', eIus', 'Iustum', 'Iudicium', etc., but '**i**llius' with short **i**.

St. Paul in Carinthia MS. 3 i (25. 2. 36; XXV. a. 3; XXV$\frac{d}{67}$). Same type. saec. VII/VIII.

(*a*) ꝗ used indifferently: 'sapienꝗa', 'nocꝗbus'; 'scienꝗa', 'repenꝗna'.
(*b*) Occasionally long initially: 'In', but '**i**pse', '**i**llum', 'e**i**us' with short **i**.

[1] Verona XL is in precisely the same script as Paris 9427. By means of internal evidence the French origin of the Paris manuscript is established beyond a doubt. Graphic features point to France also as the home of the script, since it resembles French cursive much more than Italian. Then, too, the style of ornamentation and the orthography—the use of **ci** for assibilated **ti**—strongly favour France. These considerations seem so grave that I feel justified in differing with Traube according to whom the Veronese manuscript was written in Verona. See *Vorlesungen und Abhandlungen*, II. 28. There seems to be a slight inconsistency in this passage for the same manuscript is spoken of as a 'Kursivschrift eigener Art' and then again as an example of 'Scriptura Luxoviensis'.

(32) *Ivrea I. Same type. saec. VII/VIII.

(*a*) ꞇ used for assibilated and unassibilated **ti**: 'inimiciꞇas' and 'occulꞇs', 'silenꞇo' and 'uꞇlis'. The ordinary **ti** is also used for soft **ti**: 'etiam'. The ligature ꞇ occurs for **ci**: 'quantoꞇus', 'amiꞇꞇas'.
(*b*) Initially and medially: 'In', 'Iterum', 'Illius', 'Idolatriam', 'Ipse', 'Illos'; 'aIt', 'huIus', 'conIugum', etc., yet 'cu**i**us', with short **i**.

*London Add. MS. 11878. Same type. saec. VIII in.

(*a*) ꞇ used indifferently: 'temptaꞇonis', 'uꞇ', 'senꞇt'.
(*b*) Initially: 'In'; medially not always: 'eIus' but 'cu**i**us'.

*London Add. MS. 29972.[1] Same type. saec. VIII in.

(*a*) ꞇ used indifferently: 'quoꞇens', 'menꞇmur', 'ꞇbi'. The ordinary form of **ti** is also used for assibilated **ti**: 'etiam'.
(*b*) Initially the rule; medially occasionally: 'In', 'cuIus', etc., but also 'cu**i**us'.

Fulda Bonifatianus 2. A similar type of writing but somewhat more recent than that of the preceding manuscripts.

(*a*) ꞇ used indifferently: 'raꞇo' and 'niꞇtur', 'desperaꞇonis' and 'praesenꞇs'. Frequently **ci** is used for soft **ti**: 'uicia'. A corrector changed it to 'uitia'.
(*b*) Often long in the word 'in', but not always.

Wolfenbüttel Weissenb. 99. Similar type. saec. VIII in.

(*a*) ꞇ used indifferently: 'ressurecꞇonem', 'uꞇque'; 'laetiꞇam', 'Iusꞇ'. ꞇ occurs for **ci**, e.g. 'suspiꞇonem'.
(*b*) Initially: 'In', 'Ihm̅', 'Iam', 'Iusti', even 'Ille', yet 'ipsius' with short **i**.

*Munich 29033 (fragment). Similar type. saec. VIII.

(Formerly served as fly-leaves of Munich 14102).

(*a*) ꞇ used indifferently: 'temptaꞇo', 'mitꞇt', 'confesꞇm', 'bapꞇsta'; **ci** occurs for assibilated **ti**: spacium. Also ꞇ used for **ci**: deliꞇosa.
(*b*) Often long initially: 'Iter', 'Ingressus', 'Iam', 'Iussit'; but 'ille', 'ipse', 'iustus' with short **i**.

(33) *Admont (Abbey) Fragm. Prophet.[2] Similar type. saec. VIII.

(*a*) ꞇ used indifferently: 'adflicꞇonis', 'sabbaꞇ', 'porꞇs', 'uicꞇmam', etc.; **ci** occurs for soft **ti**: 'poenitenciam', 'contricione', 'oblacionem' (corrected to 'oblationem').
(*b*) Initially often; occasionally also medially: 'In', 'Ipsa', 'Iuxta', 'maIestate'; but 'ibi', 'illut', 'ipse', 'maiestas' with short **i**.

[1] Similar writing may be seen in Vatic. Regin. lat. 317, e.g. the additions on fols. 31v, 180, 180v, etc.

[2] The fragments show two contemporaneous hands. The usage cited is true only of one scribe, the other does not employ the **ti**-ligature nor the same form of **a**. His writing makes a more recent impression and most likely represents the more modern style. The same scribe, I believe, wrote the Biblical fragments now in Munich (MS. 29158).

Würzburg Mp. Theol. fol. 64[a]. Similar type. saec. VIII.

(*a*) ꝗ used indifferently: 'genꝗum', 'tribulaꝗone', 'genꝗbus', 'ulꝗmum'; **ci** occurs for soft **ti**: 'cognicio', 'tribulacione', 'persecucionem', 'adnunciate', etc.
(*b*) Initially occasionally long, more often short: 'In', but also 'in', 'iudicium', 'huius' with short **i**.

*Vienna 847, fols. 1v, 5v, 6v. saec. VIII.

(*a*) ꝗ occurs for the hard sound: 'peccanꝗ'; **ci** is often used for assibilated **ti**: 'accio', 'legacio'.
(*b*) Initially and medially: 'In', 'Iusticiam', etc.

*Paris 12168. ‹‹ type. *c.* a. 750. The angularity of the two parts of **a** is characteristic of this group.

(*a*) One scribe regularly used ꝗ for unassibilated sound: 'resꝗꝗt', 'procreaꝗs', and ordinary **ti** for assibilated: 'otium', 'potius'.[1] But **ci** often occurs for soft **ti**. Another scribe (after fol. 68) uses ꝗ indifferently. It is evident that the first scribe was trying to make a strict distinction between assibilated and unassibilated **ti**. Curiously enough, the form he chose for hard **ti** became in other schools the regular form for soft **ti**.
(*b*) Commonly in the word **in**, otherwise often short: 'ita', 'iudas'.

*London Add. MS. 31031. Same type.[2] *c.* a. 750. (*34*)

(*a*) ꝗ often for unassibilated **ti**: 'adsꝗꝗs', 'ꝗbi', 'peccasꝗ'; **ci** very often for assibilated **ti**: 'iniusꝗcie', 'explanacio', etc.
(*b*) Usually short. This cursive element is slowly being eliminated from the book-hand.

Laon 423. Same type. *c.* a. 750.

(*a*) The first scribe (fols. 1–17) has ꝗ for unassibilated **ti** and ordinary **ti** for assibilated: 'supersꝗtiose', 'inuesꝗgatione', etc. The other scribes use ꝗ indifferently. Here it may be fair to suppose that the first scribe was consciously making a distinction between the two sounds of **ti**.[3]

Laon 137. Same type. *c.* a. 750.

(*a*) ꝗ is used indifferently, although it seems that here and there an effort was made to have it represent only the hard sound, e.g. 'pesꝗlentia', 'resꝗtutione'.

*St. Gall 214. The **l**-type. saec. VIII.

The characteristic letter is **l**, which has a distinct bend in the middle, somewhat like broken **c**, The script is related to the Corbie tcb type. See p. 29.
(*a*) ꝗ not used. Ordinary **ti** is used for assibilated and unassibilated **ti**, but **ci** often occurs for the soft sound: 'cicius', 'perdicione'.
(*b*) Initially often, but 'in', 'impleri', 'ignorat'; occasionally also medially: 'cuIus', 'eIus'.

[1] My attention was called by Professor W. M. Lindsay to this regularity on the part of the first scribe.

[2] To judge from a small facsimile, the Cambridge MS. Corpus Christi College K 8 belongs in this class of manuscripts.

[3] Knowledge of this and the next manuscript I owe to the kindness of Professor W. M. Lindsay.

***London Harley 5041. Same type. saec. VIII.**

(*a*) ꝗ not used. Ordinary **ti** for assibilated and unassibilated sound.
(*b*) Used occasionally: 'Iam', 'maIor'. Often short, even in the word 'in'.

Château de Troussures [now Paris Nouv. acq. lat. 1063]. Same type. saec. VIII.

Nov. Testam. See catalogue of sale, pl. 2 (Paris, Leclerc, 1909).
(35) (*a*) ꝗ occurs for hard sound: 'ꝗbi'; **ci** is used for assibilated **ti**: 'narracio', 'depraecacio'.
(*b*) Initial **i** has a somewhat longer form: 'In'.

***Paris 14086. Similar script. saec. VIII.**

(*a*) ꝗ occasionally for assibilated sound: 'praesumpꝗonis'; but **ci** is very frequent for soft **ti**: 'senciant', 'paenitenciam', etc.
(*b*) Initially.

***Berne 611. Similar script. saec. VIII.**

(*a*) ꝗ is used indifferently: 'legenꝗum', 'praeposiꝗonum', 'ponꝗfex'; **ci** very often occurs for soft **ti**: 'noticiam', 'monicione', 'quociens'. Ordinary **ti** is also used for the soft sound.
(*b*) Initially as a rule; medially occasionally: 'In', 'huIus', 'cuIus'; but also 'eius' with short **i**. Here and there the **i**-longa extends below the line: 'ejus', 'jejunij'.

***Bamberg B.V. 13. Similar script. saec. VIII/IX.**

(*a*) No ꝗ. No distinction between the two sounds.
(*b*) No **i**-longa.

***Paris 12598. saec. VIII ex.**

(*a*) ꝗ used for unassibilated **ti, ci** often occurring for assibilated: 'ꝗbi', 'peꝗcionibus', 'adfleccione'.
(*b*) Found here and there initially and even medially: 'eIus', 'IeIuniis'; but as a rule **i**-longa is not used.

***Vienna 1616. saec. VIII ex.**

(*a*) ꝗ used for unassibilated **ti**: 'uꝗ', 'bapꝗzatus', 'castitaꝗs'; **ci** often occurs for assibilated **ti**: 'tristicia', 'poncio', 'gencium', 'damnacionis', etc.
(*b*) Initially, but 'illa' with short **i**; medially as a rule: 'maIestas', 'huIus', 'IeIunii', 'IeIunare', etc.

Épinal 68. saec. VIII (a. 744). A type of pre-Caroline minuscule out of which the Caroline developed. The cursive elements are few; the general impression is that of a modified semi-uncial.

(36) (*a*) ꝗ seldom occurs: 'imperiꝗssimis'; no distinction is made, but **ci** is often used for soft **ti**: 'laeticia', 'uiciis', 'uiciata', etc.
(*b*) Initially and medially by one hand: 'In', 'Iam', 'eIusdem', etc.; short **i** initially and medially, by another. The cursive portion has **i**-longa. The use of **i**-longa in the body of the word, at the end of a syllable, e.g. 'lacrImarum', recalls certain semi-uncial manuscripts and Merovingian cursive. There are a number of manuscripts of the type of Épinal 68.

*Oxford Bodl. Douce f. 1 (fragments). saec. VIII post med.

This script is the immediate precursor of the **ıcb** type, which is manifestly only a further development of it. Very typical is the letter **a** which in combination is often suprascript and has the first curve turned leftward at the top. Otherwise the **a** is shaped like two adjacent **c**'s. The **b** has already the form found in the Corbie manuscripts of the **ıcb** type.

(*a*) **ꝗ** used indifferently: 'potenꝗam', 'securitaꝗs'. Ordinary **ti** is often used for the assibilated sound. **ꝗ** occurs for **ci**, e.g. 'faꝗat'.
(*b*) not used: 'in', 'huius', 'maiestatem'—all with short **i**.

*Vatic. Regin. lat. 316. Same script. saec. VIII post med.

The manuscript is in uncial, but several lines occur in this type of minuscule on fols. 2^{v} and 46.

(*a*) **ꝗ** used: 'substanꝗalem', 'temptaꝗone'; **ci** occurs for soft **ti**: 'tercia'.
(*b*) A slightly longer form of **i** occurs initially: 'In'.

Brussels 9850–2. Corbie script,[1] ıcb type. saec. VIII ex.

Most of the manuscripts of this type are of the early ninth century, a few are of the end of the eighth. The script is very conventional and shows a high point of development. (*37*)

(*a*) **ꝗ** used indifferently: 'paꝗenꝗssima'.
(*b*) Initially often, but not medially.

*Paris 3836. Same type. saec. VIII ex.

(*a*) **ꝗ** used indifferently: 'senꝗendum', 'probaꝗs'; **ci** often occurs for assibilated **ti**: 'racione', 'penetenciam', etc.
(*b*) Not used regularly.

*Paris 8921. Same type. saec. VIII ex.

(*a*) **ꝗ** is not used. However, it is evident that the distinction between the two sounds is striven after. When the **ti** is assibilated the **i** is extended below the line (as later in Visigothic manuscripts); when it is unassibilated the usual form of the **i** is retained. This distinction is observable in many parts of the manuscript. I cite these examples: fol. 31^{v} 'an**ti**ocensis' but 'cottinensis'; fol. 32^{v} 'e**ti**am' but 'extiterit'; fol. 45 'deuo**ti**onis', 'persecu**ti**onis' but 'multis' (yet I noted 'nescien**ti**bus'); fol. 138^{v} 'Lauren**ti**us' but 'surentinus'; 'proiecti**ti**us' but 'hostiensis'; fol. 140^{v} 'e**ti**am' but 'sanctitas'. **ci** is not infrequently used for assibilated **ti**.
(*b*) Often initially and medially: 'huIus', 'cuIus', etc.

Turin D.V. 3. Same type. saec. VIII ex.

(*a*) **ꝗ** occurs for unassibilated **ti**: 'omnipotenꝗs', 'prosequenꝗs'; **ci** is used for assibilated **ti**: 'milicia', 'pocius', 'racioni', 'graciarum', etc.
(*b*) Initially: 'In', 'Iohannis'; not medially: 'huius', 'cuius'.

*Paris 11627. Same type. saec. VIII/IX.

(*a*) No **ꝗ**. No distinction.
(*b*) Often used, but not regularly.

[1] The name originated with Traube.

*Paris 11681. Same type. saec. VIII/IX.

(*a*) No ꝗ. No distinction.
(*b*) Only occasionally.

*Paris 12134. Same type. saec. VIII/IX.

(*a*) No ꝗ. No distinction.
(*b*) Often initially.

(*38*) *Paris 12135. Same type. saec. VIII/IX.

(*a*) No ꝗ. No distinction.
(*b*) Occasionally.

*Paris 12155. Same type. saec. VIII/IX.

(*a*) No ꝗ. No distinction.
(*b*) Used irregularly.

*Paris 12217. Same type. saec. VIII/IX.

(*a*) No ꝗ. No distinction. **ci** occurs for soft **ti**.
(*b*) Hardly used.

*Paris 13048. Same type. saec. VIII/IX.

(*a*) No ꝗ. No distinction.
(*b*) Often initially, but irregularly.

*Paris 13440. Same type. saec. IX in.

(*a*) No ꝗ. No distinction.
(*b*) Rarely used.

*Paris 11529–30. Same type. saec. IX in.

(*a*) No ꝗ. No distinction.
(*b*) Often used, but not regularly.

*Paris 17451. Same type. saec. IX in.

(*a*) No ꝗ. No distinction.

*Paris Nouv. acq. lat. 1628, fols. 15–16. Same type. saec. IX in.

(*a*) No ꝗ. No distinction.

*Bamberg B. III. 4 fly-leaf. Same type. saec. IX in.

(*a*) No ꝗ. **ci** occurs for soft **ti**.

*London Harley 3063. Same type. saec. IX in.

(*a*) No ꝗ. No distinction.
(*b*) Used initially; not medially.

There are doubtless many other French manuscripts of the pre-Caroline or early Caroline epoch—it would hardly be necessary to enumerate them even

if I were able to do so—which employ ti indifferently. Gradually, however, this cursive element disappears altogether from the book-script. The **i**-longa, especially in the word 'in' or otherwise at the beginning of a word, stays longer (*39*)
than ti. But it too was practically rejected, although it crops up here and there at all times.

Early Italian minuscule

*Milan Ambros. Josephus on papyrus. (North Italy.) saec. VII.

(*a*) ti used indifferently: 'repetitione'. No distinction is made between soft and hard **ti**.
(*b*) Regularly initially: 'In', 'Ipse', 'Itaque'; even 'Illud', 'Ille', 'Ibi'; medially regularly for the semi-vocal sound: 'peIor', 'huIus', 'cuIus', 'aIt', 'InIurias', etc.

*Milan Ambros. C. 105 inf. (Bobbio.) saec. VII/VIII.

(*a*) ti used indifferently: 'praetio', 'meritis', 'reperti'. No distinction.
(*b*) Initially and medially: 'In', 'Ipsa', 'maIorem', etc.

*Naples IV. A. 8. (Bobbio.) saec. VII/VIII.

(*a*) ti used indifferently: 'munitionem', 'statim', 'Innocentius', 'iacentibus'. No distinction.
(*b*) Initially and medially: 'In', 'Iacentibus', 'proIecerunt'.

*Vienna 17 [now Naples Lat. 1]. (Bobbio.) saec. VII/VIII. See preceding manuscript which belongs in the same group.

*Milan Ambros. D. 268 inf. (Bobbio.) saec. VIII in.

(*a*) ti used indifferently: 'etiam', 'uirtutis', 'mentis', 'contentioni'. No distinction.
(*b*) Initially and medially: 'Ihs̄', 'Illud', 'cuIus', 'maIestatem', 'aIt'. Where the scribe had made it short initially, the corrector made it long.

*Milan Ambros. C. 98 inf. (Bobbio.) saec. VIII.

(*a*) ti used indifferently: 'dignatione', 'sapientibus'. No distinction.
(*b*) Initially the rule, even 'Illo', 'Ipso', 'Ih̄', 'Ibi', etc. Medially not always: 'InIuria', 'huIus', 'maIestate', 'maIor'; but also 'huius', 'eius'.

*Vatic. lat. 5763. (Bobbio.) saec. VIII. (*40*)

(*a*) ti used indifferently: 'notitia', 'continent'. No distinction.
(*b*) Initially: 'Ignem', 'Inter', 'Iudea'; medially not always: 'cuIus', but 'ejus' and 'eius'.

Wolfenbüttel Weissenb. 64. (Bobbio.) saec. VIII.

This manuscript belonged with the preceding.

(*a*) ti used indifferently: 'totius', 'alternatio', 'gratia', 'noctis', 'ultimum', 'tiberis'. No distinction.
(*b*) Initially the rule: 'Id', 'Ipse', 'Igne'; also used medially: 'cuIus'.

Turin A. II. 2. (Bobbio.) saec. VIII.

(*a*) ti used indifferently: 'praetii', 'uitio', 'citia', 'tibi', 'gentis'.
(*b*) Initially: 'In', 'Iustis', 'Ipse', but 'ille'; medially: 'huIus', 'IeIuniis', 'deInceps', but 'ejus'.

Turin G.V. 26. fol. 5v. (Bobbio.[1]) saec. VIII.

(*a*) ꜩ used indifferently: 'essenꜩa', 'extanꜩbus'.
(*b*) Long in 'in' (no other words occur).

*Milan Ambros. L. 99 sup. (Bobbio.) saec. VIII.

(*a*) ꜩ used indifferently: 'stulꜩꜩa', 'disꜩncꜩonem'. No distinction.
(*b*) Initially and medially: 'In', 'Ipsa', even 'Illos'; 'huIus', 'subIectis', 'aIunt', etc.

*Milan Ambros. B. 31 sup. (Bobbio?) saec. IX in.

(*a*) ꜩ is used for assibilated **ti**, but ordinary **ti** is also thus used: 'raꜩonis', but 'fluctio', 'tertia', 'sapientia'. No strict distinction.
(*b*) Initially and medially: 'In', 'InIuria', 'cuIus'.

*Verona I, fol. 403v, 404v. (Verona.) saec. VII.

An interesting example of north Italian cursive. Very characteristic is the letter **n** which somewhat resembles our capital **M**.

(*41*) (*a*) ꜩ occurs: 'temperanꜩa'. No **ti**-distinction: 'nequitia'.[2]
(*b*) Initially, medially (regardless of sound) and even finally: 'Iniquitas', 'Ita', 'Illi'; 'subIecti,' 'erIt', 'nequitIa'; 'meI', 'deI', 'fierI', 'subiectI'.[3]

*Verona III. (Verona.) saec. VIII in.

A curious minuscule derived from half-uncial and the cursive noted in Verona I, fols. 403v, 404v. It has the same form of **n**.

(*a*) ꜩ not used.
(*b*) Initially in the word 'in'.

*Verona XXXIII. (Verona.) saec. VIII in.

An excellent example of half-uncial passing into minuscule.

(*a*) ꜩ not used.
(*b*) Not used.

*Verona XLII. (Verona.[4]) saec. VIII in.

Half-uncial passing into minuscule.

(*a*) ꜩ rarely used, e.g. at end of lines: Iusꜩfi|cationis.
(*b*) Initially and medially: 'In', 'Ille', 'eIus'.

[1] A good example of Bobbio cursive may be seen in Milan Ambros. S. 45 sup. (Bobbio), p. 44, to which Professor Lindsay has kindly called my attention.

[2] The word 'otium' is spelled 'ozium', the **z** having the same form as in the word 'zelus'. Assibilated **ti** must accordingly have had the pronunciation of **z**.

[3] A similar use of **i**-longa is to be noted in Milan Ambros. O 210 sup. p. 46v written in a very old type of cursive. The peculiar form of **n** found in the Veronese manuscript is also to be seen on this page. The **ti**-ligature is used indifferently: 'ueneraꜩone', 'saluꜩs', 'menꜩs'. Examples of **i**-longa are: 'Iam', 'subIacere', 'huIus', 'oratIone', 'deuotIone', 'coelestI'.

[4] The manuscript has the Veronese **ss** which resembles **ns**.

*Verona II, fol. I^{v}. (Verona.) saec. VIII. Cursive.

Characteristic letters are: **l, p, r, g,** and the ligature **nt.**

(*a*) **ti** used indifferently: 'na**ti**ones', 'gen**ti**bus', 'polluis**ti**s'. No distinction.
(*b*) Initially: 'In'.

*Verona IV, fols. 6, 6^{v}. (Verona.) saec. VIII. Similar cursive.

(*a*) **ti** used indifferently: 'men**ti**s', '**ti**bi', 'uinc**ti**', 'pronun**ti**ans', etc. No distinction.
(*b*) Initially often: 'In', 'Iusto', 'Iudaei', 'Iussit', but 'illas', 'ignis'.

*Verona XXXVII, fol. 169^{v}. (Verona.) saec. VIII. Similar cursive. (42)

(*a*) **ti** used indifferently: 'ter**ti**o', 'dedica**ti**onem', 'la**ti**tudinem', 'can**ti**co'. No distinction. The ligature occurs for **ci:** 'prouin**ci**ae'.
(*b*) Initially: 'In', 'Ioachim', 'Iudae'.

*Verona XXXVIII, fol. 118. (Verona.) saec. VIII in.

Transition script. This well-known page furnishes one of the earliest examples of Veronese minuscule with the typical **g, r, p,** and **l.**

(*a*) **ti** not used.
(*b*) Initially and medially: 'In', 'Ignes', 'Illi', 'Ita', 'eIus', 'proIecta'.

*Verona LXII. (Verona.) saec. VIII.

Calligraphic minuscule which is manifestly derived from the above mentioned Veronese cursive. It has the characteristic **l, p, r, g,** the ligatures **nt, ae, ss** (resembling **ns**), and the superior **a.**

(*a*) **ti** used indifferently: 'nup**ti**is', 'leon**ti**o', 'meri**ti**s', 'legi**ti**mam', 'con**ti**nen**ti**ae'. No distinction.
(*b*) Not used: 'in', 'coniugium', etc., with short **i.**

*Verona LV. (Verona.) saec. VIII.

(*a*) **ti** used indifferently: 'mundi**ti**a', 'ui**ti**a', '**ti**morem', 'per**ti**naciae'. No distinction.
(*b*) Initially often, but not regularly: 'In', 'Ita', 'Iudicium', but also 'iustus', 'iustitiae', 'ignis', 'iram', 'illa', etc.

*Verona LXI, fol. 1. (Verona.) saec. VIII.

(*a*) **ti** not used.
(*b*) Initially and medially: 'In', 'eIus', 'conIunctio', 'aIt'.

*Verona CLXIII. (Verona.) saec. VIII.

(*a*) **ti** occurs occasionally. It is used indifferently: 'gra**ti**a', 'rogan**ti**', 'po**ti**us', 'adduc**ti**s'.
(*b*) Initially and medially: 'In', 'Iuuat', 'Iacit', 'cuIus', 'IeIunas'.

*Verona XV, marginalia. (Verona.) saec. VIII.

(*a*) **ti** used indifferently: '**ti**bi', 'facien**ti**bus'.
(*b*) Initially and medially: 'In', 'Iacobi', 'maIori'.

(*43*) *Carlsruhe Reich. LVII. (Verona.[1]) saec. VIII.

(*a*) **ti** used indifferently, more often for soft **ti**: 'e**ti**am', 'egyp**ti**is', 'ciuita**ti**'.
(*b*) Used irregularly: 'In', 'Inter', but 'ingressu', 'imperium', 'cuius' with short **i**.

*Paris 653 (Verona?) saec. VIII/IX. See Pl. **2** (*pl. 2*).

(*a*) **ti** used by one hand (fols. 1–6ᵛ) for assibilated **ti**: 'gra**ti**am', 'ignoran**ti**a', but 'par**ti**s' Distinction made. The new hand on fol. 6ᵛ knows neither **ti** nor the **ti**-distinction: 'e**ti**am' 'uoca**ti**'.
(*b*) Used by the first scribe (who knows **ti**): 'In', 'Ipse', 'Ihm̄', 'Ita', etc. The second scribe does not use it.

*Vercelli CLXXXIII. (Vercelli?) saec. VIII. See Pl. **1** (*pl. 1*)[2]

(*a*) **ti** used indifferently: 'ui**ti**a', 'u**ti**', 'mul**ti**'. No distinction.
(*b*) Initially always: 'In', 'Ipso', 'Illi', 'Ibi', etc.; medially regularly for the semi-vocal sound: 'eIus', 'huIus', 'cuIus'; also when 'in' occurs in the body of a composite word, e.g. 'deInde'. See discussion on p. 12.

*Vercelli CCII. (Vercelli?) saec. IX in.

(*a*) **ti** used indifferently: 'ra**ti**one', 'mul**ti**'. No distinction.
(*b*) Usually in the word 'in', otherwise not employed: 'In', but 'ius', 'ita', 'cuius', etc.

(*44*) *Vercelli CXLVIII. (Vercelli?) saec. IX.

(*a*) **ti** regularly reserved for assibilated **ti**: and ordinary **ti** for unassibilated. Distinction made.
(*b*) Initially often: 'In', 'Iam', but 'illum', 'ihm̄'; medially not used.

*Novara 84. (North Italy.) saec. VIII/IX.

(*a*) **ti** used indifferently: 'peniten**ti**a', 'na**ti**uita**ti**s'. No distinction.
(*b*) Usual with 'in', otherwise rarely used: 'In', but 'iam', 'ita', 'huius'.

Milan Trivulziana 688. (Novara.) saec. VIII/IX.

(*a*) **ti** used indifferently: 'li**ti**gia'; ordinary **ti** for soft sound: 'cautioni'; **ci** for soft **ti**: 'admonicionem'.
(*b*) Initially frequent though not always: 'In', 'Iudiciis', 'Iuret', but 'index'.

*Paris Baluze 270. (North Italy.) saec. VIII/IX.

(*a*) **ti** used indifferently: 'ra**ti**o', 'mul**ti**s'.
(*b*) Rarely used: 'In' but also 'in' with short **i**.

[1] The manuscript has the curious **ss** resembling **ns**—a feature to be noted in several Veronese manuscripts.

[2] Knowledge of this palaeographically most interesting manuscript I owe to the kindness of Father Ehrle, Prefect of the Vatican library. Through the great courtesy of Mgr. M. Vattasso I have the privilege of reproducing the manuscript. Several full-page facsimiles of this manuscript as well as of others from the chapter library of Vercelli will be given by Mgr. Vattasso in a forthcoming work. We have no positive evidence that this and the following two manuscripts were actually written in Vercelli. Since they are manifestly of north Italian origin, the probability is that they were. I mention in passing that the marginalia of Vercelli CLVIII are in a hand which is not Italian. I take it for Visigothic. The rules for **i**-longa are, as may be expected, carefully observed.

Breslau Rehdig. R. 169, fol. 92^{v}. (Aquileia?) saec. VIII ex.

(*a*) ꝗ used before consonants: 'ꝗberii'. **ci** is used for assibilated **ti**: 'tercie', 'nupcie'.
(*b*) Initially the rule: 'Illum', 'circumIbat', 'Ihs̄', etc.

Modena O.I.N. 11. saec. VIII/IX.

(*a*) ꝗ used indifferently. No distinction.
(*b*) Initially: 'In', 'Iudaica'.

*Lucca 490. saec. VIII/IX.

(*a*) ꝗ used indifferently: 'Iusꝗꝗam', 'mitꝗtur', 'ꝗmeas', etc. No distinction.
(*b*) Not used.

*Rome Sessor. 55 (2099), fols. 89 to end. saec. VIII ex.

(*a*) ꝗ used indifferently: 'enunꝗare', 'isꝗs', 'disꝗincꝗone'. No distinction.
(*b*) Not used as a rule: 'in', 'indicaret', 'coniungas'.

*Rome Sessor. 94 (1524), pt. I = pp. 1–32. saec. VIII/IX. (*45*)

(*a*) ꝗ used indifferently, but preferably for soft **ti**: 'uiꝗa', 'facultaꝗbus'. No strict distinction: 'pretiosus', 'fortia'.
(*b*) Initially and medially: 'Iam' (corrector changed to 'iam'), 'IeIuniis', 'cuIus', etc.

*Rome Sessor. 66 (2098). saec. IX.

(*a*) ꝗ where used has soft sound, but no strict distinction is observed between assibilated and unassibilated **ti**: 'innocenꝗam', but 'definitione'.
(*b*) Initially the rule; medially rarely.

*Rome Sessor. 40 (1258). saec. IX.

(*a*) ꝗ used for assibilated **ti**. Distinction observed: 'scienꝗa', 'adtingeret'.
(*b*) Initially and medially: 'In', 'Ire', but 'illius'; 'hujus', 'eIus', etc.

*Rome Sessor. 41 (1479). saec. IX.

(*a*) ꝗ for assibilated **ti**. Distinction observed.
(*b*) Initially, the rule; but 'ipse', 'illi'; medially not always: 'huIus' and 'huius', 'maior'.

*Rome Sessor. 96 (1565). saec. IX.

(*a*) ꝗ for assibilated **ti**. Distinction made: 'propheꝗam', 'tibi'.
(*b*) Not regularly used: 'In', but also 'in', 'huius', 'adiunxit', etc.

*Rome Sessor. 63 (2102). saec. IX.

(*a*) ꝗ for assibilated **ti**. Distinction usually observed: 'poꝗus', 'tanti'.
(*b*) As a rule not used.

In the more recent manuscripts of this school—for the above named Sessoriani are supposedly all from Nonantola—ꝗ and the **ti**-distinction and

i-longa are all given up.[1] The same is true of the manuscripts of Vercelli, Novara, Bobbio, Verona, Lucca, and other Italian centres. These elements disappear as soon as the Caroline minuscule prevails.

(*46*) *Roman School*

No very ancient minuscule manuscripts are known. Those that are posterior to the ninth century lack the ligature **ʒ** and observe no **ti**-distinction. The **i**-longa is not seldom used initially.

The Beneventan or South Italian School[2]

(*a*) I. In oldest minuscule manuscripts (saec. VIII) **ʒ** is used indifferently, e.g. Monte Cassino 753: 'uiʒis' and 'mitʒtur'; Bamberg HJ.IV. 15: 'noʒʒam'.

II. In Paris 7530 saec. VIII ex. **ʒ** is regularly reserved for assibilated **ti**, and the distinction is strictly observed. Although in some manuscripts of the ninth century insecurity is still to be noted (e.g. Vatic. 3320, where a later corrector often changed **tio** to **ʒ**o, and Naples VI.B. 12) the majority of the manuscripts show perfect knowledge of the two uses of **ti**. From the ninth to the fourteenth century the form **ʒ** is regularly used for assibilated, and the normal form for unassibilated **ti**. *This is one of the main rules of the Beneventan script.* A scribe rarely wrote ordinary **ti** for **ʒ**. I have noted but few cases, e.g. Rome Vallicell. D. 5, saec. XI in.: 'unguentiam'; Vatic. lat. 595: 'petiit', changed by corrector to 'pʒit', and some cases in Floren. Laur. 68. 2.[3] Occasionally too, we find **ci** for **ti**. This occurs so seldom that it is without doubt the result of slavish copying from an original in which **ci** stood for assibilated **ti**—and such spelling was certainly not unusual in the schools north of the Beneventan zone. Examples are: Monte Cassino 5: 'precio' corrected to 'preʒo'; Monte Cassino 295: 'uicia' corrected to 'uiʒa'; Vatic. lat. 3973: 'ueneciis', and Vatic. Bor-
(*47*) gian. 339: 'cicius'. On the other hand, there is nothing surprising if we find the ligature **ʒ** for **ci**. I noted 'perniʒe' in Monte Cassino 187, saec. IX. An eleventh-century corrector wrote **ci** for the ligature.

(*b*) For the usage of **i**-longa in Beneventan manuscripts see pp. 10–11.

[1] Is it possible that we have a revival of the practice in the manuscript *Bologna Univ. 1604 (Nonantola) saec. XI/XII, or is it a case of copying? I noted 'rationis' (with **i** drawn down) but 'utique' (with short **i**).

[2] The following summary is based upon an examination of over 300 Beneventan manuscripts.

[3] Cf. Andresen, *In Taciti Historias studia critica et palaeographica*, I (1899), 8.

Visigothic Minuscule

(*a*) The frequent occurrence of ꞇ is noticeable only in the oldest manuscripts, e.g. Verona LXXXIX (where it is used indifferently) and Autun 27+Paris Nouv. acq. lat. 1628–9 (where there is a tendency to reserve the ligature for the assibilated sound). In manuscripts of the ninth or tenth century ꞇ is found here and there at the end of a line to save space. It does not form part of the calligraphic hand. The distinction between assibilated and unassibilated **ti** was in time graphically represented. As this question is of importance in dating Visigothic manuscripts, it has been treated separately and at greater length below. See Part IV.

(*b*) For the usage of **i**-longa in Visigothic manuscripts see above, pp. 9–10. The manuscript evidence is given in Part IV.

German Schools

Early minuscule manuscripts from German centres have as a rule neither ꞇ nor the **ti**-distinction, nor the **i**-longa—owing most likely to Caroline influence. Nevertheless in several manuscripts of the transition period ꞇ is found, along with other cursive features such as **ri** and **te**. Its presence, therefore, may safely be taken as a hint of the date of the manuscript.

I noted ꞇ sparingly used in the following manuscripts.

*Munich 4547.[1] (Kysila-group.) saec. VIII/IX.

(*a*) used for hard sound: 'ꞇmeret' (fol. 11), 'ueritaꞇs' (fol. 12), 'inmaculaꞇ' (fol. 12), 'ꞇbi' (fol. 22), etc.
(*b*) **i**-longa is not used.

*Munich 4549. (Same group.) saec. VIII/IX. *(48)*

(*a*) ꞇ used indifferently: 'uiꞇis', 'impaꞇenꞇae', 'menꞇ', 'curaꞇs', 'laꞇtat', etc.
(*b*) Initially here and there; not medially.

*Munich 4542. (Same group.) saec. VIII/IX.

(*a*) ꞇ occurs for the assibilated sound, but chiefly the ordinary **ti**: 'sapienꞇam' (fol. 139^{v}), 'corrupꞇonem' (fol. 132^{v}), but next line: 'corruptione', with ordinary **ti**.
(*b*) Initially in the word 'in'; not medially.

*Munich 14421. saec. VIII/IX.

(*a*) ꞇ like the ligature **te** is found chiefly at the end of the line, and is used indifferently:

[1] Dr. Wilhelm of the University of Munich places the Kysila-group of manuscripts in the region of Utrecht. This judgement is based upon liturgical and philological evidence furnished by the manuscripts themselves.

'stulꝗ' (fol. 9v), 'dixeriꝗs' (fol. 12v), 'ueritaꝗs' (fol. 15v), 'laetiꝗa' (fol. 24), 'captiuitaꝗs' (fol. 43 in middle of line), etc.
(*b*) Not used.

*Munich 4564. saec. IX. Hand A is calligraphic, B more cursive.

(*a*) Not used by hand A. Hand B used ꝗ indifferently: 'cotꝗdiae', 'oraꝗone' (fol. 220), 'benediciꝗs', 'faciaꝗs' (fol. 220v), 'turbaꝗonem' (fol. 221v).
(*b*) Not used.

*Munich 6277. saec. IX.

(*a*) ꝗ used indifferently: 'operaꝗo', 'perꝗmescat', 'inꝗmo' (fol. 50), 'iustiꝗe', 'niꝗtur', 'desperationem' with ordinary **ti** (fol. 50v), etc.
(*b*) Not used.

*Munich 6402. saec. IX.

(*a*) Where found ꝗ usually has the assibilated sound: 'porꝗo' (fol. 45), 'graꝗa' (fol. 51v), 'eꝗam', 'generaꝗo' (fol. 52), etc. But 'talenꝗ' (fol. 53v). Ordinary **ti** is chiefly used for either sound, yet **ci** occurs for **ti**: 'praecio', 'praeciosi' (fol. 61).
(*b*) Here and there it crops up, but manifestly due to the exemplar: 'maIor' and 'maior' (fol. 53v).

*Munich 4719m. saec. IX.

(*a*) ꝗ used indifferently: 'contestaꝗo', 'perseueraꝗ', 'optaꝗo', 'obstinaꝗs'.
(*b*) Not used.

(*49*) In manuscripts of the St. Gall, Reichenau, and Chur districts no **ti**-distinction is observed. In many of them, however, **ci** takes the place of assibilated **ti**—a practice already noted in numerous French manuscripts, which probably served as models for the Swiss.[1] The ligature ꝗ occurs only here and there, used indifferently. As a rule **i**-longa is not employed; occasionally it is found at the beginning of a word, and less frequently in the middle. The following early examples have been examined:[2] § St. Gall 70, § 238,[3] 44, 914, 185, § 731, § 348,[3] § 722; Berne 376;[3] § Zurich Cantonsbibl. CXL,[3] § Cantonsbibl. (Rheinau) 30; § Einsiedeln 27, § 347,[3] 199,[3] § 281[3] and 157.[3]

Insular Schools[4]

(*a*) The form of the **ti**-ligature found in Insular manuscripts, as has been mentioned above, differs from ꝗ in that the upper loop or curve is missing (see p. 18). The form could easily have arisen from semi-uncial **t** combining

[1] Historical and graphic considerations suggest Burgundian influence. Further investigation may disclose relations between Luxeuil and Chur or some other Swiss centre. I suspect that the MSS. Berne 611 and St. Gall 214 are Swiss products formed under the influence of Luxeuil.

[2] Manuscripts preceded by § have **ci** for soft **ti**.

[3] In this manuscript ꝗ used indifferently is occasionally found, especially at the end of a line.

[4] Cf. facs. in Lindsay, *Early Irish Minuscule Script* (Oxford, 1910).

with **i**. The absence of the form ꝗ in pure Insular products may be regarded as one of the many proofs of the peculiar origin—in which cursive played no part—of the Insular writing. The **ti**-ligature, where found, is used indifferently. No distinction between the assibilated and unassibilated sounds is made.

(*b*) It is fair to say that **i**-longa—which, as has been shown, is of cursive origin—is often found initially, though not with any apparent regularity; (*50*)
medially it seems to be less frequent.[1]

I give a few examples. For the **ti**-ligature I use bold face.

*Bodl. Douce 140, fol. 100^{v}. (*a*) 'can**ti**cum', (*b*) not used.
The Book of Dimma. (*a*) 'fueri**ti**s', (*b*) used initially, often.
The Book of Mulling. (*a*) 'uul**ti**s', (*b*) used initially, often.
*Vatic. Pal. lat. 68. (*a*) 'adnun**ti**auit', 'demergen**ti**s', (*b*) used in 'in'.
*Vatic. lat. 491. (*a*) 'gra**ti**as', 'pieta**ti**s', (*b*) not used.
*London Cotton Tib. C. II. (*a*) 'potesta**ti**', (*b*) used with 'in'.
*Paris 10837. (*a*) '**ti**morem', 'agapi**ti**'.
*Vatic. Pal. lat. 235. (*a*) '**ti**bi', 'fon**ti**bus', (*b*) not used.
*Vienna 16. (*a*) 'repeti**ti**one', '**ti**bi', (*b*) 'In' long. Insular influenced by Italian cursive.
Turin F. IV. 1 fasc. 6. (*a*) 'indigna**ti**onem', '**ti**bi', 'mor**ti**s'. (*b*) 'In' long.

We have seen, then, that the **ti**-ligature originated in Italian cursive of the early Middle Ages. We have found it in all those types of pre-Caroline minuscule which obviously are based upon cursive, and the usage in the manuscripts corresponded to that of the documents. We missed it, on the other hand, in most of the manuscripts from about the beginning of the ninth century. This circumstance can be attributed to but one cause—the Caroline script-reform. The hypothesis is confirmed by the consideration that many manuscripts of about the year 800, written in north Italy, France, and Germany show traces of the abandoned practice. They are the manuscripts of the transition period. Still more cogent evidence is furnished by the fact that in the Beneventan centres where the Caroline influence did not reach, the **ti**-
ligature continued in use along with several other cursive features which (*51*)
elsewhere were abolished. Doubtless for similar reasons ꝗ is found in many Visigothic manuscripts, though relegated, to be sure, to a place of insignificance. The history of ꝗ, then, is a kind of epitome of the development of Latin minuscule in its important stage. We have seen, also, that the spelling **ci** for soft **ti** is a characteristic of early French, not of early Italian and that the

[1] I have found **i**-longa medially in *Palat. 202 'deInde'; *Bodl. Laud. lat. 108 'IeIunandum'. I believe that in all such cases foreign influncee is responsible for the **i**-longa.

graphic distinction of assibilated and unassibilated **ti** was regularly practiced in but two schools, the Beneventan and the Visigothic; although the usefulness of distinguishing in script the two sounds of **ti** was elsewhere recognized —as several instances clearly show—before the practice became a law of the Spanish and south Italian minuscule.

From all this the palaeographer may draw a practical hint or two for dating and placing manuscripts. For example, the regular use of ꝗ in a French manuscript is a fair sign that the manuscript was written some time before the middle of the eighth century.[1] Its sporadic appearance, on the other hand, suggests that the manuscript belongs in the period of transition, i.e. about the year 800. The frequent use of **ci** for soft **ti** in a pre-Caroline manuscript points to French origin rather than to Italian or Spanish.[2] And certain corruptions in the text due to the ligature ꝗ permit a surmise as to the probable nature of the archetype.[3]

(52) IV. **ti** IN SPANISH MANUSCRIPTS

In Visigothic calligraphy the manner of writing **ti** is of signal interest and importance. After a certain time the Spanish scribe, just as the Beneventan, used two distinct forms for assibilated and unassibilated **ti**. From evidence given below it will be seen that it is possible to fix with some degree of precision the period when the custom of making the distinction was introduced into Visigothic book-writing. In other words, a criterion for dating can be won. The assibilated and unassibilated forms differ but slightly.[4] In the case

[1] The same is true for Visigothic manuscripts.

[2] See p. 22, n. 3. An editor collating a Visigothic manuscript must be on his guard against mistaking for **c** a certain form of **t** which occurs in ligatures. Even Maffei misread **ci** where the manuscript has **ti**. Cf. Spagnolo, *L'orazionale gotico-mozarabico*, etc., *estratto dalla Rivista bibliografica italiana* (10–25 Aug. 1899), p. 8, l. 11. For 'pre**c**ium' read 'pre**t**ium'.

[3] I refer to cases where the text has **q** for **ti**, an error due most likely to copying, from an original which had ꝗ, by a scribe unaccustomed to the ligature. An instructive example is cited by Traube, *Textgeschichte der Regula S. Benedicti*, p. 85.

[4] This perhaps explains how it happened to escape the attention of palaeographers. Steffens has noted the **ti**-distinction in his description of Escor. T. II. 24 (formerly Q. II. 24). That he too failed to realize that it was as much a scribal rule in Visigothic as in Beneventan is seen from the fact that in his introduction he speaks of the **ti**-distinction in Beneventan manuscripts but not in Visigothic. I believe that Delisle's report of my observations on the subject (*Comptes-rendus de l'Académie des Inscriptions*, 1909, pp. 775–8 and *Bibliothèque de l'École des Chartes*, LXXI (1910), 233–5) is its first formulation in palaeographical literature, for there is no mention of it in Muñoz y Rivero, Ewald and Loewe, Wattenbach, or in the earlier writers on Spanish palaeography. It is a curious fact that even Paoli, with whom the question of assibilated **ti** was a matter of keen interest, made no reference to the distinction in his description of the Visigothic MS. Floren. Laur. Ashb. 17. Cf. *Collezione fiorentina*, pl. 33.

of unassibilated **ti** the normal forms of **t** and **i** are retained. In the case of
assibilated **ti** the **i** is prolonged below the line and often turned in instead of
out (cf. Pls. **5**, **6**, and **7** (*pls. 5, 6, and 7*)), the whole difference lying in the
form of the **i**, the letter **t** suffering no change. The Spanish form for assibilated **ti** (ꝗ) corresponds, then, to the Beneventan for unassibilated. But the
form ȝ, which is regularly reserved for assibilated **ti** in Beneventan calli- *(53)*
graphy, was not unknown in Spanish manuscripts. However, whereas in
Beneventan it was a constant feature of the book-hand, in Spanish it was in
time avoided. For, excepting the oldest known Visigothic manuscripts
(Verona LXXXIX and Autun 27+Paris Nouv. acq. lat. 1628–9) which employ
ȝ frequently, we find it chiefly at the end of a line, where economy of space
demanded the shorter form, or in additions entered in cursive where ȝ is
usually confined—as is the case in Italian cursive—to representing the assibilated sound.

It is needless to say that the custom of graphically distinguishing the two
kinds of **ti** in the Visigothic book-hand, which dates, as will be seen, from
about the end of the ninth century, is in no wise a reflection of a change of
pronunciation then taking place in Spain. The rule given by Isidore, Bishop
of Seville, for the orthography of such words as 'iustitia', 'militia', etc.—to
the effect that they should not be written with a **z** as they were pronounced
but with a **t** as was Latin usage—shows that three centuries prior to the introduction into calligraphy of the graphic distinction between assibilated and
unassibilated **ti**, the difference in their pronunciation was already an accom-
plished fact.[1] And we know from inscriptions that the assibilation of **ti** must
have taken place at quite an early date.[2] That the graphic distinction should
have followed centuries after the phonetic change may be natural enough—
we encounter the same phenomenon in Italy—but it is important to observe
that the distinction was practiced in cursive writing long before it was employed in calligraphic products, and that the manner of representing the distinction in Spanish cursive (ȝ for soft **ti**) was the same as that employed in
Italian cursive and in Beneventan book-hand—facts which seem to speak for
the Italian origin of the custom. This supposition becomes more convincing *(54)*
when we remember that the Spanish scribe invented a new form for denoting
assibilated **ti**, and that this form is found in Visigothic manuscripts a good
century after the Beneventan scribe was making the distinction. That the
practice of making the **ti**-distinction in Visigothic manuscripts dates from

[1] Isidor, *Etymol.* I. 27, 28. See above, p. 16, n. 6, where the passage is quoted.

[2] On the assibilation of **ti** in the Latin-speaking countries see the works cited above, p. 15 n. 3.

about the year 900 is established beyond a reasonable doubt by the evidence of over 100 manuscripts listed below.

A word as to the nature of the evidence. It is furnished by two sources: the manuscripts themselves, and facsimiles of manuscripts. As for facsimiles, in the case of some manuscripts I was dependent upon one only; in other cases, however, photographs of several pages or even of the entire manuscript were at my disposal. More manuscripts might easily have been added without modifying results,[1] but I preferred to use only those dated by recognized authorities, thus avoiding as far as possible basing an argument upon dates for which I alone was responsible. I also hesitated to use facsimiles when it was not clear whence they were taken, as in older books on Spanish palaeography. Notes furnished me by others were used only when supplemented by facsimiles.

I am aware that the evidence supplied by facsimiles of one or two pages of a manuscript is not necessarily conclusive, as it may represent (as it sometimes does) the usage of one scribe and not of another. But whereas this evidence taken by itself might seem of questionable worth, its weight as supplementary evidence when used in connection with facts gathered from the manuscripts themselves will not be gainsaid. The fact that the usage found in the facsimiles is not at all at variance with the usage noted by me in the manuscripts is a guarantee of their value. However, the brunt of the argument will be borne by the forty-five manuscripts actually examined by me—manuscripts which are fairly representative of the different phases of Spanish calligraphy.

(55) In the following list the manuscripts are arranged approximately in chronological order. In most cases my date is identical with that of others. In the few instances where the difference of opinion is essential the reasons for my date are given after the list.[2] I give first the usage of **ti**, with examples taken from the manuscript or from a facsimile. The bold-face **ti** represents the ordinary form of **t** and **i**. For the ligature ꝗ and the assibilated form of **ti** I have tried to reproduce the typical form found in the manuscript. After **ti** I give the **i**-longa usage. I also noted the use of the forked **i**-longa (shaped like a tall **y**). The form of the shafts of tall letters is given because of its value as a criterion for dating. Lastly it seemed helpful to give some literature, for the sake of quick orientation. I gave that which I had at hand, without going out of my way to make researches extraneous to the purposes of this study.

[1] I have examined photographs of at least fifty manuscripts not included in my list. In these manuscripts the **ti**-usage agreed with that of the manuscripts whose evidence is given below.

[2] See pp. 61 ff.

The references frequently cited appear under the following abbreviated forms:

Beer. *Handschriftenschätze Spaniens*, Vienna, 1894.

Beer–Diaz Jimenez. *Notícias bibliográficas y catálogo de los códices de la santa Iglesia Catedral de León*, León, 1888.

Bibl. P.L.H. Loewe–Hartel, *Bibliotheca Patrum Latinorum Hispaniensis*, Vienna, 1887.

Cat. Add. A Catalogue of the Additions to the MSS. of the British Museum.

Delisle, *Mélanges*. *Mélanges de paléographie et de bibliographie*, Paris, 1880.

Eguren. *Memoria descriptiva de los códices notables conservados en los archivos ecclesiásticos de España*, Madrid, 1859.

Exempla. Ewald et Loewe, *Exempla Scripturae Visigoticae*, Heidelberg, 1883.

Merino. *Escuela Paleográfica*, Madrid, 1780.

Muñoz. Muñoz y Rivero, *Paleografía visigoda*, Madrid, 1881.

N.A. Neues Archiv der Gesellschaft für ältere deutsche Geschichtskunde, VI (1880), 219–398 (56)
= P. Ewald, *Reise nach Spanien im Winter 1878–79*.

* Manuscripts actually examined are starred.

1. *Verona Capitol. LXXXIX. saec. VIII in.[1] ut vid.

(*a*) No **ti**-distinction: '**pa**t**i**ent**i**e', 'ut**i**que', 't**i**bi'. Noteworthy is the relatively frequent occurrence of ʒ. It is found *passim* on every page and is used indifferently: 'nequiʒe' (beginning of line), 'frucʒficet' (middle of line), 'menʒbus' (middle of line), 'conscienʒia' (middle of line). These four examples are taken from one page. In contemporary marginalia: 'iusʒʒam', etc. Later manuscripts use ʒ only occasionally at the end of lines.

(*b*) Rule observed.[2]

Cf. Maffei, *Opusc. eccles.* (*Istoria teologica* Trent, 1742), pp. 80f. and pl. IV, no. 18 (whence *Nouveau Traité*, III. 449, pl. 60); pl. IV, pts. XVII and XXI; a poor facsimile also on p. CXXXI of *Thomasii Opera omnia studio et cura Josephi Blanchini*, tom. I (Rome, 1741); Spagnolo, *L'orazionale gotico-mozarabico*, etc., *estratto dalla Rivista bibliografica italiana* (10–25 Aug. 1899); (57)
Férotin, *Liber Ordinum*, p. XV, note 2.

2. *Paris Nouv. acq. lat. 1628 (fols. 17–18). saec. VIII ut vid.

(*a*) No **ti**-distinction. In the more cursive portions ʒ is used indifferently: 'terʒa', 'evidenʒssime'.

[1] On fol. 3v (lower right-hand corner) there is a rather obscure entry of a personal character ending with the words: 'in XX anno liutprandi regis', i.e. the year 732. As the upper half of the page has the same kind of writing as the body of the manuscript, the above entry—if indeed we may regard it as chronicling an actual fact which then took place—gives us the *terminus post quem non*, and the mention of Luitprand would connect the manuscript with north Italy. It must be confessed that the first impression is that the manuscript belongs in the ninth century—it is carefully and regularly written,—but being a liturgical book, special pains may have been taken with it, which would account for the impression. Furthermore, the rather frequent occurrence of certain ligatures, especially of ʒ, also favours the earlier date. I prefer to leave the question of the date undecided. The matter deserves further investigation.

[2] For the rules of **i**-longa in Visigothic manu scripts see above, pp. 9–10.

(*b*) Rule observed. Occasionally even 'Illa'.

Cf. Delisle, ***Les vols de Libri au séminaire d'Autun*** (Bibliothèque de l'École des Chartes, LIX (1898), 386–92.[1])

3. Escorial R. II. 18. ante a. 779.

(*a*) No **ti**-distinction in minuscule portion: resurrec**ti**one, 'ter**ti**o'. In cursive parts the distinction is usually made, **ʒ** or similar forms representing the soft sound: 'Iusti**ʒ**am', 'e**ʒ**am'. Yet exceptions occur: 'segon**ti**a'.
(*b*) **i**-longa rule observed in cursive and minuscule: 'In', 'Ipsa', 'Ibi', 'cuIus'; but 'illa'. Also **i**-longa with forked top: 'acaIa'.

Cf. *Exempla*, pls. IV–VII, whence Arndt–Tangl, *Schrifttaf.*,[4] pl. 8B; *N.A.* VI. 275; *Bibl. P.L.H.*, p. 130; Steffens, *Lat. Pal.*[2], pl. 35.

4. Madrid Tolet. 2. 1 [now Vit. 14–2]. saec. VIII ex. ut vid.

Now kept in Vitrina 4[a], Sala I[a].

(*a*) No **ti**-distinction: 'pa**ti**enter', 'ter**ti**a', and 'septima'.
(*b*) Rule observed: 'Isti', 'maIor', 'caIn', 'eIus', even 'Illi'; 'caIn' with forked **i**-longa.

Cf. *Exempla*, pl. IX; *Bibl. P.L.H.*, p. 261; Muñoz, pls. VIII–IX. The date there given (tenth century, p. 119) is impossible. The date a. 708 given by Merino (p. 55) is likewise untenable. On the inscription at the end of the manuscript, which has been the cause of erroneous dating, see Berger, *Hist. de la Vulg.*, p. 13.

(58) 5. Madrid Tolet. 15. 8 [now Vit. 14–3]. saec. VIII ex. ut vid.

Now kept in Vitrina 4[a], Sala I[a].

(*a*) No **ti**-distinction: 'ter**ti**a', 'gra**ti**ssima'. In the later additions in cursive the distinction is made as in Escor. R. II. 18. The use of **ʒ** in the word 'den**ʒ**bus' (*Exempla*, pl. XII) recalls older cursive where no distinction is made and **ʒ** is used indifferently.
(*b*) Rule observed, even 'Illic', 'Ille', but 'illa' also occurs.

Cf. *Exempla*, pls. X–XII, whence Arndt–Tangl, op. cit., pl. 8C; *Bibl. P.L.H.*, p. 291, 'saec. VIII/IX'; Beer, *Codices Graeci et Latini photographice depicti*, tom. XIII (Sijthoff, Leyden, 1909), Praefatio, p. xxiv, whence Ihm, *Pal. Lat.*, pl. VII.

6. León Eccl. Cathedr. 15. saec. IX. (Clark's photos.)

(*a*) No **ti**-distinction: 'erudi**ti**onis', 'an**ti**ociam'.
(*b*) Regular, even 'Illis' and 'Illi'.

Cf. Beer–Diaz Jimenez, pp. 16 ff., who date the upper script in the tenth century: 'medio vel declinante IX. saec.', p. xvi of Prooemium to *Legis Romanae Wisigothorum fragmenta ex codice palimpsesto sanctae Legionensis ecclesiae protulit, illustravit ac sumptu publico edidit regia historiae Academia Hispana*, Matriti (1896); *Theodosiani libri XVI*, edd. Mommsen et Meyer, I. 1, p. lxx.

[1] These leaves as well as fols. 21–2 of Paris Nouv. acq. lat. 1629 formed part of Autun 27 which unfortunately I have seen only in facsimiles. Professor Lindsay kindly informs me that the distinction is usually made in the minuscule part of the manuscript, but not as in later Visigothic manuscripts, the assibilation being represented by **ʒ** or some similar form. But cases of **ʒ** for the hard sound as well as of ordinary **ti** for the soft sound also occur. It is very important to note that no distinction is made in the cursive portions.

7. *London Egerton 1934. saec. IX in. ut vid.

(*a*) No **ti**- distinction: '**citius**', '**diuitiis**', and '**antiquissima**'.
(*b*) Rule observed: 'Idem', 'Iberiam', 'huIus', even 'Ille'.

Cf. *Cat. Add.* (1854–75), p. 916; facs. in *Cat. of Anc. MSS. in Brit. Mus.* II, pl. 36.

8. *Monte Cassino 4. saec. IX. See Pl. 3 (*pl. 3*).

(*a*) No **ti**-distinction: 'sapien**ti**am', '**ti**bi'. But in cursive marginal notes entered apparently by a later hand ꝗ is regularly used for assibilated **ti**: 'senten**ti**am'.
(*b*) Rule observed. Usually 'Ille', but occasionally 'illa', 'illum'.

Cf. *Bibliotheca Casinensis*, I. 97, and facsimile. The date (saec. VII) can hardly be correct.

9. *Monte Cassino 19. saec. IX. (*59*)

(*a*) No **ti**-distinction: 'ra**ti**o' and 're**ti**nere'. But cursive additions by a later hand have ꝗ to mark assibilation.
(*b*) Rule observed, even 'Illa', also 'aIt'.

Cf. *Bibliotheca Casinensis*, I. 233, and facsimile. Their date is saec. VII, which is hardly possible.

10. Escorial & I. 14. saec. IX ut vid.

(*a*) No **ti**-distinction: 'inven**ti**one' and 'dogma**ti**bus'.
(*b*) Rule observed: 'Id', 'In', 'Ignem', 'cuIus', 'deInde', even 'Ibi'.

Cf. *Exempla*, pl. XIII; *N.A.* VI. 250; *Bibl. P.L.H.*, p. 70, and earlier Pertz's *Archiv* VIII. 815; *Rev. Bénéd.* XXVII (1910), 2.

11. Madrid Tolet. 14. 24 (now 10018). saec. IX ut vid.

(*a*) No **ti**-distinction: 'gra**ti**a', 'iumen**ti**s'.
(*b*) Rule observed, even 'Illis', 'Illorum'.

Cf. *Exempla*, pl. XVIII; *N.A.* VI. 318; *Bibl. P.L.H.*, p. 290.

12. *Paris Lat. 2994 (part II). saec. IX ut vid.

(*a*) No **ti**-distinction: 'conpara**ti**one' and 'pecca**ti**'.
(*b*) Rule observed, even 'Ille', 'pro(h)Ibeant', 'coItu'.

Cf. Delisle, *Mélanges*, p. 54, and *Facs. de l'École des Chartes*, pl. 281.

13. Paris Lat. 8093. saec. IX ut vid. (Vollmer's photos).

(*a*) No **ti**-distinction: 'sep**ti**es', 'Ingen**ti**a', and 'fluc**ti**bus'.
(*b*) Rule observed, even 'Illi'.

Cf. De Rossi, *Inscriptiones Christianae* II. 292 (where Delisle in his description dates the manuscript saec. VIII); Vollmer in *M.G.H. Auctt. Ant.*, tom. XIV, pp. xix and xl.

14. *Paris Lat. 4667 a. 828.

(*a*) No **ti**-distinction: 'Induc**ti**one' and 'u**ti**lita**ti**s'.
(*b*) Rule observed: 'Ipsius' and usually 'Ille' but also 'illis'.

Cf. *Nouveau Traité*, III. 327, and pl. 52; Delisle, *Mélanges*, p. 54; Steffens, *Lat. Pal.*[2], pl. 49; Prou, *Manuel de paléographie*[3] (1910), pl. V, no. 2.

(60) **15. Paris Lat. 12254. saec. IX ut vid.**

(*a*) No **ti**-distinction: 'lec**ti**onis', 'u**ti**lis'.
(*b*) Regular.

Cf. Delisle, *Le Cabinet des manuscrits*, III. 229 (where no mention is made of the manuscript being Visigothic. His description is: 'écriture du VIIIe siècle'). For facs. see pl. XVIII. 4.

16. León Eccl. Cathedr. 22 (CVI). post a. 839. (Vollmer's photos.)

(*a*) No **ti**-distinction: 'digna**ti**onis' and '**isti**s'.
(*b*) Rule observed.

Cf. Eguren, pp. 78–9; Beer–Diaz Jimenez, p. 23 'a. 839'; *N.A.* XXVI. 397; *M.G.H. Auctt. Ant.*, tom. XIV, p. xxxviii, 'saec. x in.', and p. xl.

17. León Eccl. Cathedr. Fragm. no. 8. saec. IX ut vid. (Vollmer's photos.)

(*a*) No **ti**-distinction: 'gra**ti**ae', 'peten**ti**'.
(*b*) Regular.

Cf. Beer–Diaz Jimenez, p. 43: 's. x' and *M.G.H. Auctt. Ant.*, tom. XIV, pp. xxxviii f.: 'saec. x'. The script is of the oldest type.

18. Barcelona Rivipullensis 46 (fly-leaves). saec. IX.

(*a*) No **ti**-distinction: 'gen**ti**um', 'composi**ti**o', and 'uagan**ti**bus'.
(*b*) Rule observed. 'Ibi' but 'ille'.

The manuscript presents several features unusual in a Visigothic manuscript, e.g. abbreviations of 'prae' and 'tur' and the Caroline symbols for 'nostri', 'per', and 'pro'.

Cf. Beer, *Die Handschriften des Klosters Santa Maria de Ripoll*, I. 33, and pl. I. (*Sitzungsberichte d. Kais. Akad. d. Wiss. in Wien*, vol. CLV (1907), 3. Abh.)

19. *Berne A. 92. 3. saec. IX ut vid.

(*a*) No **ti**-distinction: 'mali**ti**a' and 'Ira**ti**', 'damna**ti**one', 'mor**ti**ferum'.
(*b*) Rule observed.

Cf. Steffens, *Lat. Pal.*^{2}, pl. 35.

(61) **20. Madrid Univ. 31. saec. IX. (D. De Bruyne's photos of entire manuscript.)**

(*a*) No **ti**-distinction: 'le**ti**tia', 'humilia**ti**o', and 'vestimen**ti**s'. At the end of a line the ligature ꝗ is used for assibilated **ti**: 'oranꝗum', 'exultaꝗone'.
(*b*) Rule observed, even 'Illius' (often) and 'aIt'.

Cf. facs. in Merino, pl. VI; Berger, *Hist. de la Vulg.*, p. 22. The date (saec. x) in Wattenbach, *Anleit. z. lat. Pal.*^{4}, p. 22, is hardly possible.

21. *Sigüenza Capitol. Decretale 150.[1] saec. IX ut vid.

(*a*) No **ti**-distinction: 'Ius**ti**tia'. But at end of line, for economy of space, ꝗ is used for soft **ti**: 'tradiꝗonum'. Cf. preceding manuscript.

[1] These few leaves were formerly attached to the cover of 'Decretale 150' in the chapter library of Sigüenza, where they were discovered by D. De Bruyne. They contain a unique specimen of the Latin and Arabic versions of St. Paul's Epistles, and for the present are preserved in the Vatican library.

(*b*) Rule observed. 'Ihū', 'Ipsa', and 'Illa'. Also 'IudaIsmo'; 'aIs'. In the last two examples the **i**-longa splits at the top and resembles a tall **y**.

Cf. De Bruyne and Tisserant, 'Une feuille arabo-latine de l'épître aux Galates', in *Revue biblique*, July 1910 (with facsimile).

22. *Paris Nouv. acq. lat. 238. saec. IX.

(*a*) No **ti**-distinction: 'discre**ti**one' and 'sta**ti**m'.
(*b*) Rule observed, 'Illae' but also 'ille'; 'Ihū' and 'ihū'.

Cf. Delisle, *Mélanges*, pp. 60–1: 'du xe siècle'.

23. Escorial P. I. 6. saec. IX.

(*a*) No **ti**-distinction: 'contempla**ti**one' and 'dedi**ti**'.
(*b*) Rule observed.

Cf. *Exempla*, pl. XXVI: 'saec. fere decimo'; *Bibl. P.L.H.*, p. 100: 'saec. X–XI'. The script is decidedly against this recent date.

24. Albi 29. saec. IX. (*62*)

(*a*) No **ti**-distinction: 'to**ti**us', 'par**ti**bus', 'orien**ti**s'. ꝗ is used indifferently but more often for soft **ti**.
(*b*) Regular, even 'deInde', 'deInc', 'proInde'.

Cf. facs. in *Catalogue général des manuscrits des bibliothèques publiques des départements*, I (1849), 487.

25. *La Cava I (formerly 14) Danila Bible. saec. IX post med.

(*a*) No **ti**-distinction: 'genera**ti**one' and 'eun**ti**bus'.
(*b*) Rule observed: 'Ibi', 'Ibant', but 'illuc'.

Cf. facs. in Silvestre, *Paléogr. universelle*, III. pl. 141, and two plates in *Cod. Diplom. Cavens.*, tom. I, Manoscritti membranacei, p. 1, where it is put in the eighth century. For its proper date see A. Amelli, *De libri Baruch vetustissima latina versione*, etc. *Epistola ad Antonium M. Ceriani* (Monte Cassino, 1902), pp. 7 and 14: Berger, *Hist. de la Vulg.*, p. 15.

This is by far the finest product of Spanish penmanship and book-decoration known to me.

26. Madrid. Univ. 32. saec. IX ut vid. (D. De Bruyne's photos.)

(*a*) No **ti**-distinction.
(*b*) Rule observed.

Cf. facs. in Merino, pl. VI; Berger, *Hist. de la Vulg.*, pp. 15 ff.

27. Toledo Capitol. 99. 30. saec. IX.

(*a*) No **ti**-distinction: 'e**ti**am', 'at**ti**ngo'.
(*b*) Rule observed.

Cf. *Exempla*, pl. XVI.

28. *Paris Nouv. acq. lat. 2168. saec. IX ut vid.

(*a*) No **ti**-distinction: 'pestilen**ti**a'.
(*b*) Rule observed, even 'Illis'.

Cf. Delisle, *Mélanges*, p. 76: 'du xe siècle'.

29. Manchester John Rylands Library MS. Lat. 104 (116). saec. IX ex. ut vid. (Lindsay's photo.)

(*a*) No **ti**-distinction: 'Ius**ti**tia', 'men**ti**s', 'cogita**ti**one'.

(63) (*b*) Rule observed: 'Iste', 'Ipse', 'Ideo', 'Ille', but more often 'ille'; also 'ihs̄'. **i**-longa with forked top in 'aIt', 'esaIas', etc.

Cf. facs. in *New Palaeographical Society*, pl. 162.

30. *London Add. MS. 30852. saec. IX ex. ut vid.

(*a*) No **ti**-distinction: 'voca**ti**one', 'uitiorum', and '**ti**bi'.

(*b*) Rule observed, even 'Ille'.

Cf. *Cat. Add.* (1876–81), p. 121; facs. in *Cat. of Anc. MSS. of Brit. Mus.* II, pl. 37.

31. *Paris Nouv. acq. lat. 2170 (Part I). saec. IX ut vid.

(*a*) No **ti**-distinction: 'e**ti**am' and 'cunc**ti**s'.

(*b*) Rule observed.

Cf. Delisle, *Mélanges*, p. 79: 'peut remonter au xe siècle'.

32. Escorial R. II. 18 (fols 95–95v). post a. 882.

This folio contains the famous Oviedo catalogue.

(*a*) No **ti**-distinction: 'conla**ti**onum' and 'canticum'.

Cf. Muñoz, pl. IV; *N.A.* VI. 278; Becker, *Catal. Bibl. Antiq.*, p. 59; *Bibl. P.L.H.*, p. 135; Beer, pp. 376 ff.

33. Escorial P. I. 7. saec. IX ex. ut vid.[1]

(*a*) No **ti**-distinction: 'e**ti**am, 'la**ti**num', 'ius**ti**tiam'.

(*b*) Rule observed, even 'Illa'. Forked **i**-longa in 'aIt', 'esaIas'.

Cf. *Exempla*, pl. XIV; *N.A.* VI. 220, n. 4; *Bibl. P.L.H.*, p. 101.

34. Escorial T. II. 25. saec. IX ex. ut vid. (Fr. Manero's photo.)

(*a*) No **ti**-distinction: 'po**ti**us', 'mul**ti**', 'ius**ti**tie'.

(*b*) Rule observed, even 'Illis', 'proInde'. Forked **i**-longa in 'aIt'.

(64) 35. *Paris Nouv. acq. lat. 1298. saec. IX ut vid.

(*a*) No **ti**-distinction: 'e**ti**am' and 'an**ti**cam.

(*b*) Regular.

Cf. Delisle, *Mélanges*, p. 108: 'minuscule mêlée de cursive du XIe siècle'. Mixed minuscule and cursive is more in keeping with my date.

[1] This and the following manuscript have the acrostic *Adefonsi principis librum*. It has generally been assumed that this referred to Alfonso II (795–843). As the writing of these two manuscripts resembles that of some dated manuscripts of about the year 900, I am inclined to believe that Alfonso III (848–912) is meant, especially as there is historical evidence for books having been presented by the latter as well as the former. Cf. Beer, pp. 376 and 379.

36. *Paris Nouv. acq. lat. 2167. saec. IX ut vid.

(*a*) No **ti**-distinction: 'pes**ti**len**ti**a'.
(*b*) Rule observed, even 'Ihs̄' and 'Illis'.

Cf. Delisle, *Mélanges*, p. 76: 'du xe siècle'.

37. *Paris Nouv. acq. lat. 260. saec. IX ut vid.

(*a*) No **ti**-distinction: 'ui**ti**o' and 'volupta**ti**s'.
(*b*) Rule observed: 'Id', 'Ipse' but 'illo'.

Cf. Delisle, *Mélanges*, p. 114: 'du XIe siècle'.

38. *Paris Lat. 10877 (cf. Tours 615). saec. IX ex. ut vid.

(*a*) No **ti**-distinction: 'to**ti**us' and 'grega**ti**'.
(*b*) Not regular: 'incumbere', 'deinde' (with short **i**). There is something foreign about this manuscript.

Cf. Delisle, *Mélanges*, p. 54: 'probablement du xe siècle'.

39. *Paris Lat. 10876. saec. IX ex. ut vid.

(*a*) No **ti**-distinction: 'conuersa**ti**o' and 'excommunica**ti**s'.
(*b*) Not regular: 'inter', 'imperium', 'ista', 'proinde' (all with short **i**) which is a transgression of the rule. This manuscript belongs to the same school as the preceding.

Cf. Delisle, *Mélanges*, p. 54: 'probablement du xe siècle'.

40. *London Add. MS. 30854. saec. IX ex. ut vid.

(*a*) No **ti**-distinction.
(*b*) Regular; even 'Illius'.

Cf. *Cat. Add.* (1876–81), p. 121: 'x^{th} cent.'.

41. Escorial I. III. 13. saec. IX/X ut vid. (Traube's photo.)

(*a*) No **ti**-distinction.
(*b*) Regular.

Cf. *Bibl. P.L.H.*, p. 81: 'saec. x'.

42. Madrid Tolet. 14. 22 (now 10029). saec. IX/X ut vid.

(*a*) Distinction made in some parts and not in others: '**eti**am', 'paren**ti**' (no distinction); (65)
'presen**ti**a', 'na**ti**que' (with distinction). The marginalia, apparently of the same time, observe the distinction: 'depreca**ti**o'.
(*b*) Regular.

Cf. *M.G.H. Auctt. Ant.*, tom. III. 2 (1879), pp. l and lii; ibid. facs.; *N.A.* VI. 316 and 581: 'saec. x'; *Bibl. P.L.H.*, p. 284 'saec. IX/X'; *M.G.H. Auctt. Ant.*, tom. XIV, p. xxxviii.

43. *London Thompsonianus 97. [now New York Pierpont Morgan Library M. 644].[1] a. 894.

(*a*) Distinction made: 'for**ti**a' but 'duc**ti**le'.

[1] This excellently preserved manuscript (which I was privileged to examine in the library of its present owner to whom I here express my thanks) was purchased from Lord Ashburnham in 1897. The script is manifestly of the late ninth or early tenth century, and the subscription which dates it 894 (era 932) may be trusted.

(*b*) Regular, even 'Illi'.

Cf. *A descriptive catalogue of the second series of 50 manuscripts in the collection of H. Y. Thompson* (1902), p. 304.

44. Madrid Tolet. 43. 5 (now 10064). saec. IX/X ut vid.

(*a*) Distinction made; 'precedenꞇum' but 'iustissime'.
(*b*) Regular; but 'illi', also proIbendum'.

Cf. *Exempla*, pl. XVII: 's. IX si non antiquior'; *Bibl. P.L.H.*, p. 299. Reasons for my date are given below, pp. 63 f.

45. Madrid Acad. de la Hist. 20 (F. 186).[1] Loewe–Hartel, no. 22. saec. IX/X ut vid. The Bible of San Millan.

(*a*) Distinction made in first part of manuscript: 'tribulaꞇone', but 'angustia', 'canticum'. No distinction in last part of manuscript, which is by a different hand. The marginalia which are added make the distinction.
(66) (*b*) Regular, even 'Illis'. Also 'sIon', 'ebraIce', with forked **i**-longa.

Cf. *Exempla*, pl. XXV: 'saec. X'; *N.A.* VI. 332: 'saec. IX'; *Bibl. P.L.H.*, p. 500: 'saec. VIII'. According to a subscription in the manuscript its date is 662! Berger, *Hist. de la Vulg.*, p. 16. For discussion of the date see below, p. 64.

46. Madrid Tolet. 10. 25 (now 10007). a. 902.

(*a*) Distinction made by first scribe: senꞇunt' but 'celestium'. Often ȝ is used: 'exeunȝum'. No distinction by second scribe. Here the work of the corrector can be watched; he adds the tail to **i** where **t** is assibilated. On fol. 47ᵛ 'eꞇam' seems to be by second scribe. The scribe towards the end of the book uses ꞇ for assibilated **ti**. Likewise a later entry on fol. 147ᵛ makes the distinction. These valuable details I have from W. M. Lindsay.
(*b*) Regular, but 'illut', 'illo'. The second scribe has 'Itaque' occasionally with forked **i**-longa. The clubbed shafts of tall letters tend to become angular.

Cf. *Exempla*, pl. XIX; Monaci, *Facs. di antichi mss.*, pl. 88; *Bibl. P.L.H.*, p. 265.

47. Madrid Tolet. 35. 1 (now 10001). saec. IX/X ut vid.

(*a*) No **ti**-distinction: 'tertia', 'tibi'.
(*b*) Regular. Forked **i**-longa in 'aIt', 'efraIm'.

Cf. *Exempla*, pl. XXVII[a]; *Bibl. P.L.H.*, p. 296: 'saec. IX/X'.

48. León Eccl. Cathedr. 14. saec. X in. (Clark's photo.)

(*a*) No **ti**-distinction: 'tibi' and 'ratio'.
(*b*) Regular. Shafts of tall letters have angular tops.

Cf. Beer–Diaz Jimenez, p. 15.

49. Barcelona Rivipullensis 49. a. 911.

(*a*) No **ti**-distinction: 'letitia', 'abstinentie'. But ȝ is used for soft **ti** at the end of a line: 'sentenȝa'.

[1] The entire manuscript has been photographed for the Commission on the Vulgate. D. De Bruyne, one of its members, kindly allowed me to examine the photographs.

(*b*) Regular: 'Ipsa', 'Ihū', even 'Illis'.

Cf. Beer, *Die Handschriften des Klosters Santa Maria de Ripoll*, I. 34 and pls. 2 and 3 (see above, no. 18); Steffens, *Lat. Pal.*^{2}, pl. 66B (= 54 of 1st ed.). (*67*)

50. Escorial a. I. 13. saec. X in.

(*a*) Distinction made: 'Iusti**cɋ**as', 'diligen**cɋ**a'.
(*b*) Regular, even 'Illi'.

Cf. Muñoz, pl. V: 'a 912'; *Exempla*, pl. XV: 'fortasse a. 812'; *N.A.* VI. 226: 'saec. IX'; *Bibl. P.L.H.*, p. 10: 'a. 912', where the note on p. 13 contains Ewald's discussion of the date. Beer (p. 383, note and p. 384, note 3) favours 812; Traube, *Textgeschichte der Regula S. Benedicti*, p. 64 (= 662). The reasons for my date are given below, pp. 62 f.

51. Manchester John Rylands Library MS. Lat. 93. a. 914. Written at Cardeña by Gomiz. (Lindsay's photo.)

(*a*) No **ti**-distinction by original scribes: 'scien**ti**am', 'potesta**ti**bus'. But a contemporary corrector makes the distinction: 'ac**cɋ**o' (fol. 58), 'ac**cɋ**onibus' (fol. 292).
(*b*) Rule observed, but 'ille', 'ihš' (also ('Ihš'). Forked **i**-longa in 'aIt', 'hIems', 'IudaIca'.

The subscription which dates the manuscript will be published by Dr. M. R. James in his catalogue of the John Rylands MSS.

52. Escorial T. II. 24 (formerly Q. II. 24). saec. X ut vid. See Pl. 5 (*pl. 5*).

(*a*) Distinction made: 'al**cɋ**us' but 'la**ti**no', 'quaesi**cɋ**o' but 'quaes**ti**o'.
(*b*) Regular.

Cf. *Exempla*, pl. VIII (older literature given); Muñoz, pl. 3; *N.A.* VI. 272; *Bibl. P.L.H.*, p. 112; Beer, *Praefatio* to Tolet. 15. 8, p. xxiv; Steffens, *Lat. Pal.*^{2}, pl. 36 (= Suppl., pl. 17). In these works the manuscript is dated saec. VIII, saec. VIII/IX, a. 733 or 743. The grounds on which my date is based are given below, pp. 61 f.

My facsimile I owe to the courtesy of Dr. Franz Steffens to whom I here express my thanks.

53. Madrid Tolet. 15. 12 (now 10067). a. 915. (*68*)

(*a*) No **ti**-distinction by one scribe: 'e**ti**am', 'perfec**ti**onis'. Distinction made by another: 'e**cɋ**am', but 'pertimescit'. See Pl. 4 (*pl. 4*) containing a facsimile of both hands.
(*b*) Regular. One hand writes invariably 'illius'; another has 'Illo'. Also 'aIt' with forked **i**-longa. The up-strokes of the scribe who makes the **ti**-distinction are strongly clubbed and often tend to end in an angle—a feature of the early tenth century.

Cf. *Exempla*, pl. XX; *Bibl. P.L.H.*, p. 293.

54. Madrid Acad. de la Hist. 24 (F. 188). Loewe–Hartel, no. 25. a. 917 ?

(*a*) Distinction made by first scribe:[1] 'districa**cɋ**one'. No distinction at end of manuscript: 'e**ti**am', 'ra**ti**o'.
(*b*) Regular. In first part even 'Ille'. Forked **i**-longa in 'Igne'. The script is not the compact sort of the ninth century.

Cf. *Exempla*, pl. XXI; *N.A.* VI. 332; *Bibl. P.L.H.*, p. 503. The subscription which furnishes the date seems to have been tampered with. Cf. pl. in *Exempla.*

[1] These facts I learn from W. M. Lindsay. The plate in the *Exempla* reproduces the portion where no distinction is made.

55. Madrid P. 21 (now 1872). saec. x in. ut vid.

(*a*) Distinction made: 'gratias' but '**ti**tulo'.
(*b*) Regular.
Cf. *Exempla*, pl. xxviii: 'saec. x/xi'. The script is plainly against this date.

56. Escorial S. I. 16. saec. x in. ut vid.

(*a*) No **ti**-distinction: 'tris**ti**tia'.
(*b*) Regular. 'illius'. The script presents a strange appearance.
Cf. *Exempla*, pl. xxxvii: 'saec. xi ut vid.'; Eguren, p. 82. For my date see below, p. 64.

57. *Paris Nouv. acq. lat. 238 (fly-leaf). saec. x ut vid.

(*a*) Distinction made: 'positionem' but 'mar**ti**res'.
(*b*) Regular.
Cf. reference cited to no. 22.

(69) 58. *London Add. MS. 25600. a. 919.

(*a*) Distinction made: 'pudicitia', 'ius**ti**tiae', but '**ti**meant'.
(*b*) Regular, even 'Illis'.
Cf. *Cat. Add.* (1854–75), p. 208; *Facs. Pal. Soc.*, pl. 95; Arndt–Tangl, ii, pl. 36; *Cat. Anc. MSS. Brit. Mus.* ii, pl. 38.

The shafts of the letters **b, d, h, i**-longa and **l** have a prefix (or serif) at the top consisting of a small stroke made obliquely from left to right and upwards. In some manuscripts it is made at a right angle with the main shaft and often extends beyond it thus giving it the form of a mallet-head (cf. Pls. **5**, **6**, **7** (*pls.* 5, 6, 7,)). This graphic feature is noteworthy, as it is lacking in manuscripts of the preceding periods.

59. León Eccl. Cathedr. 6. a. 920. (Clark's photo.)

(*a*) Distinction made: 'editionem' but 'legeri**ti**s'.
(*b*) Regular.
Cf. Beer–Diaz Jimenez, p. 5; Berger, *Hist. de la Vulg.*, p. 17.

60. Madrid Tolet. 11. 3 [now Vit. 14–2]. a. 945. (Kept in Vitrina 2ª, Sala Iª.) (Haseloff's photo.)

(*a*) Distinction regularly made by one scribe: 'iniquum', 'uitiis' but 'ex**ti**tit'. Yet another scribe (to judge from the facsimile in Muñoz) seems unsteady in his use, for he makes the distinction in some words and not in others: 'silentium' (l. 1) but 'silen**ti**um' (l. 6); 'contemplationis' (l. 7) but 'contempla**ti**onum' (l. 4). The examples are from Muñoz's facsimile.
(*b*) Regular. The tops of tall letters have a prefix. Cf. no. 58.
Cf. Muñoz, pl. vi and p. 117.

61. *London Add. MS. 30844. saec. x ut vid.

(*a*) Distinction made: 'pretium'.
(*b*) Regular, even 'Illa'.
Cf. *Cat. Add.* (1876–81), p. 119.

62. Madrid Acad. de la Hist. 25 (F. 194). Loewe–Hartel, no. 8. a. 946. (70)

(*a*) Distinction made: 'pigritiam' but '**ti**more', 'celes**ti**a'.
(*b*) Regular, even 'Ille'; forked **i**-longa in hebraIca'.

Cf. *Exempla*, pl. XXII; *N.A.* VI. 331; *Bibl. P.L.H.*, p. 493.

63. Manchester John Rylands Library MS. Lat. 89 (99.) a. 949. Written at Cardeña (Lindsay's photo.)

(*a*) Distinction made: 'poenitentiam', 'tribulatio' but 'salu**ti**s', '**ti**more'.
(*b*) Regular. The tops of tall letters have a prefix. Cf. no. 58.

The subscription which dates and places this manuscript will be given by Dr. M. R. James in his forthcoming catalogue of the John Rylands MSS.

64. *Paris 2855 (part II). *c.* a. 951.

(*a*) Distinction made: 'actionem', but 'deser**ti**' and 'moles**ti**arum'.
(*b*) Regular, yet 'ihm̄', 'illum'.

The tops of the tall letters have a prefix. Cf. no. 58.
Cf. Delisle, *Mélanges*, p. 53, where older literature is cited; facs. see Silvestre, *Paléogr. univ.* III, pl. 206; *Facs. de l'École des Chartes*, pl. 277.

65. Escorial a. II. 9. a. 954.

(*a*) Distinction made: 'profanationibus' but 'cunc**ti**s'.
(*b*) Regular.

Script not compact. The tall shafts thicken at the top in a triangular form.

Cf. *Exempla*, pl. XXIII; *Bibl. P.L.H.*, p. 19.

66. *Paris Nouv. acq. lat. 239. saec. X.

(*a*) Distinction made: 'tris**ti**tie' but 'celes**ti**a'.

Cf. Delisle, *Mélanges*, p. 78.

67. León Eccl. Cathedr. 21 (additions on a page left blank). saec. X. (D. De Bruyne's photo.)

(*a*) Distinction made.

The script may be even more recent. It shows foreign influence, e.g. **p̄** = 'prae'; **p** with (71)
superior **o** = 'pro'; **m** with apostrophe = 'mus', etc. The Catalogue by Beer–Diaz Jimenez does not describe these additions.

68. *Florence Laur. Ashburnham 17. saec. X ex. ut vid.

(*a*) Distinction made: 'generationem' but '**ti**bi'.
(*b*) Regular, even 'Illa', 'Illius', 'Illi'.

The tops of the tall letters have a prefix. Cf. no. 58.
Cf. facs. in *Collez. fiorent.*, pl. 33; *Rivista delle bibl. e degli archivi*, XIX (1908), 5. See above p. 40, n. 4.

69. Madrid Acad. de la Hist. F. 212. Loewe–Hartel, no. 44. saec. X ex. ut vid.

(*a*) Distinction made: 'spacɉum' but 'complectitur'.

The tops of the tall letters have a prefix. Cf. no. 58.
Cf. *Exempla*, pl. XXIV: 'a. 964'; *N.A.* VI. 334: 'saec. X'; *Bibl. P.L.H.*, p. 514: 'saec. XI'.

70. *Paris Nouv. acq. lat. 2170 (last 22 leaves). saec. X ut vid.

(*a*) Distinction made: 'institucɉonis', 'oracɉone'.

Cf. Delisle, *Mélanges*, p. 79.

71. *London Add. MS. 30846. saec. X ut vid.

(*a*) Distinction made: 'supplicacɉone' but 'peccatis'.

Cf. *Cat. Add.* (1876–81), p. 120.

72. *London Add. MS. 30845. saec. X ut vid.

(*a*) Distinction made: 'cessacɉone' but 'peccatis'.

Cf. *Cat. Add.*, p. 120; facs. in *The Musical Notation of the Middle Ages* (London, 1890), pl. I.

73. Escorial d. I. 2. a. 976. (Traube's photo.)

(*a*) Distinction made: 'racɉone', 'sacerdotibus'.
(*b*) Regular. Forked i-longa in 'laici'. Tops of tall letters have prefixes.

Cf. *N.A.* VI. 238; *Bibl. P.L.H.*, p. 43; facs. in *N.A.* VIII. 357, containing a line of script and one of arabic numerals, perhaps the earliest example in a western manuscript.

(*72*) 74. *Paris Nouv. acq. lat. 2180. ante a. 992.

(*a*) Distinction made: 'ecɉam', 'iusticɉa', but 'iuventuti'.
(*b*) Regular; 'Ibi' but 'illi'.

Cf. Delisle, *Mélanges*, p. 101.

75. Escorial d. I. 1. a. 992.

(*a*) Distinction made: 'oblacɉones' but 'retinent'.
(*b*) Regular. The tops of tall letters have a prefix. Cf. no. 58.

Cf. *Exempla*, pl. XXVII*b*; *N.A.* VI. 236; *Bibl. P.L.H.*, p. 43.

76. *Paris Nouv. acq. lat. 1296. saec. X ut vid.

(*a*) Distinction made: 'aucɉo' but 'estimo', 'congestio'. This is perhaps the oldest Latin manuscript on paper; sheets of vellum are interspersed.

Cf. Delisle, *Mélanges*, p. 109: 'du XIIe siècle'.

77. *London Add. MS. 30851. saec. X/XI ut vid.

(*a*) Distinction made: 'stilancɉa'.
(*b*) Regular, even 'Illud'.

The tops of the tall letters have a prefix. Cf. no. 58.
Cf. *Cat. Add.* (1876–81), p. 120.

78. *London Add. MS. 30847. saec. XI ut vid.

(*a*) Distinction made.

Cf. *Cat. Add.* (1876–81), p. 120.

79. *Paris Nouv. acq. lat. 2179. saec. XI ut vid.

(*a*) Distinction made: 'Indignacjo' but 'quaestionarii', 'vestigia'.

Cf. Delisle, *Mélanges*, p. 95.

80. Escorial e. I. 13. saec. XI ut vid.

(*a*) Distinction made: 'geroncjus' but 'ualentinus'.

(*b*) Regular, even 'Illud'.

Tall letters are very long and have a prefix at the top. Cf. no. 58.
Cf. *Exempla*, pl. XXIX: 'saec. X/XI'.

81. *London Add. MS. 30850. saec. XI ut vid.

(*a*) Distinction made: 'oracjone' but 'uoluptati'.

Cf. *Cat. Add.* (1876–81), p. 120; facs. in *The Musical Notation of the Middle Ages*, pl. IV.

82. *Paris Nouv. acq. lat. 2178. saec. XI ut vid. (*73*)

(*a*) Distinction made: 'pacjentis.

Cf. Delisle, *Mélanges*, p. 85; facs. pl. II in catalogue of sale (1878).

83. Escorial &. II. 5. saec. XI ut vid. (Clark's photo.)

(*a*) Distinction made: 'pacjencja' but 'odisti'.

(*b*) Regular.

Cf. *Bibl. P.L.H.*, p. 75.

84. Madrid Tolet. 35. 2 (now 10110). saec. XI.

(*a*) Distinction made: 'Insurgencjum'.

Cf. *Exempla*, pl. XXX. The date 'a. 1006' is given in index on the authority of Merino. But there is much uncertainty in connection with this date. The script is very ill formed and may be older than saec. XI.

85. *Paris Nouv. acq. lat. 235. saec. XI ut vid.

(*a*) Distinction made: 'aedificacjo' but 'protinus', 'modestiam'.

The tops of the tall letters have a prefix. Cf. no. 58.
Cf. Delisle, *Mélanges*, p. 75.

86. *Paris Nouv. acq. lat. 2176. saec. XI ut vid.

(*a*) Distinction made: 'racjone' but 'multi'.

Cf. Delisle, *Mélanges*, p. 70; facs. pl. IV in catalogue of sale (1878).

87. *Paris Nouv. acq. lat. 2177. saec. XI ut vid.

(*a*) Distinction made: 'Iusticjae', 'pacjenti'.

I noted 'Iusticia' (p. 473). The use of **ci** for soft **ti** begins to creep into manuscripts during the eleventh century, and is often found after that time.—The tops of the tall letters have a prefix. Cf. no. 58.

Cf. Delisle, *Mélanges*, p. 71.

88. Escorial &. I. 3. a. 1047. (Clark's photo.)

(*a*) Distinction made: 'racȷonem' but 'con**ti**net'.

The tops of tall letters have a prefix. Cf. no. 58.

Cf. Muñoz, pl. xi, p. 121; Beer, p. 218.

(*74*) 89. *London Add. MS. 30855. saec. xi ut vid.

(*a*) Distinction made.

Cf. *Cat. Add.* (1876–81), p. 122.

90. Madrid Bibl. nacion. (Beatus super Apocalypsim.) a. 1037–65. Now kept in Vitrina 1ª, Sala Iª.

(*a*) Distinction made: 'ecȷam' but 'al**ti**tudo'.

(*b*) Regular; 'aIt' with forked **i**-longa.

Cf. Muñoz, pl. xii (where no press-mark is given).

91. Madrid Bibl. nacion. (Forum judicum from León.) a. 1058. Now kept in Vitrina 4ª, Sala Iª.

(*a*) Distinction made: 'precȷo' but 'facultatibus'.

(*b*) The tops of tall letters have a prefix. Cf. no. 58.

Cf. Muñoz, pl. xiii (no press-mark).

92. Madrid Acad. de la Hist. F. 211. Loewe–Hartel, no. 47. saec. xi ut vid.

(*a*) Distinction made: 'quaesicȷo'.

(*b*) Regular, but 'illius'. The tops of tall letters have a prefix. Cf. no. 58.

Cf. *Exempla*, pl. xxxvi.

93. Madrid Royal Private Library 2 J 5. a. 1059.

(*a*) Distinction made; 'gracȷa' but 'salu**ti**s'.

(*b*) Regular, but 'illo'. The tops of tall letters have a prefix. Cf. no. 58.

Cf. Exempla, pl. xxxii.

94. Madrid Bibl. nacion. A. 115 (now 112). saec. xi (a. 1063?)

(*a*) Distinction made: 'negocȷis'.

(*b*) Not regular: 'in' often with short **i**. Sign of decay of script. The tall letters have a prefix occasionally, as a rule they thicken at the top in the form of a triangle.

Cf. *Exempla*, pl. xxxiii, whence Arndt–Tangl[4], pl. 8d.

95. Madrid Bibl. nacion. A. 2 (now 2). saec. xi ut vid. (D. De Bruyne's photo.)

(*a*) Distinction made.

Cf. Berger, *Hist. de la Vulg.*, p. 20.

96. *Paris Nouv. acq. lat. 2171. ante a. 1067. (75)

(*a*) Distinction made: 'Ius**ti**ti am', 'forti ores'.
(*b*) Regular, but 'illum'.

Cf. Delisle, *Mélanges*, p. 68: 'première moitié du XIe siècle'; Férotin, *Le Liber Ordinum*, p. xiii.

97. León Eccl. Cathedr. 2. a. 1071. (Clark's photo.)

(*a*) Distinction made: 'ius**ti**tiam'.
(*b*) Regular.

Cf. Beer–Diaz Jimenez, p. 2.

98. *Paris Nouv. acq. lat. 2169. Completed a. 1072.

(*a*) Distinction made: 'ratione' but 'mit**ti**t', 'ques**ti**o'.
(*b*) Regular. The tops of tall letters have a prefix. Cf. no. 58.

Cf. Delisle, *Mélanges*, p. 107; Férotin, *Le Liber Ordinum*, p. xxxiii.

99. *London Add. MS. 30848. saec. XI ut vid.

(*a*) Distinction made.
(*b*) Regular: 'Illa' and 'illuc'.

Cf. *Cat. Add.* (1876–81), p. 120.

100. Madrid Acad. de la Hist. F. 192. Loewe–Hartel, no. 29. a. 1073.

(*a*) Distinction made: 'lectio' but 'noc**ti**s'.
(*b*) Regular, but 'illa'. The shafts of the tall letters have a prefix. Cf. no. 58.

Cf. *Exempla*, pl. xxxv; *N.A.* VI. 332.

101. Madrid Bibl. nacion. R. 216 (now 6367). a. 1105.

(*a*) Distinction made: 'fornicationem'.
(*b*) Regular, but 'illa'.

Cf. *Exempla*, pl. XXXVIII.

102. *London Add. MS. 11695. a. 1109 (or 1091).[1]

(*a*) Distinction made: 'condicione' but 'cons**ti**tuta'.
(*b*) Regular: 'Ipsius', even 'Illa'.

The tops of tall letters have a prefix. Cf. no. 58.

Cf. Delisle, *Mélanges*, p. 60; *Facs. Pal. Soc.*, pls. 48, 49; Arndt–Tangl^{4}, pl. 37; *Facs. de l'École des Chartes*, no. 353. Coloured facs. in Westwood's *Pal. Sacra Pict.*

103. Madrid Archiv. hist. nacion. 989–B. Vitrina 40. a. 1110. (76)

(*a*) 'palacio': **ci** is used for assibilated **ti**. The spelling on the whole is that of an ignorant notary.

Cf. facs. in Muñoz, pl. XIV (where no press mark is given).

[1] The subscription which gives us the date is not quite clear. Cf. Prou, *Manuel de paléog.*^{3} (1910), p. 101, n. 4.

104. *Rome Corsinian. 369 (formerly 40 E 6). saec. XII.

(*a*) Distinction made in Visigothic portion: 'cogniɑɉo', 'persecuɑɉonis'. The non-Visigothic hand often writes **ci** for assibilated **ti.**

In Visigothic script are fols. 144–56 and additions on fol. 106.[1] The rest of the manuscript is in ordinary minuscule by contemporaneous hand. This is the sixth example known to me of a Spanish manuscript in Italy. It has been correctly described by Zacarias García: 'Un nuevo manuscrito del comentario sobre el apocalipsis de San Beato de Liebana', in *Razón y fé* XII (August 1905), pp. 478–93. The manuscript is palaeographically very instructive. The Visigothic script in it is impure, showing a mixture of ancient and foreign elements, especially in the abbreviations. The tops of tall letters as in other recent manuscripts have a prefix. Cf. Pl. **7** (*pl.* 7).

Evidence of corrections, additions, and documents

The above evidence is instructively supplemented by a consideration of the following corrections and additions, and by the testimony of notarial documents.

In Escorial T. II. 24 (formerly Q. II. 24) on line 6 of fol. 73 (cf. *Exempla*, pl. VIII) the scribe originally wrote 'quesitio' with the assibilated form of **ti.** The word, however, should have been 'questio'. The corrector who crossed out the superfluous **i** also changed the form of the second **i.**

(77) One of the scribes of Madrid Tolet. 10. 25, a. 902, does not make the **ti**-distinction. In this part of the manuscript the activity of the corrector is plainly noticeable: he adds the tail to the **i** where **ti** has the soft sound.

The scribe or scribes of Manchester John Rylands Library MS. 93 make no distinction, but contemporary additions have it (fols. 58, 292) and a later corrector changes the ordinary form of **ti** to ɑɉ where it is assibilated, e.g. on fol. 129.

The MS. Madrid Acad. de la Hist. 20 (F. 186) shows a wavering in the matter of the **ti**-distinction. The marginalia, which seem to me by a later hand, invariably observe it. The same indecision with regard to the **ti**-usage is found in Madrid Tolet. 10. 25. The later entry on fol. 147^{v} makes the distinction.

The documents which I have been able to study in the facsimiles of Muñoz furnish data which may fairly be regarded as confirming the evidence of the manuscripts.[2]

[1] The additions, it seems, escaped the notice of García. As they occur in the non-Visigothic portion of the manuscript they furnish further evidence for his contention that the whole manuscript was written in Spain.

[2] The earliest examples of Visigothic cursive show no **ti**-distinction, as we learn from the cursive pages of Autun 27 (cf. p. 40, n. 4). There is likewise no distinction in the Escorialensis of Augustine ('Camarín de las reliquias') in the cursive part containing the *Benedictio cerei.* But this writing, as Traube has pointed out (*Nomina Sacra*, p. 191, n. 1), must not be regarded as Spanish.

In a document of 857 (Muñoz, pl. 16) ʒ is used for assibilated **ti**, but not ꞇ.[1]

In a document of 898–929 (Muñoz, pl. 17) no distinction is made, **ci** doing service for assibilated **ti**. But in a document of 904 (Muñoz, pl. 18) we have the distinction: 'preꞇo' but 'dedis**ti**s'.

It is needless to enumerate the later documents. As a rule the distinction is made as in manuscripts. Occasionally it happens that ꞇ is used indiscriminately (cf. Muñoz, pls. 22 and 41). In the more recent documents **ci** is used for assibilated **ti**. Yet in a document of 1137 (Muñoz, pl. 42) the two forms of **ti** are still strictly differentiated: 'uendiꞇones' but '**ti**bi'.

Results. Criterion for dating (78)

A study of the usage illustrated by the foregoing data gives us the following facts with regard to **ti**-forms in Visigothic manuscripts.

1. The distinction is never found in manuscripts which are indisputably of the eighth or early ninth century.

2. The distinction is invariably made in the more recent manuscripts, beginning (to use the safest limits) with the second half of the tenth century and extending to the twelfth, i.e. as long as the script lasts.

3. Certain manuscripts, written between the two periods indicated, show a wavering in usage, one scribe making the distinction and another not; or one scribe making it in some cases and not in others.

There can be but one interpretation of these facts. The custom of making the **ti**-distinction in book-script was consciously introduced. This graphic innovation, which on the face of it has something formal and conventional (since the ligature ʒ, which did service for assibilated **ti** in cursive, was rejected as unsuitable in book-hand), was in all probability introduced in connection with liturgical books, where a need was felt of facilitating the reading aloud. The form ꞇ was to tell the reader at once that he should give the soft sound of **t**. As such scribal changes, however, are adopted slowly, and reach some schools much sooner than others, it need not surprise us that scribes of one school should continue in the old way long after those of another had adopted the new one. The absence of the **ti**-distinction may therefore say less to us than its presence. Its presence is at once a hint that the manuscript is not of the oldest kind. But there are manuscripts in which one scribe makes the

[1] In the cursive portion of Escorial R. II. 18 (ante a. 779) assibilated **ti** is regularly represented by ʒ. The same is true of the additions in cursive found in many manuscripts posterior to the eighth century.

distinction and another does not.[1] These are manifestly manuscripts of the transition period, in which the struggle between the old and the new can be wit-
(79) nessed, the younger scribe adopting the innovation, the older persisting in his old-fashioned way as he had been taught. The fact that these manuscripts were written, as both the dated and the undated manuscripts show, precisely in the interval between two periods the first of which displays the invariable absence, the second the invariable presence of the distinction, is the best possible proof that the custom of making the distinction was then in the actual process of adoption by the various schools of Spain. The question as to which centre was first to practise the distinction and which were the centres more backward about doing so must be left for further investigation.

What are the more precise limits of the transition period? The earliest dated example known to me of a manuscript with the **ti**-distinction is Thompsonianus 97 [Pierpont Morgan M. 644], written, according to a subscription, in the year 894. As the form of the letters corresponds to that of other dated manuscripts of the same time, there is no reason for questioning the originality of the subscription. The latest dated example known to me of a manuscript in which the scribe shows insecurity in his usage is of the year 945.[2] As several dated manuscripts which fall between 894 and 945 show the **ti**-distinction (at least by one hand), it is fair to consider these two dates as the extreme limits of the transition period. From all this it must follow that a manuscript without the distinction is in all probability older than 894 (as many manuscripts of the type of Thompsonianus 97 still ignore the distinction); that on the other hand a manuscript with the **ti**-distinction is hardly older than 894, and in most cases much younger.

The manuscripts which may be pointed out as disputing the criterion just formulated are, I believe, so few in number that they could fairly be regarded as mere exceptions to a rule. But such manuscripts remain exceptions only if
(80) we accept their traditional dates.[3] If we can show those dates to be untenable or improbable on palaeographical grounds the validity of the **ti**-criterion will thus at once be both tested and confirmed. This I shall attempt to do. I preface my argument with a few remarks on the script as such.

Briefly, we may distinguish four stages of development:

[1] Cf. in my list [above] the numbers 42, 45, 46, 53, 54, and 60.

[2] Cf. no. 60 of list. It is only fair to note that this statement is based on a facsimile of Muñoz which is less trustworthy than a photograph. The photographs which I had of this manuscript showed the distinction regularly.

[3] Although with great hesitation, I have ventured to disagree with the date given by Delisle in the case of nos. 35 and 37 of my list. If his dates are correct, I should be at a loss to explain the **ti** usage in these manuscripts.

(*a*) The first stage is exemplified in the oldest manuscripts, saec. VIII–IX. The script has striking compactness. The pen-stroke is not fine. The shaftless letters are rather broad, the arcs of **m, n,** and **h** are low; their last stroke turns in. The separation of words is imperfect. The point of interrogation is usually a later addition. The suspensions 'bus' and 'que' are generally denoted by a semi-colon placed above **b** and **q** (cf. Pl. **3** (*pl. 3*)).

(*b*) The second stage is illustrated by the manuscripts of the end of the ninth and the beginning of the tenth century. The script is looser and larger; the shafts of tall letters are club-shaped; the shaftless letters have more height than breadth; the final stroke of **m, n, h** often turns out. The separation of words is more distinct; the interrogation point is used. The suspensions 'bus' and 'que' are represented now by means of the semi-colon, now by means of an **s**-like flourish (cf. Pl. **4** (*pl. 4*)).

(*c*) The third stage is seen in manuscripts of the tenth and eleventh centuries. The letters are better spaced; the pen-stroke is often fine. The body of the letters is rather tall and narrow. The final stroke of **m, n, h,** etc., regularly turns out. Particularly characteristic are the shafts of tall letters, which end in a little hook or mallet-head. The suspensions 'bus' and 'que' are denoted by an **s**-like flourish placed above **b** and **q,** i.e. the semi-colon of the first stage is here made in one conventionalized stroke (cf. Pls. **5** and **6** (*pls. 5 and 6*)).

(*d*) The last stage of the script is characterized by the decay and awkward- (*81*)
ness of the old forms and the employment of foreign elements (cf. Pl. **7** (*pl. 7*)).

The **ti**–*criterion tested.* We are now in a position to test the **ti**-criterion. I select first the most important exception. The MS. Escorial T. II. 24 (formerly Q. II. 24)[1] containing the Etymologies of Isidore has long enjoyed the distinction of being the oldest dated manuscript in the script (see Pl. **5** (*pl. 5*)). The traditional date is 733 or 743. A computal note in the text (fol. 68) says: 'usque in hanc presentem eram que est DCCLXXI', which is the year 733. A few lines below occurs: 'usque in hanc praefatam DCCLXXXI eram' which is the year 743. One of these dates is plainly wrong. From the calculation in the text it appears that 743 is the correct year. In the judgement of Eguren, Muñoz y Rivero, Ewald and Loewe, Beer, and Steffens, not to mention older authorities, the script did not seem to belie the date established by the computal note. Steffens gives 743 as the date of his facsimile, but he is cautious

[1] For literature see no. 52 of the list.

enough to add: 'unter der Voraussetzung, daß jene Eintragung ein Original ist und nicht etwa eine Abschrift aus einem anderen Codex.' R. Beer, in his learned Praefatio to the reproduction of the Toletanus 15. 8 compared that manuscript with Escorial T. II. 24, thus trying to determine the age of the undated manuscript by the aid of the presumably dated one. He says of our manuscript: 'litterae sunt aliquanto altiores ductusque magis tenues', thus pointing out essential differences. But when he continues and says 'sed utriusque libri scriptura, ut ex *Exempl. Scr. Visig.* tab. VIII et ex tab. 17 supplementi Steffensiani perspicere licet, in universum non est dispar', he seems to me to be withdrawing his earlier judgement just quoted. It is also plain that a certain calligraphic difference escaped Beer's notice: one manuscript uses only one form for **ti**, the other two distinct forms. But indeed a careful examination of the script of the Escorialensis will disclose other traits foreign
(82) to the oldest type of Visigothic writing. Foremost is the general impression already noted by Beer: the proportions of the letters, their relation to one another. It is plainly not the old, compact, broadly flowing writing. In the oldest manuscripts the **m** and **n** and the arch of **h** all turn inward. In the Escorialensis and the more recent manuscripts these strokes thicken at the end and turn out. In the older type the letter **ǵ** has often a rather short and curved down-stroke, in the Escorialensis and the more recent type of manuscripts it is very long. But the unfailing earmark of the recent type is the hook or mallet-shaped end of the shafts of **b**, **d**, **h**, **i**-longa, and **l**, which is unknown in the oldest manuscripts. The Escorialensis has such shafts.[1] The abbreviation sign over **b** and **q** for 'bus' and 'que' has the form of an uncial **s** as in the more recent type of manuscripts (cf. Pl. **5** (*pl. 5*)). In short, purely graphic considerations are against the traditional date of 743. I may state my conviction that the computal note is merely a copied one, and that Escorial T. II. 24 may be fairly held to confirm the value of **ti** as a criterion for dating.

The manuscript Escorial a. I. 13[2] furnishes an excellent instance of the caution with which the inscriptions and subscriptions of Spanish manuscripts must be used.[3] According to a note in cursive on fol. 186^{v} the manuscript was written 'regnante adefonso principe in era DCCCCL', i.e. in 912. Ewald has pointed out that in 912 there was no reigning Alphonse, as Alphonse III had died in 910. By assuming that the scribe inserted a superfluous C he gets era DCCCL

[1] More precisely one of the scribes of this manuscript whose writing is seen in our plate. The facsimile in the *Exempla* shows another hand which does not make this type of shaft.

[2] For literature see no. 50 of list.

[3] Other examples are not wanting. Cf. nos. 33, 34, 45, 52, 84, and 102 of list.

corresponding to 812, which agrees with the reign of Alphonse II (795–843) and thus 812 was (presumably) the date of the manuscript. Muñoz has 912. The description in the *Exempla* is 'fortasse 812', the reservation being doubt- (*83*)
less a concession by Ewald to Loewe. For according to the latter's notes as edited by Hartel the date of the manuscript was 912 and not 812. Ewald's explanation did not seem thoroughly convincing to Traube. But Beer's date is 812. In connection with one of the Codices Ovetenses mentioned in the inventory of 882 he notes: 'es ist zweifellos der heutige Escorialensis a. I. 13 "de la yglesia de Oviedo" (vgl. Loewe–Hartel, S. 10 ff.), dessen Beschreibung in allen wesentlichen Stücken mit der vorliegenden übereinstimmt. Durch diese Identifikation wird auch die Datierung (des ersten Teiles des Codex) 812 (Jahr der Alphonsischen Schenkung, nicht 912) gestützt.' But cannot the Escorialensis be a copy of a manuscript which was presented in 812 and catalogued in 882? Against this early date, however, is the script of the manuscript, which is not of the old type. The letters are somewhat irregular and awkward, which lends the script an appearance of antiquity. The shafts of tall letters thicken at the end. The upright strokes of **m** and **n** thicken below and turn out. The abbreviation sign over **b** and **q** is an **s**-like flourish. Judged by purely graphic standards the manuscript should belong at the beginning of the tenth century. As for the subscription the very nature of the error in it hints that it was copied from an original having DCCCL. The scribe unconsciously inserted the extra C because he was accustomed to writing DCCCC—a type of mistake we commit every January. Thus though the year 912 need not be the exact date when the manuscript was copied, it is more than likely that it was written after era 900, which would fully account for the presence of the **ti**-distinction, not found in the manuscripts of the beginning of the ninth century.

The manuscript Madrid Tolet. 43. 5[1] shows a cruder and less calligraphic type of writing than the manuscript just considered and that perhaps lends it an impression of antiquity. But it lacks all resemblance to the earliest kind of (*84*)
Visigothic writing, having the same features as those noted in Escorial a. I. 13. The editors of the *Exempla* date it 'saec. IX, si non antiquior'. Again I believe we have a sort of compromise between the *duumviri*. For Loewe's more precise description (in *Bibl. P.L.H.*, p. 299) makes distinct mention of the more recent character of the script. 'Die Hs gehört jedenfalls dem IX. Jahrhundert: *sie zeigt nicht die alte gedrückte Schrift wie der Toletaner Isidor* [the same

1 Cf. no. 44 of list.

script as my Pl. **3**], zeigt aber denselben Charakter wie spätere Hss.'—This manuscript makes the **ti**-distinction. It shows the more recent type of writing. Loewe's own words tend to confirm the validity of the **ti**-criterion.

The manuscript Madrid Acad. de la Hist. 20 (F. 186)[1] is another of those upon the date of which scholars have expressed the most divergent opinions. According to a subscription it was written in 662, and even this date has had its supporter. The editors of the *Exempla* put it in the tenth century, yet in their separate reports Ewald and Loewe give different dates. The former says 'saec. IX' the latter 'saec. VIII'. Again I believe that the awkwardness of the script was mistaken for antiquity. But the script is against an early date. The opinion expressed in the *Exempla* is most likely correct. The fact that the **ti**-distinction is made in one part of the volume and not in another is surely not without importance in dating this manuscript.

The manuscript Escorial S. I. 16[2] has for some inexplicable reason been put into the eleventh century by the editors of the *Exempla.* I believe that no study of its script could leave this date unchallenged. According to Eguren the manuscript is by two centuries older. To be sure Eguren is
(*85*) trying to identify the manuscript with one mentioned in the Oviedo inventory of the year 882, which may perhaps have biased him in favour of an anterior date. But even if we do not fully agree with his statement that 'the character of the script employed in this important manuscript corresponds to the first half of the ninth century' it is still much nearer the truth than the date given by Ewald and Loewe. The manuscript makes no **ti**-distinction. And if, as I believe, my date is right, it furnishes no exception to the **ti**-criterion established by our investigation.

Where there is so much dispute and uncertainty, pure palaeography will have to say the last word. I believe that in the long run we are less apt to go wrong in the matter of dating, if we respect the hints learned from a careful study of the script than if we allow ourselves to be guided purely by inner evidence. The letter is less likely to prove misleading than a subscription. The latter may be copied; but the scribe did not and could not disguise his hand. The form of the letters he made infallibly betrays his epoch.

[1] For literature see no. 45 of list.
[2] For literature see no. 56 of list.

NOTES ON THE PLATES (*86*)

Pl. 1. Vercelli CLXXXIII. saec. VIII.

An excellent example of north Italian book-cursive. Superior **a** is frequent, **i**-longa occurs regularly initially (ll. 2, 5) and also medially, **ꝗ** is used indifferently (l. 11). Noteworthy is the form of **z** (l. 11). Of the many abbreviations may be mentioned: **nī, nā, nām** = nostri, nostra, nostram: **nͦ** = nunc, **pͦ** = pro, **pͭ** = post, **qͦ** = quo, **uͦ** = vero, **t** with horizontal flourish = ter, **t** with vertical wavy stroke = tur.

Pl. 2. Paris Lat. 653. saec. VIII/IX

A specimen of transition writing. Our facsimile reproduces two hands. The first shows cursive traditions; it uses **i**-longa, **ꝗ** (for soft **ti**), the ligatures of **ri, st,** etc. Characteristic is the **r** with the shoulder extending over the following letter. The second hand lacks **i**-longa, **ꝗ,** ligatures of **ri, st,** etc., and represents the more modern tendency. Abbreviations are frequent. Noteworthy are **ns̄r** = noster (5 times), **nēr** = noster, **n̄m̄** = nostrum (also **nr̄m**), **nōris** = nostris, **n̄** = nostro (once), **uēri** = vestri; **mīa** and **m̄ā** = misericordia. For some of these details I am indebted to Dr. A. Souter.

Pl. 3. Monte Cassino 4. saec. IX in.

Visigothic writing of the first period. The **ti**-distinction is not made (ll. 1, 2, etc.) in the text. An addition in the margin has **ꝗ** for soft **ti** (l. 3). Note the abbreviation of 'bus' and 'que'. The last stroke of **m, n,** and **h** turns in. The tall letters have simple shafts. Observe that a Cassinese scribe of the eleventh century transcribed the Visigothic marginal entry in cursive.

Pl. 4. Madrid Tolet. 15. 12 [now 10067]. a. 915.

A manuscript of the transition period. Our facsimile shows two hands. Col. 1 represents the more modern style, with **cꝗ** for soft **ti** (ll. 1, 2, 6). The vertical strokes of **m** and **n** thicken and turn out, the tall letters end in thick clubs, the letters are rather well spaced. The **us**-symbol (*87*)
is made in one **s**-like flourish. The hand of col. 2 shows the old school. The **ti**-distinction is not made (ll. 13 and 14). The letters are not so well spaced. **m, n,** and **h** recall the oldest type. The tall letters have simple shafts. The **us**-symbol is made in two strokes. The plate is taken from Ewald and Loewe.

Pl. 5. Escorial. T. II. 24 (formerly Q. II. 24). saec. X.

The palaeographical features to which attention should be called are: (1) the general spacing and height of letters. (2) The vertical strokes of **m, n, i,** etc., which thicken and turn out. (3) The prefix at the end of tall letters. (4) The **s**-like stroke for **us.** (5) The use of **cꝗ** for soft **ti.** These graphic peculiarities place the manuscript in the tenth century.

Pl. 6. Escorial d. I. 1. a. 992.

Our facsimile illustrates the third stage of Visigothic calligraphy, when the script had already reached the highest point and was beginning to decline. The graphic features noted in Pl. **5** (*pl.* 5) also characterize this manuscript, only the writing is more formed and more regular. The plate is taken from Ewald and Loewe.

Pl. 7. Rome Corsinian. 369. saec. XII.

A specimen of Visigothic writing in its last stage, showing the decay of traditional forms. The abbreviation of **tur** and the **us**-symbol show the continental influence to which the script succumbed.

The Naples Manuscript of Festus; its Home and Date

(917) THE traditional belief that Rallus brought the manuscript from Illyria seems to be based on hearsay evidence, which scholars are inclined to regard with scepticism, since it emanates from Giombatista Pio, a not altogether reliable source in the case of the Festus MS. (Müller, Praefatio to his edition, p. ii, n. 2; P. de Nolhac, *La bibliothèque de Fulvio Orsini*, p. 213; Sabbadini, *Le scoperte*, etc., p. 145). If there may be a legitimate doubt as to whether or not the manuscript came to Italy from Illyria, there can, on the other hand, thanks to the aid of palaeography, be no doubt that the manuscript did not originate in Illyria.

Unfortunately we are not in a position to compare our manuscript of Festus with manuscripts known to have been written in Illyria during the eleventh or twelfth century. But we have a not inconsiderable number of manuscripts which were executed in Dalmatia, the maritime province to the south-west of Illyria. These manuscripts are in the *Littera Beneventana*. In fact the Dalmatian manuscripts show that peculiar kind of Beneventan writing which is found in the manuscripts and documents of Bari and its vicinity. In other words, the Dalmatian scribes manifestly took as their models the manuscripts of their nearest neighbours across the Adriatic. It seems then not unreasonable to suppose that a manuscript written in Illyria during the eleventh–twelfth centuries would have also shown that type of Beneventan writing. Be this as it may, the Festus MS. is not in Beneventan. It furnishes an unmistakable example of the type of minuscule which flourished in Rome and its vicinity. In fact a careful comparison of the Festus MS. with, say, Vatic. lat. 378, which was written at Rome toward the end of the eleventh century, discloses such striking similarities as to render it highly probable that the manuscript of Festus was written in Rome itself. In support of this view mention may be made of the following features common to both manuscripts:

1. The general impression; the awkwardness of the script; the coarse pen-strokes.
2. The form of **r**, with the stem slanting to the right; the use of capital **S** at the end of the line; the two forms of **d**, the uncial form having the shaft bent back above the loop in a horizontal line, so as to resemble an **o**

From *Berliner Philologische Wochenschrift*, 1911, no. 29, cols. 917–18.

with a long fore-stroke.

3. The use of rustic capitals for colophons, captions, and for the first letter of a sentence. *(918)*
4. The form of the abbreviation-stroke, a horizontal line traced from left to right and ending in a hook bent downward.
5. The manner of abbreviating the syllables 'bis', 'mus', 'mur', 'que', 'runt', 'rum', 'tur', 'tus'.
6. The use of the characteristic initials with interlaced vine-pattern upon a coloured background, the pattern itself being left uncoloured.

On the date of the Festus MS. different views have been expressed. According to Thewrewk (Preface to the facsimile, p. 1) Mommsen and Hülsen favour the tenth century, O. Müller and Keil the eleventh; Janelli dates it 'saec. XI vel XII' (Müller, Praef. p. iv). The MS. Vatic. lat. 378 must have been written toward the end of the eleventh century, since the entry recording the death of Leo Ostiensis is a later addition. Our manuscript of Festus seems older or at least as old as Vatic. lat. 378, and may be considered of the second half of the eleventh century.

The Date of Codex Rehdigeranus

(569) In view of the forthcoming new edition of the Codex Rehdigeranus (Breslau MS. R 169) of the Gospels (*l*), a few words on the subject of its date and script may be of interest.[1]

The Codex Rehdigeranus is written in bastard uncials of a style found in a number of eighth-century manuscripts, of which the Ambrosian Gregory (MS. B. 159 sup.) from Bobbio, written about A.D. 750 at the command of Abbot Anastasius, is perhaps most like our manuscript (see *Pal. Society*, I. 121).[2] In the strong contrast between fine and shaded strokes, in the tapering off of the heavy vertical strokes in a fine hair-line, the uncials of the Rehdigeranus bear some resemblance to Greek uncials of the Slavonic type. The scribe is not expert; his letters lack regularity and finish; he is manifestly unaccustomed to the uncial hand.

(570) He probably wrote in the first half of the eighth century—hardly before that, and surely not much later. The use of the abbreviation $\overline{\text{QNM}}$ = quoniam, the omission of **N** in the middle of a word in the middle of the line (RESPŌDIT, fol. 273^{v}), the occasional use of **i**-longa initially (IUSTI, IUDAEI, IN, etc.), the fairly frequent separation of words, and the whole character of the script make a date anterior to the year 700 quite unlikely. On the other hand, the original scribe must antedate the year 800 since the uncial additions on fol. 273^{v} and the cursive insertion on fol. 92^{v} are still of the eighth century.

The cursive script on the page containing the Capitulare Evangelii (Morin in *Rev. Bénéd.* XIX. 1 ff.) possesses unmistakable earmarks of north Italian notarial products. It is interesting to note that **ci** occurs often for assibilated **ti** ('abumina**ci**onem', 'desola**ci**onis'), a spelling which at that time must have been common in Aquileia, Ravenna, and neighbouring towns.

From *The Journal of Theological Studies*, XIV (1913), 569–70.

[1] The new edition has been undertaken by Dr. Heinrich Vogels of the University of Munich, who generously supplied me with photographs and with such information as was necessary for forming a palaeographical judgement.

[2] A similar, though somewhat older, style of unicals we have in codex *q* (Munich MS. 6224, saec. VII, from Freising; see *Old Lat. Bibl. Texts*, no. III). The liturgical additions in cursive (facs. in Chroust's *Mon. Pal.*, ser. I, Lief. VI, pl. I) bear such a striking resemblance to the cursive addition in *l* (fol. 92^{v}), likewise liturgical in character, as to seem to be the work of one hand.

The corrector who made the extensive addition in uncials on fol. 273v and added *passim* the then modern punctuation may reasonably be assigned to the latter part of the eighth century. Of palaeographical interest is his regular use of a line surmounted by a dot to indicate omitted **m**, and his employment of three dots (·.·) arranged in a triangle, with base atop, as the point of interrogation—a style of interrogation sign not peculiar to the corrector of our manuscript, for it is found in some other Italian manuscripts. The value of the three dots thus arranged—as will be shown elsewhere—is precisely the same as that of the ordinary point of interrogation made of three strokes (or curves). Both signs indicate the modulation of voice required in an interrogative sentence, and signify an up, followed by a down, followed by an up again, so that ·.· is the equivalent of ∿.

(v)

The Beneventan Script

HISTORY OF THE SOUTH ITALIAN MINUSCULE

PREFACE AND INTRODUCTION

> Absit tamen ut hac in re magisterii partes mihi arrogem. Quippe in republica litteraria omnes liberi sumus. Leges ac regulas proponere omnibus licet, imponere non licet. Praevalent istae, si veritate ac recto judicio fulciantur: sin minus, ab eruditis et recte sentientibus merito reprobantur.
>
> J. MABILLON

THE present work is an essay in regional palaeography. Its inception goes back to my student days at the University of Munich. My master, Ludwig Traube, had proposed to me the thesis 'Monte Cassino as a centre for the transmission of Latin classics'. After spending some time on this subject it became clear that adequate treatment of it would be possible only after acquiring such a knowledge of the peculiar script used at Monte Cassino as would enable me to make sound and independent judgements with regard to the dates of Monte Cassino manuscripts, that is, manuscripts written in the Beneventan or south Italian minuscule. Thus I conceived the idea of making a careful study of the script employed throughout the lower half of the Italian peninsula.

Traube made no objection to my working on a subject of my own choice; but with characteristic generosity put at my disposal his entire library, his very large collection of facsimiles, and even some of his own notes. Owing to my ill health I had not the fortune to put into Traube's hands the completed study. But I had at least the satisfaction of knowing that he approved of the results reached before his death. All who knew Traube know that he was like a father to his pupils. No one can feel more keenly than I the loss my work has suffered by want of his guidance and criticism; and the best verdict I could hope for upon this book would be that it was at least conceived in Traube's spirit.

The claim the present work may make upon the attention of scholars is that
(vi) the results embodied in it are drawn almost entirely from the original sources, the manuscripts themselves. It is not the merit but the good fortune of the

Oxford, Clarendon Press, 1914, pp. v–xi, 1–21.

author that he has been able to investigate nearly all the extant material in his field; for through the support both of individuals and of institutions, he has been privileged in quite extraordinary measure, in being given the opportunity to visit all the libraries containing manuscripts that concerned him, and to devote ample time upon them unhindered. But it is none the less true that this book stands upon the shoulders of its predecessors; and it is thanks to the pioneer labours of those who preceded me that I could take full advantage of the opportunity I had. The works of the illustrious Monte Cassino scholars Caravita, Tosti, Amelli, and Piscicelli Taeggi have made my own possible.

Caravita wrote before the new era in palaeography ushered in by Delisle and Traube, and his work is weak on the palaeographical side. He is at sea when confronted by manuscripts not written in the south Italian hand. And even in the case of south Italian manuscripts his dates are not always reliable. His classification of the manuscripts into strict groups is often arbitrary and sometimes clearly mistaken. There is also some confusion in the press-marks. But these defects may be passed over in view of the great services he rendered in making such rich stores of material accessible to scholars. What has been said of Caravita may fairly be said of the great catalogue of Monte Cassino manuscripts, the *Bibliotheca Casinensis*, which we owe to the untiring diligence of Tosti, Amelli, and their coadjutors. In giving a facsimile of each manuscript described in the first four volumes of the catalogue its editors put palaeographers under great obligation. Yet the student who depends solely upon this catalogue for his knowledge of Beneventan writing cannot avoid wrong impressions, since the reproductions, being in lithograph, want that accuracy which can only be achieved by a mechanical process. But neither (vii)
Caravita nor the editors of the *Bibliotheca Casinensis* aimed at making contributions to palaeography. The publication which, on the palaeographical side, is our chief, indeed our only, source of information regarding the south Italian script came from the pen of Dom Odorisio Piscicelli Taeggi, formerly of Monte Cassino, now of Bari. His *Paleografia artistica di Montecassino* is, as the title suggests, primarily interested in the artistic aspect of the Monte Cassino manuscripts. Yet the short and well-written preface to the section entitled *Longobardo-Cassinese* is the most important palaeographical contribution we have on the subject, and all our textbooks base on it. But the work is expensive and not easily accessible; and the chromo-lithograph facsimiles, although executed with admirable care, and most valuable for giving an idea of the colours used by the miniaturists, are open to the same objection as those in the *Bibliotheca Casinensis*. They can lay no claim to absolute accuracy.

Another study deserving of mention is Professor Rodolico's 'Genesi e svolgimento della scrittura Longobardo-Cassinese'. It marks in several respects an advance upon Piscicelli Taeggi. It too is limited in its scope to the study of the manuscripts preserved at Monte Cassino; but it furnishes some new observations and rectifies some old errors. It contains, to be sure, some faulty and premature conclusions, but these would undoubtedly have been revised had the author extended his researches over a larger field. The short paper entitled *Della scrittura Longobarda nelle sue diverse fasi* (Rome, 1906), by A. Morinello, would not have been mentioned here but for the fact that it appears as an authority in one of the best textbooks on palaeography. It is only fair to the author to state that the pamphlet, which is simply an account
(viii) of six manuscripts preserved at Naples, was meant for private circulation, and
makes no pretension to being a contribution to the science.

The aim of the present work has been to give a history of the south Italian minuscule, and to deal with the various problems it presents. In treating some questions briefly and others at great length, I have been guided by the palaeographical importance of each question discussed. In the historical introduction, Monte Cassino may perhaps appear to occupy too much space, but this was inevitable in view of the importance of Monte Cassino both as a seat of learning and as a scriptorium. It seemed important to treat fully the subject of the name, to point out the hopeless confusion which arises from the ambiguous term Lombardic, and to justify the claims of the name Beneventan. Another question of importance was the demarcation of the Beneventan zone. I have given a list of all the centres whence Beneventan manuscripts are known to have come, and also a list of the manuscripts which are to be connected with each centre. The use of Beneventan writing in Dalmatia is of interest both to the palaeographer and to the student of western culture. The Italian origin of our script needed no elaborate demonstration, as it is admitted now on all sides, yet it seemed necessary to discuss in detail the theory that the Visigothic script influenced the development of the Beneventan and to show that this view is unsupported by facts. In the chapter on abbreviations I consciously transgressed the limits of my subject proper and gave a short sketch of the development of abbreviations in Latin manuscripts. I did this partly to render more intelligible the discussion of the Beneventan abbreviations, and partly to make Traube's results accessible in English. This chapter may be found to be the most useful in the book. In dealing with such a mass of details as that presented by the abbreviations found in hundreds of manu-
(ix) scripts, it was necessary to suppress everything which tended to blur the clear

outline of the development. It will be seen that a careful study of the development of several abbreviations has furnished trustworthy, objective dating criteria. In the discussion of the Beneventan sign of interrogation an attempt has been made, I believe for the first time, to touch upon a subject which will in the future receive more careful attention from palaeographers. The Beneventan method of punctuating interrogative sentences throws considerable light on the manner in which such sentences were read. It also provides the palaeographer with a most interesting touchstone for detecting Beneventan influence. In formulating the rules and traditions of the script I have tried to show what is essentially Beneventan. Given the Beneventan alphabet and a knowledge of the rules, any one could write correct Beneventan—a fact which I have tested by applying the rules myself in connection with a fragment which was mistaken for Beneventan.

The Appendix demands a few words of explanation. It contains a list of over 600 Beneventan manuscripts, if fragments are included. Its value lies in the fact that it includes only genuine south Italian products. Nearly all the manuscripts mentioned have been examined by me either in the original or in facsimile. In the case of the few manuscripts which I have not seen, I have stated in each case on whose authority the manuscript was included. Owing to the promiscuous use of the term Lombardic and the rather vague appreciation of what is and what is not Beneventan, it was impossible to admit without verification manuscripts elsewhere described as Lombardic, Cassinese, or even Beneventan. This will explain the omission from my list of a number of manuscripts which might be suspected to be south Italian products. The type of minuscule closely resembling the Beneventan, which was in use in north Italy during the ninth century, does not come within the scope of the present (x)
study, and I have for that reason excluded such manuscripts as Ivrea XCIX, Milan Ambros. B. 31 sup., Bamberg B. III. 30, Rome Sessor. 40 (1258), and many others. It would have added greatly to the value of the list if references had been given to published facsimiles and literature. But a complete and adequate bibliographical study I was unable to give here, and it must be reserved for a future occasion, should it be found advisable to publish such a study. It often happens that an apparently insignificant fact proves of importance in reconstructing the history of a manuscript. Hence it seemed necessary (except, for obvious reasons, in the case of Monte Cassino) to take account of manuscripts which showed only a line or two of Beneventan, or a Beneventan fly-leaf. It would perhaps have been more scientific not to assign dates to the manuscripts in the list, especially as some of them were examined

by me several years ago and it is likely I should now modify my judgement in some cases. But the discrepancy, I believe, would never be very material; so that on the whole it seemed best to consult the convenience of the student rather than my own reputation for strictly accurate dating. Where my dates differ from those of Caravita and others, this is not due to oversight on my part but to difference of opinion. The list will doubtless receive many additions, but that it is as full as it is, is owing to the help I had from Traube, from the works of the Monte Cassino scholars mentioned above, and from those of Bannister, Bethmann, Ebner, Ehrensberger, Loewe–Hartel, Reifferscheid, and Schenkl.

It has taken me many years to do this work—I prefer not to think how many —and it would have taken me much longer but for the assistance accorded me on all sides. First and foremost I am indebted to Traube—a debt which has reference not only to the present book but to any future work in palaeo-
(xi) graphy as well. Next after Traube I owe profound gratitude to Father Ehrle, the Prefect of the Vatican Library, whom to know is an ethical education. During the years I was privileged to work in the Vatican Library his interest, encouragement, and advice never failed me. My work has likewise profited greatly from the unstinted assistance of the Vatican Scriptores, to all of whom I here express my thanks: to Dott. Carusi, Abbé Liebaert, Mgr. Mercati, Professor Nogara, Mgr. Stornaiolo, and Mgr. Vattasso. My debt to Monte Cassino is second only to that I owe to the Vatican. To the former Librarian of the Abbey, P. Ambrogio Amelli, as well as to the present Keeper of the Archives, Dom Simplicio de Sortis, I am deeply obliged, for the liberality with which they allowed me to make use of their treasures. And I am grateful as well for the hospitality I enjoyed at the hands of Abbot Krug and his successor. My sojourns at Monte Cassino, one of the most beautiful and venerable shrines of western Christendom, have been experiences not easily forgotten.[1]

I have reserved for the last the expression of my indebtedness to James Loeb, to whom I have been privileged to dedicate this book. From the time I left America to begin my studies abroad, he has never ceased to aid and encourage my work in every possible way; and that I have been able to pursue my investigations uninterruptedly is in very large measure due to his generosity. No one knows better than the author the shortcomings of this book; but such as it is, it could never have been printed had not Traube been my master and James Loeb my friend.

[1] In the original there follows a long list of acknowledgements.

INTRODUCTION (*1*)

The history of a script which lasted five centuries is indissolubly bound up with the history of the region in which it was used. Such a script would of necessity receive some impress of the intellectual and political movements of its locality, and thus act as a register, as well as a medium, of culture. The study of such a script does well then to take cognizance of the *milieu* of its development; and will become more fruitful by extending its inquiry to the books written in the script, to the centres prominent for copying activity, and to the personages, literary and political, who fostered the culture they inherited.

This is not the place for a history of the culture of southern Italy. Yet a brief sketch of the main events affecting the region in the Middle Ages seems indispensable, and will, I hope, suffice for an introduction to the chapters following. I shall content myself with grouping the incidents to be narrated around the vicissitudes of the mother house of occidental monasticism, Monte Cassino. She was for the period the great centre of light and learning, the leader and model of all the smaller schools. And owing to her geographical situation and extensive feudal possessions no event of real importance in southern Italy left her untouched.

In the history of Western culture southern Italy has played if not a leading certainly a significant part. It has well been pointed out that from the beginning her mission was to preserve and hand on what she got from others. It was a little Greek colony in southern Italy that brought the alphabet to Rome. When Rome fell and the German barbarians swept over Italy, it was a son of the extreme south who did much to save profane learning from impending destruction. A south Italian abbey became the mother house of the order
which more than any other institution offered for centuries an asylum to (*2*)
learning and the arts. It was, again, largely through southern Italy that the wisdom of the East was made accessible to the West. Contact with Greek culture southern Italy probably never lost; and new treasures were opened up by the translation movement that began under the Normans in Sicily, and was continued by their Suabian and Angevin successors. It was from a Calabrian that the first humanist learned his Greek; and it was a Sicilian who, in the memorable year 1423, brought back with him from Constantinople classics unread for a thousand years.

Harassed and exploited by one barbarian foe after another, Italy lay, at the end of the fifth century, impoverished and exhausted. Her art and learning had sunk so low that they might perhaps have perished in the tumult of the invasions which followed, had they not found asylum in the monasteries. The nobler spirits of the time flocked in great numbers into the religious houses. Civic and political virtue had apparently died out. The affairs of this world presented a sickening aspect; and men and women felt that there was no other path to the better life than through the gates of the cloister.

It is no wonder then, that the three prominent men with whose works the annals of the Middle Ages may be said to begin had each spent a greater or smaller portion of his life within the walls of a monastery. St. Benedict, Cassiodorus, and Gregory the Great had all been monks; and each did distinct service for the monasticism of the West: the first by furnishing a Rule suited to the needs of the Occident; the second by encouraging the monks to foster liberal learning; the last by protecting and championing the cause of the monastic order.

In 529 St. Benedict founded Monte Cassino, and there he wrote his famous *Regula*. Following in the footsteps of St. Basil he composed a Rule which events have proved to be precisely suited to the Western genius. It is characterized by mildness and common sense, and differs from its predecessors,
(3) which were based on eastern models, in the 'elimination of austerity and in the sinking of the individual in the community'.

In founding the Benedictine Order St. Benedict built better than he knew. He hardly foresaw—and it was certainly not his intention—that his monasteries would become the chief instruments for the transmission of pagan as well as Christian literature. His interest lay in the cultivation not of learning but of piety. His aim was salvation, not knowledge. Yet his Rule left an opening for the seven arts by providing for a library and by demanding of each monk that he should spend two hours daily in reading—during Lent even three hours, and on Sundays and holidays all the time not devoted to divine service. The famous 48th chapter of the Rule says:

> Otiositas inimica est animae; et ideo certis temporibus occupari debent fratres in labore manuum, certis iterum horis in lectione divina.... In quibus diebus quadragesimae accipiant omnes singulos codices de bibliotheca, quos per ordinem ex integro legant.

St. Benedict doubtless referred to the reading of Scripture and the Fathers; but as each monk was given during Lent a separate manuscript—and at times the abbey had no less than 200 monks—a large library was indispensable; and this necessitated copying activity.

The impulse to cherish the learning of the past came in the main from Cassiodorus. Nearly all his life had been spent in political activity, as minister of Theodoric and his successors. Towards its close he retired to his own estate in the extreme south of Italy. In Vivarium near Squillace he founded a monastery which in a measure was to take the place of the Christian university he had dreamed of establishing in Rome. In the seclusion of his monastery he developed remarkable literary activity. In writing his *Institutiones divinarum et saecularium litterarum*, an encyclopaedia of sacred and profane learning, he did great service to mankind. For he completed the work of St. Benedict by making the writing of books, the preservation of authors, a sacred duty and an act of piety.

Hardly had the Goths been expelled from Italy when fresh hordes of bar- (*4*)
barians poured down from the north. This time a people came who were destined to stay. A little over a decade after the Lombards entered Italy we find them besieging Naples. In 581 they plundered and sacked Monte Cassino. The monks fled to Rome, where Pope Pelagius gave them a home near the Lateran. Here they remained for over 130 years. Of their doings during this time we know, however, very little. Under Gregory the Great they certainly received every possible encouragement. There is a fitness in the fact that the Patriarch of Western monasticism should have found his biographer in the greatest of the popes. Considering the popularity of Gregory's *Dialogues*, it is not easy to overestimate the prestige which accrued to the Benedictine Order from the Pope's admiration of its founder. The marvellously rapid extension of the order may be largely due to this very circumstance.

Concerning the monks of Monte Cassino during the seventh century the annals are silent. All we know is that they remained in Rome. The tradition was vague even in the eleventh century. The catalogues of abbots which we find in eleventh-century manuscripts lack the precise dates of the abbots of the seventh century. It is in the beginning of the eighth century that we again touch facts. In the year 717 or 718 Petronax of Brescia, a strong and influential man, was asked by Pope Gregory III to take the monks back to the monastery which had been abandoned for over a century. With gifts from Rome and generous assistance from the neighbouring abbey of St. Vincent on the Volturno, Monte Cassino soon began to prosper, and once more men from different parts of the world sought peace within its cloisters. Some of the books presented to the monks by Pope Gregory's successor, Zacharias, are perhaps still to be found among the extant palimpsests of Monte Cassino-

During this period of reconstruction, at least at the beginning of it, condi-

tions were hardly favourable to literary activity. From one witness of the time,
(5) the Anglo-Saxon Willibald, we learn that even the discipline was lax. This wealthy and pious man, whose religious zeal had led him to make the pilgrimage to the Holy Land, must have been of influence in the abbey, for he was given positions of responsibility there. The presence of this Englishman may have prepared the way for the authors of his native land, Bede and Alcuin, whose popularity became great in the abbey, as elsewhere.

At the same time with Willibald there lived in Monte Cassino a Spanish Presbyter, Diapertus by name. His sojourn is, as far as I know, the first and only evidence of direct contact with Spain.

The fame of the abbey had brought to her during the same century another illustrious stranger, the Bavarian Sturmius, later first abbot of Fulda. It was St. Boniface who sent him to the mother house to learn the true monastic discipline at its source. Relations of this sort could not have been without beneficial consequences to the abbey.

The prestige of the abbey is again witnessed in the invitation sent by Duke Odilo of Bavaria to monks of Monte Cassino to come and settle at Mondsee near Salzburg. A similar invitation came a little over two centuries later from the King of Hungary.

Two personages of the eighth century bring southern Italy into connection with Gaul. Ambrosius Autpertus, a native of Gaul, spent the last decades of his life in the Benedictine abbey of St. Vincent on the Volturno. It is interesting to note that one of the earliest copies of his Commentary on the Apocalypse is actually one of the oldest specimens we have of Beneventan writing (Benevento III 9). Again, at the end of the century Monte Cassino was visited by Adalhard of Corbie, then one of the most prominent monasteries in Gaul. This visit may not have been without its influence on our script; for Corbie was then already in possession of a highly developed minuscule, which was far from being the case in Monte Cassino.

(6) Thus the mother house prospered and grew in fame, and during the abbacy of Theodemar (778–97) it was accorded quite unusual honours. It had before received into its fold Ratchis, King of the Lombards, and Carloman, brother of Pippin. In 787 Charlemagne himself paid a visit to the shrine of St. Benedict. Later, at his own request, a copy of the Rule was sent him, which was a literal reproduction of the autograph brought back by the monks from Rome. But what gave even more enduring lustre to the abbacy of Theodemar was the sojourn at Monte Cassino of Paulus Diaconus. One of the most learned men

of his time, our only source for the early history of the Lombards, Paulus Diaconus had for political reasons left his monastery in the north and become a monk at Monte Cassino before 782. Under his influence the abbey grew into an important school. Pupils came from far and wide. Stephen II of Naples had his clerics sent to Monte Cassino to sit at the feet of the great man. The merit of Paulus did not escape Charlemagne, in whose court the scholar spent some time; but after 787 we find him again at Monte Cassino, where he remained until his death. The stimulus he gave to learning lingered on long after he passed away. Practically all our oldest manuscripts in the writing discussed in this book date from the time when Paulus Diaconus was in Monte Cassino; and their contents evince an interest in profane as well as Christian literature. We have Cassiodorus' *Institutiones*, Gregory of Tours' *De cursu stellarum*, Isidore's *Etymologiae*, and a large collection of grammatical treatises, viz. the manuscripts Bamberg HJ. IV. 15, Cava 2, and Paris lat. 7530.

During the ninth century southern Italy felt a reflection of the renaissance that had taken place in France. Monte Cassino can boast of the writers Hildericus, Autpertus, and Bertharius. At the same time Ursus, Bishop of Benevento, made an abridgement of Priscian, a contemporary manuscript of which we may have in Rome Casanat. 1086. Other ninth-century manuscripts also show an interest in grammar. The city of Benevento was reputed to have thirty-two teachers of profane learning (*philosophi*) at the time when Louis II visited it. We have only the word of the Anonymous Salernitanus for this, (7)
but the story must have some basis of truth.

A new enemy put an end to these peaceful activities. The Saracens had swept everything before them. Masters of Palermo by the year 831, Tarentum and Bari fell into their hands between 840 and 850. In the next two decades everything south of Rome and east of the Abruzzi was in their possession. The Greeks were too weak, the Lombards too much divided among themselves, to offer adequate resistance. Not before Louis II came in 871 was Bari relieved of its thirty years' yoke. No sooner had he left the country than the Saracens were threatening Benevento and Salerno.

On the 22nd of October 883 the prosperous rule of Abbot Bertharius was cut short by the appearance of the enemy at Monte Cassino. The Saracens sacked and plundered the abbey. The abbot fell into their hands. The monks who managed to escape fled to Teano near Capua. One of their number was Erchempert, who after Paulus Diaconus continues the history of the Lombards to the year 889. As a historian he is superior to his contemporaries; and he is our main source for the sad and turbulent events of the ninth century.

Further misfortunes soon overtook the fugitive monks. The monastery at Teano was burned down, and in it perished their most precious treasure, the Rule which St. Benedict had written with his own hand. The monks sought refuge in Capua, where they lived for over half a century. Their sojourn here marks a new epoch of the script. For a generation they made good use of peace and security. They produced a number of manuscripts, the first in fact which evince distinct progress in calligraphy and ornamentation. But the monks of St. Benedict did not remain untouched by the moral degeneration of the tenth century. Like other Italian monasteries, theirs also stood in need of the reform which came from Cluny; and though Cassinese tradition is silent on the subject there can be little doubt that at least indirectly they were
(8) influenced by Odo's reforms, since we know from another source that the Cassinese abbots Balduin and Aligern were pupils of Odo.

Owing to troubles which arose with the Capuan princes, Aligern in 949 led the monks back to Monte Cassino. From now on, the abbey was destined to enjoy almost two centuries of ever-increasing prosperity. It was while Aligern was abbot that St. Nilus visited Monte Cassino and established his monks in the neighbouring monastery of Vallelucio. His sojourn here as well as in Capua and Gaeta is of interest because it may be supposed that the meeting of Greek and Latin monks was mutually beneficial. We cannot say what specific gain the Latins had therefrom, but we are certain that the Greeks learnt from their Latin hosts that peculiar style of initial decoration which we find in so many south Italian Greek manuscripts and which distinguishes them at once from Greek manuscripts of the Levant.

When Aligern's abbacy, which lasted twenty-seven years (949–86), came to an end he was succeeded by Manso, a relative of the Capuan princes, through whose influence alone he gained his position. As he was not the choice of the monks, his election bred dissension. Some of the bravest of them left the abbey rather than submit, among these being John of Benevento and Theobald, both destined later to become abbots of Monte Cassino, and Liutius, the future provost of S. Maria di Albaneta. These three made a journey to the Holy Land; the other seceding monks went to Lombardy and founded monasteries there.

In the tenth century, admittedly the darkest of the Middle Ages, the flame of learning was still kept alive in southern Italy. From extant manuscripts we can discern the interest felt in the classics, medicine, history, poetry, and canon law. The number of interesting books read and copied is by no means

small. Among them I may mention Virgil, Livy, Josephus, the fables of Hyginus, Solinus; Dioscorides, Galen, and an extraordinary compendium of the medical knowledge of the period; Paulus' commentary on St. Benedict's
Rule, the works of St. Gregory, collections of canons, writings of the Fathers, (9)
etc. (see the tenth-century manuscripts reproduced in *Scriptura Beneventana*,[1] pls. 31–55).

The works of several writers of the period have come down to us. At the beginning of the century we encounter two curious authors, Auxilius, a Gaul by birth, and Eugenius Vulgarius, probably an Italian grammarian. Their work—which throws lurid light upon a disgraceful episode in papal history—we have in a Beneventan manuscript (Bamberg P. III. 20) which I venture to regard as contemporaneous. John, deacon of Naples, continues the *Gesta Episcoporum* of his city. From him we have also a life of Bishop Athanasius I and an account of the transfer of the relics of St. Severinus. In Naples too we witness the interesting literary activity of Duke John and his consort. At his request the Presbyter Leo collected and had copied the works of numerous writers, among whom are mentioned Livy, Josephus, and Dionysius. To Leo we also owe a translation of the *Vita Alexandri Magni*, which he had brought from Constantinople (see below, p. 82[2]). In secular history the work of Paulus Diaconus and Erchempert is continued, with far less skill and acumen, by the anonymous monk of Salerno. Another historical treatise, of no great significance in itself, should be mentioned, the *Historia miscella* of Landolfus Sagax, which continues the *Historia Romana* of Paulus Diaconus to the year 813. The author lived and wrote about the year 1000, probably in Naples. A contemporaneous manuscript of his work (Vatic. Pal. lat. 909) though not, as has been stated, an autograph, is in existence.

The year 1000 came and went without bringing the dreaded end of terrestrial things. On the contrary it ushered in an era of extraordinary political and intellectual activity. Three events stand out with especial prominence. The Normans, that wonderful people from the north, arrive in southern Italy and soon become its conquerors. The German emperors take an unusually active
part in Italian affairs. Lastly, the temporal power of the popes sees a remark- (10)
able increase. The Roman pontiff defies the German emperor and takes part in the struggle for the possession of Italy. In the long contest the powers are grouped now in this way, now in that; and Monte Cassino, rich and strong, is an important factor throughout. From the middle of the century she throws

[1] [Oxford, Clarendon Press, 1929. Ed.]

[2] [Not reprinted in this volume. Ed.]

in her lot with the papacy and becomes one of its main stays. It is not mere accident that within a generation two Cassinese abbots become popes, that several abbots and even monks receive the cardinal's hat, and that the greatest pope of the century is the close friend of the greatest abbot of Monte Cassino. Nothing again, as has well been shown, is more indicative of the relation between the abbey and the Roman See than the fact that another Pope, Nicholas II, made Abbot Desiderius his apostolic vicar in the entire lower half of the peninsula. That under these circumstances the monastery should grow in fame as well as in fortune goes without saying. But it is not these events alone that made the century memorable in the annals of Monte Cassino. Its destinies were guided by men of remarkable ability and they had the secret of gathering about them the best talent of their age.

The century which was to witness the golden era in the history of Monte Cassino was fittingly begun under the abbots Atenolf (1011–22) and Theobald (1022–35). Leo Ostiensis tells us that up to their time the abbey had been but poorly supplied with books. From now on, the zeal with which books were copied, the care expended upon the work, and the imposing size and beauty of the manuscripts give earnest of the perfect products to follow in the Desiderian period.

Even as provost in S. Liberatore, a monastery at the foot of Mt. Majella in the Abruzzi, Theobald had been instrumental in having over thirty books copied as he tells us in his will made in 1019 (see below, pp. 79 f.[1]). As Abbot of Monte Cassino his interest did not abate. From a catalogue entered in two manuscripts of the time, probably at his command, we learn what were the
(*11*) very books which he ordered to be written. A number of them are also mentioned by the chronicler Leo. Besides Augustine and Gregory, we note that history was read, the *Historia Romana*, the *Historia Langobardorum*. The list includes the encyclopaedia of Hrabanus Maurus, the *Leges Langobardorum*, and others (see below, pp. 80 f.[2]).

After the death of Theobald the monastery was once more harassed by the Capuan princes. This time help came from without, and the fact is important, for it marks the beginning of German influence in the abbey. The Emperor Conrad came to the rescue and brought with him a German abbot to take charge of the monks. With Richerius (1038–55), who came to Monte Cassino from the monastery of Leno near Brescia, where he had been abbot, fresh zeal entered into the life of Monte Cassino. Some two decades later another Ger-

[1] [Not reprinted in this volume. Ed.]

[2] [Not reprinted in this volume. See, however, below, p. 90. Ed.]

man played a prominent part in the affairs of the monastery—Frederick of Lorraine. Having sought refuge there from the wrath of the emperor he was elected abbot in 1056, to become Pope as Stephen IX two years later. The presence of Germans in Monte Cassino and the fact that they held positions of importance must have left its mark on the abbey. As a matter of fact, after Frederick's abbacy a style of initial decoration comes into vogue which is manifestly of German origin. And it seems a reasonable hypothesis which would connect the famous manuscript of the *Annals* and *Histories* of Tacitus with the two German abbots of Monte Cassino. For Tacitus, as we know, was read in Germany during centuries when apparently no trace of him existed in Italy. The eleventh-century manuscript of Widukind's *Res gestae Saxonicae* which we find in Monte Cassino (MS. 298) may have a similar origin.

The next abbot is the great Desiderius (1058–87). Dauferius—such was his real name—was born at Benevento of noble stock. From his boyhood the religious life strongly appealed to him. But owing to parental objections he had to run away to become a monk. A quiet monastic life, however, was not to be his lot. His character and abilities placed him in positions of eminence not of his seeking. Thus when Frederick of Lorraine was made Pope, the *(12)*
abbacy fell upon Desiderius. As friend of his predecessor, now become Stephen IX, and of Hildebrand, later Gregory VII, he was naturally a staunch supporter of papal policy. But he was also the political friend of the Normans. Under his rule Monte Cassino saw its era of true greatness. Gifts and grants received from popes and emperors had in the past greatly swelled the revenues of the abbey—she had possessions along the Adriatic, in Apulia, in the Abruzzi, even in Lombardy. Under the leadership of Desiderius her fortunes became still more imposing. This is not the place to describe the part he played in the affairs of southern Italy. What interests us here is the fact that under him learning and the arts received a powerful impulse. Not only did he renew and embellish the buildings of the abbey, but he erected a magnificent new basilica, decorated with mosaics by workmen brought over from Constantinople—an event in the history of Italian art. It is an old observation that the temper of an age is reflected in its calligraphic products. The manuscripts copied under Desiderius—many of which have come down to us—mark the highest achievement in Beneventan penmanship. And the literary interest of the period may be judged to some extent by the books then produced. The ancient Chronicle of Monte Cassino gives a long and interesting list of the books copied in the abbacy of Desiderius. It contains chiefly theological and

liturgical works, but there are several histories: Josephus, Gregory of Tours, Paulus Diaconus, Erchempert, and others; there are also several classics: *De natura deorum* of Cicero, the *Institutiones* and *Novellae* of Justinian, the *Fasti* of Ovid, Virgil's *Eclogues*, Terence, Horace, Seneca, the grammatical works of Theodorus and Donatus (see below, pp. 81 f.[1]).

Himself a learned writer, Desiderius gathered about him and encouraged literary ability of every sort. Alfanus, later Bishop of Salerno, noted as physician, poet, and theologian, was an intimate friend of the abbot, and is supposed to have had great influence with him. Besides Alfanus, Monte Cassino
(*13*) had at that time Pandolf of Capua, the mathematician and astronomer, Guaiferius, the poet of the abbey, and Alberic, author of a *Liber de dictamine* and a charming life of S. Scholastica. Here should also be mentioned Johannes Caietanus (later Pope Gelasius II) who, as secretary to Pope Urban II, is known to have revived the *cursus*. But the three literary men who have most interest for us are the monks Amatus and Leo, and the physician Constantinus Africanus. To Amatus we are indebted for the earliest account of the Normans. The original of his work is lost; we have it only in an early French translation discovered during the last century by Champollion Figeac. Constantinus Africanus came to Italy as a fugitive from Carthage, where his enemies had accused him of being a magician. Versed in the philosophies, sciences, and languages of the East, Constantinus was a perfect store-house of learning. He lived in Monte Cassino, where he translated many medical works into Latin. He also visited Salerno. His sojourn in southern Italy doubtless added much to the fame of the school of medicine in Salerno.

Leo Ostiensis stands out as one of the most pleasing figures of his time. He is known chiefly as the author—at least in large part—of one of the best chronicles written during the Middle Ages, that of Monte Cassino. He entered the abbey as a boy and while still young had attracted the attention of Abbot Desiderius. As keeper of the archives he was fully equipped for the task imposed upon him by Oderisius, the successor of Desiderius. Despite the fact that the chief aim of the history was to make good the claims of the abbey to the multifarious grants and privileges bestowed or presumably bestowed upon it during its long career, Leo managed to endow his performance with the dignity and seriousness of objective history. He relates events simply, faithfully, and well; he treats of men and affairs with tact and candour. He did not finish his task, for he was made cardinal, and ecclesiastical affairs preoccupied him. In the oldest manuscript of the Chronicle, which lies in Munich—

[1] [Not reprinted in this volume; see, however, below pp. 87 f. Ed.]

CLM 4623—the palaeographer may examine with delight the writing of Leo (*14*) himself; and the historian may have the pleasure of seeing the work in the making, for the manuscript has in the margin and between the lines the very corrections of the author.

The end of the eleventh and the beginning of the twelfth century are times of strife and confusion. To the conflict over the investitures was added the papal schism. Monte Cassino felt the effects of these troubles. And there was something more: its prominence and prosperity in worldly affairs reacted unfavourably upon its general tone. The times of Oderisius and his successors during the early twelfth century usher in a new era, the beginning of the decline. With monastic discipline relaxed, with abbots taking part in battles, with politics forming the chief interest, nothing good could be expected. Monte Cassino took the wrong side in the papal schism, and she had to suffer when Innocent II, by the aid of the emperor, became pope.

The figure which may be said to incorporate the virtues and vices of this time is Petrus Diaconus. An indefatigable worker, clever, versatile, and of easy address, his talents won him position, and he was charged by Abbot Rainaldus to continue the history of Monte Cassino which Leo had left at the year 1075. Peter's work was as different from Leo's as was his whole character. His one aim was to glorify himself and his abbey; and to attain this end he did not hesitate to invent documents. His numerous forgeries—some of which had long been recognized as such—have recently been exposed with masterly skill, and Peter stands condemned as a garbler of facts and inventor of falsehoods. As he is his own biographer we cannot be altogether sure even of the events of his life, but this much is quite indisputable: he was a voluminous writer. Besides continuing the Chronicle of Monte Cassino to the year 1138, he has left us a work on the illustrious men of his monastery, one on its saints, and important registers of Cassinese documents, not to mention numerous hagiographic and theological works.

With Petrus Diaconus and the monk Alberic, who wrote a *Vision of Heaven* (*15*) *and Hell* which is in some ways a forerunner of Dante's, we take leave of the last striking figures in the literary annals of Monte Cassino—excepting perhaps that of the French abbot Bernard Ayglerius († 1282) who wrote a commentary of the Rule of St. Benedict, a contemporary manuscript of which has come down (Monte Cassino 440).

Outside of Monte Cassino evidence is not lacking of considerable culture. Aversa is praised by Alfanus as another Athens; Benevento, St. Vincent on the Volturno, Cava, Naples, Salerno, and Bari have their writers, chroniclers, and annalists. But if we look for the great centre of literary activity in the twelfth century we must turn to Sicily. In Palermo, at the court of the Normans, we witness a unique and fascinating spectacle. We find there men from all parts of the world. The new rulers were as wise and tolerant as they were brave. Wherever they saw talent they sought to attract it. And this policy, which served them well in the affairs of government, they carried over into the domain of letters. Thus at the court Greek and Arab, Lombard and Hebrew scholars worked in amity and gave of their best. Under these circumstances Palermo naturally became a great centre for the exchange of ideas, more especially for the spread of eastern ideas. The many Latin translations of Greek and Oriental works that we owe to Sicily bear witness to this intellectual activity. Even in previous centuries, as we have seen, translations of hagiographic and medical works were undertaken in southern Italy. What we witness now in Palermo is a concentrated movement which extended its interests into various branches. What King Roger began Frederic II and his successors continued.

We have come to a new epoch in south Italian history. A civic sense was gradually wakening in the different communes. The Benedictine houses were plainly losing their old supremacy as seats of learning. Inner and outer causes contributed to the decline. They can boast of few writers and thinkers of
(16) eminence. The rise of important lay schools, the new universities of Salerno and Naples, certainly contributed to the diminution of Benedictine prestige. But this was not the only cause. Even as a religious order the Benedictines no longer answered to the needs of the time, as may be seen from the vast extension of the mendicant orders. With the decline of the Benedictine monasteries our script also declines. For the Beneventan script is primarily a Benedictine script.

II

So much for the historical background of our script. We have tried to touch upon the main events, and have made brief mention of the chief literary figures and their works, which constitute the first and most certain test of intellectual life. We should now apply another measure—we should ask what writers were particularly read and copied, and how faithfully their texts were transmitted. It is by applying a test of this sort upon the centres of southern Italy that we first appreciate how much we owe to them for the preservation of ancient and medieval writers. But such a task must be left to a more competent hand. Here only a few of the outstanding facts can be given.

More than one of our most cherished classics has been saved from destruction by the hand of a Beneventan scribe. Varro's *De lingua latina* exists only in two Beneventan manuscripts, Florence Laur. 51. 10 saec. xi ex. and Paris lat. 7530 saec. viii ex., both written in Monte Cassino. The Cassinese have always cherished an affection for Varro as one of their own. Tacitus' *Historiae* (i–v) and *Annales* (xi–xvi) depend upon the single Laurentianus 68. 2 saec. xi med., written in Monte Cassino. The same manuscript is our unique source for Apuleius' *Metamorphoses* and *Florida*. The copy of the text which was made in the thirteenth century (Florence Laur. 29. 2) is also in Beneventan and comes most likely from Monte Cassino. To have handed on to posterity the works of Varro, Tacitus, and Apuleius is distinction enough for any centre. But we are indebted to Beneventan transmission for some other works.

The most important manuscript for Seneca's *Dialogues* is Milan Ambros. (17)
C. 90 inf. saec. xi ex., from Monte Cassino. Hyginus' *Fabulae* existed only in one Beneventan manuscript of the early tenth century, a few fragments of which are still to be seen in Munich (CLM 6437). Our knowledge of the Scholion of Varius' *Thyestes* we owe to two Beneventan manuscripts, Paris lat. 7530 and Rome Casanat. 1086 saec. ix, written in Benevento. Servius' *De metris Horatianis* depends solely upon Paris lat. 7530. The new thirty-four lines of Juvenal discovered by Winstedt are found only in the Beneventan manuscript Oxford Bodl. Canon. Class. lat. 41 saec. xi/xii.

The value of Beneventan transmission is also seen in cases where different families of a text exist. Vatic. lat. 3342 saec. x has the best text of Solinus. For the text of Ovid two Beneventan manuscripts are of value: Vatic. lat. 3262 saec. xi ex., containing the *Fasti*, and Eton Bl. 6. 5 saec. xi, the *Heroides* and *Remedia Amoris*. As for Cicero, Vatic. lat. 3227 saec. xii in. has the best text of the *Somnium Scipionis* and is the most familiar representative of the Italian family for the *Philippics*. For *De legibus*, Leyden 118 is important. The same manuscript contains the *De natura deorum* and *De divinatione*. It is doubtless the very manuscript which was copied in Monte Cassino at the order of Abbot Desiderius. The Laurentianus 51. 10 is, apart from Poggio's Cluniacensis, our only source for Cicero, *Pro Cluentio*. Although the Monte Cassino manuscript of Frontinus is not in Beneventan, the original probably was. At any rate it is Monte Cassino that has saved this unique work.

Altogether the classics found in Beneventan writing are by no means few. We have Apuleius (Florence Laur. 68. 2 saec. xi and 29. 2 saec. xiii), Auctor ad Herennium (Florence Laur. 51. 10 saec. xi ex., London Add. MS. 11916 saec. xi ex.), Caesar (Florence Laur. 68. 6 saec. xii/xiii), Cicero (Florence Laur.

51. 10, Leyden 118 saec. XI ex., Vatic. lat. 3227 saec. XII in., Vatic. Ottob.
lat. 1406 saec. XI ex.), Germanicus (Madrid 19 (A. 16) saec. XI),[1] Hyginus
(Munich 6437 saec. X in.), Juvenal (Oxford Bodl. Canon. Class. lat. 41 saec.
(*18*) XI/XII), Livy (Prague Univ. 1224 fragm. saec. X), Macrobius (Vatic. Ottob.
lat. 1939 saec. XI ex.), Ovid (Eton Bl. 6. 5 saec. XI, Vatic. lat. 3262 saec. XI ex.,
Naples IV. F. 3 saec. XII), Sallust (Vatic. lat. 3327 saec. XII/XIII), Seneca (Milan
Ambros. C. 90 inf. saec. XI ex.), Solinus (Vatic. lat. 3342 saec. X, Monte Cas-
sino 391 saec. XI), Statius (Eton Bl. 6. 5 saec. XI, Vatic. lat. 3281 saec. XII),
Tacitus (Florence Laur. 68. 2 saec. XI med.), Pompeius Trogus, Justin's Epi-
tome (Florence Laur. 66. 21 saec. XI ex.), Varro (Florence Laur. 51. 10 saec.
XI ex., Paris lat. 7530 saec. VIII ex.), Vegetius (Vatic. Pal. lat. 909 saec. X/XI),
Virgil (Vienna 58, Paris lat. 10308, Vatic. lat. 1573 and 3253, Oxford Bodl.
Canon. Class. lat. 50, and Monte Cassino (*sine numero*) debris of *Aen.* III–XII),
besides the grammarians Servius (Paris lat. 7530, Vienna 27, Vatic. lat. 3317),
Priscian (Vatic. lat. 3313, Rome Casanat. 1086, both saec. IX), and anonymous
treatises in Paris lat. 7530.

It goes without saying that the region which contained the famous school
of Salerno did not lack medical manuscripts. In Beneventan writing over a
dozen have come to my notice, and it is an interesting fact that some of these
are older than the date usually given to the beginning of the Salernitan school.
Healing the sick was an act of piety. Consequently both St. Benedict's Rule
and Cassiodorus' *Institutiones* encourage the study of medicine. And we learn
that the Cassinese abbots Bertharius, Aligern, and Desiderius, and Archbishop Alfanus of Salerno had each composed or compiled works in medicine.
In his monastery at Vivarium Cassiodorus had, as he himself explicitly tells
us (cap. 31), certain works of Hippocrates, Galen, and Dioscorides, both in
the original and in Latin translation. It is an instructive fact that the Greek
works mentioned by Cassiodorus are the very ones of which Latin versions
were known in south Italy, as may be seen from extant Beneventan manuscripts. These prove conclusively that the Greek physicians were known in
south Italy before Constantinus Africanus came to live there. The Beneventan
medical manuscripts known to me are: Florence Laur. 73. 41 saec. IX in.
(*19*) Pseudo-Apuleius, Pseudo-Dioscorides, etc.; Monte Cassino 69 saec. IX ex.
Excerpta varia; Monte Cassino 97 saec. X in. Pseudo-Apuleius, Pseudo-

[1] Madrid 19 (A. 16) is here included on the authority of P. v. Winterfeld. Loewe did not describe the manuscript as Cassinese, and Professor B. L. Ullman, who kindly examined the manuscript for me, was not inclined to consider it Beneventan either.

Dioscorides, etc.; Glasgow Univ. V. 3. 2 saec. x in. Galen, etc.; Munich 337 saec. x Dioscorides; Vienna 68 saec. x ex. Priscianus, Aurelianus, etc.; Monte Cassino 225 saec. xi ex. *Varia*; Monte Cassino 351 saec. xi ex. Paulus of Aegina, *De curatione totius corporis*; Turin K. IV. 3 saec. xi ex. *Miscellanea Herbaria* (destroyed in fire of 1904); Rome Angelican. 1496 (V. 3. 3) saec. xi ex. palimpsest, primary script Benev.; Paris Nouv. acq. lat. 1628, fols. 19–26 saec. xi ex.; Copenhagen Old Royal Collection 1653 saec. xi ex. Muscio (Soranus), Oribasius; Vatic. Barb. lat. 160 (IX. 29) saec. xi *Herbarium*, Priscianus, Galen, Oribasius; Rome Basilicanus H. 44 saec. xii/xiii *Liber de medicina*. Of these the Munich and Copenhagen manuscripts are particularly interesting.

If we turn to medieval writings we find, as we should expect, that as regards historical and liturgical works which had their origin in south Italian soil, the Beneventan tradition is either our only authority or a very important witness. I refer to such local histories as the *Gesta Episcoporum Neapolitanorum* or the Chronicle of Monte Cassino, to such works as Paulus Diaconus' Commentary on St. Benedict's Rule, or the biographies of local saints. Of works not obviously connected with southern Italy, a few may be cited in the transmission of which Beneventan manuscripts are important.

One of our chief sources for early Christian liturgy is the description of a journey to Jerusalem made about A.D. 540—the approximate date assigned to it by recent criticism—by a certain Aetheria of Aquitaine. The *Itinerarium Aetheriae*, formerly known in literature as *Peregrinatio Silviae*, exists only in a Monte Cassino manuscript of the eleventh century, discovered by Gamurrini and now preserved in Arezzo. The manuscript also contains another unique work, Hilary's *Tractatus de mysteriis*, which is probably the very book ordered by Abbot Desiderius.

The *Acta Archelai* of Hegemonius, an anti-Manichaean document of great interest both to the historian and the theologian, is known to us chiefly in a (*20*)
Latin translation. The *editio princeps* (1698) of this work rested solely upon the Beneventan manuscript Monte Cassino 371 saec. xi/xii. For previous to Traube's discovery, which made Beeson's excellent edition possible, the Beneventan manuscript was the only complete one known.

A work of Gregory of Tours already mentioned, *De cursu stellarum*, which has become known in the last century in its complete form, has come down only in a Beneventan manuscript of the eighth century, Bamberg HJ. IV. 15. The same manuscript is one of our oldest witnesses to Cassiodorus' *Institutiones*. The defence of Pope Formosus, which we have in the curious writings of Auxilius and Eugenius Vulgarius mentioned above, has come down through the tenth-century Beneventan manuscript Bamberg P. III. 20. The oldest papal Register in existence, that of John VIII, is a copy made by some monk of Monte Cassino, whence the book came to the Vatican archives. The Beneventan manuscript of Cyprian (Monte Cassino 204 saec. XI) is important for the text of the Epistles and *Testimonia* and is indispensable for reconstructing the archetype. The oldest manuscript of Corippus' *Iohannis*—it has been lost since the sixteenth century—was one of the books written under Abbot Desiderius.

History was a favourite subject in our region. Besides local historians like Paulus Diaconus and Erchempert we find Sallust, Livy, Tacitus, Orosius, Justin's Epitome, Hegesippus, Victor Vitensis, Bede, and Anastasius. To these must be added Gregory of Tours's *History of the Franks* and Widukind's *Res gestae Saxonicae*. For the last two the Beneventan texts are of marked importance. South Italian manuscripts are also valuable for the transmission of Roman law (*Epitome Iuliani*), of canon law (Vatic. lat. 5845 saec. X), of medieval glossaries, of the medieval novel (Flor. Laurent. 66. 40 saec. IX ex.).

Of the numerous Biblical manuscripts in Beneventan writing none holds a pre-eminent position. But it is interesting to note that the text of the best Vulgate manuscripts, the Amiatinus and Lindisfarnensis, is probably derived
(*21*) from manuscripts brought to England from south Italy. The Fuldensis we know was written in Capua.

This survey, brief and summary as it is, will, I hope, at least have given some idea of the importance of the south Italian centres in the transmission of ancient and medieval works.

The main works consulted for this chapter are first the sources: 'Leonis Marsicani et Petri Diaconi chronica monasterii Casinensis' (ed. Wattenbach in *Mon. Germ. Hist. SS.* VII. 551 ff.) and Petrus Diaconus, *Liber illustrium virorum archisterii Casinensis* (edited and annotated by J. B. Marus, Rome, 1655); secondly the books on the history of Monte Cassino: Gattula, *Historia abbatiae Cassinensis* (Venice, 1733) and *Accessiones ad historiam abbatiae Cassinensis* (Venice, 1734); Tosti, *Storia della badia di Monte Cassino* (Naples, 1842–3); and Caravita, *I codici e le arti a Monte Cassino* (Monte Cassino, 1869–70); thirdly the following works of reference and publications treating different phases of south Italian history and culture: Amari, *Storia dei Musulmani di Sicilia* (Florence, 1854–72); Balzani, *Le Cronache italiane nel medio evo*, 2nd ed. (Milan, 1900); Batiffol, *L'abbaye de Rossano* (Paris, 1891); Capasso, *Monumenta ad Neapolitani ducatus historiam pertinentia* (Naples, 1881–92); Caspar, *Petrus Diaconus und die Monte Cassineser Fälschungen* (Berlin, 1909); Chapman, 'La restauration du Mont-Cassin par l'abbé Pétronax,' in *Rev. Bénédictine*, XXI (1904), 74 ff., and *Notes on the Early History of the Vulgate Gospels* (Oxford, 1908); De Renzi, *Storia documentata della scuola medica di Salerno*, 2nd ed. (Naples, 1857); Franz, *M. Aurelius Cassiodorius Senator* (Breslau, 1872); Freeman, *Historical Essays*, 3rd ser., 2nd ed.; Gay, *L'Italie méridionale et l'Empire byzantin* (Paris, 1904); Giacosa, *Magistri Salernitani nondum editi* (Turin, 1901); Giesebrecht, *De litterarum studiis apud Italos primis medii aevi saeculis* (Berlin, 1845); Hartwig, 'Die Uebersetzungsliteratur Unteritaliens in der normannisch-staufischen Epoche', in *Centralbl. f. Bibliothekswesen*, iii (1886), 161 ff.; 223 ff.; 505 f.; Haskins and Lockwood, 'The Sicilian Translators of the 12th Century', etc., in *Harvard Studies in Class. Philology*, XXI (1910), 75 ff.; Hirsch, 'Desiderius von Monte Cassino als Papst Victor III', in *Forschungen zur deutschen Geschichte*, VII (1867), 3 ff.; Lake, 'The Greek Monasteries in South Italy', in *Journal of Theol. Studies*, IV (1903), nos. 15 and 16; Mabillon, *Annales ordinis Sancti Benedicti*; Manitius, *Geschichte der lat. Literatur des Mittelalters*, I (Munich, 1911); Montalembert (Count de), *The Monks of the West*, vol. I (London, 1896), with an introduction by F. A. Gasquet; Ozanam, *Documents inédits pour servir à l'histoire littéraire de l'Italie depuis le viii*^{e} *siècle jusqu'au xiii*^{e} (Paris, 1850); Rose, 'Die Lücke im Diogenes Laertius und der alte Uebersetzer', in *Hermes*, I (1866), 367 ff.; Schipa, *Alfano I arcivescovo di Salerno* (Salerno, 1880); Tiraboschi, *Storia della letteratura italiana*, 2nd ed. (Modena, 1787–94); Traube, *Textgeschichte der Regula S. Benedicti*, 2nd ed. (Munich, 1911); *Vorlesungen und Abhandlungen*, vol. II (Munich, 1911), and his notes on Monte Cassino as a centre for the transmission of Roman authors; Wattenbach, *Deutschlands Geschichtsquellen*, I (7th ed.), II (6th ed.).

The Unique Manuscript of Apuleius' Metamorphoses *(Laurentian. 68. 2) and its Oldest Transcript (Laurentian. 29. 2)*

(*150*) THE chief works of Tacitus and Apuleius have come down to us in a single Beneventan—i.e. south Italian—manuscript of the eleventh century. The *Annals* (books XI–XVI) and *Histories* (books I–V) of Tacitus, and the *Apologia*, *Metamorphoses*, and *Florida* of Apuleius, depend solely on the authority of the famous Florentine manuscript preserved in the Laurentian Library under the press-mark 68. 2. Any new light that can be thrown on such a manuscript is of interest to classical scholars. With the portion of the manuscript containing the works of Tacitus the writer has dealt at some length in a paper read in April 1913, in London before the International Congress of Historical Studies, which paper will be published shortly. Here it is proposed to deal with the portion containing the works of Apuleius, and with the oldest extant transcript of this portion, which is also in Beneventan writing, and is likewise preserved in the Laurentian Library under the press-mark 29. 2. In the critical apparatus of Apuleius Laur. 68. 2 is cited as *F*, and Laur. 29. 2 as *φ*.

THE TWO PARTS OF LAUR. 68. 2

Before proceeding to the main subject a few words should be said on the relations of the two portions of Laur. 68. 2.

The manuscript is composed of two distinct parts: fols. 1–103 contain Tacitus; fols. 104–91 contain Apuleius. The two parts did not form one volume originally, and C. Paoli had observed that in an earlier binding the works of Apuleius preceded those of Tacitus.[1] We do not know when the works of Tacitus and Apuleius were first joined under one cover. When Professor H. E. Butler says in his preface to the Oxford edition of the *Apologia*[2] that 'the only mention of the works of Tacitus at Monte Cassino suggests

From *The Classical Quarterly*, XIV (1920), 150–5.

[1] Cf. Rostagno, *Praefatio*, p. 11, in the facsimile edition of Tacitus (68. 2) in *Codd. Graeci et Latini photographice depicti*, vol. VII, pars. 2 (Leyden, 1902).

[2] H. E. Butler and A. S. Owen, *Apulei Apologia*, pp. xxxi f. (Oxford, 1914).

that they were bound up with the poems of Homer' he is giving currency to an erroneous and discarded interpretation of an item in a catalogue in the Chronicle of Monte Cassino.[1] Professor Butler further says that the hands of the Tacitus and Apuleius portions are identical. Professor Rostagno in his *Praefatio* (p. xvi) expresses himself more cautiously, and says that they are very much alike. That the two hands are not identical may be seen from the (*151*)
following points of difference (let *T* represent the scribe of Tacitus and *F* the scribe of Apuleius):[2]

T used ·,· as the punctuation at the end of a paragraph; *F*, on the other hand, uses the simple point (.). *T* frequently uses two horizontal lines to indicate abbreviation (**c̿** = con, **e̿** = est, **n̿** = non, **u̿** = uer, etc.); whereas *F* invariably uses the single horizontal stroke. Final **r** is short in *T*; in *F* it descends below the line. In *T* the down-stroke of **p** has a curious and characteristic inclination to the left in the familiar 'pro'-symbol (ꝓ), so much so that the symbol somewhat resembles the letter **x**;[3] in *F* this pronounced difference between ordinary **p** and the **p** in the 'pro'-symbol does not exist. The form of assibilated **ti** (as in 'spatia') is different in *T* and *F*. In *F* the upper loop of this 8-shaped ligature is considerably to the right of the lower loop. This is much less marked in *T*. These differences are enough to prove that *T* and *F* are not identical: that in MS. Laur. 68. 2 one scribe wrote the Tacitus and quite another scribe the Apuleius. There is moreover a marked difference in the general impression made by *T* and *F*. The latter represents a further stage of development. If the Tacitus was copied, as script and historical considerations go to show, about the middle of the eleventh century the Apuleius may reasonably be ascribed to the end of that century. So much for the relation between the Tacitus and Apuleius portions of MS. Laur. 68. 2.

ON THE MANUSCRIPTS OF APULEIUS

Ever since H. Keil made the discovery that all the manuscripts of Apuleius' *Metamorphoses* suffer from a lacuna in book VIII, caused by a partially torn page in Laur. 68. 2, it has been universally recognized that all manuscripts

[1] See F. Haase's edition of Tacitus I, p. lxix, and M. Manitius, *Philologisches aus alten Bibliothekscatalogen*, p. 68, in *Rheinisches Museum*, xlvii (1892), Ergänzungsheft.

[2] Facsimiles of *F* will be found in R. Helm's edition of the *Florida* (Leipzig, 1910). Of *T* we have a complete facsimile reproduction in the Leyden series, and E. Chatelain reproduces a page in his *Paléographie des classiques latins*, p. 146.

[3] This is very striking where ordinary **p** and the 'pro'-symbol come together. Cf. col. 2, ll. 2 and 3 of fol. 38, the page reproduced by Chatelain.

are derived from the single source, Laur. 68. 2.[1] Corroborative evidence has since been adduced by R. Helm, who showed that in a certain passage in the *Apologia*, where, owing to extreme thinness of parchment in *F*, a letter **u** shows through between the words 'inducat' and 'animum', some manuscripts have 'inducatu animum', and others, resorting to conjecture, give 'inducat in animum'.[2] Of all the transcripts of *F* only one is of importance, and that is *ϕ*, or Laur. 29. 2. It is important to us for two reasons: it was written before its exemplar *F* was as badly defaced as it is now, so that for a number of readings we depend entirely on *ϕ*, since *F* has become illegible. Whether or not in such cases *ϕ* is to be trusted implicitly we shall see presently. The other reason is that *ϕ* is the oldest manuscript in which the lacuna in *F* referred to above is supplied. This supplement could be derived from a manuscript of
(*152*) Apuleius now lost, or from the portion torn out of *F*, which had been recovered, or it may be the result of clever conjecturing. That the last is the most likely is the conclusion reached by the writer after a careful examination of *F* (fols. 160^{r} and 160^{v}) and *ϕ* (fols. 53^{r} and 53^{v}).

No one who has compared a page of text in *ϕ* with the same text in *F* will for a moment maintain that *ϕ* is a painfully accurate copy of its exemplar. A careful comparison of the text on the torn folio (160^{r} and 160^{v}) in *F* with the corresponding folio (53^{r} and 53^{v}) in *ϕ* has convinced me that the scribe of *ϕ* differed from the average scribe in that he tried to make sense of what he was copying, and that when his exemplar seemed faulty or dubious or had what seemed to him archaic spelling he did not hesitate to change or emend. He did not copy word for word, but carried entire phrases or clauses in his mind, with the result that he made gratuitous modifications and transpositions. Nor did he try his utmost to decipher all that was possible. For when he came to the faded writing at the foot of fol. 159^{v} in *F* (*Metam.* VIII. 6, ed. Helm, 180, 23–4) he left blank spaces for the words that were difficult to read. He wrote (top of fol. 53^{r}):

> ipse fecerat auide circumplexus, omnia quidem lu-
> gentium officia ——————— affinxit sed sole la-
> crime procedere noluerunt. Sic ———————
> ——————————— lamentabamur, etc.

A much later hand (the hand that supplied the other lacuna) inserted 'sollerter' after 'officia'. Even today, after a lapse of seven centuries, when the original from which *ϕ* copied is certainly less and not more legible than it was

[1] H. Keil, *Observationes in Catonis et Varronis de re rustica libros* (Halle, 1849), pp. 77 f.

[2] See his preface (pp. xxix f.) to the Teubner edition of the *Florida*.

in the thirteenth century, when ϕ was written, we can still discern 's.l..rter'. Yet the scribe of ϕ apparently made no effort to write what was in *F*. And of the large omission after 'sic' a careful inspection of *F* still reveals 'ad $\overline{\text{nri}}$ (= nostri) s.......dinem q(ui) u.re.[1]' This goes to show that the scribe of ϕ was not painstaking. Nor was he a conscientious scribe. For he did not hesitate to write what he did not actually see, as may be seen from his inserting a word between 'uulnera' and 'lancea',[2] where *F* has 'non sunt tota dentium uul.... lancea mali Thrasilli', etc. The gap which occurs between 'uul' and 'lancea' is at the beginning of a line, and it is mathematically demonstrable that only four letters preceded 'lancea'. They are, of course, 'nera'. But the scribe of ϕ added 'sed' before 'lancea' because the sense seemed to him to require it, and he did not stop to measure the space to see if it could possibly have been there. This helps one to form an idea of his fidelity to his exemplar. That he takes other liberties with his original may be seen from his constantly writing 'Tharsillus' for *F*'s 'Thrasillus', and 'Alepolemus' for 'Tlepolemus'. We must not suppose that the scribe of ϕ failed to distinguish between **a** and **t**, which in Beneventan are liable to confusion. He saw that *F* had **t** in 'Tlepolemus', but apparently regarded it as an error for **a** by the scribe of *F*. The scribe of ϕ *(153)*
invariably changes the better spelling **ae** (the **e** with cedilla of *F*) to **e**, and the unassimilated form of compound verbs to the assimilated ('adfixit' to 'affixit', 'subcumbens' to 'succumbens', 'adquiescas' to 'acquiescas', etc.). *F* has 'bacchata', ϕ 'bachata'; *F* 'adhibere', ϕ 'adibere'; *F* 'hilaro', ϕ 'hylaro'; *F* has 'formonsus', ϕ 'formosus'; *F* 'charites', ϕ 'carites'. Here and there ϕ inverts the order in *F* or makes slight additions. Where *F* has 'uerum religiosae necessitati', ϕ has 'uerum etiam necessitati religiose'; *F* has 'iterans', ϕ 'reiterans'; *F* 'mortis meae', ϕ 'mee mortis'; *F* 'nullo lumine conscio', ϕ 'nullo conscio lumine'. Where *F* has (*Met.* VIII. 10, Helm 185, 9) the impossible 'nec ecce est mihi', the scribe of ϕ, without the least interruption in the flow of his writing, gives us the correct 'necesse est mihi'.

Further illustration of the method followed by the scribe of ϕ is to be had from an examination of his treatment of the lacuna which occurs in folio 160^{r}–160^{v} of his exemplar (*Met.* VIII. 7–8, ed. Helm 182, 7–15). Where *F* has 'vultu non quidem hilaro, uerum ...lo sereniore', the scribe of ϕ promptly supplied 'pau'. Again, where *F* has 'luctu ac maerore carpebat animum .. .. tos totasque noctes insumebat l....... ....derio', the scribe of ϕ supplied

[1] Professor E. Rostagno very kindly examined this passage for me in both manuscripts.

[2] See fol. 160^{v}, col. 1, ll. 6–7. This leaf is reproduced in Helm's edition of the *Florida* (Leipzig, 1910).

after 'animum' the words 'et dies to', which is obviously right. But he did not venture to supply the next omission, though the ending 'derio' must have suggested 'desiderio'. This restraint on his part must be placed to his credit. And a few lines above, where *F* has 'iubebatur, uiuentium ..nia', the scribe of ϕ makes no effort to guess the missing two letters, but leaves space for them and writes 'ma'—his misreading of 'nia'.

The above comparison of two pages in *F* (fols. 160^{r}–160^{v}) with the corresponding two pages of ϕ (fols. 53^{r}–53^{v}) is sufficient to enable us to form an estimate of the degree of confidence one may attach to those readings which, owing to their faded condition in *F*, depend solely on the authority of the first hand in ϕ. And here palaeography may give a word of warning. The pages in *F* which are now illegible, or almost so, were already hard to read in the thirteenth century. It seems that the manner of preparing the parchment at Monte Cassino in the eleventh century was such as to reduce the absorbing quality of the flesh side of the parchment. This accounts for the numerous eleventh-century manuscripts from Monte Cassino in which two sides of legible script alternate with two that are faded. The ink on the hair-side of the skin has weathered the centuries well, but has scaled off the flesh-side of the parchment. That the defacement took place within a couple of centuries after the manuscripts were written may be seen from the fact that eleventh-century manuscripts had to be retouched in the thirteenth century. An excellent example is furnished by Laur. 68. 2 itself, which on fols. 102^{v} and 103^{r} (the end of the Tacitus) shows thirteenth-century Beneventan letters covering the faded letters of the eleventh century.[1]

(*154*) THE DATE OF ϕ

The trustworthiness of ϕ has been impugned to some extent by Professor Rossbach's claim that it is a humanistic copy purposely written to resemble Beneventan. Professor Rossbach has expressed this view of ϕ on a number of occasions,[2] and has recently reiterated it in his review of Butler and Owen's edition of Apuleius' *Apologia* (Oxford, 1914).[3] This view cannot be left unchallenged. Ever since Bandini, in 1764, in his catalogue of Laurentian Latin manuscripts ascribed ϕ to the twelfth century, scholars have been in the habit of using that date. Some editors, it is true (as Van der Vliet and Helm), influenced, perhaps, by Professor Rossbach's arguments, refrained from com-

[1] Cf. E. A. Lowe, *The Beneventan Script*, pp. 286 f.

[2] Cf. *Berliner Philologische Wochenschrift*, XVII (1897), col. 1041; ibid. XX (1900), col. 1479.

[3] Ibid. XXXVI (1916), col. 936.

mitting themselves. In my book on the Beneventan script, where ϕ is cited a number of times, it is regularly ascribed to the thirteenth century. Thus it is clear that I regard ϕ as a genuine Beneventan manuscript and not a humanistic *tour de force*.

If we examine the grounds on which Professor Rossbach bases his view, we find that his suspicions were aroused by the fact that the opening leaves of ϕ are in ordinary minuscule, and the so-called Lombardic writing does not begin before fol. 5. But there is nothing peculiar or striking in this to anyone familiar with the manuscripts of southern Italy. It is not at all rare to find both Beneventan and ordinary minuscule written by contemporary scribes in one and the same manuscript. If a scribe who had learned his writing outside of the Beneventan zone happened to be collaborating on a manuscript with a Beneventan scribe, the result had to be a manuscript of the mixed character of ϕ. Further details and evidence will be found in chapter v of *The Beneventan Script*, where the whole question is treated at length.

The next point adduced by Professor Rossbach is the strange look of the script, which to him is an all-too-careful and yet insufficiently exact copy of Beneventan. The unfamiliar aspect of ϕ, however, is due to the fact that it was written at a time when Beneventan was losing ground, when its century-old traditions were beginning to totter, and when innovations borrowed from ordinary minuscule were being freely adopted. This accounts for the frequent use of ordinary minuscule **a**, for the use of the horizontal stroke as well as the 3-stroke for omitted **m**, for the lapses in the use of **i**-longa, the **fi**-ligature and the Beneventan interrogation-point. But in all this ϕ does not stand alone. A number of other thirteenth-century manuscripts show a similar mixture of style and uncertainty in usage, an excellent case in point being furnished by the patristic MS. Rome Sessorian. 32 (2093). Another reason why the script of ϕ seems unfamiliar lies in the roundness of its characters. This type of writing was common in Bari and its vicinity, and it is quite likely that the scribe of ϕ came from that region. Professor Rossbach finds corroboration in the greyish tint of the ink and the clearness of the parchment. Here I must plead ignorance. Although I have examined nearly all extant Beneventan *(155)*
manuscripts, I have not found that ink or parchment are safe or helpful criteria. They may easily become so by the aid of chemistry and the microscope. Further evidence for his view Professor Rossbach finds in the abbreviations of ϕ, which, he claims, are fewer in number than in genuine Beneventan products. Assuming the truth of the statement, it would seem to make an unconvincing argument. But it is not true. As a simple test, I noted all the

abbreviations of *F*, a genuine Beneventan product, on fols. 160[r] and 160[v], and all the abbreviations in the corresponding text of *ϕ* (fols. 53[r] and 53[v]), and find that *ϕ*, far from having less abbreviations than *F*, has actually dozens more on each page.

According to Professor Rossbach, *ϕ* is one of a class of Renaissance manuscripts which reproduce the features of the exemplar, and are a stumbling block to the uninitiated. The latter part of the statement is apparently true; but to say that *ϕ* reproduces the features of its exemplar *F* is absurd. *F* is an eleventh-century manuscript, with characters and abbreviations typical of that century; *ϕ*, on the other hand, has both the script and the abbreviations of a distinctly later century. If *ϕ* is imitating *F*, why does it have **n̄o** (non) where *F* has **n̄**; **an̄iam** (animam) where *F* has **am̄am**; **c̄o** (con) where *F* has **c**; **ub̄** with superscript 2 (uerbis) where *F* has **ub̄**; **q̧** (quod) where *F* has **qđ**; **ł** (uel) where *F* has **uł**; the monogram for 'quidem' where *F* has three letters? And how account for the numerous abbreviations in *ϕ* which are altogether absent from *F*? How does it happen that these abbreviations are the very symbols we find in twelfth-and thirteenth-century Beneventan manuscripts? The explanation is simple enough: *ϕ* is a Beneventan manuscript of about the year 1200. For if a man imitate a script he must decide upon the period he is to imitate. If one insists that *ϕ* is an imitation, it must be not of an eleventh-century exemplar, but of a thirteenth-century exemplar.[1] As no such exemplar existed, *ϕ* is no imitation. I need not point out that a humanist wishing to imitate Beneventan would hardly choose his model from the worst period of the script, when a model from the best period was at hand in the very manuscript he wished to copy. When Professor Rossbach further cites the *Guelferbytanus* of Tibullus, the *Leidensis Perizonianus* of Tacitus, and the *Leidensis Vossianus* of the *Periochae* of Livy as examples of similar Renaissance imitations ('von ähnlich geschriebenen Codices') one must admit that the three manuscripts mentioned are Renaissance products, and that they do attempt to revive an earlier stage of writing; but it must also be stated that no one with knowledge of Latin manuscripts can fail to detect the Renaissance earmarks in their script and decoration. The very opposite is true of *ϕ*: no one with experience of Latin manuscripts is likely to question its bona fide antiquity.[2]

[1] Not only are script and abbreviations in *ϕ* typical of the thirteenth century, but all other graphic features are true to type.

[2] I have recently consulted the opinion of Professor Rostagno and Professor Schiaparelli, two excellent connoisseurs of Italian manuscripts. They both ascribe *ϕ* to the twelfth century.

On the Oldest Extant Manuscript of the Combined Abstrusa *and* Abolita *Glossaries*

As a contributory step toward a new edition of Du Cange's *Glossarium mediae et infimae latinitatis*, planned by the International Association of Academies, the British Academy has undertaken to publish a critical edition of medieval glossaries. The most important of these glossaries, because it constitutes the parent-compilation from which subsequent compilers of glossaries drew their material, is that pair known as *Abstrusa* and *Abolita*, found combined in the Vatican MS. 3321, which is the oldest extant manuscript of purely Latin glossaries. It is with the date and home of this manuscript that the present note is concerned. *(189)*

The manuscript was used by Arevalo for his edition of the works of Isidore.[1] The first one to use the glossaries was Angelo Mai, the great discoverer of palimpsests.[2] He referred to it as 'codicem unum mirabilem litteris grandibus saeculi ferme VI'. The first careful description of the manuscript we owe to A. Wilmanns.[3] It was left to Gustav Loewe to point out the important position which this manuscript occupies among glossaries: 'Omnium codicum glossas mere latinas exhibentium uetustissimus esse uidetur Vaticanus 3321'.[4] The complete text of the glossaries was published by Loewe's colleague, G. Goetz, in the *Corpus glossariorum latinorum*, IV. 3–198 (Leipzig, 1889). During the past few years the subject of medieval Latin glossaries has received fresh treatment at the hands of Professor W. M. Lindsay. He has dealt with the manuscript in question in this journal, vol. XI (1917), pp. 120 ff. A good facsimile of the manuscript is given by Chatelain.[5]

The manuscript contains 234 leaves, measuring 155 by 210 mm., with 30 lines to a page. The fly-leaves A and B are from an eighth-century uncial manuscript of homilies, in two columns. The binding is in modern vellum, showing the arms of Cardinal Pitra (1869–89). The manuscript belonged to

From *The Classical Quarterly*, XV (1921), 189–91.

[1] *S. Isidori Hispalensis episcopi opera omnia*, II. 270 (Rome, 1797).

[2] *Class. Auct.* VI. 501–51 (Rome, 1843). He printed excerpts from this manuscript along with excerpts from seven other glossaries preserved in Vatican manuscripts.

[3] *Rheinisches Museum*, XXIV (1869), 381 ff.

[4] *Prodromus corporis glossariorum*, pp. 143 f. (Leipzig, 1876).

[5] *Uncialis scriptura*, pl. XLVB.

the Sicilian humanist, Panormita (1394–1471), later to Fulvio Orsini (1529–1600), who bequeathed it, with the rest of his manuscripts, to the Vatican Library.[1] The parchment is thick, and not very well prepared. Quires are signed in the middle of the lower margin of the last page. The outside pages of each quire show the flesh side of the vellum. The ruling is on the flesh side.

Abbreviations are frequent. This is partly due to the nature of the subject matter. Besides the Nomina Sacra, which are normal, there occur: **B;** = bus. **Q;** = que. **A:**[2] = aut. **AVT:** = autem. **E** = est. **Id** = id est. **ISL** = Israhel.
(190) **IT** = item. **N** = non. **NR** = noster. **ꝑ** = per. **ꝓ** = pro. **QM** = quoniam. **R** (with stroke above letter, or intersecting the right leg) = rum. **T** (with horizontal stroke) = tur. **V** (with horizontal stroke) = uel. Recurrent phrases like 'inter . . et . . quid interest' are abbreviated in various ways, and many arbitrary abbreviations are used at the end of lines where the scribe was crowded for space. Omissions are indicated by means of **HD** in the text and corresponding **HS** in the lower margin, placed either before or after the supplied word.[3] All these additions—and there are many of them—are in contemporary uncial writing. Words are not always separated. Two correctors are contemporary, and use uncials, a third uses ordinary minuscule of the tenth century (fol. 90). Marginalia were added by a humanistic hand of the fifteenth century.

On the date of the manuscript scholars have expressed very divergent views. Angelo Mai was ready to assign this 'wonderful codex' to the sixth century.[4] Loewe and Goetz attribute it to the seventh.[4] This is also the date given by Traube.[5] But Reifferscheid,[6] Chatelain, and Lindsay[7] ascribe the manuscript to the eighth century, which seems to me the more correct date. The number and kind of abbreviations used and the form of the letters **T**, **L**, and especially of **LL** coming together, with the two shafts joined at the top by one horizontal hair-line, conform very well with eighth-century usage, but not so well with seventh-century usage. If the manuscript cannot, on the one hand, be

[1] The last page has the entry: 'ANT. PANORMITAE.' The paper fly-leaf has the entry: 'Lexicon di voce sacre et profane con alcune operette de Isidoro Ispalense, et altri, scritto di lettere maiuscole, in 4°, in carta pergamena tocco dal Panormita Ful. Vrs.' This entry is not Fulvio Orsini's, as is commonly supposed, but the work of an eighteenth-century library official, whose entries are found in other manuscripts of the Orsini collection. P. de Nolhac gives a facsimile of this hand (which he too mistook for Fulvio Orsini's) in his excellent book, *La Bibliothèque de Fulvio Orsini*, Specimen VIII, and 'Note sur la planche' (Paris, 1887).

[2] I omit the horizontal stroke above the letters.

[3] On fol. 188v **HS** occurs after the supplied line instead of before it. This is very old usage, and is rarely found after the seventh century.

[4] Op. cit.

[5] *Textgeschichte der Regula S. Benedicti* (1st ed.), p. 104.

[6] *Bibliotheca patr. lat. Ital.* I. 545.

[7] Op. cit.

moved back to the seventh century, neither can it be pushed forward to the ninth: the use of $\overline{\mathbf{T}}$ for 'tur' and the very imperfect separation of words prevent us from regarding the manuscript as more recent than the eighth century.[1] The general impression of the script also favours the eighth. Moreover, the fact that all the contemporary additions and corrections are in uncial would seem to argue for the first half rather than for the second half of that century. Compared with the Autun Gospels (MS. 3) of the year 754[2] our manuscript makes an older impression; compared with the Milan MS. of Gregory (Ambros. B. 159 sup.)[3] written about 750, it makes a somewhat more recent impression. This discrepancy may be due to the fact that the Autun MS. was written in France, the Milan MS. in Bobbio, north Italy, while our manuscript may actually come from south Italy, or the vicinity of Rome.

There is nothing to indicate where the manuscript was written. The two fly-leaves in uncial letters, taken from another manuscript, the contemporary addition STEPHANUS ARHIPBR BIBAT (!), the later minuscule additions do not throw any new light; nor does the portrait on fol. 1^{v}, of a teacher, a cleric, seated on his throne (it recalls the well-known portrait of the seated Vergil, in the Codex Romanus), help us to place the manuscript. The manuscript was certainly written in Italy. One is tempted to connect it with south Italy, because pieces of parchment, with Beneventan writing, were used to strengthen the binding, and traces of this writing are still seen on the paper fly-leaf. Also the fact that a manuscript with a somewhat similar text is still preserved at Monte Cassino (MS. 439 saec. x) and is written in the south Italian minuscule, tends to favour the same locality. Against this, it must be borne in mind that there are no additions in Beneventan writing, and all the minuscule additions at the beginning and end of the volume are in ordinary minuscule. While it is true that ordinary minuscule was used in the Beneventan zone during the entire period when Beneventan was the ruling script in southern *(191)*
Italy,[4] as many manuscripts attest, it would none the less be odd for a manuscript of south Italian origin to have all its additions in ordinary minuscule and none in Beneventan. This consideration leaves open the possibility that the manuscript is a product of some scriptorium north of the Beneventan zone. It shows no resemblance to the manuscripts of famous north Italian centres like Bobbio and Verona. Of schools in central Italy we know too little to help us in forming a judgement. As the famous Naples manuscript of Festus

[1] The use of **HS** *after* the supplied line on fol. 188^{v} argues for the older date; see n. 3, p. 100 above.

[2] Steffens, *Lat. Paläog.*[2], pl. 37; Zangemeister–Wattenbach, *Exempla Cod. Lat.*, etc. Suppl., pl. LXI.

[3] *Palaeographical Society*, I, pl. 121.

[4] Cf. *The Beneventan Script*, pp. 84 ff.

was written, as has been shown, in Rome or its vicinity,[1] it is not at all unlikely that this important compilation of glossaries, which shows much dependence on Festus, may also come from a centre in Rome or its vicinity.

To sum up: the manuscript is certainly Italian. It is probably south Italian, though there is a possibility of its being central Italian, or even Roman. The most probable date is about the middle of the eighth century, before 750 rather than after.

[1] Cf. *Berliner Philologische Wochenschrift*, no. 29 (1911), cols. 917 f. [above, pp. 66 f.]

The Palaeography of the Morgan Fragment (3)

DESCRIPTION OF THE FRAGMENT

Contents—size—vellum—binding

THE Morgan fragment of Pliny the Younger contains the end of book II and the beginning of book III of the *Letters* (II. XX. 13–III. V. 4). The fragment consists of six vellum leaves, or twelve pages, which apparently formed part of a gathering or quire of the original volume.

The leaves measure $11\frac{3}{8}$ by 7 in. (286 × 180 mm.); the written space measures $7\frac{1}{4}$ by $4\frac{3}{8}$ in. (175 × 114 mm.); outer margin; $1\frac{7}{8}$ in. (50 mm.); inner, $\frac{3}{4}$ in. (18 mm.); upper margin, $1\frac{3}{4}$ in. (45 mm.); lower; $2\frac{1}{4}$ in. (60 mm.).

The vellum is well prepared and of medium thickness. The leaves are bound in a modern pliable vellum binding with three blank vellum fly-leaves in front and seven in back, all modern. On the inside of the front cover is the book-plate of John Pierpont Morgan, showing the Morgan arms with the device: *Onward and Upward*. Under the book-plate is the pressmark M. 462.

Ruling

There are twenty-seven horizontal lines to a page and two vertical bounding lines. The lines were ruled with a hard point on the flesh side, each opened sheet being ruled separately: fols. 48^v and 53^r, 49^r and 52^v, 50^v and 51^r. The horizontal lines were guided by knife-slits made in the outside margins quite close to the text space; the two vertical lines were guided by two slits in the upper margin and two in the lower. The horizontal lines were drawn across the open sheets and extended occasionally beyond the slits, more often just beyond the perpendicular bounding lines. The written space was kept inside the vertical bounding lines except for the initial letter of each epistle; the first letter of the address and the first letter of the epistle proper projected into the left margin. Here and there the scribe transgressed beyond the bounding line. On the whole, however, he observed the limits and seemed to prefer to leave a blank before the bounding line rather than to crowd the syllable into the space or go beyond the vertical line.

From *A Sixth-Century Fragment of the Letters of Pliny the Younger* (with E. K. Rand): Washington, Carnegie Institution, 1922, pp. 3–22. [See Pls. **8** to **21**.]

Relation of the six leaves to the rest of the manuscript

One might suppose that the six leaves once formed a complete gathering of the original book, especially as the first and last pages, fols. 48^{r} and 53^{v}, have a darker appearance, as though they had been the outside leaves of a gathering that had been affected by exposure. But this darker appearance is sufficiently accounted for by the fact that both pages are on the hair side of the parch-
(4) ment, and the hair side is always darker than the flesh side. Quires of six leaves or trinions are not unknown. Examples of them may be found in our oldest manuscripts. But they are the exception.[1] The customary quire is a gathering of eight leaves, forming a quaternion proper. It would be natural, therefore, to suppose that our fragment did not constitute a complete gathering in itself but formed part of a quaternion. The supposition is confirmed by the following considerations:

In the first place, if our six leaves were once a part of a quaternion, the two leaves needed to complete them must have formed the outside sheet, since our fragment furnishes a continuous text without any lacuna whatever. Now, in the formation of quires, sheets were so arranged that hair side faced hair side, and flesh side flesh side. This arrangement is dictated by a sense of uniformity. As the hair side is usually much darker than the flesh side the juxtaposition of hair and flesh sides would offend the eye. So, in the case of our six leaves, fols. 48^{v} and 53^{r}, presenting the flesh side, face fols. 49^{r} and 52^{v} likewise on the flesh side; and fols. 49^{v} and 52^{r}, presenting the hair side, face fols. 50^{r} and 51^{v} likewise on the hair side. The inside pages 50^{v} and 51^{r}, which face each other, are both flesh side, and the outside pages 48^{r} and 53^{v} are both hair side, as may be seen from the accompanying diagram.

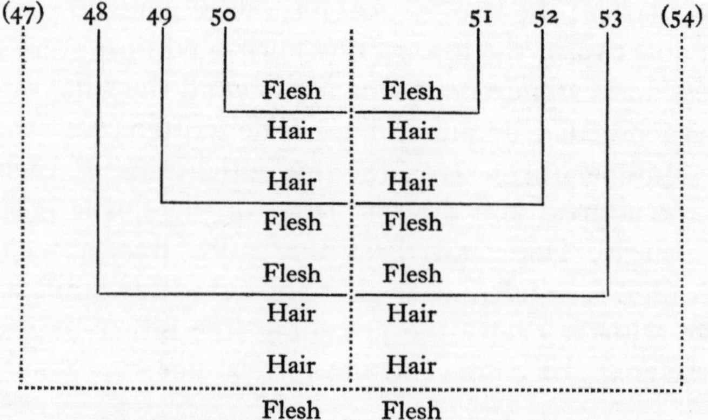

[1] For example, in the fifth-century manuscript of Livy in Paris (MS. lat. 5730) the forty third and forty-fifth quires are composed of six leaves, while the rest are all quires of eight.

From this arrangement it is evident that if our fragment once formed part of a quaternion the missing sheet was so folded that its hair side faced the present outside sheet and its flesh side was on the outside of the whole gathering. Now, it was by far the more usual practice in our oldest uncial manu- (5)
scripts to have the flesh side on the outside of the quire.[1] And as our fragment belongs to the oldest class of uncial manuscripts, the manner of arranging the sheets of quires seems to favour the supposition that two outside leaves are missing. The hypothesis is, moreover, strengthened by another consideration. According to the foliation supplied by the fifteenth-century Arabic numerals, the leaf which must have followed our fragment bore the number 54, the leaf preceding it having the number 47. If we assume that our fragment was a complete gathering, we are obliged to explain why the next gathering began on a leaf bearing an even number (54), which is abnormal. We do not have to contend with this difficulty if we assume that fols. 47 and 54 formed the outside sheet of our fragment, for six quires of eight leaves and one of six would give precisely 54 leaves. It seems, therefore, reasonable to assume that our fragment is not a complete unit, but formed part of a quaternion, the outside sheet of which is missing.

Original size of the manuscript

In the fifteenth century, as the previous demonstration has made clear, our fragment was preceded by 47 leaves that are missing today. With this clue in our possession it can be demonstrated that the manuscript began with the first book of the *Letters*. We start with the fact that not all the 47 folios (or 94 pages) which preceded our 6 leaves were devoted to the text of the *Letters*. For, from the contents of our 6 leaves we know that each book must have been preceded by an index of addresses and first lines. The indexes for books I and II, if arranged in general like that of book III, must have occupied 4 pages.[2]

[1] In an examination of all the uncial manuscripts in the Bibliothèque Nationale of Paris, it was found that out of twenty manuscripts that may be ascribed to the fifth and sixth centuries only two had the hair side on the outside of the quires. Out of thirty written approximately between A.D. 600 and 800, about half showed the same practice, the other half having the hair side outside. Thus the practice of our oldest Latin scribes agrees with that of the Greek: see C. R. Gregory, 'Les Cahiers des manuscrits grecs' in *Comptes Rendus de l'Académie des Inscriptions et Belles-Lettres* (1885), p. 261. I am informed by Professor Hyvernat, of the Catholic University of Washington, that the same custom is observed by Coptic scribes.

[2] The confused arrangement of the indexes for books I and II in the Codex Bellovacensis may well have been found in the manuscript of which the Morgan fragment is a part. The space required for the indexes, however, would not have greatly differed from that taken by the index of book III in both the Morgan fragment and the Codex Bellovacensis.

We also learn from our fragment that space must be allowed for a colophon at the end of each book. One page for the colophons of books I and II is a reasonable allowance. Accordingly it follows that out of the 94 pages preceding our fragment 5 were not devoted to text, or in other words that only 89 pages were thus devoted.

Now, if we compare pages in our manuscript with pages of a printed text we find that the average page in our manuscript corresponds to about 19 lines of the Teubner edition of 1912. If we multiply 89 by 19 we get 1691. This number of lines of the size of the Teubner edition should, if our calculation be correct, contain the text of the *Letters* preceding our fragment. The average page of the Teubner edition of 1912 of the part which interests us contains a little over 29 lines. If we divide 1691 by 29 we get 58·3. Just 58 pages of Teubner text are occupied by the 47 leaves which preceded our fragment. So close a conformity is sufficient to prove our point. We have possibly allowed too much space for indexes and colophons, especially if the former
(6) covered less ground for books I and II than for book III. Further, owing to the abbreviation of 'que' and 'bus', and particularly of official titles, we cannot expect a closer agreement.

It is not worth while to attempt a more elaborate calculation. With the edges matching so nearly, it is obvious that the original manuscript as known and used in the fifteenth century could not have contained some other work, however brief, before book I of Pliny's *Letters*. If the manuscript contained the entire ten books it consisted of about 260 leaves. This sum is obtained by counting the number of lines in the Teubner edition of 1912, dividing this sum by 19, and adding thereto pages for colophons and indexes. It would be too bold to suppose that this calculation necessarily gives us the original size of the manuscript, since the manuscript may have had less than ten books, or it may, on the other hand, have had other works. But if it contained only the ten books of the *Letters*, then 260 folios is an approximately correct estimate of its size.

It is hard to believe that only six leaves of the original manuscript have escaped destruction. The fact that the outside sheet (fols. 48^{r} and 53^{v}) is not much worn nor badly soiled suggests that the gathering of six leaves must have been torn from the manuscript not so very long ago and that the remaining portions may some day be found.

Disposition

The pages in our manuscript are written in long lines,[1] in *scriptura continua*, with hardly any punctuation.

Each page begins with a large letter, even though that letter occur in the body of a word (cf. fols. 48^{r}, 51^{v}, 52^{r}).[2]

Each epistle begins with a large letter. The line containing the address which precedes each epistle also begins with a large letter. In both cases the large letter projects into the left margin.

The running title at the top of each page is in small rustic capitals.[3] On the verso of each folio stands the word EPISTULARUM; on the recto of the following folio stands the number of the book, e.g. LIB. II, LIB. III.

To judge by our fragment, each book was preceded by an index of addresses
and initial lines written in alternating lines of black and red uncials. Alternat- (7)
ing lines of black and red rustic capitals of a large size were used in the colophon.[4]

Ornamentation

As in all our oldest Latin manuscripts, the ornamentation is of the simplest kind. Such as it is, it is mostly found at the end and beginning of books. In our case the colophon is enclosed between two scrolls of vine-tendrils terminating in an ivy-leaf at both ends. The lettering in the colophon and in the running title is set off by means of ticking above and below the line.

Red is used for decorative purposes in the middle line of the colophon, in the scroll of vine-tendrils, in the ticking, and in the border at the end of the index on fol. 49. Red was also used, to judge by our fragment, in the first three

[1] Many of our oldest Latin manuscripts have two and even three columns on a page, a practice evidently taken over from the roll. But very ancient manuscripts are not wanting which are written in long lines, e.g. the Codex Vindobonensis of Livy, the Codex Bobiensis of the Gospels, or the manuscript of Pliny's *Natural History* preserved at St. Paul in Carinthia.

[2] This is an earmark of great antiquity. It is found, for example, in the Berlin and Vatican Schedae Vergilianae in square capitals (Berlin lat. 2° 416 and Rome Vatic. lat. 3256 reproduced in Zangemeister and Wattenbach's *Exempla Codicum Latinorum*, etc., pl. 14, and in Steffens, *Lateinische Paläographie*², pl. 12B), in the Vienna, Paris, and Lateran manuscripts of Livy, in the Codex Corbeiensis of the Gospels, and here and there in the palimpsest manuscript of Cicero's *De Re Publica* and in other manuscripts.

[3] In many of our oldest manuscripts uncials are employed. The Pliny palimpsest of St. Paul in Carinthia agrees with our manuscript in using rustic capitals. For facsimiles see J. Sillig, *C. Plini Secundi Naturalis Historiae libri xxxvi*, vol. VI (Gotha, 1855), and Chatelain, *Paléographie des Classiques Latins*, pl. CXXXVI.

[4] In this respect, too, the Pliny palimpsest of St. Paul in Carinthia agrees with our fragment. Most of the oldest manuscripts, however, have the colophon in the same type of writing as the text.

lines of a new book,[1] in the addresses in the index, and in the addresses preceding each letter.

Corrections

The original scribe made a number of corrections. The omitted line of the index on fol. 49 was added between the lines, probably by the scribe himself, using a finer pen; likewise the omitted line on fol. 52^v, ll. 7–8. A number of slight corrections come either from the scribe or from a contemporary reader; the others are by a somewhat later hand, which is probably not more recent than the seventh century.[2] The method of correcting varies. As a rule, the correct letter is added above the line over the wrong letter; occasionally it is written over an erasure. An omitted letter is also added above the line over the space where it should be inserted. Deletion of single letters is indicated by a dot placed over the letter and a horizontal or an oblique line drawn through it. This double use of expunction and cancellation is not uncommon in our oldest manuscripts. For details on the subject of corrections, see the notes on pp. 23–34.[3]

There is a ninth-century addition on fol. 53 and one of the fifteenth century on fol. 51. On fol. 49, in the upper margin, a fifteenth-century hand using a stilus or hard point scribbled a few words, now difficult to decipher.[4] Presumably the same hand drew a bearded head with a halo. Another relatively recent hand, using lead, wrote in the left margin of fol. 53^v the monogram QR[5] and the roman numerals i, ii, iii under one another. These numerals,
(8) as Professor Rand correctly saw, refer to the works of Pliny the Elder enumerated in the text. Further activity by this hand, the date of which it is impossible to determine, may be seen, for example, on fol. 49^v, ll. 8, 10, 15; fol. 52, ll. 4, 10, 13, 21, 22; fol. 53, ll. 12, 15, 16, 17, 20, 27; fol. 53^v, ll. 5, 10, 15.

Syllabification

Syllables are divided after a vowel or diphthong except where such a division involves beginning the next syllable with a group of consonants.[6] In that

[1] This is also the case in the Paris manuscript of Livy of the fifth century, in the Codex Bezae of the Gospels (published in facsimile by the University of Cambridge in 1899), in the Pliny palimpsest of St. Paul in Carinthia, and in many other manuscripts of the oldest type.

[2] The strokes over the two consecutive i's on fol. 53^v, l. 23, were made by a hand that can hardly be older than the thirteenth century.

[3] [Not reprinted in this volume. Ed.]

[4] I venture to read 'dominus meus . . . in te deus'.

[5] This doubtless stands for 'Quaere' (= 'investigate'), a frequent marginal note in manuscripts of all ages. A number of instances of Q for 'quaere' are given by A. C. Clark, *The Descent of Manuscripts* (Oxford, 1918), p. 35.

[6] Such a division as 'ut|or' on fol. 51^r, l. 10, is due entirely to thoughtless copying. The scribe probably took 'ut' for a word.

case the consonants are distributed between the two syllables, one consonant going with one syllable and the other with the following, except when the group contains more than two successive consonants, in which case the first consonant goes with the first syllable, the rest with the following syllable. That the scribe is controlled by this mechanical rule and not by considerations of pronunciation is obvious from the division SAN|CTISSIMUM and other examples found below. The method followed by him is made amply clear by the examples which occur in our twelve pages:[1]

fol. 48r, line 1, con—suleret
2, sescen—ties
3, ex—ta
7, fal—si
fol. 49v, line 3, spu—rinnam
5, senesce—re
7, distin—ctius
12, se—nibus
13, con—ueniunt
15, spurin—na
18, circum—agit
20, mi—lia
24, prae—sentibus
25, grauan—tur
fol. 50r, line 1, singu—laris
4, an—tiquitatis
5, au—dias
9, ite—rum
11, scri—bit
12, ly—rica
15, scri—bentis
17, octa—ua
19, uehe—menter
20, exer—citationis
21, se—nectute
22, paulis—per
23, le—gentem
fol. 50v, line 2, de—lectatur
3, co—moedis
4, uolupta—tes
5, ali—quid
6, lon—gum
11, senec—tute
12, uo—to
13, ingres—surus
14, ae—tatis
15, in—terim
16, ho—rum
20, re—xit
21, me—ruit
22, eun—dem (9)
25, epis—tulam
fol. 51r, line 2, mi—hi
4, arria—nus

1 For further details on syllabification in our oldest Latin manuscripts, see Th. Mommsen, 'Livii Codex Veronensis', in *Abhandlungen der k. Akad. d. Wiss. zu Berlin, phil.-hist. Cl.* (1868), p. 163, n. 2, and pp. 165–6; Mommsen-Studemund, *Analecta Liviana* (Leipzig, 1873), p. 3; Brandt, 'Der St. Galler Palimpsest', in *Sitzungsberichte der phil.-hist. Cl. der k. Akad. der Wiss. in Wien*, CVIII (1885), 245–6; L. Traube, 'Palaeographische Forschungen IV', in *Abhandlungen d. k. Bayer. Akad. d. Wiss.*, III. Cl., XXIV. 1 (1906), 27; A. W. Van Buren, 'The Palimpsest of Cicero's *De Re Publica*', in *Archaeological Institute of America, Supplementary Papers of the American School of Classical Studies in Rome*, II (1908), 89 ff.; C. Wessely, in his preface to the facsimile edition of the Vienna Livy (MS. lat. 15), published in the Leyden series, *Codices graeci et latini*, etc., tom. XI. See also W. G. Hale, 'Syllabification in Roman speech', in *Harvard Studies in Classical Philology*, VII (1896), 249–71, and W. Dennison, 'Syllabification in Latin Inscriptions', in *Classical Philology*, I (1906), 47–68.

6, facultati—bus
7, super—sunt
8, gra—uitate
9, consi—lio
10, ut—or
13, ar—dentius
23, con—feras
24, habe—bis
27, concu—piscat
fol. 51^{v}, line 3, san—ctissimum
5, memo—riam
10, pater—nus
11, contige—rit
12, lau—de
14, hones—tis
15, refe—rat
17, contuber—nium
21, circumspi—ciendus
22, scho—lae
24, nos—tro
27, praecep—tor
fol. 52^{r}, line 2, demon—strare
5, iudi—cio
6, gra—uis
8, quan—tum
9, cre—dere
12, mag—nasque
13, ge—nitore
16, nes[cis]—se
19, nomi—na
20, fauen—tibus
23, dis—citur
fol. 52^{v}, line 1, uidean—tur
3, con—silium
5, concu—pisco
6, pecu—nia
7, excucuris—sem
10, se—natu
12, ne—cessitatibus
19, postulaue—runt
21, bae—bium
23, claris—sima
25, in—quam
26, excusa—tionis
fol. 53^{r}, line 1, com (*or* con)—pulit
5, ueni—ebat
7, iniu—rias
8, ex—secutos
10, prae—terea
12, aduoca—tione
13, con—seruandum
15, com—paratum
16, sub—uertas
17, cumu—les
18, obliga—ti
23, tris—tissimum
fol. 53^{v}, line 2, facili—orem
3, si—quis
5, offi—ciorum
7, praepara—tur
8, super—est
10, sim—plicitas
11, compro—bantis
14, diligen—ter
20, cog—nitio
22, milita—ret
26, exsol—uit

Orthography

The spelling found in our six leaves is remarkably correct. It compares favourably with the best spelling encountered in our oldest Latin manuscripts of the fourth and fifth centuries. The diphthong **ae** is regularly distinguished from **e.** The interchange of **b** and **u, d** and **t, o** and **u,** so common in later manuscripts, is rare here: the confusion between **b** and **u** occurs once ('comprouasse', fol. 52^{v}, l. 1); the omission of **h** occurs once ('pulcritudo', fol. 51^{v}, l. 26); the use of **k** for **c** occurs twice ('karet', fol. 51^{r}, l. 14, and 'karitas', fol. 52^{r}, l. 5). The scribe uses the correct forms in 'adolescet' (fol. 51^{v}, l. 14) and 'adulescenti' (fol. 51^{v}, l. 24); he writes 'auonculi' (fol. 53^{v}, l. 15), 'exsistat' (fol. 51^{v}, l. 9), and 'exsecutos' (fol. 53^{r}, l. 8). In the case of composite words he has the assimilated form in some, and in others the unassimilated form, as the following examples go to show:

fol. 48^{r}, line	3, inpleturus	fol. 48^{r}, line	7, improbissimum
49^{r},	13a, adnotasse	48^{v},	23, composuisse
	19, adsumo	50^{r},	1, ascendit
50^{r},	1, adsumit		6, imbuare
	27, adponitur		22, accubat
50^{v},	3, adficitur	51^{r},	2, optulissem
51^{r},	19, adstruere		3, suppeteret
	21, adstruere		16, ascendere
	26, adpetat	51^{v},	16, accipiat
51^{v},	9, exsistat	52^{v},	1, comprouasse
	12, inlustri		11, collegae
	14, inbutus		17, impetrassent
52^{r},	18, admonebitur	53^{r},	8, accusationibus
52^{v},	20, inplorantes		15, comparatum
	22, adlegantes	53^{v},	1, computabam
	24, adsensio		5, accusare
	27, adtulisse		11, comprobantis
53^{r},	8, exsecutos		23, composuit

Abbreviations

Very few abbreviated words occur in our twelve pages. Those that are found are subject to strict rules. What is true of the twelve pages was doubtless true of the entire manuscript, inasmuch as the sparing use of abbreviations in conformity with certain definite rules is a characteristic of all our oldest manuscripts.[1] The abbreviations found in our fragment may conveniently be grouped as follows:

[1] That is, manuscripts written before the eighth century. The number of abbreviations increases considerably during the eighth century. Previously the only symbols found in calligraphic majuscule manuscripts are the 'Nomina Sacra' (*deus, dominus, Iesus, Christus, spiritus, sanctus*), which constantly occur in Christian literature, and such suspensions as are met with in our fragment. A familiar exception is the manuscript of Gaius, preserved in the Chapter library of Verona, MS. xv (13). This is full of abbreviations not found in contemporary manuscripts containing purely literary or religious texts. Cf. W. Studemund, *Gaii Institutionum Commentarii Quattuor*, etc. (Leipzig, 1874); and F. Steffens, *Lateinische*

1. Suspensions which might occur in any ancient manuscript or inscription, e.g.:

B· = BUS
Q· = QUE[1]
·C̄· = GAIUS[2]
P· C· = PATRES CONSCRIPTI

2. Technical or recurrent terms which occur in the colophons at the end of each book and at the end of letters, as:

·EXP· = EXPLICIT
·INC· = INCIPIT
LIB· = LIBER
$\overline{\text{VAL}}$· = VALE[3]

(11) 3. Purely arbitrary suspensions which occur only in the index of addresses preceding each book, suspensions which would never occur in the body of the text, as: SUETON TRANQUE,[4] UESTRIC SPURINN.

4. Omitted **M** at the end of a line, omitted **N** at the end of a line, the omission being indicated by means of a horizontal stroke, thickened at either end, which is placed over the space immediately following the final vowel.[5] This omission may occur in the middle of a word but only at the end of a line.

Authenticity of the six leaves

The sudden appearance in America of a portion of a very ancient classical manuscript unknown to modern editors may easily arouse suspicion in the minds of some scholars. Our experience with the 'Anonymus Cortesianus' has taught us to be wary,[6] and it is natural to demand proof establishing the

Paläographie[2], pl. 18 (pl. 8 of the Supplement). The Oxyrhynchus papyrus of Cicero's speeches is non-calligraphic and therefore not subject to the rule governing calligraphic products. The same is true of marginal notes to calligraphic texts. See W. M. Lindsay, *Notae Latinae* (Cambridge, 1915), pp. 1–2.

[1] Found only at the end of words in our fragment. Its use in the body of a word is, however, very ancient.

[2] The C invariably has the two dots as well as the superior horizontal stroke.

[3] The abbreviation is indicated by a stroke above the letters as well as by a dot after them.

[4] An ancestor of our manuscript must have had TRANQ., which was wrongly expanded to TRANQUE.

[5] This is a sign of antiquity. After the sixth century the **M** or **N** stroke is usually placed above the vowel. The practice of confining the omission of **M** or **N** to the end of a line is a characteristic of our very oldest manuscripts. Later manuscripts omit **M** or **N** in the middle of a line and in the middle of a word. No distinction is made in our manuscript between omitted **M** and omitted **N**. Some ancient manuscripts make a distinction. Cf. Traube, *Nomina Sacra*, pp. 179, 181, 183, 185, final column of each page; and W. M. Lindsay, *Notae Latinae*, pp. 342 and 345.

[6] The fraudulent character of the alleged discovery was exposed in masterly fashion by Ludwig Traube in his 'Palaeographische Forschungen IV', published in the *Abhandlungen der*

genuineness of the new fragment.[1] As to the six leaves of the Morgan Pliny, it may be said unhesitatingly that no one with experience of ancient Latin manuscripts could entertain any doubt as to their genuineness. The look and feel of the parchment, the ink, the script, the titles, colophons, ornamentation, corrections, and later additions, all bear the indisputable marks of genuine antiquity.

But it may be objected that a clever forger possessing a knowledge of palaeography would be able to reproduce all these features of ancient manuscripts. This objection can hardly be sustained. It is difficult to believe that any modern could reproduce faithfully all the characteristics of sixth-century uncials and fifteenth-century notarial writing without unconsciously falling into some error and betraying his modernity. Besides, there is one consideration which to my mind establishes the genuineness of our fragment beyond a peradventure. We have seen above that the leaves of our manuscript are so arranged that hair side faces hair side and flesh side faces flesh side. The visible effect of this arrangement is that two pages of clear writing alternate with two pages of faded writing, the faded appearance being caused by the ink scaling off from the less porous surface of the flesh side of the vellum.[2]
As a matter of fact, the flesh side of the vellum showed faded writing long *(12)*
before modern times. To judge by the retouched characters on fol. 53^r it would seem that the original writing had become illegible by the eighth or ninth century.[3] Still, a considerable period of time would, so far as we know, be necessary for this process. It is highly improbable that a forger could devise this method of giving his forgery the appearance of antiquity, and even if he attempted it, it is safe to say that the present effect would not be produced in the time that elapsed before the book was sold to Mr. Morgan.

But let us assume, for the sake of argument, that the Morgan fragment is a modern forgery. We are then constrained to credit the forger not only with a knowledge of palaeography which is simply faultless, but, as will be shown in the second part, with a minute acquaintance with the criticism and the history of the text. And this forger did not try to attain fame or academic

Bayerischen Akademie der Wissenschaften, III. Klasse, XXIV. Band, I. Abteilung (Munich, 1904).

[1] Cf. E. T. Merrill, 'On the Use by Aldus of his Manuscripts of Pliny's *Letters*', in *Classical Philology*, XIV (1919), 34.

[2] That the hair side of the vellum retained the ink better than the flesh side may be seen from an examination of facsimiles in the Leyden series *Codices graeci et latini photographice depicti*.

[3] That the ink could scale off the flesh side of the vellum in less than three centuries is proved by the condition of the famous Tacitus manuscript in Beneventan script in the Laurentian Library. It was written in the eleventh century and shows retouched characters of the thirteenth. See fols. 102, 103 in the facsimile edition in the Leyden series mentioned in the previous note.

standing by his nefarious doings, as was the case with the Roman author of the forged 'Anonymus Cortesianus', for nothing was heard of this Morgan fragment till it had reached the library of the American collector. If his motive was monetary gain he chose a long and arduous path to attain it. It is hardly conceivable that he should take the trouble to make all the errors and omissions found in our twelve pages and all the additions and corrections representing different ages, different styles, when less than half the number would have served to give the forged document an air of verisimilitude. The assumption that the Morgan fragment is a forgery thus becomes highly unreasonable. When you add to this the fact that there is nothing in the twelve pages that in any way arouses suspicion, the conclusion is inevitable that the Morgan fragment is a genuine relic of antiquity.

Archetype

As to the original from which our manuscript was copied, very little can be said. The six leaves before us furnish scanty material on which to build any theory. The errors which occur are not sufficient to warrant any conclusion as to the script of the archetype. One item of information, however, we do get: an omission on fol. 52^{v} goes to show that the manuscript from which our scribe copied was written in lines of twenty-five letters or thereabouts.[1] The scribe first wrote EXCUCURIS|SEM COMMEATU. Discovering his error of omission, he erased SEM at the beginning of line 8 and added it at the end of line 7 (intruding upon margin-space in order to do so), and then supplied, in somewhat smaller letters, the omitted words ACCEPTO UT PRAEFECTUS AERARI.
(13) As there are no *homoioteleuta* to account for the omission, it is almost certain that it was caused by the inadvertent skipping of a line.[2] The omitted letters number twenty-five.

A glance at the abbreviations used in the index of addresses on fols. 48^{v}–49^{r} teaches that the original from which our manuscript was copied must have had its names abbreviated in exactly the same form. There is no other way of explaining why the scribe first wrote AD IULIUM SERUIANUM (fol. 49, l. 12), and then erased the final UM and put a point after SERUIAN.

[1] On the subject of omissions and the clues they often furnish, see the exhaustive treatise by A. C. Clark entitled *The Descent of Manuscripts* (Oxford, 1918).

[2] Our scribe's method is as patient as it is unreflecting. Apparently he does not commit to memory small intelligible units of text, but is copying word for word, or in some places even letter for letter.

THE DATE AND LATER HISTORY OF THE MANUSCRIPT

Our manuscript was written in Italy at the end of the fifth or more probably at the beginning of the sixth century.

The manuscripts with which we can compare it come, with scarcely an exception, from Italy; for it is only of more recent uncial manuscripts (those of the seventh and eighth centuries) that we can say with certainty that they originate in other than Italian centres. The only exception which occurs to one is the Codex Bobiensis (*k*) of the Gospels of the fifth century, which may actually have been written in Africa, though this is far from certain. As for our fragment, the details of its script, as well as the ornamentation, disposition of the page, the ink, the parchment, all find their parallels in authenticated Italian products; and this similarity in details is borne out by the general impression of the whole.

The manuscript may be dated at about the year A.D. 500, for the reason that the script is not quite so old as that of our oldest fifth-century uncial manuscripts, and yet decidedly older than that of the Codex Fuldensis of the Gospels (*F*) written in or before A.D. 546.

On the dating of uncial manuscripts

In dating uncial manuscripts we must proceed warily, since the data on which our judgements are based are meagre in the extreme and rather difficult to formulate.

The history of uncial writing still remains to be written. The chief value of excellent works like Chatelain's *Uncialis Scriptura* or Zangemeister and Wattenbach's *Exempla Codicum Latinorum Litteris Maiusculis Scriptorum* lies in the mass of material they offer to the student. This could not well be otherwise, since clear-cut, objective criteria for dating uncial manuscripts have not yet been formulated; and that is due to the fact that of our four hundred or more uncial manuscripts, ranging from the fourth to the eighth century, very
few, indeed, can be dated with precision, and of these virtually none is in the *(14)*
oldest class. Yet a few guide-posts there are. By means of those it ought to be possible not only to throw light on the development of this script, but also to determine the features peculiar to the different periods of its history. This task, of course, cannot be attempted here; it may, however, not be out of place to call attention to certain salient facts.

The student of manuscripts knows that a law of evolution is observable in writing as in other aspects of human endeavour. The process of evolution is from the less to the more complex, from the less to the more differentiated, from the simple to the more ornate form. Guided by these general considerations, he would find that his uncial manuscripts naturally fall into two groups. One group is manifestly the older; in orthography, punctuation, and abbreviation it bears close resemblance to inscriptions of the classical or Roman period. The other group is as manifestly composed of the more recent manuscripts: this may be inferred from the corrupt or barbarous spelling, from the use of abbreviations unfamiliar in the classical period but very common in the Middle Ages, or from the presence of punctuation, which the oldest manuscripts invariably lack. The manuscripts of the first group show letters that are simple and unadorned and words unseparated from each other. Those of the second group show a type of ornate writing, the letters having serifs or hair-lines and flourishes, and the words being well separated. There can be no reasonable doubt that this rough classification is correct as far as it goes; but it must remain rough and permit large play for subjective judgement.

A scientific classification, however, can rest only on objective criteria—criteria which, once recognized, are acceptable to all. Such criteria are made possible by the presence of dated manuscripts. Now, if by a dated manuscript we mean a manuscript of which we know, through a subscription or some other entry, that it was written in a certain year, there is not a single dated manuscript in uncial writing which is older than the seventh century—the oldest manuscript with a *precise* date known to me being the manuscript of St. Augustine written in the abbey of Luxeuil in A.D. 669.[1] But there are a few manuscripts of which we can say with certainty that they were written either before or after some given date. And these manuscripts which furnish us with a *terminus ante quem* or *post quem*, as the case may be, are extremely important to us as being the only relatively safe landmarks for following development in a field that is both remote and shadowy.

The Codex Fuldensis of the Gospels, mentioned above, is our first landmark of importance.[2] It was read by Bishop Victor of Capua in the years A.D. 546 and 547, as is testified by two entries, probably autograph. From this it follows that the manuscript was written before A.D. 546. We may surmise—
(15) and I think correctly—that it was shortly before 546, if not in that very year. In any case the Codex Fuldensis furnishes a precise *terminus ante quem*.

The other landmark of importance is furnished by a Berlin fragment containing a computation for finding the correct date for Easter Sunday.[2]

[1] See below, p. 119. [2] See below, p. 118.

Internal evidence makes it clear that this *Computus Paschalis* first saw light shortly after A.D. 447. The presumption is that the Berlin leaves represent a very early copy, if not the original, of this composition. In no case can these leaves be regarded as a much later copy of the original, as the following purely palaeographical considerations, that is, considerations of style and form of letters, will go to show.

Let us assume, as we do in geometry, for the sake of argument, that the Fulda manuscript and the Berlin fragment were both written about the year 500—a date representing, roughly speaking, the middle point in the period of about one hundred years which separates the extreme limits of the dates possible for either of these two manuscripts, as the following diagram illustrates:

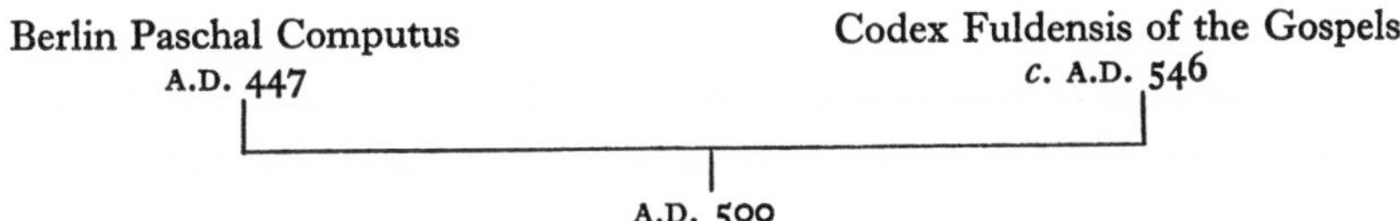

If our hypothesis be correct, then the script of these two manuscripts, as well as other palaeographical features, would offer striking similarities if not close resemblance. As a matter of fact, a careful comparison of the two manuscripts discloses differences so marked as to render our assumption absurd. The Berlin fragment is obviously much older than the Fulda manuscript. It would be rash to specify the exact interval of time that separates these two manuscripts, yet if we remember the slow development of types of writing the conclusion seems justified that at least several generations of evolution lie between the two manuscripts. If this be correct, we are forced to push the date of each as far forward or back as the ascertained limit will permit, namely, the Fulda manuscript to the year 546 and the Berlin fragment to the year 447. Thus, apparently, considerations of form and style (purely palaeographical considerations) confirm the dates derived from examination of the internal evidence, and the Berlin and Fulda manuscripts may, in effect, be considered two dated manuscripts, two definite guide-posts.

If the preceding conclusion accords with fact, then we may accept the traditional date (*c.* A.D. 371) of the Codex Vercellensis of the Gospels. The famous Vatican palimpsest of Cicero's *De Re Publica* seems more properly placed in the fourth than in the fifth century; and the older portion of the Bodleian manuscript of Jerome's translation of the *Chronicle* of Eusebius, dated after the year A.D. 442, becomes another guide-post in the history of uncial writing, since a comparison with the Berlin fragment of about A.D. 447

(16) convinces one that the Bodleian manuscript cannot have been written much after the date of its archetype, which is A.D. 442.

Dated uncial manuscripts

Asked to enumerate the landmarks which may serve as helpful guides in uncial writing prior to the year 800, we should hardly go far wrong if we tabulate them in the following order:[1]

1. Codex Vercellensis of the Gospels (*a*) *c.* a. 371

Traube, loc. cit., no. 327; Zangemeister–Wattenbach, pl. XX.

2. Bodleian Manuscript (Auct. T. 2. 26) of Jerome's translation of the Chronicle of Eusebius (older portion) post a. 442

Traube, loc. cit., no. 164; J. K. Fotheringham, *The Bodleian Manuscript of Jerome's Version of the Chronicle of Eusebius Reproduced in Collotype* (Oxford, 1905), pp. 25–6; Steffens[2], pl. 17; also Schwartz in *Berliner Philologische Wochenschrift*, XXVI (1906), col. 746.

3. Berlin Computus Paschalis (MS. lat. 4°. 298) *c.* a. 447

Traube, loc. cit., no. 13; Th. Mommsen, 'Zeitzer Ostertafel vom Jahre 447' in *Abhandl. der Berliner Akad. aus dem Jahre 1862* (Berlin, 1863), 539 ff.; 'Liber Paschalis Codicis Cicensis A. CCCCXLVII' in *Monumenta Germaniae Historica, Auctores Antiquissimi*, IX. I. 502 ff.; Zangemeister–Wattenbach, pl. XXIII.

4. Codex Fuldensis of the Gospels (*F*), Fulda MS. Bonifat. 1, read by Bishop Victor of Capua ante a. 546

Traube, loc. cit., no. 47; E. Ranke, *Codex Fuldensis, Novum Testamentum Latine interprete Hieronymo ex manuscripto Victoris Capuani* (Marburg and Leipzig, 1868); Zangemeister–Wattenbach, pl. XXXIV; Steffens[2], pl. 21*a*.

5. Codex Theodosianus (Turin MS. A. II. 2) a. 438–*c.* a. 550

Manuscripts containing the Theodosian Code cannot be earlier than A.D. 438, when this body of law was promulgated, nor much later than the middle of the sixth century, when the Justinian Code supplanted the Theodosian and made it useless to copy it.

Traube, loc. cit., no. 311; idem, 'Enarratio tabularum' in *Theodosiani libri xvi*, edited by Th. Mommsen and P. M. Meyer (Berlin, 1905); Zangemeister–Wattenbach, pls. XXV-XXVIII; C. Cipolla, *Codici Bobbiesi*, pls. VII, VIII. See also *Oxyrh. Papyri*, XV (1922), no. 1813, pl. I.

[1] For the pertinent literature on the manuscripts in the following list the student is referred to Traube's *Vorlesungen und Abhandlungen*, I. 171–261 (Munich, 1909), and the index in vol. III (Munich, 1920). The chief works of facsimiles referred to below are: Zangemeister and Wattenbach, *Exempla Codicum Latinorum Litteris Maiusculis Scriptorum* (Heidelberg, 1876 and 1879); E. Chatelain, *Paléographie des classiques latins* (Paris, 1884–1900), and *Uncialis Scriptura Codicum Latinorum Novis Exemplis Illustrata* (Paris, 1901–2); and Steffens, *Lateinische Paläographie*[2] (Trier, 1909). (Second edition in French appeared in 1910.)

6. The Toulouse Manuscript (No. 364) and Paris MS. lat. 8901, containing Canons, written at Albi a. 600–66

Traube, loc. cit., no. 304; F. Schulte, 'Iter Gallicum' in *Sitzungsberichte der K. Akad. der Wiss., Wien, Phil.-hist. Kl.*, LIX (1868), 422, facs. 5; C. H. Turner, 'Chapters in the history of Latin manuscripts: II. A group of manuscripts of Canons at Toulouse, Albi, and Paris' in *Journal of Theological Studies*, II (1901), 266 ff.; and Traube's descriptions in A. E. Burn *Facsimiles of the Creeds from Early Manuscripts* (= vol. XXXVI of the publications of the Henry Bradshaw Society).

7. The Morgan Manuscript [M. 334] of St. Augustine's Homilies, written in the Abbey of Luxeuil. Later at Beauvais and Château de Troussures a. 669

Traube, loc. cit., no. 307; L. Delisle, 'Notice sur un manuscrit de l'abbaye de Luxeuil copié en 625' in *Notices et Extraits des manuscrits de la Bibliothèque nationale*, XXXI. 2 (1886), 149 ff.; J. Havet, 'Questions mérovingiennes: III. La date d'un manuscrit de Luxeuil' in *Bibliothèque de l'École des Chartes*, XLVI (1885), 429 ff.

8. The Berne Manuscript (No. 219 B) of Jerome's translation of the Chronicle of Eusebius, written in France, possibly at Fleury a. 699

Traube, loc. cit., no. 16; Zangemeister–Wattenbach, pl. LIX; J. R. Sinner, *Catalogus codicum manuscriptorum bibliothecae Bernensis* (Berne, 1760), pp. 64–7; A. Schöne, *Eusebii chronicorum libri duo*, II (Berlin, 1866), p. XXVII; J. K. Fotheringham, *The Bodleian Manuscript of Jerome's Version of the Chronicle of Eusebius* (Oxford, 1905), p. 4.

9. Brussels Fragment of a Psalter and Varia Patristica (MS. 1221 = 9850–52) (*17*)
written for St. Medardus in Soissons in the time of Childebert III a. 695–711

Traube, loc. cit., no. 27; L. Delisle, 'Notice sur un manuscrit mérovingien de Saint-Médard de Soissons' in *Revue archéologique*, nouv. sér. XLI (1881), 257 ff. and pl. IX; idem, 'Notice sur un manuscrit mérovingien de la Bibliothèque Royale de Belgique—, n° 9850–52' in *Notices et extraits des manuscrits*, etc., XXXI. 1 (1884), 33–47, pls. 1, 2, 4; J. Van den Gheyn, *Catalogue des manuscrits de la Bibliothèque Royale de Belgique*, II (1902), 224–6.

10. Codex Amiatinus of the Bible (Florence Laur. Am. 1) written in England ante a. 716

Traube, loc. cit., no. 44; Zangemeister–Wattenbach, pl. XXXV; Steffens[2], pl. 21B; E. H. Zimmermann, *Vorkarolingische Miniaturen* (Berlin, 1916), pl. 222; but particularly G. B. de Rossi, *La Bibbia offerta da Ceolfrido abbate al sepolcro di S. Pietro, codice antichissimo tra i superstiti delle biblioteche della sede apostolica* — Al Sommo Pontefice Leone XIII, omaggio giubilare della biblioteca Vaticana (Rome, 1888), no. V.

11. The Trèves Prosper (MS. 36, olim S. Matthiae) a. 719

Traube, loc. cit., no. 306; Zangemeister–Wattenbach, pl. XLIX; M. Keuffer, *Beschreibendes Verzeichnis der Handschriften der Stadtbibliothek zu Trier*, I (1888), 38 ff.

12. The Milan Manuscript (Ambros. B. 159 sup.) of Gregory's Dialogi, written at Bobbio in the abbacy of Anastasius *c.* a. 750

Traube, loc. cit., no. 102; *Palaeographical Society*, pl. 121; E. H. Zimmermann, *Vorkarolingische Miniaturen* (Berlin, 1916), pls. 14–16, Text, pp. 10, 41, 152; A. Reifferscheid, *Bibliotheca patrum latinorum italica*, II. 38 f.

13. The Bodleian Acts of the Apostles (MS. Selden supra 30) written in the Isle of Thanet ante a. 752

Traube, loc. cit., no. 165; Smith's *Dictionary of the Bible*, IV (New York, 1876), 3458*b*; S. Berger, *Histoire de la Vulgate* (Paris, 1893), p. 44; Wordsworth and White, *Novum Testamentum*, II (1905), p. vii.

14. The Autun Manuscript (No. 3) of the Gospels, written at Vosevium a. 754

Traube, loc. cit., no. 3; Zangemeister–Wattenbach, pl. LXI; Steffens[2], pl. 37.

15. Codex Beneventanus of the Gospels (London Brit. Mus. Add. MS. 5463) written at Benevento a. 739–60

Traube, loc. cit., no. 88; *Palaeographical Society*, pl. 236; *Catalogue of the Ancient Manuscripts in the British Museum*, II, pl. 7.

16. The Lucca Manuscript (No. 490) of the Liber Pontificalis post a. 787

Traube, loc. cit., no. 92; J. D. Mansi, 'De insigni codice Caroli Magni aetate scripto' in *Raccolta di opuscoli scientifici e filologici*, tom. XLV (Venice, 1751), ed. A. Calogiera, pp. 78–80; Th. Mommsen, *Gesta pontificum romanorum*, I (1899) in *Monumenta Germaniae Historica*; Steffens[2], pl. 48.

Guided by the above manuscripts, we may proceed to determine the place which the Morgan Pliny occupies in the series of uncial manuscripts. The student of manuscripts recognizes at a glance that the Morgan fragment is, as has been said, distinctly older than the Codex Fuldensis of about the year 546. But how much older? Is it to be compared in antiquity with such venerable monuments as the palimpsest of Cicero's *De Re Publica*, with products like the Berlin *Computus Paschalis* or the Bodleian *Chronicle* of Eusebius? If we examine carefully the characteristics of our oldest group of fourth- and fifth-century manuscripts and compare them with those of the Morgan manuscript we shall see that the latter, though sharing some of the features found in manuscripts of the oldest group, lacks others and in turn shows features peculiar to manuscripts of a later group.

Oldest group of uncial manuscripts

Our oldest group would naturally be composed of those uncial manuscripts which bear the closest resemblance to the above-mentioned manuscripts of the fourth and fifth centuries, and I should include in that group such manuscripts as these:

A. OF CLASSICAL AUTHORS (*18*)

1. Rome, Vatic. lat. 5757.—Cicero, De Re Publica, palimpsest.

Traube, loc. cit., nos. 269–70; Zangemeister–Wattenbach, pl. XVII; E. Chatelain, *Paléographie des classiques latins*, pl. XXXIX. 2; *Palaeographical Society*, pl. 160; Steffens[2], pl. 15. For a complete facsimile edition of the manuscript see *Codices e Vaticanis selecti phototypice expressi*, vol. XXIII (Vatican City, 1934); Ehrle–Liebaert, *Specimina codicum latinorum Vaticanorum* (Bonn, 1912), pl. 4.

2. Rome, Vatic. lat. 5750+Milan, Ambros. E. 147 sup.—Scholia Bobiensia in Ciceronem, palimpsest.

Traube, loc. cit., nos. 265–68; Zangemeister-Wattenbach, pl. XXXI; *Palaeographical Society*, pl. 112; complete facsimile edition in *Codices e Vaticanis selecti*, etc., vol. VII (Milan, 1906); Ehrle–Liebaert, *Specimina codicum latinorum Vaticanorum*, pl. 5A.

3. Vienna, 15.—Livy, fifth decade (five books).

Traube, loc. cit., no. 359; Zangemeister–Wattenbach, pl. XVIII; E. Chatelain, *Paléographie des classiques latins*, pl. CXX; complete facsimile edition in *Codices graeci et latini photographice depicti*, tom. IX (Leyden, 1907).

4. Paris, lat. 5730.—Livy, third decade.

Traube, loc. cit., no. 183; Zangemeister-Wattenbach, pl. XIX; *Palaeographical Society*, pls. 31 and 32; E. Chatelain, *Paléographie des classiques latins*, pl. CXVI; *Reproductions des manuscrits et miniatures de la Bibliothèque nationale*, ed. H. Omont, vol. I (Paris, 1907).

5. Verona, XL (38).—Livy, first decade, 6 palimpsest leaves.

Traube, loc. cit., nos. 349–50. Th. Mommsen, *Analecta Liviana* (Leipzig, 1873); E. Chatelain, *Paléographie des classiques latins*, pl. CVI.

6. Rome, Vatic. lat. 10696.—Livy, fourth decade, Lateran fragments.

Traube, loc. cit., no. 277; M. Vattasso, 'Frammenti d'un Livio del V°. secolo recentemente scoperti, Codice Vaticano Latino 10696' in *Studi e Testi*, vol. XVIII (Rome, 1906); Ehrle–Liebaert, *Specimina codicum latinorum Vaticanorum*, pl. 5B.

7. Bamberg, Class. 35*a*.—Livy, fourth decade, fragments.

Traube, loc. cit., no. 7; idem, 'Palaeographische Forschungen IV, Bamberger Fragmente der vierten Dekade des Livius' in *Abhandlungen der Königlich Bayerischen Akademie der Wissenschaften*, III. Klasse, XXIV. Band, I. Abteilung (Munich, 1904).

8. Vienna, lat. 1*a*.—Pliny, Historia Naturalis, fragments.

Traube, loc. cit., no. 357; E. Chatelain, *Paléographie des classiques latins*, pl. CXXXVII. I.

9. St. Paul in Carinthia, XXV.a.3.—Pliny, Historia Naturalis, palimpsest.

Traube, loc. cit., no. 231; E. Chatelain, loc. cit., pl. CXXXVI. Chatelain cites the manuscript under the press-mark XXV 2/67.

10. Turin, A. II. 2.—Theodosian Codex, fragments, palimpsest.

Traube, loc. cit., no. 311; Zangemeister-Wattenbach, pl. xxv; Cipolla, *Codici Bobbiesi*, pl. vii.

B. OF CHRISTIAN AUTHORS

1. Vercelli, Cathedral Library.—Gospels (*a*) ascribed to Bishop Eusebius (†371).

Traube, loc. cit., no. 327; Zangemeister–Wattenbach, pl. xx.

2. Paris, lat. 17225.—Corbie Gospels (ff^{2}).

Traube, loc. cit., nos. 214; *Palaeographical Society*, pl. 87; E. Chatelain, *Uncialis Scriptura*, pl. ii; Reusens, *Éléments de paléographie*, pl. iii (Louvain, 1899).

3. Constance–Weingarten Biblical fragments.—Prophets, fragments scattered in the libraries of Stuttgart, Darmstadt, Fulda, and St. Paul in Carinthia.

Traube, loc. cit., no. 302; Zangemeister–Wattenbach, pl. xxi; complete facsimile reproduction of the fragments in *Codices graeci et latini photographice depicti*, Supplementum ix (Leyden, 1912), with introduction by P. Lehmann.

4. Berlin, lat. 4°. 298.—Computus Paschalis of *c.* a. 447.

Traube, loc. cit., no. 13; see above, p. 118, no. 3.

5. Turin, G. VII. 15.—Bobbio Gospels (*k*).

Traube, loc. cit., no. 324; *Old Latin Biblical Texts*, vol. ii (Oxford, 1886); F. Carta, C. Cipolla, C. Frati, *Monumenta palaeographica sacra*, pl. v. 2; R. Beer, 'Über den ältesten Handschriftenbestand des Klosters Bobbio' in *Anzeiger der Kais. Akad. der Wiss. in Wien*, 1911, no. xi, pp. 91 ff.; C. Cipolla, *Codici Bobbiesi*, pls. xiv–xv; complete facsimile reproduction of the manuscript, with preface by C. Cipolla: *Il codice Evangelico* k *della Biblioteca Universitaria Nazionale di Torino* (Turin, 1913).

6. Turin, F. IV. 27+Milan, D. 519. inf.+Rome, Vatic. lat. 10959.—Cyprian, Epistolae, fragments.

Traube, loc. cit., no. 320; E. Chatelain, *Uncialis Scriptura*, pl. iv. 2; C. Cipolla, *Codici Bobbiesi*, pl. xiii; Ehrle–Liebaert, *Specimina codicum latinorum Vaticanorum*, pl. 5d.

7. Turin, G. V. 37.—Cyprian, de opere et eleemosynis.

Traube, loc. cit., no. 323; Carta, Cipolla e Frati, *Monumenta palaeographica sacra*, pl. v. 1; Cipolla, *Codici Bobbiesi*, pl. xii.

(*19*) 8. Oxford, Bodleian Auct. T. 2. 26.—Eusebius-Hieronymus, Chronicle, post a. 442.

Traube, loc. cit., no. 164; see above, p. 118, no. 2.

9. Petrograd [Leningrad] Q. v. I. 3 (Corbie).—Varia of St. Augustine.

Traube, loc. cit., no. 240; E. Chatelain, *Uncialis scriptura*, pl. iii; A. Staerk, *Les Manuscrits latins du* V^e *au* XIIIe *siècle conservés à la bibliothèque impériale de Saint-Petersbourg* (St. Petersburg, 1910), vol. II, pl. 2.

10. St. Gall, 1394.—Gospels (*n*).

Traube, loc. cit., no. 60; *Old Latin Biblical Texts*, vol. II (Oxford, 1886); *Palaeographical Society*, II, pl. 50; Steffens[1], pl. 15; E. Chatelain, *Uncialis Scriptura*, pl. I. 1; A. Chroust, *Monumenta Palaeographica*, XVII, pl. 3.

Characteristics of the oldest uncial manuscripts

The main characteristics of the manuscripts included in the above list, which is by no means complete, may briefly be described thus:

1. General effect of compactness. This is the result of *scriptura continua*, which knows no separation of words and no punctuation. See the facsimiles cited above.

2. Precision in the mode of shading. The alternation of stressed and unstressed strokes is very regular. The two arcs of O are shaded not in the middle, as in Greek uncials, but in the lower left and upper right parts of the letter, so that the space enclosed by the two arcs resembles an ellipse leaning to the left at an angle of about 45°, thus O. What is true of the O is true of other curved strokes. The strokes are often very short, mere touches of pen to parchment, like brush work. Often they are unconnected, thus giving a mere suggestion of the form. The attack or fore-stroke as well as the finishing stroke is a very fine, oblique hair-line.[1]

3. Absence of long ascending or descending strokes. The letters lie virtually between two lines (instead of between four as in later uncials), the upper and lower shafts of letters like h l p q projecting but slightly beyond the head and base lines.

4. The broadness of the letters m n u

5. The relative narrowness of the letters f l p s t

6. The manner of forming b e l m n p s t

B with the lower bow considerably larger than the upper, which often has the form of a mere comma.

E with the tongue or horizontal stroke placed not in the middle, as in later uncial manuscripts, but high above it, and extending beyond the upper curve. The loop is often left open.

L with very small base.

M with the initial stroke tending to be a straight line instead of the well-rounded bow of later uncials.

N with the oblique connecting stroke shaded.

P with the loop very small and often open.

[1] In later uncials the fore-stroke is often a horizontal hair-line.

S with a rather longish form and shallow curves, as compared with the broad form and ample curves of later uncials.

T with a very small, sinuous horizontal top stroke (except at the beginning of a line when it often has an exaggerated extension to the left).

7. Extreme fineness of parchment, at least in parts of the manuscript.

(*20*) 8. Perforation of parchment along furrows made by the pen.

9. Quires signed by means of roman numerals often preceded by the letter **Q**· (= Quaternio) in the lower right corner of the last page of each gathering.

10. Running titles, in abbreviated form, usually in smaller uncials than the text.

11. Colophons, in which red and black ink alternate, usually in large-sized uncials.

12. Use of a capital, i.e. a larger-sized letter at the beginning of each page or of each column in the page, even if the beginning falls in the middle of a word.

13. Lack of all but the simplest ornamentation, e.g. scroll or ivy-leaf.

14. The restricted use of abbreviations. Besides **B**· and **Q**· and such suspensions as occur in classical inscriptions only the contracted forms of the *Nomina Sacra* are found.

15. Omission of **M** and **N** allowed only at the end of a line, the omission being marked by means of a simple horizontal line (somewhat hooked at each end) placed above the line after the final vowel and not directly over it as in later uncial manuscripts.

16. Absence of nearly all punctuation.

17. The use of **hd** in the text where an omission has occurred, and **hs** *after* the supplied omission in the lower margin, or the same symbols reversed if the supplement is entered in the upper margin.

If we now turn to the Morgan Pliny we observe that it lacks a number of the characteristics enumerated above as belonging to the oldest type of uncial manuscripts. The parchment is not of the very thin sort. There has been no corrosion along the furrows made by the pen. The running title and colophons are in rustic capitals, not in uncials. The manner of forming such letters as **bemrst** differs from that employed in the oldest group.

B with the lower bow not so markedly larger than the upper.
E with the horizontal stroke placed nearer the middle.
M with the left bow tending to become a distinct curve.
R S T have gained in breadth and proportionately lost in height.

Date of the Morgan manuscript

Inasmuch as these palaeographical differences mark a tendency which reaches fuller development in later uncial manuscripts, it is clear that their presence in our manuscript is a sign of its more recent character as compared with manuscripts of the oldest type. Just as our manuscript is clearly older than the Codex Fuldensis of about the year 546, so it is clearly more recent than the Berlin *Computus Paschalis* of about the year 447. Its proper place is at the end of the oldest series of uncial manuscripts, which begins with the Cicero palimpsest. Its closest neighbours are, I believe, the Pliny palimpsest of St. Paul in Carinthia and the *Codex Theodosianus* of Turin. If we conclude by saying that the Morgan manuscript was written about the year 500 we shall probably not be far from the truth.

Later history of the Morgan manuscript (*21*)

The vicissitudes of a manuscript often throw light upon the history of the text contained in the manuscript. And the palaeographer knows that any scratch or scribbling, any *probatio pennae* or casual entry, may become important in tracing the wanderings of a manuscript.

In the six leaves that have been saved of our Morgan manuscript we have two entries. One is of a neutral character and does not take us further, but the other is very clear and tells an unequivocal story.

The unimportant entry occurs in the lower margin of fol. 53^{r}. The words 'uir erat in terra', which are apparently the beginning of the book of Job, are written in Carolingian characters of the ninth century. As these characters were used during the ninth century in northern Italy as well as in France, it is impossible to say where this entry was made. If in France, then the manuscript of Pliny must have left its Italian home before the ninth century.[1]

That it had crossed the Alps by the beginning of the fifteenth century we know from the second entry. Nay, we learn more precise details. We learn that our manuscript had found a home in France, in the town of Meaux or its vicinity. The entry is found in the upper margin of fol. 51^{r} and doubtless represents a *probatio pennae* on the part of a notary. It runs thus:

> A tous ceulz qui ces p*resent*es l*ett*res verront et orront
> Jeh*an* de Sannemeres garde du scel de la provoste de
> Meaulx & Francois Beloy clerc Jure de p*ar* le Roy
> nostre sire a ce faire Salut sachient tuit que p*ar*.

The above note is made in the regular French notarial hand of the fourteenth and fifteenth centuries.[2] The formula of greeting with which the

[1] This supposition will be strengthened by Professor Rand; see p. 53. [Not reprinted in this volume. Ed.]

[2] Compare, for example, the facsimile of a French deed of sale at Roye, 24 November 1433 reproduced in *Recueil de fac-similés à l'usage de l'École des Chartes*. Premier fascicule (Paris, 1880), no. 1.

document opens is in the precise form in which it occurs in numberless charters of the period. All efforts to identify Jehan de Sannemeres, keeper of the seal of the *provosté* of Meaux, and François Beloy, sworn clerk in behalf of the King, have so far proved fruitless.[1]

Conclusion

Our manuscript, then, was written in Italy about the year 500. It is quite possible that it had crossed the Alps by the ninth century or even before. It is certain that by the fifteenth century it had found asylum in France. When and under what circumstances it got back to Italy will be shown by Professor Rand in the pages that follow.

So it is France that has saved this, the oldest extant witness of Pliny's
(22) *Letters*, for modern times. To medieval France we are, in fact, indebted for the preservation of more than one ancient classical manuscript. The oldest manuscript of the third decade of Livy was at Corbie in Charlemagne's time, when it was loaned to Tours and a copy of it made there. Both copy and original have come down to us. Sallust's *Histories* were saved (though not in complete form) for our generation by the abbey of Fleury. The famous Schedae Vergilianae, in square capitals, as well as the Codex Romanus of Virgil, in rustic capitals, belonged to the monastery of St. Denis. Lyons preserved the *Codex Theodosianus*. It was again some French centre that rescued Pomponius Mela from destruction. The oldest fragments of Ovid's *Pontica*, the oldest fragments of the first decade of Livy, the oldest manuscript of Pliny's *Natural History*—all palimpsests—were in some French centre in the Middle Ages, as may be seen from the indisputably eighth-century French writing which covers the ancient texts. The student of Latin literature knows that the manuscript tradition of Lucretius, Suetonius, Caesar, Catullus, Tibullus, and Propertius—to mention only the greatest names—shows that we are indebted primarily to Gallia Christiana for the preservation of these authors.

[1] No mention of either of these is to be found in Dom Toussaints du Plessis' *Histoire de l'église de Meaux*. For documents with similar opening formulas, see ibid. ii (Paris, 1731), 191, 258, 269, 273.

Two Fragments of Virgil with the Greek Translation (*154*)

OUR knowledge of the extent to which Latin letters were studied in the non-Latin-speaking provinces of Rome is so meagre that any Latin fragment found in those provinces assumes a peculiar interest. Two such fragments have recently come to my knowledge: one in the Rainer collection of the Nationalbibliothek of Vienna, the other in the Ambrosiana of Milan.[1] Both fragments come from Egypt, and both contain verses from the *Aeneid*, with the Greek translation opposite the Latin.

The Ambrosian fragment is palimpsest, the Virgilian verses (*Aen.* i. 588–94) lying buried under an Arabic text of hagiographic character. As the authorities of the Ambrosiana propose to publish an exhaustive study of the entire palimpsest (which seems of extraordinary interest), it will suffice here to state that the script of both the Latin and the Greek is in sloping uncials of
perhaps the end of the fifth or of the beginning of the sixth century.[2] In the (*155*)
first line of the fragment one reads easily: RESTITIT AENEAS. . . .]ΠΕCΤΗ: AINEIAC. . . . In the last line my hasty examination showed TUM SIC REGINAM. . . TOTE ΟΥΤωC BACIΛ. . . .

The Rainer fragment agrees with the Ambrosian in having the Latin text in the left column and the Greek in the right column. But it differs from it in that the verses of Virgil do not occupy a whole line, but are spread over several lines of uneven length, the Greek in each case corresponding exactly to the Latin. The fragment is manifestly a school vocabulary similar to the one from Oxyrhynchus[3] which is now preserved in the University Library of Cambridge.[4] And, like this fragment, it is written on rather coarse parchment in crudely shaped uncial characters of the early sixth century, and contains

From *The Classical Review*, XXXVI (1922), 154–5.

[1] Sincere thanks are due to Professor C. Wessely for permission to examine all the Latin fragments in the Rainer collection, and to Mgr. Gramatica, Prefect of the Ambrosiana, for permission to publish my find.

[2] Facsimiles of similar writing may be seen in *Papiri greci e latini* (Pubblicazioni della Società Italiana), vol. I, no. 6 (= Protoevangelium Iacobi), and vol. I, no. 55 (= Index of the Digests).

[3] Grenfell and Hunt, *Oxyr. Papyri*, VIII, no. 1099.

[4] Add. MS. 5896. A vocabulary to Cicero's *Catil.* II, similarly arranged, is found in another papyrus from Egypt, published in *Rylands Papyri*, no. 61. Have we not an analogously constructed Biblical vocabulary in the famous Graeco-Latin manuscript in the Bodleian, known as the Laudian Acts (Bodleian MS. Laud. Gr. 35)? Facsimiles in *Palaeogr. Society*, pl. 80.

parts of lines 673–4 of book V of the *Aeneid*. The flesh side of the parchment is practically illegible. On the hair side it is still possible to read:

[ ]	TAOY]
[ ]	ΠΡΟϾ
INANEM	MATAIAN
QUALUDO	HC[ ]
INDUTUS	[ ]

The translation of INANEM suggests that the vocabulary was not of the highest order.

The soil of Egypt has produced very few literary fragments in Latin.[1] We have bits of Virgil, Cicero, Sallust, Livy, and a rather good-sized fragment of the Epitome of Livy; some other historical scraps still unidentified; a Latin paraphrase of a Greek fable, as well as nineteen lines of a Latin translation of Babrius. In point of number texts of Virgil predominate.[2] If the excavations up to date have yielded a harvest that is at all typical,[3] then it would appear that Virgil held a high place in the Latin education of Egyptians, perhaps not unlike the place which he occupies in our own classical training. The Ambrosian and Rainer fragments are insignificant in themselves. Their importance lies in the testimony they bear.

[1] See the excellent article by W. Schubart in *Klio*, XIII (1913), 27 ff. To the details which he gives on p. 37 must now be added *Oxyr. Pap.* XI, no. 1379 (Livy); *Amherst Pap.* no. 26 (Babrius).

[2] See *Oxyr. Pap.* I, No. 31; VIII, no. 1098 and no. 1099; *Tebtunis Papyri*, II, p. 334 (a line from the *Georgics* (IV. 1–2) repeated six times, doubtless as an exercise in writing; *Papiri greci e latini* (Pub. Soc. Ital.), I, no. 21; these with the two fragments under discussion make a total of seven.

[3] A full list of Latin fragments found in Egypt is given by Arthur Stein in *Untersuchungen zur Geschichte und Verwaltung Ägyptens unter römischer Herrschaft* (Stuttgart, 1915), pp. 207–10.

On the African Origin of Codex Palatinus of the Gospels (e)

IN his lucid and interesting account of the recovery of a lost leaf of Codex (*401*) Palatinus (*e*) of the Latin Gospels Professor A. Souter raises the question of the origin of the manuscript and comes to the conclusion that the manuscript was written in Africa.[1] I think something may be said in support of this view, but the grounds on which Professor Souter bases his conclusion need examining. Nothing is more important in Latin palaeography than to ascertain the characteristics which distinguish the various schools of writing. The present note is concerned with the question of the African school. Did such a school exist in the fifth and sixth centuries and, if so, what were its distinguishing features?

Whenever there is a suspicion that a given manuscript may come from Africa it is sound palaeography to resort at once to Codex Bobiensis (*k*) of the Gospels[2] to see if striking similarities are to be observed. For, if any Latin (*402*) manuscript of the Bible comes from Africa, Codex *k* is that manuscript. Not only is the form of its uncial characters 'exotic', as Traube expressed it (taking the Italian uncials as the normal), but the many curious symbols for the 'Nomina Sacra' which abound in *k* are found in no other Latin manuscript.[3] This in itself renders *k* a provincial product. When to peculiarity of script and of abbreviations we add peculiarity of text the surmise that we are dealing with a provincial product changes to conviction. Now we know that the text of *k* is African. We naturally infer that the script is also. This hypothesis, moreover, receives corroboration from the circumstance that the two manuscripts which most closely resemble it graphically contain works of an African Father, St. Cyprian.[4] The general angularity of curved letters found in *k* is

From *The Journal of Theological Studies*, XXIII (1922), 401–4.

[1] *J.T.S.* XXIII (1922), 285.

[2] MS. Turin G. VII. 15. For facsimiles see C. Cipolla, *Codici Bobbiesi*, pls. XIV–XV and the complete reproduction of the manuscript: *Il codice Evangelico* k *della Biblioteca Universitaria Nazionale di Torino* (Turin, 1913). Also *Old Latin Biblical Texts*, vol. II (Oxford, 1886); and *J.T.S.* V (1903), 88 ff.

[3] See L. Traube, *Nomina Sacra*, pp. 138 ff.

[4] I refer to MS. Turin F. IV. 27 (+Milan D. 519 inf.+Vatic. lat. 10959) and the fragment, Orléans 192 (169), fol. 1 reproduced in Chatelain, *Uncialis Scriptura*, pl. VA. The Turin manuscript is reproduced in Chatelain, op. cit., pl. IV, and in Cipolla, *Cod. Bob.*, pl. XIII. Facsimile of the Vatican fragment of the Turin manuscript in Ehrle–Liebaert, *Specimina cod. lat. Vatic.*, pl. 5D.

also to be seen in these two manuscripts of Cyprian. And the peculiarly shaped **m,** with the first stroke a markedly straight line, as in half-uncials, is especially noteworthy. Another characteristic letter is **e** with the tongue rather coarsely drawn, not at all like the **e** of such genuine Italian manuscripts as the Puteanus of Livy (MS. Paris lat. 5730)[1] and the Codex Vercellensis (*a*) of the Gospels,[2] written about the same time as *k* and the Cyprian manuscripts mentioned. And the stroke indicating omitted **m** or **n** at the end of a line is placed in *k* and the two Cyprian manuscripts not *after* the vowel, as is usual in Italian manuscripts of this period, but directly *over* it. If we were right in regarding *k* as of African origin then the similarity between *k* and the two manuscripts of Cyprian (an African writer) is tantamount to confirmation of the African origin of these two Cyprian manuscripts also. If this reasoning is correct, *k* and the two Cyprian manuscripts constitute our first touchstone for testing African origin, at least for uncial manuscripts of about the fifth century.

How does the case stand with regard to the Codex Palatinus? The first point to bear in mind is that it is not as old an uncial manuscript as either *k* or the two Cyprian manuscripts. It is perhaps by a century more recent. This
(*403*) may account for the absence in *e* of the peculiar forms found in *k*. But are there no features in *e* which point to Africa as its home? Professor Souter gives three: '(1) the fact that the initial letter of each column, whether it be at the beginning of a word or not, is always a very large capital; (2) the horizontal stroke beyond the end of a line indicating omitted **m** or **n** is neither a horizontal stroke pure and simple (with or without a . or ,) nor a gracefully curved line (with or without a . or ,), but a horizontal stroke with a short angular hook at each end, thus ⟷; (3) the letter **G** is not represented by a **C** with a faint oblique stroke at the foot, but by an additional curl of the lower part of the curve of the **C** itself.' Let us examine these three features in their order.

1. If the use of capitals at the beginning of each page or column is an African feature we should find it in *k* and the Cyprian manuscripts. This is not the case, however. On the other hand, this feature, if it be African, should be absent in non-African manuscripts. What are the facts? We find capitals at the beginning of each page or each column used regularly in the following manuscripts:

[1] Facsimiles in Chatelain, *Pal. des class. lat.*, pl. CXVI; *Pal. Soc.*, pls. 31, 32; Zangemeister–Wattenbach, *Exempla*, pl. XIX, and elsewhere; the entire manuscript is reproduced on a reduced scale by Berthaud of Paris.

[2] Facsimile in Ehrle–Liebaert, *Specimina*, pl. 5c.

A. *Classical Works*

1. Vatic. lat. 3256+Berlin lat. fol. 416—Virgil. Square capitals saec. IV.
2. Vienna 16[1]—Lucan. Rustic cap. saec. IV.
3. Vatic. lat. 10696—Livy. Uncial saec. V.
4. Paris lat. 5730[2]—Livy. Uncial saec. V.
5. Vienna 15—Livy. Uncial saec. V.
6. Vienna 1[a]—Pliny Hist. Nat. Uncial saec. V.
7. St. Paul in Carinthia XXV. 2. 36—Pliny, Hist. Nat. Uncial saec. V.
8. Vienna 1—Ulpianus, Instit. Uncial saec. V.
9. Verona XV (13)—Gaius, Instit. Uncial saec. V.
10. New York, Morgan MS. M. 462—Pliny, Epist. Uncial saec. V.

B. *Christian Works*

1. Paris lat. 17725—Gospels (ff^{2}). Uncial saec. V.
2. Milan Ambros. C. 73 inf.—Gospels. Uncial saec. V.
3. Vienna 1235[3]—Gospels. Uncial saec. V.
4. Verona XXVIII (26)—August. Uncial saec. V.
5. Petrograd Q. v. I. 3—August. Uncial saec. V.
6. Würzburg Th. Q. 2—Hieron. Uncial saec. V.
7. St. Paul in Carinthia XXV. 3. 19—Ambros. Uncial saec. V.
8. Verona XIII (11)—Hilarius. Uncial saec. V.

The above list, it will be seen, includes only the oldest of the Latin manu- (*404*)
scripts which show the feature under discussion. No one will venture to claim these manuscripts for Africa on the strength of this feature. Some of them obviously originated in Italy, with which country their whole past history is bound up. Others are so like them as to justify their being ascribed to Italy.

2. The shape of the **m** or **n** stroke found in *e* is, I fear, no criterion. It is found in Vienna 1235 [Naples Lat. 3] and in other manuscripts that have no connection with Africa.

3. The **G** found in Codex Palatinus is a form taken from Rustic capitals. The scribe of *e* is guilty here of mixing types of writing. It is hard to find another uncial manuscript with this form of **G.** It is not found in *k* nor in the two Cyprian manuscripts referred to above. There is no ground whatever for considering it African.

Although it must be granted that the palaeographical arguments adduced

[1] The manuscript is now in Naples [Lat. 2]. Facsimiles in *Mon. Pal. Vindob.*, vol. II, pls. 27–8.

[2] Only here and there, e.g. fol. 257v, col. ii, begins with a capital though in the middle of a word.

[3] Now in Naples [Lat. 3].

by Professor Souter do not establish the African theory, there is one external feature which connects the Palatinus with *k* and the Cyprian manuscripts and thus supports that theory. The feature is sufficiently peculiar to merit attention. I refer to the trick which the scribe of *e* has of writing his letters not on the line or just a little above the line (as is usual with scribes) but partly above and partly below the line, so that the ruled line appears to cut through the lower portion of the letters. This feature is very marked in the Turin Cyprian manuscript. It is also seen here and there in *k*, and, unless I err, in the Orléans fragment of Cyprian as well. The leaf of the Palatinus examined by me in the British Museum shows the same unusual feature. Now this feature is very rare in Latin manuscripts, and *e* shares this feature with *k* (the African text of the Gospels) and two manuscripts of Cyprian, an African writer. It is, of course, possible that this agreement is merely accidental. It is more reasonable, however, to ascribe it to the common African origin of the manuscripts in question. If the above is correct, our main source of information of African palaeography during the earliest period is to be found in *k* and *e* and the Cyprian manuscripts mentioned above.

Codex Palatinus of the Gospels was preserved in the eighteenth century in the Bishop's Palace at Trent. For over a century it found a home in the Imperial and Royal Library of Vienna (MS. 1185). As a result of the war the precious book is again at Trent.[1] *Habent sua fata libelli.*

[1] See H. Tietze, *Die Entführung von Wiener Kuntswerken nach Italien* (Vienna, 1919), pp. 38 and 51.

Note on the Genuineness of the New Plautus Fragment

A FRAGMENT of Plautus (*Cistellaria*, 123–47, 158–82), written in purple ink, (*24*) discovered at Hiersemann's of Leipzig and acquired by the Staatsbibliothek of Berlin, was published in 1919 by Professor H. Degering[1] and discussed in this review by Professor Lindsay soon afterwards.[2] It will be recalled that the fragment was found on the inside of the wooden cover of a twelfth-century manuscript of Ovid's *Metamorphoses* (the cover itself being in Venetian leather of the sixteenth century), that some scribbling on a fly-leaf connects the manuscript with Friuli, and that the present whereabouts of the Ovid manuscript are shrouded in mystery. The genuineness of the Plautus fragment has now been impugned. In a paper read before the Paris Academy, the eminent palaeographer, Professor Chatelain, subjected the fragment to a searching examination, and concluded that neither its text nor its palaeography could be regarded as authentic.[3]

Although one may not agree with all the details of Professor Chatelain's strictures,[4] it is undeniable that the cumulative effect of his criticism is disconcerting. While I hesitate to endorse his condemnation without having seen the original, I confess that such opinion as I am able to form from a study of the facsimile is unfavourable to the fragment. For suspicion is aroused not only by the mysterious disappearance of the Ovid manuscript, but by the following graphic features of the fragment itself:

1. Unusual colour of ink; the use of purple ink for a text is unprecedented.
2. Lack of sure touch in forming letters (not the awkwardness of a beginner, or of a style still unperfected), and lack of definite script-direction or *ductus*.
3. Singular variety in size and form of letters.
4. Great unevenness in spacing between letters, and between lines (the latter, however, may be the result of shrinking, due to moisture or paste).

From *The Classical Review*, XXXVII (1923), 24.

[1] *Sitzungsber. d. Preuß. Akad. d. Wiss.*, 1919, pp. 468–76 (and facsimile), 497–503.

[2] Vol. XXXIII (1919), 152.

[3] 'Comptes rendus de l'Académie des Inscriptions et Belles Lettres,' pp. 223–9 (*Bulletin*, Mai–Juin, 1922): 'Un prétendu fragment de Plaute en onciale du IVe siècle.'

[4] Letter **a** with roundish bow is not unknown in very old uncial; cf. the Bodleian Chronicle of Jerome (Auct T. 2. 26), saec. V, or the Florentine Pandects, saec. VI. Nor do the objections to the 'boucle antérieure' of the letter **u** and of the cross-stroke of **t** seem convincing.

5. Lack of alignment in the initial letters of lines. (Apparently the bounding line which invariably guides such alignment is missing. If so, the fragment possesses another extraordinary feature.)

Though further investigation may rehabilitate the fragment, the date ascribed to it by its editor is in any case centuries wide of the mark. As the fragment lacks all the earmarks of our oldest uncial manuscripts,[1] a date like the fourth century is impossible. If genuine, it is not older than the sixth century. That the fragment once formed part of an *édition de luxe*, written for a royal personage, is unthinkable. Such books were produced by expert scribes, not by botchers.

[1] See the guides given by Chatelain in his *Uncialis Scriptura* and the writer's observations in *A Sixth-Century Fragment of the Letters of Pliny the Younger*, pp. 19 f. (Washington, 1922) [this volume, pp. 123 f.]

On the Date of the Codex Toletanus

THE sixth volume of the *Collectanea Biblica Latina* is a memorable publica- (267)
tion from the pen of Dom Henry Quentin, entitled 'Mémoire sur l'établissement du texte de la Vulgate' (Rome and Paris, 1922). Its treatment of the
difficult problems involved in the text of the Bible is calculated to arouse a
great deal of discussion, by reason both of the method employed and the
results reached. I have no right to speak upon textual problems, but one who
has worked upon Visigothic manuscripts cannot fail to be interested in the
new date Dom Quentin assigns to the famous Codex Toletanus (MS.
Madrid Tolet. 2. 1).[1]

His date is furnished by a subscription at the end of the manuscript, which
contains these facts:[2] Servandus, Bishop of Seville, was the *auctor possessorque*
of this volume of the Old and New Testament. He made a present of it to his (268)
intimate friend and companion, John, who became Bishop of Cordova, and
this John, in his turn, dedicated the volume, *compte perfectum*, to St. Mary's
of Seville, on the 10th Kalends of January in the era 1026, i.e. on 23 December of the year 988. The unusual phrase 'auctor possessorque' Dom Quentin
interprets to mean that Servandus had the book written for him. This view
is not shared by Berger, who explains 'auctor' in the sense that Servandus had
a clear title to the volume.[3] The phrase 'compte perfectum' signifies for Dom
Quentin that the volume presented to Bishop John was unfinished, and that
he himself had it 'nicely completed' before offering it to St. Mary's. It is
important to bear in mind that the first phrase has received two interpreta-
tions, and that the second phrase makes it reasonable to suppose that there
were two distinct stages in the making of the volume. Historically there is no
fault to find with the subscription. In 988 we do find a Bishop Servandus in
Seville and a Bishop John in Cordova.[4]

The reason scholars like Berger,[5] Ewald and Loewe,[6] C. U. Clark,[7] and Dom De Bruyne[8] have found it impossible to accept the subscription at its

From *Revue Bénédictine*, xxxv (1923), 267–71.

[1] Dom Quentin, op. cit., pp. 316–23.

[2] S. Berger, *Histoire de la Vulgate*, p. 13; Muñoz y Rivero, *Paleografía visigoda*, p. 119 and pl. 9; Ewald and Loewe, *Exempla scripturae Visigoticae*, p. 7 and tab. IX; Dom Quentin, op. cit., p. 322.

[3] S. Berger, op. cit., p. 14.

[4] Gams, *Series episcoporum*, pp. 3 and 28.

[5] Loc. cit.

[6] Loc. cit.

[7] *Collectanea Hispanica*, p. 45.

[8] *Revue Bénédictine*, xxxv (1923), Bull. de litt. lat. no. 146.

face value is that the script of the manuscript clearly favours a much earlier date.[1] Remembering how frequently scribal notes at the end of Visigothic manuscripts have proven unreliable guides for dating,[2] they did not hesitate to put their faith in palaeography. And, as a matter of fact, the specimen of the script of the Toletanus given in Ewald and Loewe's collection[3] has all the earmarks of what palaeographers have accepted as the early stage of Visigothic writing.[4] I refer to the striking compactness, the broad proportions of the shaftless letters, the arcs of **m, n,** and **h** being low with the last stroke turning inwards, the use of the semi-colon above **b** and **q** for 'bus' and 'que', and the poor separation of words. And, on the other hand, the same specimen
(*269*) of the Toletanus has not the slightest resemblance to the dated tenth-century manuscripts whose dates are above suspicion.[5] In these manuscripts 'the letters are better spaced; the pen-stroke is often fine. The body of the letters is rather tall and narrow. The final stroke of **m, n, h,** etc., regularly turns outward. Particularly characteristic are the shafts of tall letters, which end in a little hook or mallet-head. The suspensions 'bus' and 'que' are denoted by an **s**-like flourish placed above **b** and **q,** i.e. the semi-colon of the first period is here made in one conventionalized stroke.'[6]

Far from assigning the script of the Toletanus to the end of the tenth century, scholars have been ready to assign it to the end of the eighth. Thus two centuries separate Dom Quentin's date from the accepted one—a margin of error which will be conceded to be excessive, even in an inexact science like palaeography. For those, however, who hold, on palaeographical grounds, that the Toletanus was written nearly two centuries before 988, the problem is greatly complicated by the fact that Dom Quentin finds support for his date in palaeography itself. He points out that the curious capitals used in the subscription are identical with the capitals used in the incipits and rubrics at the beginning of Acts (fol. 358[r]). He gives facsimiles of both.[7]

[1] This is also the opinion expressed in my *Studia Palaeographica* (= Sitzungsberichte der K. Bayer. Akad. der Wiss. (1910), 12. Abhandlung), p. 57 [this volume, p. 44].

[2] Cf. *Studia Palaeographica*, p. 82, n. 3 [this volume, p. 62, n. 3].

[3] Op. cit., pl. IX.

[4] Cf. C. U. Clark, *Collectanea Hispanica*, pp. 106 f.

[5] A list of dated manuscripts is given by C. U. Clark on p. 65. His plate 24 reproduces a manuscript which is dated by a subscription (a. 977) which Loewe accepted as genuine, likewise Clark. Instructive are plates XXIII and XXIV in Ewald and Loewe. The Cassiodorus MS. of a. 949 and that of Gregory of a. 914 are reproduced in Dr. James's *Catalogue of the John Rylands Library of Manchester*, pls. 120–2 and 109–11; the British Museum Add. MS. 25600 (a. 919) is reproduced in *Palaeogr. Society*, I. 95, in *Catal. of Ancient MSS. in the B.M.* II. 38; Arndt–Tang-[4], pl. 36; Reusens, *Éléments de Pal.*, pl. 12B.

[6] Cf. *Studia Palaeographica*, p. 80 [this volume, p. 61].

[7] Op. cit., pp. 318 and 319, facs. 30 and 31.

When one compares these two facsimiles, it is impossible not to recognize that there is no difference between them. Those who, like Berger, refuse to believe that the manuscript was written for Servandus, are driven to assume that the writing of the subscription is a faultless imitation of the script used by the rubricator. But why such pains should have been taken to imitate the rubricator's script remains unexplained. The motive is certainly not apparent. It is clear, then, that another explanation must be sought.

Without a careful examination of the original, it seems hazardous to the writer to reject Dom Quentin's date summarily. To be sure, the specimen in Ewald and Loewe hardly permits of two opinions. It clearly shows us Visigothic writing of the early stage, saec.viii–ix, and not of the late tenth cen- (270)
tury. But if some hurried notes made in 1911 on a few photographs kindly lent me by Dom De Bruyne are to be trusted, the manuscript has parts which are not so ancient as the specimen in Ewald and Loewe; for I found two features which belong to the later stage of writing: namely, the **ti**-distinction and the use of the interrogation-mark (with the two kinds of questions distinguished). Are we to suppose that the manuscript was begun in the ninth century, and lay in an unfinished state, without rubrics and colophons, for several generations, till it was completed and ornamented by the order of Bishop John in 988? Such a supposition would account for the special reference to 'compte perfectum' of the subscription, and would explain the identity of the scripts used in the notes and in the titles and colophons.

An examination of plate xx of Ewald and Loewe, containing a specimen of Madrid Tolet. 15. 12 (Isidorus) of the year 915, teaches us that two types of writing, the old and the new, might be practised in the same scriptorium side by side. The left-hand column shows the modern scribe, the right-hand column (after the subscription) shows the older scribe. The former has all the new features, the **ti**-distinction among them. The latter is manifestly old-fashioned, and his performance recalls Visigothic writing of the first stage.[1] Now the question naturally arises, if it is possible, in the year 915, to have a scribe writing in the style we have considered the earliest stage, is it not also possible to find survivals of this style in the year 988? *A priori*, one is inclined to rule out the possibility. It certainly seems highly improbable, and particularly so in the case of this manuscript, which, according to the subscription, was in the possession of one bishop, perhaps even written at his order, and

[1] It is interesting to observe that this scribe uses the peculiar form of uncial **M** which we find in the subscription and rubrics of the Toletanus. See col. ii, l. 11, from bottom, the word *Mundi*.

made the object of a special dedication by another bishop. Such a manuscript, it stands to reason, must come out of a scriptorium where progressive influences were at work. The older scribe of Tolet. 15. 12 was apparently more than a generation behind the progress that had been made in Visigothic writing; since, in the celebrated Beatus MS. of 894,[1] we have a clear example
(271) of the more modern style (with the **ti**-distinction, interrogation-mark, etc.). To suppose that a style which was already out of date in 894, a survival of which we find in the year 915, could be handed on for practically three more generations, is hardly reasonable. And for that reason, the present writer cannot accept the verdict that the Codex Toletanus in all its parts is a product of the tenth century. Parts manifestly go back to an older period. Whether other parts, which show more modern features, may be assigned to the year 988, it is impossible to say without seeing the original. In any case, the jolt given to Visigothic palaeographers by Dom Quentin's date of the Toletanus, will administer a very wholesome shock, and will, I trust, lead to further intensive investigation of such matters as abbreviation, punctuation, and decoration, which may prove valuable and trustworthy guides in the dating of this interesting and difficult script.

[1] Formerly in the library of Henry Yates Thompson of London, now in that of J. P. Morgan in New York [M. 644]. Cf. C. U. Clark, op. cit., p. 39, no. 570.

A Hand-list of Half-uncial Manuscripts

INTRODUCTION

THE advisability of bringing out a list of half-uncial manuscripts was sug- (34)
gested by Traube's list of uncial manuscripts. The study of uncial writing has been immensely furthered by that list. Without it, investigations in this field would be rendered extremely difficult. It seems reasonable to suppose that a similar list of half-uncial manuscripts, even though incomplete, would also serve a useful purpose. Half-uncial writing was practised at the same time, often in the same place, as uncial. By having a list of extant manuscripts or fragments of manuscripts in half-uncial writing, as a companion to Traube's list, one would be afforded a fairly accurate survey of the authors read and copied from the fourth to the ninth century. Moreover, such a list would furnish the palaeographer with a guide to the raw material for the study of the half-uncial script. The history of this script, its origin, and the peculiarities which characterize its different schools, are outside the scope of this paper. The most desirable approach to the solution of these problems will be found to lie in the intensive study of such important centres as Verona, Bobbio, Lyons, and Corbie.

That the present list is provisional and incomplete goes without saying. Even Traube's uncial list of about 400 manuscripts can now be augmented by some seventy-five items. Additions to the present list are therefore to be expected and will, of course, be gratefully received. But I am also bound to add that such a degree of completeness as has been attained is due largely to the labours of others. I refer particularly to Chatelain's *Uncialis Scriptura* and *Les Palimpsestes latins*; Traube's *Nomina sacra*; Lindsay's Index of Manuscripts in his *Notae Latinae* and the printed list of Liebaert's negatives preserved at the Vatican.

Such merit as the list has it derives from the fact that nearly all the manu- (35)
scripts recorded have been examined; and where that was impossible facsimiles have been used. In only a very few cases has it been necessary to cite the authority of others without verification. A few items included in this list have elsewhere been described as uncial or minuscule. This necessitates a word of explanation as to the criterion I have employed. I am not here

From *Miscellanea Fr. Ehrle*, IV (1924), 34–6.

concerned with the futile discussion as to whether half-uncial is not in reality minuscule. The name 'half-uncial' stands for a definite type and calls up a clear and distinct image. It is therefore useful and scientific. To use the indefinite and wider term 'minuscule' is to put a premium on vagueness, and therefore to court confusion. The same objection must be urged against the name 'mixed' script.

My rule for what is and what is not half-uncial is a rough and ready one. If all the manuscripts which we are accustomed to classify as half-uncial were like the Basilican Hilary of 509–10, or the Veronese Sulpicius Severus of 517 or the Cassinese Ambrosiaster of about 570, then there would be no difficulty whatever. These manuscripts represent what may be termed the *canonical* half-uncial. And of course, all manuscripts like them are half-uncial. But there are many deviations from this norm, chiefly owing to the presence of uncial elements. The rule adopted in this list has been to call a script half-uncial if it has four distinctly non-uncial elements, as for example letters **b**, **d**, **m**, and **r**, or **b**, **g**, **m**, and **s**, or some such combination. I have excluded from my list manuscripts which show only one or two such forms, as for example the Codex Bezae and the Codex Claromontanus, with half-uncial **b** and **d**, and the Codex Laudianus, with half-uncial **b**. These are uncial manuscripts, aside from the one or two letters just mentioned which they regularly have in the half-uncial form. In fact these manuscripts represent, as I hope to show elsewhere, a type by themselves. But the Formula Fabiana of the Rainer Museum of Vienna has the half-uncial forms of **b**, **d**, **m**, **r**, and **s**, and thus has, according to my rough rule, deviated sufficiently from the uncial to be classified as half-uncial.[1] A manuscript like this has no place in a list of uncial manuscripts, for the uncial alphabet is a very clear and distinct one, and does
(36) not permit of so wide a margin of variation.[2] On the other hand, there are some eighth-century manuscripts, which show a curious mixture of uncial and half-uncial forms, which renders classification rather arbitrary. In other cases again it is difficult to say whether the manuscript is half-uncial or early minuscule. When such a manuscript has been included here, its precarious position has been indicated.

It is impossible for one who is not a connoisseur of medieval and especially

[1] This manuscript and others like it are of a type which to my mind represents the early stage of half-uncial writing—a type designated by Professor Schiaparelli (*La scrittura latina*, p. 150) as 'semi-onciale arcaica o rustica', of which he gives a very complete list.

[2] This statement takes it for granted that uncial is senior to half-uncial, as a distinct type of calligraphy. Professor Schiaparelli's view, according to which the uncial type was evolved from archaic half-uncial, presents difficulties which it would be out of place to discuss here.

of patristic literature to do justice to the bibliography of the manuscripts listed below.[1] I have had to content myself with citing palaeographical publications only. But I believe that no collection of facsimiles of any importance has been overlooked. The plates cited reproduce half-uncial writing. Facsimiles of other scripts found in the same manuscript have been disregarded, except where facsimiles of the half-uncial portion are lacking. Traube and Lindsay had used many half-uncial manuscripts for their studies on abbreviations. It is often instructive to see what company a manuscript keeps in its use of this or that abbreviated form; and it therefore seemed advisable to include references to Traube's *Nomina Sacra*. It was impossible to cite Lindsay's work in the same way, because his *Notae Latinae* has not the same kind of index; but the index given shows that Lindsay had used a great many of these manuscripts. References to facsimiles in older literature have been intentionally omitted, because the reproductions are inexact, and have an antiquarian rather than a palaeographical value.

[1] This list is not reprinted here. [Ed.]

The Palaeography of the Bobbio Missal

(62) *M* = Main hand of Missal proper, penitential, etc.

M^2 = Uncial hand which wrote the Mass *pro principe*, fols. 251–3. See Pl. **22**, no. 24 (*pl. 1, no. 24*).

A = Uncalligraphic additions on fols. 1–8^{v}, 286, 292^{v}–295^{v}, 299–300^{v}.

a = Uncalligraphic additions on fols. 253^{v}–254, 291^{v}–292.

THE PLATES

The illustrations on Pl. **22** (*pl. 1*) are taken from the following folios:

fols.	fols.	fols.	fols.
1 = 92^{v}	7 = 14^{v}	13 = 230	19 = 55
2 = 224	8 = 35	14 = 64, 155	20 = 56^{v}
3 = 188	9 = 25, 83^{v}	15 = 25	21 = 5^{v}, 2^{v}, 2, 300
4 = 137, 59	10 = 56^{v}	16 = 234^{v}, 211	22 = 104^{v}
5 = 221	11 = 23, 244	17 = 84^{v}	23 = 296^{v}
6 = 137	12 = 40^{v}	18 = 55, 54	24 = 252

The last four initials on Pl. **23** (*pl. 2*) are from the inserted Mass *pro principe*. The preceding initial **R** is from *A*; all the rest from *M*.

(63) INTRODUCTORY

FOR the liturgical student, the Bobbio Missal occupies a similar position to that held, in the field of Biblical criticism, by the Codex Bezae. It is an outstanding problem; an enigma which, after long entreaty, still refuses to give up its secret. It first appears in literature at the end of the seventeenth century, a year after Mabillon discovered it at Bobbio. The preface he wrote for his edition of the Missal, published in 1687, is a masterpiece of exposition, and continues even at this distance to be worthy of our serious consideration. In our own time, the origin and composition of the Missal have been dealt with by such eminent scholars as Mgr. Duchesne, Dom Cagin, Edmund Bishop, Dom Wilmart, Ludwig Traube, and Dom Morin.[1] To Léopold Delisle we

From *The Bobbio Missal* (by Dom A. Wilmart, E. A. Lowe, H. A. Wilson): Henry Bradshaw Society, LXI (London, 1924), 62–106. [See Pls. **22** and **23**.]

[1] I name these authorities in chronological order. For the full title of their works see section VI of Dom Wilmart's study 'Notice du Missel de Bobbio' (Henry Bradshaw Society LXI. 3–58), pp. 39 f.

owe the first minute palaeographical description of the manuscript,[1] to Dom Wilmart the most complete and searching analysis of its contents. Dom Wilmart's study, which appeared in Cabrol's *Dictionnaire*,[2] is of such high importance that it is reproduced, by his generous permission, in the present volume. Since the appearance of his first article, Dom Wilmart has twice returned to the Missal, each time throwing fresh light upon the problems it presents.[3] Perhaps the most suggestive palaeographical account of the manuscript was written by the greatest palaeographer of our day, Ludwig Traube. His discussion of its date and origin, in A. E. Burn's *Facsimiles of the Creeds*,[4] is, like all that came from Traube's pen, full of charm and insight.

Having said so much, it would appear both hazardous and presuming to enter upon further discussion of the manuscript. The single excuse must be afforded by the fact that since Traube's day, thanks to the generosity of the late Dr. J. Wickham Legg, it has become possible for every student to have
before him the complete facsimile edition of this valuable book;[5] and thus to *(64)*
undertake that extensive and exhaustive study which formerly was beyond the power of most. While it is still impossible to give a clear and definite verdict upon the most important phase of the problem, namely, the question of origin, yet the student of palaeography, by close and careful study, should be able to call attention to all the differentiating features of the manuscript, and to indicate the schools with which it shows closest affinity. As the study of palaeography advances, as a greater knowledge of individual centres facilitates our efforts to localize manuscripts, more light will doubtless be forthcoming upon the problem in hand. Meanwhile, the most useful service palaeography can render toward the understanding of this intriguing volume is to throw into high relief the distinctive features it possesses. For this purpose, it will be necessary to go rather at length into the script, abbreviations and orthography of the manuscript. For convenience in discussion, it should be stated that the Missal proper is written by one hand, designated as *M*; that the few pages in uncial—the Mass *pro principe*, written by another hand—are referred to as M^2; and that the pages containing added matter, in two different styles of crude writing, one showing distinct majuscule and the other as distinct minuscule traits, are referred to as *A* and *a*.

[1] *Cabinet des manuscrits*, III. 224 f.

[2] *Dictionnaire d'archéologie chrétienne et de liturgie*, fascicule XV, cols. 939–62 (1908), where a complete bibliography of the Missal is given. [See above, p. 142, n. 1. Ed.]

[3] 'Une curieuse instruction liturgique du Missel de Bobbio', published in the now defunct *Revue Charlemagne*, II (1912), 1–16; and 'Le palimpseste du Missel de Bobbio', in *Revue Bénédictine* (1921), pp. 1–18.

[4] *Henry Bradshaw Society*, vol. XXXVI (London, 1909).

[5] Ibid., vol. LIII.

(65) DESCRIPTION OF THE MANUSCRIPT

Name

The manuscript known as the 'Bobbio Missal' was discovered in Bobbio in 1686 by Mabillon, through whom it passed into the library of his abbey of Saint-Germain-des-Prés,[1] and thence, along with other manuscripts, to the Bibliothèque nationale of Paris, where it now bears the pressmark MS. lat. 13246.

Size

The manuscript, the cover of which is modern, consists of 300 folios.[2] But in marking the folios, fol. 38 has been omitted, and fol. 206 occurs twice. The folios measure 18×9 cm. ($7 \times 3\frac{1}{2}$ in.) and the written space measures 13×7 cm. ($5\frac{1}{4} \times 2\frac{3}{4}$ in.).

Ruling

There are, normally, 21 or 22 ruled lines to a page, except in the Mass *pro principe*, where there are 28, and in the added portions in cursive, where the number varies from page to page. The ruling is done with a dry point, guided by slits in the margin. The horizontal lines are bounded by two pairs of parallel vertical lines, which are unusually close together for bounding lines.

Ink

The ink has stood the test of time remarkably well. The writing on the flesh side is quite as legible as that on the hair side. But differences in the colour of the ink are noticeable in the added portions. Thus, the ink on fols. 291^{v}–2 is a drab gray; on fols. 292^{v}–4^{v}, l. 6, of a darkish hue; on fols. 294^{v}, l. 7–295^{v}, it is a chestnut colour. These differences are not due to the varying effect of time on the same ink (since the hands are coeval), but are the result of carelessness in mixing the ink.

Parchment

The parchment is not of uniform quality, being fine in some parts and coarse in others. A different kind of parchment is noticeable in the partial gathering formed by fols. 251–4 which contain the inserted Mass *pro principe* written in a style unlike the rest of the manuscript.

[1] Our manuscript formed no. 1488 of the Fonds of Saint-Germain-des-Prés.

[2] Not 301, the number given by Delisle in *Cabinet des manuscrits* III. 225.

Quires (66)

Quire-marks are wanting. If they ever existed, no vestiges of them remain. The outer sheet of each quire is folded flesh side out. In the table that follows, the order of quires is indicated by letters, the number of leaves in each quire by arabic superior numerals. The leaves that are merely slips are enclosed in parentheses.[1]

	fols.		fols.		fols.
A^8	1–8	N^8	110–17	BB^8	200–6 *bis* (203, 204)
B^{11}	9–19 (11)	O^8	118–25	CC^{14}	207–20 (207, 220)
C^9	20–8 (24)	P^8	126–33	DD^8	221–8
D^8	29–36	Q^8	134–41	EE^8	229–36 (232, 233)
E^8	37–45 (41, 42)[2]	R^{10}	142–51	FF^8	237–44
F^8	46–53	S^6	152–7	GG^{12}	245–56
G^{12}	54–65	T^8	158–65	HH^8	257–64
H^{11}	66–76 (71)	V^8	166–73 (169, 170)	II^8	265–72
I^8	77–84	X^8	174–81	KK^3	273–5 (274)
K^8	85–92 (88, 89)	Y^2	182–3	LL^8	276–83 (279, 280)
L^8	93–100	Z^8	184–91 (187, 188)	MM^{12}	284–95 (289, 290)
M^9	101–9 (105)[3]	AA^8	192–9	NN^5	296–300 (296)[4]

It will be seen from the above that there is no uniformity in the composition of the quires. In fact, the variety is quite extraordinary, and is of a piece with other extraordinary features of the manuscript, which seem to point to some out-of-the-way village as its home.

SCRIPT (67)

A difficulty confronts us at the very start. What name are we to give the script of our Missal?[5] For it cannot be called uncial, since it frequently has

[1] The manuscript is so tightly bound that it is very difficult to see how the quires were formed. But the description which follows is doubtless correct, since it agrees with the collations independently made by the late Dr. Bannister and by Dom Wilmart.

[2] No. 38 does not exist, and no. 206 occurs twice.

[3] This results in hair side facing flesh side in the middle of the quire, which is unusual.

[4] On the composition of this quire, see the careful description by Dom Wilmart in *Revue Bénédictine* (1921), pp. 11 f.

[5] Mabillon, in the Preface to his edition (p. 275), called the script majuscule: 'scriptus est codex . . . litteris maiusculis'; Delisle, *Cabinet*, III. 225, calls it uncial; so does Traube in Burn's *Facsimiles of the Creeds*: 'Die Schrift ist in der Hs. selbst Unciale' (p. 46); yet Traube's list of uncial manuscripts expressly omits the Bobbio Missal on the ground that the half-uncial elements predominate (*Vorlesungen und Abhandlungen*, I. 221); Dom Wilmart, on the other hand, in his classic article on the Missal (cols. 941 and 942) speaks of the script as semi-uncial. Professor Lindsay, in his *Notae Latinae* (p. 443), describes the script as 'uncial of Luxeuil?' but in the Appendix (p. 476) speaks of it as 'rude uncial, half-uncial and minuscule'.

forms (e.g. of **a, b, c, m, s, t**) that are foreign to uncial. Nor can it be called half-uncial, since it has forms (e.g. of **b, d, r, s**) not found in half-uncial writing. Nor, again, would it be correct to speak of it as early minuscule, for it can be shown that the scribe regarded it as something different, since he used a script which we should describe as minuscule when making additions, or when crowded for space at the end of a page or passage, as on fols. 43, 56, 72, 82^{v}, 92^{v}, 202, 211^{v}, 224 l. 12, 249^{v}, and 278^{v}.[1] In other words, he regarded the script of the body of the Missal as a majuscule script. This impression is confirmed by the fact that the only leaves of the Missal proper which were filled in by another scribe, probably of another centre—they contain the inserted Mass *pro principe*—are in uncial writing, i.e. a majuscule script. Another reason for believing that the mixed script of the Missal was considered a majuscule or major script is furnished by the circumstance that nearly all the titles and rubrics are in the same script as the text of the Missal.

Thus, there is no fixed traditional name by which we may call the script of the Missal. It is a *mixed* type, a transition script. As such, however, it is not unique. A number of eighth- and ninth-century manuscripts are known whose script presents a medley of types.[2] Our manuscript must be viewed as one of this class. The problem is further complicated by the fact that we are not confronted by the performance of a trained scribe belonging to a recognized
(68) school. The strong admixture of personal idiosyncrasies,[3] the shaky hand here and there as of one suffering from illness or old age,[4] goes to show that what we have before us is the work of a private individual—a cleric who made a copy of the service book of which he stood in need, and which, to judge from its size, he probably carried about with him in his travels.

Letters

Upon analysis of the script, the following facts emerge:

The letters **F**, **G**, **N**, and **R** occur only in uncial form.[5]

[1] See pl. **22**, no. 1 (*pl. 1, no. 1*).

[2] Mixed alphabets are found in Vatic. lat. 5750 (upper script), Verona X (8), Verona LII (50), Carlsruhe (Reich.) 253, Paris lat. 4884, Munich 14197, to mention only a few instances. It is interesting to note that Insular manuscripts of the majuscule type show a mixed script which may be responsible for the spread of the custom. The influence of Insular models on a scribe attempting to write minuscule may be seen in the Munich MS. 14653.

[3] Witness his odd way of forming **o** with the two arcs faultily joined, **S** with an excrescence at either end, **R** with a peculiar bend of the right leg, and **l** with the broken back. See pl. **22**, nos. 11, 6, 13, 10 (*pl. 1, nos. 11, 6, 13, 10*).

[4] See fols. 56^{v} *ad fin.* and 57^{r}. If the manuscript is the work of an old man, then it is more recent than it looks.

[5] Trifling exceptions, occurring at the end of a line or a page, or in a space left vacant, are ignored in this statement.

The letters **a**, **b**, **d**, **l**, and **s** have both uncial forms and half-uncial or minuscule forms.[1]

The letters **c**, **e**, **m**, **t** (**c** and **e** with the broken back) are clearly minuscule, recalling the French rather than any other type.

The letters **h**, **i** (also **i**-longa), **k**, **p**, **q**, and **x** are minuscule of a neutral type.

The letters **u**, **y**, and **z** are noteworthy; **u** and **y** have the two forms.

a Two forms, uncial and half-uncial, the uncial being more common. Though the two forms may occur on the same page, yet there are whole sections of the Missal in which either one or the other form predominates.[2]

b Two forms; the uncial predominates. The half-uncial recalls Burgundian models; the shaft is frequently topped by a cross-stroke, as in **h** and **l**.[3] See Pl. **22**, no. **3** (*pl. I. no. 3*).

c Two forms, the round-backed and the broken-backed. The latter is less frequent. It recalls forms found in eighth-century French and Swiss minuscule manuscripts. The round-backed form often descends below the (*69*) line, when followed by **h**, **l**, or **o**.[4] The combination of the dropped **c** with a following **l** is very characteristic (see below under Ligatures). The top of the **c** often has a hair-line, like a horn, extending from the end of the curve toward the right.[5] See Pl. **22**, no. **4** (*pl. I, no. 4*).

d Two forms, uncial and half-uncial, the latter not so frequent. The stem occasionally descends below the line as in early French minuscule. See Pl. **22**, no. **5** (*pl. I, no. 5*).

e Two forms, the round-backed and the knobbed or pointed-backed. The latter form is less frequent, and recalls forms found in eighth-century French and Swiss minuscule manuscripts. See Pl. **22**, nos. **4** and **6** (*pl. I, nos. 4 and 6*).

[1] In the case of **a**, **b**, and **s** the scribe seems to be reproducing half-uncial models.

[2] This may be due to copying from different exemplars. How else explain the almost exclusive use of half-uncial **a** in the Lesson on fols. 56^{v}–57, and of uncial **a** in the parts preceding or following?

[3] The same feature is seen in Berne 645, Paris Nouv. acq. lat. 1619, Bamberg B. V. 13.

[4] The same characteristic is found in St. Gall 226, the well-known eighth-century uncial manuscript of Isidorus on papyrus, and in Vienna 563 (upper script) containing patristic excerpts. There is reason for believing that both manuscripts come from Gaul, although Beer and Zimmermann (*Vorkarolingische Miniaturen*, p. 150) seem to favour Bobbio as the home of the Vienna manuscript.

[5] The same is true of **g** and **s**. This peculiar feature is found in the upper script of the palimpsest, Vatic. Reg. lat. 2077 (facs. in Chatelain, *Paléographie des classiques latins*, pl. 32).

f Uncial form.

g Uncial form.[1] Here and there it is surmounted by the hornlike stroke, as in letter **c** described above. See Pl. **22**, no. **7** (*pl. 1, no. 7*).

h Occasionally the shaft is surmounted by a horizontal cross-stroke as in **b** and **l**.

i A short and a long form. The latter is used without strict regularity, at the beginning of words, and occasionally in the body, to represent the **y**-sound. Here and there the shaft has the top cross-stroke. In a number of instances the long form of the letter descends below the line, as it does in French manuscripts.[2] See Pl. **22**, no. **9** (*pl. 1, no. 9*).

k Normal form.

(*70*) **l** Uncial and minuscule forms. The shaft is frequently surmounted by a horizontal top-stroke. Here and there it has the broken form found in Merovingian manuscripts See Pl. **22**, nos. **3** and **10** (*pl. 1, nos. 3* and *10*).

m Normal half-uncial or early minuscule form.

n Uncial form. The third stroke frequently resembles an elongated comma, which meets the oblique second stroke not on the base-line, but some distance above it. This characteristic is encountered in many north Italian manuscripts and in some French ones.[4] See Pl. **22**, no. **11** (*pl. 1, no. 11*).

o The form is frequently irregular, the bows failing to join properly, so that they overlap, either at the top or the bottom. Here and there the letter is heart-shaped. See Pl. **22**, no. **11** (*pl. 1, no. 11*). Dotted **o** is used in exclamation, but not exclusively so (cf. fols. 25v and 234).

p Normal form.

q The bow is sometimes left open at the top. Elsewhere it joins the shaft so

[1] The minuscule form occurs in the word 'angeli' on fols. 28 and 35, at the end of a section, where space is limited. It resembles the French form. The same is the case in the word 'gloria' on fol. 224, l. 12. See pl. **22**, nos. **2** and **8** (*pl. 1, nos. 2 and 8*).

[2] See, e.g. fol. 45v, l. 15 ('Zebedei'), fol. 83v, l. 21, fol. 172, l. 8 ('cuius'), fol. 189v, l. 16 ('mei'), fol. 264, l. 16 ('eius').

[3] The most aggravated examples of this deformity will be found in the British Museum MS. Harley 5041. Manuscripts like Paris Nouv. acq. lat. 1619, Autun 20, St. Gall 214, Berne 611, Brit. Mus. Add. MS. 24143, also have this feature. More details will be found in Lindsay's *Palaeographia Latina*, I, p. 12, and p. 34, par. 69.

[4] Conspicuous examples are Rome Vatic. Ottob. 66, Rome Vitt. Emanuele 1372 (Sess. 39, pt. 7), Vitt. Eman. 2106 (Sess. 58), Vitt. Eman. 2109 (Sess. 128), Verona LX (58), Verona LXI (59), Milan Ambros. B. 159 sup. (Bobbio), probably all of Italian origin; and Paris lat. 2206, Orléans 192 (169), fols. 21–7, Lyons 600 (517), Paris lat. 1732, pt. ii, St. Gall 1395, pp. 412–15, which are all probably of French origin. But the resemblance of the N in the latter manuscripts is not so close to the Missal's N as is the N in the former group from Italy.

as to look heart-shaped. Capital **Q** recalls Merovingian models. See Pl. **22**, no. **12** (*pl. 1, no. 12*).

r Uncial form. Frequently the bow is compressed rather than round. Here and there the right leg bends like a knee, as if about to execute a kick. This unusual form is frequently used by the hand that wrote the additions. See Pl. **22**, nos. **13** and **21** (*pl. 1, nos. 13* and *21*).

s Two forms, uncial and half-uncial. Though the former is somewhat more common, the two are used indifferently, occurring side by side in the same word. This strongly recalls the usage in early Irish and English manuscripts. The upper curve of the **s** is frequently surmounted by the horn-like stroke mentioned above, under **c** and **g**. See Pl. **22**, no. **6** (*pl. 1, no. 6*).

t Minuscule form, with the left branch of the cross-stroke usually bent down (*71*)
in a curve to join the stem. The loop sometimes extends to the base-line.

u Besides the normal form, a **v**-shaped form occurs here and there. Very rarely the sickle-shaped **u** is used. See Pl. **22**, no. **14** (*pl. 1, no. 14*).

x The normal form, in three strokes. See Pl. **22**, no. **15** (*pl. 1, no. 15*).

y Chiefly on the line, with both strokes curving to the right. Both the dotted and the undotted form occur. Both forms often extend below the line. See Pl. **22**, no. **16** (*pl. 1, no. 16*).

z Normally projects above the head-line; occasionally high above it, recalling types found in French manuscripts. See Pl. **22**, no. **14** (*pl. 1, no. 14*).

Ligatures and Combinations

The common ligatures are **ae, ns, us, ur**, and **nt**. The last two are practically confined to the end of a line, the others may be found anywhere in the line. **e** with cedilla, which is but another graphic form of **ae**, occurs only occasionally.[1] The ligature **ae** has the normal form with the back of uncial **a** doing duty as the back of **e**. In **ns** and **us** the **s** has the half-uncial form. See Pl. **22**, no. **18** (*pl. 1, no. 18*).

As regards combinations, attention should be called to the characteristic form of **c**, followed by **l** or a vowel, when the **c** is somewhat lowered as if better to hold the following letter. The combination **cl**, as has been said, is a noteworthy feature of the manuscript. See Pl. **22**, no. **19** (*pl. 1, no. 19*).

[1] See the last word on fol. 84^{v}. Here there can be no doubt that the cedilla is by first hand. See Pl. **22**, no. **17**, (*pl. 1 no. 17*).

SCRIPT OF THE ADDED PORTIONS

Whereas the added portions of our Missal may possess little or no importance for the student of liturgy, for the palaeographer and for the student of romance philology, they are of extraordinary interest. If we subject them to a careful examination, we shall see that *A* (fols. 1–8, 286, 292^{v}–95^{v}, and 299^{v}–300^{v}) is written in a script which contains uncial elements[1] recurring with
(72) considerable constancy and regularity;[2] while the remaining pages of the added portions, which I have called *a* (fols. 253^{v}–4 and 291^{v}–2), show a marked absence of uncial elements. Their script, in a general way, recalls Merovingian minuscule of a cursive type.

But that *A* and *a* come from the same pen cannot be for a moment doubted. The curious form of **t**, with the top suggesting a mushroom, and the peculiar and unmistakable form of **di**, with an **i**-stroke obliquely intersecting the stem and bow of **d** at the base-line, are sufficient to establish the identity of the two beyond a doubt. See Pl. **22**, no. **21** (*pl. 1, no. 21*).

But what, then, is the relation of *A* and *a* to the hand that wrote the Missal proper? The first impression, it must be confessed, is one of distinct dissimilarity. This might be accounted for by the circumstance that *M* is an attempt at calligraphy, while *A* and *a* are obviously written in great haste, now crowded, now sprawling, in utter disregard of appearances. An inspection of single letters shows that the mushroom-shaped **t** found in *A* and *a* never occurs in *M*, not even at the end of lines, where the scribe was crowded for space; while, on the other hand, the form of **t** found in *M* does not occur in the pages of *A* and *a*. These facts strengthen the first general impression that the hand of *M* is not the same as the hand of *A* and *a*. And yet, much can be said in favour of their identity. Certain curious forms of **a**, **c**, **o**, **r**, and **s**, which occur frequently in parts of *A* and *a*,[3] also crop up here and there, as if by inadvertence, in the pages of *M*.[4] I refer to **a**, with the bow resembling a beak pointing to the left; **c** with the broken back; **o** with the two arcs either intersecting or failing to join at the top or base-line; **r** with the bow compressed or flattened, and the right limb bent at the knee, as if administering a kick; **s** with the hornlike-stroke surmounting the upper curve. The evidence afforded by these letters seems very weighty; it is not easy to brush it

[1] The uncial forms of **m** and **n** occur on fols. 299^{v}–300^{v}, but not on fols. 292^{v}–295^{v}.

[2] The presence of uncial elements in such hasty writing is the point that matters. The fact that not infrequent lapses into minuscule occur is relatively unimportant.

[3] See Pl. **22**, no. **21** (*pl. 1, no. 21*).

[4] See Pl. **22**, nos. **9**, **11**, **13**, and **6** (*pl. 1, nos. 9, 11, 13, and 6*).

aside. The 'kicking **r**', in particular, is so individual a trait that it is hard to believe it was made use of by two different scribes. But despite all this, the dissimilarity of the two **t**'s presents an objection to the theory of identity which seems unanswerable.

The strong individual characteristics displayed by *M* and *A* are even more marked in *a*. The general impression made by the crowded and undisciplined lines of these additions defies description. All one can say is that one finds them rather more Merovingian than Italian in appearance.[1] The particular (73)
items that lend support to this impression are: **g**, with the lower bow pressed out of shape; **d**, with the stem descending well below the line; and **c**, with the broken back. Even the form of **r**, with the right shoulder awkwardly hovering over the following letter—which Traube connected with a group of manuscripts of Rhaetian origin—is also found in French eighth-century products. The form of **di**, with the oblique intersecting stroke, a distinguishing trait common to *A* and *a*, is not known to me in any manuscripts or charters of the seventh or eighth century. But here, again, the impression is Merovingian rather than Italian.[2]

PRIMARY SCRIPT OF THE PALIMPSEST LEAVES

The last five folios of our manuscript (fols. 296–300) are palimpsest, and form a separate quire. A careful study of them was made by Dom Wilmart, who was the first to ascertain that the original text which made way for the liturgical matter was Ambrose on Luke.[3] Dom Wilmart was also the first to

[1] We know what genuine Bobbio cursive looks like. Examples will be found in Cipolla's *Codici Bobbiesi*; Steffens, *Lat. Pal.*[2], pls. 25B, 27, 33, 34; Chatelain, *Paléog. des class. latins*, pl. XXX. These are quite unlike the cursive in our manuscript.

[2] To be sure, final **d** with intersecting stroke is found in manuscripts and charters of the seventh and eighth centuries to represent **de, di, dum,** or any similar suspension. But no example of **d** followed by a stroke in the precise form found in the additions of the Bobbio Missal is known to me in pre-Caroline manuscripts. The nearest approach to it may be seen in the Insular manuscript Turin, F. IV. 1, fasc. 7 (Cipolla, *Codici Bobbiesi*, pl. 37, col. ii, l. 4: 'egrediebatur').

[3] Cf. *Revue Bénédictine*, XXXIII (1921), 1–18. On p. 13 of this article Dom Wilmart mentions the one ancient manuscript of this text known to him, namely, Milan Ambros. H. 78 sup.+ Turin G. V. 15, in half-uncial of the sixth century, from the library of Bobbio. I have recently come across an older fragment, in uncial of the fifth or early sixth century, in Zurich. I refer to the palimpsest leaves (17 and 18) in the miscellany MS. 79B. (For the identification of the lower text I am indebted to Dom Morin's written catalogue). The Zurich leaves come from St. Gall, for the upper script contains part of the glossary found in the palimpsest MS. St. Gall 908. Traube's conjecture (*Vorles. und Abh.* I. 260, n. 1) is fully borne out by the facts: the same hand is at work in both manuscripts, and both have two columns of twenty-seven lines to the page. In order to write this glossary stray leaves of older manuscripts were used. According to Scherrer (*Verzeichniss der Handschriften der Stiftsbibliothek von St. Gallen*, p. 324), nine ancient manuscripts went

go minutely into the question of the home and date of the original leaves. It
(74) is this aspect of the question which interests us here. Any precise fact with regard to the primary script may throw some light on the history of the Missal.

The primary script of the palimpsest leaves is a half-uncial of that peculiar variety which Traube called 'quarter-uncial'.[1] The Fleury Augustinus (Orléans MS. 192 (169), fols. 32–3) and the Autun palimpsest of the Interpretatio Gai Institutionum (MS. 24) are calligraphic examples of this type of half-uncial; while the grammatical treatises (Sacerdos, etc.) in part III of the miscellany formerly known as Vienna MS. 16 which is now at Naples [Lat. 2], and the marginalia in the celebrated Fragmenta Prophetarum known as the Constance–Weingarten fragments, are examples of a more cursive variety of the same type. The half-uncial of our five leaves partakes of the characteristics of both these varieties—it is neat and calligraphic, and it has a number of cursive features[2]—and may represent an intervening stage of development. See Pl. **22**, no. **23** (*pl. 1, no. 23*).

If we are right in thinking that a certain affinity exists between our leaves and the four manuscripts mentioned above,[3] it is important to see if anything can be ascertained as to the origin of these manuscripts. Of Vienna 16 this much is established. It comes from Bobbio, and doubtless formed part of the oldest collection of Bobbio manuscripts of which we have any knowledge. R. Beer tried to prove that this manuscript actually belonged to Cassiodorus' Library at Vivarium.[4] Of the marginalia in the Weingarten Fragments nothing positive is known beyond the fact, pointed out by Dom Morin, that the liturgical lections correspond in one case with usage in the district of Milan.[5] This is an interesting connection and may have a bearing on the
(75) origin of the marginalia. The Autun palimpsest was found at Autun.[6] The

to the making of MS. 908. As far as I could judge from photographs (kindly sent me by the Revd. P. Dold, of Beuron Abbey), neither the upper nor the lower scripts in MS. 908 recalls scripts in Bobbio palimpsests. The St. Gall palimpsests deserve a separate monograph.

[1] *Vorlesungen und Abhandlungen*, II. 27.

[2] Dom Wilmart, op. cit., p. 4, recognizes this when he says: 'Cette fine écriture a tous les traits de l'ancienne et pure semionciale, rapprochée de la cursive jusqu'à l'extrême limite, sans cesser néanmoins d'être une écriture littéraire.'

[3] Facsimiles (1) of the Fleury leaves are given by Delisle in *Mémoire sur l'école calligraphique de Tours*, pl. V; by Reusens, *Éléments de paléographie*, pl. IV. 1; by Chatelain, *Uncialis scriptura*, pl. LXIV. 2; (2) of the Autun palimpsest in Chatelain, op. cit., pl. LXI; (3) of Vienna 16, part III, in Beer, *Monumenta Palaeographica Vindobonensia*, II, pls. 35–8; (4) of the Weingarten fragments in Zangemeister–Wattenbach, *Exempla Codicum Latinorum litteris maiusculis scriptorum*, pl. XXI, and a complete facsimile reproduction in *Codices Graeci et Latini photographice depicti*, supplement vol. IX, with introduction by P. Lehmann.

[4] Op. cit., pp. 17 f.

[5] Dom Morin's view is given by Professor Lehmann in the preface to the facsimile edition just mentioned.

[6] The ninth-century probatio pennae: *memor nostri, sancte Benigne* (fol. 110v) points to Autun.

secondary script is certainly of local origin, and Traube thought the same might be true of the primary script.[1] There is nothing, I think, that can be urged against this view either on historical or palaeographical grounds. As to the Fleury fragment, Traube was ready to regard it as a product of Fleury.[2] If his views are correct—they are based not on the script alone, but on a study of abbreviations and other features as well—then the type of half-uncial under consideration was practised in Gaul as well as in Italy.[3] And this is apparently confirmed by the eighth manuscript with which Dom Wilmart compares our leaves.[4] I refer to the Milan palimpsest Ambros. O. 136 sup., a singular palimpsest in which a religious text makes way for a classical author.[5] Dom Wilmart places this manuscript in one group with Vienna 16 and Turin G. V. 4 (destroyed in the fire of 1904),[6] and expresses the opinion that the three manuscripts probably all come from Bobbio. This is doubtless true of the Vienna and Turin manuscripts. But of the Milan palimpsest we know for a fact that it was acquired in France. It never formed part of the Bobbio collection, for it entered into the Ambrosiana through its first prefect, Antonio Olgiati, who brought it from Avignon.[7] As it is of French provenance it is very probably also of French origin. At any rate, the half-uncial script in this manuscript seems different from that in genuine Bobbio palimpsests.

From all this it is fairly clear that the palimpsest leaves in our Missal do not give us a clear lead. The probability is that they are Italian; but the possibility of French origin is not to be excluded.

To anyone familiar with the oldest Latin manuscripts this type of half-uncial has all the marks of great antiquity. If our dated half-uncial manu- (76)
scripts are any guide at all—and for the present they are the most reliable guides we have[8]—then it seems more reasonable to assign our five leaves to

[1] Traube, *Nomina Sacra*, p. 243: 'und mag in Autun geschrieben sein, wo Chatelain ihn entdeckte.'

[2] Traube, *Nomina Sacra*, p. 153, and *Vorles. und Abh.* II. 27.

[3] It is undeniable that early French minuscule of certain schools derives directly from this type of half-uncial. See below, p. 178.

[4] *Rev. Bénéd.* XXXIII (1921), 8.

[5] Chatelain, *Paléographie des classiques latins*, pl. LXXXI.

[6] Fortunately a facsimile exists in Cipolla's *Codici Bobbiesi*, pl. XXXV.

[7] Olgiati's entry on the inside front cover reads: *Hunc codicem notis adspersum Avenione uehendum curavimus*. Similar entries are found in other Ambrosian manuscripts. A list of Ambrosian manuscripts from France was published in *Mélanges Chatelain* (pp. 588–97) in a paper entitled 'Manoscritti di provenienza francese nella Biblioteca Ambrosiana di Milano', by the present Pope (A. Ratti), formerly Prefect of the Ambrosiana.

[8] They are the familiar manuscripts: (1) Archivio di S. Pietro D. 182 of the year 509–10 known as the Codex Basilicanus of Hilary, facsimiles of which are found in Zangemeister-Wattenbach, pl. LII; *Palaeographical Society*, I, pl. 136; *Archivio Paleografico Italiano*, I, pls. 93–5; Steffens, *Lateinische Paläographie*², pl. 20; Ehrle–Liebaert, *Specimina Codicum Latinorum*, pl. 6A. (2) Verona XXXVIII (36), of the year 517,

the fifth century than to the sixth. It is to the fifth century that a connoisseur like Professor Chatelain assigns the first seven manuscripts with which Dom Wilmart compares these leaves.[1] This much, however, is beyond dispute: the library that had these five leaves at its disposal possessed a discarded manuscript (or parts of it) of great antiquity. The most important centres where such very ancient scraps were utilized as palimpsests are Bobbio, Verona, St. Gall, Autun, Fleury, Luxeuil, Lorsch. Our leaves may hail from any one of these, or from a less well-known centre. They may have been used for a second time in the library where they had been preserved, but the ignorant spelling and uncalligraphic writing of the secondary text make it seem probable that the old leaves were given to a wandering cleric who needed a few sheets of parchment to make some additions to his Missal—the book that was always with him.

ABBREVIATIONS

In considering the abbreviations found in this manuscript, it is necessary to bear in mind that there are certain differences to be noted in the three parts *M*, *A*, and *a*. There are abbreviations in one which are not found in another, and differences exist in the different sections of the added portions themselves. In order to set off the abbreviations which the scribe used normally, these are put in a list separate from the technical abbreviations proper to a liturgical book. It is the literary abbreviations that seem likely to serve as an aid in dating and placing the manuscript.

(77) N.B.—*The various strokes which in the original mark abbreviated words are omitted here in the interest of economy. Save in exceptional cases no attempt is made to reproduce them.*

The Nomina Sacra are regular: **ds**, **di** = deus, dei; **dns**, **dni** = dominus, domini;[2] **ihs**, **ihu** = Iesus, Iesu; **xps**, **xpi** = Christus,[3] Christi; **sps**, **spui**, **spm** = spiritus, spiritui, spiritum;[4] **scs**, **sci** = sanctus, sancti.

containing Sulpicius Severus. Facsimiles in Sickel, *Monumenta Graphica Medii Aevi*, VIII, pl. 2; Arndt–Tangl, *Schrifttafeln*, pl. 34A; Zangemeister–Wattenbach, pl. XXXII; E. Monaci, *Facsimili*, pl. 82; *Monumenta Palaeographica Sacra*, pl. IV; *New Pal. Soc.* II, pl. 6; Zimmermann, *Vorkarolingische Miniaturen*, pl. 1B. (3) Monte Cassino CL (346), before the year 570, containing Ambrosiaster. Facsimiles in Zangemeister–Wattenbach, pl. LIII; Steffens,[2] pl. 23C; Thompson, *Introduction to Greek and Latin Palaeography*, facs. no. 100.

[1] Wilmart's article, p. 6.

[2] Occasionally in the final phrase 'per dominum', etc., **dn** is used for **dnm** (fol. 286); and, on fol. 6v of the added portion, **dom** = dominum.

[3] Similarly in the final phrase on fol. 268v 'Christum' is rendered by **xm**.

[4] The form 'sptibus' occurs on fol. 109; and the derivative form 'spitalem' on fol. 276.

The ancient suspensions '-bus' and '-que' are abbreviated by means of **b** and **q**, followed by the semi-colon: **b ;** = bus ; **q ;** = que. The syllable '-rum' at the end of a line is indicated, as in our oldest extant manuscripts, by means of a stroke through the right limb of **R**, thus: **R̸** = rum. Omitted **m** is marked by a stroke, similar to the regular abbreviation-stroke, placed over, or slightly to the right of the vowel preceding the **m**. The omission is not confined to the end of a line, but may occur anywhere. Omitted **n** is marked in the same way. It is, however, chiefly found at the end of a line.[1] All the above observations hold good for the added portions of the Missal as well.

LITERARY ABBREVIATIONS

M (= main hand)		*A* and *a* (= added portions)
anno		an
autem		aut
est		ē
incipit	= INCP	
Israhel	= isrl	isrl ihsrl (fol. 294)
meus	= ms	
nomen	= nom	
non	= no n (occasionally)	n̄
noster, etc.	= nr, no, nm, nis, nra, nri, nre, nro, nrum, nris, nros, nras;[2] the sporadic Visigothic forms: nse, nsis, nsras, nsis, nsm.[3] See below *uester*	nr, no, ntri, ntrom (fol. 286) (78)
omnes	= oms, omns (fol. 278v)	
omnis	= omns	
omnipotens, etc.	= omps, omptis, ompm; also (acc.) opm (fol. 285v) and ompot (fol. 116v)	
patrem		patr
per	= ꝑ (the most frequent form, in both the main text and the additions) ꝓ (frequent in the main text, also in certain parts	ꝑ ꝓ

[1] In the added portions it is also found medially.

[2] The **nri-** and **ni-**types are found side by side on the same page. The **ni-**type, being the elder, is preferred in the recurrent phrase 'per *dominum nostrum Iesum*', etc.

[3] The exact text and folios where these forms occur will be found below, p. 161, n. 1.

LITERARY ABBREVIATIONS—*continued*

	M (= main hand)		*A* and *a* (= added portions)
	per (*cont.*)	of the additions: fol. 6ᵛ ff., 253ᵛ f.; 293ᵛ ff.[1] See Pl. 22, no. 20 *pl. 1, no. 20*).	p̄ (in certain added portions, fols. 8, 8ᵛ, 294ᵛ) p′ (in some added portions, probably taken from an Insular exemplar)[2]
(79)	prae		p̄
	prius		p̄
	pro	= p with a sinuous stroke through the shaft; once only in main text (fol. 281ᵛ)[3]	ꝓ and p̄ (fols. 2ᵛ, l. 6; 5, ll. 5 and 8; 7, l. 14; 8ᵛ, l. 6. Normally, this signifies 'prae')
	propter	= propt	
	quae		q̄
	qui (que)		q (with stroke through shaft)[4]
	qui		q̇ (fols. 292ᵛ ff.)
	quia	= qa (fol. 152ᵛ, end of line) with stroke through shaft of q	qa (fol. 6ᵛ)[5] with stroke through shaft of q
	quid		qd (stroke through q)
	quis		qs (stroke through q)
	quod		qd (stroke through d, or q; Q with stroke through tail)
(80)	quoniam	= qnm qn (only on fols. 44 and 210ᵛ)	qnm
	saeculum, etc.	= sclm, scli, sclo, scla, scloꝝ, sclis	scli
	sunt		s
	uester, etc.	= ur, uri, ura, uro; and the Visigothic forms usm and us (= uestris)[6]	

[1] This form is regularly used in Visigothic script during its entire duration, and frequently in eighth-century French manuscripts. On the other hand, it is rare in Italian manuscripts.

[2] On fol. 8, l. 13, this form of 'per' is manifestly taken over from the copy, and, owing to its unfamiliarity, is changed to **p** with a more or less horizontal stroke over it. Other instances occur on fol. 286 ('super', and 'per').

[3] The bow of the **p** is not continued to form the loop to the left of the shaft in the usual way. Instead, a horizontal stroke intersects the shaft, and curls upward on the left side. The rarity of this form suggests that it comes from the exemplar.

[4] I omit the form 'qebus', with stroke through shaft of **q**, found on fols. 1ᵛ, 5, and 5ᵛ. The stroke probably stands for omitted **u**, instead of **ui**.

[5] **qa**, with stroke over **q**, occurs on fol. 6ᵛ. This may be due to phonetic confusion: **quea** = quia.

[6] See below, p. 161, n. 1.

LITERARY ABBREVIATIONS—*continued*

M (= main hand)		*A* and *a* (= added portions)
Syllables found in abbreviated form are:		
-lus	= L with stroke through base ('angelus', fol. 32)	
-men	= m̄ (in 'nomen', fol. 86)	m̄
-mus	= ms (only used by M[2])	m̸ (m with a stroke through the continuation of the last leg)
-rum	= ꝶ (in 'numerorum', fol. 32, 'verum', fol. 58ᵛ, 'iterum', fols. 104ᵛ, 155ᵛ)	
-ter	= t (in 'jugiter', fol. 79, 'pater', fols. 106, 243ᵛ, 273; 'personaliter')	t

The hand *M*[2] which wrote the five pages (fols. 251–3) of pure uncial has
the following abbreviations: **B** = bus, **Q** = que, **DD** = David, **DS** = deus,
ILL = illo, **OMPS** = omnipotens, **ꝑ** = per, **SCLI** = saeculi, **-MS** = -mus (*81*)
(verb ending). These forms are in all respects identical with those used by the
scribe of the main text, except that the latter uses two forms of 'per' (ꝑ and **ꝑ**),
and nowhere abbreviates the syllable '-mus'.[1]

LITURGICAL ABBREVIATIONS

The list which follows contains the abbreviated forms of recurrent liturgical phrases and rubrics. These are as a rule arbitrary suspensions, which, under ordinary circumstances, it would be useless to record. But considering the importance of the Bobbio Missal, and the difficulty in fixing its home, it seems best to include even apparently useless data, for the discovery of another liturgical volume with more or less identical arbitrary forms might throw unexpected light on our problem. Where a number of forms of an abbreviation are used, the more frequent are given first.

Small capitals are used for abbreviations found in titles and rubrics.

angelus, i	= angl, an
annos	= an, ann (in penitential only)
antiphona	= AN

[1] The form of 'per' found on fol. 251ᵛ, l. 6, is obviously added by another hand, probably that of the main scribe.

apostoli = APOS[1]
archangeli = archan
baptismum = baptis
benedictio = BEN, BENE, BENED
capitulum = CAPL, CAPT, CAPTL, CAPLT (in addition)
celebrantes = celebr
collectio = COLL, COLLEC, COL, COLLECT
confessor = conf, confes
contestatio = CONTES, CONT, CONTEST, CONTESTA, CONTE
cottidiana = COTTIDIAN
defuncti = DEFUN
depositione = DP, DEP
diaconus = DIAC, DIACO, diacon (penitential only)
(82) dixit, dicitur[2], dicens, dicis = D (with oblique stroke through the body of D)
diebus = d, dib (in the phrase 'diebus illis dixit Iesus')
dignum = dig, dign (fol. 24)
dilectissimi = dli, dl (used in connection with 'fratres'; see below, 'karissimi')
discipulis = d, discp, discip, disp, dis
ecclesiae = aecle
epistula = EPIS, EPS (fols. 167, 175^{v}, 179^{v})
evangelium = AEVAN, AEVANG, AEVANGL, AEVG, AEVAG, AEV
faciendum = FACIEN
famuli, o, um = faml, fal (famulo). In both cases the abbreviation-stroke intersects the **l**.
fratres = ff, f (also in additions)
ille = ll (in all cases, sing. and pl., masc. and fem., where the pronoun stands for a name to be supplied in the prayer); il (nom. sing., dat. and acc. pl.); ill (nom., gen. and dat. sing., gen. pl.); l (gen. dat. acc. and abl. sing., gen. and acc. pl.)
interpretatio = INTP (in the additions)
Iohannem = IOHAN, IOHA, IOHANN ('secundum Iohannem')
item = IT
iustum = i (in the phrase 'vere dignum et iustum')[3]
karissimi = k, ki (in 'fratres karissimi', cf. 'dilectissimi', above)

[1] The regular form in the title before the Lesson from the Apostles. The form 'aps' for the genitive occurs on fol. 179^{v}. The added line on fol. 209 has 'aposli'. The form 'apos' is found in a number of eighth-century manuscripts in Insular and early French minuscule.

[2] On fol. 212^{v}, 'dicitur' is expressed by dic, without abbreviation-stroke.

[3] The usual form is short **i** with abbreviation-stroke above. In at least five cases the stroke is over **i**-longa. In three cases it intersects **i**-longa.

laudant = lau, laud ('quem laudant angeli', etc.)
lectio = LIC, LICT
legenda = LEG, L, LEGE
libera = l (in the phrase 'miserere et libera')
magis = mag, mg, ma ('magis gratis . . . miserere et libera me')
maiestatem = m ('per quem maiestatem tuam laudant')
martyris = mar, marty
Mattheum = MATTH, MATH, MATTHE ('secundum Mattheum')
miserere = m, miser (see above, 'magis', etc.) *(83)*
missa = M, MIS
nomina = NOM, NO, NOMI ('post nomina')
oratio = OR, ORA, ORATI
pacem = P ('ad pacem')
paeniteat = pen, pe (in the penitential only)
pane et aqua = p, pane et a (penitential only)
post = P (in the phrase 'post nomina')
praefatio = PREF
presbyter = PRBT[1]
prophetae = PROPH
psalmos = pl [p]salm (in penitential only)
quadragesima = QUADR, QUADRA
quadragesimas = quadrag (penitential only)
quaesumus = QS
respondet = RP
romanos = ROM ('epis ad Rom.')
sacerdos = sacr (in penitential only)
sacerdotis = sacer
sapientiae = SAPIEN ('liber Sap.')
secundum = S ('secundum Lucam, Matt.', etc.), an oblique stroke intersects capital S,[2] secund (in additions only, fol. 6^{v})[3]
signum = sig
tempore = tpr (in additions only)
virginis = VIRG

The preceding lists show that there are on the whole few abbreviations in either *M* or *M*². The two kinds of 'noster' symbols, the **ni-** and **nri**-types, are found side by side, a fact which bears upon the question of the date of our

[1] In added rubrics on fols. 86 f.

[2] This is the only form of abbreviation used. Written out in full, the word occurs on fols. 101 and 173.

[3] The suspension-stroke used is identical with the stroke used with **d** throughout the added portions.

manuscript.[1] There are a few instances of Visigothic forms, the significance of which is touched upon below. Attention should also be drawn to the very frequent use of that form of the 'per' symbol which is often found in French manuscripts and documents of the Merovingian period, and is the regular 'per' symbol in Visigothic writing from the eighth to the twelfth century. Note-
(84) worthy, too, is the precise shape of the symbol—the wavy line to the left of the shaft, not the simple sinuous continuation of the bow. 'Prae' and 'pro' are not abbreviated. 'Quoniam' is consistently represented by **qnm**. Only twice does another form, **qn**, occur.

When we turn to the abbreviations of the added portions we are struck by their number and variety. In fact, differences are noticeable in the different parts of *A*; and the supposition which naturally occurs to one is, that the variations, since they are all used by one and the same scribe, must be due to differences in the exemplar. The section 'Benedictio olei', which contains the Insular abbreviation for 'per', is presumably copied from an Irish original. Moreover, there seems to be great confusion in the manner of abbreviating 'per', 'prae', and 'pro'. Whereas 'noster' usually appears in the forms found in the Missal proper, the use of 'ntri', 'ntrom', on one page, is probably not accidental. If, as seems likely, these forms are due to the exemplar, then the latter was more likely French than Italian.[2]

As to the technical abbreviations, whether or not the numerous forms found in our list will ever throw any light on the origin of our manuscript it is impossible to say till the technical abbreviations of other missals are printed and compared with them. Meanwhile, attention may be drawn to three examples which do not vary in their form: **apos** for 'apostoli', **epis** for 'epistula', and **S** (**S** with an oblique stroke through it) for 'secundum'. 'Apos' is the form regularly found in the Luxeuil Lectionary (Paris 9427) and in the Calendar of St. Willibrord (Paris 10837).[3] No parallel for this form of 'secundum', as used in the phrase 'secundum Mattheum, secundum Lucam', etc., has come to my notice. But small **s**, with a cross-stroke, is a recognized and familiar Insular abbreviation for 'secundum'. A centre like Luxeuil, where Irish and French elements met, could very easily account for the form of these two abbreviations. But Luxeuil, it need hardly be said, is only one of many centres that answer that description.

[1] See below, pp. 175 and 177.

[2] On the use of 'noster' see Lindsay, *Notae Latinae*, p. 148, ¶ 189; see also p. 154, ¶ 196 for instances of **nt** = noster.

[3] Also in the MSS. Würzburg Mp. Th. Q. 24 (Anglo-Saxon); Paris 12634, fol. 148v; Wolfenbüttel Weiss. 99 has both 'epis' and 'apos'.

A consideration of the abbreviations found in the Missal makes it quite clear that no uniformity of style existed in the centre where our manuscript was written. As in the script, so in the abbreviations, the Missal represents a transition stage; and there is nothing in the abbreviations to connect them (*85*) unmistakably with a distinct school. While it is true that certain forms of 'per' in the added portions suggest Insular sources, yet the Insular and north Italian abbreviation symbols which are found in a considerable number of eighth-century manuscripts from Bobbio are entirely lacking in our manuscript. Visigothic symptoms are present here and there in the manuscript; but the few cases of the Spanish forms of 'noster' and 'uester' cannot be regarded as conclusive evidence. These are merely individual indications of indirect Spanish influence, and may betray the Spanish ancestry of this or that particular part of the Missal; but they do not signify either Spanish origin or a Spanish exemplar for the whole. And excepting these forms, no typical Visigothic abbreviations occur.[1]

Thus it will be seen that the abbreviations are of a mixed character, which may perhaps be best described as in the main Merovingian, but with slight borrowings from Visigothic and Insular sources.

ORTHOGRAPHY

The errors in spelling found in our manuscript are many and varied. It has long been realized that they are of unusual interest to the student of Romance languages; and as a matter of fact, two studies have already been published dealing with some sections of the added portions.[2] An examination of the spelling of *M*, *A*, and *a* shows clearly that all these parts contain the same (*86*)

[1] For the convenience of the student of Liturgy, I append the passages in which the Spanish forms of 'noster' and 'uester' occur.

fol. 141 'ad dominum deum *usm*' in Lesson from Joel 2: 12–13 [293]

fol. 181 'quia lampades *nse* extinguuntur' in Lesson from Matt. 25: 1–13 [369]

fol. 181v 'da eius patrocinio peccatis *nsis* indulgencia' in Collect of Mass for one Virgin [371]

fol. 283v 'Inlumina quaesumus domine tenebras *nsras*' in Evening Prayers [565]

fol. 284 'propiciare domine uespertinis supplicacionibus *nsis*' in Evening Prayers [568]

fol. 298 'credo in Iesum Christum . . . et dominum *nsm*' in Symbolum fidei duodecinarium [591]

fol. 257 Possibly, 'quid cogitatis in cordibus *us*' in Lesson from Luke 5: 17–26 [500] should be classed among the Visigothic forms

The form **us** is hardly the contraction 'u(estri)s', but rather the syllabic suspension u(e)s(tris)'.

[2] See Section III, part 2, of the preceding article by Dom Wilmart [cf. above, p. 142, n. 1]. Unfortunately the studies by P. Meyer and Boucherie were made half a century ago. It is high time that a new attempt be made by competent hands. My own summary treatment has had the advantage of a revision by C. T. Onions, which is here gratefully acknowledged.

type of errors. The difference noted is not of kind but of degree, since *A* and *a*, being much more carelessly written than *M*, contain a larger proportion of faulty spellings. Thus the additions furnish the richer quarry of corrupt forms.

In the table that follows, the forms found in *M*, the Missal and penitential, etc., are printed in ordinary type, while small type is used to indicate forms found in *A* and *a*, the additions in uncalligraphic writing. The specimens chosen from the Missal, though they are not exhaustive, are, however, representative; while the specimens from *A* and *a*, owing to the very instructive philological material they furnish, have been given with greater fulness. It is hoped that the present survey, which must perforce be tentative in its nature, will show the need of a minute and exhaustive treatment of this side of the manuscript. From such a treatment more precise information should be forthcoming as to the locality where our Missal originated.

a for **e**: consumarit 33, 30; spaciosam 37, 19; gehende (= gehenna) 142, 16; mala 159, 25.

novissima 3, 13; pasares 2, 2; alemetum (= elementum) 180, 13.

a for **u**: virgalis 59, 27; pias (corr. to pius) 141, 22.[1]

a for **au**: Agustini 10, 29; 69, 18; Pali 127, 21 (in added title); ad (= aut) 166, 3; aguria 175, 8.

atem (= autem) 4, 13.

ae for **ĕ** passim: aevigilabunt 8, 8; aededit 10, 9; aedocti 13, 21; aeclesia 169, 16; volumtariae 175, 32; diae, diaem 178, 2.

cociaens (= quotiens) 2, 1; usquae 3, 12; diaes 179, 15.

ae for **ĭ**:[2] aemitando 15, 17; tuae (= tui) 160, 4.

filiae 2, 1; filiaes 3, 11; sequaetur 5, 9; tuae 5, 9; oliae (= olei), nacariae, filiae 173, 16.

e for **a**:

genere 7, 1; Ienuarium[3] 179, 12.

e for **ae** passim (in accented and unaccented syllables): emolor 8, 17; celis 15, 10; presta 14, 2; 170, 13; etatem 169, 20; egypti 170, 25; premia 171, 7.

letaris 4, 23.

(87) **e** for **ĭ** passim (in accented and unaccented syllables): calices 169, 7; omne

[1] Due probably to some graphic confusion.

[2] Apparently confined to unstressed syllables.

[3] Instances of this spelling in pagan and Christian inscriptions of Italy it is unnecessary to cite, but it is not confined to Italy. Le Blant, *Inscriptions chrétiennes de la Gaule*, no. 325, reproduces a lost epitaph from Amiens, which has UBI FICIT GENARIVS DIES XV (mentioned by Bonnet, *Le Latin de Grégoire de Tours*, p. 96, n. 2).

170, 19; forte 170, 26; vives 171, 5; 171, 10; homenem 175, 40; cenere 176, 18.

sene 2, 3; lebrum 178, 12.

e for **ĭ** (= **y**):

senagoga 2, 7; egeptom 2, 28; marteres 4, 9; paraletecos 153, 16; 153, 18; tebus (= typus) 153, 19; presbeteratum 178, 16.

e for **oe**: ceperunt 8, 5; federis 169, 25.

e (or **ae**) omitted before **st**: stimatur 13, 12; stas 21, 23; stote 21, 38; 88, 40; stu 29, 35.

e prosthetic (before **sc, sp, st**): externitur 59, 25; expernere 147, 35; expectacolum 149, 25.

espes 3, 28; estulti 3, 31; espolias 4, 25; exelera 5, 6.

e inserted:

senexteros, senestera 1, 1–3.

i for **a**:

creaturi 173, 16; conburit 176, 23.[1]

i for **ae**: qui 41, 22.

dimonis 153, 25; 178, 14; qui 179, 2; 179, 4.

i for **ĕ** passim (in accented and unaccented syllables): faciim 9, 2; disideria 15, 6; maniat 169, 19; meriamur 172, 18; quadropidia 174, 12; sagriligium 175, 7; 175, 18; cantit 176, 5; 176, 9; scopit 176, 22.

autim 1, 13; rignum 2, 11.

i for soft **g**: iuieter (= iugiter) 152, 18 (*M*[2]).

i for **u**: sidodis[2] (= synodus) 175, 23.

i for **y** passim: mistirium 12, 2; martirum 100, 16; sinagoge 158, 7; 158, 12.

elemosina 1, 1.

i for **z**:

babteiatus 179, 12.[3]

i prosthetic: istopore 40, 27.

ispiritales 4, 4; iscalam 7, 7.

i inserted: dispergiens 93, 16.

Moyise 3, 15; transfierit 4, 21; axsiendit 179, 16; logientem 180, 4.

i in hiatus:

diiabulus 1, 8; 2, 19; 3, 19; 153, 21; 180, 7; subdiiaconatus 178, 14; 178, 15.

[1] These seem to possess no significance, being probably mere blunders of the eye.

[2] Due probably to some confusion other than phonetic.

[3] Cf. Carnoy, *Le Latin d'Espagne*, p. 157.

o for **a**:[1] fomolatum 169, 14.

honc 173, 14.

(88) **o** for **ŭ** : oxurem 92, 3; ambolare 172, 18; clericos 173, 22; copidus 175, 12.

passim, fructos, adtolet 1, 15; sicot, lopos 1, 16; ot 4, 21; sul et lona 177, 30.

ou for **au**:

temsourus 1, 6.

u for **a**:[2] munum 121, 16.

u for **au**: cludos 37, 20.

u for **ğ**:[3] fraumentis 89, 12.

u for **ŏ** passim: ignusces 15, 31; oxurem 92, 3; humicidium 173, 22; redimtur, salvatur 177, 5.

arbur 1, 13; tuti 3, 14; sul et lona 177, 30.

u (omitted before **i**): hic 167, 11.

y for **i**: ephyfania (twice) 34, 30–1; chyrografa 39, 2; syciram (= siceram) 95, 13; cuy (usually in the final phrase 'cui merito') 30, 34; 51, 33; 51, 42; 104, 12; 128, 22 ('deus cuy redditur'); 128, 33 ('cuy abraham'); 131, 3; 135, 33; 142, 18; 143, 3; 146, 6; 159, 10; 161, 33; 163, 26.[4]

b for **p**: obproprium 8, 9; obtatas 168, 3.

lubis 1, 18; habut (= apud) 3, 10; labedibus 4, 6; tebus (= typus) 153, 19; procebetabit 178, 27; abrilis 179, 8; 179, 12; 179, 14; 179, 15.

[1] Of no significance, apparently.

[2] Doubtless of graphic, not phonetic, significance.

[3] Seems rather French or Spanish than Italian. Cf. Grandgent, *Vulgar Latin*, § 268; Meyer-Lübke, *Grundriss*, I. 472.

[4] The spelling 'cuy' occurs no less than fourteen times in our manuscript, which is most remarkable in so early a manuscript. While the use of **i** for **y** is a common phenomenon of Latin manuscripts, y for **i** is, to my knowledge, rarely found in Italian manuscripts or charters of our period. In Merovingian charters, on the other hand, and in Merovingian cursive additions (saec. VIII) found in French manuscripts one frequently encounters **y** for **i**, even in common everyday words. To give a few examples: a charter of the year 703 (Lauer-Samaran, *Les Diplômes originaux des Mérovingiens*, pl. 29) has 2 cases; of the year 710 (pl. 31) 1 case = 'ubyque'; of the same year (pl. 32) 1 case = 'marctyni'; of the year 716 (pl. 34) 15 cases = 'habyre' (2), 'iobymmus', 'exygendum', 'exygire', 'nysi', 'sybymed', 'racionabyliter uby' (2), 'ibydem' (3), 'rigny'; of the same year (pl. 35) 5 cases = 'uby', 'ibydem', 'habyre' (2), 'ubycumque'. In the famous Lyons Psalter (MS. 425 olim 351 + Paris Nouv. Acq. lat. 1585) additions in Merovingian cursive abound. The cases of y for **i** are: 'Christyanus' (70^{v}), 'myhy' (twice fol. 71^{v}), 'recypiant', 'scytum' (74). Cf. Delisle, *Mélanges*, pp. 34–5. On fol. 103^{v} of the Paris MS. lat. 256 from St. Denis the column in Merovingian cursive has 4 cases of **y** for **i**. In Paris Nouv. acq. lat. 1594 from Lyons a Merovingian note on fol. 35 has 'deregy' = 'dirigi' = 'dirige'. Cf. Delisle, *MSS. Libri et Barrois*, pl. I. 6. A Merovingian note on fol. 121^{v} of Autun 107 has 'adsum[p]sisty'. A Merovingian fragment from Chartres has 'hyc'. Cf. Le Blant, *Inscriptions chrétiennes de la Gaule*, no. 215, pl. 24, no. 144. On the use of y in later French charters ('loy', 'foy', 'Remy', etc.) see *Bibliothèque de l'École des Chartes*, XXXVII (1876), 17.

b for **u**: malibolis 15, 3; habete 76, 28; sibi (= sive) 162, 4; iubenilem 169, 20. (*89*)

sibi (= sive) 1, 3.

b omitted: edomata 174, 25.

suverteretur 2, 24; so (= sub) 4, 10.

c for **ch**: Racel 30, 19; 168, 13; 168, 25.

patriarcas[1] 3, 15; corus 178, 6.

c for **g**: neclexerit 176, 2; 176, 14; 176, 16.

macus 7, 6; faticare 153, 27; abdinaco, pelaco 177, 15; pacanorum 177, 17.

c for **qu**: relicum 110, 17; secuntur 115, 27; longincus 119, 29; condam 151, 20 (M^2).

cociaens (= quotiens) 2, 1; co 7, 9; 178, 10.

c for **z**:[2]

temsauricas 5, 9; Lacarus 6, 11; Nacariae 173, 16.

c omitted: autor[3] 22, 4; 172, 25.

notes 2, 21; letur 178, 12.

ch for **c**: archanum 32, 6; chana 34, 12.

ci for **ti** passim: insipiencie, emolacionem 8, 17.

avaricia 1, 8; iusticiae 1, 12; persicociones 1, 17.

d for **n**:[4] gehendam 142, 12; 142, 16; sidodis 175, 23.

d for **s**:

adse 2, 3; 2, 5.

d for final **t**:

Nixiad, faciad 1, 1; inquid 4, 9; quod 6, 23 (thrice); 7, 1.

d for medial **t**: condemnat 157, 13.

[1] But cf. 'patriarhe' 3, 16.

[2] In *Palaeographia Latina*, I (1922), 61, Professor Lindsay takes another view: he regards the **c** as a form of **z**. This, however, is untenable in view of the recurrence of precisely the same form of **c** in words like 'facta' and 'cesares' on the same page as 'Lacarus' (fol. 8 *ad fin.*). Paul Meyer, in his edition of this passage, *Romania* (1872), 483–90, made the same error. The correct reading is given by Delisle, *Cabinet des manuscrits*, III. 225 (and pl. XV. 7). The substitution of **c** for **z** is extraordinary. The reverse process, namely, the use of **z** for **c**, is met with in an inscription from Spalato: cf. *C.I.L.* III. 12894, ZONIUGI = CONIUGI. In this connection mention may be made of an analogous confusion: **ga** for **Ia** and **dia** in the words 'Iacob' and 'diaboli' (spelt 'Gacop' and 'gabole') are found in the Merovingian (saec. VIII) cursive addition of liturgical character in Paris lat. 256 (fol. 103v) from the Library of St. Denis. The text and additions are indubitably French. A facsimile of the upper half of fol. 103v is given by Delisle, *Cabinet*, pl. XI. Here **ga**: **Ia** or **dia**~**ca**: **za** in the Bobbio Missal.

[3] The **c** is added above the line, the scribe having first written 'autor'.

[4] For the opposite, **nd** > **nn** see Pirson, *La Langue des inscriptions latines de la Gaule*, p. 91 f. Apparently a Celtic phenomenon.

d added: ad (= a) 175, 23.

d omitted: amitti 9, 12; a (= ad) 16, 19.

di (intervocalic) for **i**:

madias (= maias) 179, 17.

di for **z**: exorcidio 73, 38.

f for **ph**: Filippensis 86, 7; Farisei 122, 7.

(90) **g** for **c**: logam 151, 24 (M^2); plagatus 155, 14; sagriligium 175, 7; 175, 18.

garetatem 3, 32; sagreligium 178, 24; 178, 26; furngacionem 178, 27.

g for **i** (= **j**): congugio 175, 22.

magestates 173, 13; Isage 178, 12.

g omitted (intervocalic):

frioreteca 153, 19.

g omitted (before **n**):

renum 2, 25; 6, 17; 179, 3; conovit 3, 5; 7, 2; rinum 3, 18; renom 3, 26; manetodine 4, 20; benenote 5, 7; dinetur 5, 19; renavit 6, 21; renanti 179, 10; dinatus 173, 19; anussentem 180, 3.

h omitted passim: abeas 10, 4.

eretici 1, 3; proibetur 4, 2; os 5, 16.

h superfluous passim: hoccultis 14, 3; hurit 16, 7; homnes 72, 32; havete 76, 28.

honus (= unus) 2, 3; huhic 4, 17.

h for **ch**: brahium 14, 19; brahio 170, 26.

h for **sch**:

pahe (= pasche) 178, 6.

k for **c**: karissimi, kari (passim); kariant (= careant) 123, 28.

l for **r**: palma 88, 9.

m for **n**: cumlatis 9, 9; volumtate 175, 1; 175, 32; 176, 3.

volumtatem 2, 3; foramem acos, tramsire 2, 26; cumcludi 180, 8.

m for **o**:

infructumsi 2, 9.

m superfluous:[1] opem 13, 25; de adventum 16, 9; ab errorem 17, 5; ambolom 114, 32.

passim: tiniam et 1, 4; eclesiam est 2, 1; in agrom 2, 11; peccatam que 3, 9; sub modiom aut 4, 10; temsauricas 5, 9; hominems 178, 22.

m (final) omitted[1] passim: ad iustitia 8, 10; oblacione 11, 12; dudo 23, 13; innixo 114, 18; in supplicio aeternom 144, 9.

[1] Cf. Bonnet, *Le Latin de Grégoire de Tours*, p. 154.

Christo colemus 1, 2; corpus autem nostro 2, 1; elu (= illum) 4, 24; baptismo 6, 8.

n for **m**:

lanpadas 3, 30.

n superfluous:

estunte 1, 18; terran sancta 3, 21; Nineven 6, 18.

n omitted:

no (= non) 3, 33; 179, 6; demostrat 3, 4; 3, 15; 4, 13; 4, 18.

p for **b**: obproprium 8, 9; suplimi 12, 18; opproprium 88, 22; 88, 25; 95, 32; (*91*) plaspemare 157, 14.

patepolo 177, 21.

p for **ph**: iosep 34, 11; blaspemat 155, 3.

p for **t**:

cuptidiano 153, 20.

ph for **p**: sphongiam 65, 3.

p (before **t** and **s**) omitted: saltirium 106, 18; temtas 156, 9; sallebat 157, 3; sumsit 158, 35; temtacionis 165, 3; salmos 176, 5–6; redimtur 177, 5.

sumti 173, 18; 174, 1; diinces 179, 22.

qu for **c**:[1] de quo rus (= decorus) 41, 11; illiquo 152, 20 (M^2); quoinquinat 136, 36.

qu for **ch**: quorus 41, 26; 43, 25; 43, 33.

r for **l**: frivoras (corr. to frivolas) 107, 23; terorem (= tellurem) 154, 10.

s (final) for **n**: nos 136, 26.

nos 3, 11.

s (or **ss**) for **sc**:

ssilicet 4, 12; sussetavit 7, 12; asindat 173, 12; anussentem 180, 3.

s (final) superfluous: agminas 14, 18; Iesus 14, 27; 14, 31; nocturnis 171, 30; sententias 174, 25; talis 175, 24.

quamdios 5, 14; 5, 17; sub reges 179, 11.

s (final) omitted:

domino 6, 10; illio 153, 10; de profondi 177, 18; men 179, 1.

s for **x**:

crucefisus 179, 14–15.

t for **d**: edomata 174, 35; quatropidia 175, 28.

aliut 4, 3; set 4, 10; retet (= reddit) 5, 10; sit 180, 2.

t (final) for **s**:

heresit (= haeresis) 3, 20.

[1] Cf. **qu** for **ch**.

t for **th**: corintius 8, 13; catolice 10, 10; tronum 135, 36; marta 145, 38.

temsaurezate 1, 5; 5, 9.

th for **t**: thobae 142, 39; 160, 28.

t superfluous passim: est (= es) 18, 21; 24, 12.

t (final) omitted passim: es 16, 33; 23, 25; pos 98, 31.

au 1, 9; face 1, 13; potes 2, 6; sun 6, 23; docun 178, 22; pus 179, 15.

u for **b**:

tivi 5, 1; cevum (= cibum) 179, 1.

u for **ph**:[1]

proveta 6, 21; 6, 22; 176, 12; 177, 16.

x for **s**: sinextris 42, 39; 64, 20; externitur 59, 25; expernere 147, 35; expectacolum 149, 25.

senextera 1, 1; dixtera 1, 1; 1, 2.

(92) **x** for **sc**:[2]

nixiad (= nesciat) 1, 1; 1, 4; dixipolis 2, 15; 2, 25; 178, 20; 179, 16; asxendirit 2, 15; 7, 6; 179, 16; axendirunt 2, 17; verexibantur 3, 9; naxitur 4, 1; isxitare 4, 6; exelera 5, 6; dixindat 173, 13; 177, 20; 179, 8.

z for **g**: evanzelizare 28, 2.[3]

Simplification is not common in the Missal, but very common in the additions, e.g.:

b for **bb**:

habas = abbas 6, 16.

c for **cc**: aeclesia 10, 6 et passim in Missal; in additions:

2, 17; 2, 19; 4, 15; 178, 11; ece 1, 15; ociduntur 2, 2; 6, 16; 7, 10; acepere 2, 7; 178, 17; pecata 177, 22–3; 180, 6.

d for **dd**:[4]

aducit 5, 8; adidit 6, 10.

f for **ff**:

ofererint 178, 1.

l for **ll**:

ilis 2, 3; elam 2, 13; elu = illum 4, 24; cf. 4, 25; 153, 21; 153, 27; 177, 11; 178, 1; 178, 3; 179, 2; novelum 3, 4; inteleguntur 4, 7; tole 5, 14; 178, 18; galurum 177, 26.

m for **mm**: comunione 14, 7; 175, 23; 176, 35–6; camino 16, 5.

cometat 179, 21; comonionem 180, 6.

[1] Cf. Traube, *Vorlesungen und Abhandlungen*, II. 59.

[2] J. M. Burnam, *Palaeographia Iberica*, 1, pl. 1, cites similar spelling in a Spanish manuscript, Paris lat. 4667.

[3] Cf. Carnoy, *Le Latin d'Espagne*, p. 156: 'septuazinta'.

[4] The contrary **dd** for **d** occurs: 'addam' 177, 21.

n for **nn**:[1] inenarrabile 39, 14.

none 2, 2; Iuhanem 4, 1–2; anus 5, 22; 6, 5; 6, 8; 6, 10; 6, 20; 179, 13; mana 7, 10; Susana 177, 16.

p for **pp**: opresserit 174, 37.

opresores 5, 16.

r for **rr**:[2]

resorecionem 153, 14; 177, 21; 178, 7; 179, 15; torentes 177, 17; corupta 179, 1; corere 179, 23.

s for **ss**:[3]

pasares 2, 2; pasionem 2, 13; 2, 22; 153, 12; posemus 3, 25; eset 4, 16; 5, 20; 135, 5 (added by *A*); mesam 177, 25; 178, 2; 178, 4; necesitas 177, 26; 179, 2.

t for **tt**:

atendis 5, 1; permitates 153, 28; cometat, dimete 179, 21.

The chief facts to be gathered from the above list may be summarized as follows: *(93)*

1. The various sections of the manuscript (*M*, *A*, *a*) are, as far as spelling goes, all of one piece.

2. The most frequent confusion occurs in **e** and **i**, and **o** and **u**. The correct use of the diphthong **ae** is found here and there, but as a rule its place is taken by **e**, occasionally by **i**. On the other hand, **ae** often takes the place of **e**, and occasionally of **i**.

3. **ci** quite regularly takes the place of assibilated **ti**.

4. Final **m** is frequently omitted where it belongs and added where it does not belong—a confusion due, it would seem, to pronunciation rather than to syntax.

5. Final **t** is frequently omitted where it belongs and added where it does not belong.

6. **x** and **sc** apparently represented the sound of **s**.

7. Extremely curious and puzzling is the confusion of **ca** for **za**,[4] which occurs thrice, and the spelling 'transfierit' for 'transferret'.

8. Lastly, the spelling 'cuy' for 'cui', which occurs fourteen times in the Missal. It is to my knowledge unexampled in Latin manuscripts of this period.

In a manuscript full of corrupt spelling it is curious to encounter so many unassimilated forms of the verb, both in the Missal and in the additions.

[1] The contrary **nn** for **n**: 'pannes' 180, 12.

[2] The contrary **rr** for **r**: 'suverterretur' 2, 24.

[3] The contrary **ss** for **s**: 'monss' 4, 20.

[4] It is possible that the confusion is graphic rather than phonetic.

Unless we assume that they are taken over from the exemplar, it would be difficult to account for this anomaly. In the first ten pages of the Missal there occur: 'conmendat' 8, 15–16; 'adtendite' 8, 20; 'inrogas' 9, 16; 'inlibatur' 10, 5; 'adstancium' 10, 12; 'inmacolatam' 12, 10; 12, 16. In the added portion one meets with 'adtolet' 2, 21; 'inponet' 4, 11 (cf. 113, 8); 'adtendis' 4, 26; 'adnunciantem' 179, 9; 'inperatore' 179, 14, etc.

Pending the judgement of experts on the spelling in this manuscript, it would be rash to venture an opinion. It may, however, be permissible to call attention to the fact that Visigothic symptoms are practically absent.[1] And the same may be said of Bobbio symptoms. For the orthography of the not incon-
(94) siderable number of seventh- and eighth-century manuscripts which are known to have come from Bobbio and other north Italian centres does not present quite the same types of error in spelling as our Missal. Especially noticeable is the absence of **ci** for soft **ti**, and of the use of **y** in common Latin words. And if we turn to charters we find the same is true. If the Latin forms of the Bobbio Missal be compared with eighth-century north Italian charters from the neighbourhood of Milan[2]—that is, not far from Bobbio—the difference will be found to be very marked. And there can be no doubt that these charters, in their vulgar forms, present a true picture of local pronunciation, just as the vulgar forms in the Missal furnish a true picture of the mode of speech in the region where the Missal was written. This difference, it would seem, is incompatible with the theory that the Bobbio Missal originated somewhere in north Italy.

On the other hand, if we turn to Merovingian manuscripts of the seventh and eighth centuries, we find that their orthography bears distinct resemblance to that of our manuscript. Not only do they have the same kind of confusion in the vowel sounds that we find in our manuscript, but they show the same partiality for the use of **ci** for assibilated **ti**.[3] Furthermore, in the cursive additions of some of these manuscripts,[4] written in Merovingian characters of the eighth century, and in the Merovingian charters of the seventh and eighth centuries, we have the same general orthographic picture,

[1] Such a form as 'stote' for 'estote' (fol. 142^{v}, l. 4) recalls Spanish methods; likewise the form 'Racel' for 'Rachel', but these instances are negligible.

[2] See the excellent collection of eighth-century charters in G. Bonelli's *Codice Paleografico Lombardo*, Milan, 1908.

[3] It is true that Milan F. 84 sup. and Vienna 563 have **ci** for **ti**, but the latter manuscript seems to me French, and the former is a direct copy from a French original, as the decorative initials show.

[4] See above, p. 162, n. 3.

including the use of **ci** for soft **ti** and the occasional substitution of **y** for **i** in simple Latin words, as well as the improper omission and addition of final **m**.[1]

All these considerations, taken together, tend to direct our eyes rather towards some part of France than towards Italy for the home of our Missal. But it would be useless to disguise from ourselves the fact that the accessible material with which we may compare the Missal cannot be regarded as exhaustive; and that manuscripts from other regions, bearing closer resemblance to the orthography of our manuscript, may yet come to light.

SYLLABIFICATION (95)

As a rule, our scribe divides words in the normal Latin way, that is, after the vowel, except where several consonants follow the vowel, in which case he divides as follows: 'doc-ti', 'om-nes', 'cog-nita', 'celes-ti', 'bap-tismum', 'confes-sionis'; even 'tran-sirit' (209^{v}). But occasionally he indulges in such grotesquely irregular divisions as: 's-plendor' (36), 's-criptum' (41), 'hierus-alem' (57), 's-pelunce' (64), 's-tans' (75), 'sangu-enis' (181^{v}), 's-cabillum (259^{v}), 'sacri-s' (295).[2]

GRAMMATICAL

That the traditional rules of Latin grammar were little respected by the half-educated scribe of our Missal is made quite clear by the syntax exemplified in the entire manuscript. While the scribe of the Missal proper is more or less on his guard and shows some sense of decorum, the scribe of the additions—whether he be the same or a different man—quite lets go of himself in his hastily scribbled performance. If we study the additions we notice that in imparisyllabic nouns of the third declension the genitive is used for the nominative: 'castus hominis' 3, 22; 'Iulius Caesares' 6, 20; that the accusative absolute is used for the ablative absolute: 'uisam tempestatem' 2, 22; 'uxorem ductam' 3, 10; 'persumtas (= praesumptas) duas horas' 178, 8; that total confusion reigns in the use of the cases with either preposition or verb. This is true of the Missal proper as well; thus we find: 'aceruo pucolum' 67, 7; 'hab altarem' 3, 5;[3] 'sub modiam aut so vasu' 4, 10; 'de dies malus' 4, 22;

[1] See, for example, Delisle, *Cabinet des manuscrits*, pl. xi. 3 (Paris lat. 256, fol. 103^{v}); Ehrle–Liebaert, *Specimina*, pl. 18 (Vatic. Reg. 317, fol. 136^{v}); and the forthcoming *Codices Lugdunenses antiquissimi*, pl. v (Lyons 425).

[2] In nearly all these instances **s**-impura seems to be the stumbling-block. Pronunciation may explain the vagary. It is hard to imagine an Italian scribe capable of such irregularities.

[3] It seems probable that errors of this type, in which **m** is wrongly added or omitted, were due rather to phonetic than to grammatical confusion.

'hab elum' 5, 2; 'ex vergene sanctam' 6, 6; 'cum asinam' 6, 21; 'di celom' 7, 10; 'christo colemus' 1, 2; 'sunt xxx filius et xl filias' 6, 1; 'de v. panis et duobus pisces' 151, 1, etc. In the story of the seven brothers who had had the same wife, the Vulgate and the old-Latin versions read 'omnes' (one reads 'septem') 'enim habuerunt eam' (Matt. 22 : 28), but our text (3, 14) has 'tuti (= toti)'. It would be interesting to know where this varia lectio hails from, and whether it is indicative of any locality.

(96)

PUNCTUATION

There is no strict system of punctuation used. Yet it is clear that an attempt was made to mark off liturgical phrases by means of points placed medially or high. These points, however, do not always correspond to what would seem to us suitable division. Another punctuation is also found here and there, shaped like arabic figure nine with the loop very open at the top. This is really a form of dot and comma (;) made in one stroke, without removing the pen. See Pl. **22**, no. 22 (*pl. 22, no. 22*).

ORNAMENTATION

The decorative initials are simple in design and crude in execution. The colours used are mainly red, brown, and green. The plaited work in the letter **D** on fol. 219 has some gold; but it is quite possible that the gold was added later. In general it may be said that the style of the initials has closer affinity with the French than with other schools. Pl. **23** (*pl. 2*) shows all the important initials occurring in the manuscript.[1]

EXEMPLAR

There is ground for believing that our Missal was copied from an exemplar having the same number of lines to the page. This hypothesis alone adequately explains why there is a singular lack of uniformity in the treatment of the final line on a page. For example: fol. 125^{r} has, like most of the other folios, twenty-two ruled lines, yet the scribe ventured to add part of an extra line because he did not wish to stop in the middle of 'sur-rexit'. But he did not hesitate to end fol. 126^{v} in the middle of 'pecca/tis'. More than half of the last line of fol. 126^{r} is left blank. The same is true of part of the last line on

[1] Through the courtesy of Professor Lehmann, it was possible to submit this plate to an expert on pre-Caroline ornamentation, who was not told from what manuscript the initials were taken. This expert seemed quite confident that their style was French.

fols. 127^{r}, 127^{v}, 128^{r}, 129^{v}, 130^{r}, 130^{v}. The word PRO which begins fol. 131^{r} could easily have been written on the last line of fol. 130^{v}. On fol. 133^{r} there was ample room for 'saule' after 'sibi' but the scribe preferred to leave a blank and write 'saule' on the next page. These examples are chosen at random. They are typical. Their like will be found on nearly every page.[1]

Something more may be learnt of the exemplar from an examination of the (97)
errors found in the Missal. A number of these errors point to an exemplar written in a script in which **a** and **u** could be confused. Thus we find on

Fol.				
Fol. 40^{v}	beutitudine	(27, 28)	*corr. to*	beatitudine
93^{v}	uirgalis	(59, 27)	*for*	uirgulis
199^{v}	munum	(121, 16)	,,	manum
233	pias	(141, 22)	,,	pius[2]
251	logam	(151, 24)	,,	locum[3]
251^{v}	ueternum	(151, 26)	,,	aeternum[3]

Other errors show the confusion of **s** with **f,** and **r** with **s**:

Fol.				
Fol. 65	insaniam	(42, 39)	*for*	infamiam
217	suerit	(132, 27)	*corr. to*	fuerit
243	patemus	(147, 4)	*for*	patimur
243	corregimus	(147, 9)	,,	corrigimur
246	generatur	(148, 29)	,,	generatus
252	hos	(152, 5)	,,	Hur[3]

On fol. 130^{v} in the phrase 'filium tuum de celis nobis misisti' (82, 27) the scribe first wrote 'cecis', an error that suggests an exemplar in which **c** and **l** were similar. This similarity is, in fact, found in certain types of Merovingian minuscules in which **c** and **l** have the broken-backed forms.[4] Other errors, again, must have arisen from misinterpretation of abbreviations in the exemplar. On fols. 177–8 the manuscript has 'proxima ita in rem tempora protulerunt' (108, 41). This makes nonsense. The correct reading is found in the Liber Mozarabicus Sacramentorum (no. 1002) which has 'etatis nostre tempora protulerunt'. In order to get 'ita in rem' from the correct reading we must predicate an exemplar with 'etati nostre' written thus: 'etati$\overline{\text{nre}}$' with abbreviation-stroke over **nre** to denote 'nostre'. The confusion of **e** with **i** is common and explains 'ita'. The **t** that follows was evidently overlooked.

[1] Fols. 241–7 furnish instructive examples.

[2] The note in the edition is incorrect. It should read: **u** made over **a**.

[3] This example comes from the inserted Mass 'pro principe' written in contemporary uncials, but by a hand other than the main scribe's.

[4] See *Palaeographia Latina*, I, 13–14, 34, sections 12, 16, 69.

Faulty division of the following four letters would give $\mathbf{i\overline{nre}}$ = 'in rem'. On fol. 245[v] the meaningless 'inconpensa' is most likely due to the scribe's failure to notice the horizontal stroke in $\overline{\mathbf{p}}$ which stands for 'pre'.

The above errors seem to warrant a conclusion or two regarding the script
(98) and date of the exemplar. The use of the **nri**-type of 'noster' is more congruous with eighth-century methods than with those of the seventh when the **ni**-type was in vogue. As for abbreviated 'prae' it is very uncommon in the seventh century and does not come into frequent use before the second half of the eighth century. These facts should be taken into consideration in arriving at an estimate of the date of the Missal itself. The errors due to the confusion of letters cited above clearly pre-suppose an exemplar written in a minuscule script. It seems more reasonable to ascribe such an exemplar to the eighth than to the seventh century.

DATE

Mabillon assigned the Bobbio Missal to the seventh century. It was, as he expressed it, a thousand years old. That was in 1687. This opinion has seemed acceptable to Delisle, to Traube, and to Dom Wilmart. It is not difficult to understand why the manuscript was dated in the seventh century. There is a certain crudity and simplicity about it, which suggested antiquity. It seemed less modern, in script and ornamentation, than such well-known liturgical books as the Missale Gothicum, the Missale Francorum, or the Missale Gallicanum vetus.[1] But the more one studies our Missal, the more one is inclined to doubt the traditional view. To the present writer, the manuscript cannot be older than the eighth century. This date is supported by the following considerations:

1. The mixed character of the script (see above, pp. 145 f.). No examples of mixed script are known which can with safety be assigned to the seventh century. Dated seventh-century manuscripts like the Homilies of St. Augustine, from Luxeuil, of 669,[2] and the Berne copy (no. 219) of Jerome's Chronicle, from Fleury, of 699,[3] bear no resemblance to our manuscript. The only dated manuscripts which possess at least some

[1] For literature and facsimiles see the bibliography in Traube's *Vorles. und Abhandl.* I. 235, 236, 237 (nos. 285, 288, 291); to this add Zimmermann, *Vorkarolingische Miniaturen*, pls. 44–7, 99–101, 101*–101****.

[2] Facsimile in L. Delisle, 'Notice sur un manuscrit de l'abbaye de Luxeuil copié en 625' (*Notices et extraits des manuscrits de la Bibliothèque Nationale*, XXXI. 2 (1886), 149 ff.).

[3] Facsimiles in Zangemeister and Wattenbach, *Exempla codicum Latinorum*, etc., pl. LIX; *New Palaeographical Society*, I, pl. 230.

points of similarity are the Autun Gospels, from Vosevium,[1] of the (99)
year 754, and the Bobbio Gregory, written about 750 for Abbot Anastasius.[2]

The use of **e** with cedilla for **ae**.

The use of the ligatures **ns** and **us**, in the middle and not merely at the end of a line.

The character of the minuscule writing used by our scribe when crowded for space. See above, p. 146.

2. The preponderance of the **nri**- over the **ni**-type of the abbreviation of 'noster'.

   The promiscuous use of the two 'per'-symbols, and their very frequent occurrence.

   The occurrence of **q** with sinuous stroke through the shaft, for 'que', a feature of eighth-century Merovingian manuscripts.

   The frequent omission of **m** anywhere in the line or even in the body of a word.

   The fact that 'omnis' and 'meus' are abbreviated.

3. The frequent separation of words, and the use of a form of punctuation (ς) other than the mere point (a flourish like a figure 9 with the upper loop open).
4. The number and kind of orthographic errors.
5. The probable nature of the exemplar. (See above, pp. 173 f.)

ORIGIN

When we turn from the question of date to that of origin, the problem becomes much more complicated. It is the part of candour to state at the outset that the precise home of our manuscript cannot be fixed on the available evidence. Any attempt at more than general localization must be in the nature of a surmise. For the present, it is only possible to indicate broadly the region where a book like our Missal could have been written. Perhaps the best way of weighing the claims of the various countries coming under consideration would be to summarize and comment upon the views held by the authorities referred to at the beginning of this study.[3]

[1] Facsimiles in Zangemeister and Wattenbach, op. cit., pl. LXI; Steffens, *Lateinische Paläographie*, pl. 37; Zimmermann, *Vorkarolingische Miniaturen*, pls. 78–84.

[2] MS. Milan Ambros. B. 159 sup., reproduced in *Palaeogr. Society*, I, pl. 121; Zimmermann, op. cit., pls. 14–16.

[3] The precise references will be found in Dom Wilmart's article cited above, p. 142, n. 1.

(*100*) Mabillon called the Missal 'Sacramentarium Gallicanum'. The liturgical grounds for thinking it Gallican are stated with great clearness and cogency in his admirable preface. He ventures the guess that the Missal may have been used in the province of Besançon, in which the monastery of Luxeuil was situated. And as St. Columban, who founded Luxeuil, also founded Bobbio, a thread of relationship is presumably established between the place where the Missal originated and the place where it was found. Moreover, the name Bertulfus, entered in the margin of the Missal, is identified by Mabillon with the Bobbio abbot of that name († 639). As Bertulfus is known to have gone to Bobbio from Luxeuil, in 626, Mabillon's theory of the Missal's origin gains in plausibility. What Mabillon uttered as conjecture was treated as undisputed fact by Forbes, who, in republishing the Missal, calls it 'Missale Vesontionense'. There were those who did not share Mabillon's view of the origin of the Missal. Mgr. Duchesne adduced arguments, historical and liturgical, on behalf of the district of Milan. Dom Cagin came out for Bobbio, and in this stand he had later the stout support of Edmund Bishop, a liturgical student of extraordinary learning and discernment. Dom Wilmart, whose exhaustive study of the Missal lends great weight and authority to his view, did not at first venture beyond the statement that the Missal came from some part of France. Afterwards, he came to the conclusion, which he expressed in his article published in the *Revue Charlemagne*, that a region situated between Milan and Burgundy—a region like Coire—would best satisfy the exigencies of the case. But in his last article, in the *Revue Bénédictine*,[1] after a careful study of the palimpsest leaves, he comes to a different conclusion. The palimpsest leaves, he argues, are in north Italian script: the hand that wrote over the palimpsest is the same as the hand of the Missal proper, therefore the Missal must have been written in north Italy, and that in a centre near Bobbio, but not in Bobbio itself, thus accounting for the presence of mixed Irish liturgical elements and the entire absence of Irish graphic symptoms. In 1914 Dom Morin attacked the problem of origin;[2] and by a skilful grouping of the evidence, and by bringing into high relief the Mozarabic elements in the Missal, he made plausible the suggestion that the ancient Septimania, or
(*101*) that part of France whose chief centre is Narbonne, offered the most likely field for the mingling of Gallican, Mozarabic, and Milanese rites exhibited in the Missal. The additions furnished him with further evidence in support of this view. Traube, in his carefully balanced statement, did not lay so much stress on the Spanish connections. Had he realized that the typical forms of

[1] *Rev. Bénéd.* (1921), pp. 15–18.

[2] Ibid., issue of April, 1914.

'noster' and 'vester' occur half a dozen times, and that the Spanish form of the 'per'-symbol appears frequently, in the Missal proper, and not only in the additions and in final phrases, as he thought, he might have attached more importance to the Spanish symptoms. Had he, furthermore, known that **nri**, **nro** preponderate over **ni**, **no**, as abbreviations of 'nostri', 'nostro', etc., he would doubtless have dated the manuscript in the eighth rather than in the seventh century. Traube was more impressed by the Irish colouring of the Missal. Bobbio was the natural home for such a product; yet Bobbio had to be ruled out, because of the absence of those Irish or north Italian features, or a mixture of the two, which are present in genuine Bobbio products. If Bobbio, St. Columban's Italian foundation, is given up, one naturally thinks of his foundation in Gaul, namely, Luxeuil, especially since the script of Luxeuil, unlike that of Bobbio, suffered no modification, so far as we know, as a result of Irish influence. And there was nothing in the script, abbreviations or orthography of the Missal or additions, incompatible with the theory that it originated in Luxeuil. Traube, like Mabillon, was ready to attach significance to the presence of the name Bertulfus in the margin of the Missal. If the Missal came from Luxeuil, Traube believed that it accompanied Bertulfus when he moved to Bobbio in 626. But Traube's concluding remarks are more cautious, and deserve quotation.[1]

> If [he says] we wish to restrict ourselves to the limits of probability, we may say the Parisinus is a work scarcely calligraphic, and difficult to localize and date; probably the manuscript belongs to France as an example of the barbarous seventh century. Irish influences, reflected in the contents and the orthography, might point to Luxeuil or to a centre which enjoyed conditions similar to those of this Irish monastery in France. If it be said with still greater caution the manuscript belonged to Bobbio, but was written by a scribe accustomed, not to the script of Bobbio, but to the French, the appendices could rightly be cited against the argument, since they also do not use the script of Bobbio.

To sum up. The reasons which are, or could be, given in support of Bobbio *(102)*
or vicinity as the home of our Missal are:

1. The fact that the Missal was found there.
2. The presumably Irish authorship of the compilation.
3. The fact that Ambrose has a place in the Canon.
4. The character of the primary script of the palimpsest leaves.[2]

[1] I cite the English version given in Burn's *Facsimiles of the Creeds*, p. 30.

[2] One might add the form of **N** found in the Missal—a form also found in a number of north Italian manuscripts. See above, p. 148, n. 4.

The reasons against Bobbio proper are these:

1. No Bobbio saints occur in the Missal.
2. There are no references to the monastery or to monks.
3. There are no traces of the peculiar Bobbio script, abbreviations, or decoration; the orthography is unlike that found in authentic Bobbio products.
4. The Missal is not registered in the inventory of 1461.

If it was worth while to preserve a service-book that was out of use, it was also worth while to record its existence. To the candid critic, the arguments *contra* Bobbio must appear more weighty than those *pro* Bobbio. But it has been argued that if the Missal did not come from Bobbio, perhaps it was copied near Bobbio from a Bobbio exemplar; for when the scribe of the Missal was out of clean parchment, he resorted to scraps of an older manuscript which could only have come from north Italy. The whole argument hinges on the truth of this last statement. The scrap is written in a beautiful small-sized half-uncial which Traube called quarter-uncial.[1] It is certainly as old as the sixth century. But do we know enough of half-uncial writing to say what is Italian and what Burgundian? The manuscript which in my opinion shows the nearest likeness to the half-uncial leaves in our Missal is the Orléans fragment of St. Augustine (MS. 192 (169), fols. 32–3), which Traube thought might have been written at Fleury.[2] Dom Wilmart prefers to believe that it got to Fleury from Italy. This may be the case, but it cannot be considered as evidence. I am aware that there are extant examples of quarter-uncial which come from Bobbio, but does this exclude the possibility that the same type of writing was practised in the important centres of Gaul?
(103) In fact, there is reason to believe that the tradition of this type was better cherished in France than in Italy; for at the dawn of Latin minuscule writing in the eighth century there emerges a minuscule script in France which shows distinct signs of having been worked out by men thoroughly versed in the tradition of the type of half-uncial under discussion. This was not the case in north Italy.

But even if we assume that the half-uncial of our palimpsest was a type confined to northern Italy, why could not a manuscript in this writing have emigrated to some part of France or elsewhere? This is just what Dom Wilmart must suppose, in order to account for the existence of the Fleury fragment at Orléans. As a matter of fact, a careful scrutiny of extant Latin palimpsests

[1] See Pl. **22**, no. 23 (*pl. 1, no. 23*).

[2] The primary script of St. Gall 912 (Psalter) also shows resemblance to our leaves.

shows that not a few ancient manuscripts of the fifth or sixth century were converted into palimpsests in France. I can think of three, at least, that show an ancient text buried under scriptura Luxoviensis of the early eighth century.[1] I fear the present state of our knowledge does not warrant the drawing of a conclusion one way or the other from the nature of the primary script of our palimpsest.

Perhaps at this point comment might be made upon the conjecture that the name Bertulfus, entered in the margin, connects our manuscript with Bobbio, and refers to the seventh-century Abbot Bertulfus, of that house. Considering the casual way in which the entry is made, it appears improbable that any more significance attaches to Bertulfus than to the other five names which are entered at the foot of various pages. All these names are jotted down by the same crude, uncalligraphic hand that wrote the additions. As there is no reason which explains why any one of them, more than another, was written into the manuscript, so there is no evidence for supposing that any one of them, more than another, has historical significance. In any case, whether the Bertulfus mentioned is the abbot of that name or no, Traube's surmise that the Missal might have been brought from Luxeuil to Bobbio by Bertulfus in 626 is untenable on palaeographical grounds; for if we compare our Missal with a genuine Luxeuil product like the manuscript of St. Augustine, of the year 669, now in the Pierpont Morgan library of New York, we are left in no manner of doubt of the greater antiquity of the latter manuscript.

Of the six names thus entered—Bertulfus, Elderatus, Munubertus, Daco- *(104)*
lena, Bonolo, and Aquilina[2]—not much can be made. Traube pointed out that the unusual name Dacolenus is found in a charter of Moissac of the year 680. For the name Aquilina there is also French evidence.[3] Names in '-linus' or '-lenus' are not unknown in north Italy. But one is struck with their unusually frequent occurrence in southern France. Two out of the five names in our list have this ending; but this may easily be pure accident, and the argument is not one to be pressed. Whether or no the names of the saints

[1] I refer to St. Paul in Carinthia XXV. 2. 36 of Pliny; Verona XL (38) of Livy; Wolfenbüttel Aug. Quart. 13. 11 of Ovid. The list of early French palimpsests is not a small one, but it would be out of place to discuss them here.

[2] They are entered at the foot of fols. 197^v, 208^v, 213^v, 268^v, 271^v, 284. The faded entry at the foot of fol. 270 was most likely that of another name. Neither Delisle nor Dom Wilmart mentions Aquilina. These entries are all by one hand—the scribe's own, I believe.

[3] I owe this knowledge to the courtesy of M. Henri Omont, who writes: 'Le nom d'Aquilina se trouve dans un diplôme de Clotaire III rapporté par la Chronique de Bèze (cf. G. Pertz, *Diplom.* I. 39–41, nos. 42 and 43). *Aequilina silva* (forêt d'Iveline) se trouve dans un diplôme de Pépin (Tardif no. 62).' Letter of 22 Dec. 1920.

invoked in the incantations on fol. 254 really throw any light on the home of the Missal or of its possessor, it is not for a layman to say. The saints are: Severus, Anatolius, Aridius, and Donatus. Dom Morin pointed out that two churches of Agde were dedicated to Anatolius and Severus respectively. The latter he would identify with the Abbot of Agde, of about 500; the former with the Bishop of Lodève, at about the first half of the seventh century. Upon the other two saints the learned Benedictines have no conjecture to offer. But if St. Aridius is either the Lyons († 611) or the Limoges († 591) saint of that name—and I find no Aridius in Italy—the fact would constitute another crumb of evidence in favour of France—or at least in favour of the French origin of the incantations. A St. Donatus († 660) was Bishop of Besançon. Moreover, the circumstance that the Penitential at the end of the Missal is almost pure Burgundian favours French origin, or at least French connection.

If, in conclusion, we turn to palaeography proper, we find it easier to say to which regions the Missal does not belong, palaeographically speaking, than to which it does. But it is of some importance to state even the negative side clearly: script, abbreviations, orthography, and decoration point away from purely Insular or purely Visigothic centres. The few instances of the Spanish forms of 'noster' and 'vester' are not, as has been seen, conclusive evidence of direct Visigothic influence. Nor is the use of ꝑ for 'per'. The few instances of
(105) the Insular form of 'per' (pʼ) and the misspellings of Irish flavour, both confined to the additions, may be due to an Insular exemplar, direct or indirect, for those particular additions. But our manuscript could have been written either in northern Italy or in France. The palaeographical arguments in favour of northern Italy have been weighed and found, to my mind, wanting[1] —perhaps only because of the partial nature of the evidence at our command. The arguments in favour of some French centre—and these seem the most convincing to me—are to be gleaned from a few details in the preceding chapters dealing with script, abbreviations, orthography, and decoration. I lay particular stress on the use of ꝑ for 'per', on the spelling 'cuy' for 'cui', and on the rather Merovingian appearance of the additional portions. To say, however, that our Missal was written in one Frankish centre rather than another would be to go beyond the warrant given us by the present data.

If palaeography were not, in the hands of certain experts, rapidly becoming an exact science, competent to fix within a decade the date of an undated

[1] See above, pp. 159–61, 169–71.

manuscript, and to determine its home with enviable confidence,[1] I should be tempted to sum up the impression made upon me by the Missal in some such unscientific language as this:

A little over twelve hundred years ago, in an obscure village somewhere on this side of the Alps, in a district where French was the spoken language, near a convent of nuns, an old cleric once copied a service-book. His hand was not very steady, but he wrote with a will, and meant to do a good job. His parchment was not of the best, and his penmanship showed that he was no master of the craft. He had two kinds of ink: ordinary dark for the text, and red for the rubrics. He used the red as unskilfully as the black. He had little time, busy priest that he was, for over-care or refinements to bestow on titles and rubrics. But he could not deny himself the pleasure of some ornamentation,
so when he could he copied a decorative initial, with results pathetic in their *(106)*
crudity. The old scribe was trying to follow his original page for page. When he came to passages he knew by heart, such as lessons from the gospels or prophets, he often cast a mere glance at his copy, and trusted his memory for the rest. He was a simple, downright man—no purist in spelling or grammar. He wrote as he spoke, with **ci** for **ti**, soft **ġ** for **j**, and vice versa; and he had small regard for case or verb endings. Coming from a modest place, he could not afford many books, so he crowded into his Missal much more than properly belonged there. And when his parchment went back on him, he borrowed fortuitous scraps.

In the centuries that elapsed between the writing of the Missal and its discovery by Mabillon, many a priceless manuscript treasure has been destroyed and lost to us for ever. By some strange freak of fate, this homely copy by an obscure, unnamed cleric has survived to puzzle and to edify us.

[1] A case in point is Dr. E. H. Zimmermann's important publication entitled *Vorkarolingische Miniaturen* (Berlin, 1916), which in its dating and placing of manuscripts is unwarrantably precise and therefore misleading. Its four volumes of plates are beyond all praise, but the volume of text is marred by contradictory statements and by a failure to draw a sharp distinction between fact and conjecture. For a sound corrective see Dr. A. Haseloff's critical review in *Repertorium für Kunstwissenschaft*, XLII. 164–220.

The Codex Bezae and Lyons

(270) THE origin of the Codex Bezae remains one of the outstanding problems of Biblical criticism. We are little nearer a definite solution today than we were ten years ago, when the present writer ventured—perhaps a little more boldly than he would today—the theory 'that the Codex Bezae was a provincial product, that it originated in a non-Italian centre, that Greek tradition prevailed in that centre, that from the time of its execution to about A.D. 800 the Codex was preserved in a centre (or centres) where Greek was the literary and ecclesiastical language; and that from about 800 onwards it existed in
(271) some western or Latin-writing centre', etc.[1] While much of this must remain mere theory, and some of it seems as reasonable today as it did when it was written, it must be confessed that the objections raised by Mgr. Mercati against the theory that the manuscript originated in a Greek-writing centre are so weighty and convincing as to render that hypothesis untenable. For it is perfectly true, as Mgr. Mercati points out,[2] that the ornamentation of the Codex Bezae, the wording of the colophons, the manner of abbreviating the running titles, and the position of the quire-marks, are in keeping with Latin and not with Greek scribal tradition. But to infer from this that the Codex Bezae was written in a Latin centre, say in south Italy, would be to ignore all the non-Latin features of the manuscript. Perhaps the truth lies elsewhere.

But the present note is concerned not with the origin but with the provenance of the manuscript.

In his letter of presentation to the University of Cambridge, dated 6 December 1581, Theodore Beza states that the manuscript came from the monastery of St. Irenaeus at Lyons. From his note prefixed to the manuscript we learn that it had been found there in 1562.[3] As there is no reason whatever for doubting this statement, it may be taken to represent a fact. If so, the first fact we have to deal with takes us to Lyons. There are some other crumbs of

From *The Journal of Theological Studies*, xxv (1924), 270–4. [See Pls. **24** and **25**.]

[1] *Journal of Theological Studies*, xiv (1913), 385.

[2] Ibid. xv (1914), 448 ff.

[3] The letter and the note are given in the complete facsimile edition published by the University of Cambridge, in two volumes, in 1899. The text is printed in F. H. Scrivener, *Bezae Codex Cantabrigiensis* (Cambridge, 1864), pp. vi and viii.

circumstantial evidence which go to confirm the Lyonese provenance of the manuscript. This evidence has been dealt with in lucid and, to me, convincing fashion, by the learned Benedictine scholar, Henri Quentin, in an article entitled, 'Le codex Bezae à Lyon au IXe siècle.—Les citations du Nouveau Testament dans le Martyrologe d'Adon'.[1] In an appendix to this article, Dom Quentin shows that Mariano Vittori,[2] in the notes to his edition of St. Jerome, cites certain interesting Biblical readings from a Greek manuscript, variously designated thus:[3]

1. antiquissimus quidam graecus codex, quem Tridentum attulit Claremontanensis episcopus anno domini 1546: this is apropos of the reading in John 21 : 22 ἐὰν αὐτὸν θέλω μένειν οὕτως.
2. et ita etiam scriptum est in antiquissimo codice Lugdunensi: this (272)
apropos of the reading in Matt. 1 : 23 καὶ καλέσεις.
3. Desunt etiam (scilicet Matt. 9 : 13 εἰς μετάνοιαν) apud graecum codicem Vaticanum qui scriptus est iam sunt mille anni et ultra, et apud alterum antiquissimum librum graecum Claremontanensem.

The three citations obviously refer to one and the same manuscript. The two readings and one omission in question are characteristic of Codex Bezae. The 'codex antiquissimus' of Vittori is, it would seem, no other than the Codex Bezae itself. The first citation, though lacking a reference to the home of the manuscript, tells the interesting fact that it had been brought to the Council of Trent by the Bishop of Clermont.[4] The second reference shows that Vittori, or his authorities, knew that the manuscript belonged to Lyons. The last reference betrays a confusion arising from the circumstance that the manuscript had been used on a public occasion by a Bishop of Clermont. The 'Codex Lugdunensis' quite naturally became a 'Codex Claremontanensis'.

Whereas it can surprise no one to learn that the Codex Bezae was known as a Lyons manuscript some two decades before it was discovered at St. Irenaeus, it is highly interesting to learn that there is good ground for believing that the manuscript existed in Lyons fully seven centuries earlier. This contention Dom Quentin makes highly probable by analysing the Biblical

[1] *Revue Bénédictine*, xxxiii (1906), 1–25. Allusion to this article is found in Sir Frederic Kenyon's *Handbook to the Textual Criticism of the New Testament*[2] (1912), p. 89, n. 1; and in Professor A. Souter's *The Text and Canon of the New Testament* (1913), p. 25, n. 2.

[2] Bishop of Rieti from 2 to 29 June 1572.

[3] I have not verified these readings. Dom Quentin cites from the Antwerp edition of 1578 (tom. i, p. 570, cols. 1 and 2; p. 631, col. 1). Professor Souter cites from the Paris edition of 1609 (tom. i, pp. 509, 510) and states that its first edition appeared in Rome in 1566.

[4] Guillaume III Duprat, Bishop of Clermont, 1528–60, founder of the Clermont College of Paris.

citations of Adon's Martyrology, which, according to the best authorities, was composed at Lyons between 850 and 860, and depends in parts on Florus Diaconus, Adon's celebrated contemporary at Lyons. Dom Quentin points out that a number of citations show great affinity with the Codex Bezae, and concludes that the Codex Bezae is the most probable source of these readings. Considering that Adon's Martyrology was doubtless written at Lyons, it seems reasonable to suppose that its citations, which recall the unique and peculiar readings of Codex Bezae, are direct borrowings from that codex. The fact that the manuscript was, in modern times, discovered at Lyons, would seem to lend further support to Dom Quentin's theory.

To these fragments of literary evidence it is possible to add two palaeographical items which point quite conclusively in the same direction. I refer to the use, in the added portion of the Codex Bezae, of blue ink, and of a peculiar three-shaped form of interrogation-mark (see Plate **124** a).

The use of blue ink in Latin manuscripts is extremely rare. When, therefore, I came upon the blue ink in the added ninth-century portion of the
(273) Codex Bezae—it occurs in the colophon at the end of St. Mark on the Greek side of the text, fol. 348^{v}—I knew I was in possession of a clue which might prove useful in throwing light on the provenance or later history of the manuscript. It was from Delisle's careful description of the important ninth-century manuscript Lyons 484 (414) that I learned of my second example of blue ink.[1] This manuscript contains Commentaries on the Pauline Epistles, taken from the works of St. Augustine. The excerpts were made by Florus Diaconus, a well-known literary and ecclesiastical figure of Lyons in the middle of the ninth century—the very Florus on whom Adon depended for parts of his Martyrology, mentioned above. An inspection of the manuscript amply bore out the observations made by Delisle. Blue ink is used on nearly every page where normally red would be used, that is, in the marginal rubrics, at the beginning of sections, and especially in the citations from St. Paul. This manuscript was regarded by Delisle as Florus's autograph. And for part of it at least this may very easily be true. In any case, there can be no dispute as to its origin. It is a pure Lyons product. There is one other Lyons manuscript in which blue is used, alternately with red, to set off the first word of sections. I refer to the manuscript of Jerome, Lyons 600 (517), in uncial writing of the early eighth century, which is probably a local product, though there is no

[1] L. Delisle, 'Notices sur plusieurs anciens manuscrits de la bibliothèque de Lyon', in *Notices et Extraits des manuscrits*, XXIX, pt. 2 (1880), 402.

positive proof of it.[1] Part of this manuscript is now at Paris (Nouv. acq. lat. 446).

The one other case of blue ink known to me—here again alternating with red—is likewise in a French manuscript, Rom. Vatic. Regin. 317, the famous Missale Gothicum, which seems to have been written for Autun, but has every mark of being a Luxeuil product.[2] These three instances may seem very meagre data from which to draw definite conclusions. But proper weight must be given to the fact that the usage in question is exceptional in Latin manuscripts, and that these three exceptions are all French, and two of them are Lyonese.

Experience with Beneventan manuscripts has shown that the sign of interrogation, if at all characteristic, can be useful in disclosing unexpected relationships.[3] I have for years been on the look-out for other instances of the peculiar question-mark which is characteristic of the Codex Bezae. Though many manuscripts have been inspected in the meantime, very few examples have come to light. Inquiries among scholars in the same field have not raised
by one my number of instances. It may, then, fairly be considered as excep- *(274)*
tional a feature of Latin manuscripts as is the blue ink.

This peculiar sign of interrogation has come to my notice in the following five manuscripts:[4]

1. Lyons 484 (414). Florus's excerpts from St. Augustine, minuscule saec. IX. By original hand, probably that of Florus (*passim*).
2. Lyons 478 (408). St. Augustine, uncial, saec. VI. By the scribe of the added first quire in ninth-century uncials (fol. 6ᵛ).
3. Lyons 604 (521). St. Augustine, half-uncial, saec. VII. Added by the ninth-century corrector, who made the annotations supposed to come from Florus himself[5] (e.g. fol. 74). Part of this manuscript is in Paris (N.a. lat. 1594).

[1] Facsimiles of this and other Lyons manuscripts in uncial and half-uncial script are given in the third issue of the Lyons publication entitled *Documents paléographiques, typographiques, iconographiques* (Lyons, 1924).

[2] See H. M. Bannister's Introduction to his edition of the Missale Gothicum in vol. LII of the *Henry Bradshaw Society* (London, 1917).

[3] *The Beneventan Script*, pp. 258 ff. (Oxford, 1914).

[4] Of course this sign may exist in several other ninth-century Lyons manuscripts unexamined by me, but it is only its presence in manuscripts unconnected with Lyons that would weaken the force of the argument.

[5] The theory that these annotations are by Florus Diaconus originates, I believe, with the late Dr. S. Tafel who planned an extensive study of the School of Lyons. I find these annotations attributed to Florus in Dr. Zimmermann's *Vorkarolingische Miniaturen*, p. 167 (Berlin, 1916). The work of this annotator may be seen on pls. II, VIII, IX, XVI, XXXIII, XXXIV in the collection of Lyons facsimiles mentioned in note 1 of this page. Pl. XXXVII reproduces a page from the Codex Bezae showing the interrogation-sign under discussion.

4. Paris 9550. Eucherius of Lyons, uncial, saec. VII. Added by a ninth-century corrector, who made other annotations supposed to come from Florus himself (e.g. fol. 67).
5. Lyons 431 (357). Evangeliary, minuscule, saec. IX. Added by a ninth-century corrector (e.g. fols. 64^{v}, 97, 97^{v}, *et passim*).

All these five manuscripts are connected with Lyons. The last came to Lyons from Venissie,[1] a locality near by. The fourth contains the work of a Lyons bishop and has the annotations which, whether Florus's own work or not, are in any case from the hand of a Lyonese scholar. The same annotator worked over Lyons 604, 478, and 484, the remaining three examples. Lyons 484 has the important distinction of containing both the peculiar question-mark and the blue ink for rubrics—the very two palaeographical features for which the Codex Bezae is remarkable. In view of this palaeographical evidence, it seems highly probable that the Codex Bezae was in Lyons when the added pages were written (perhaps by Florus himself, who may very easily have brought the book with him from afar). Taken in connection with the literary evidence given above, this seems to make probability touch certainty.

[1] According to an entry in the manuscript which is printed in full in *Catalogue général des manuscrits, etc.*, XXX, pt. 1, p. 110.

Some Facts about our Oldest Latin Manuscripts

A FEW years ago Professor Souter made the suggestion that the curious custom of beginning each page of a manuscript, or each column of a page, with a large letter might be of African origin. He was struck with this feature while examining a fragment, newly acquired for the British Museum, of the celebrated Codex Palatinus of the Gospels (formerly at Vienna, MS. 1185, now at Trent), which is supposed to give us the African text of the New Testament.[1] In reply to the suggestion, the present writer submitted a list of eighteen manuscripts in which this usage is illustrated.[2] As most of the manuscripts are manifestly Italian, the African origin of the practice was shown to be untenable. Quite recently another theory has been put forward, localizing the practice within still narrower limits. According to Professor Weinberger, the use of a capital at the beginning of each page would seem to be a peculiarity of manuscripts coming from Cassiodore's library at Vivarium; and he proceeded to use this feature as a touchstone for detecting *Codices Vivarienses*.[3] Impressed by the unusual interest attaching to this feature, I began to assemble all the instances I had, and to look for others. I collected a list of nearly fifty items, an inspection of which showed me at once that in registering the phenomenon under discussion I had unwittingly drawn up a list of very ancient manuscripts. The list does not, to be sure, hold all our oldest manuscripts, but most of those it holds are, as will be seen, among the oldest. In other words, the use of a large letter at the beginning of each page is clearly a custom of very great antiquity. This being so, it seemed useful to interrogate these manuscripts further, in order to ascertain what other practices they have of interest to palaeographers. (*197*)

From *The Classical Quarterly*, XIX (1925), 197–208.

---

[1] *Journal of Theological Studies*, XXIII (1922), 284 ff.

[2] Ibid., p. 403.

[3] W. Weinberger, 'Handschriften von Vivarium' in *Miscellanea Francesco Ehrle*, IV. 77 ff. (Rome, 1924). Here five new items are added to my list of eighteen; but my own notes on Palat. Lat. 1631 do not quite bear out Professor Weinberger's observations. According to Mgr. Mercati, who was good enough to examine the manuscript for me anew, the large letter is found only on a few pages. The rule is for pages to begin with the ordinary sized letter. The occasional use of the large letter may be taken as a hint that the Codex Palatinus is more recent than the Codex Vaticanus (no. 2 of our list).

Most of our oldest Latin manuscripts, especially of the classics, have been carefully studied and minutely described in prefaces and special articles by scholars like Mommsen, Studemund, Ehrle, Hauler, Chatelain, Traube, and others. And equally great experts have given us exact details about the oldest manuscripts of the Bible. But, so far as I know, there exists no single study which collects, verifies, and correlates the palaeographical data embedded in these various dissertations. While such a comprehensive study must still remain a desideratum, it may be serviceable to make an attempt, even of a tentative and partial kind, in the direction of bringing together some facts concerning our oldest Latin manuscripts. I therefore propose to examine this series of nearly fifty manuscripts, and to focus attention upon a few of the features they present. These are:

1. The use of a capital at the beginning of each page or column, irrespective of its position in the word or sentence.
2. The manner of indicating omitted **m** and **n** at the end of a line.
3. The use of running titles in the top margin.
4. The size and disposition of the written space.
5. The manner of signing quires.

(*198*) A few remarks about the material examined will be needed by way of preface. Though the list of manuscripts and fragments of manuscripts illustrating the phenomenon which is the point of departure for this article can make no claim to exhaustiveness, it is probably fairly complete. For my notes on manuscripts in rustic capitals and uncial and half-uncial script cover, I believe, the great majority of such manuscripts of which we have knowledge. Three of those in my list are known to me only through facsimiles: the Turin

(*198*)

No.	Press-mark	Contents	Script	Date Saec.	Large letters begin	Omission of final *m* indicated by	Omission of final *n* indicated by
1	Vatic. 3256 (St. Denis) +Berlin 2° 416	Virgil (*Frag.*)	Square capitals	V	Each page; huge capitals amounting to ornamental initials	∸	—
2	Vatic. 3225	Virgil	Rustic	IV	Each page	—	— (once, fol. 70)

* The asterisk indicates that the manuscript is palimpsest.

Italics are reserved for manuscripts in which the initial letter occurs sporadically, or is found regularly in one part of the manuscript and not in another.

Frag. (in the column marked 'Contents') indicates that the evidence for the use of the initial large letter is

manuscript destroyed in the fire of 1904, the manuscript from Leningrad, and the one from León. The others I have had in my hands, and was able to examine them with some care.[1] Certain palimpsests, owing to the use of reagents, are now very difficult to decipher. In such cases I have had to accept earlier results obtained by others who saw more and better. Other manuscripts have suffered from the ravages of time or the binder's shears, and having lost *(199)*
their margins, lack all, or nearly all, data as to quire marks, running titles, size of written space, or manner of indicating omitted **m** or **n.** In such cases the absence of data is indicated by dotted lines. It seemed instructive to have the facts presented in tabular form, as certain relations emerge from a table, which might otherwise remain unobserved. The order followed is roughly chronological by authors and scripts. Ten items are in square or rustic capitals, thirty-six in uncials, and one in semi-uncial. The manuscripts in rustic (and square) capitals have been given precedence over those in uncial and half-uncial, simply because as a script rustic writing is older than uncial. This does not, however, mean that all the manuscripts in rustic capitals are older than those in uncials. As a matter of fact there is ground for believing that several of those in rustic capitals are not so old as the oldest uncial manuscripts on the list. I have intentionally divided the twenty-six classical items from the twenty-one Biblical and patristic ones, so as to bring out at a glance what extant manuscripts of classic or Christian writers show the curious custom of the initial large letter on each page.

[1] For various kind services in supplying me with new observations or verifying my own I am indebted to Mgr. Mercati, Mgr. Carusi, Professor D'Elia, Professor Schiaparelli, Professor Maleyn, and especially to Dom C. Mohlberg, who at a great cost of time carefully inspected a number of palimpsests for me.

(199)

m and *n* distinguished	Running title	Size of written space	No. of lines	No. of columns	Quire marks	Miscellaneous remarks	No.
Yes	None	250×265 mm.	20	1	None occur on the extant folios	The MS. has the earliest known initials	1
No	Apparently rustic capitals, only vestiges remain (teste Mohlberg)	160×160	21	1	Roman numerals (teste Mohlberg)	Rests of quire mark XUIII (?) are seen on fol. 7^{v}. Rests of running title on fols. 35 (LIB III), 71, 72	2

furnished by a fragment. The fragment may be typical of the whole manuscript, but it is, of course, possible that parts now lost did not show the practice in question.

Quire marks are found, unless otherwise stated, in the lower right corner of the final page of the gathering.

No.	Press-mark	Contents	Script	Date	Large letters begin	Omission of final *m* indicated by	Omission of final *n* indicated by
3	Florence Laur. 39. 1 (Bobbio)	Virgil	Rustic	V, ante A.D. 494	Many pages, but not all	—	
4	Vatic. Palat. 1631 (Lorsch?)	Virgil	Rustic	V	Only a few pages		
5	*Naples IV. A. 8 (Bobbio) +Naples Lat. 2 (olim Vienna 16)	Lucan (*Frag.*)	Very large Rustic	IV	Each page	—	
6	*Vatic. 5750 (Bobbio)	Persius-Juvenal (*Frag.*)	Rustic	V	Each page		
7	*Orléans 192 (Fleury) +Berlin 4° 364 +Regin. 1283B	Sallust (*Frag.*)	Rustic	V	Each column	—	—
8	*Vatic. Regin. 2077	Cicero	Rustic	IV	Each column; the first letter only a trifle larger	—	—
9	*Turin A. II. 2* (Bobbio)	Cicero (*Frag.*)	Rustic	IV	Each page	—	—
10	*Vatic. Palat. 24	Livy Book 91 (*Frag.*)	Rustic	V	First column regularly, but occasionally both columns	—	—
11	*Verona XL (38) (Luxeuil)	Livy First decade	Uncial	V	Each column	—	
12	Paris 5730 (Avellino)	Livy Third decade	Uncial	V	Many columns, but not all	—	
(200) 13	Vatic. 10696	Livy Fourth decade (*Frag.*)	Uncial	V	Each column	—	—
14	Vienna 15 (Lorsch)	Livy Fifth decade	Uncial	V	Each page	—	—
15	*Vatic. 5757 (Bobbio)	Cicero *De Rep.*	Uncial	IV/V	Each column, but only on some pages	—	—
16	Vienna 1[a]	Pliny *Hist. Nat.* (*Frag.*)	Uncial	V	Each column	—	—
17	*Rome Vitt. Eman. 2099 (Sessor. 55) (Nonantola)	Pliny *Hist. Nat.*	Uncial	V	Each page		
18	*St. Paul in Carinthia XXV. 2. 36 (olim XXV. a. 3)	Pliny *Hist. Nat.*	Uncial	V ex.	Each page	—	

m and *n* distinguished	Running title	Size of written space	No. of lines	No. of columns	Quire marks	Miscellaneous remarks	No.
	In small rustic capitals	170×120	29	1			3
		205×185	23	1			4
	In rustic capitals	180×230	15	1	None occur in the extant fragment	I regard this script as rustic, not square capitals. The MS. has very wide margins	5
	In small rustic capitals	170×155	26	1	....	Final letter on the page is large	6
No	....	180×180	21	2	....		7
No	In small rustic capitals	*Circa* 170×170	20	2	....		8
No	In small rustic capitals	*Circa* 150×140	13	1		Very wide margins	9
Yes	In small rustic capitals (?)	140×105	30	2	....	Words are divided at end of lines in the Greek style	10
	Small uncials	195×160 —180	30	2	q XXXIII	A few pages have the last letter large	11
	Small uncials	180—185 ×*c.*170	26	2	Roman numeral preceded by a bracket		12
No	Small uncials	205×190	30	2	q XV		13 (*201*)
No	Small uncials	245×145	29	1	q XUIII		14
No	Small uncials	170×160	15	2	q XIII		15
	....	....	*c.* 35	2	....		16
			21				17
	Small rustic capitals	145×80	26	1	q XII	Last letter is large on a number of pages	18

No.	Press ma k	Contents	Script	Date	Large letters begin	Omission of final *m* indicated by	Omission of final *n* indicated by
19	New York Morgan MS. M. 462 (Meaux)	The Younger Pliny *Epist.*	Uncial	v/vi	Each page	—	—
20	*Vatic. 5750 (Bobbio) +Milan E. 147 sup.	Fronto	Uncial	v	Each column	—	—
21	*Paris 12161 (Corbie)	Asper (*Frag.*)	Uncial	v ex.	Each page	—	—
22	Vienna I	Ulpian (*Frag.*)	Uncial	v ex.	Each page		
23	*Verona XV (13)	Gaius	Uncial	v ex.	Each page	—̣	—
24	*Vatic. 5766 (Bobbio) +Turin A. II. 2	Fragm. ante-Justinian.	Uncial	v	Each page	—	—
25	Florence Laur. s.n.	Justinian Digests	Uncial	vi	Each page in part of the MS., even in Greek text	—̣	—
26	*Verona LXII (60)	Fragm. Codicis Justiniani	Uncial	vi	Each column		
27	Paris 17225 (Corbie)	Gospels Codex Corbeiensis	Uncial	v	Each column, with some exceptions	—	—
28	Naples Lat. 3 (olim Vienna 1235)	Gospels Cod. Purpureus	Uncial	v ex.	Each page	—	—
29	Trent s.n. (olim Vienna 1185) +Dublin Trin. Coll. 1709 (N. IV. 18) +London Add. MS. 40107	Gospels Codex Palatinus Purpureus	Uncial	v ex.	Each column	—	—
30	*Vatic. 5763 (Bobbio) +Wolfenbüttel Weiss. 64	Job Judges	Uncial	v ex.	Each page	—	
31	*Milan Ambros. C. 73 inf. (Bobbio)	Luke (*Frag.*)	Uncial	v ex.	First column	—	—

m and *n* distinguished	Running title	Size of written space	No. of lines	No. of columns	Quire marks	Miscellaneous remarks	No
No	Small rustic capitals	170×140	27	1			19
No	Small uncials	168×165	25	2	Roman numeral preceded by q		20
No	Small uncials	150×100	25	1	....		21
	Small rustic capitals			1			22
Yes, as a rule	None	235×195	24	1		Words are divided in Greek as well as in Latin style. Final letter is large on fols. 10, 13, 110, 134, 142, 195	23
No	Small uncials	190×185	32	1	Numerals		24
Yes	None	255×250	24	2	Numerals in left corner of first page of quire	Some pages end with a capital (fols. 122, 122v, 126, etc.). Words are divided in the Greek style	25
		240×200	50	2	Roman and Greek numerals		26
No	Small uncials	170×170	24	2	Roman numerals with or without preceding q		27
No	Small uncials	*Circa* 140×140	14	1	Roman numerals preceeded by Q		28
No	Square capitals	*Circa* 215×180	20	2			29
No	....	170×170	18	1	Roman numeral preceded by q		30
No	Small uncials	180×180	26	2			31

No.	Press-mark	Contents	Script	Date	Large letters begin	Omission of final *m* indicated by	Omission of final *n* indicated by
32	*Paris 6400 G (Fleury)	Acts and Apocalypse (*Frag.*)	Uncial	V	Each page	—	—
(*202*) 33	Paris Gr. 107	Epist. S. Pauli Codex Claromontanus	Uncial	V/VI	Each page between fols. 1–70^r with lapses on fols. 46–51	—	
34	*Naples Lat. 2 (Bobbio) (olim Vienna 16)	Apocr. Epist. Apost. (*Frag.*)	Uncial	V		—	
35	*León Cathedr. 15	Old Testament	Half-uncial	VII	Each column	—	
36	Paris 10592 (Lyons)	Cyprian	Uncial	V ex.	Each column on fols. 1–8^v, 148–155^v	—	—
37	St. Gall 213	Lactantius	Uncial	V	Each page		
38	Verona XIII (11)	Hilar. on Psalms	Uncial	V ex.	Each column	–̣ or —	–̣ or —
39	St. Paul in Carinthia XXV. 3. 19	Ambrose	Uncial	VI in.	Each column on fols. 39–93^r	–̣	—
40	Würzburg M.p. th. q.2	Hieronymus on Ecclesiastes	Uncial	V	Each page	~	⌐
41	Verona XVII (15)	Hieronymus Epistles	Uncial	VI ex.	Each page, in part of the MS.	–̣	—
42	Verona XXVIII (26)	Augustine Civ. Dei	Uncial	V med.	Each page	—	—
43	Leningrad Q. v. I. 3 (Corbie)	Augustine	Uncial	V	Each column	—	—
44	Paris 12634 (Corbie)	Augustine Regula	Uncial	VI/VII in.	Many pages	–̣	—
45	*Vatic. 5766 (Bobbio)	Cassian	Uncial	VIII	Most pages, but not all	—	—
46	Verona LI (49)	Maximus Arrianus	Uncial	VI in.	Most pages	—	—
47	St. Gall 912	Glossary	Uncial	VIII in.	Many pages between pp. 1–71		

m and *n* distinguished	Running title	Size of written space	No. of lines	No. of columns	Quire marks	Miscellaneous remarks	No.
	....	195×190	23	1	....		32
No	Small uncials	150×140	21	1	None	Here and there lines end with large letters	33 (*203*)
	Small uncials (visible traces)		18	2			34
				2			35
No	Small uncials	170×155	25	2	By letter fols. 9 to 147ᵛ)	The leaves which have the initial large letter are independent of the body of the MS.	36
	Small uncial		31	1			37
No	Small uncials	180×125	26	2			38
Yes	Small uncials	175×170	21	2	Roman numerals		39
Yes		180×170	25	1			40
Yes	Small uncials (on certain pages, but after fol. 270 on every page)	*Circa* 205×185	20	1	Roman numerals		41
No	None	195×120	30	1	Roman numerals preceded by q		42
No	None	210×190	28	2	Roman numerals		43
Yes	None	180×130	26 and 20 (fols. 85 to 165)	1	Roman numerals preceded by q		44
No	Uncial	225×130	35	1	Numeral in lower left corner (89ᵛ)		45
No	None	*Circa* 220×165	25	1	Roman numeral preceded by ꝗ		46
		120×95	14	2			47

(202)
I (*a*) THE LARGE LETTER AT THE BEGINNING OF EACH PAGE

It is hardly necessary to insist on the great antiquity of this practice. It has not escaped the attention of scholars.[1] A glance at the above list shows that twenty-one of the forty-seven manuscripts enumerated are palimpsests (the examples being furnished, of course, by the primary script); that ten items are in *scriptura capitalis*, this number forming a third of all the extant manuscripts in capitals known to us. That all ten of these contain classical authors
(203) is what we should expect. The fact that the majority of the manuscripts in the list contain classical authors and date for the most part from the fifth century, confirms the antiquity of the practice and suggests that its origin was pagan.[2]

Thus the antiquity of the practice is beyond reasonable doubt; but the time and manner of its inception can only be the subject of surmise. It is absent, so far as I know, from extant papyrus rolls. As for the purpose it served, that, obviously, could only be ornamental, since the use of a capital in the middle of a word can have no other significance. And these two statements, taken together, seem to me to throw out a hint that the practice was born about the time when the literary treasures of the past began to be transferred from papyrus roll to vellum codex—that is, during the fourth century. A papyrus roll was to the scribe no more than a monotonous succession of columns,
(204) which did not lend themselves to the idea of embellishment; the codex differed from the roll chiefly in that it was possible to have a book conveniently open at any desired page. Thus the page became the unit, and derived an individuality denied to the columns of the roll. Perhaps the large initial represents the scribe's first recognition of this fact, and his dawning impulse to lend a touch of beauty to his page.

An important characteristic of the initial large letter is that it is contained within the space allotted for writing, differing thus from the capital used to mark the beginning of a paragraph, which normally projects into the margin. When we find, in the famous manuscript of Virgil, in square capitals, Vatic. 3256 (no. 1 of our list), each page beginning with a capital not strictly

[1] e.g. Mommsen, Jordan, Studemund, Hauler, Traube, and Vattasso remark upon it in their discussions of Vatic. 5766, Palat. 24, Regin. 1283, Verona XL, Verona XV, Rome Sessor. 55, Bamberg and Lateran Livy Fragments (cf. *Abhandl. der Berlin. Akad.*, 1859, pp. 384–5; 1868, pp. 31–206, 207–15; 1869, p. 162; *Hermes* V, 1871, p. 399; *Gai Instit. Commentarii*, 1874; *Comment. Woelfflinianae*, 1896, p. 309; 'Palaeographische Forschungen', IV, *Abh. der kgl. bayerisch. Akad.* XXIV, Bd. I, 1904, p. 27; *Studi e Testi*, XVIII. 4).

[2] It is a curious fact that all the oldest manuscripts of Livy exemplify the practice. The absence of the Bambergensis from our list is due to the absence of the necessary data, the beginnings of the pages having been lost.

contained within the limits of the written space, we may take this fact as evidence of the relatively more recent date of the manuscript—an ascription borne out by its practice of distinguishing between omitted **m** and omitted **n** at the end of lines (see below). And when we notice that these large capitals in the Virgil manuscript have ornamental elements—they are in fact the earliest ornamental initials known to us—we may fairly conclude that we have here a natural development of the practice of putting a single large capital at the beginning of each page.

If we cannot say with any precision when the practice in question began, there is evidence that it started to lose ground as early as the fifth century. This hypothesis alone accounts for the irregular use of the initial capital in such manuscripts as the Codex Mediceus (no. 3) and Codex Palatinus (no. 4) of Virgil, the famous Codex Puteanus of Livy (no. 12). When we meet with the same irregularity in the Cicero palimpsest (no. 15) and in the Palatine fragment of Livy (no. 10), it is probably for the same reason. Although the last manuscript has two columns on a page, only one out of the four extant pages has a capital at the beginning of both columns, the others only at the top of the first column. The facts that a distinction is made between omitted **m** and **n** at the end of lines, and that the method of syllabification is Greek, also indicate that the manuscript is of the fifth century rather than earlier. And when, in the Codex Claromontanus of the Epistles, we find the use of the initial capital in the first seventy folios and not in the rest of the manuscript, though it was all written by the same scribe, we may feel assured that we are no longer in the presence of a regular scribal practice, but rather of a belated survival. It may easily be that these seventy folios went back to an archetype showing this feature. That the Claromontanus has a composite character is sufficiently proved by the text of the Epistle to the Hebrews, which, Professor Clark tells me, is linguistically quite unlike the rest of the Epistles. A graphic proof of this difference is furnished by the use of ordinary ink in the citations which occur in this Epistle, whereas red ink is used in citations occurring in the rest of the manuscript.

Manuscripts in which one scribe uses the initial capital and another does not probably belong to the transition period. The use of the initial capital by one or more scribes of the Florentine Digests I am inclined to regard as a survival of the practice outside of Italy—if I am right in thinking the manuscript has a Byzantine origin. As a curiosity I may mention that it is even used in the Greek text.

The occurrence of the initial capital on certain folios of the Cyprian manuscript (no. 36) is explained by the fact that those leaves (they are at the front and the back of the manuscript) come from an altogether different manuscript from the rest of the codex, and represent an older scribal tradition. The bulk of the manuscript I am inclined to regard as a product of the school of Lyons, and regret that it was not included in the collection of the oldest Lyons manuscripts just published.[1] The manuscript has the familiar annotations attributed to Florus.

A custom of this kind does not die out everywhere at the same time; and the
(*205*) presence of the feature in a seventh-century half-uncial manuscript from Spain (no. 35) is instructive as bearing testimony to the way in which ancient Italian scribal usage survived in the lands on the periphery of the empire. Again, there would always be slavishly copying scribes to reproduce the feature unreflectingly ages after it had actually ceased to be the regular practice. Thus its presence in the eighth-century manuscript of Cassian (no. 45) or in an eighth-century glossary (no. 47) suggests that the archetypes of these manuscripts probably date from the fifth or sixth century.[2]

Finally, as for the suggestion that the school of Vivarium is the home of the practice of using a larger letter at the beginning of each page, this much may be said: if there is any truth in the supposition, then practically all the manuscripts in our list come from Vivarium. But this conclusion is, on the face of it, improbable, not to say absurd, and, so far as evidence goes, quite unsupported by facts at our command. The valid conclusions to be drawn from a consideration of our list are that the practice in question is of Italian origin, and that it is of great antiquity. But despite the fact that the practice cannot be narrowly localized it has more than antiquarian interest, since it may be useful in giving a hint of the date, origin, or archetype of a manuscript which illustrates the practice. That the practice was known to the best calligraphers of the fourth and fifth centuries may be gathered from the fact that it is found

[1] E. A. Lowe, *Codices Lugdunenses antiquissimi: La plus ancienne École calligraphique de France* (Lyons, 1924).

[2] To the examples in my list may be added a few others that have since come to my notice: (1) Vienna 563 is palimpsest. The primary script, in fifth-century uncials, contains the Evangelium Nicodemi. Here most pages, though not all, begin with a larger letter. (2) The practice is illustrated in the vellum fragment of Genesis from Egypt (*Oxy. Pap.*, no. 1073, vol. VIII, pl. VI), if the extant leaf may be taken as typical. (3) In Paris 12205, containing St. Augustine in seventh-century uncials, one scribe begins each page with an ordinary letter (this scribe uses the curious g with the split tail), while another scribe regularly has a large letter (fols. 77 ff. and 143–57). The latter is either reproducing an ancient original slavishly, or he is clinging to a custom long since become obsolete. (4) In Vatic. Ottob. 319, another seventh-century uncial manuscript of St. Augustine, we get echoes of the custom, for here and there the scribe indulges in a large letter at the beginning of the page, which he doubtless takes over unthinkingly from his original.

in *éditions de luxe*, as witness the *Codices purpurei* of the Bible, and the magnificent manuscripts of the Latin classics, with the sumptuous margins, contained in our list (nos. 1, 5, 9, 13, 28, 29).

(*b*) USE OF A LARGE LETTER AT THE END OF A PAGE

The use of the initial letter at the head of a page or column has a curious corollary in the use of a large letter at the end of page or column as well. Instances are found in nos. 6, 11, 18, and 23. In the Codex Claromontanus (no. 33) the letters **c**, **e**, **o**, **r**, and **s** at the end of lines are occasionally written large.

II. OMISSION OF **m** AND **n** AT END OF LINE

In describing the fifth-century Fleury fragments of Jerome's *Chronicle*, Traube made the correct observation that the practice of marking omitted **n** at the end of a line is not so old as the practice of marking omitted **m**; and that the distinction between omitted **m** and omitted **n** is still more recent.[1] The evidence furnished by the oldest manuscripts in our list completely and fully confirms his observations. I am so much convinced of the validity of this test that I do not hesitate to apply it as corroborative evidence in the
cases of the Vatican Virgil in square capitals (no. 1) and the Palatine fragment (*206*)
of Livy in rustic capitals (no. 10), and to assign them to the fifth rather than to an earlier century. By the same token the Gaius of Verona (no. 23) cannot be older than the fifth century. When omitted **m** and **n** are differentiated, the **m** is indicated by a stroke over a dot, the **n** by the simple stroke. Noteworthy is the nuance employed by the scribe of Würzburg M.p. th. q. 2 (no. 40), his **n**-stroke turning up at the left and down at the right, while the **m**-stroke turns up at the right end. Normally in our oldest manuscripts the stroke for omitted **m** and **n** follows the vowel, and is strictly confined to the end of lines.

III. RUNNING TITLES

The importance of collecting data on the use of running titles was first pointed out by Karl Dziatzko in his *Untersuchungen über ausgewählte Kapitel*

[1] L. Traube, *Hieronymi chronicorum codicis Floriacensis fragmenta*, etc., p. vi (= *Codd. Gr. et Lat. photogr. depicti*. Suppl. vol. 1 (Leyden, 1902)). Some statistics of the omission of **m** and **n** will be found in Traube's *Nomina Sacra*, pp. 179, 181, 183, 185. But my own observations do not always agree with his. Where divergencies occur I have verified the facts set down in the table.

des antiken Buchwesens (Leipzig, 1900), pp. 178 ff. In this work he made the interesting suggestion that the presence or absence of running titles could be used as a test for dating the oldest Latin manuscripts. He pointed out that running titles did not exist in papyrus rolls; that they are first found in vellum codices, and that even in codices their use could hardly have been general at the end of the fourth century, for in a letter of St. Augustine to St. Jerome, written in 397, the former complains that he was unable to tell the name of a work of St. Jerome's he had just received because it lacked a front title. From this it would follow that manuscripts with running titles by first hand cannot, roughly speaking, go much back beyond the fifth century.[1] In other words, the presence of running titles, providing they are not later additions, furnishes an approximate *terminus post quem*. This view seems sound, and should command universal agreement. But when Dziatzko makes the statement (p. 183) that manuscripts lacking running titles must be older than manuscripts which possess them (by first hand) he goes too far. His position seems to me to be open to criticism on both general and specific grounds. In the first place, it is never safe to draw conclusions as to dates from the absence of this or that given feature, since the absence may be accounted for on other grounds. It is the positive and not the negative fact that is decisive in such questions. In the second place, the data on which Dziatzko built his theory and based his classification were unreliable. It is almost impossible to conduct fruitful palaeographical investigations of this type if one is limited to the use of facsimiles. I venture to think that Dziatzko's whole discussion would have followed different lines had he been able to consult the manuscripts themselves. He would also in that case have been far more cautious in the application of his test, and his classification of the oldest manuscripts would have been very different.[2]

The few facts to be gleaned from an examination of our list are as follows:

1. Nearly all the manuscripts show running titles.
2. These titles are usually written by the scribe or a contemporary hand.
3. They are usually in the same type of script as the text, though somewhat smaller.

[1] This may throw some light on the date of the Gospel Harmony which fell into the hands of Victor, Bishop of Capua (†554). It had neither running titles nor front title, as we learn from the opening words of his preface to his Harmony: 'Dum fortuito in manus meas incideret unum ex quattuor evangelium compositum, et absente titulo, non inuenirem nomen auctoris', etc. Migne, *Patrologia Latina*, LXVIII, col. 251.

[2] Mgr. M. Vattasso expresses a similar criticism when he says that Dziatzko's discussion is not exhaustive, and that the whole question merits going into again (*Studi e Testi*, XVIII (1906), 4, where the Lateran Livy fragments are discussed).

4. The use of a different type of script in the title first appears in manuscripts of the end of the fifth or beginning of the sixth century (nos. 18, 19, 22).

Running titles are lacking in three out of the ten items in capitals. In one of the ten it is no longer possible to say whether they were there or not. In six cases their presence is clear. In the oldest uncial manuscripts in the list their presence is the rule, their absence the exception. If Dziatzko's test held good, then the absence of the titles in Vatic. 3256 (no. 1) would be a sign that (207)
it is older than the other manuscripts in rustic capitals which show the titles. But if this is so, then the Laurentian Digests of the sixth century and other manifestly sixth-century manuscripts (nos. 25, 44, and 46) because they lack the titles, are also older than all the manuscripts in uncials and rustic capitals which show them, which is on the face of it absurd.

IV. SIZE AND DISPOSITION OF PAGE

It is open to question whether statistics on the size of page and number of columns in a page, considering that they are furnished by so small a list of manuscripts, are susceptible of any scientific interpretation. But a résumé of the facts is perhaps not without interest. Our table seems to indicate that two columns were preferred to long lines in the oldest manuscripts. That all the works in verse were written in long lines and not in two columns requires no special explanation, and accounts for long lines in six out of the ten items in capitals. Of the remaining four manuscripts, which contain prose works, only one is in long lines. The evidence of the uncial manuscripts seems to point in the same direction. Of the four very ancient manuscripts of Livy in our list only one is written in long lines. I may mention in passing that the Bamberg fragments of Livy in uncials of the fifth (or outgoing fourth) century[1] show three columns to the page. The oldest manuscript of the Gospels in our list (no. 27) is written in two columns. And the same is true of the Codex Vercellensis (not in our list), which is probably of the end of the fourth century. This tendency was probably more marked during the period when papyrus rolls were being replaced by vellum codices. Since a copy normally tends to reproduce its exemplar, it is clear that the nearer we approach the period when the roll was being replaced by the codex the more frequent would be the manuscripts written in more than one column.

As to the size of the written spaces, the figures in our table go to confirm an observation made long ago by scholars—namely, that the oldest manuscripts

[1] See above, p. 196, n. 2.

show a tendency to use the square format. It is almost hopeless to try to deduce any general observations from the present size of pages, since in most manuscripts the margins have been cut away, in some cases more, in some less. But the written space has remained what it was, and lends itself to exact tabulation. I am not prepared to vouch for the absolute accuracy of my data, but I think the measurements fairly correct. It will be seen that thirteen manuscripts in the list have a written space that is practically a perfect square (nos. 2, 7, 8, 12, 20, 24, 25, 27, 28, 30, 31, 32, 39), and in the case of ten manuscripts the space is almost square (nos. 1, 4, 6, 9, 11, 13, 15, 33, 36, 40). If we consider only the length of the written space, seventeen centimetres or thereabouts seems to be the most popular length.

Our statistics dealing with the number of lines on a page permit of no generalizations. Six manuscripts have 26 lines, 5 have 25, 5 have 21, 4 have 30, 3 have 24, and 4 have 20 lines. One very ancient manuscript (no. 9) has as few as 13 lines, another (no. 15) has 15. But the small number is no indication of age. For the eighth-century glossary from St. Gall (no. 47) has no more than 14 lines.

V. QUIRE SIGNATURES

Our table confirms the observation that ancient Latin manuscripts have their gatherings signed in the lower right-hand corner of the last page of each
(208) quire. This is true of all but one manuscript in our list. The exception is the Florentine Codex of the *Digests*, in which the signatures are found on the first page of the quire, in the lower left-hand corner. But this manuscript does not reflect pure Latin tradition, and is unusual in more than one respect. The usual way of signing is by Roman numerals. Only one manuscript in the list (no. 36) uses letters instead of numerals. This departure from the customary may be due to its being a provincial product.[1] The Roman numeral is as a rule preceded by the letter **q**, standing for 'quaternio', the abbreviation being indicated either by an oblique stroke through the shaft of the **q**, or a horizontal stroke over it, or by a mere dot after it.

It will be interesting to see to what extent the above observations will be confirmed by further investigation of the oldest Latin manuscripts.

[1] The quire-marks are found between fols. 9 and 147^{v}, the part of the manuscript which was probably written at Lyons. Fols. 1–8 and 148–55 come from a different manuscript.

The Vatican Manuscript of the Gelasian Sacramentary and its Supplement at Paris

THE importance of the Gelasian Sacramentary in the history of western (*357*)
liturgy is a commonplace to students of Christian worship.[1] It is the earliest Roman mass-book that has come down to us. It has not, however, reached us in its original form, but with modifications and additions made by generation after generation, in an effort to adapt it for the use of countries remote from Rome. It is only through these adapted missals that we can today form an idea of the early Roman mass-book. The oldest of them happens to be the one that was current in Gaul; and although an interval of not less than two and a half centuries separates it from the missal which tradition connects with Pope Gelasius (492–6), it is none the less the oldest extant witness of the Gelasianum. The matter dealt with in this article directly concerns this oldest copy of the Gallic Gelasianum, which, like two other very ancient liturgical treasures, the Gothicum and the Missale Francorum,[2] is preserved in the Regina collection of the Vatican Library, where it bears the number 316.[3] It is a curious fact that, apart from the Leoninum, which is not a missal in the proper sense, and the Monte Cassino palimpsest,[4] all our oldest liturgical witnesses come from France: for to the Gelasianum, Gothicum, and Missale Francorum must also be added the Missale Gallicanum Vetus, the Mone Missal, and the Bobbio Missal, all of them products of the eighth century.[5]

The present paper deals but secondarily with the Vatican manuscript of the Gelasianum. Its primary object is to call attention to two quires which once

From *The Journal of Theological Studies*, XXVII (1926), 357–73.

[1] See Edmund Bishop's stimulating and masterly article entitled 'The Earliest Roman Mass Book', published in his *Liturgica Historica*, pp. 39–61 (Oxford, 1918); and the preface to H. A. Wilson's *The Gelasian Sacramentary* (Oxford, 1894). For fuller literature the student may now be referred to Dom Cabrol's article 'Gélasien' in the *Dictionnaire d'Archéologie chrétienne et de Liturgie* (Paris, 1924).

[2] MSS. Vatic. Regin. 317 and 257. Traube in his list of uncial manuscripts gives the most important literature: *Vorles. und Abhandl.* I. 236–7 (Munich, 1909).

[3] See Traube, loc. cit., and the article by Dom Cabrol, cited in n. 1, which also contains an excellent facsimile.

[4] MSS. Verona LXXXV (80) and Monte Cassino CCLXXI: Traube, loc. cit., nos. 356 and 117.

[5] MSS. Vatic. Pal. 493, Carlsruhe 253, and Paris lat. 13246: Traube, loc. cit., nos. 285, 69; *Henry Bradshaw Publications*, vols. LIII (1917), LVIII (1920), and LXI (1924).

(358) formed part of this Vatican manuscript. They are at present embedded in a miscellany in the Bibliothèque Nationale which bears the pressmark MS. lat. 7193, and occupies fols. 41–56 of that manuscript. The Paris quarto catalogue describes the miscellany as 'Codex membranaceus olim Colbertinus'; so this scrap-book belonged to J. B. Colbert, Minister of Louis XIV. Under item 5 our leaves are thus described: 'Formulae exorcismorum: litteris uncialibus octavo saeculo exaratae.'[1] Traube's list of uncial manuscripts adds nothing to the information given in the catalogue;[2] the catalogue itself omits to mention that, besides the Exorcisms, the leaves contain a Penitential and the Breviarius Apostolorum. Of these three parts, the Penitential only has been exploited. It was first published in 1851 by Wasserschleben, not without errors,[3] and again, but far from accurately, in 1898 by Schmitz, who makes the preposterous statement that its script is Visigothic.[4] If any other scholars refer to the contents of these two quires, I am unaware of it.

I first examined the quires in 1921, when I was struck with the resemblance of the writing to that of Reginensis 316. It was not until 1925, upon a request from Dom De Bruyne for new instances of *membra disiecta* of manuscripts,[5] that it occurred to me to verify the impression registered in 1921. I found it fully reaffirmed. The form of the uncial characters, the shape of the small initials, seemed the same in both; and the alternate use of red and green in titles, and the use of a ᴦ surmounted by one or more dots running up from right to left obliquely to mark the end of certain sections, were features common to both. There was also identity in the style of abbreviations. On looking for other agreements, I found that both the Paris leaves and the Vatican manuscript have twenty-three lines to the page, and the parallel vertical bounding lines are at the same distance apart in both manuscripts. The dimensions of the full page vary, to be sure, by 2–3 millimeters, owing doubtless to the binder's shears, but the written space is practically identical, being 128 × 216 mm. in the Reginensis and 130 × 216 mm. in the Paris leaves.[6]

[1] *Catalogus Codicum Manuscriptorum Bibliothecae Regiae*, III. 324 (Paris, 1744).

[2] Traube, loc. cit., no. 290.

[3] F. W. H. Wasserschleben, *Die Bussordnungen der abendländischen Kirche*, pp. 412 ff. (Halle, 1851).

[4] H. J. Schmitz, *Die Bussbücher und die Bussdisziplin der Kirche*, pp. 326 ff. (this is vol. II of *Die Bussbücher und das kanonische Bussverfahren* (Düsseldorf, 1898)).

[5] See the series inaugurated in the *Revue Bénédictine*, XXXVI (1924), 121 ff. and continued in XXXVII (1925), 165 ff.

[6] These measurements were taken in 1921, and may not hold for each and every page. The Prefect of the Vatican Library was good enough to verify my data, and his report bears out what is said above of the Reginensis. For the facsimiles here reproduced my thanks are due to Mgr. Mercati, M. Omont, and the Clarendon Press.

And lastly, I ascertained that the Reginensis ends with a gathering marked (359)
xxxiiii; the Paris quires are marked xxxv and xxxvi; these quire marks being entered in both manuscripts by the original scribe, and in both occupying the same position on the page.

If there can thus be no shadow of a doubt that the Paris quires were originally meant to follow the last folio of the Reginensis, it is not difficult to see why their connection has heretofore escaped attention. It is because the Gelasian Sacramentary as it stands in the Reginensis is complete, apart from a few pages of the index, which are missing at the head of the volume.[1] It would not occur to any one that a manuscript ending with a colophon which reads: EXPLICIT LIBER SACRAMENTORUM $\overline{\text{DO}}$ GRACIAS. SICUT NAUIGANTIBUS DULCIS EST PORTUS SCRIPTORI NOUISSIMUS UERSUS, and this followed by a page left blank—the last page of the manuscript—could be in any way incomplete at the end. Yet it is at the end of the Vatican manuscript that the Paris leaves belong; the quire-marks prove that. Moreover, the final prayers in the Reginensis with the title 'Ad poenitenciam dandam' suggest the Penitential which was meant to follow. Like the Penitential itself these prayers must be an addition, for they are not registered in the index.[2] It seems clear that the Paris leaves constitute a planned supplement to the Sacramentary. And inasmuch as even the 'additamenta' of so important a liturgical monument are not without considerable interest, it seems justifiable to publish them entire. Perhaps in the hands of another Edmund Bishop they may be found to throw new light on the history of the Gelasian Sacramentary itself.

The Paris leaves open with prayers entitled 'Exorcismus contra inerguminos', which occupy the whole of the quire marked xxxv. Part of these prayers, I believe, see the light here for the first time.[3] I must leave it, however, to the expert in these matters to bring out their due importance. Quire xxxvi begins with a Penitential which, as stated above, has twice been published.[4] I give it here exactly as it is in the manuscript, abbreviations and all. That it belongs along with the Penitential in the Bobbio Missal to the class known as the Burgundian is clear at first sight. The curious error 'uacuus' for 'uagus' found in the phrase 'more cain uagus et profugus sit', in article 3,

[1] The index begins with the 46th mass of the third book. The missing pages constituted the first quire. Neither Muratori's nor Wilson's edition reproduces the truncated index. One must go back to Tommasi's to see it.

[2] The last item in the index reads: 'item alia pro salute uiuorum'. It is no. ciii in the index, but cvi in the text.

[3] I have had the advantage of consulting such experts as the Revd. H. A. Wilson and Dom Wilmart. In the opinion of the latter the long exorcism with which the Supplement opens is unique and unedited.

[4] See above, p. 204, nn. 3 and 4.

(360) at once connects our Penitential[1] with that found in the Brussels MS. 8780–93, where the same error occurs[2]. The French origin of the Penitential appears from other items; and, as Schmitz has pointed out, it forms a member of the group which have a common basis of forty-one articles. The Penitential occupies the first six leaves of this quire.

The final two leaves are devoted to the so-called 'Breviarius Apostolorum'. It does not appear that this text was known to Duchesne.[3] D'Achery's text depends on a more recent witness, and Gerbert did not use any manuscript so old as ours, which, unless I err, is the oldest extant.[4] The transcription of the full Supplement follows.

[fol. 41] [5]EXORCISMUS[6] CONTRA INERGUMINOS[5]

Deus[7] caelorum, deus angelorum, deus archangelorum, deus patriarcharum, deus prophetarum, deus apostolorum, deus martyrum deus confessorum, deus uirginum deus omnium sanctorum, deus abraham deus isaac deus iacob, deus qui dedisti uitam post mortem Domine deus sancte pater omnipotens, te inuoco quia tu dignus es inuocari Ego pono manum meam carnalem Tu tuam sanctam de caelis spiritalem supermitte super famulo tuo illo Ut non
(361) lateat, hic serpens inimicus Sic percuciatur in uirtute claritatis tuae. Quomodo percussisti duas ciuitates sodomam et gomorram. Sic percutiatur hic maledictus seductor saeculi. Exprobrator gencium Laqueus mortis . filius tene-

[1] This error is corrected without comment in Wasserschleben's edition, op. cit., p. 412.

[2] The modern pressmark is Brussels 2493. The manuscript is written in pre-Caroline minuscule of a gauche type and must come from one of the lesser centres of northern France. Facsimiles are given by Zimmermann, *Vorkarolingische Miniaturen*, pl. 121, who assigns the manuscript to about 780.

[3] L. Duchesne, 'Martyrolog. Hieronym.' in *Acta Sanctorum*, November, tom. II, pars. I, Prolegom., pp. lxxv ff. (Brussels, 1894).

[4] L. d'Achery, *Spicilegium Veterum aliquot Scriptorum*, 2nd edition, II. 25 f. (Paris, 1724); Gerbert, *Monumenta Veteris Liturgiae Alemannicae*, I. 453 f. (1777–9). D'Achery's text depends upon the Gellone Sacramentary, Gerbert's on a Reichenau manuscript.

[5–5] The title is in the same uncial script as the text which follows, but the letters are coloured, blocks of red alternating with blocks of green—a favourite practice in this school of writing.

[6] The abbreviations found in this and the following prayers are here given *in extenso*, those in the Penitential and Breviarius are retained.

[7] With this may be compared no. cxliiii in the Gregorian Sacramentary, ed. Wilson, p. 229. Dom Wilmart suggests the following comparisons: Martène, *De Antiq. Eccl. Rit.* I. 15 ff., II. 329 ff. and 332 ff. With the next prayer (*Domine sancte pater*, etc.) compare Wilson, p. 230. Dom Wilmart's references are Martène (ed. Bassano, 1788), III, cap. IX, ordo i and ordo iii = tom. II. 347 and 351; Gerbert, *Monum. Vet. Liturg. Alem.* II. 128, 130 f.; Muratori, *Lit. Rom. Vet.* II. 239. For *Nec te latet*, etc., cf. Wilson, p. 162, and Martène, I, cap. I, art. XVIII, ordo X = tom. I. 69, 72, 77, and Muratori, II. 61, 155. For the next cf. Martène, III, cap. ix, ordo iii = tom. ii. 353, col. I, where too it follows *Nec te latet*. For the last prayer (*Omnipotens*, etc.) cf. Martène, III, cap. IX, ordo iii = tom. II. 351, col. 2; Gerbert, II. 133.

brarum Audi tanta uirtute. Tanta maiestate || [fol. 41v] per quem te adiuro. Adiuro te per regem caelorum[1] per christum creatorem per iesum saluatorem, animarum nostrarum per illum te adiuro damnate. Non per aurum neque per argentum neque per lapidibus praeciosis. Per deum te adiuro. Qui petrum mergentem manum porrexit et te inuenit in monumentum latere. Et tu eum prostratus adorasti et dixisti ei. Quid nobis et tibi iesus nazareni fili dei altissimi. Ante . tempus uenisti perdere nos. Et si nos perdere uis mitte nos in gregem porcorum et ubicumque nomen . tuum audierimus gementes . et trementes exibimus et dabimus honorem. Da illi honorem maledicte satanas illuc te collige. in profundum . maris in gregem porcorum . in deserta loca . ubi non aratur . nec semi- || [fol. 42] natur . nec nomen . illius potens inuocatur. Illuc te collige damnate. Cessent nequiciae tuae. Cessent . fallaciae tuae. Cessent conpaginaciones tuae Cessent machinae tuae. Cessent pestilenciae tuae. Cessent et fantasiae tuae. Seperate . ab hanc plasma Quomodo seperatum est. Caelum a terra Lux a tenebras Iusticia . ab iniquitate Uita a morte Sic te et tu sepera damnate. Non communicabis in escam Non in putum Non uigilantem Nec dormientem. Nec sedentem Nec ambulantem Nec tacentem Nec in publicum. Nec in priuatum . non communicabis. Non facies cotidianas . non tercianas. Non quartanas . non adgrediens in biuio Non in triuio Non in quatruuio Non occupauis linguam Nec guttorem . nec || [fol. 42v] sub guttere. Nec intestinum minimum Nec in maiorem.damnate.interdicitur tibi duodecem . oras diei et duodicem hore noctes in quibus non facias . quod ad tuis uoluntatibus perteneat. Sanguilappie[2] multis formis persuasor malorum Accusator ueritatis Umbra uacua Inflate Inanis Filius tenebrarum. Angelorum iniquitas. Proiectus es de caelo maledicti satanas meritis tuis Inmundissimi dęmoniorum uictus es damnate. Uincit te qui uinci non potest. Uincit te. A et ω. Uincit te ille qui scit numerum capillorum famulorum famularum suarum qui nouit numerum stillarum . uincit te qui firmauit caelum et terram mare et . omnia . quae in eis sunt Ille tibi imperat . non caro et sanguis . nec pompa saeculi . deus tibi imperat pater et filius et spiritus sanctus Ille tibi imperat qui ieiunauit. || [fol. 43] . XL . diebus . et XL.noctibus Et quartum diem Lazarum.de monumento suscitauit . qui dixit ad discipulos suos Ite in nomine meo, manus inponite Daemonia expellite Paralyticos curate Mortuos suscitate Surdi audiant Claudi ambulent Et omnem ualitudinem curate quod gratis accepistis gratis date. Nulla tibi gracia aguntur Iam . conpleti sunt sex milia annorum in co oportit tibi inmundissime daemoniorum finem habere In gregem porcorum in deserta loca ubi non aratur nec seminatur uentrem (362)

[1] *o* ex *u* m. 1. [2] *lap* sup. ras.

tuum et pectore Tu terribilis non euadebis poenas quas tibi praeparatae sunt Occurunt te a quattuor cardinibus mundi In illius uirtutibus impero qui aperit . quod . nemo claudit et claudit quod nemo aperit. In illius uirtutibus te adiuro qui fecit caelum || [fol. 43^{v}] et terram. Caecum inluminantem surdum audientem mutum loquentem . ille tibi imperat inmundissime spiritus a quo tu dixisti . ut tibi fierint panes de lapidibus. Et ille tibi dixit non in solo pane uiuit homo sed in omne uerbo dei Ille tibi imperat maledicti satanas qui aqua uinum fecit in canna gallilea. Qui pauit in heremo quinque milia uirorum extra numero mulierum et infantum de quinque panibus et duobus piscibus unde exsuperauerunt duodecem cophani fragmentorum quod est typus XII. apostolorum Audi tanta uirtute tanta maiestate per quem te adiuro Adiuro te per regem caelorum per christum creatorem per iesum saluatorem animarum nostrarum per illum te adiuro damnate Non per aurum neque per argentum neque per lapidibus praeciosis. Per deum te adiuro qui petrum mergentem manum porrexit. Tanta gloria. || [fol. 44] Tanta claritate . adiurasse te maledicti satanas apparisce inlebisce . angustiaris quomodo angustiatur saeculus exorcidiaris. Non cantaueris non tibi cantica cantentur per trea testimonia te adiuro. Adiuro te per patrem . et filium . et spiritum sanctum ut citius hinc exorcizatus abscedas ubi ergo tu latebis quando dominus noster iesus christus discendit cum multitudinem angelorum quattuor tubę canebunt a quattuor cardinibus mundi. Totus mundus ardebit ab oriente usque ad occidentem. dominus de caelo discendit confringere terram . et tunc apparebunt corpora sanctorum. Petrę mouebuntur de loca ipsorum et sol in sanguinem conuertitur. Dominus caelum plicauit tamquam librum in manu sua et tu ubi latebis . maledicte satanas Numquid hoc dicturus eris quod tibi hoc non fuerit imperatum . hoc tibi signum || [fol. 44^{v}] erit in diem iudicii quod tu non dissipauis in aeternum. Inuentum uenisti Inuentum exi. Integrare linque exi ab eo . quomo\`do´[1] exiuit coruus de arca noe. Sic exiit et non rediit . sic tu exi maledicte satanas. Hic locum non habebis nec refrigerium tibi tormenta super tormenta . poenas super poenas . plagas super placas. Ferriculi calentes . praeparati sunt te flagellis calentibus castigare maledicte satanas meritis tuis. Inmundissime . daemoniorum non facias . nec pauore . nec tremore . nec transuaricabis . nec impedis competentem uitam.uitam aeternam Non persuadebis hominem . ad malum faciendum . non moechabis[2] non uiolabis . non mortem tradas Non permittas septem nequitiores tibi qui peius faciant quam tu non deuersis languoribus doloribus In illius membrorum non || [fol. 45] occupauis quod tuum non est . non habites ubi

[1] *do* inter lin. m. 1. [2] *moe* sup. ras.

spiritus sanctus habitat per eundem dominum nostrum iesum christum te adiuro qui uenturus est iudicare . uiuos et mortuus et saeculum per ignem.

Domine sancte pater omnipotens aeternę deus osanna in excelsis pater (*363*)
domini . nostri . iesu christi qui illum refugam tyrannum gehennę deputasti qui unigenitum tuum in hunc mundum misisti. Ut illum rugientem leonem contereret uelociter. Adtende et accelera ut eripias hominem tuis formatum manibus A ruina et daemonio meridiano. da domine terrorem tuum super bestiam quae exterminat uineam tuam. Da fiduciam seruis tuis. Contra nequissimum draconem . fortiter stare. Ne contempnat . sperantes in te. Nec[1] dicat sicut in faraone iam dixit. deum non noui nec israel demitto. Urguat illum domine dextera tua potens discedere a famulis tuis ne diucius prae || [fol. 45v] sumat captiuum tenere hominem quem tu ad imaginem tuam facere dignatus es Adiuro te ergo serpens antique per iudicem uiuorum et mortuorum per factorem mundi per eum qui habit potestatem mittere . te in gehennam. Ut ab hoc famulo dei illo qui ad ęcclesiae praesepia concurrit cum excercito furoris tui festinos discedas. Coniuro te non meam infirmitatem sed uirtute spiritus sancti ut desinas ab his quos omnipotens deus ad imaginem suam fecit. Cede . cede non mihi sed mysteriis christi. Illius enim te perurguet potestas qui te adfigens cruce suę subiugauit. Illius brachium contremisce. Qui diuictis gemitibus inferni animas ad lucem produxit. Sit tibi ter`r´or[2] corpus hominis. Sit tibi formido imago dei nec resistas . nec moreris discedere . ab homine quoniam `con´placuit[3] christo ut in hominem habitaret . et ne in || [fol. 46] firmissimum condemnandum putes. Imperat tibi dominus Imperat tibi maiestas christi Imperat tibi deus pater imperat tibi filius et spiritus sanctus. Imperat tibi apostolorum fides sancti petri et pauli et ceterorum apostolorum. Imperat tibi martyrum sanguis. Imperat tibi indulgencia confessorum Imperat tibi sacramentum crucis. Imperat tibi mysteriorum uirtus. Ex`i´[4] transgressor exi seductor pleni omni dolo et fallacia Veritates inimici Innocencium persecutor Da locum durissime . da locum impiissime Da locum christo in quo nihil inuenisti de operibus tuis. Qui te expoliauit qui regnum tuum destruxit. Qui te uinctum ligauit et uasa tua disrupit Qui te proiecit in tenebras. exteriores ubi tibi cum ministris tuis erat praeparatus interitus sed quid nunc turbolente recogitas quid temerarie[5] retractas Reus|| [fol. 46v] omnipotente deo cuius statuta transgressus es. Reus filio eius iesu christo quem et temptare ausus es et crucefigere praesumsisti Reus humano

1 sup. ras. 2 *r* inter lin. m. 1. 3 *con* inter lin. m. 1. 4 *i* sup. lin.
5 *e* ex *i* m. 1.

generi . cui mors tuis persuasionibus uenit . adiuro ergo te draco nequissime In nomine agni inmaculati qui ambulat . super aspidem et basiliscum. Qui conculcat leonem et draconem ut discedas ab homine Discedas ab ecclesia dei Contremisce Et effuge inuocato nomen domini illius quem inferi trement.
(364) Cui uirtutes caelorum et potestatis et dominaciones subiectae sunt. Quem cerubin et seraphin indeffessis uocibus laudant. Imperat tibi uerbum caro factum. Imperat tibi natus ex uirgine Imperat tibi iesus nazarenus qui te cum discipulis contempneris elisum et prostratum exire iussit ab homine . quo pręsente . cum te ab homi-|| [fol. 47] ne[1] seperasset nec porcorum grege pręsumebas contingere. Recide ergo nunc adiuratus in nomine eius ab homine quem ipse plasmauit. Durum tibi est christo uelle resistere . durum tibi est contra stimulum calcitrare quia quicquid tardius exis supplicium tuum crescit. Quoniam non hominem contempnis sed illum qui dominator uiuorum et mortuorum est cui uniuersitas tacit qui uenturus est iudicare saeculum per ignem per

Nec te lateat satanas inmineri tibi poenas inmineri tibi tormenta diem iudicii . diem supplicii sempiterni diem qui uenturus est uelut clybanus ardens in quo tibi atque angelis tuis sempiternus est praeparatus interitus et ideo pro tua nequicia damnate atque damnandae Da honore deo uiuo da honore iesu christo filio eius Da honore spiritui . sancto paraclyto In cuius uirtute || [fol. 47^v] praecipio tibi quicumque es spiritus inmundi Ut exias et recidas ab hoc famulo dei illo et eum deo suo reddas quoniam dominus noster iesus christus eum ad suam graciam et benedictionem uocare dignatus est. Te domine supplices exoramus ut uisitacione tua sancta erigas famulum tuum illum . nec aduersario liceat usque ad animae temptacionem sicut in iob terminum pone . ne inimicus de anima ista incipiat triumphare Unde ergo maledicte recognosce sentenciam tuam et da honore deo uiuo et uero et recede ab hoc famulo dei illo tibi ergo praecipio maledicte inmunde spiritus hostis humani generis per deum patrem omnipotentem inuisibilem et inconpręhensibelem atque inmortalem qui fecit caelum et terram mare et omnia quae in eis sunt Ut omnes uirtus aduersarii omnes exercitus diaboli[2] omnis incursus inimici. || [fol. 48] omnis fantasma satane eradicare et effugare ab hoc famulo dei illo ita ut in eo ultra locum non habiat contrarii uirtutes admixtio Sed tu deus omnipotens propicius adesto ut corporibus daemoniis obsessus totam nequiciam diabulicam[1] tuam potenciam sint purgati per hoc signum sanctae crucis quem nos damus tu maledicti diabule numquam audeas uiolare per ᵭominum nostrum iesum christum

[1] [n painted red Ed.] [2] signum + superpos. m. 1.

qui uenturus est in spiritu sancto iudicare uiuos et mortuos et saeculum per ignem.

Domine sancte pater omnipotens aeternae deus qui peccancium non uis animas perire sed culpas conteri Respice propicius super hunc famulum illum qui peccatorum merito expulsus a facie tua potestati est subiectus satane Reminiscere miseracionum tuarum et expelle ab eo . omnem inimici infestacionem atque angustias satane mun-|| [fol. 48v]datum. Ad pristinam sanitatem reforma puritatem. Sit illud pristinum templum sanctum . quod . fuit in (365) baptismum inhabitet in eo spiritus sanctus per dominum nostrum iesum christum qui uenturus est iudicare saeculum per ignem.

Omnipotens et misericors deus pater domini nostri iesu christi te supplices deprȩcamur. Impera diabulo qui hunc famulum tuum illum detenet ut ab eo recidat. Et libera eos qui crediderunt in uerbum liberatorem dominum nostrum iesum christum ut expurgati ab omni labe iniquitates maiestate tuae pura mente deseruiant consecuti graciam spiritus sancti . qui cum patre et filio uiuet et regnat in saecula saeculorum amen.

[*There follow five blank lines, and in the centre of the lower margin is the quire-mark xxxv, by the original scribe. Vatic. Regin. 316 ends with quire xxxiiii.*]

[IUDICIUM POENITENTIALE][1]

[fol. 49] [1] Siquis uero homicidiū casu fecerit id .ē. non uolens .VII. añ peniteat III ex ipsis in pane et aqua [2] Siquis ad homicidiū faciendū consenserit . et factus fuerit .VII. añ paeniteat .III ex ipsis in pane et aqua Si autē uoluit et non potuit .III añ paeñt. [3] Siquis uero clericus homicidiū uoluntariae fecerit .X. añ exul paeñt. Post hos . añs recipiatur in patria sua . si bene egerit paeñt in pane et aqua testimoniū conprobatus ep̄s uel sacerdotib; cū quos paenituit et cui conmissus fuit. Satisfaciat parentib; eius quē occidit uiciū filii reddens quaecūq; uultis faciam uobis. Si autē non satisfecerit parentib; illius numquā recipiatur in patria sua sed more cain uacuus[2] et profugus sit sup̱ terrā [4] Siquis uero coactus pro qua'li'bet necessitate aut nesciens p̱iurauerit|| [fol. 49v] III. añ . peñt .I. ex his . in pane et aqua [5] Siquis p̱iurauerit sciens . ā. p̱ cubiditatē .VII. añ peñt et helimosinas iuxta uires et p̱sonā faciat et numquam iuret postea [6] Siquis furtum capitule commiserit . id .ē. quadrupede uel casas effrigerit . ā . quolibet. Meliore prȩsidio furauerit .VII. añ peñt III ex his in pane et aqua Qui uero de minoris rēs furtū fecerit . III añ

[1] The Penitential begins a new quire and a new page, but lacks a title. There has been some error of transposition in the order. The text as given in Wasserschleben, pp. 412 ff. and Schmitz, II. 326 ff. has errors of various sorts.

[2] *vagus* perperam W.

peñt et qđ furaū si potest reddat [7] Siquis adulteriū cōmiserit id .ē. cum
uxorē alterius ā sponsa .ł. uirginitate corruperit . si clericus .III. añ peñet .I.
ex his in pane et aqua si diāc IIII. II ex his in pañ et aqua si pręsbt .VII. III ex
his in pān et aq̄. [8] Siquis furnicauerit cū scīmoniale ł đo decata cognoscat[1]
se adulteriū ꝑpetrasse sic̄ in superiore sentencia unusquisq; iuxta ordinē
su-|| [fol. 50]ū peñt [9] Siquis sepulcrū uiolauerit .V. añ peñt III ex his in pañ
(366) et aq̄. [10] Siquis corpus . ł sanguines dñi neglexerit . ā inde ꝑdiderit . añ
integr̄ peñt in pañ et aqua Si ꝑ ebrietatē ā crapula illut euomerit trib; qua-
dragensimis in pañ et aq̄. peñt Si uero ꝑ infirmitate una tantū modo ebđ peñt
[11] Siquis clericus . ł uxor sua infante obpraesserint III añ peñt .I. ex his in
pañ et aq̄. [12] Siquis uero . maledicus id .ē. emissor tempestati fuerit .VII
añ peñt III ex his in pañ et aq̄. [13] Siquis . sē . quolibet uoluntate membro
truncauerit .III. añ peñt .I. ex his in pañ. et aq̄. [14] Siquis āt usuras undecūq:
exegerit III añ peñt .I. ex his in pañ et aq̄ [15] Siquis ꝑ potestate . ā quolibet
ingenio res alienas malo ordine inauaserit . ł tulerit superiore sentencia similit̄
peñt et elimosinas . || [fol. 50ᵛ] multas faciat. [16] Siquis sacrilegiū fecerit id
.ē. quos auruspicis uocant . qui auguria colunt si ꝑ aues ā quocūq: malo
ingenio auguriauerit III añ peñt in pañ et aq̄. [17] Siquis auriolis quos diuinis
uocant aliquas diuinaciones fecerit q‹ et h'. daemonū .ē. V. añ peñt .III. ex his
in pane . \`e´t aqua [18] Siquis aliū[2] ꝑ ira ꝑcusserit et sanguinē fuderit .XL.
diebus peñt. Diaconus .VI. menses pręsb . añ in pañ . et aq̄. [19] Siquis cupidus
.ā. auarus fuerit ā supb: .ā. inuidus . ā ebriosus . ā fratrē suū hodio habuerit .
ł alia his similia .q̄. denumerare longū .ē. \`III q:´[3] peñt cū pañ et aq̄ . [4]et iuxta
uires suas aelimosinas faciat[4] [20] Siquis sortes quas scor̄ contra racionē
uocant . ł alias sortes habuerit uel pro qualecumq: malo ingenio sortitus fuerit
ł [5]auguri[5] auerit .III añ peñt [21] Siquis [6]ad || [fol. 51] fontes . ł ad arbores[6] . ā ad
cancellus uel ubicūq: excepto in ecclesia . ā \`in´ ipsius atria uota uouerit ā
soluerit III añ peñt in pañ et aq̄ . quia et hoc sacrileg\`i´ū .ē. ł daemonū. Qui
uero ibidē aederit . ā biberit .I. añ in pañ et aq̄ . peñt. [22] Siquis clericus .
postquā se dō uouit . iter̄ ad alterū habitū sic̄ canes ad uomitū reuersus fuerit
ł uxorē duxerit .X. añ pēnteant ambo .III ex his in pañ et aq̄ et nūquā postea
in coniugio copulentur qđ si noluerit ▒ sc̄a senodus ł sedis apostolica
separare ▒ eos a cōmunione et conuiuio omniū catholicor̄ Similit̄ et mulier
postquā se dō uouit si tale scelus admiserit pari sen\`ten´cia subiaceat [23]
Siquis falsitatē commiserit .VII. añ peñt III. ex his in pañ et aq̄. Qui āt consen-

[1] *o* ex *u* m. I.

[2] *autem* perperam Wasserschleben et Schmitz.

[3] inter lin.

[4–4] sup. ras. m. I.

[5–5] *auguri* sup. ras. m. I.

[6–6] *ad arbores uel ad fontes* perperam W. et Sch.

serit .v. añ peñt [24] Siquis uenaciones quas . || [fol. 51v] cumq: exercuerit .
clericus añ . diac̄ .II. sacerdos .III. peñt. [25] Siquis cū quadrupede furnicatus
fuerit clericus II. añ peñt diac̄ III sacerdos .v. tres ex his in pañ et aq̄ [26]
Siquis qđ in Kāl ianuarias multi faciunt in ceruolū qđ dr̄ ā uecula uadit III
añ peñt quia et hoc daemonū est. [27] Siqua mulier uoluntaria . aborsum
fecerit III añ in pañ et aqua peñt [28] Siquis matimathecus fuerit id .ē. ꝑ
inuocacionē daemonū hominū mentes tulerit . ā debacantes fecerit .v. añ
peñt III ex his in pañ et aqua [29] Siquis uirginē ł uiduā raptus fuerit III añ (367)
cū pañ . et aq̄ peñt [30] Siquis dilaturas fecerit qđ de`te´stabile .ē. superiora
uersi sentencia . accipiat. [31] Siquis seruū .ā. quēcūq: hominē qualibet
ingenio in captiuitatē duxerit . ā transmiserit .III. || [fol. 52] añ in pañ et aqua
peñt et preciū reddat [32] Siquis . domū . ł areā cuiuscūq: uoluntate igne
cremauerit parē superiorem sentenciā subiacet. [33] Siquis de ministerio
scāe . ęclesiae . ł qualecūq: opus quolibet modo fraudauerit . ł neglexerit .VII
añ peñt et qđ tulit si potē reddat. [34] Siquis sacerdos ł quislibet clericus . ā
cū sacrata dō puella inebrientur si ꝑ ignoranciā VII. dieb: si ꝑ neglegenciā .XV.
dieb: si ꝑ contemptu XL. dieb: in pañ et aq̄ . peñt. Laici uero si ꝑ ignorancia
.IIII dieb: si ꝑ neglegencia .VII. dieb: si ꝑ contemptu XV. dieb: in pañ et aq̄ .
peñt et elimosina facī [35] Et qui cogit . hominē ut inebrietur simili modo ut
ebrius peñt [36] Siquis morticinū ł sanguinē commederit si ꝑ ignoranciā XX
dieb: si ꝑ sciencia XL. dieb: peñt [37] Siquis sacerdos || [fol. 52v] ā . diaconus
aut monachus fornicauerit . sicut sodomitę fecerunt .X. añ peñt III ex ipsis
in pañ et aq̄ VII. uero aliis absteneat se a uino et carnib: et non maneat cum
alio in sempiterno. Clerici uero saeculares uel laici .VII. añ . peñt . II. ex ipsis
in pañ et aq̄ [38] Qui concupiscit mentē furnicare sed non potuit .I. añ pent .
[39] Qui ꝑ turpiloquiū . ł aspectu tactu ł osculo quoinquinatus id est pollutus
fuerit tamen ñ uoluit furnicare corporalit̄ XX. ł XL dieb: iuxta qualitatē peñt
Si āt inpugnacione cogitaciones uioleñt quoinquinat' .VII dieb: peñt. [40]
Qui in somnis uoluntate pollutus est . surgat canatq: ienua flectendo VII
psalmos in crastino cum pañ et aq̄ uiuat ł XXX. psāl flectendo uniuscuiusq: in
fiñ canat [41] Volens in somno || [fol. 53] peccare siue pollutus siue uoluntate
.XV. psāl canat . peccans . non pollutus XXIIII ps̄. [42] Siquis laicus cū quadrupede . furnicauerit .I. añ si uxorē habit peñt si āt non habet dimidio [43]
Sic et qui uxorem ñ habens et propriis membres se ipsum uiolauerit . añ
peñt in pañ et aq̄. [44] Siquis corpus suum titille in consurgendo . furnicare
XL. noctes peñt . et si pollutus fuerit titillacione .LXX dieb: et suppositus .VII.
[45] Qui patrē ā matrē suam `in´pulsauerit impius ā . sacrilegus . iudicandus
.ē. peñt tempus quamdiu in impietate . steterit [46] Qui facit furnicaonē in

ęcclesia penetencia .ē. omnib: 'dieb:' uitę suę praebeat . obsequiū domui dī [47] Sicuius paruolus sine baptismo in negligencia mortuus fuerit .III. añ peñt . in primo añ .c'. pañ et aqua in duos alius sine dilicias || [fol. 53v] [48] Qui ꝑiuriū fecerit .VII. ān peñt. Qui ducit . aliū in ꝑiuriū ignorantē .VII. ān peñt. Qui . āt . ductus in ꝑiuriū ignorans et p'ea recognuscit .I. 'añ' peñt Qui uero suscipiat' qđ in ꝑiuriū deducit' . tamen iurat . ꝑ consensu .II. añ peñt [49] Siquis sacrificiū ꝑdiderit et nescit ubi sit .I. añ peñt in pañ et aq̄. [50] Siquis negligenciā fecerit . erga sacrificiū . ut siccet' et a uermib: consumat'
(368) medio añ peñt in pañ et aq̄ [51] Siquis sacerdus qui offerit . sacrificiū et si ei ceciderit sacrificiū de manu illius usq: ad t̄rā et non inuenerit omne qđcūq: in loco ubi ceciderit conburet . igne et abscondet cinere illa sub altare . ita ut ñ conculcetur et ipse peñt medio añ . et si inuenerit scupa mundetur et conburet igne et abscondat . in t̄ra similit̄ et ipse .XX. dieb: peñt Si āt usq: ad altare . uno die . [52] Clericus || [fol. 54] semel furnicans .I. añ c' pañ . et aq̄ . et duos alios absteneat se a uino et car̄ Si ā in consuetudine . multo tempore fuerit III añ c' pañ et aq̄ peñt et officiū clericatus amittat . et quattuor alios absteneat se a uino et carne . si . āt . filiū genuerit .IIII. añ peñt . [53] Paruoli infantes furnicacione imitantes et inritantes se inuicē si ñ quoinquinantur pollucione .XX dieb: peñt. Si uero frequent̄ XL dieb: peñt [54] Siquis puer . qui peccatū . cū pecode commiserit .C. dieb: peñt. [55] Siquis puer paruulus. obpraessus a seniori suo .XX. añ habens . aetate . ebdomada peñt. Si consentit .XX. dieb: peñt. [56] Vir ꝑ semetipsū inquinans .C. dieb: peñt. Reiterans añ peñt [57] Viri inter faemora furnicantes .I. añ peñt reiterans .II. [58] Siquis uero in t̄ra[1] furnicantes si pueri s̄ .II. añ pent. Si uiri .III Si itera-|| [fol. 54v]uerint .VI. si āt in consuetudine uertunt paenitencia . addatur [59] Siquis . cum alio iram tenit . in corde homicida iudicetur Si ñ uult reconciliare fratri suo quē hodio habuit . Tamdiu . in pañ et aq̄ peñt usq: dū reconcilietur ei . [60] De capitalib: āt peccatis . id .ē. homicidiū. Adulteriū Ꝑiuriū Furnicacionē Inmundiciā Laici .III. añ peñt . Clerici .V. Subdiaconi .VI. Diaconi .VII. Praes̄bi .X. Eps̄i .XII. [61] De minorib: uero peccatis id .ē. furtū falsū testimoniū et ceteris similib: peccatis . Laici . añ. Clerici .II. Subdiaconi .III. Diaconi .IIII. Praes̄bi .V. ep̄i .VI. finit . iudicium peñt . amen. ∴∴

[*The rest of the page, a space of seven lines, has been left blank. The new section follows without title.*]

[1] *Sic* MS., *terga* W. et Sch.

[BREUIARIUS APOSTOLORUM]

[fol. 55] Simon . qui interpraetatur . oboediens . petrus . agnoscens filius iohannis frāt . andreae.dicetur.ortus uico bethsaida prouinciae.gallileae. Qui propt̄ simonē magū licet . dī occulto nutu romam ꝑuenit ibiq: praedicans euangeliū XXV annor̄ eiusdē urbē tenuit pontificatū .VI autē . et .XXX anno post passionē . dn̄i sub nerone caesare ut uoluit . cruci suspensus .ē. Cuius nataliciū .III. k̄l iūl celb̄t.

Paulus qui int̄prętatur pius . ortus ex tribu beniamin . apostolus genciū . hic .II. post ascensione dn̄i an̄ baptizatus et sub nerone roma eodē die quo et petrus capite truncatus ibiq: sepultus est.

Andreas qui int̄praetatur uirilis uel decorus frat̄ petri hic praedicaū scitiam (369)
et 'a'chaiā Ibiq: in ciuitate patras cruce suspensus occubuit . pridie . k̄l decembris.

Iacob: qui || [fol. 55v] int̄praetatur subplantator. filius zebedei . frater iōh. Hic spaniae . et occidentalia loca praedicatur et sub herode . gladio caesus occubuit . sepultus .ē. in achaiā . marmarica . VIII k̄l decembris.

Iohannis qui int̄praetatur . gracia dī apostoł et . euangelista . filius zebedei . frat̄ iacobi . delectus dn̄i pręd icatur asię . et in effeso .VI. k̄l ian̄ sepultus .ē. nāt 'eius' alia VIII k̄l iūl quando et sc̄i iōh baptistae . cęlebra ▒ tur.

Thomas qui int̄praetatur . abysus didimus hoc .ē. xp̄i similis hic partes et medis prędicatur et distinans orientalē plagā ibiq: euangeliū prędicaū. Lancea enim ibi transfixus occubuit . in calaminicę . indię ciuitatē ibiq: sepultus .ē. in honore XII. k̄l ian̄.

Philippus qui int̄prętatur . os . lampadis a bethsaida ciūit ortus . ē . unde et petrus galli'i's prędicaū xp̄m Deinde in frigię prouinciae . crucefixus .ē.|| [fol. 56] et lapidatus obiit. Ibique cum filiab: suis . quiescit . cuius nāt k̄l mādi cęlēb.

Iacob: frat̄ dn̄i hierusolimor̄ primus ep̄s . hic dū hierusalē xp̄m dī filiū prędicaret . de templo a iudaeis pręcipitatus . lapidib:q: obpremitur . ibiq: iuxta templū humat' eius nāt . et ordinacio eius VI k̄l iān colitur.

Bartholomeus apostolus nom̄ ex siria lingua suscipit . et int̄prętatur . filius suspendentes aquas liconiam praedicaū ad ultemū in albano maiores arminiae urbe uiuens a barbaris decoriatus atq: ꝑ iussū reges astrages decollatus sicq: t̄rae conditus .VIII k̄l septem̄b.

Matheus apostolus et euangelista qui int̄prętatur . donatus hic etiā ex tribu sua leui sumpsit cognomentū ex publicano a xp̄o elictus. Primū quidē in iudęa euangelizaū postmodū in macidonia et passus in ꝑsida requiescit in montib: pastor̄ XI k̄l octobris.

Simon zelotes Qui int̄prętatur zelus hic prius dictus .ē. || [fol. 56v] cananeus zelo dī feruens. Par 'in' cognomento petri et similis in honore hic accepit aegypti principatū et post iacobū iustū cathedrā dicet' tenuisse hierusolimor̄ post annos . cxx meruit sub adriano p̱ crucē sustenire martyriū passiones. Iacit in porforo eius nataliciū cęlebratur . v. k̄l nouem̄b.

Iudas qui int̄prętat' confessor Iacobi frāt in mesopotamia . atq: interiorib: ponti prędicauit Sepultus .ē. in merito arminię urbe cuius festiuitas caelebratur .v. k̄l nouembris.

Mathias de septuaginta discipulos unus et pro iuda scarioth .XII. int̄ apostolos subrogatus elictus . sorte et solus sine cognomento . cui datur euangelii praedicacio in iudaea ∻∻

[*The remaining five lines are blank. At the foot of the page, in the centre of the margin, the quire-mark xxxvi is entered by the hand that wrote the text.*]

(370) Perhaps it would not be out of place to say a few words about the date and home of the celebrated manuscript to which the Supplement once belonged. The date guessed at by Morin, who was perhaps the first scholar to describe and use the Reginensis, is, in my opinion, very near the true one.[1] Writing in 1651, he spoke of it as nine hundred years old.[2] And scholars like Bona and Tommasi accepted his judgement.[3] A greater antiquity was attributed to the manuscript by Delisle,[4] who thought it might be assignable either to the end of the seventh or the beginning of the eighth century. Given the great authority of Delisle's opinion, this view has had very wide acceptance. It has been adopted by the last editor of the manuscript, the Revd. H. A. Wilson, and also by Edmund Bishop and Dom Cabrol.[5] But Delisle's view can hardly be right. No student of uncial script who is familiar with dated eighth-century manuscripts, nor any expert in the decorative initials found in French manuscripts of the pre-Caroline period, would concur in this view. In the opinion

[1] J. Morinus, *Commentarius Historicus de Disciplina in Administratione Sacramenti Poenitentiae*, etc. (Paris, 1651). The manuscripts exploited for this work are described in an appendix at the end. On p. 52 he discusses our manuscript.

[2] His exact words are so interesting and instructive as to merit quotation in full: 'Antiquissimus omnium codicum quos nancisci nobis contigit, ille est quem in opere nostro Petauianum saepius vocauimus à Possessore, viro amplissimo, D. Petauio Parlamenti Senatore integerrimo, qui perhumanè, illum nobis dedit vtendum. Illius character nongentis annis non videtur inferior. Est enim scriptus literis majoribus, et quadratis quae vnciales aliqui vocant' (op. cit., p. 52).

[3] J. Bona, *Rerum Liturgicarum Libri duo*, ed. R. Sala, III. 99; J. M. Thomasius, *Codices Sacramentorum nongentis annis vetustiores* (Rome, 1680). See the preface, p. 1 (unnumbered), where Morinus is cited.

[4] L. Delisle, *Notice sur vingt manuscrits du Vatican*, pp. 7 ff. (Paris, 1877); *Mémoire sur d'anciens Sacramentaires*, p. 68 (Paris, 1886).

[5] See the works cited above, p. 203 n. 1.

of Dr. Zimmermann, no mean authority on the art of this period, the middle of the eighth century is the correct date.[1] Till we have surer criteria this date seems more acceptable than the earlier one. I base this judgement on the ground that similar initials, and similar colours for titles, are to be found in manuscripts that are clearly of the second half of the eighth century, and also because the peculiar types of uncials employed in this manuscript are found as titles in a number of French minuscule manuscripts which are, by common consent, of the second half of the eighth century.[2] Lastly, the number and kind of abbreviations favour the later rather than the earlier date.[3] Further support I find in the fact that in the two sections where the Greek text is written in Latin uncials, the interlinear Latin translation, which is (*371*)
without the least doubt contemporary, is written in a type of pre-Caroline minuscule which is the immediate precursor of the **ab**-type,[4] and that type flourished in the last few decades of the reign of Charlemagne. What is true of the date of the Sacramentary is also true of the Supplement, as the two parts are manifestly contemporary, and even seem to be the work of the same scribe (see accompanying plates).

When the Paris leaves were detached from the Sacramentary proper, we shall probably never know. The obvious occasion that suggests itself is when the manuscript was taken apart for binding. The colophon on the penultimate page of the Reginensis suggested that the manuscript was complete, without the two extra quires, which may thereupon have been left out of the rebound manuscript. I say rebound, for it is inconceivable that so beautiful and well preserved a manuscript could have existed for centuries in loose quires. The earliest scholars to use the Reginensis found it in its present state. Tommasi would not have neglected to mention the Supplement if he had found it, and this is still more true of Morinus, since his work was directly concerned with Penitentials. In fact, Morinus's own words make it quite clear that when the

[1] H. Zimmermann, *Vorkarolingische Miniaturen*, pp. 217 f. and pls. 135–8.

[2] See the manuscripts enumerated at the close of the article.

[3] The following abbreviations are seen in the Paris leaves. Forms found only in the Penitential are marked (P). I omit the horizontal abbreviation stroke over words. **a** = aut or autem (P), **at** = autem, **co** = con, **c** = cum (P), **dr** = dicitur, **eps, epi, epsi** = episcopus, -i, **.e.** = est (later typical of the Tours school), **h'** = hoc (P), **srl** = israel, **n** = non, **ni, nm** = nostri, nostrum, **nom** = nomen, **omnips, omnps** = omnipotens, **oma** = omnia, **ꝑ** = per, **p̓** = post, **q** = quae, **ꝗ** = quia (P), **qnm, quo** = quoniam, **qd** = quod, **sic** = sicut, **s** = sunt, **t** = ter, **t'** = tur or tus (P), **ł** = vel. The Nomina Sacra have their normal forms. The forms **aq et pan** = aqua et pane, **ans, an** = annos, and **pen** or **pent** = paeniteat, occur only in (P).

[4] A facsimile may be seen in Delisle's *Mémoire*, cited above, pl. IV, and in Ehrle–Liebaert, *Specimina codicum Latinorum*, pl. 20.

manuscript was still in Paris, in the possession of Senator Petau, it ended precisely as it does today.[1]

One would give a great deal to be able to ascertain the scriptorium that produced this manuscript of the Gelasianum. For the present, that is still beyond us. It is certainly a French product, as internal and external evidence amply attest. The presence of Saint Denis in the Canon of the Mass and his precedence over Saints Hilary and Martin gave rise to the view that it was a Paris book, written for the Abbey of Saint Denis. This seemed highly probable to an authority like Duchesne,[2] and Traube in his list of uncial manuscripts, probably following Duchesne, gives Saint Denis as the 'Bibliotheksheimat'.[3]
(372) The manuscript lacks the familiar Saint Denis *ex libris*, and there is no other external mark connecting it with that abbey. Yet there is palaeographical evidence favouring a Saint Denis origin; it would, however, take us too far afield to examine it now in detail. Here it will suffice to point out that certain curious features found in the half-uncial manuscripts Paris lat. 2706 (Saint Augustine)[4] and Paris Nouv. acq. lat. 1619 (Oribasius),[5] both eighth-century French manuscripts, are shared by the Reginensis. The first of these manuscripts has the Saint Denis *ex libris*, the second the mention of Abbot Hilduin[6] as a *probatio pennae*. Strictly speaking these entries establish only later provenance, not origin. The reason no one has claimed these two manuscripts for Saint Denis is because to do so would upset our notions of pre-Caroline French script. For the accepted view of them is that they come from some centre in the north-east of France, to which quarter, too, more recent opinion has assigned the peculiar minuscule which is found in two parts of the Gelasianum, placed interlineally over the Greek, to which reference was made.[7] If this view is correct, one would naturally think of Corbie; but I am inclined to exclude Corbie, for the reason that quite different and easily recognizable types prevailed there in the period to which our manuscript belongs.[8] Had Angilbert been its abbot a generation or so earlier, St. Riquier would have seemed to me a suitable centre whence such a manuscript might come,[9]

[1] J. Morinus, op. cit., IV, cap. 18 = p. 211, where it is explicitly stated that our manuscript (his 'antiquissimus Petavianus') ended with the Ordo *Ad Poenitentiam dandam*.

[2] L. Duchesne, *Les Origines du Culte chrétien* (2nd ed.), p. 119.

[3] L. Traube, *Vorles. und Abh.* I. 237.

[4] Cf. Zimmermann, op. cit., pl. 129.

[5] Cf. Delisle, *Catalogue des manuscrits des fonds Libri et Barrois*, pl. V. 2; and Zimmermann, op. cit., pl. 115B.

[6] A celebrated abbot of that name presided over St. Denis in 814. The *probatio pennae* may well belong to about that period.

[7] See W. M. Lindsay, *Notae Latinae*, p. 472; Zimmermann, op. cit., pp. 213 ff.

[8] See P. Liebaert in *Palaeographia Latina* (ed. Lindsay), I. 62 ff. (1922).

[9] See Edmund Bishop's stimulating and illuminating article in *Liturgica Historica*, pp. 314 ff.

considering its wealth and prestige at that time, and the fact that its inventory of 831 mentions no less than nineteen Gelasian sacramentaries.[1] But whether St. Riquier, in the middle of the eighth century, was a sufficiently important school of writing is doubtful. And if one thing is more certain than another, it is that this beautiful, dignified, and well-preserved copy of the Gelasianum is the product of a great school of writing, with all appliances and means to boot. It could not have come from one of the lesser and little-known centres. Furthermore, the centre whence it came must have been familiar with Anglo-Saxon and Irish manuscripts, as may be seen from some of the decorative elements employed, and from the actual form of certain initials. That the Reginensis belonged to Alexandre Petau, Senator of Paris, before it came into (*373*)
the possession of the Queen of Sweden, and that the scrap-book containing the Supplement belonged to Minister Colbert, are facts that offer us no assistance in solving our problem. It would seem that the last word will some day have to be said by pure palaeography.

To assist in its solution I here mention the few manuscripts known to me which are written in the same type of uncial characters as Reginensis 316. They are:

Paris lat. 6413, Isidorus, Sententiae, De natura rerum.
Paris lat. 10399, fol. 4, 5, 46+ } Eusebius-Rufinus, Historia Ecclesiastica.
Paris lat. 10400, fol. 27 }
Oxford Bodl. Laud. Misc. 126, Augustinus, Epist. and De trinitate.[2]

To these should be added Paris lat. 18282, Euseb.-Rufinus, Hist. Eccles., and Paris lat. 12240 and 12241 in which, however, only the titles are in the type of uncial under discussion, the text being in minuscule. The latter two manuscripts contain volumes II and III of Cassiodorus's work on the Psalms, volume I being found in Paris lat. 12239, written in a different type of minuscule, namely, the Corbie type to which Liebaert gave the name *en*.[3] The three volumes all come from the library of Corbie, but volume I is older than the other two and in a different script. Inasmuch as Reginensis 316 has some writing in a peculiar type of contemporary minuscule it is useful to mention here what other manuscripts show the same script. They are:

Autun 20, Gregorius, Dialogi, and Augustinus, Enchiridion.
Montpellier 3, Evangelia.

[1] Cf. G. Becker, *Catalogi Antiqui*, p. 28, items 217–35.

[2] Facsimiles in *New Palaeographical Society*, pls. 83–5; Chatelain, *Uncialis Scriptura*, pls. 52, 96; Zimmermann, op. cit., pls. 138–41.

[3] Facsimile in Lindsay's *Pal. Lat.* I, pl. 2.

Oxford, Bodl. Douce f. 1, Sacram. Gelasianum (fragm.).[1]
Paris lat. 4808 (fol. 121), Enigmata Symphosii.

Whoever is fortunate enough to fix the precise home of any of the above manuscripts will, I believe, either have discovered, or be on the way to discovering, the centre whence comes the oldest extant copy of the oldest Roman mass-book.

[1] Facsimile in Wilson's *Gelasian Sacramentary*, p. lvii. It is a fact worth noting that Reginensis 316 and the Douce fragment, the oldest witnesses, both came from the same school of writing. It is to some neighbouring school, moreover, that we must assign, on palaeographical grounds, the index in Reims MS. 8; the lost Sacramentary which began with this index must have been practically identical with the Reginensis. Cf. A. Wilmart, *Revue Bénédictine*, Oct. 1913, pp. 437–50.

A New Manuscript Fragment of Bede's 'Historia Ecclesiastica'

STUDENTS of Bede will be interested to learn of the existence of a fragment (*244*) of a manuscript, heretofore unused, of the *Historia Ecclesiastica Gentis Anglorum*. Unfortunately the new witness consists of only a single leaf, but its antiquity is such as to render it worthy of the attention of scholars. The leaf contains part of the letter of Pope Vitalian to King Oswy (bk. III. 29) and the last chapter of book III; the initial words being: *munuscula a vestra celsitudine*, the final words: *domum redire laetantes. Finit amen.* (I. 198–200, ed. Plummer.) It so happens that the last half-dozen lines of book III are almost entirely lost in the Cotton MS. C. II. Till recently the fragment formed part of the famous collection of manuscripts created by the zeal of Sir Thomas Phillipps. Whether the leaf in question came to England with the Meermann manuscripts which Sir Thomas had acquired in 1824, or was picked up in England, which is the more likely alternative, I am unable to say. It is now, however, no longer at Cheltenham, but in the possession of A. Chester Beatty, Esq., the oldest of whose manuscripts all come from the Phillipps collection, amongst them being the unique manuscript of the *Carmen Apologeticum* of Commodianus. It is with the kind permission of the owner, and through the courtesy of Mr. Eric G. Millar, who is preparing a catalogue of the Beatty manuscripts, that the present note is written.[1]

When the Revd. Dr. Plummer published his classic edition of Bede's history[2] —would that the other works of Bede could find such a competent editor—he based his text on the four manuscripts which he considered the oldest, namely: the Moore manuscript, in the Cambridge University Library, Kk. V. 16 (*M*),[3] the British Museum MS. Cotton Tiber. A. XIV (*B*),[4] the British Museum MS. Cotton Tiber. C. II (*C*),[5] and the manuscript [11] from the Namur Municipal (*245*) Library (*N*).[6]

From *The English Historical Review*, XLI (1926), 244–6.

[1] [Both manuscripts have changed hands again. The Bede fragment is now Pierpont Morgan Library, M.826; the Commodian codex is Brit. Mus., Add. MS. 43460. Ed.]

[2] Oxford, at the Clarendon Press, 1896.

[3] Cf. *Palaeographical Society*, pls. 139, 140.

[4] Cf. *Catalogue of Ancient Manuscripts at the British Museum*, II, pl. 20.

[5] Cf. *Pal. Soc.*, pl. 141; *Catal. of Anc. MSS. at Brit. Mus.* II, pl. 19; Zimmermann, *Vorkarolingische Miniaturen*, pls. 291–2; Reusens, *Éléments de paléographie*, pl. 11.

[6] No facsimile exists. On the manuscript see Plummer's paper entitled 'Mémoire sur un

As might have been expected, the majority of the oldest witnesses, three out of four, are in Anglo-Saxon characters, only one manuscript (*N*) being in ordinary minuscule. As its text is inferior to the others, so is it also of more recent date. Experts now ascribe it to the ninth rather than to the eighth century. The Moore Bede is remarkable for its age; it is almost contemporary with the author, the date ascribed to it being about 737, and Bede died in 735. Curiously enough, this, the oldest extant manuscript of Bede, was not written in England, but in one of the English foundations on the Continent. *B* and *C*, however, are pure English products. Though not so old as *M*, they may reasonably be assigned to the latter part of the eighth century. Another manuscript of about this period, in Anglo-Saxon characters somewhat resembling those of *B*, is a manuscript which Plummer did not use for his edition, Leningrad Q. v. I, no. 18[1] which once belonged to the abbey of Corbie, whence it was removed during the Revolution.[2]

To these four eighth-century witnesses in Anglo-Saxon script must now be added a fifth: the leaf which forms the subject of this note. In the Phillipps collection it bore the press-mark 36275. It was evidently not seen by Schenkl, who did not scorn to mention fragments in his *Bibliotheca Patrum Latinorum Britannica*, nor, so far as I can learn, was it known to Potthast, Wattenbach, Manitius, or earlier scholars. The manuscript from which it came must have been a stately volume. The page was divided into two columns, measuring about 12 by 4 in., with 31 lines to the column. A little of the lower margin still remains; nothing of the upper; in fact, part of the first line of script has been cut away. The parchment has the rough feel peculiar to English and Irish manuscripts of the period. The writing is a bold, well-formed Anglo-Saxon minuscule, with some, though not very close, resemblance to the script of *C*. There are the usual abbreviations of the Nomina Sacra, of '-bus', '-que', 'per', 'prae', 'pro', and the characteristic insular symbols for 'con', 'eius', 'enim', and the Anglo-Saxon sign for '-tur' (**t** with a vertical stroke intersecting the right side of the horizontal beam). Citations from scripture are marked
(*246*) by a point and a comma (. ,) to the left of the cited passages, as is the custom in many Anglo-Saxon manuscripts. But documents cited are not specially marked in the margin, as they are, for instance, in the Moore manuscript.

A collation of the fragment with Plummer's edition has shown that its text

manuscrit de l'Histoire ecclésiastique du peuple anglais de Bède, dit le Vénérable', in tome xix of *Annales de la Société Archéologique de Namur*.

[1] See facsimiles in Arndt–Tangl, *Schrifttafeln*[4], pl. 9; A. Staerk, *Les Manuscrits latins du V au XIII*^{e} *siècle conservés à la Bibliothèque impériale de Saint-Pétersbourg*, I, pl. XIV; II, pl. L; Zimmermann, op. cit., pl. 332.

[2] [See retraction in *C.L.A.* xi. 1621 (Oxford, 1966) Ed.].

is not remarkable for correctness. It has a number of trifling misspellings, transpositions, and some manifest errors. One error is of interest, as it serves to indicate the affiliation of the manuscript with Plummer's *M*-group. In III. 29 (I. 198, l. 13, ed. Plummer) the correct reading is 'cum hic esset defunctus', whereas our fragment shares with *M* the impossible reading 'cur'. As 'cum' and 'cur' are not usually confused in Anglo-Saxon script, this error must go back to a common ancestor.

The existence of several eighth-century manuscripts, in Anglo-Saxon script, of the *Historia Gentis Anglorum*, is eloquent of Bede's popularity at home. That copies reached the Continent almost during the author's lifetime, is proven by the Moore manuscript. There is also evidence that Bede's history was read at Würzburg in the eighth century. For it is found in a catalogue of books entered in a manuscript which existed at Würzburg in that century.[1]

[1] I refer to the Bodleian MS. Laud Misc. 126. A facsimile of the catalogue is to be seen in *New Palaeogr. Soc.*, pl. 83. The catalogue deserves a separate article which, it is hoped, will shortly appear. [See below, pp. 239 ff. Ed.]

A Note on the Codex Bezae

(9) PROFESSOR ROPES, in his important book on the text of the Acts, has come out for a Sicilian origin for the Codex Bezae. And the chairman of our club, in the third issue of the *Bulletin*, has invited members to express themselves freely on the new hypothesis. He was even optimistic enough to think it probable that new light might be thrown on the question from the side of palaeography and linguistics. Now given the total absence of ancient Sicilian manuscripts which might serve as a basis for comparison, a palaeographer would be rash indeed if he ventured either to endorse or reject an hypothesis built up exclusively on historical and ecclesiastical considerations. Accordingly, the present writer has felt he had no warrant for an expression of opinion. His only excuse for saying anything now is the appearance of Professor Sneyders de Vogel's interesting paper in which he takes issue with Professor Ropes and adduces arguments favouring a French origin for the Codex Bezae. His philological arguments are based on a number of orthographical errors found in the Codex; they afford him convincing proof, on the one hand, that the manuscript could not have been written in Sicily, on the other that in all probability its origin was Franco-Provençal, in other words, that it came from the region of Lyons and Vienne. But so cautious a scholar as Professor Sneyders de Vogel did not fail to recognize the hypothetical grounds of his own conclusions. His last paragraph reads:

> Si notre raisonnement est juste et que ces mots représentent réellement la prononciation du scribe, le Codex Bezae est postérieur à l'époque où la voyelle finale s'est amuïe, c'est à dire qu'il ne peut dater que du septième siècle au plus tôt. Si d'autres considérations nous obligent à attribuer notre manuscrit à une époque antérieure, notre raisonnement basé sur ces graphies perd toute sa valeur et il faudra les expliquer comme des erreurs du scribe qui ne tirent pas à consequence.

(*10*) It is precisely because considerations of a palaeographical nature do exist which oblige us to attribute our manuscript to an earlier epoch that the writer is impelled to enter into the discussion and to give his reasons for regarding the Codex Bezae as one of our very oldest Biblical manuscripts. If some one attempted to assign a manuscript to the third or fourth century a sceptic

From *Bulletin of the Bezan Club*, IV (1927), 9–14.

might justifiably question the existence of adequate grounds for the ascription, since not a single definitely dated third- or fourth-century manuscript has come down to us. But when we approach the sixth and still more the seventh century we find terra firma under foot: we have reached a period for which dated manuscripts and charters exist in sufficient number to furnish us with clear, objective criteria for judging both cursive and calligraphic writing of those two centuries.

Now it so happens that we actually possess three dated manuscripts of the seventh century, all fortunately written in France. Were the Codex Bezae a French product of the seventh century there would be some similarity between it and these manuscripts, but none exists. The Bezan codex is both utterly different from the Toulouse manuscript of Canons written at Albi between 600 and 666, the manuscript of the Homilies of St. Augustine written in 669 at Luxeuil, and the manuscript of St. Jerome's Chronicle written probably at Fleury before 699; and it is distinctly older than any of these. But not only is the Codex Bezae manifestly older than the above-named seventh-century manuscripts, it has every appearance of being considerably more ancient than the famous Codex Fuldensis of the Gospel Harmony written in Italy, read and annotated by Victor, Bishop of Capua, in the year 546. In fact, the Codex Bezae must be pushed back to a still remoter antiquity, for a comparison with the Basilican Hilary in the Chapter-Library of St. Peter's written at Cagliari, partly in half-uncial, partly in uncial, before the year 509–10, shows that the Bezan Codex possesses the older characteristics. Thus tested by the criteria which extant dated manuscripts furnish, the Codex
Bezae seems to belong to a period anterior to the year 500. An excellent (*11*)
palaeographer like Professor Burkitt did not hesitate to ascribe it to the fifth century; an expert in Biblical studies like Dom Chapman argued in favour of the early part of that century; and another Benedictine savant, Dom Wilmart, whose practical knowledge of Latin manuscripts is equalled by very few, admitted the possibility of an ascription to the fourth century—such is the powerful impression of antiquity made by the Codex Bezae upon those who have worked upon it and lived with it.

But it may be objected by those who find it hard to accept so early a date that the Bezan scribe was consciously imitating a much older exemplar, and thus imparted to his copy an air of greater antiquity than it really possesses. Such things have been done. There are archaistic manuscripts as there are archaistic statues. The Utrecht Psalter is a case in point. But such experiments are never so perfect as to deceive utterly. At one point or another the imita-

tive character is betrayed. The opposite, however, is true of the Codex Bezae: its genuineness grows on one the more one examines it, and its great antiquity is strikingly confirmed by the added lines at the foot of fols. 59[v]–60, which supply an accidental omission due to *homoioteleuton*. These lines, on both the Greek and Latin sides, are written not in a stiff, formal book-script, but in an easy-going semi-cursive. There can be no question of imitation here. The script of the added lines was as unpremeditated as was their omission. They were not written by the scribe but by a later reader or corrector (Scrivener's G). A comparison with the cursive lines entered in the Basilican Hilary in the year 509–10 leaves not a shadow of doubt as to the older character of the Bezan cursive. For equally ancient Latin cursive one would have to go to the Strassburg papyrus letter of recommendation commonly ascribed to the fourth century. The two lines of Greek cursive are as cleverly written as the Latin. They make an impression of great antiquity upon those best qualified
(12) to judge, papyrologists like Professor Hunt and M. Seymour de Ricci, the former considering the fifth century possible, the latter finding even the fourth admissible.

So much for the date of the manuscript judged by purely graphic tests. We have one other very important aid in the problem of dating our oldest manuscripts, I mean abbreviations. The scholar who more than any other understood their significance was Traube, and I like to quote his own words:

> Ego cum aetatem codicis sciscitor, statim me ad compendia vertor, quorum consideratio in arte nostra plurimum solet conferre. . . . Compendia historiam suam habent.

When we examine the abbreviations used in the Codex Bezae on the Latin side—the Greek side is here uninstructive—we find full confirmation of the date derived from a study of the script. More than that: a careful analysis throws some light on the exemplar, which was evidently not all of a piece or of one period. For the abbreviation-symbols designating 'dominus' used by the Bezan scribe in Acts—they are of the **dns-dni**-type—represent a later stage in the development of the abbreviated forms of the Nomina Sacra than the symbols **dms-dmi**, etc., found in the four Gospels. Whereas in John, Luke, and Mark we find only the **dms**-type, in Matthew the more recent **dns**-type is also admitted. Now it is a fact that our oldest Biblical manuscripts of the Old-Latin version—I refer to Vercellensis, Veronensis, Corbiensis, the Fulda Weingarten fragments, the Sangallensis—all agree in using the **dms**-type of symbol for 'dominus'. It is also a fact that our oldest manuscripts of the Vulgate, both the Fuldensis written before 546 and the even older

Sangallensis in half-uncial which I regard as of the fifth century, are ignorant of the **dms**-type and consistently employ the **dns**-type, which as everyone knows is the type that henceforth prevailed. Thus it is clear that the presence of **dms** for 'dominus' in the Codex Bezae is corroborative evidence of its age. A number of Biblical manuscripts that employ the **dms**-type have another
curious feature in common: instead of abbreviating the words 'deus', 'dei' *(13)*
by means of **ds, di,** they write the Nomen Sacrum in full, but distinguish it by means of a horizontal stroke above the word. This feature is also met with in the Codex Bezae, and its occurrence is not haphazard or accidental: it is practically confined to the parts of the manuscript in which **dms** is used for 'dominus'. It is found sixty-nine times in Luke, and only twice in Acts. Evidently the Codex Bezae must have been written in the transition period when the type **dms** was slowly giving place to **dns** and this must have been, judging from dated manuscripts, before the sixth century.

In so far, then, as Professor Sneyders de Vogel's hypothesis depends on the possibility of assigning the Codex Bezae to so late a period as the seventh century it is, viewed from the angle of palaeography, untenable. But even if his theory allowed the Codex Bezae to retain its venerable position in the fifth century one would still be at a loss how to account for the marked differences which exist between it, a supposedly Franco-Provençal product, and the oldest extant Lyons manuscripts, some of which presumably are of Lyonese origin and are assignable to the fifth and sixth centuries.

As to the home of the Codex Bezae, let us confess frankly that it still remains a fascinating puzzle. Lyons, south Italy, Sardinia, Sicily, Dacia, or some part of Africa, any of these may be right. I have argued against Lyons; it is possible to bring objections against south Italy and Sardinia; Sicily and Dacia seem reasonable enough hypotheses, but they are mere guesses; and palaeographically at least something may be said in favour of a mixed community in Africa. For if one thing is clearer than another it is that the Codex Bezae belonged to a mixed community in which Greek was the liturgical language, and Latin was also used. Yet neither seems to have been the native tongue of the Bezan scribe who wrote his Latin with a pen cut for writing Greek; and if his Greek letters strike one as somewhat odd, his Latin characters are
still queerer. If, on the one hand, his method of signing quires and of marking *(14)*
omissions and transpositions is in keeping with Greek usage, on the other hand his running titles, his colophons, and the ornamentations at the ends of books are redolent of a Latin scriptorium. The Latin script he employs is unusual in Latin calligraphy. For parallels we must go to legal fragments

found in Egypt and to inscriptions found in outlying districts of the Roman empire. In short, it is the work of a provincial, ignorant of old Latin traditions. Scholars are agreed that in discussing the origin of the Codex Bezae one must always bear in mind its connection with the Claromontanus of the Pauline epistles. It is hardly a mere coincidence that both these Graeco-Latin manuscripts are written in what I call the **bd**-uncials, considering that there is not a third calligraphic manuscript in existence written in the same script. Nor is it likely to be mere chance that both these manuscripts have survived in France. Two leaves of the Codex Claromontanus are palimpsest (fols. 162–3), and the remarkable fact is that the primary script contains a portion of Euripides' *Phaethon*. There is a famous palimpsest in the Palatine collection of the Vatican (MS. lat. 24): under an early-eighth-century text of the Old Testament lie buried parts of seven ancient texts, some Greek amongst the Latin, and one text, Seneca, is written in a type of **bd**-uncials which strongly recalls, as Studemund long ago noted, the script of the Codex Bezae. Perhaps if we knew more about this palimpsest, which richly deserves a special monograph, some light might be shed on the origin of the Codex Bezae. One other clue may be worth following up. The Codex Bezae was certainly used at Lyons in the ninth century. There is some ground for believing that the added leaves were written by Florus himself. As he was a scholar who had travelled much, he may have brought the manuscript from some distant land. Is there anything in his life or in his writings to give us a further hint?

A New Fragment in the B-Type

THE abbey of St. Peter's at Corbie in Picardy has played a very important (*43*) role in the preservation of ancient and medieval manuscripts. This has been common knowledge ever since the days of Mabillon and the authors of the *Nouveau Traité*, most of whose illustrations were drawn from Corbie manuscripts. Delisle's admirable studies have served to emphasize still more the importance of Corbie as a literary centre (L. Delisle, in *Bibliothèque de l'école des chartes*, XXI [1860], 393 ff., 498 ff., and in *Cabinet des manuscrits*, II [1874], 104 ff. and 427 ff.). But it was Traube who unfolded for us the full significance of Corbie as a scriptorium.[1] When Delisle wrote his *Cabinet des manuscrits* he was still labouring under the 'Lombardic' misapprehension, and it did not seem unlikely to him that the so-called 'Lombardic' manuscripts from Corbie, written in the script now known as the **ab**-type, originated in Italy. Traube, following in the footsteps of the great Maffei, discarded the equivocal terminology and its pseudo-historical implications, and by allowing these wonderful manuscripts to tell their own plain tale, came to recognize in them a peculiar and practically local type, which he called 'the old script of Corbie'. He was thus the first to stake out the claims of Corbie and neighbouring centres, and to make a clearing, as it were, in the 'selva selvaggia' of pre-Caroline minuscule scripts. Traube's 'old script of Corbie' is a distinct type. A partial list of manuscripts in this type was given by me in 'Studia Palaeographica' (*Sitzungsberichte* of the Munich Academy, 1910, Abhandlung (*44*) 12, pp. 36 ff.).[2] A practically complete list is found in Professor Lindsay's paper entitled 'The Old Script of Corbie, its Abbreviation Symbols' (in *Revue des Bibliothèques*, XXII [1912], 411 ff.).[3] But Traube's designation

From *Palaeographia Latina*, v (Oxford, 1927), 43–7. [See Pl. **26**.]

[1] L. Traube, 'Perrona Scottorum' in Munich Academy *Sitzungsberichte*, 1900, p. 493, where Leningrad F. v. XIV. 1 is described as written 'in der ältesten (Schrift) von Corbie, die in dieser Gegend geherrschet haben muss'. A similar observation is found in his earlier work, 'O Roma nobilis' in the Munich Academy *Abhandlungen*, XIX [1892], 331, Anm. 5. Here Traube speaks of the Corbie script as French half-cursive.

[2] [This volume, pp. 29 f.]

[3] To be added are two items mentioned by Lindsay, *Notae Latinae*, p. xi, n. 1, and one from Oxford: Bordeaux, Bibl. Publique, MS. 28 St. Augustine; Cologne, Hist. Archiv GB. Kasten B. 140, 141; Oxford, Bodleian, Canonici Patr. lat. 112 Athanasius, etc., in ordinary minuscule with additions and corrections in **ab**-type, e.g. fols. 11, 36v *et passim*. The contents of this Oxford manuscript correspond exactly with item 225 of the Corbie catalogue

has proved inadequate, since Corbie did not have one old script but several. The type that Traube had in mind happens to have two letters, **a** and **b**, in a form which differentiates the type from all others. It accordingly seemed more precise and therefore more scientific to name this particular script the 'Corbie **ab**-type', a nomenclature adopted in my *Studia Palaeographica* and accepted by Professors Lindsay, Lehmann, Zimmermann, Rand, Dom Wilmart, and others. If further justification were needed for giving up the term coined by Traube, it is now supplied by Liebaert's discovery, recently enlarged upon by M. Lauer, that an entirely different type—a type of ordinary minuscule—was practised at Corbie during the second half of the eighth century. This type possesses fully as good a right to be called 'the old script of Corbie' as does the **ab**-type. (Cf. P. Liebaert, 'Some Early Scripts of the Corbie Scriptorium' in *Pal. Lat.* I [1922], pp. 62 ff. and pls. II–V; P. Lauer, 'La Réforme carolingienne de l'écriture latine' in *Extraits des mémoires présentés par divers savants à l'Académie des Inscriptions et Belles Lettres*, tome XIII, 1924.)

It is perhaps worth stating that, in speaking of the **ab**-type as a Corbie type, we are using a terminology which must not be construed too literally. If it is taken to mean that the type originated at Corbie and was confined to
(45) that centre, the designation is clearly misleading. We have no evidence to show that Corbie created the type, and there is good ground for believing that the type was practised in other places, e.g. Saint Riquier, Soissons, Arras, perhaps also Beauvais and other centres in the north and near Paris. The justification for the expression 'Corbie **ab**-type' lies in the circumstance that the majority of the manuscripts in the **ab**-type were actually preserved to us by the monastery of Corbie, so that it is reasonable to suppose that Corbie played a leading part in the development of this interesting script.

Palaeographers are aware that Autun 20 (Gregory's *Dialogues*; Augustine's *Enchiridion*), Montpellier (Bibl. Ville) 3 (Gospels), Oxford Bodl. Douce f. 1 (Gelasian Sacramentary) and Vatic. Regin. 316 (Gelasian Sacramentary) form a group by themselves.[1] These manuscripts are written in a script which we

as printed in Becker's *Catalogi bibl. antiqui* p. 282. The fly-leaf of Reims MS. 8, containing the Index Liturgicus of Saint-Thierry, is in a type between the **ab**- and the **b**-type which deserves a separate note (cf. A. Wilmart in *Rev. Bénédictine*, 1913, pp. 437 ff.). [See also *Revue des Bibliothèques*, XXIV. 24: W. M. Lindsay (ed. *PL*)].

[1] Cf. *Stud. Pal.* p. 36 and *Rev. des Bibliothèques*, loc. cit., p. 414. The late S. Tafel also discussed these manuscripts in the now defunct *Revue Charlemagne* II (1912), 105 ff. Facsimiles of the Montpellier manuscript are in the Liebaert collection. Of the Reginensis a plate exists in Delisle, *Mémoire sur d'anciens Sacramentaires* (pl. IV) and in Ehrle–Liebaert, *Specimina codd. Lat.* (pl. 20). The manuscript itself is in uncials of the eighth century. It is the minuscule additions on fols. 8ᵛ, 45ᵛ, and 46 that interest us here.

call the **b**-type, and which is clearly the immediate forerunner, perhaps the direct ancestor of the **ab**-type. They have nearly all the distinguishing features of the latter type, including the curiously shaped **b**, with the short horizontal tag to the right of the stem and the long open bow; but they lack the typical **a** shaped like undotted **i** followed by **c**, and they have instead an **a** shaped like two adjacent **c**'s or contiguous **oc**. When, however, **a** combines with the letter which follows, the top of the first stroke of **a** bends to the left (as in the **ab**-type). It is the frequent use of this **a** in combination, and its frequent position above the line that constitute characteristic features of this group. If we are correct in assuming that the **ab**-script flourished at the end of the eighth and the beginning of the ninth century, then the **b**-type must have been in use during the early decades of the second half of the eighth century, hardly earlier than the middle of the century.

The fragment which forms the subject of this note is written in the **b**-type, *(46)*
and thus forms the fifth member of the above group.[1] It is a single leaf bound up in the miscellany, Paris. lat. 4808, as fol. 121. The approximate size of the written space is 240 × 145 mm. There are twenty-nine long lines to the page. See Pl. **26** (*pl. ix*).

The leaf contains the initial seventy-four verses of Symphosius 'Enigmata', not however divided into verses, but running on like a prose text. The library of Corbie, as is well known, possessed a manuscript in which Symphosius was represented.[2] I refer to Leningrad MS. F. v. XIV. 1, which, as Traube has shown, must have been written at St. Riquier, whence it was borrowed by someone at Corbie (cf. Traube, 'O Roma nobilis', pp. 29 ff. = *Abhandlungen* of the Munich Academy, XIX. 2 [1891], 325 ff.). It is in the **ab**-type and unless I err, also has twenty-nine lines to the page.[3] The two manuscripts do not

The Oxford fragment is reproduced in Wilson, *The Gelasian Sacramentary* (Oxford, 1894), p. lvii.

[1] Related to this small group of minuscule manuscripts is a small group of uncial and half-uncial manuscripts of extraordinary interest to liturgiologists and palaeographers, which should be dealt with exhaustively by competent hands. The scholar who can fix the date and determine the origin of these manuscripts will have thrown much needed light on a very puzzling palaeographical problem. [Cf. *Notae Latinae*, p. xi: W. M. Lindsay (ed. *PL.*)].

[2] See G. Becker, *Catalogi bibl. ant.* no. 136, item 170, which reads: 'Fortunati de diversis rebus; in laudem sancte Marie liber unus bis scriptus; de vita sancti Martini libri IV; multa alia de diversis; de virginitate laudanda in sanctis veteris et novi Testamenti; enigmata Althelmi episcopi et *Symphosii scholastici*; versus Probe' (= Delisle, *Cabinet des MSS.* II. 436). Copies of Symphosius existed in the Middle Ages in the libraries of Reichenau, St. Gall, Passau, Bobbio, Murbach, Lorsch, Fleury (?), Corbie and in an unidentified library. Cf. Becker, loc. cit., nos. 6. 364; 10. 2; 22. 393; 28. 37; 32. 422–3; 33. 74; 37. 417; 38. 73; 45. 4; 121. 58, 72, 91; 130. 170.

[3] The manuscript is important for the text of Fortunatus, Aldhelm and a collection of ancient Christian inscriptions, and has been used by Leo, De Rossi, and Ehwald, as well as by Riese

offer an identical text, but seem to represent two different recensions. The Paris fragment was carefully described by J. Klein in *Rheinisches Museum*, XXII [1868], 525 ff. and was used by A. Riese in his 'Anthologia latina' I. I. 222 (app. crit.). The Paris catalogue of 1744 describes the fragment rather
(47) vaguely, thus: 'Aenigmata nonnulla versibus expressa et longobardico charactere exarata (*Catalogus codd. MSS. Bibl. Regiae*, pars tertia, tom. IV (Paris, 1744), p. 3).

It may be mentioned in conclusion that the miscellany Paris lat. 4808 has another interest for palaeographers, since it contains on fols. 53–65 (Eucherius) a portion of the sixth-century uncial manuscript to which fols. 1–23 (Julii Honorii Cosmographia) of Paris lat. 2769 also once belonged. Traube was evidently unaware that the two parts came from one manuscript (Traube, *Vorles. und Abhandl.* I. 213). The credit of making the fact public belongs to Dom De Bruyne, who has put us all under obligation to him by publishing the series of articles entitled 'Membra disiecta' (*Revue Bénédictine*, XXXIV [1924], 121, etc.). In the last of the series brief comment will be found on Paris lat. 2769 and 4808, where I have tried to point out that those who are searching for 'Codices Vivarienses' would do well to study carefully this dismembered manuscript.

and others. It is described in *Neues Archiv*, V (1897), 255. Facsimiles in Staerk's work on the manuscripts of St. Petersburg, II, pl. 27, and in Arndt–Tangl, *Schrifttafeln*, pl. 6.

An Uncial (Palimpsest) Manuscript of Mutianus in the Collection of A. Chester Beatty

THE purpose of this note is to call the attention of scholars to a palimpsest of (29)
Mutianus and to a new and remarkable collection of manuscripts.

A Latin translation of John Chrysostom's Commentary on the Epistle to the Hebrews apparently did not exist before the time of Cassiodorus,[1] who found it necessary to have one made for the use of his monks at Vivarium. The translator was Mutianus, as we learn from chap. viii of the *Institutiones* which Cassiodorus wrote about 544.[2] That Mutianus's version was well known in the Middle Ages and read in many centres is to be gathered from the mention of it in numerous early catalogues from the ninth century onwards.[3] Thus it is found at St. Gall, Lorsch, Bobbio, Pomposa, St. Riquier, St. Vaast, Durham, Cluny, Tournay, Limoges, to mention only the best-known libraries. No contemporary copy of Mutianus has come down. Heretofore the oldest extant witnesses known to scholars were manuscripts of the ninth century.[4] Recently, however, a copy has come to light which is little more than a century removed from the original. This copy is, unfortunately, a palimpsest, and so well has the primary text been obliterated that no traces of it were discerned by expert observers like Schenkl and Lindsay.[5] I myself had the manuscript in my hands in 1920 and never suspected it of being
palimpsest.[6] It is to Mr. Eric G. Millar of the British Museum that the credit (30)

From *The Journal of Theological Studies*, XXIX (1927–8), 29–33.

[1] See E. Riggenbach, *Die ältesten lateinischen Kommentare zum Hebräerbrief*, Zahn's *Forsch. zur Gesch. d. neutestamentlichen Kanons*, VIII. 1 (1907), 2, to which Professor Souter kindly called my attention.

[2] 'Ad Hebraeos vero epistolam quam sanctus Iohannes Constantinopolitanus episcopus triginta quattuor homiliis Attico sermone tractavit, Mutianum virum disertissimum transferre fecimus in Latinum ne Epistolarum ordo continuus indecoro termino subito rumperetur' (Migne, *Patr. Lat.* 70, col. 1120).

[3] The index to G. Becker's *Catalogi bibliothecarum antiqui* (Bonn, 1885), p. 315 merely informs one that the version is found in many libraries. For more precise reference see Riggenbach, loc. cit.

[4] On Professor Souter's authority Riggenbach mentions the following manuscripts: Verona 54 (52), Milan Ambros. A. 135 inf., Cologne 61, and Cues 19.

[5] Cf. H. Schenkl, *Bibliotheca Patrum Latinorum Britannica*, I. 2 (Vienna, 1892), 114 f., and W. M. Lindsay, *Notae Latinae* (Cambridge, 1915), p. 452.

[6] It was also unknown to Traube or we should find it in his list of uncial manuscripts in *Vorlesungen und Abhandlungen*, I (Munich, 1909), 181, to which should also be added Cheltenham 22229, a leaf from an eighth-century manuscript of the gospels written in France.

of discovery belongs.[1] It was made, as I learn, quite accidentally. He happened to turn a leaf so that it came directly in front of his electric lamp, the light from which was so powerful that it brought out the palimpsest-character in astonishingly clear fashion. A few leaves were treated with reagents and were found to contain a commentary on the Epistle to the Hebrews which was soon identified as that of Mutianus Scholasticus. This instructive and happy experience should lead to interesting finds on the part of other librarians.

The text of Mutianus was written in a clear, bold type of Italian uncial characters of about the end of the seventh century. The manuscript formed a stately volume in which each page measured 365 × 266 mm. ($14\frac{3}{8} \times 10\frac{1}{2}$ in.), and was divided into two columns of thirty-one lines, with an interval of 18·5 mm. ($\frac{3}{4}$ in.) between the columns, the written space measuring 307 × 209 mm. ($12\frac{1}{8} \times 8\frac{1}{4}$ in.).

It is possible that the library in which this uncial manuscript happened to be a century or so after it was written had a minuscule copy of Mutianus, rendering the older one obsolete, or it may be that there was a great scarcity of parchment and hardly any interest in Mutianus—whatever the cause may have been, about the end of the eighth century the uncial text of Mutianus was erased to make room for a minuscule copy of various works of St. Augustine and the *Carmen Apologeticum* of Commodianus.

The manuscript in which the text of Mutianus lies buried is well known to patristic scholars under the press-mark of Cheltenham 12261.[2] In 1924 it passed from the Phillips collection in Cheltenham to the Beatty collection in London, where it bears the number 3 [now Brit. Mus. Add. MS. 43460]. It consists of 197 leaves of which fols. 1–111 are palimpsest. These 111 leaves formed $55\frac{1}{2}$ leaves of the original uncial manuscript. Whether or not scholars will ever be able to collate the oldest extant witness to Mutianus, still for the most part invisible, must depend on the owner's willingness to submit the palimpsest to treatment by reagents, which would, of course, involve disfiguring the best part of the manuscript.[3] Fortunately, scientists are at work on the problem of finding a process of photography which will effectively reproduce the underscript without the aid of chemical reagents. Such a discovery would be a boon indeed to palaeography as well as to letters.[4]

[1] The palimpsest is described in the catalogue cited in full below, p. 236, n. 3.

[2] Described by Schenkl, loc. cit.

[3] The facsimile in the Beatty catalogue shows that the text could be easily deciphered if reagents were applied.

[4] The most successful efforts so far have been made by the monks of Beuron.

The manuscript which contains the submerged text of Mutianus is of great
value quite apart from the uncial underscript, for the eighth-century minus- (*31*)
cule script gives us the best text of St. Augustine's *De Utilitate Credendi* and
the unique text of Commodianus' *Carmen Apologeticum.*[1] It is a curious fact
that the text of Commodianus's *Instructiones* is preserved in a manuscript
which is also unique and which also formerly belonged to the Phillipps collection (no. 1825) and is now at Berlin (no. 167).[2] It is quite probable that the
two manuscripts actually hail from the same general region.[3] The poems of
Commodianus were evidently little read in the Middle Ages. One finds no
mention of them in medieval catalogues,[4] and, as has been said, only two
ancient copies have actually reached us. Now Berlin 167 originated, as script
and abbreviations go to show, in some north Italian centre, which was probably Verona.[5] While there is nothing to connect our palimpsest with Verona,
there can be no doubt that it formed part of the old library of S. Silvestro of
Nonantola, near Modena, where it may have been written.[6] The oldest manuscripts of Nonantola present an interesting literary and palaeographical problem which still awaits solution.[7] A number of them are written in a type of
minuscule so like early Beneventan as to be practically indistinguishable from
it. This may, of course, be explained as a simple migration of manuscripts
from the south to the north. There is some historical support for this theory:
for Anselm, the first Abbot of Nonantola, when exiled by King Desiderius
(†774), is said to have gone to Monte Cassino whence he brought back many
books.[8] But the Chronicle of Monte Cassino does not record his visit, and the
manuscripts of Nonantola are, on the whole, so much superior to south
Italian products of the same time (Paris Lat. 7530, Cava 2, Casanatensis 641)[9]
as to make it seem unlikely that they come from the same school. Moreover, (*32*)
the uncial manuscripts of Nonantola nearly all show features which are

[1] See J. Zycha's preface to his edition in the Vienna *Corpus Scriptorum Ecclesiasticorum Latinorum*, XXV (1891), sect. VI, pt. I, and Dombart's preface to vol. XV in the same series. A new edition is expected from Dr. J. Martin of Würzburg. Cf. his *Commodianea* in the Vienna *Sitzungsberichte*, CLXXXI. 6 (1917).

[2] See V. Rose, *Die lateinischen Meermann-Handschriften des Sir Thomas Phillipps in der Königl. Bibliothek zu Berlin* (Berlin, 1892), p. 374.

[3] Professor Lindsay (*Notae Latinae*, p. 452) was ready to regard the two poems as parts of one manuscript, but this is impossible as the two differ not only in script but also in size.

[4] At least they are not found in the catalogues published by G. Becker cited above, p. 233, n. 3.

[5] Cf. Lindsay, op. cit., p. 447. The form of g is remarkably like that found in many Veronese manuscripts.

[6] See Millar's description of the manuscript in the new catalogue.

[7] On the dispersal of the Nonantola library see I. Giorgi in *Archivio delle Biblioteche e degli archivi*, VI (1896), 54 ff.

[8] See Muratori, *Antiquitates Italicae*, IV. 944 and Waitz, *Mon. Germ. Hist.*, *SS. Rerum Langobardicarum et Italicarum*, pp. 503 and 517.

[9] See the facsimiles in Traube's *Quellen und Untersuchungen*, III. 3 (Munich, 1908).

distinctly north Italian.[1] What is true of them is probably true of the early minuscule manuscripts. They were written either at Nonantola or at some other north Italian centre. The resemblance which their script bears to early Beneventan seems perfectly natural if it be remembered that 'the Beneventan is, in reality, nothing more than a continuation in south Italy of the traditional Italian school' and that 'a Beneventan script becomes apparent only by contrast with those scripts which succumbed to the Caroline reform'.[2] Anyone desiring to study the Codices Nonantolani will in the future have to resort to the Beatty collection, which contains no less than eight manuscripts which give evidence of having belonged to Nonantola.

This brings me to the second part of my note—the Beatty collection. A catalogue of a portion of the collection has just appeared.[3] It consists of a pair of magnificent volumes, one of text and one of plates, which describe and illustrate forty-three Latin manuscripts, ranging from the eighth to the thirteenth century. Five more similar pairs of volumes are promised: two to deal with later Latin manuscripts, two with Oriental, and one with Greek, Coptic, etc. The task of describing the Western manuscripts has been entrusted to the able hands of E. G. Millar. Such is the careful and scholarly work bestowed on the first forty-three manuscripts that the catalogue at once takes rank amongst the finest in existence. It is also one of the most beautiful; and for this credit is due to Emery Walker, Ltd., and to the Oxford University Press. In fact, lovers of ancient manuscripts have rarely been put under so great an obligation by a catalogue, and they are indebted to Mr. Beatty for a generosity bordering on munificence in the illustrations. The forty-three manuscripts described are accorded no less than ninety-nine monochrome and three coloured folio-size plates, which are as splendid specimens of the art of mechanical reproduction as can anywhere be found.

Nearly all of Mr. Beatty's manuscripts have been purchased in the last half-dozen years. All the oldest and several of the finest come from the Phillipps collection—twenty-five in all. Not since 1889, when Berlin acquired the handsome lot of Meerman Phillippici (nos. 1338–2010), have such inroads been made upon the oldest section of the Cheltenham collection. The twenty-five Phillippici acquired by Mr. Beatty are sufficiently important

[1] I refer especially to the form of N. The Codices Sessoriani in uncial script are enumerated in Traube's *Vorles. u. Abh.* I. 228–9.

[2] E. A. Lowe, *The Beneventan Script* (Oxford, 1914), p. 95.

[3] *The Library of A. Chester Beatty: A Descriptive Catalogue of the Western Manuscripts*, by Eric George Millar, vol. I, manuscripts 1–43 (Oxford, 1927).

to warrant giving a list of them with their past and present press-marks.[1]

Beatty	Phillipps	Contents	Date and provenance	(33)
1	36275	Bede, *Hist. Eccl.*	saec. VIII (Anglo-Saxon)	
2	8400	Homiliary	saec. VIII ex. (Ottobeuren)	
3	12261	Augustine, Commodianus	saec. VIII ex. (Nonantola)	
4	12260	Epistola Datiani, Fulgentius, etc.	saec. VIII–IX (Nonantola)	
5	12264	Augustine, *Sermons*	saec. VIII–IX (Nonantola)	
6	12263	Eugippius, *Exc. from Aug.*	saec. VIII–IX (Nonantola)	
7	12262	Bede, *Comment. Can. Epist.*	saec. VIII–IX (Nonantola)	
9	2165 and 21787	Gospels	saec. IX (Franco-Saxon)	
10	14122	Gospels (fragm.)	saec. IX ex. (Franco-Saxon)	
11	10190	Ansegisi, *Capitula*	saec. ix ex. (Tours)	
12	6546	Canons of Councils	saec. IX–X (Nonantola)	
13	389	Canons of Councils	saec. X (Germany)	
14	390	Canons of Councils	saec. X (Germany)	
15	3075	Eutropius	saec. X (Nonantola)	
16	3674	Gregory, *Dialogues*	saec. X (France)	
*17	12348	Gospels	*c.* 1000 (Flanders)	
18	934 and 2708	Gregory, *Homilies*	saec. XI–XII (France)	
*22	4769	Bible	saec. XII (Walsingham Priory)	
23	3535 or 3534	Lectionary	saec. XII (Flanders, S. Trond)	
24	21948	Minor Prophets, glossed	saec. XII (Flanders, Anchin?)	
*29	3344	Job, glossed	saec. XII (Flanders)	
31	1092	Bede on *Luke*	saec. XII (Germany, Gladbach)	
32	4597	Psalter with Peter Lombard	saec. XII (Germany)	
33	385	Suetonius	saec. XII ex. (France?)	
*43	12269	Augustine, *City of God*	saec. XI–XII (Nonantola)	

Apart from the manuscripts of the Phillipps collection Mr. Beatty has drawn widely from other sources. His collection contains examples of some of the finest medieval schools of France, Germany, Flanders, and England, the last country being represented by magnificent manuscripts from Bury St. Edmunds and St. Augustine's, Canterbury. Very beautiful are the two

[1] [Of the manuscripts listed above only those marked with an asterisk have remained in the Chester Beatty Library, Dublin, after the collector's death. Ed.]

manuscripts from the school of Tours (the ninth-century Gospels formerly in the possession of Henry Yates Thompson and the Capitula Ansegisi) and from the Franco-Saxon school. Striking, too, is the tenth-century Evangeliarium (MS. 42) from Germany. Of the later period, mention should be made of the remarkable initials in the manuscript of St. Augustine's *City of God* (MS. 43), and the exquisitely beautiful leaves from a Psalter illuminated by W. De Brailes, in England, about 1240.[1] In fact, there is hardly a manuscript in the collection that does not gladden the heart of a student of manuscripts.

[1] The description of these leaves as well as of the Tours gospels from H. Yates Thompson's collection is by the great connoisseur of medieval art, Sidney G. Cockerell.

An Eighth-Century List of Books in a Bodleian Manuscript from Würzburg and its probable Relation to the Laudian Acts

Of the various collections of manuscripts in the Bodleian Library none is so (3)
important as the collection presented by Archbishop Laud.[1] Among the Laudian manuscripts by far the most valuable are those composing the group which comes from St. Kilian's in Würzburg. And of these Würzburg manuscripts the oldest is the eighth-century copy of St. Augustine's *De Trinitate*, now MS. Laud. Misc. 126.[2] On a page originally left blank, at the end of this
manuscript (fol. 260^r) an Anglo-Saxon hand of about the year 800 entered (4)
a small list of books.[3] This list, the subject of the present note, is worthy of study for two reasons: first, it refers, in all probability, to the books of the episcopal library of Würzburg, and thus gives us an idea of what that library was like at the end of the eighth century, that is, about two generations after the Anglo-Saxon Boniface placed his compatriot Burchard in charge of the newly established bishopric of Würzburg; and second, because of the light which this ancient catalogue may throw on a former home of the famous

From *Speculum*, III (1928), 3–15. [See Pls. **27** to **30**.]

[1] The bulk of Laud's manuscripts came to Oxford in four instalments. The figures as given by W. D. Macray in *Annals of the Bodleian Library* (Oxford, 1890), pp. 83 ff., are 462 volumes in 1635, 181 in 1636, 575 in 1639, and 81 in 1640. But according to more recent authority the first instalment (22 May 1635) consisted of 467 manuscripts, 46 being from Würzburg, and 5 rolls and 2 charters; the second (16 June 1636) of 183 manuscripts; the third (28 June 1639) of 554 manuscripts, among them the famous Graeco-Latin codex of the *Acts* and the Peterborough *Chronicle*; the fourth (6 Nov. 1640) of 47 manuscripts. Cf. E. W. B. Nicholson's note in *A Summary Catalogue of Western Manuscripts in the Bodleian Library at Oxford* (Oxford, 1922), II. 1, pp. 13 ff. The entries found inside the Laudian MSS. (see facs. on Pl. **28**A (*pl. II. 1*)) are apt to be erroneously regarded as furnishing the date when the particular manuscript was donated.

[2] For facsimiles see Chatelain, *Uncialis Scriptura*, pls. 52 and 96; E. H. Zimmermann, *Vorkarolingische Miniaturen*, pls. 138–41 and p. 218; *New Palaeographical Society*, ser. II, pls. 83–5. There is a summary and somewhat inaccurate description of the manuscript in H. O. Coxe, *Catalogus Codicum Manuscriptorum Bibliothecae Bodleianae*, II. 1 = *Catal. Codd. MSS. Laudianorum: Codices Latini* (Oxford, 1858), cols. 128, 129.

[3] For some inexplicable reason this list has never been published. A few items are mentioned by Coxe in the catalogue just cited. P. Lehmann alludes to it in his excellent study, *Franciscus Modius als Handschriftenforscher* (Munich, 1908), p. 65, n. 1. The editors of the *New Palaeographical Society* (loc. cit.) give a facsimile of a portion of the list and make a number of interesting observations.

Graeco-Latin manuscript of the Acts known to Biblical scholars as *E* or the Laudian Acts (Bodleian MS. Laud. Gr. 35).[1]

The manuscript Laud. Misc. 126 is written partly in uncials and partly in half-uncials of a distinct type which flourished in the Frankish realm during the eighth century.[2] The ornamentation, which consists of birds and fishes, is as characteristic as the script; the frequent use of green ink in titles is also a feature peculiar to this type. North-eastern France has been suggested as the home of this style of decoration.[3] The French origin of the manuscript is further confirmed by the few words found on fol. 259ᵛ, after the last colophon at the very end of the original text, written in pre-Caroline minuscule of the unmistakably French style which preceded the so-called Corbie type.[4] Accordingly, the manuscript which contains the ancient catalogue under discussion came to Würzburg from France. Nor is it the only Würzburg
(5) manuscript of French provenance. In the famous Würzburg palimpsest (MS. Mp. th. fol. 64a) we find, over the Pentateuch and Prophets in fifth-century uncials, St. Augustine's *Commentary on the Psalms* written in a French type of pre-Caroline minuscule to which has been given the name of 'Luxeuil'.[5] The important Munich MS. of the *Breviarium Alarici* (Cod. Lat. Monac. 22501), written in uncial characters of the seventh century, formerly belonged to the Cathedral Library of Würzburg, but its place of origin must be France, to judge from the script and the history of the text.[6]

From a note entered on the fly-leaf (fol. 1ᵛ) of this eighth-century manu-

[1] For a description, see Coxe, op. cit. I (1853), 517; facsimiles are in J. O. Westwood, *Palaeographia Sacra Pictoria*, pl. x. 1; C. Tischendorf, *Monumenta Sacra Inedita*, IX (1870); *Palaeographical Society*, I, pl. 80; F. H. A. Scrivener, *A Plain Introduction to the Criticism of the New Testament* (4th ed. by E. Miller, Cambridge, 1894), facs. 25; W. A. Copinger, *The Bible and its Transmission* (London, 1897), pl. XIII. Further literature in L. Traube, *Vorlesungen und Abhandlungen*, I (Munich, 1909), 210.

[2] The entire quires marked iii, vi, xi, xii, and the last page of quire x are written in half-uncial; the rest of the manuscript is in uncial. For other manuscripts written in this type of uncial see the writer's article, 'The Vatican MS. of the Gelasian Sacramentary and its Supplement at Paris', *Journal of Theological Studies*, XXVII (1926), 373 [this volume, p. 219].

[3] Cf. Zimmermann, op. cit., p. 81.

[4] I refer to the words: 'speraui iam teneo illi sunt'.

[5] A. Chroust, *Monumenta Palaeographica*, Lieferung v, pl. 4, has a good facsimile. The manuscript which gives the name to the type is Paris, B.N. Lat. 9427 containing the Gallican Lectionary which Mabillon discovered at Luxeuil. For other manuscripts in this style of pre-Caroline minuscule see my 'Studia Palaeographica', *Sitzungsberichte d. kgl. bayer. Akademie d. Wiss.*, philos.-philol. u. hist. Kl. (Munich, 1910), Abh. 12, pp. 31 f. [this volume pp. 25 f.]. The Luxeuil type is fully illustrated by Zimmermann, op. cit., pls. 44–74.

[6] Facsimiles in Silvestre, *Paléographie Universelle*, pl. 112; Zangemeister–Wattenbach, *Exempla Codicum Lat. Litteris Majusculis Scriptorum*, pls. 27, 28; Traube, 'Enarratio Tabularum', pls. IV, VI, in Mommsen's *Theodosiani Libri XVI* (Berlin, 1905); Zimmermann, op. cit., pl. 38; E. A. Lowe, *Codices Lugdunenses Antiquissimi* (Lyons, 1924), facs. suppl. 1.

script of St. Augustine, it appears that it reached St. Kilian's within a century after it was written. The note is in ordinary minuscule of the ninth century and runs as follows:

> Si mors quod absit inopinata super familiarem amicum nostrum ingruerit, adiuro per deum omnipotentem illum in cuius liber iste de sancta trinitate beati augustini peruenerit manus, faciat eum sancto kiliano restitui.[1]

The presence of this note at the opening of the manuscript suggests that the librarian of St. Kilian's set great store by the volume. The final words 'faciat eum sancto kiliano restitui' bear witness to the practice of lending books. Thanks to the record in the catalogue itself of two instances of this practice, we are able to make a shrewd guess concerning the library which the catalogue represents.

In printing the catalogue, I preserve the original spelling, order and relative position of the columns. I have, however, for convenience' sake, printed the extended forms, since the accompanying facsimile (Pl. **27** (*pl. 1*)) makes a letter-for-letter transcript unnecessary. To simplify reference, I have also (*6*) numbered items and have put in square brackets, after certain items, the name of the author or of the work to which, in my opinion, it most probably refers. Apart from a few items, identification with extant manuscripts is quite out of the question. But I have thought it useful to call attention to extant Würzburg manuscripts not later than the year 900, which might reasonably be copies of items in the list.

1. Actus apostulorum
2. pastoralem [*Gregorius M.*]
3. dialogorum [*Gregorius M.*]
4. commentarium AD HOLZKIRIHHUN
5. historia anglorum [*Beda*]
6. epistola sancti hieronimi
7. liber doctrinę christiane [*Augustinus*]
8. sancti augustini de fide
9. sancti ambrosi de fide
10. liber orosi [*Historia adv. gentes*]
11. liber arnouii [*Arnobius Contra haereses* or *Super Psalmos*]
12. iuuenci super euangelia
13. liber super effeseos [*Hieronymus*]

[1] This entry is printed by Coxe, loc. cit., col. 129, and by the editors of *New Pal. Soc.*, whose folio number 16 is a printer's error for 1b (1 verso) and whose 'dominum' is an incorrect expansion of **dm**.

14. episcopal<e>
15. decreta pontificum
16. liber augustini de quantitate animę
17. liber iunili [*Instructiones*?]
18. official<e> [*Isidorus, De officiis*, possibly Amalarius]
19. enceridion [*Augustinus*]
20. liber prosperi [*De vita contemplativa*]
21. moralia in iob libri xxiii [*Gregorius M.*]
22. summum bonum [*Isidorus*]
23–4. lectionari duo
25. glosa
26. liber althelmi [*De laudibus virginitatis*?]
27. liber de trinitate [*Augustinus*]
28–9. liber esaiae duo
30. catalogus hieronimi presbyteri de auctoribus librorum
31. grammatica sancti augustini et sancti bonifati
32. epistulae sancti pauli

(7) ad fultu

33. speculum [*Augustinus*]
34. omelia sancti gregorii maiora pars
35. liber prouerbium
36. beatitudines [*Chromatius*?]

In any attempt to identify items in the list with extant Würzburg manuscripts the date of the catalogue is an important consideration. For if my date, about A.D. 800, is correct, then there are only six or seven identifiable items, namely 1, 2, 4, 15, 27, 32, and 34. All other Würzburg manuscripts which could be brought into relationship with the list seem to me to be considerably later than the year 800. Some of these, however, deserve mention here as being possible early copies of books registered in the list. This possibility is converted to probability by the circumstance that many of the manuscripts are either themselves in Anglo-Saxon characters or are obviously copied from Insular exemplars.

Item 1. Presumably Bodleian MS. Laud. Gr. 35, of which more will be said below.

Item 2. Bodleian MS. Laud. Misc. 263 has the Würzburg shelfmark. It is written in Anglo-Saxon script of the early ninth century. Würzburg M. p. th. f. 42, in ordinary minuscule of the ninth century, also contains Gregory's *Regula Pastoralis*. The fly-leaf is in Anglo-Saxon and a corrector used the Anglo-Saxon method of supplying omissions (fol. 2^{r}).

Item 3. Würzburg M.p. th. f. 19, in Anglo-Saxon letters (except fols. 1^{v}–14^{v}), saec. IX in. This copy of the *Dialogues* might be contemporary with our list, but I rather doubt it.

Item 4. The anonymous commentary was in its place when the list was made. The entry which records that it was borrowed was made by a different librarian. Judging from its position between the books of the Pope who sent the first mission to England and the book of the first English historian one may venture the guess that it was another book with English associations. Such a book is Würzburg M. p. th. q. 2, containing St. Jerome's *Commentary on Ecclesiastes* in fifth-century uncials, which, before it got to Würzburg, had belonged to Abbess Cuthsuuitha, as is attested by the inscription in beautiful Anglo-Saxon majuscule characters on the front fly-leaf. The only abbess by this name of whom history knows was in charge of a nunnery in or near Worcester about the year 700, which fits in admirably with the date of the inscription.[1] In view (*8*)
of the English atmosphere suggested by the first few entries in the catalogue this identification has something in its favour.[2]

Item 7. The Bodleian MS. Laud. Misc. 121, saec. IX, from Würzburg, is in ordinary minuscule, but in part manifestly under Insular influence (see fols. 72 ff. On fol. 4 ħr occurs for 'autem').

Item 11. In view of the preceding item, Arnobius *Contra haereses* seems highly probable here, but Arnobius *Super Psalmos* is not to be excluded considering that the next item is a commentary on part of the Bible.

Item 15. Würzburg still possesses three very old manuscripts of canons. Of these ,M.p. th. f. 3, in Anglo-Saxon script, might be identified with our item; but M.p. th. f. 72, containing the Dionysio-Hadriana, is written in Anglo-Saxon characters of the Würzburg-Fulda region but of a later date than our catalogue. Later, too, is M.p. th. f. 146, written in ordinary minuscule but under Anglo-Saxon influence.[3] It should be added that Bodleian MS. Laud. Misc. 436, in Anglo-Saxon characters of the early ninth century, contains the *Concordia Canonum* by Cresconius. The manuscript probably comes from Würzburg.

Item 18. This probably refers to Isidore's *De Ecclesiasticis Officiis*, in which case it could be identified with Würzburg, M.p. th. q. 18, written in Insular characters of the end of the eighth century; or else to a very early copy of the work by Amalarius which in the tenth century manuscript Boulogne 82 in Insular script is actually entitled, as I learn from W. J. Anderson, *Liber Officialis*. This, however, would necessitate pushing forward the date of the catalogue by at least two decades.

[1] On Cuthsuuitha, see W. G. Searle, *Onomasticon Anglo-Saxonicum* (Cambridge, 1897), p. 150, who refers to documents printed by Birch (*Cartularium Saxonicum*, 85, 122) and Kemble (*Codex Diplomaticus Aevi Saxonici*, 36, 53).

[2] Facsimiles of this manuscript in Chroust, *Monum. Pal.*, ser. I, Lief. V, pls. 2, 3.

[3] A facsimile of M. p. th. f. 72 is given by Chroust, loc. cit., pl. 6.

Item 21. A manuscript of Gregory's *Moralia* in Anglo-Saxon script of the ninth century still exists in Würzburg M.p. th. f. 149a, but it contains only books 32–35; M.p. th. f. 150, in ordinary minuscule of the ninth century, shows Insular influence but contains only excerpts from the *Moralia*.

Item 26. The most obvious reference would be to *De laudibus virginitatis*. It exists in Würzburg Mp. th. f. 21, written in the time of Bishop Gozbald (842–55). The
(9) script is ordinary minuscule but the abbreviations show that it was copied from an Anglo-Saxon original.[1] But it is quite possible that Aldhelm's *Metrica* and *Aenigmata* are here meant. The place of this item next to the item *Glosa* would support such an identification.

Item 27. Probably refers to the eighth-century copy of St. Augustine *On the Trinity* which came to Würzburg from France and is now Bodleian MS. Laud. Misc. 126, on the last page of which was entered the catalogue under discussion.

Item 31. St. Boniface's *Grammar* is a very rare manuscript. Apparently a single copy has survived, and is now preserved in the Vatican Library, MS. Pal. lat. 1746, from Lorsch.[2] This manuscript begins with St. Augustine's *Grammar* and ends with St. Boniface's. The presumption is that the manuscript in our list contained the same group of works as the Palatinus. The ancient Würzburg librarian thought it sufficient to mention the first and last authors.[3]

Item 32. The Pauline Epistles are found in Würzburg M.p. th. f. 12 and M.p. th. f. 69, both in Insular script of about the year 800, and in Bodleian MS. Laud. Lat. 108 in Anglo-Saxon script of the ninth century.[4]

Item 34. Of Gregory's *Homilies* many manuscripts must have existed. Würzburg still possesses several. M.p. th. f. 45 is written in Anglo-Saxon characters of about the year 800 and might thus be the volume referred to in our catalogue. M.p. th. f. 43, in Insular script (Irish?) seems of the ninth century. M.p. th. f. 47 and M.p. th. f. 59, both in Anglo-Saxon script, are apparently of the ninth century. Bodleian MS. Laud. Misc. 275 from Würzburg is in a German type of ordinary minuscule (ninth century), but under Anglo-Saxon influence.

Item 36. This may refer to Chromatius' Sermon on the eight Beatitudes, printed in Migne, *Patrol. Lat.* xx. 323 ff.

[1] A facsimile is in Chroust, loc. cit., pl. 9.

[2] See *Neues Archiv*, VIII (1883), 320. Mr. C. H. Beeson of Chicago believes he has found two more copies in Paris manuscripts.

[3] The Palatinus was used by A. Mai in *Class. Auct. e Vatic. Codd. editi* VII (Rome, 1835), 475 ff., and by Arevalo in his *Isidoriana*, II. 370 (Migne, *Patrol. Lat.* LXXXI. 879), who gives its full contents as follows: *Artes S. Augustini, Regula Augustini de nomine et aliis partibus orationis, Ars Donati quam Paulus Diaconus exponit, S. Ysidori episcopi de grammatica et partibus eius et figuris, Dynamius grammaticus ad discipulum suum, Grammatica Juliani episcopi Toletani, Grammatica et ars Tacuini, Alia ars siue grammatica Juliani Toletani, Ars Asperi de octo partibus orationis, Ars domni Bonifacii arciepiscopi et martyris*. For a similar, though not precisely identical, collection see items 416, 417 of the tenth-century Lorsch catalogue in Becker's *Catalogi Bibliothecarum Antiqui*, p. 110.

[4] For facsimiles see E. S. Buchanan, 'The Epistles of St. Paul from the Codex Laudianus', *Sacred Latin Texts: No. II* (London, 1914).

An analysis of the above list shows that five items refer to Biblical books (*10*)
(1, 28, 29, 32, 35), four to books by Gregory (2, 3, 21, 34), one to Bede's works (5), three (possibly four) to Jerome (6, 13, 30, and possibly 4), seven to Augustine (7, 8, 16, 19, 27, 31, 33), one each to Ambrose (9), Orosius (10), Arnobius (11), Juvencus (12); three at least are liturgical (14, 23, 24), one is canon law (15), one Junilius (17), one Prosper (20), one (possibly two) Isidorus (22 and probably 18), one a glossary (25), one Aldhelm (26), one Boniface (31) and one a book on the Beatitudes (36).

It can hardly be denied that the order in the catalogue, if it is not altogether haphazard, is peculiar. The first entry, distinguished by a capital letter, is, curiously enough, a volume of the Acts. No other medieval catalogue beginning with the Acts is known to me.[1] The second entry is Gregory's *Cura Pastoralis*, the third his *Dialogi*. These are followed by an anonymous Commentary and by Bede's *Historia Ecclesiastica*, called here by its short title. Strange that these books, unless similarity of format connects them, or unless some other special reason exists, should come before the works of the great doctors of the Church, Sts. Augustine, Jerome, Ambrose. One is struck with the fact that a number of items are given without the author, as if the books were too familiar to require it, amongst them the works of Sts. Jerome, Augustine, Gregory, Isidore, and Bede. Considering the position of three Biblical volumes toward the end of the list, it strikes one as odd that the catalogue opens with a manuscript of the Acts.

The whole of the above catalogue is written in Anglo-Saxon characters, excepting the words AD HOLZKIRIHHUN, which are added by a German hand after the fourth item, *commentarium*. There can be no doubt what the added phrase signifies. It records the loan of the book to Holzkirchen. Similarly, the phrase *ad fultu*, which is entered in small Anglo-Saxon characters above the entries in the second column, makes note of the fact that the four books in
that column had been borrowed by the monastery of Fulda. Fulda and Holz- (*11*)
kirchen were close together, the latter was in fact a dependency of the former.[2] In his study on the humanist Modius, mentioned above,[3] Professor Lehmann expressed the view that our catalogue referred to the library of Fulda. But he was misled by imperfect copies furnished to him, which failed to note the

[1] No instances occur in G. Becker's *Catalogi Bibliothecarum Antiqui* (Bonn, 1885), and none is known to my friend Professor Lehmann, whose knowledge of medieval catalogues is very extensive. I here wish to acknowledge my gratitude to Professor Lehmann and to Dom Wilmart for suggestions which they were good enough to give me.

[2] As early as 775 the monastery of Holzkirchen was the property of Fulda. Cf. A. Hauck, *Kirchengeschichte Deutschlands*, II (3rd and 4th edd., 1912), 584 f. and 823.

[3] p. 239, n. 3.

precise position of the phrase 'ad fultu'. Its position over the second column makes it clear that Fulda, like Holzkirchen, was borrowing books from another library. What library was it that put Fulda and Holzkirchen under this obligation?

One or two hints we may gather from the catalogue itself. We note, in the first place, that the list does not include St. Benedict's Rule, nor any other monastic Rule; on the other hand, it contains such items as *lectionari* and *episcopale*, books which strongly suggest that we are dealing with the chapter library of a bishopric, and not with a monastic library. From the use of Anglo-Saxon script in the catalogue and additions, from the presence in the list of all the important Anglo-Saxon writers (Bede, Aldhelm, Boniface), and in fact from the whole arrangement, we may gather that the library in question was situated in a centre where Anglo-Saxon influence was strong. By the arrangement, I mean the prominent position given to Gregory, the Pope who instituted the Christian Church in England, and to the Venerable Bede, both of whom take precedence over Augustine and Jerome. Finally, this ecclesiastical library, which was under Anglo-Saxon influence, must have enjoyed very friendly relations with the monasteries of Fulda and Holzkirchen.

Considering that the manuscript containing the catalogue actually belonged to Würzburg in the ninth century, one naturally thinks of Würzburg; and, in reality, no other place corresponds to the above conditions quite so well. Both the monastery at Fulda and the episcopal see at Würzburg owe their existence to the zeal and energy of the Anglo-Saxon missionary Boniface.[1] Fulda was his favourite abbey, and the bishopric of Würzburg he entrusted to his faithful follower, the Anglo-Saxon Burchard. Under these circum-
(*12*) stances it goes without saying that close and friendly relations existed between Fulda and Würzburg, the exchange of books being one manifestation of the intellectual commerce between the two seats of learning. Extant manuscripts from Fulda and Würzburg, written in Anglo-Saxon characters, show that the script that Boniface and Burchard brought with them to Germany continued to flourish there for nearly a whole century after their arrival. Considering then that our catalogue belongs to a library of the Fulda district, that it represents an episcopal library under Anglo-Saxon influence, and that Würzburg is the first place with which we can definitely connect the manuscript containing it, we are probably correct in concluding that the above list of manuscripts refers to the ancient library of St. Kilian's at Würzburg.[2]

[1] The reader is referred to Hauck's work just cited.

[2] The editors of the *New Pal. Society* (loc. cit.) concede the possibility that the list refers to Würzburg.

As for the age of the catalogue, a *terminus ad quem* is furnished by the writing itself, which to all appearances is hardly much posterior to the year 800. This approximate date is also confirmed by internal evidence. The catalogue mentions no work of the Anglo-Saxon Alcuin, who died in 804. The *terminus a quo* is supplied by the history of Würzburg. The bishopric was not in existence before the year 741, so our catalogue is more recent than that date. But it is probably posterior to the year 787, because the fly-leaf at the beginning of the volume (fol. 1^{r}) contains, in similar if not identical script, a copy of Charlemagne's famous letter *De Litteris Colendis* addressed to Abbot Baugulf of Fulda in 787.[1] It may accordingly be safe to say that our catalogue was entered in the Würzburg manuscript toward the end of the eighth century.

And this brings me to my second point: may not *Actus Apostolorum* in the catalogue actually refer to the well-known Codex *E*(*e*)?[2] I am inclined to think that it does. The identification, I realize, is pure conjecture, but something, I think, may be said for it. If we take the view that the arrangement in the list is not an accidental one but reflects Anglo-Saxon predilection for the works of Pope Gregory and Bede, then the place occupied by the volume of (*13*)
Acts is best explained by similar historical association. And this fits in well with the history of the manuscript as it is commonly reconstructed. That history, though sometimes stated so dogmatically as to make it appear that every assertion is attested by documentary evidence, is in truth mostly conjectural.[3] Briefly, it is this: the manuscript was written in seventh-century uncial characters, probably somewhere in Sardinia, for it contains, at the end of the volume, a copy of an edict in seventh-century Greek cursive which mentions *Fl. Pancratius, dux Sardiniae*—a local title used between 534 and 749. It must have left Sardinia early, for by the beginning of the eighth century we find it in England: Biblical scholars seem to be agreed that the Venerable Bede, in his *Retractationes in Acta*, written between 731 and 735, used a text that can be no other than Codex *E*.[4] It is usually stated that it was brought

[1] See the edition in *Monumenta Germaniae Historica, Leges*, II. 79, and C. H. Beeson's *A Primer of Medieval Latin* (Chicago, 1925), pp. 152 f. A discussion of this letter will be found in Professor Lehmann's forthcoming study on Fulda.

[2] See above, p. 240, n. 1.

[3] See the example cited by Dr. Craster in *The Bodleian Quarterly*, II (1919), no. 23, p. 289. In F. G. Kenyon, *Our Bible and the Ancient Manuscripts* (2nd ed., 1896), pp. 145 f., one gets the impression that the manuscript never left England; but the same writer gives a very cautious and accurate account of the manuscript in his *Handbook to the Textual Criticism of the New Testament* (2nd ed., 1912), pp. 100 f.

[4] There are over seventy citations from Acts in which Bede agrees with *E*, and in some readings Bede and *E* agree against all other witnesses. Cf. H. J. Vogels, *Handbuch der neutestamentlichen Textkritik* (Münster i. W., 1923), p. 52. But it is a curious fact that not a single correction or pen-trial is in the Anglo-Saxon script.

to England by Theodore of Tarsus, though there is no evidence for that.
Professor Ropes's suggestion that it was one of the books acquired in Italy
by Benedict Biscop or Ceolfrid has more historical foundation,[1] since there
is a record that books were brought back to England by both of these inveterate travellers.[2] The manuscript must have left England during the eighth
century, for the additions which were made to it are all in continental writing
(*14*) and some of them, like the Creed, go back to the eighth century.[3] Dr. Craster
has pointed out reasons for thinking that the manuscript first went to Italy
and was still there in the fourteenth century.[4] But the usual opinion is that it
went from England to Germany, having been taken thither by one of the
missionaries. It was in Germany that Archbishop Laud's agents, taking advantage of the turbulent conditions during the Thirty Years War, acquired
so many of the Latin manuscripts which he presented to Oxford.[5] As the
oldest of these came from Würzburg, the natural supposition is that our
manuscript of Acts also came from Würzburg, because such a manuscript,
for which there was no practical use, could have been preserved only in a

[1] J. H. Ropes, *The Text of Acts* (London: Macmillan, 1926), p. lxxxv (being vol. III of *The Beginnings of Christianity*, edited by Foakes-Jackson and Kirsopp Lake).

[2] The *Historia Abbatum Auctore Baeda* (ed. C. Plummer), p. 369, speaks of piles of books brought back by Benedict Biscop: *innumerabilem librorum omnis generis copiam adportauit.* In the same history (p. 379) we read of Ceolfrid: *bibliothecam utriusque monasterii, quam Benedictus abbas magna caepit instantia, ipse non minori geminauit industria; ita ut tres pandectes nouae translationis, ad unum uetustae translationis quem de Roma adtulerat, ipse super adiungeret*, etc. See also the *Historia Abbatum Auctore Anonymo* (ed. C. Plummer), p. 395.

[3] A 'probatio pennae' in ordinary minuscule, saec. IX, X, occurs on fol. 1^{r}, on fol. 2^{v}, top margin, and another by a different hand on fol. 10^{v}; on fols. 10^{v}, 11^{r}, 94^{v}, 144^{v}, occur interlinear transliterations of the Greek text. The Latin script seems of about the year 900. *Kaí* is reproduced by *κι*, which is noteworthy and may be of use in fixing the home of the manuscript in the tenth century. The pen-trials on fol. 226^{v} are of different dates: 'iacobus prsbr grecus' is in well-formed Caroline of the ninth century; ερρωcθε 'ualete' may be of the tenth; two other entries, partially erased, are of the same date. The ungainly insertion in the top margin of fol. 226^{v} 'beatus b.tus qui metuit' may be saec. VIII ex. The same hand made entries on fol. 227 verso and recto. The 18 lines of uncial which contain the Creed seem to me an eighth-century addition. The form of the letter **G** with the cauda turning up instead of down and the form of **X** recall French types. The text of the Creed is 'Old Roman' and not 'Textus Receptus'. Cf. A. E. Burn, 'Facsimiles of the Creeds from Early Manuscripts', *Henry Bradshaw Society* XXXVI (London, 1909), 2. See Pls. **28–30** (*pls. II, III*)

[4] Cf. *Bodleian Quarterly*, II (7 Nov. 1919), 290: 'The omission of **g** before **i** in "&dimoloiarũ (= etymologiarum)" in the note on fol. 2^{v} is characteristically Romance (cf. the Italian "loica" derived from "logica"). . . . A fourteenth-century note on fol. 224^{v} recording a lacuna in the text has more of an Italian than a German look.' See Pl. **29** (*pl. II*). It should be observed that the fourteenth-century entry consists of only four words ('Nota hic est defectus')—hardly enough for forming a definitive judgement—and that the scribe who omitted **g** before **i** in the pen-trial on fol. 2^{v} also wrote **td** for **t**. Perhaps carelessness pure and simple accounts both for the superfluous **d** and for the missing **g**.

[5] Cf. *Centralblatt für Bibliothekswesen*, XVI. 243.

centre which had a taste for very ancient manuscripts, and Würzburg was certainly such a centre, as one may judge from extant remains. Heretofore, the connection between Codex *E* and Germany in the eighth century has rested on mere assumption. But the manuscript itself contains actual evidence of its residence in Germany in that century. On fol. 226v there is a note, scratched in with a stylus, in the column to the right of the Creed, under the pen-trials *ϵρρωcθϵ* ualete . . . *ϵρρωσθϵ*. This note is written in clear round uncial characters of the eighth century.[1] If one holds up the parchment to the proper light one can read without difficulty MARIAE UIR[GINIS] / GAMUNDUM. If this *(15)* reading is correct, and I have not the slightest doubt that it is,[2] then Codex *E* must have been at St. Mary's of Gamundum when that note was written. Gamundum, Gamundium, Gamundiae can be no other than Hornbach, situated in the diocese of Metz.[3] About the year 727 Pirmin, the founder of Reichenau, also founded a monastery at Hornbach, and its church was dedicated to the Virgin.[4] He lived at Hornbach till his death, about 753, and there is a tradition that tells of a visit which St. Boniface paid him at Hornbach.[5] If Codex *E* ever came into the possession of St. Boniface it would not require a flight of the imagination to see how it got from Fulda to Würzburg, whose first bishop was Burchard, a disciple of Boniface.

Apart from the small kernel of fact contained in the note which connects

[1] Dr. Kirsopp Lake, in 1913, called my attention to the existence of a note written with a stylus. J. H. Ropes gives the credit for the discovery to E. W. B. Nicholson, but the latter acknowledges his own indebtedness to Dr. Lake (cf. *Summary Catalogue of Western MSS.*, etc., II [Oxford, 1922], 48). Nicholson does not say what the note contained but he describes the script as 'Latin majuscules' which 'might very well be written at Canterbury in the late 7th c.' According to Dr. Craster (cf. *Bodleian Quarterly*, II [1919], 289), the credit belongs to R. L. Poole.

[2] I am aware that Dr. Craster reads GAEMUNDUM. The letter E presumably is written in ligature, for there is no room for a full letter between A and M. But apart from the objection that in the eighth century on the Continent ligatures of AE are not found in the middle of a word (though they are found at the ends of lines, to save space, even in our oldest manuscripts), a careful inspection shows that what has been taken for a scratching with the stylus is in fact a little crease in the parchment. See Pl. **30** (*pl. III*).

[3] U. Chevalier, *Répertoire des Sources Historiques du Moyen-Âge, Topo-Bibliographie*, col. 1262, gives Hornbach as the only equivalent for Gamundiae, -um. All other places by that name are manifestly out of the question in this connection.

[4] 'Viro sancto arrisit prae caeteris locus, in confinio dioeceseon Trevirensis et Metensis, ob duorum confluxum rivulorum Gamundium sive Gamundiae, aliis *Hornbach* appellatus cuius amoenitate et opportunitate sic captus est Pirminius, ut requiem sibi perpetuam illic statuerit. Expurgato a sordidis venatorum usibus loco, monasterium insigne condidit cum aede sacra in honorem et memoriam beatissimae Virginis Mariae.' (Cf. *Gallia Christiana*, XIII, cols. 830E–831A).

[5] See the Life of St. Pirmin edited by Holder-Egger in *Monumenta Germaniae Historica, SS.* XV, pars i, p. 29.

the manuscript with Hornbach, most of the steps in the foregoing reconstruction, are, it must be admitted, conjectural. Yet I venture to think that this mixture of fact and surmise furnishes as probable a story of the wanderings of this curious manuscript as we can get at present; and it also satisfactorily accounts for the peculiar prominence given to a manuscript of Acts in an eighth-century catalogue of a library which to all appearances is the episcopal library of Würzburg.

More Facts about our Oldest Latin Manuscripts

(43) IN an article entitled 'Some Facts about our Oldest Latin Manuscripts', which appeared in this journal,[1] the present writer put together a group of forty-seven manuscripts which had this one feature in common, that each page or each column of a page they contained began with a large letter, regardless of whether that letter occurred in the middle of a sentence, or even in the middle of a word. It so happened that the list thus drawn up was composed almost entirely of very ancient manuscripts; indeed, it contained a very large proportion of the oldest manuscripts extant. In the circumstances it seemed useful to note down the behaviour of these manuscripts with respect to four other features—namely, the manner of indicating the omission of **m** and **n** at the end of lines, the use of running titles in the top margin, the size and arrangement of the written space, and the manner of signing quires.

The data furnished by the forty-seven manuscripts made possible observations under these several heads, and the drawing of certain conclusions—which, however, were necessarily incomplete and tentative, because the observations were based upon an examination of only part of our oldest manuscripts. In the tables which follow I propose to fill in the gap and set down an array of a further hundred-odd manuscripts comprising nearly all extant Latin manuscripts of the fifth and sixth centuries, well enough preserved to furnish me with the data to be investigated.

As to the arrangement of the tables: while in a general way the chronological order is followed, it seemed interesting, as before, to make a division between classical or non-Christian books and those which contain Biblical or patristic writings. In the first list of forty-seven manuscripts honours were about even between the two classes; but in the present list the growing tendency to neglect the classics becomes manifest. Out of 103 items only thirteen are classical or non-Christian. Again, in the class containing Christian works, I have not followed the strictly chronological order, preferring to put the Biblical manuscripts in a group, as also those of certain of the Church Fathers, in order to bring out at a glance whatever features, of size or material arrangement, they had in common. I have tried to be as chronological as I could.

From *The Classical Quarterly*, XXII (1928), 43–62.

[1] *Classical Quarterly*, XIX (1925), 197–208 [this volume pp. 187–202].

As most of these manuscripts are unfortunately undated, it may seem bold to claim that any arrangement could be chronological. In our present state of knowledge, or ignorance, judgements in the matter of dating must be to a large extent subjective. Yet objective criteria do exist—a fact which those

(*44*)

No.	Press-mark	Contents	Script	Date	Omitted m	Omitted n	Running titles
48	*St. Gall 1394 (pp. 7–49) +248 (pp. 196–212) +275	Virgil (Primary Script)	Square capitals	IV			Smaller square capitals
49	Vatic. 3867 (St. Denis)	Vergilius Romanus	Rustic capitals	IV/V	—		Smaller rustic
50	*Verona XL (38)	Virgil (Primary Script)	Rustic	IV/V	—		Smaller rustic (?)
51	*Milan, Ambr. G. 82 sup. (Bobbio)	Plautus (Primary Script)	Rustic	IV/V			Smaller rustic
52	Vatic. 3226	Terentius Bembinus	Rustic	IV/V	None	None	Full size red rustic
53	*Milan, Ambr. R. 57 sup. (Bobbio)	Cicero (Primary Script)	Rustic	V			Smaller rustic
54	Bamberg, Class. 35a	Livy, Fourth Decade (*Frag.*)	Uncial	V ex.	—	—	
55	**London, Add. 17212 (S. Maria Deipara, Nitrian Desert)	Licinianus (*Frag.*)	Uncial	V	—	—	Smaller uncia
56	Vatic. Urbin. 1154	Probus	Uncial	V ex.	−̣	—	
57	Paris 9643 (Lyons)	Codex Theod.	Uncial	VI^1	−̣	−̣	
58	Milan, Ambr. C. 105 inf. (Bobbio)	Hegesippus	Half-uncial	VI^1	−̣	—	Smaller half-uncial on F.S. only
59	Cassel, Theol. F. 65 (Fulda)	Hegesippus	Half-uncial	VI^2	—	—	Smaller half-uncial
60	*Milan, Ambr. E. 147 sup.+Vatic. 5750 (Bobbio)	Symmachus (Primary script)	Half-uncial	VI ex.	−̣†	−̣†	Smaller half-uncial
61	Vercelli, Cathedr. (Cod. Vercellensis)	Gospels (*a*) (antehieron.)	Uncial	IV (*circa* 371)	−̣	−̣ or —	Smaller uncial
62	Turin G. VII. 15 (Bobbio)	Gospels (*k*) (antehieron.)	Uncial	IV/V	—	—	Smaller uncial
63	Stuttgart (Const.–Weing. Fragm.)‡	Prophets (antehieron.)	Uncial	V	None§	None§	Smaller uncial

In the above table an asterisk (*) preceding a press-mark indicates that the manuscript is palimpsest, in whole or in part.

F.S. means on the flesh side of the leaf. H.S. means on the hair side of the leaf.

R. = red; Rt. = right; b.-ll. = bounding-lines.

† Teste O. Seeck.

‡ Complete press-marks: Stuttgart, Landesbibl. H.B. II. 20, 54; VII. 1, 8, 12, 25, 28, 29, 30, 39, 45; XI. 30; XIV. 14, 15+5 leaves and a strip in the Hofbibl.+Darmstadt 895, 896+Fulda Aa 1, 11, 13, 15, 24+St. Paul in Carinthia XXV. a/11 and a/16 (single leaves).

§ Teste P. Lehmann.

most conversant with the manuscripts themselves are readiest to admit—and if we are guided by the criteria furnished us by the few dated monuments[1] we cannot go very far astray. I venture to think that very few will disagree radically with the dates in these lists.

(45)

Quire marks	Measurements	No. of columns	No. of lines	Colophons	Nomina Sacra	Miscellaneous remarks	No.
	Circa **225×270**	1	19	Two lines of capitals		Very wide margins	48
	333×332 **240×250**	1	18	Rustic, occasional red		Red for first line of books	49
	260×205 **130×170**	1	13			Sloping **bd**– uncial marginalia	50
Small R. uncial letter F.S. (added later)	262×241 **175×175**	1	19	Rustic			51
Rom. num. H.S.	160×185 **113×132**	1	25	Rustic		Double bounding-lines ruled on F.S.	52
	275×255	3	24				53
	290×250 **197×205**	3	35			Wide margins	54
	235×172 **158×158**	2	24				55
Rom. num. F.S.	265×160 **155×105**	1	25	Uncial, alternate red lines		Single bounding-lines. Wide margins	56
Rom. num.	280×220 **215×195**	1	30	Chapter headings in rustic			57
Rom. num. on F.S.	298×245 **210×180**	2	25			Single bounding-lines	58
Rom. num. on F.S.	280×215 **238×173**	1	36	Rustic	b̄ = bus	Single bounding-lines. Ruling on H.S.	59
	Circa 295×255 **223×185**	1	28			Capitals begin page even in mid-word. Ruling on F.S.	60
Rom. num.	255×160 **170×105**	2	24	Uncial, alternate red lines	·dm̅s̅·, dn̅e̅ de̅i̅	Citations indented	61
Rom. num. H.S.	190×160 **135×120**	1	14	Uncial, whole page; lines: black, red, red, black	dōm̄ de̅i̅	Single b.-ll. Ruling both hair and flesh. Peculiar abbreviation of Nomina Sacra	62
Probably Rom. num.§	280×250 **173×185**	3	23	Uncial, alternate red lines	dm̅s̅, de̅i̅, de̅o̅	De luxe MS.: no abbreviation except Nomina Sacra. New books begin with R. lines	63

In the column marked 'Measurements' the figures are always given in the order length by width; those in ordinary type indicate page size, those in bold face type the written space; all measurements are in millimetres.

In the 'Quire marks' column the examples given are typical, and are taken from the manuscript for illustration.

[1] For a list of these, as well as for a description of the features characterizing our oldest manuscripts, see E. A. Lowe and E. K. Rand, *A Sixth-Century Fragment of the Letters of Pliny the Younger*, pp. 13–20 (Washington, 1922) [this volume, pp. 115–25].

No.	Press-mark	Contents	Script	Date	Omitted m	Omitted n	Running titles
64	*Würzburg M.p. th. f. 64a	Pentateuch and Proph. (antehieron.) (Primary Script)	Uncial	V	—	—	Smaller uncial
65	St. Gall 1394‖ (pp. 50–89)	Gospels (*n*) (antehieron.)	Uncial	V	—̣	—	Small uncial, chapter number in R. Greek letter
66	Berlin, Th. lat. fol. 485¶ + Quedlinburg frag.	Kings (*Frag.*)	Uncial	V	—̣		Smaller uncial
67	Cambridge, University Nn. II. 41 (Cod. Bezae)	Gospels and Acts (*d*) (antehieron.)	**bd**-Uncial	V	—	—	Smaller uncial
68	*St. Gall 912	Jeremiah (Primary Script)	Uncial	V	—	None	
69	*Munich 6225 (fols. 76–115) (Freising)	Pentateuch (antehieron.) (*Frag.*) (Primary Script)	Uncial	V ex.	—	—	?
70	Vatic. 7223 (Part I, fols. 1–66)	Matthew (*h*) (antehieron.)	Uncial	V ex.	—	—	Smaller uncial
71	St. Gall 1395†	Gospels	Half-uncial	V ex.	—		Smaller half-uncial
72	Paris 10439 (Chartres)	John (ch. I–VI = antehieron.)	Uncial	V ex.	— Often —̣	—̣	
73	*Autun 21 + Paris N.a.l. 1628 (fols. 5–14)	Gospels (Primary Script)	Uncial	V/VI	—	—	Smaller uncial
74	Sarezzano,§ now at Florence	Gospels (antehieron.) (*Frag.*)	Uncial	V/VI (*circa* 500)	—̣	—	Smaller uncial
75	Lyons 425 (351) + Paris N.a.l. 1585	Psalter	Uncial	V/VI	⊤	—̣	
76	Paris 11947 (St. Germain)	Psalterium Argenteum	Uncial	V/VI	—		

‖ + St. Gall 172 (pp. 257 f.) + Stadtbibl. Vad. 70 (fol. 278) + Chur 2 leaves.

¶ Teste Schultze.

Quire marks	Measure-ments	No. of columns	No. of lines	Colophons	Nomina Sacra	Miscellaneous remarks	No.
	275 × 227 **165 × 150**	2	25		$\overline{dms}$	Twelve-leaved quires. Very wide margins	64
Rom. num.	300 × 260 **215 × 195**	2	24	Uncial, very simple. No *Explicit* or *Incipit*	$\overline{dms}$· $\overline{dei}$	Single bounding-lines. Citations marked by > in left margin opposite each line	65
		2	26		·$\overline{dns}$· $\overline{deo}$	First three lines of first column of each page in R.	66
Gk. num. with stroke above on H.S.	260 × 220 **185 × 145**	1	33	Uncial; Matthew and John alternate lines red; Luke alternate words red	$\overline{dms}$ and $\overline{dns}$, $\overline{dei}$	Single b.-ll. Citations not specially indicated. First three lines of each book red	67 (47)
	Circa 200 × 200 **141 × 102**	1	15		$\overline{dmi}$	Capitals begin each page	68
	234 × 195	2	25–7	Big capitals, red and black	$\overline{dms}$ $\overline{deo}$ $\overline{stm}$	Columns begin with capitals. R. some lines in Exod., Levit., and Deut.	69
.$\overline{III}$. or VII F.S.	240 × 200 **185 × 145**	2	23	Uncial; alternate red lines	$\overline{dns}$	Single bounding-lines. Purplish ink for first line of new chapter preceded by number in rustic	70
Rom. num. F.S.	230 × 175 **155 × 140**	2	25	Uncial	$\overline{dni}$	Double bounding-lines	71
.XVI. F.S.	72 × 56 **47 × 34**	1	11		$\overline{dno}$	Single bounding-lines	72
Rom. num.‡	295 × 150	2	24	Rustic; red and black‡	$\overline{dns}$	Citations indented. First line of chapters R.‡	73
Rom. num.	300 × 250 **180 × 175**	2	16	Apparently none; but chapter headings marked in margin by Greek uncial letter with stroke above it	$\overline{dms}$	Writing between two ruled lines	74
Rom. num. F.S.	290 × 255 **205 × 205**	1	13		$\overline{dms}$ and $\overline{dns}$, $\overline{deus}$	Writing between two ruled lines. Double bounding-lines. Nomina Sacra in red	75
$\overline{uIII}$· F.S.	275 × 215 **200 × 180**	1	18		$\overline{dms}$ and $\overline{dns}$, $\overline{deus}$	Double bounding-lines. Gold for Nomina Sacra	76

† +St. Gall 414+Stadtbibl. 292+St. Paul in Carinthia XXV. d. 65+Zürich C 79b+Zürich, Staatsarchiv A.G. 19, No.II. ‡ Teste A. Royet. § Teste A. Amelli.

No.	Press-mark	Contents	Script	Date	Omitted m	Omitted n	Running titles
77	Verona VI (6) (Cod. Purpureus)	Gospels (antehieron.)	Uncial	V/VI	-̣	—	Smaller uncial
78	Verona IV (4) (fols. 3–5)	Wisdom	Half-uncial	V/VI	—		Smaller half-uncial
79	*Vienna 16 (Part II = fols. 42*, 43–56, 71–5) now Naples, Lat. 2 (Bobbio)	Acts (antehieron.), James, Peter (Primary Script)	Half-uncial	V/VI	—	—	None
80	Fulda, Bonif. 1 (Cod. Fuldensis)	Gospel Harmony and N.T.	Uncial	*ante* 546	-̣	None	Small rustic
81	London, Harley 1775	Gospels (*z*)	Uncial	VI	-̣	-̣	Small rustic, not on all pages
82	Orléans 19 (16) (fols. 11–18)	Ecclesiasticus, Song of Songs	Uncial	VI^{2}	-̣		
(48) 83	Vatic. 7223 (Part II = fols. 67–end)	Mark, Luke, John	Uncial	VI^{2}	-̣	-̣	Smaller uncial
84	Verona I (1)	Greek-Latin Psalter	Uncial	VI^{2}	-̣		
85	Milan, Ambr. C. 39 inf.	Gospels (*M*)	Uncial	VI^{2}	— -̣ —.	—	Smaller uncial
86	Verona IV (4) (frag. 1 = fols. 1–2)	Levit. XVI; Deut. XXX	Half-uncial	VI ex.	-̣		
87	Munich 6436† (Part 1) + Univ. 4° 928 + Göttweig (Freising)	Pauline Epistles	Uncial	VI ex.	— -̣ once	— probably	Exists, on F.S. only
88	Cambridge, C.C.C. 286§ (Canterbury)	Gospels (*X*)	Uncial	VI ex.	-̣	None	Smaller uncial
89	Orléans 19 (16) (fols. 19–25)‖	Prophets	Uncial	VI/VII	-̣	—	

† Teste A. De Bruyne.
§ Teste E. C. Hoskyns.

Quire marks	Measurements	No. of columns	No. of lines	Colophons	Nomina Sacra	Miscellaneous remarks	No.
No traces	270×230 **165×150**	2	18	Uncial	dm̄s, dn̄s, dēi	Writing between two ruled lines. Single bounding lines	77
	293×173 **230×120**	1	30		dn̄s	Written space very oblong	78
Rom. Num.	229×175 **170×125**	1	25 (or 24)	Uncial	dn̄s	d, s, r, occasionally uncial	79
Rom. num.	290×140 **190×80** very oblong	1	35	Rustic	dn̄s	Single bounding-lines. Citations marked by < in left margin opposite each line. Syllabification corrected to Greek, Anglo-Saxon marginalia	80
Rom. num. F.S.	*Circa* 180×120 **130×80**	1	25	Square capitals; alternate red lines	dn̄s s̄rh̄l	Citations marked by > in left margin opposite each line. Initial line or lines of new books R.	81
	(Reconstructed) *circa* **186×130**	2	30	Rustic		Ruling on hair side. Rubricated headings in Song of Songs	82
·III· or XXX q F.S.	240×200 **185×145**	2	23	Uncial		Single bounding-lines. Red: first line of chapter and first three lines of new books	83 (49)
÷ q· III ÷ F.S.	270×200 **210×140**	1	26	Uncial, but probably added later		Double bounding-lines. Greek written with Latin letters	84
XXX F.S.	275×170 **185×111**	1	25	Curious capitals, alternate red lines	dn̄s	Single bounding-lines	85
|XIII F.S.	356×290 **260×245**	1	32				86
Rom. num. above Greek num., e.g. III/Γ	260×175 **210×150**	1	32		dn̄i	Citations indented; and when one begins in mid-line < is put before first word (cf. Lyons 483). First three lines of epistles R.	87
Rom. num. preceded by 'Q' on F.S.	255×195 **184×130**	2	25	Rustic, alternate red lines		Double b.-ll. Ruling F.S.	88
	355×245 **285×220**	2	38			Double bounding-lines	89

|| +The Hague, Museum Meermanno-Westreenianum 10B 1, fols. 26–30, 31–2.

No.	Press-mark	Contents	Script	Date	Omitted m	Omitted n	Running titles
90	Würzburg M. p. th. q. 1a	St. Kilian's Gospels	Uncial	VI/VII	—		Smaller uncial
91	*Milan, Ambr. G. 82 sup. (Bobbio)	Kings (Secondary Script)	Half-uncial	VI/VII			
92	London, Add. 40165	Cyprian (*Frag.*)	Uncial	IV	—	—	Smaller uncial
93	Brescia, Quirin. H. VI. 11¶	Cyprian (*Frag.*)	Uncial	V	—̣ —	—̣ —	Smaller uncial
94	Turin F. IV. 27 +Milan D. 519 inf. (fly-leaves) +Vatic. 10959 (Bobbio)	Cyprian	Uncial	V	—	—	Smaller uncial
95	Turin G. V. 37 (Bobbio)	Cyprian	Uncial	V	—	—	Smaller uncial
96	Orléans 192 (169) (fol. 1) (Fleury)	Cyprian	Uncial	V	—		Smaller uncial
97	Bologna, Univ. 701 (509)	Lactantius	Uncial	V²	—	—	Smaller uncial
98	Orléans 192 (169) (fols. 40–1) (Fleury)	Lactantius	Uncial	V²	—	—	Smaller uncial
99	*Paris 13246 (fols. 296–300ᵛ)	Ambrose (Primary Script)	Half-uncial	V	—	—	
(50) 100	Paris 2630 (St. Denis)	Hilary	Uncial	V	—	—	Smaller uncial
101	Paris 152 (fols. 9–16) (Lyons)	Hilary	Uncial	V²	—	None	Smaller uncial
102	Verona XIV (12)	Hilary	Uncial	V ex.	—		Smaller uncial
103	Paris 8907 (Chartres)	Hilary, Ambrose, etc.	Uncial	V/VI	—	—	Smaller uncial
104	Lyons 452 (381) +Paris, N.al. 1593	Hilary	Uncial	V/VI	—	—	Smaller uncial
105	Vatic., Basilic. D. 182 (Cagliari)	Hilary	Half-uncial	VI in. (*ante* 509/10)	—	—	

¶ Teste G. Mercati.

Quire marks	Measurements	No. of columns	No. of lines	Colophons	Nomina Sacra	Miscellaneous remarks	No.
q̄ VII q XIII qū XIIII under Rt. col.	206 × 172 **150 × 125**	2	26	Mixed capitals; some red		Red used at beginning of chapters	90
	263 × 243 **165 × 170**	1	19	Uncial	dn̄s	Citations indented. Running foot rubric	91
	305 × 225 (Reconstructed) **220 × 200**	4	33		dm̄s	Single b.-ll.; wide margins. Citations in red, indented	92
	280 × 210 written space almost square	2	27		dm̄s and dōm	Single b.-ll. Titles indented. Chapters numbered at left in red Greek uncial	93
	275 × 230 **165 × 165**	2	23	Uncial, very simple	dm̄i	Single b.-ll.; ruled line cuts through letters. Very wide margins. Bright red at beginning of books	94
Rom. num. F.S.	200 × 165 **130 × 112**	2	20	Uncial, alternate red lines	dm̄s, deō	Double bounding-lines. Citations indented	95
	190 × 155	2	26		deō	African	96
Rom. num. F.S.	290 × 255 **230 × 200**	2	33	Uncial, whole page, alternate red lines	dn̄o, dei	Single bounding-lines. Citations indented	97
	270 × 200 **223 × 185**	2	32				98
	225 × 85††	1	*Circa* 30–32††		dn̄s	Citations indented	99
Rom. num. F.S.	Big 4° **200 × 183**	2	28	Uncial, alternate red lines	dn̄s, sc̄tm	Single b.-ll. pricking in centre for horizontal ruling. Citations indented. First line of new book red	100 (51)
None	272 × 230 **170 × 178**	2	23	Uncial	dn̄s	Ruling on hair side, single b.-ll. Citations indented	101
Rom. num. F.S.	310 × 275 **205 × 205**	2	21	Uncial, alternate red lines	dn̄s	Single bounding-lines. Citations indented. De luxe MS.	102
Rom. num. F.S.	350 × 260 **240 × 210**	2	32	Uncial, alternate red lines; alternate R. letters in *Feliciter*	dn̄m (dm̄s once)	Single b.-ll.; citations indented. Three red lines begin books	103
A, B, C, or ·q· XI, etc. F.S.	290 × 250 **220 × 202**	2	25	Uncial. Both *Finit* and *Explicit*	dn̄s	Double bounding-lines. Citations indented	104
q XXXIIII	270 × 205 **210 × 155**	1	30	Uncial and half-uncial			105

†† Teste A. Wilmart.

No.	Press-mark	Contents	Script	Date	Omitted m	Omitted n	Running titles
106	Vienna 2160* +St. Florian +Vatic. Barberini s.n.	Hilary	Half-uncial	VI	–̣	—	Smaller half-uncial
107	*St. Gall 722	Hilary	Half-uncial	VI	÷		Apparently none
108	Paris, N.a.l. 1592 (Tours)	Hilary	Uncial	VI ex.	–̣	—	Small rustic
109	Oxford, Bodleian Auct. T. II. 26	Eusebius-Jerome	Uncial	*post* 442	—	—	Column headings, small uncial
110	Paris 6400B† (Fleury)	Jerome	Uncial	V	—	—	None
111	Paris 2235	Jerome	Uncial	VI	–̣	—	
112	Bamberg B. IV. 21	Jerome, Augustine	Half-uncial	VI	–̣	None	Small uncial
113	Orléans 192 (169) (fols. 29–30) (Fleury?)	Pseudo-Jerome	Uncial	VI^2	–̣	None	
114	Orléans 192 (169) (fols. 21–7) (Fleury?)	Jerome	Uncial	VI/VII	–̣	—	
115	Verona XXII (20)	Jerome	Half-uncial	VI ex.	÷	— rare	Smaller half-uncial
116	Orléans 192 (169) (fols. 32–33) +Paris 13368 (fol. 256) +N.a.l. 2199 (fol. 1) (Fleury)	Augustine	Quarter-uncial	V	—	—	None
117	Orléans 192 (169) (fol. 38)	Augustine	Uncial	VI in.			
(52) 118	Rome, Vitt. Em. 2094 (Sessor. 13) (Nonantola)	Augustine	Uncial	VI	–̣	—	Smaller uncial
119	Lyons 478 (408)	Augustine	Uncial	VI	–̣	—	

† (Fols. 1–8, 285–90)+Leyden, Voss. Lat. 4° 110a (fols. 167–72)+Vatic. Regin. 1709A.

Quire marks	Measurements	No. of columns	No. of lines	Colophons	Nomina Sacra	Miscellaneous remarks	No.
q lIII	287 × 204 **210 × 130**	I	27–34, average 30	Half-uncial		Citations marked by > in left margin opposite each line	106
uII or XVI F.S.	255 × 162 **195 × 120**	I	27	Half-uncial. *Finit* and *Explicit*		Single bounding-lines	107
Uncial then minusc. letters	280 × 250 **180 × 175**	I	22	Rustic	dni	Single bounding-lines. First line of new book red	108
·uII· ·Δ·, etc. F.S.	325 × 185 **167 × 125**	Several	30		dns (dom once), isl, ilm	MS. required special ruling which is on H.S.; groove faces groove. tm (= tamen), t (= tur) in contemporary marginalia	109
Rom. num. F.S.	205 × 170 **150 × 145**	Several	26				110
Letter middle lower margin F.S.	Square 4° **208 × 170**	I	36	Square capitals (hand A), rustic (hand B), sometimes with alternate red lines	dni	Citations marked by > or — in left margin opposite each line. Here and there half-uncial letters	111
	290 × 210 **233 × 160**	I	34–5	Capitals and uncial	dns	Single bounding-lines	112
	213 × 130	I	27			Single bounding-lines	113
? = | = i H.S.	290 × 200 **260 × 190+**	I	35			Ruling on H.S.	114
XIIII or XX F.S.	222 × 197 **173 × 150**	I	25			Single bounding-lines	115
	258 × 156 **180 × 100**	I	23			Citations marked by > in left margin opposite each line. Interesting marginalia	116
	230 × 160+ **195 × 160+**	I	25				117
q XXVIII F.S.	330 × 225 **255 × 175**	I	32	Rustic, alternate lines red	Nom. Sac. regular. No other abbreviation	Single bounding-lines. Citations marked by ε or > > in left margin opposite each line. First three lines of books and first line of chapters red	118 (53)
In lower left corner of first page of each quire F.S.	260 × 215 **198 × 182**	I	28	Uncial; *Finit* for *Explicit*	dns	First two lines of new book in red	119

No.	Press-mark	Contents	Script	Date	Omitted m	Omitted n	Running titles
120	Paris 13367 (Corbie)	Augustine	Half-uncial	VI	—	—	None
121	*Rome, Vitt. Em. 2099 (Sessor. 55) (Nonantola)	Augustine (Secondary Script)	Half (½)-uncial	VI^{2}	—		
122	Turin G. V. 26 (Bobbio)	Augustine	Half-uncial	VI^{2}	—		
123	Milan, Ambr. G. 58 sup. (fols. 74–5) (Bobbio)	Augustine	Uncial	VI^{2}	-̣		
124	Vatic. Palat. 210	Augustine	Uncial	VI/VII	-̣		
125	Paris 12214 + Leningrad Q. v. I. 4 (Corbie)	Augustine	Half-uncial	VI/VII	Unc. g — ½ unc. g ÷	hand — hand None	Rustic on F.S. only
126	Paris 9533	Augustine	Half-uncial	VI/VII	∸	—	Cursive add., but probably contemporary
127	Würzburg M. p. th. q. 3	Priscillian	Uncial	V/VI	(Hand -̣ (Hand -̣	A) — B) -̣	
128	Vienna 847	Rufinus	Uncial	V/VI	—	—	Occasional title (see colophons)
129	Paris 8084 (fols. 1–155)	Prudentius	Rustic	VI (ante 527)	—		Smaller rustic
130	Ravenna s.n.§	Ambrose	Half-uncial	VI in.	∸	—	Small half-uncial on F.S. only
(54) 131	Verona XXXVIII (36)	Sulpicius Severus	Half-uncial	A.D. 517	÷ also ∸ —		Smaller half-uncial

† Possibly a later addition, but was doubtless originally there, too.

Quire marks	Measure-ments	No. of columns	No. of lines	Colophons	Nomina Sacra	Miscellaneous remarks	No.
Rom. num.+ abbrev. for *contuli* F.S.	245×195 **167×147**	1	25	Uncial and half-uncial; *Explicit* black, *Incipit* red	dni	Single bounding-lines. Citations usually indented, and always marked by ε in left margin opposite each line. First line of book in R.	120
q+Rom. num., then +unc. letters F.S.	280×200 **225×170**	1	43	Uncial, alternate lines red	dni	First line of books red	121
q ui or /q xiii F.S.	215×143 **175×110**	1	21–2	Uncial	n̊, n̊ (= nostro, -i), cf. Lyons 483	Single bounding-lines	122
	200×160	1	29	Uncial, alternate lines red			123
Rom. num. F.S.	240×180 **195×135**	1	33	Some in rustic		Citations from earlier work of St. Augustine in half-uncial	124
Rom. num. F.S.	260×220 **197×165**	2	29	Rustic and square capitals; *Explicit* and *Finit*	dni	Single bounding-lines. First line of new book in red uncial. Probably copied from uncial exemplar. Contemporary slanting uncial and half-uncial marginalia, with ancient abbreviations	125
None visible	260×175 **190×130**	1	26	Half-uncial, alternate red lines	dns b³ = *bus*	Single bounding-lines on F.S. Citations marked by εε in left margin opposite each line. Probably of Visigothic origin	126
Rom. num.† F.S.	215×157 **175×105**	1	21	Rustic or uncial; *Finit* for *Explicit*	dns and dms	Citations indented. Red for first three lines of books	127
: II : F.S.	192×172 **125×125**	1	14–15	None: rubrics and *Incipit* in top margin uncial		Writing between two ruled lines. First two lines of MS. and first line of new sections in red	128
q II F.S.	302×280‡ **205×185**	1	20			Double bounding-lines	129
(First part) q· xiii· (second part) letters	(Present size) 300×225 **205×175**	2	28	Bold half-uncial	dns	Ruling on H.S. Citations in smaller half-uncial and indented	130
q |||| xi |||| Right side, but 'q' almost in centre F.S.	255×220 **200×190**	1	20	Half-uncial, some red; *Finit* and *Explicit*		Ruling on F.S.	131 (55)

‡ Teste *Pal. Soc.*, ser. 1, pl. 29. § Teste G. Mercati.

No.	Press-mark	Contents	Script	Date	Omitted m	Omitted n	Running titles
132	*Autun 24 +Paris, N.a.l. 1629 (fols. 17–20)	Cassian (Secondary script)	Half-uncial	VI	—	—	None
133	Lyons 483 (413)	Origen	Half-uncial	VI	—	—	
134	Paris 12097 (Corbie)	Canons; Catalogue of Popes	Half-uncial	VI (537–55)	÷ also —		None
135	*Verona LV (53)	Didascalia Apost. (Primary Script)	Half-uncial	VI	−̣	—	
136	Florence, Laur. 65. 1	Orosius	Uncial	VI[1]	−̣	—	Smaller uncial
137	Paris 2769 (fols. 1–23) +4808 (fols. 53–65)	Eucherius; Cosmographia	Uncial	VI	−̣	None	
138	Vatic. 5704	Epiphanius	Uncial	VI[2]	—	—	None
139	Paris 10593	Basilius, Rufinus	Uncial	VI[2]	−̣	None	Rustic on first and last pages of quire only
140	Monte Cassino CL (346)	Ambrosiaster	Half-uncial	Ante A.D. 570	−̣	None	
141	Vatic. 3375†	Eugippius	Half-uncial	VI ex.	−̣		None
142	Milan, Ambr. H. 78 sup. +Turin G. V. 15 (Bobbio)	Ambrose	Half-uncial	VI ex.	—		None

† Teste E. Carusi.

Quire marks	Measurements	No. of columns	No. of lines	Colophons	Nomina Sacra	Miscellaneous remarks	No.
Rom. num. F.S.	241 × 151 **175 × 100**	1	21	Half-uncial			132
q xxxviiii F.S.	290 × 225 **200 × 160**	1	21	Half-uncial; *Finit* and *Explicit*	dms n̊ (cf. Turin G. V. 26) is = iesus	Single bounding-lines. ʒ at beginning and end of citation; ʒʒ if a second citation occurs on same page (cf. Munich 6436). Contemporary slanting mixed uncial and half-uncial marginalia	133
q IIII F.S.	280 × 210 **235 × 180**	1	33	None	dno, interesting abbrev.	Single bounding-lines. 'Islands' of uncial in the text	134
	255 × 155 **205 × 125**	1	35				135
Rom. num. F.S.	243 × 215 **175 × 160**	1	25	Square capitals, alternate red lines	scts	Capitals often begin a page, even in mid-sentence. Single bounding-lines. First line of new book in red. Marginal rubrics and sloping **bd-** uncial marginalia	136
None visible	245 × 180‡ **190 × 145**	1	31	Red rustic; occasional red rustic headings	dni	Single bounding-lines Ruling F.S.	137
q xxxuiiii right corner, but spread out F.S.	280 × 220 **250 × 160**	1	23	Uncial mixed with rustic, alternate red lines	dno	Single bounding-lines	138
/vi F.S.	260 × 180 **202 × 132**	1	28	Square caps, sometimes alternate lines red, sometimes all red	dni, N̊ (= non) Add. in uncial	Single bounding-lines. First line of books red. Rustic rubrics where running title should be. Interesting ancient abbreviation in marginalia	139
Rom. num.	299 × 215 **240 × 175**	1	30	'Argumentum' in rustic	dns	Citations indented and marked by ~ in left margin opposite each line. Has slanting uncial marginalia	140
Rom. num. F.S.	343 × 250 **240 × 190**	1	38–40	None		Some contemporary slanting uncial marginalia	141
q xxxi F.S.	242 × 203 **173 × 153**	1	23	Rustic; *Finit* for *Explicit*	dns	Single bounding-lines. Citations marked by ~ in left margin opposite each line. Many marginalia, with ancient abbreviations	142

‡ The page-size of Paris 4808 is 260 × 190.

No.	Press-mark	Contents	Script	Date	Omitted m	Omitted n	Running titles
143	Milan, Ambros. O. 210 sup. (fols. 1–46) (Bobbio)	Vigilius Tapsensis, etc.	Half-uncial	vi/vii	— —̣	—	None
(56) 144	Verona XXXVII (35)	Clement	Half-uncial	vi^2	—	None	A line ruled and traces visible; probably small half-uncial
145	Verona XXXIX (37)	Cassiodorus	Uncial	vi/vii	÷ — —̣	—	
146	Milan, Ambr. D. 36 sup. (Bobbio)	Prudentius	Uncial	vi/vii	—̣	—	Cut away, if any
147	Vercelli, Cathedr. 158	Clement	Uncial	vi/vii	—̣		Smaller uncial
148	Turin, Archivio di Stato J. b. II. 27 (Bobbio)	Lactantius, etc.	Uncial	vi/vii	—	—	
149	Vatic. Regin. 267 (fols. 1^v–98^v) (Fleury)	Fulgentius	Uncial	vi/vii	—	—	
150	Vatic. Regin. 267 (fols. 99–end) (Fleury)	Fulgentius	Half-uncial	vi/vii	—̣ —	None	

I. THE LARGE LETTER AT THE BEGINNING OF EACH PAGE

Before I remark upon the data contained in the above tables, I wish to make a few additions that have since come to my notice of other manuscripts which exhibit the feature of a large letter at the beginning of each page, and to point out the practical value it may have to an editor of an ancient text. Through the kindness of Professor F. C. Burkitt I am in a position to add St. Gall 912,[1] the Old-Latin version of Jeremiah (no. 68), and Munich 6225, an Old-Latin version of the Pentateuch (no. 69). With these two should be put Milan, Ambr. E. 147 sup., Symmachus, in half-uncial (no. 60). In these three manu-

[1] References to literature and to published facsimiles of most of the manuscripts mentioned in this article will be found in Traube's *Vorlesungen und Abhandlungen*, I. 161–261, and in *Miscellanea Ehrle*, XV. 34–61.

Quire marks	Measurements	No. of columns	No. of lines	Colophons	Nomina Sacra	Miscellaneous remarks	No.
Q̄ IIII	247×197 **205×165**	1	31–3	Ornamental rustic (not oldest type) or half-uncial	dn̄s		143
Rom. num., then letters F.S.	324×246 **200×180**	2	25	Half-uncial		Single bounding-lines	144 (57)
≡ q v toward Rt. F.S.	280×225 **215×175**	1	25	Big uncial, alternate red lines, pyramidal		Single bounding-lines	145
VIII ε F.S.	225×145 **185×110**	1	28	Mixed capitals		Double bounding-lines	146
XI	250×215 **200×170**	1	23	Uncial, alternate red lines	dn̄s	First three lines of books in red. Visigothic marginalia	147
q IIII F.S.	232×210 **205×185**	1	24	Uncial, red		Here and there capitals begin a page even in mid-sentence. Single b.-ll. First line or first few words of books in red	148
Rom. num. F.S.	270×190 **200×135**	1	23	Capitals (hardly rustic, perhaps square), alternate red lines		Many pages begin with capitals. Single bounding-lines. < < to left of citations	149
Rom. num. F.S.	270×190 *circa* **205×140**	1	33–4	Rustic, sometimes alternate red lines		Single bounding-lines	150

scripts the use of the capital letter at the beginning of the page is still a living practice. In the following manuscripts its presence is due either to inadvertence or to faithful copying from a much older exemplar: I refer to the Florence Orosius (no. 136) and the Turin Lactantius (no. 148), which show this feature here and there; to the Regina MS. of Fulgentius (no. 149), which has it frequently in the uncial section but not in the half-uncial; and to three other manuscripts not included in the list, since they are more recent than the year 600—namely, the famous Escorial manuscript of St. Augustine's *De baptismo* (uncial, saec. VII), which has it on many pages; the Paris MS. 12205 of the *Regulae monasticae*, etc., also in uncial of the seventh century, where it occurs only in certain quires (fols. 77–92^v and 143–57); and the Boulogne MS. 47 (42) of Jerome on Matthew, written in eighth-century pre-Caroline minuscule of a type used in northern France. I do not think there can be any other explanation of the presence of the large letter in the Boulogne St. Jerome. One of the scribes faithfully reproduced his original page by page,[1] as is shown by the fact that some pages are overcrowded,[2] while on others he plainly spread out as he came to the end.[3] A corrector carefully cancelled[4] or erased[5] the meaningless capital at the beginning of a page and put a smaller one in its place. This manuscript, therefore, is as good—if it be a correct copy—as the fifth- or sixth-century exemplar from which it was copied.[6] It is not likely that there existed a middle member with this curious feature. Any manuscripts, therefore, in which capital letters rise up unexpectedly in the text doubtless go back to a very old archetype in which this feature was normal, and their value as witnesses must be assessed accordingly.

II. OMISSION OF **m** AND **n** AT END OF LINE

The practice of omitting **m** at the end of a line to save space is not indigenous in Latin manuscripts, but is an importation of a Greek custom which goes back to pre-Christian times.[7] There is no sign of the practice in the oldest Latin papyri fragments that have come down to us. The earliest dated Latin example is furnished by an inscription of the time of Pope Damasus (366–84) engraved by Philocalus, scribe and stone-cutter. What we find in this inscription doubtless reflects the usage of his scriptorium. Traube suggested that the
(58) custom was introduced into Latin centres in the course of translating Scripture from Greek into Latin, which seems a reasonable hypothesis.[7]

When a Greek scribe came to the end of a line and had to write the letter N to finish the word or syllable, he made use of the device of indicating that letter by a horizontal stroke instead, in order not to go beyond the written space. In Latin, however, the analogous letter is not N but **M**. This explains why the Latin practice is apparently at first confined to the **m**, the omission of **n** being a later extension.[8]

The data furnished in our present list bear out in a general way the observations made on the first forty-seven manuscripts. An examination of these additional hundred-odd manuscripts makes it perfectly clear that the oldest

[1] He wrote fols. 1–67^{v}.

[2] E.g. fol. 21^{v}.

[3] Fols. 26, 30, 51 *et passim*.

[4] E.g. fols. 26^{v}, 30^{v}, 51^{v}, etc.

[5] Fols. 5^{v}, 6^{v}, 12, 14^{v}, etc.

[6] C. H. Turner used this manuscript for the purpose of comparing it with the Worcester leaves in eighth-century uncial. Cf. *Early Worcester MSS.*, p. xv (Oxford, 1916).

[7] L. Traube, *Nomina Sacra*, p. 241.

[8] Traube, *Hieronymi Chronicorum Codicis Floriacensis Fragmenta*, p. vii (Leyden, 1902); published in *Codices Graeci et Latini photographice depicti*, Suppl. I.

way of marking the omission of **m** or **n** is by the simple stroke. Yet it cannot be denied that the use of a stroke with a point beneath it is also of very great antiquity, since it is found in such manuscripts as the Codex Vercellensis (no. 61) and the Brescia Cyprian (no. 93). It thus unfortunately becomes useless as a dating criterion. Another fact which emerges with some definiteness is that the habit of making the distinction between **m** and **n** grows more frequent the nearer we approach the year 600. The earliest instances of the distinction are furnished by the Vatican Virgil in square capitals and the Palatine Livy (nos. 1 and 10 of our first list). The practice may be expressed statistically thus: Out of seventy-two manuscripts from the fourth to the end of the fifth century only nine make the distinction, whereas out of forty-four manuscripts of the sixth century twenty-one make the distinction. In the earlier manuscripts, one in every eight, roughly speaking, may be said to make the distinction; in the later, it is one in every two. A few manuscripts are in a class by themselves as regards their manner of distinguishing **m** from **n**. In the Codex Fuldensis (no. 80) we find two consecutive dots under the stroke for **m** and a mere stroke for **n**. In the Lyons Psalter, however, **m** is indicated by the horizontal stroke over two dots underneath each other, the **n** by a stroke over a single dot. Of the peculiar style employed in the Würzburg Jerome (no. 40) mention was made in the previous article. Our table shows cases in which different forms of the **m**-stroke occur in different parts of the manuscript. Thus in Milan, Ambr. C. 39 inf. (no. 85) three varieties of the stroke occur: the ordinary horizontal line, the stroke over a dot, and the stroke to the left of a dot. In Verona XXXVIII (36) (no. 131) of the year 517 we find ÷ ∸ —, and ÷ ⨪ — in Verona XXXIX (no. 145). Two modes of indicating omitted **m** deserve special attention: (1) the use of a line surmounted by a point for **m**, a usage which was destined to become characteristic of Visigothic manuscripts—this is found once in the Pauline Epistles, Munich 6436 (no. 87) which has other Spanish symptoms, in the Verona Sulpicius Severus (no. 131) of the year 517, in the Ravenna Ambrose (no. 130) also in sixth-century half-uncial, and in the Paris MS. 9533 of Augustine (no. 126) which has unmistakable Visigothic features; (2) the other is the use of a sign like our division sign (÷)—this is found in the Verona MSS. XXXVIII, XXII, and XXXIX (nos. 131, 115, 145), in the Paris MSS. 12097 and 12214 (nos. 134 and 125), both apparently of French origin, and in St. Gall 722 (no. 107) of Hilary (all of these six manuscripts being of the sixth century). Nearly all manuscripts mark the omission of **n** by the single stroke. In a few, however, the stroke above a dot is found, the oldest example being the Codex Vercellensis (no. 61). Many scribes carefully avoid the omission of **n** and prefer to insert it outside the space allotted for text even though they make regular use of the **m**-stroke. On the whole, it must be admitted that the practice with regard to **m** and **n** omission signs has proven less helpful as a dating criterion than had been anticipated.

(59) III. RUNNING TITLES

The observations made under this head in the previous article (pp. 206–7) are born out by the manuscripts in the present list. Running titles are found even in the oldest items; and Dziatzko's dictum remains untenable—that is, the absence of running titles cannot be used as a criterion of antiquity. What remains abundantly clear is that the use of a different type of script for the running title from that used in the text is first noticeable in manuscripts of the end of the fifth or the beginning of the sixth century (nos. 18, 19, 29, 80, 81). As corroborative evidence this fact should be useful in arriving at the date of a manuscript, since it furnishes a *terminus a quo*. The earliest five manuscripts showing a different type of script in their titles are all written in uncial, the titles being in small rustic—that is, in a type which already counted as an ancient script. Similarly, the half-uncial Jerome of the sixth century at Bamberg (no. 112) had its running titles in the older script, namely uncial. In a few manuscripts one observes the interesting custom of placing the running titles on the flesh side of the leaves only (nos. 58, 87, 125, 130). An explanation of this custom which suggests itself is that the running titles were entered as soon as the sheets were ruled, which, as far as my present data indicate, was normally done on the flesh side.

IV. SIZE AND DISPOSITION OF PAGE

In the former list of forty-seven manuscripts six had a written space which is perfectly square, and in the present there are seven. All of these manuscripts are earlier than the sixth century, thus confirming the impression gained from the previous list that the oldest manuscripts preferred the square format. Of manuscripts having a written surface which is *nearly* square—that is, with less than an inch difference between height and width—the present list has twenty-four, so that one out of every four manuscripts is almost square. In the former list of forty-odd manuscripts prior to the year 600, eighteen such items are found. Two manuscripts have a format which is distinctly oblong—namely, the Codex Fuldensis and the Verona fragment of the Book of Wisdom (nos. 80 and 78).

In the matter of dividing his writing space the earlier scribe may be said to show a preference for two columns. Barring poetry, most of our books that go back to the fifth century are in two columns. Manuscripts with more than two columns are rare. The Cyprian fragments in the British Museum have actually four columns. Three manuscripts in our list have three columns to the page; two of these are classical—the Cicero in rustic capitals from Bobbio (no. 53) and the Bamberg fragment of Livy (no. 54), and one is Biblical—the Constance-Weingarten fragments of the Prophets (no. 63). Our earliest copies of the Gospels are nearly always written in two columns. This is not the case with the other books of the Bible, which are very often in long lines.

As to the number of lines on a page, the smallest found in our table is eleven (no. 72); two manuscripts show thirteen (nos. 50 and 75). The largest number is forty-three (no. 121). The great majority (namely, fifty-nine) of the manuscripts show a preference for the twenties. The favourite number, to judge by our list, was twenty-five, found in fourteen manuscripts out of the fifty-nine. To base any generalizations on the above data would be hazardous.

V. QUIRE SIGNATURES

Here too, the additional evidence furnished by our 103 manuscripts only goes to support the earlier observations. The ancient custom manifestly is to place the quire mark in the extreme right-hand corner of the lower margin of the last page. It is not till we get to the seventh and eighth centuries that *(60)*
the tendency to move the quire mark toward the centre appears, though exceptions occur—for instance, Paris 2235 (no. 111) has it in the middle. This is also the case in the still older manuscript (not included in our list) of the Codex Carolinus of the Pauline Epistles in Gothic and Latin (Wolfenbüttel, Weiss. 64). For some unknown reason Lyons 478 (no. 119) has the quire marks on the left-hand corner of the first page, in which respect it resembles the Florentine Digests, to which attention was called in the first list (no. 25). Normally the quire signature consists of a Roman numeral, often under a gamma-shaped bracket. In many manuscripts the numeral is preceded by **q** (signifying 'quaternio'), variously abbreviated. Although the use of Roman numerals continues to be the normal practice, the use of letters is found from the end of the fifth century onward (examples are furnished by no. 36 of the first list, and by nos. 104, 108, 111, 121, 130, 144 of the present list). A few manuscripts show peculiar features. In the Bodleian Jerome (no. 109) the first quires are marked with Roman numerals, the subsequent ones with Greek; in the Pauline Epistles from Freising (no. 87) we find the odd practice

of placing the Roman numeral above the Greek; in the extant leaves of the Codex Carolinus (mentioned above) the form of the letter E signing the quire is Gothic, not Latin; in the Codex Bezae (no. 67) Greek numerals alone are used, but they are placed, it should be noted, in the lower right-hand corner of the last page of the quire, which is normal in Latin but not in Greek manuscripts. In one sixth-century manuscript of our list (no. 120) the quire mark is followed by the reversed letter **c** = con(tuli).[1]

VI. COLOPHONS

The first fact that strikes one in scanning our list is that in our oldest manuscripts the style of the colophon is very simple, with few or no ornamental features. The second fact is that the letters used, though generally of a larger size, are of the same script as the main text. During the first half of the sixth century the new practice comes in of using a more ancient type of script for the colophon than was used in the text. Perhaps the earliest dated example is the Basilican Hilary of the year 509–10, which has in its colophon both uncial and half-uncial lines. The Codex Fuldensis (no. 80), written before 546 in uncial, uses rustic letters for the colophon; the Codex Harleianus (no. 81) of the same age, also in uncial, uses square capitals for its colophons. The contemporary Bamberg Jerome (no. 112) has capitals and uncials in the colophons.

In our oldest manuscripts the words 'Explicit' and 'Incipit' are not used at all. It will be seen from our table that in a number of manuscripts the word 'Finit' is used instead of 'Explicit', a practice which may throw some light on the history of the text. Statistics on this point have been given by Professor Lindsay.[2]

As regards the ornamental side of the colophon, a device which early became popular with scribes was the use of red in alternate lines or in alternate words, as well as in alternate strands of the rope-like pattern often enclosing the colophon. This practice goes back to very ancient times: it is found, for example, in the Codex Bezae (no. 67) and in the Constance-Weingarten fragments (no. 63).

VII. NOMINA SACRA

In the column marked 'Nomina Sacra' I have noted chiefly the data for 'dominus', since there was a clear development in the manner of abbreviating

[1] The word 'contuli' occurs in some other manuscripts at the ends of quires. It is generally written out; occasionally it occurs in Tironian symbols.

[2] W. M. Lindsay, *Palaeographia Latina*, II (1923), 5–10.

this word, which renders it an important dating criterion. Where I fail to (*61*) indicate how 'dominus' was abbreviated it may be taken for granted that the form used was $\overline{\mathbf{dns}}$, $\overline{\mathbf{dni}}$, etc. The unabbreviated form of 'deus', surmounted by a stroke to call attention to the sacred word, is a feature found only in our oldest Biblical and Patristic manuscripts, and thus seemed worth tabulating in this column. Here and there a few other interesting 'Nomina Sacra' have been included without the least attempt at giving the various forms of that word found in the manuscript. In my first list of forty-seven manuscripts no data were given under this head. To fill the gap the reader is referred to Traube's *Nomina Sacra*, pp. 178–85.

VIII. CITATIONS

With few exceptions the method of marking a citation in manuscripts of the fourth and fifth centuries is by indentation, which varies in width from one to three letters. The exceptions are the Fragmenta Sangallensia (codex *n*) of the Gospels (no. 65), the Würzburg Jerome (no. 40), and the St. Augustine in quarter-uncial from Fleury (no. 116), in which citations are indicated by a small mark placed in the margin at the left of each line. This is the method usually adopted by scribes of the sixth century and later. It is interesting to note that in the Codex Claromontanus, the Graeco-Latin manuscript of the Pauline Epistles (no. 33), the rule is to mark citation by indentation, except in the Epistle to the Hebrews, which differs from the rest of the manuscript in more than one respect (cf. former article, p. 197). Scribes employed various means to call attention to a citation. In the London fourth-century Cyprian (no. 92) the cited passages are in red; in the uncial manuscript of St. Augustine, Vatic. Palat. 210 (no. 124), citations are in half-uncial; in the Ravenna Ambrose (no. 130), written in half-uncial, they are in a smaller type of half-uncial. A few manuscripts use two methods at once—namely, indentation and quotation marks—e.g. Paris 13367 (no. 120) and Monte Cassino CL (no. 140), both of the sixth century. An entirely different style is found in Lyons 483 of Origen (no. 133)—a manuscript remarkable for other peculiar features—where the citations are set off as in modern times by marks before and after the quotation. These are usually single, but if a second citation occurs on the same page it has double quotation marks. In Munich 6436, the Pauline Epistles, probably of Spanish origin (no. 87), indentation is used; but if the citation begins in the body of a line a single quotation mark is placed immediately before its first word.

IX. RULING

The matter of how sheets were ruled and how many were ruled at a time clearly deserves more attention than it has yet received. How useful minutiae of this sort may become as aids in dating manuscripts, especially manuscripts from a single school, has lately been demonstrated by Professor Rand.[1] It is also not unlikely that a careful study of the methods followed in different scriptoriums may furnish new and unsuspected touchstones for localizing manuscripts. Unfortunately my data on the subject of ruling are incomplete; but such facts as I have show that in practically all our oldest manuscripts the outside pages of each quire (that is, fol. 1^r and fol. 8^v of the normal gathering) received the direct impression of the stylus, and that these outside pages were the flesh side of the skin (see column marked 'Quire marks)'. In a number of very ancient manuscripts, however, the ruling is on the hair side. They are the Codex Bobiensis (no. 62), *k* of the Gospels, of supposedly African origin; the Codex Bezae (no. 67), *d* of the Gospels and Acts, whose palaeography is as eccentric as its text; the Ravenna Ambrose (no. 130) in which other appar-
(62) ently un-Italian characteristics are noticeable; the Paris Hilary from Lyons (no. 101), probably a local product; and the Orléans fragments of Ecclesiasticus and of Jerome (nos. 82 and 114), which may also come from some centre situated outside the main current.

To insure greater regularity in the size of letters, a few manuscripts, manifestly copies *de luxe*, have ruling for the headline as well as for the baseline. They are the Sarezzano and Verona purple Gospels, the Lyons Psalter, and the Vienna Rufinus (nos. 74, 77, 75, 128). This feature, it may be mentioned in passing, is found in the famous illuminated Greek Codex Purpureus, the Vienna Genesis. Another fact which emerges is that the vertical bounding-lines which confine the written space were, in our oldest manuscripts, single lines. The use of double bounding-lines seems to be a later practice.

The foregoing observations, brief as they are, may fairly be said to corroborate the tentative conclusions reached in the former paper. I do not flatter myself that anything startlingly new has emerged from the facts presented; certainly no dating criteria have been established capable of mechanical application. Yet the two articles will have been written to some purpose if any useful hints have been thrown out here and there, and if the data collected and set down in tabular form will make it easier for scholars to discern what some of the facts about our oldest Latin manuscripts really are.

[1] *Palaeographia Latina*, v (1927), 52–77.

Codex Bezae: The Date of Corrector G

In Scrivener's painstaking and very useful introduction, the activity of the (32)
corrector whom he calls *G* is assigned to the eleventh century.[1] If this is not a mere clerical error it is one of the most curious palaeographical lapses on record. Eor the correct date is fully five centuries earlier. Sanday, Burkitt, and Kenyon long ago called attention to the untenability of Scrivener's date. If he were right, then the value of a very large number of corrections would be of minor significance. If the date suggested by modern palaeographers be right, then these corrections win greatly in importance. It is perhaps, therefore, of some use to state the grounds for the date nowadays accepted. According to Scrivener's observation, the work of corrector *G* is found in 283 places, his activity being confined chiefly to the Latin side. Most of his corrections consist of a letter or two, or a word here and there. Fortunately, however, one of his additions is the insertion of two omitted lines, on both the Greek and Latin sides (fols. 59b and 60a; Matt. 18 : 18).[2] It is these two lines which furnish the main material for forming an idea of his date. Experts on Greek manuscripts are agreed upon the great antiquity of the two lines of Greek script. Professor A. S. Hunt saw no reason for dating it later than the fifth century. M. Seymour de Ricci was inclined to make it older still. Sir Frederick Kenyon did not regard it as more recent than the seventh century. Inasmuch as one hand wrote the Latin and the Greek, the Latin forms help us to test the validity of the opinions entertained regarding the Greek. Several letters on the Latin side stamp the script at once as still belonging to imperial times. If we compare this semi-cursive script with Ravenna charters of the sixth century it is at once manifest that our two lines represent a script of an earlier period. The ancient-looking letters which strike the eye are the cup-
shaped **u**; the uncial **g** whose first stroke coincides with the head-line; the **r** (33)
with the first two strokes resembling Greek *gamma*, and the last stroke shaped like the first half of letter **u**.[2] The latest manuscript in which such an **r** is still found is perhaps the Florentine Digest of the sixth century, but that manuscript does not contain the ancient shape of **u** and **g** found in our two

From *Bulletin of the Bezan Club*, v (1928), 32–3.

[1] *Bezae Codex Cantabrigiensis*, p. xxvi (Cambridge, 1864). [See Pls. **61b** and **63a** (Vol. II).]

lines. We must go back to the well-known fourth century papyrus letter from Egypt,[1] preserved at Strassburg, to find a similar **u** and **g**. Moreover, the whole *ductus* of the two Latin lines is in keeping with the ancient appearance of the few characters I have singled out. It would seem reasonable then to assign hand *G*, roughly, to a period between 500 and 550. This approximate date is probably as close to the truth as it is possible for us to get on the basis of the extant material with which we can compare this hand.

The hand that wrote these two lines also added the reading 'facit eam moechari' on fol. 14a (Matt. 5 : 32), supplied the omission 'harundinem quassatam' on fol. 37a (Matt. 12 : 20)—which omission is also supplied on the Greek side—and added (*inter alia multa*) the following other corrections:

'intelleximus'	on fol. 46a (Matt. 13 : 51)
'coinquinant'	on fol. 51a (Matt. 15 : 18, 19)
'uiuentis'	on fol. 54a (Matt. 16 : 16)
'meus'	on fol. 54a (Matt. 16 : 17)
'facit aut prae[stat]'	on fol. 58a (Matt. 17 : 24)
'per'	on fol. 63a (Matt. 19 : 8)
'causa'	on fol. 63a (Matt. 19 : 9)

The hand that wrote these marginal additions, which I have selected only from the beginning of the manuscript, is the same hand that wrote the reading 'uox', as Scrivener correctly observed, in the margin of fol. 419a (Acts 2 : 2), as a variant of 'echo', which variant, I understand, is of considerable interest to the textual critic.

[1] Cf. F. Steffens, *Lateinische Paläographie*², pl. 13.

Regula S. Benedicti: Specimina Selecta e Codice Antiquissimo Oxoniensi (7)

[INTRODUCTION]

THE Rule of St. Benedict has come down to us in two recensions. Their true relation to each other was first taught us by Traube. In a memorable treatise dealing with the history of the manuscript tradition of the Rule[1]—a model of what such studies should be—he proved conclusively that one recension gave us the author's own words and that the other was a revised and interpolated text. The St. Gall MS. 914 is the chief representative of the first class: it is the faithful copy made by two Reichenau monks for their teacher from the model copy of the Rule made at Charlemagne's request in 787 from the very book written by St. Benedict.[2] The Bodleian MS. Hatton 48 is the chief representative of the revised and interpolated text, that is, of the *textus receptus*, which was current in the West up to the ninth century. It not only holds the place of seniority in this class, but is, in fact, the oldest copy of the Rule now in existence. For that reason alone it merits special study. It also happens to be the only manuscript of the Rule written in uncial characters. The fact that these uncial characters were penned in England, where uncials were not common, renders the Hatton manuscript of peculiar interest both to the historian and to the palaeographer. The former will see in the manuscript another witness to the continuation of the influence of the Roman mission in England; the palaeographer will find in it confirmation of the fact that English scribes evinced great aptitude for penmanship from the earliest times and learnt to use the traditional Italian scripts as expertly as they used the script taught them by their nearer masters from Ireland—the type out of which grew their national scripts.

Size, composition, etc.

The manuscript consists of fols. 76+i, measuring 305 mm.×215 mm.,

From the facsimile edition (Oxford, Clarendon Press, 1929), pp. 7–15. [See Pls. **31** to **36**.]

[1] L. Traube, *Textgeschichte der Regula S. Benedicti*, 1st ed., 1898: 2nd ed. by H. Plenkers, 1910; published in the *Abhandlungen* of the Bavarian Academy.

[2] This text was printed by the monks of Monte Cassino in *Regulae Sancti Benedicti traditio codicum mss. casinensium a praestantissimo teste usque repetita codice sangallensi 914 nunc primum omnibus numeris expresso*, etc. (Monte Cassino, 1900).

about $12\times 8\frac{1}{2}$ in., with a written space of 210×155–60 mm., $8\frac{3}{8}\times 6\frac{1}{8}$ in., arranged in two columns of 22 lines between single bounding-lines and ruled with a hard point two folios at a time after the quire had been formed (i.e. direct impression of the stylus on fols. 1^r, 3^r, 5^r, 7^r). Occasionally a bifolium was ruled before it was placed in its gathering. Pinpricks guided the lineation, the outside bounding lines running along these pinpricks; the inside bounding lines were guided by two pinpricks at the top and bottom respectively. The hair-side is on the outside of the quire. Except when cancels occur in a gathering, flesh-side faces flesh and hair-side hair. The quires are of eight leaves, except the last, which is composed of six. Cancels occur between fols. 1–2, 5–6, 11–12, 14–15, 49–50, 54–5, 66–7, 69–70; two leaves have been cut away at the end of the manuscript, making the last quire appear a binio instead of a ternio, which it really was. Quires, except the first, are everywhere signed by means of **q** under the first column followed by the number of the quire under the second column of writing, as in our Pl. **32** (*pl. II*); the arrangement is reversed in the first quire. Both the **q** and the Roman numeral are adorned with a set of three parallel graded lines above and below; the uncial
(*8*) form of **q** is used everywhere except in the eighth quire, where it is a capital. Parchment is stiffish and not of fine quality; it has not that suède-like feel which one finds in many English and Irish manuscripts. It has been thoroughly scraped on both sides, so that often it is difficult to tell flesh- from hair-side; and the skin, unfortunately, shows the writing through. The first five lines of fol. 1^v, col. 2, were left blank because the two lines in red on col. 1 of fol. 1^r showed through. The ink is of an excellent black colour with a tinge of brown where it is worn or has run. The red used for chapter-headings is vermilion, which is tarnished in many places. Imperfect parts of the skin were used, imperfections occurring not only at the edge but in the very middle of a column (e.g. fols. 41 and 63). The binding of boards covered with white leather is probably of the twelfth century; the back is modern, but a portion of the old back has been laid down inside the front cover.

Writing

The whole manuscript is the work of an expert scribe who used a broad pen for the text and a finer pen for the chapter-headings and most of the corrections. Though beautifully written, his uncial characters are not of the ancient type.[1] The very heavy down-strokes, the artificial bow of **A**, the

[1] The characteristics of this type are enumerated in E. A. Lowe and E. K. Rand, *A Sixth-Century Fragment of the Letters of Pliny the Younger*, pp. 19 f. (Washington, 1922) [this volume, p. 123 f].

angular finish to the tail of **G** are clear marks of the latest stage of uncials. The scribe's natural script was doubtless the Anglo-Saxon, two lines of which have somehow crept in, and are to be seen in the title of chapter xxxiii (the plate reproduced by Traube). As imitation uncial it deserves the highest praise. The scribe has caught something of the ancient, orderly succession of letters, where each occupies its allotted place on the line. There is a massive dignity and solidity in the characters which he uses, and the work is so well done that one gains the conviction that many other manuscripts in uncial characters must have issued from the same school. **A** has two forms; the upper bow of **B** is beautifully small, as in very ancient uncials; **C, E, F, G, L, N, S, T, X** have the characteristic triangular-shaped finish to one or more strokes. The letters with curved bows are generously rounded. The scribe employs ligatures, but only at the ends of lines, thereby showing his understanding of what is fitting in uncial writing. The most frequent are **AE, NT, UNT, UI, NI, OR, ON, UT, UL, UE, US** (the **S** having the half-uncial form); the less frequent, **OS, UB, UR, NS, UF, UP, RE**; the least, **NC** and **NE**, not found in ancient uncial manuscripts. Letters **S** and **T** rise above their fellows, but only at the ends of lines. The half-uncial form of **S** occurs here and there at line-ends. In the red chapter-headings two forms of **A** and two forms of **G** occur, and two forms of **Q** in the quire-marks.

Punctuation

The system of punctuation is very simple. It consists of a medial point which is used for the full-stop as well as for shorter pauses. The scribe may have copied from an exemplar divided in cola and commata. Citations from the Bible are not distinguished in any way. The form of the medial point is
triangular, which is in keeping with the style of writing. It is, in fact, identical (9)
with the ends of certain strokes of **E, F, G, L, S, T**. Pairs of **s**-like flourishes occur occasionally at the end of a chapter, and almost regularly after chapter-headings.

Abbreviations

The scribe's knowledge of abbreviation is probably greater than is displayed in the manuscript, for every now and then, when crowded at the end of a line, he surprises one by dropping into compendia which are unusual in an uncial manuscript. Being a good scribe, he has a sense of what is fitting and therefore avoids these forms in the body of his text. Here the only forms he permits himself are the well-known Nomina Sacra 'Dominus', 'Deus', 'Christus',

Spiritus Sanctus'. He does not once abbreviate 'noster'; and 'Israel' is also written out. Even such forms as '-bus' and '-que', sanctioned by the earliest traditions, he abbreviates only at line-ends, using a semicolon run together in the shape of a 3 to indicate the suspension. The omission of **M** is relegated strictly to the line-end or the syllable near the line-end. Found elsewhere it is the work of the corrector. The omission of final **N** is avoided; where it occurs at the end of the line past the space allotted to writing, it is crowded in as best may be. Apart from the Nomina Sacra and final **M**, the abbreviations encountered, and that only at the end of lines, are the following (here given in the order of their frequency):

$\overline{\textbf{qd}}$ = quod (fols. 8, 10^{v}, 12, 14^{v}, 40, 47^{v}, 53, 58, 59^{v}, 61^{v}, 64, 71^{v}).
$\bar{\textbf{p}}$ = prae (fols. 4, 18, 21^{v}, 68^{v}, 71).
ꝓ = pro (fols. 37^{v}, 38^{v}, 45^{v}, 54^{v}, 56^{v}).
p' = per (fols. 49^{v}, 55, 61^{v}, 70^{v}).
$\bar{\textbf{u}}$ = uel (fols. 23, 48, 51^{v}).
$\bar{\textbf{n}}$ = non (fol. 34^{v}).
$\bar{\textbf{s}}$ = sunt (fol. 30).
$\overline{\textbf{frs}}$ = fratres (fol. 38^{v}, by the rubricator).

All of these are abbreviations of some antiquity, but they would hardly be found in a non-technical Italian uncial manuscript of this period. The scribe's nationality is betrayed by one of the abbreviations—the curious 'per'-symbol seen in our Pl. 35B (*pl. V.* 2). The first corrector, who, as we shall see, is no other than the scribe himself, once makes use of **h'** for 'autem' (fol. 68), which is another unmistakably Insular abbreviation.[1]

Syllabification

The scribe does not show that clear sense of word-division which one finds in the normal uncial manuscript written in Italy. He is not in touch with the good ancient tradition, and proceeds inconsistently. Thus he divides

'scrip-tura' and 'scri-ptum'
'fac-tis' and 'ample-ctatur'
'o-mni' and 'om-nia'.

(*10*) He also permits himself the impossible divisions

'p-salmodiae' and 'lingu-am'.

[1] On abbreviations see L. Traube, *Nomina Sacra* (Munich, 1907), and W. M. Lindsay, *Notae Latinae* (Cambridge, 1915).

Spelling

In his spelling the scribe is neither consistent nor impeccable. In words with prefixes he not infrequently has the unassimilated form, e.g. 'adplicet', 'inritatus', 'inpigerunt', 'conplens', 'conputare', 'inprobus'; but he also has the assimilated forms, as 'attingere', 'corrupti', etc. Of errors in orthography the most instructive, as we shall see, are those in which he uses a single **s** for **ss**, or **ss** for **s**, as 'misas', 'praemiso', 'uicissimo'. There are confusions of **e** and **i**, e.g. 'tacete', 'trea', 'suscipit' for 'suscepit', etc.; of **o** and **u**, e.g. 'oraturio' (*passim*); of **d** and **t**, e.g. 'idem' for 'item'; of **b** and **p**, e.g. 'obproprium', 'puplicanus'; of **e** and **ae**, e.g. 'estimet' and 'aeclesiis', 'praecaeptum', 'caetero'. There is misuse of **h**, e.g. 'abituros', 'eminam', 'ebdomada', and 'abhominabiles'. He allows himself such spellings as 'psaltyrii', 'antefana', 'antefonis', 'penticusten', even 'pesticosten', 'rennuatur', 'prumtus'.

Ornamentation

The manuscript contains as many as 75 coloured initials of the unmistakably Anglo-Saxon type. A selected group of them was reproduced by Astle.[1] They are outlined in black and filled with red. The surrounding dots are also red. Here and there the artist employs little groups of three dots, and, what is more curious, a horizontal dotted line traversing the inner space of a letter, or seeming to block it in vertically and horizontally—a feature which recalls in some respects the Canterbury Psalter. Red is also used regularly for the chapter-headings and the numbers marking the twelve steps of humility. A Maltese cross, also in red, is found over the initial **A** at the very beginning of the Preface (Pl. **31** (*pl. I*)). It should be noted that the first letter after the initial is invariably larger than the letters in the text proper; this is an ancient practice of Irish and English scribes, as may be seen in the Book of Kells, Bangor Antiphonary, Lindisfarne Gospels, and the Martyrology of St. Willibrord.[2] Here and there red dots embellish the letter after the initial. A touch of green occurs in capital **D** on fol. 5. On fols. 7v and 75 smaller letters nestle inside the initial.

Corrections and additions

There are a very large number of corrections in the manuscript. They are for the most part the work of a corrector whose hand is seen on practically

[1] Th. Astle, *The Origin and Progress of Writing*, pl. VIII (London, 1784; 2nd ed., 1803).

[2] Cf. Sir Edward Sullivan, *The Book of Kells*[3] (1927); E. G. Millar, *The Lindisfarne Gospels* (1923); F. E. Warren, *The Antiphonary of Bangor*, H. Bradshaw Society, vol. IV (1893); H. A. Wilson, *The Calendar of St. Willibrord*, H. Bradshaw Society, vol. LV (1918).

every page. The similarity of his writing to that of the rubricator is so manifest as to require no proof. On careful analysis, one comes to the conclusion that this corrector is not only identical with the rubricator but with the scribe himself. The difference in appearance between the script of the text and the script of the rubricator and corrector is not due so much to difference of form as to the difference resulting from the use of differently cut pens; the scribe's pen was cut very much more broadly than the rubricator's, causing the down-
(11) strokes of the former to seem very much heavier. Both scribe and rubricator use the same three types of **A**. The rubricator's **G** usually ends in a fine curve, but here and there he indulges in that superfluous triangular finial which is the normal manner of ending the **G** in the text. This is also true of the *hasta* of the letter **E** used by the rubricator: here and there it has the triangular finish, as in the text. The **B**'s in the text and the **B**'s used by the rubricator are identical, and this may be said of nearly all other letters. Over and above the correction of single letters, there are about forty-five instances of where one or more words have been added, either interlinearly or in the margins. The critical marks used to denote the insertion of single letters are two dots arranged like a colon in the text where the letters belong, and two dots before the letters inserted above the line. Variant readings or larger omissions are denoted by means of a line under a dot or two lines under a dot in the text where the omission or variant occurs, and the same sign in the margin before the inserted word or words. Once, on fol. 49^{v}, the omission and insertion are marked by a line with two dots underneath; on fol. 48 by means of two lines under two dots. Occasionally omission or correction is marked by the horizontal flourish. In order to mark deletion the corrector either encloses between colons the passage to be omitted, as on fol. 31^{v}; or he places two dots over a line on each and every word to be omitted, as on fol. 53; or he simply draws an oblique line through the cancelled letters, as on fol. 66. Transposition is marked by means of a dot over a line before the words to be transposed (see fol. 49^{v}). An early corrector places a **z** (= ζήτει) over the incorrect *tamen* on fol. 51 and in the margin opposite the ungrammatical 'reseruato sibi' on fol. 63^{v}.

Next in point of time is the hand that added the syllable 'lib' on fol. 8 and the two and a half lines in Anglo-Saxon script of the ninth century on fol. 49^{v} illustrated on our Pl. **35B** (*pl. V. 2*).

Next is a tenth-century ordinary minuscule hand, which wrote 'ab' on fol. 8 and 'adsumat' on fol. 37.

Lastly, there is a thirteenth-century corrector, whose activity is restricted to the first sixteen folios, where his rough-shod methods are easily recognized by the brown ink he used in dividing the *scriptura continua* into words, and changing **e**'s to **i**'s and **i**'s to **e**'s, adding **es** on fol. 3 and making the unnecessary addition of 'ibus ue' on fol. 4. Evidently the text was not to his liking, for he tired of his task of correction and no trace of him is found after fol. 16^{r}.

Four entries which can only be considered as *probationes pennae* occur in chronological order as follows: on fol. 42^{v}, top margin, a tenth- or eleventh-century hand, using ordinary minuscule, wrote 'cniht ic drink', reproduced in our Pl. **35A** (*pl. V. 1*). On fol. 44^{v} (Pl. **34** (*pl. IV*)) may be seen the entry 'aegelmaer', a name which is found in somewhat modified spelling in early Saxon charters.[1] This hand also added 'menes' on the same page, and seems of about the year 1000. On fol. 59^{v}, the Nomina Sacra 'ih̄s xp̄s' are by an eleventh-century hand. Lastly, a sixteenth-century hand wrote on the top margin of fol. 9 'Thomas bryne'. Here mention might be made of the neums inserted on fol. 20^{v} over 'secundus hu[militatis gradus]'; on fol. 23^{v} in the margin; on fol. 29^{v} over the word 'prima' in chapter xvi; and on fol. 62 over (*12*)
'nomen [sanctorum]', and on fol. 44^{v} reproduced in our Pl. **34** (*pl. IV*), where the music, as Dom Beyssac kindly informs me, has no reference whatever to the words in this chapter; and this was also the view held by H. M. Bannister.

Errors

Whereas his penmanship is of a distinctly high order, the same cannot be said for the scribe's accuracy in copying or for his knowledge of Latin. Some of his errors are manifestly due to nodding. He wrote 'praeceta' for 'praecepta' (fol. 9), 'neglant' for 'neglegant' (fol. 55), 'tun' for 'tunc' (fol. 61^{v}), also 'septe' for 'septem'. Other errors are due to the eye wandering and being distracted by a neighbouring letter or letters, e.g. for 'singula lecta' he writes 'singula lectula' (fol. 34), for 'curam gerat' he writes 'curat gerat' (fol. 39), and for 'perturbat' he first wrote 'purturbat' (fol. 47). Very curious are the errors 'A c̄o pascha' for 'A s̄c̄o pascha' (fol. 29), and 'recauendum' for 'praecauendum' (fol. 74^{v}), which are the initial words of chapters 15 and 69 respectively. This type of error is easily accounted for if we suppose that the scribe was copying from a manuscript in which the initial letter or letters of chapters had not yet been filled in by the illuminator. Certain errors in spelling, such as 'misa' for 'missa', may be due to faithful repro-

[1] See Aegelmaer = Aethelmaer, in W. G. Searle, *Onomasticon Anglo-Saxonicum*, pp. 42 f. E. W. B. Nicholson calls attention to the fact that an abbot Elmerus ruled at St. Augustine's, Canterbury, from 1006 to 1022 (*Early Bodleian Music*, III, p. xx).

duction of what was in his original, on which they thus shed some light, for it is a characteristically Insular weakness.

Date and origin

The foregoing observations will perhaps suffice to give an idea of the methods pursued by our scribe. It remains to see whether they permit of any conclusion as regards date and origin. It is abundantly clear that our manuscript was written by a monk who was more interested in the form than in the content, and his penmanship furnishes undeniable testimony of the fact that uncial script was practised with signal success in England. To determine the period when this manuscript was copied we are dependent solely upon palaeographical considerations. The use of *scriptura continua*, the strict adherence to the rule of reserving all ligatures, omission of **m**, and unusual abbreviations to the end of a line, the great simplicity of the punctuation and ornamentation, the great regularity with which the letters follow each other, all speak for a period hardly more recent than the beginning of the eighth century. Our manuscript has, in fact, an older appearance than the Brussels MS. 9850–2, written in uncial characters at Soissons between 695 and 711. On the other hand, a seventh-century date seems unlikely, in view of the ornate character of some of the letters, the manner of signing the quires, and the use of such abbreviations as **pꝛ**, **p̄**, **ꝓ**, **n̄**, **q̄d**, **s̄**, and **ū**. A date then somewhere about A.D. 700 is probably not wide of the mark.

As to the home of the manuscript, something can be said for Canterbury. To begin with, there is some material connection with Canterbury afforded by the end fly-leaf, which is strikingly like eleventh-century products from that centre. On Pl. **36**A (*pl. V. 3*) a portion of the fly-leaf may be compared with a genuine Canterbury document (Pl. **36**B (*pl. V. 4*)). Secondly, there is some resemblance between a great many letters in our manuscript and the uncials in the Cotton Psalter (British Museum, Cotton MS. Vespasian A. I)
(*13*) from Canterbury,[1] only that the Hatton manuscript is written by a more expert scribe. There is also some agreement, which seems hardly a mere coincidence, in the manner of ruling the sheets after folding. One might, perhaps, also claim some family resemblance between the dotted squares which contain the capitals at the beginning of each verse in the Cotton Psalter and the attempted blocking-in with dotted rectangles of some of the initials in the Hatton manuscript. That uncial writing was practised in Kent may be seen from the Cotton charter supposed to be of the year 679 (Cotton MS. Augustus II. 2).[2]

[1] References to facsimiles will be found in the list of uncial manuscripts given below.

[2] See the list below.

As for the original from which the Hatton manuscript was copied, an error like 'tamen' for 'tantum', apparently found only in our manuscript,[1] suggests an Insular exemplar (an early corrector has a *z* (= ζήτει) over the word), and the meaningless 'hiemis tempore sc̄o' (on fol. 25) for the correct 'hiemis tempore suprascripto' probably has a similar origin. It is quite likely that the exemplar was written in 'scriptura continua', in short verses of about twelve to thirteen letters. One is tempted to make that inference from the circumstance that several omissions contain thirteen or twice-thirteen letters, although it must be admitted that a number of omissions do not fit this unit.[2] In one case, however, where the Hatton manuscript stands alone in its class in making the omission of 'aut quasi tueri' (fol. 74v), the letters count 13. On the other hand, it should be stated that at no point at the end of a page is the scribe found to be crowding or spreading, as scribes usually do when they follow their copy page by page.

When this copy of the Rule left its original home is unknown. It once belonged to Christopher, Lord Hatton († 1670). It was bought for the Bodleian of Robert Scot in 1671. Its earlier press-mark was Hatton 93. Traces of pre-Bodleian shelf-marks are still seen on the old leather binding.[3]

LIST OF ENGLISH UNCIAL MANUSCRIPTS AND CHARTERS *(14)*

Inasmuch as the use of uncial writing by English scribes is by no means a common phenomenon and since some genuinely English uncial manuscripts have been wrongly attributed to Italian scribes, it may be of some use to conclude this brief study with a list of manuscripts and charters written in uncial script, which may, with a fair degree of certainty, be claimed for England. They are given in alphabetical order, with some references to published facsimiles—which are, however, by no means complete.

1. AVRANCHES: MSS. 48+66+71. FLY-LEAVES. EVANGELIA. Part of Leningrad O. v. I. 1. See below.

[Facsimile in *C.L.A.* vi. 730 (Ms. 66, 1v). Ed.]

[1] Neither P. E. Schmidt's nor E. Woelfflin's edition mentions this variant. Schmidt made very incomplete use of our manuscript, so that his apparatus criticus is not trustworthy as far as the Hatton manuscript is concerned.

[2] On the subject of omissions and their value in textual criticism, see the classic work by A. C. Clark, *The Descent of Manuscripts* (Oxford, 1918).

[3] This observation is found among the notes left by E. W. B. Nicholson, formerly Bodley's Librarian.

2. DURHAM: CHAPTER LIBRARY, A. II. 16. EVANGELIA. From north England. Uncial and insular book-hand, saec. VIII.

New Palaeographical Society, I, pls. 54, 55, 56 (fols. 12ʳ (uncial), 28ʳ (insular), 121ʳ (insular)). Zimmermann, *Vorkarolingische Miniaturen*, pl. 327 (fol. 37ʳ uncial and insular). H. D. Hughes, *A History of Durham Cathedral Library*, reduced facs. opposite p. 20 (fol. 109).

3. — CHAPTER LIBRARY, A. II. 17. EVANGELIA. Insular majuscule. From north England, saec. VIII in. Fols. 103–11 (St. Luke) are in uncial, *c.* A.D. 700.

(i) Iusnlar Majuscule:

New Pal. Soc. I, pl. 30 (fol 51ʳ). Zimmermann, *Vorkarol. Min.*, pls. 221–2 (fols. 1ʳ, 383ᵛ, 69ʳ). H. D. Hughes, op. cit., reduced facs. opposite p. 20 (fol. 2).

(ii) Uncial:

New Pal. Soc. I, pl. 157 (fol. 109ʳ). Akin to Codex Amiatinus in Florence and to the added leaves of the Utrecht Psalter.

4. FLORENCE: BIBLIOTECA MEDICEA LAURENZIANA, AMIATINUS I. BIBLIA SACRA (CODEX AMIATINUS). Written at Jarrow, Northumbria. English uncial, *c.* A.D. 700.

Silvestre, *Paléographie Universelle*, pl. 81 (= 235) = cxiv. *Pal. Soc.* II, pls. 65–6. Zangemeister–Wattenbach, *Exempla codicum Latinorum*, etc., pl. XXXV (fol. 86ᵛ). Steffens, *Lateinische Paläographie*¹, pl. 28 (= *Lat. Pal.*², pl. 21B) (dedication page). Thompson, *Introduction to Greek and Latin Palaeography*, no. 93. Zimmermann, *Vorkarol. Min.*, pls. 222*, 222** (fols. 796ᵛ, 805ʳ), and text fig. 24 (Cassiodorus frontispiece). Quentin, *Mémoire sur l'établissement du texte de la Vulgate, Collectanea Biblica Latina*, VI, frontispiece (fol. vʳ frontispiece), figs. 74–81 (fols. 857ʳ, 801ʳ, viiʳ, 2ᵛ–iiiʳ, ivʳ, 1003ᵛ, 796ᵛ, 886ᵛ). Sunyol, *Introducció a la Paleografia Musical Gregoriana*, p. 341 (copy of Steffens). E. G. Millar, *The Lindisfarne Gospels*, pl. 37 (fol. 5ʳ = Cassiodorus frontispiece). Further literature in Traube's *Vorlesungen u. Abbandlungen*, I. 183 f., 260 n.

5. HEREFORD: CATHEDRAL LIBRARY, P. II. 10. TWO FLY-LEAVES (A+Z). COMMENTARY ON MATTHEW. English uncial, saec. VIII.

[Facsimile in *C.L.A.* ii. 158 (fol. Aᵛ). Ed.]

6. LENINGRAD: F. v. I. 3. PHILIPPUS IN IOB; with Hieronymus as an interlinear gloss. From Corbie. The main text in late uncial, saec. VIII; the interlinear gloss in insular, saec. VIII.

Staerk, *MSS. latins ... de Saint-Pétersbourg*, I, pl. ix (fol. 39ʳ) (insular). Staerk, *MSS. latins ... de Saint-Pétersbourg*, II, pl. XXVIII (fol. 38ʳ) (shows both scripts).

— O. v. I. 1. EVANGELIA. Probably from England. Uncial, saec. VIII. Part of this manuscript in Avranches 48+66+71. See above, no. 1.

Staerk, *MSS. latins*, etc. I, pl. VII (fol. 1ᵛ); II, pl. XXV (fol. 1ʳ).

7. LONDON: BRITISH MUSEUM, COTTON MS. VESPASIAN A. I. CANTERBURY PSALTER. Uncial, saec. VIII.

Astle, op. cit., pl. IX. 2; Westwood, *Facsimiles of Miniatures*, etc., pl. III; *Palaeographia Sacra Pictoria*, pl. XL; *Pal. Soc.* I, pl. 18; *Catalogue of Ancient MSS. in the Brit. Mus.* II, pls. 12–15; *Facsimiles of Biblical MSS. in the Brit. Mus.*, pl. X; Zimmermann, *Vorkarol. Min.*, pls. 286–8. G. F. Warner, *Illuminated MSS. in the British Museum*, ser. IV, pl. I. See also Traube, op. cit., p. 193.

8. — BRITISH MUSEUM, ADDITIONAL MS. 37518. FLY-LEAVES. LITURGICA. Insular uncial, saec. VIII.

New Pal. Soc. I, pl. 132 (fol. 116ᵛ).

9. — BRITISH MUSEUM, ADDITIONAL MS. 37777. ONE LEAF. BIBLIA SACRA. Written in north England. Uncial, *c.* A.D. 700. Akin to Codex Amiatinus and Stonyhurst St. John.

New Pal. Soc. I, pls. 158, 159 (complete facsimile).

10. — BRITISH MUSEUM, COTTON MS. AUGUSTUS II. 2. CHARTER OF HLO- (*15*)
THARI OF KENT. A.D. 679.

E. A. Bond, *Facsimiles of Charters in the British Museum*, I, pl. I (1873).

11. — BRITISH MUSEUM, COTTON MS. AUGUSTUS II. 29. CHARTER OF OETHILRED. A.D. 692 or 693.

Ibid., pl. 2.

12. — BRITISH MUSEUM, COTTON MS. AUGUSTUS II. 3. CHARTER OF AETHILBALD. A.D. 736.

Ibid., pl. 7.

13. OXFORD: BODLEIAN LIBRARY, HATTON 48 [4118]. REGULA SANCTI BENEDICTI. Probably written at St. Augustine's, Canterbury. Uncial, saec. VII–VIII.

Traube, *Textgeschichte d. Reg. S. Ben.* (1910) (fol. 40ᵛ). *New Pal. Soc.* II, pl. 82 (fol. 30), saec. VIII. Nicholson, *Early Bodleian Music*, pl. 4 (fol. 44ᵛ), saec. VII ex.

14. — BODLEIAN LIBRARY, SELDEN SUPRA 30 [3418]. ACTUS APOSTOLORUM. Written in Thanet, came from Canterbury. Uncial, saec. VIII in. (*ante* A.D. 752).

New Pal. Soc. II, pl. 56 (pp. 30, 90). Nicholson, *Early Bodleian Music*, pl. 5 (p. 102).

15. PARIS: BIBLIOTHÈQUE NATIONALE, MS. LAT. 281+298. EVANGELIARIUM (CODEX BIGOTIANUS). From north France, Fécamp. English uncial and ornamental capitals with Insular ornamentation, *c.* A.D. 800.

Delisle, *Cabinet des MSS.*, pl. X. 1 (ornamental capitals), 2 (uncial). Zimmermann, *Vorkarol. Min.*, pl. 285 (fols. 86ʳ, 137ʳ).

16. — BIBLIOTHÈQUE NATIONALE, MS. LAT. 9561. ISIDORUS AND GREGORY. English uncial. From St. Bertin. English initials and abbreviations.

Chatelain, *Uncialis Scriptura*, pl. 48 (fol. 7).

17. STOCKHOLM: KUNGL. BIBLIOTEKET, A. 135. EVANGELIA (CODEX AUREUS). From Canterbury. Uncial, saec. VIII ex., with Anglo-Saxon minuscule inscriptions, *c.* A.D. 850.

Zimmermann, *Vorkarol. Min.*, pls. 204a, 280–6 (fols. 104^{r}, 6^{r}, 8^{r}, 9^{v}*, 150^{v}*, 11^{r}*, 1^{r}, 5^{v}), pl. 284 (fol. 11^{r} shows both scripts).

18. STONYHURST: COLLEGE LIBRARY, s.n. EVANGELIUM IOHANNIS (St. Cuthbert's Gospel of St. John). Written in north England. Uncial, *c.* A.D. 700. Same type as the Codex Amiatinus.

Westwood, *Palaeographia Sacra Pictoria*, pl. 11. *Pal. Soc.* I, pl. 17. E. Johnston, *Writing and Illuminating and Lettering*, p. 442, pl. v.

19. UTRECHT: UNIVERSITY LIBRARY, MS. SCR. ECCL. 484 (UTRECHT 32) (*olim* COTTON MS. CLAUDIUS C. VII).

(i) The Utrecht Psalter. Ornamental rustic capitals.

Birch, *Complete Autotype Facsimile*, 1873. Birch, *The Utrecht Psalter*, pl. I (Psalm XI) 1876. Arndt-Tangl, *Schrifttafeln*, pl. 33, saec. IX in. P. Durrieu in *Mélanges Havet* (Paris, 1895), illustrations only. Herbert, *Illuminated MSS.*, pl. XII. Millar, *English Illuminated MSS.*, pl. I (Psalms XXX, LXVIII). A. Boinet, *Miniature Carolingienne*, pls. 61–5. Copies of the Utrecht Psalter are—London: British Museum Harley 603. Cambridge: Trinity College R. 17. I. Paris: Bibliothèque Nationale Lat. 8846.

(ii) Evangelia appended to the Utrecht Psalter (fols. 93–105). Written in north England. Uncial, saec. VIII. Same type as the Codex Amiatinus.

Birch, *Complete Autotype Facsimile*, 1873.

30. WORCESTER: CATHEDRAL LIBRARY, s.n. PATERIUS. Written in England. Uncial, saec. VIII.

C. H. Turner, *Early Worcester MSS.* (Oxford, 1916) (complete facsimile).

The Unique Manuscript of Tacitus' Histories (257)

(FLORENCE LAUR. 68. 2)

AMONG the letters of Pliny the Younger, there are few, I believe, that interest us more than those addressed to his friend Cornelius Tacitus. One of these is particularly interesting by reason of a prophecy it contains touching the future of Tacitus' *Histories*. Collecting material for this work, Tacitus had asked his friend to send him certain information about his career. Pliny's response to the request begins with the familiar words:

> Auguror, nec me fallit augurium, historias tuas immortales futuras, quo magis illis (ingenue fatebor) inseri cupio. (7, 33)

Pliny's prophecy has been fulfilled; and as long as our civilization retains its Western character, the great and sombre historian of the early Caesars will doubtless have his honourable place. Different generations will put a different value upon him in the future, as they have done in the past. And in the same age he will affect different temperaments differently; but his writings bid fair to remain a κτῆμα εἰς ἀεί.

It would be out of place here to inquire into the extent of his influence (258) upon modern European literature.[1] Traces of it are manifest in the political writings of Machiavelli, Guicciardini, Giannotti, in the essays of Montaigne, in the dramas of Corneille, Racine, and Alfieri. But however much Tacitus may have occupied the minds of men of letters since the Renaissance, no such interest in his work was shown in the Middle Ages or in antiquity.[2] For a time his historical works were even in danger of being almost lost to us.

As far as we can judge, Tacitus seems to have been little appreciated by his immediate posterity. The historian Vopiscus informs us that the Emperor Tacitus (275–6) had decreed that the writings of his ancestor (for the emperor claimed descent from the historian) should be copied at regular intervals and deposited in all public archives and libraries.[3] From this we can only infer

From *Casinensia* (Monte Cassino, 1929), pp. 257–72. [See Pls. **37** and **38**.]

[1] This has been admirably done by Felice Ramorino in his essay: *Cornelio Tacito nella storia della coltura* (Milan, 1895).

[2] See F. Haverfield, 'Tacitus During the Late Roman Period and the Middle Ages' in *Journal of Roman Studies*, VI (1916), 196–201. For this reference I am indebted to Professor A. C. Clark.

[3] 'Cornelium Tacitum, scriptorem historiae augustae, quod parentem suum eundem diceret,

that the works of Tacitus had fallen into neglect; and we may assume that the imperial decree had no effect upon the taste of the time. There were various reasons why Tacitus was unpopular. For one thing he was cordially disliked by Christians and Jews because he had been unflattering and hostile to both of them. Tertullian (*Ad nationes* I. 11) speaks of Tacitus as the prince of garrulous liars, 'ille mendaciorum loquacissimus'. Such a characterization by one of the much-read early Christian writers was not calculated to add to the popularity of Tacitus in later centuries, when practically all literature was Christian literature. Perhaps the last of the ancients who appreciated Tacitus was the historian Ammianus Marcellinus, who continued the story of the Caesars where Tacitus had left off. Sulpicius Severus borrows much from Tacitus; and in his Christian history of the world the Spanish presbyter
(259) Orosius cites and combats the Roman historian. But it is a significant fact that the grammarians of the late empire without exception ignore the existence of Tacitus. They cite no examples from his works. And in the sixth century Cassiodorus (*Variae*, 5. 2) speaking of Baltic amber mentioned in the *Germania* (45), refers to Tacitus as a certain Cornelius, 'quodam Cornelio scribente'.[1] During many centuries after Cassiodorus, Tacitus had shrunk to a mere name in Italy. So far as I know we find no trace of any knowledge of him in Italian medieval writers. And no ancient catalogue known to us, whether of an Italian or transalpine library, mentions works of Tacitus.

It was in the eleventh century that a south Italian scribe copied part of the *Histories* and the end of the *Annals*. Had that copy been destroyed, this part of Tacitus' writings would have been irretrievably lost to posterity. For, like some other cherished classics—one thinks of Varro's *De lingua latina*, Catullus' poems, Cicero's correspondence with Atticus, his *Orator* and *De oratore*, the fifth decade of Livy, Pliny's correspondence with Trajan—, the survival of this part of Tacitus as well as of the rest of his works depended upon a single thread.[2]

Much has been written on our manuscript of Tacitus. After the excellent monographs of Professor G. Andresen, who had lived long and lovingly with the manuscript and won from it more secrets than any other scholar,[3] and the exhaustive and learned preface to the facsimile edition by Professor

in omnibus bibliothecis conlocari iussit et, ne lectorum incuria deperiret, librum per annos singulos decies scribi publicitus in cunctis archiis iussit et in bibliothecis poni': Flavius Vopiscus, *Tacitus*, 10. 2.

[1] Haverfield, loc. cit., p. 199.

[2] Cf. Sabbadini, *Le scoperte dei codici latini e greci*, etc., pp. 211 f.

[3] G. Andresen, *In Taciti historias studia critica et palaeographica* (*Wissenschaftliche Beilage zum Jahresbericht des Askanischen Gymnasium zu Berlin*), Part I—1899; Part II—1900.

Rostagno,[1] it is difficult to say anything new about the manuscript that is of importance. But even crumbs of information are not unwelcome in the case of so important a witness. I shall therefore re-examine the questions of origin, date, and archetype, and inquire into the causes which led to the making of a copy in southern Italy in the eleventh century, in the hope of obtaining clearer ideas on these several heads. At the same time, I should like to seize this opportunity to state the grounds for the conjecture regarding our manu- (*260*)
script made by me elsewhere,[2] a conjecture accepted by Professor Clark and the late Professor Haverfield.[3]

The Laurentian manuscript of Tacitus known as Mediceus II (modern press-mark, Plut. 68. num. 2) contains books XI–XVI of the *Annals* and books I–V of the *Histories*,[4] and is written in Beneventan or so-called Lombardic characters, that is, in the south Italian minuscule. The consensus of opinion among scholars is that the manuscript originated in Monte Cassino in the second half of the eleventh century, while the great Abbot Desiderius, who later became Pope Victor III, presided over the monastery (1058–87). We possess a catalogue of the books written under this abbot,[5] and one of its items has long been supposed to refer to the manuscript of Tacitus under discussion. This is the opinion of Wattenbach in his edition of the Chronicle of Monte Cassino, of Oscar Hecker in *Boccacciofunde*, of E. Rostagno in his preface to the facsimile edition in the Leyden series, of M. Schanz in his *Geschichte der römischen Litteratur*, and lastly of H. Goelzer, in his recent large edition of the *Histories*.[6] The learned editor of the *Bibliotheca Casinensis* seems to share this view.[7]

The catalogue in question occurs in the Chronicle of Monte Cassino, begun by the monk Leo, and continued by the monk Petrus Diaconus. It is one of the best chronicles produced in the Middle Ages. The item in the catalogue which is supposed to refer to Tacitus runs thus: 'Historiam Cornelii cum Omero'.

As has been remarked above, there is no medieval catalogue known to us, which makes unambiguous mention of Tacitus. But there is a Corbie cata-

[1] Henricus Rostagno in *Codices graeci et latini photographice depicti*, vol. VII, pars 2 (Leyden, 1902).

[2] E. A. Lowe, *The Beneventan Script*, p. 11 (Oxford, 1914) [this volume, pp. 82 f.]

[3] Loc. cit., p. 200.

[4] The beginning of book XI is missing and book XVI lacks the end. Facsimiles in Chatelain, *Paléographie des classiques latins*, pl. 146; *The Legacy of the Middle Ages*, facs. 32 (Oxford, 1926); and in the Leyden series mentioned above.

[5] *Chronica Monasterii Casinensis*, III. 63, ed. Wattenbach, pp. 746 f. See also Th. Gottlieb, *Ueber mittelalterliche Bibliotheken*, p. 416 and the writer's *Ben. Script*, pp. 81 f.

[6] Paris, Hachette, 1920, 2 vols.

[7] Vol. I, p. XI.

logue which has this item: 'Liber Cornelii de bello troiano'.[1] And, in a Saint
(261) Riquier catalogue of the year 831 we have: 'historiam Homeri ubi dicit et Dares Phrygius'.[2] From the juxtaposition in the Monte Cassino catalogue of the *Historia Cornelii* with Homer, it is clear that the history referred to is that of the siege of Troy. In other words, the item has reference to the apocryphal work *De excidio Troiae* supposed to have been written by the Phrygian Dares and translated into Latin by Cornelius Nepos. The Cornelius, then, of the Monte Cassino catalogue is not Tacitus but Cornelius Nepos. That this is the true interpretation of the Monte Cassino catalogue is further shown by a number of other catalogues in which the translation of Dares is mentioned together with some other work on Troy, either in prose or verse, usually the other apocryphal work on the Trojan war attributed to the Cretan Dictys. The instances have been collected by Manitius.[3] Friedrich Haase in his edition of Tacitus (I, p. LXIX) long ago called attention to the erroneous identification of Cornelius with Tacitus in the catalogue of Desiderian books. And Manitius, in his work just cited, retracted his former view, which approved of the identification. In fact, even Wattenbach had a suspicion that the identification was doubtful, for in his notes on the passage of the chronicle, he calls attention to the remarkable agreement with the item in the Corbie catalogue, to which reference has been made. It is important to call attention to this error, for it is certain to be repeated in the future having found lodgement in such standard works as those above cited.

From what has just been said, it follows that the Monte Cassino catalogue can no longer be cited as evidence for the date and origin of our manuscript. But if history does not bear out the connection between Abbot Desiderius and our Tacitus, perhaps palaeography does. Let us begin by inquiring if our manuscript bears any resemblance to manuscripts written in the time of Desiderius. This is not difficult, as we fortunately possess a number of genuine
(262) Desiderian products. One of them has been reproduced in the Leyden series. I refer to the Codex Heinsianus (Leyden 118) of Cicero's *De natura deorum*.[4] A comparison between the Laurentian Tacitus and the Heinsianus of Cicero —to take a case which anyone may verify for himself, as complete reproductions of both the manuscripts are in all the larger libraries—a comparison between these two will show that in general appearance the Heinsianus makes

[1] G. Becker, *Catalogi Antiqui*, n. 136, item 340.

[2] Ibid., n. 11, item 192. Examples could easily be multiplied. Paris Nouv. acq. lat. 1423, saec. XIII begins: 'incipit historia Cornelii ad Salustium Crispum in Trojanorum hystoria'. See Delisle, *Manuscrits latins et français*, I. 206.

[3] M. Manitius, *Philologisches aus alten Bibliothekskatalogen*, pp. 121 f. (Frankfurt, 1892).

[4] *Codd. gr. et lat.* XVII (Leyden, 1912).

a more recent impression. The letters have the regular, uniform, somewhat stiff forms which are characteristic of the manuscripts written under Desiderius. The Tacitus manuscript, on the other hand, shows a freer style of writing recalling an earlier generation. The impression made by the script as a whole is fully borne out by an examination of details. An excellent test letter is final **r**. In Desiderian and in later manuscripts, final **r** descends below the line. In most pre-Desiderian manuscripts the letter is short. Next to the script, abbreviations offer the best test of the date of a manuscript. Now the Tacitus manuscript has a set of abbreviations which represent an earlier stage, as compared with those in the Heinsianus.[1] Whereas the latter makes continual use of the system of abbreviating by means of suprascript letters, e.g. $\overset{a}{\mathbf{c}}$ (cra), $\overset{a}{\mathbf{g}}$ (gra), $\overset{a}{\mathbf{p}}$ (pra), $\overset{i}{\mathbf{p}}$ (pri), $\overset{a}{\mathbf{t}}$ (tra), $\overset{o}{\mathbf{t}}$ (tro), the former rarely uses such abbreviations. Absence of abbreviations, to be sure, is not conclusive evidence. A scribe may know symbols and not use them. But we may not suppose that this particular system is avoided in the Tacitus manuscript, for it is otherwise full of abbreviations, and doubtless represents the scribe's complete equipment.[2] If we compare single abbreviations, we get the same result. The Tacitus manuscript gives the older form, the Heinsianus the more recent. To take a few telling examples: the Tacitus has **am̄o**, the Heinsianus **aīō**, for 'animo'; the Tacitus usually preserves the **m** in the abbreviation of 'omnis' (**om̄is**), the Heinsianus omits it as a rule (**oīs̄**). The Tacitus abbreviates the syllable 'uer' by a horizontal stroke over the **u**, the Heinsianus by a 2-shaped sign. The Tacitus never omits the **n** in the third declension ending 'ione (natione)', the Heinsianus does (**naōtie**). The Tacitus never omits 'er' in the syllable 'der', the Heinsianus does. In all these cases the Tacitus manuscript represents the older, pre-Desiderian tradition.[3] The abbreviations, then, as well *(263)*
as the script, are against assigning the manuscript to the period of Desiderius. If we next examine the punctuation signs, we notice that the Tacitus manuscript has the freer, pre-Desiderian form of the points.

The Beneventan script is rich in dated manuscripts of the eleventh century. We know of several that were written under Abbot Theobald, i.e. between 1022 and 1035.[4] But our manuscript of Tacitus does not quite fit into this period. Its script, abbreviations, and general appearance represent a somewhat more developed stage. Accordingly the manuscript must have been written about the middle of the century, i.e. in the period between the

[1] A very full list of them is given by O. Plasberg in his Preface to the facsimile edition.

[2] [See this volume, p. 93. Ed.]

[3] See *Ben. Script*, ch. VIII.

[4] See *Scriptura Beneventana*, pls. 59, 60, 61, 62, and *Ben. Script*, pp. 342 ff.

Theobaldan and the Desiderian. Nearly all of this period happens to coincide with the abbacy of Richerius, who presided over Monte Cassino between 1038 and 1055. Richerius was a German. And hardly two years after his death another German became head of Monte Cassino, Frederick of Lorraine, later Stephen IX. The date of the Tacitus manuscript, then, falls during what we may call the period of German ascendancy at Monte Cassino. An abbot is quite likely to influence the literary life of his community. A forceful personality is certain to do so, and these German abbots must have been men of strong character to attain office of highest distinction in a foreign land.

The chronicler of Monte Cassino who gives us a list of the Desiderian manuscripts included neither Tacitus nor Apuleius—the two are actually bound together in our manuscript and were written at about the same time. Petrus Diaconus, the author of this part of the chronicle, who prided himself on his knowledge of Roman authors, could hardly have failed to give Desiderius credit for two such manuscripts, had he known them to be Desiderian. Their absence from the list is doubtless due to the simple fact that they were not Desiderian.[1]

So much for the date of the manuscript. The accepted opinion with regard
(*264*) to its home is true, though not always on the grounds that are advanced. The manuscript was written at Monte Cassino. Having seen nearly all the extant manuscripts in this type of script, I find that it is easier to say that such and such a manuscript was not written at Monte Cassino, than to say that it was. In other words, the script is not always a safe guide. I think it important to call attention to this fact, because some scholars have not hesitated to attribute manuscripts to Monte Cassino on the sole ground of the character of the writing. I believe that such judgements are rash. At least, for my part, I must confess that I am often unable to decide from the mere writing, whether a manuscript was written at Monte Cassino, Cava, Naples, or Benevento. But our manuscript of Tacitus, quite apart from its resemblance to other Monte Cassino manuscripts, has a *probatio pennae* which definitely connects it with Monte Cassino. On fol. 103^{v}, i.e. on the last page of the Tacitus manuscript, in a column left blank, a twelfth-century hand wrote 'Abbas raynaldus . . .'. Professor Rostagno was the first to recognize the importance of this entry, and correctly surmised from it connection with Monte Cassino. Monte Cassino had, in fact, two abbots named Raynaldus during the twelfth century. As the name is not uncommon, it could be objected that this Raynaldus may

[1] For the list of Desiderian manuscripts see *Ben. Script*, pp. 81 f.

have belonged to some other monastery. The supposition becomes improbable when we consider another instance, which has come to my notice. In the well-known manuscript of Cicero's *Philippics*, Vatic. lat. 3227, written in Beneventan characters of about the year 1100, we find thrice the probatio pennae *Raynaldus dei gratia*. Of course, to be supplied is some word like 'abbas', 'praesul', or 'episcopus'. There can be little doubt that the manuscript was written at Monte Cassino, since in the right margin of fol. 24^{r} the scribe amused himself by writing the word 'Casinum' in capital letters. So the *Raynaldus dei gratia* of the Vatican manuscript from Monte Cassino may justly be regarded as a variation of the *probatio pennae* in the Tacitus manuscript. I believe there is another feature which connects the manuscript with Monte Cassino. In examining the 230-odd manuscripts still at Monte Cassino one is impressed with the fact that in a very large number of Cassinese manuscripts of the eleventh century the ink has almost disappeared on one side (the flesh side) of the parchment, rendering those pages almost illegible. This was probably due to some fault in preparing the parchment. The writing on the flesh side of these manuscripts must have grown pale before two centuries had elapsed; for in a number of the manuscripts a thirteenth-century Beneventan hand retraced the characters of the eleventh. Throughout our manuscript of Tacitus we find similar faded writing on the flesh side. On fols. 102^{v} (*265*)
and 103 we have clear examples of the thirteenth century attempt at restoration[1] (see Pl. **38A** (*pl. IIa*)).

There is one other consideration which speaks for the Cassinese origin of our manuscript. When we ask what other manuscripts in Beneventan writing are preserved in the Laurentian library, we learn that they are nearly all of classical authors, and one of them at least can be shown to come from Monte Cassino. The manuscript of Justin's *Epitome* (Laur. 66. 21) has a less familiar Monte Cassino ex-libris: 'iste liber est ecclesie Casinensis'.[2] The manuscript of Hegesippus (Laur. 66. 1) has the unmistakable marks of the Codices Theobaldini (1022–35). The manuscript of Varro (Laur. 51. 10) has a *Nota* opposite the word 'Casinum' in the text, from which Spengel argued—I think rightly—that the manuscript was of Cassinese origin.[3] This entry, the script, and the authenticated presence of Varro's works in Monte Cassino render it fairly certain that the Laurentian Varro originally belonged to Monte Cassino.

[1] This circumstance in itself would be sufficient to disprove the preposterous contention advanced by Hochart and some others that the Laurentian manuscript is a humanistic forgery.

[2] See *Ben. Script*, p. 71.

[3] See L. Spengel in *Abhandlungen d. Bayer. Akad. der Wissen.* VII. 2, p. 434.

The manuscripts of Varro, Tacitus, and Apuleius probably left Monte Cassino at the same time. They were rescued, as the phrase goes, by some humanist, who was probably none other than Boccaccio. To Petrarch the works of Tacitus and Varro were only known in name. The first to use these authors was Boccaccio; and this good fortune was granted him towards the end of his life.[1] There can be no doubt that he possessed the Beneventan manuscripts of Tacitus and Varro which are now in the Laurentian library. This may be seen, on the one hand, from the copies of these manuscripts which he left in the Convent of S. Spirito in Florence, which correspond perfectly with the original; and from the fact that Boccaccio's citations from Varro and Tacitus, in his *Genealogia deorum* and *De claris mulieribus*, as Pierre de Nolhac has shown, are taken only from books preserved in the Beneventan manuscripts, and from no others.[2]

(*266*) How these manuscripts came into Boccaccio's hands we do not know, but we can make a shrewd guess. We have reason to believe they were not presented to him during his visits to Monte Cassino. Attracted by the fame of the abbey, as he told his pupil Benvenuto da Imola, he paid it a visit. He found the library shamefully neglected, without bolt or lock, grass growing in the windows, dust thick on the books, monks using the precious manuscripts for turning out prayer-books, which they sold for a few soldi to women and children. Grieved unto tears he left the library 'dolens et illacrymans recessit'.[3] But none of this, I fear, is to be taken seriously. It all sounds uncommonly like an apology. He seems to be anxious to show that it was only an act of simple piety to remove the precious classics to a place of safety, say to Florence. The letter which he wrote in 1371 to the Calabrian abbot Niccolò di Montefalcone requesting the return of a quire from the Tacitus, suggests that he probably had accomplices.[4] But no one can doubt that the Tacitus manuscript was dishonestly obtained after reading Poggio's letter of 27 September 1427 to Niccolò Niccoli: 'Cornelium Tacitum cum venerit, observabo penes me occulte. Scio enim omnem illam cantilenam, et unde exierit et per quem, et quis eum sibi vendicet: sed nil dubites, non exibit a me ne verbo quidem.'[5] The manuscript which was written at Monte Cassino left its original home

[1] See G. Minozzi, *Montecassino nella Storia del Rinascimento*, I (Rome, 1925), where the visits are discussed at great length.

[2] P. De Nolhac, 'Boccace et Tacite' in *Mélanges d'archéologie et d'histoire*, XII (1892), 130 ff.

[3] See L. Tosti, *Storia della Badia di Monte Cassino*, III. 92 ff., and E. Rostagno in his preface to the facsimile edition, pp. iii f.

[4] P. de Nolhac, loc. cit.; G. Voigt, *Die Wiederbelebung des classischen Alterthums*, p. 250; Rostagno, loc. cit., p. vi, n. 3.

[5] Rostagno, ibid., p. iii.

sometime before 1370, and its home has been Florence since the end of the fourteenth century. So much then for the date, origin, and vicissitudes of the Laurentian manuscript of Tacitus' *Histories*. Let us now inquire briefly into the fortunes of the manuscripts of the rest of Tacitus' works. Perhaps by so doing we may be in a better position to appreciate the reasons which led to the revival of interest in Tacitus at Monte Cassino in the middle of the eleventh century.

It is a well-known fact that the first books of the *Annals*, which are found
in the Laurentian MS. 68. I (Medic. I), came to Italy from Germany. Ori- (*267*)
ginally the book belonged to the Westphalian monastery of Corvey. In some mysterious way the book disappeared in 1508. Pope Leo X, who rightly or wrongly became its owner, sent a Brief in 1517 to the Archbishop of Mainz, which refers to the complaint made by the German monks, who asked for the restoration of their property. In it occurs this delightful passage: 'and we have sent back to the said abbot and monks of the monastery of Corvey a corrected and printed copy, elegantly bound (*non inornate ligatum*), which is to take the place of the one which they have lost; and in order that they may realize that this loss has been rather to their advantage than disadvantage, we send them *pro ecclesia monasterii eorum indulgentiam perpetuam*'.[1]

But we owe to Germany not only the first books of the *Annals*, but also the *Germania* and the *Agricola*. It was from Hersfeld in Hessen that Enoch of Ascoli in 1455 brought those works to Italy.[2] Eight leaves of this manuscript were discovered a few years ago in Jesi, in a private library.[3]

It is not hard to understand why Tacitus should have remained known to Germans. By furnishing them with an account of their own primitive history, he became a source of perennial interest. It was only natural for the German medieval chronicler to draw upon Tacitus for facts about ancient Germany. According to Manitius, a recognized authority in medieval literature, the whole of Tacitus was known to Einhardt,[4] the Fulda monk who was Charlemagne's biographer. This, however, is a statement that needs interpretation. Rudolf, another monk of Fulda, was acquainted with Tacitus' *Germania*, as may be seen from his *Translatio S. Alexandri*. Again, in the *Annales Fuldenses*, there is a passage (ad a. 852) in which Tacitus' *Annals* are cited. And Widukind of Corvey, the historian of the Saxons, is supposed to have used Tacitus

[1] The full papal Brief is printed by F. Philippi in *Philologus*, XLV (1886), 377 ff.

[2] Sabbadini, *Le scoperte dei cod. lat. e greci*, etc., I. 140; II. 254.

[3] Cf. C. Annibaldi, *L'Agricola e la Germania di Cornelio Tacito* (Città di Castello, 1907).

[4] M. Manitius in *Neues Archiv*, VII (1882), 527 ff., and *Geschichte d. lat. Literatur d. Mittelalters*, I. 643 ff.

(*268*) besides Sallust and Livy. Scholars have conjectured that our extant Hersfeld and Corvey manuscripts of Tacitus were probably copied from a Fulda exemplar.

If it is true that Tacitus was read and cited in Germany during the Middle Ages, we are not surprised to learn that the minor works of Tacitus and part of the *Annals* were, at the beginning of the Renaissance, found in Germany and nowhere else. In view of the known interest of Germans in the author of the *Germania* it does not seem rash to conjecture that our unique manuscript of Tacitus' *Histories* and the latter part of the *Annals*, which, to judge from its palaeography, falls, as has been shown, during the period of German rule at Monte Cassino, owes its existence at Monte Cassino to the interest felt by the German abbot Richerius in the author who had written about his forebears. It is probably no mere coincidence that the Monte Cassino manuscript of Widukind's *Res gestae saxonicae* (MS. 298) seems also to belong to the period of Abbot Richerius.

Whether the manuscript of Tacitus is a copy of an exemplar brought from Germany, or of an ancient but forgotten volume leading a dishonoured existence among the unused books of the abbey, it is impossible to tell. That books from Germany occasionally got to Monte Cassino is certain. The celebrated collection of grammatical works found in Paris lat. 7530, which was written at Monte Cassino toward the end of the eighth century (it contains a fragment of Varro) must have been copied, at least in part, from an original that came from Germany. It has a German gloss which the Italian scribe copied; and it has here and there abbreviations which show Anglo-Saxon influence.[1] The two facts point to some such abbey as Fulda. Now it happens that a visitor from Fulda is actually recorded in the Chronicle of Monte Cassino. We are told that Boniface sent Sturmius to Monte Cassino to study the monastic discipline at its source. Sturmius later became Abbot of Fulda. It is reasonable to suppose that he did not come empty-handed. Paris lat. 7530 may easily be a copy of one of the books he brought with him. There is, moreover, proof that German influence continued to be felt at Monte Cassino even in the time of Abbot Desiderius. This evidence is capable of ocular
(*269*) demonstration. I refer to the influence which the school of Ratisbon exercised upon the illuminators of Monte Cassino.[2] In the collection of Homilies written

[1] Cf. W. M. Lindsay, *Notae Latinae*, p. xv; E. A. Lowe, *Scriptura Beneventana*, pl. 9.

[2] E. Bertaux in *L'Art dans l'Italie Méridionale*, p. 275 (Paris, 1904), has some general observations on the subject of Cassinese indebtedness to Germany. But it was F. von Baldass who first called attention to the direct relation of the Ratisbon school to the Cassinese. See *Anzeiger d. philos.-histor. Kl. d. Kais. Akademie d. Wissen. in Wien*, XLVIII (1911), n. XXV.

by the scribe Leo in 1072 for Abbot Desiderius,[1] we find a type of initials heretofore unknown in Cassinese manuscripts,[2] a type which is directly borrowed from the Ratisbon School. In fact, certain initials in this manuscript are unmistakable copies of a German model still extant. Before the German ascendancy of the middle of the eleventh century at Monte Cassino, we do not encounter the type of initial in which the space enclosed by the letter-form is filled with narrow intertwined bands of conventionalized leaves. Once introduced this type becomes part and parcel of the Cassinese artists' equipment. This result could not have been achieved by a manuscript 'quelconque'. It took a codex of some importance to do this. As a matter of fact we still possess one such German manuscript that must have served as a model at Monte Cassino. This manuscript is the Gospel-book of Emperor Henry written in eleventh-century Caroline minuscule, and decorated in the Ratisbon style of ornamentation.[3] It is preserved in the Ottobonian collection of the Vatican (MS. 74).[4] From internal evidence we learn that this copy of the Gospels was written for the German emperor Henry, probably Henry II (973–1024).[5] It is a beautiful book worthy of an emperor's library. The Chronicle of Monte Cassino distinctly tells us that Queen Agnes, wife of Henry III, when she paid her long visit to Monte Cassino in 1073 made munificent gifts to the abbey, among them being a beautiful book of the (*270*)
Gospels.[6] In the Vatican volume just mentioned there are additions in Beneventan writing, proving conclusively that it was used in south Italy. There can be no doubt where in south Italy. We need only examine the illuminated decorations of the German volume, and compare them with the initial decorations of the volumes written by Leo, the famous Cassinese scribe,[7] to be convinced that Monte Cassino possessed either this very volume or at least one like it, from which its artists drew inspiration and appropriated features which particularly appealed to them, not, however, without adding something peculiarly their own.

While it is true, as we have seen, that interest in Tacitus dates from the

[1] MS. Monte Cassino 99; cf. *Script. Benev.*, pls. 67, 68.

[2] It is not found in Monte Cassino MS. 339, which is Desiderian.

[3] See G. Swarzenski, *Die Regensburger Buchmalerei*, p. 123 (Leipzig, 1901); S. Beissel, *Vatikanische Miniaturen*, pp. 35 ff., pl. XVIII.

[4] Facs. in *Archivio paleografico italiano*, IV. 32–8; see especially pl. 37.

[5] Scholars are at variance as to which Emperor Henry is meant. Gaudenzi in *Arch. pal. ital.* cited above favours Henry IV (1084–1105), Beissel and Swarzenski prefer Henry II though Henry III (1046–55) is not out of the question.

[6] Cf. *Chron. Monast. Casin.* III. 31 (ed. Wattenbach, p. 722).

[7] I refer to MSS. Monte Cassino 99 and Vatic. Lat. 1202; see *Script Benev.*, pls. 67, 68, 70, 71.

German regime at Monte Cassino during the eleventh century, it should be pointed out that this interest did not die out with the German influence in the abbey, for it can be shown that monks of Monte Cassino used this volume of Tacitus in the thirteenth century, i.e. fully a hundred years before Boccaccio found it there. The evidence lies in the thirteenth-century Cassinese characters we find on certain pages carefully replacing the original eleventh-century characters which had grown so pale as to be well-nigh illegible (see plate). There is only one conclusion that can be drawn from these efforts at restoration in the thirteenth century: it is that an interest in these books of Tacitus still lived on within the walls of the abbey. That the manuscript lay within easy reach of scribes in the twelfth century may be seen from the circumstance that one of the blank pages was used for trying out new pens. I refer to the probatio pennae *Abbas raynaldus* discussed above.

Of the original from which our manuscript was copied little can be said with certainty. The numerous instances of faulty words due to misunderstanding of the *scriptura continua* of the archetype suggest that the Monte
(*271*) Cassino scribe copied directly from an ancient exemplar. For such meaningless and un-Latin divisions and combinations as:

Amo enissimis	for Amoenissimis
militi aeterrebantur	,, militiae terrebantur
qua esentias	,, quae sentias

could hardly have been handed on from copy to copy without causing some reader or corrector to insert 'Require' or 'Nota' in the margin to call attention to the corruptions.[1] If it be correct to assume that there was no middle link between the eleventh century copy and the ancient exemplar in *scriptura continua*, can anything further be surmised as to the age and script of that exemplar? A number of errors due to misreading of certain letters suggest that the archetype was in rustic capitals. For the frequent confusion of **I** with **F** or **I** with **T** can only occur in copying from an exemplar in rustic capitals. I give a few examples of such errors:[2]

Hist.	II. 56. 3	omne Ias nefasque	= omne fas
	II. 95. 5	Iecisset	= fecisset
	III. 83. 7	Iacies	= facies
Ann.	XV. 45. 10	Ierebatur	= ferebatur
Hist.	V. 1. 4	superiori unam	= super fortunam
	I. 31. 2	euentior te	= euenit forte

[1] For other examples see Andresen's study cited above, II. 24.

[2] Other examples in Andresen, loc. cit. II. 8–9.

Professor Andresen, whom nothing of importance in our manuscript seems to have escaped, points out that in the celebrated passage (*Annals*, xv. 44) 'quos per flagitia invisos vulgus Christianos appellabat. Auctor nominis eius Christus', etc., the scribe of our manuscript originally wrote 'Chrestianos', which he (or a corrector) later changed to 'Christianos'.[1] The confusion of **E** with **I** is frequent in copying from an exemplar written in rustic capitals. But one finds it difficult to believe that our scribe could have made such an error in so familiar a word as 'Christiani'. The only reasonable explanation for his writing 'Chrestiani' (with an **E**) is that his original had an **E** which he automatically reproduced. This fact not only throws light on the fidelity with which the eleventh-century scribe reproduces his ancient original, but it suggests that the original must go back to a time when 'Chrestiani' was still a common spelling. We know that Tertullian (*Apol.* 3) complains of the misspelling with **e** as does Lactantius (*Div. Inst.* iv. 7. 5); and in one place (*272*)
(Acts xi: 26) the Sinaiticus, a manuscript of the fourth century, has *XPHCTIANOYC* (fol. 107). But Orosius (vii. 6. 15) in quoting Suetonius (*Claudius* 25. 4) has 'Christo' in the words 'Iudaeos impulsore Chresto' of Suetonius.

Whether the silent correction is due to the author or to a scribe it is impossible to tell. If Orosius had left it 'Chresto' it is more than likely that a scribe would sooner or later have changed the spelling to the more familiar and to him more correct form. This surmise is supported by an examination of the oldest manuscripts of Lactantius. In *Div. Inst.* iv. 7. 5 Lactantius says: 'sed exponenda huius nominis ratio est propter ignorantium errorem, qui eum inmutata littera Chrestum solent dicere'. Here the St. Gall palimpsest (saec. v) leaves us in the lurch, as a quire is missing, but the Bologna MS. (701), which certainly is not more recent than the sixth century, has the abbreviated form of 'Christum', i.e. $\overline{\mathbf{xpm}}$, thus showing what a Christian scribe was apt to do with the *nomen sacrum* even if by so doing the point of the sentence is destroyed.

That the Palatine manuscript of the eleventh century also writes $\overline{\mathbf{xpm}}$ in this passage does not surprise us in the least, when we consider that the writing of the *nomina sacra* in their contracted form had been a rule of centuries' standing. But the scribe of Tacitus in *Annals*, xv. 44, writes the word 'Christus' out in full. It seems highly improbable that this *nomen sacrum* would have remained in its original uncontracted form had copies made by Christian scribes intervened between the ancient archetype and our eleventh-

[1] *Wochenschrift für klass. Phil.* (1902), cols. 780 f.

century copy. But it may be asked: has not the uncontracted form survived in the eleventh-century copy? It has. But only because our scribe was copying faithfully from an exemplar written in *scriptura continua*. His attention being fully occupied with the task of forming good Latin words he allowed the 'illicit' form to creep into his text. I may be wrong, but this circumstance is to me another argument in favour of the supposition that the eleventh-century manuscript was copied directly from an ancient text of pagan origin.

Our extant classical manuscripts and fragments of manuscripts in rustic capitals—about a score all told—seem to have been written before the year 500. If what has been said above of the exemplar corresponds to the facts of the case, then our manuscript of Tacitus must have been copied from an original that goes back to the fifth century or even further.

A List of the Oldest Extant Manuscripts of Saint Augustine (235)

WITH A NOTE ON THE CODEX BAMBERGENSIS

IT is an interesting fact that in both pagan and Christian literature the oldest extant remains are of the giants and the favourites. Just as the most ancient classical Latin manuscripts are of Virgil, Terence, Lucan, Persius, Juvenal, Sallust, Cicero, and Livy, so, too, the oldest manuscripts of Christian learning, apart from Holy Scripture, contain Cyprian, Lactantius, Ambrose, Hilary, Prudentius, Jerome, and St. Augustine; and in point of numbers St. Augustine heads the list. This, of course, may be mere chance, but it is more likely to be chance aided by human selection. In any case, the survival of so many Augustinian manuscripts of great antiquity is a noteworthy fact. If the works that are preserved in the oldest manuscripts may be taken as a guide, it would appear that the treatise on the Psalms enjoyed the greatest popularity.

I propose in this article first to give a list of manuscripts of St. Augustine written in uncial or half-uncial characters, with references to published facsimiles; and then to make some palaeographical observations on one of the oldest of the Augustinian manuscripts, namely the Bambergensis.

The list is arranged alphabetically by libraries. The date next to a manuscript is, of course, approximate, and represents my present view. Though the list can lay no claim to being complete, it will, I think, be found to contain nearly all the oldest extant codices. Titles of works cited for the first time in the references are given in full, and afterwards in an abbreviated form. Facsimiles based on hand drawings are, for the most part, ignored. The contents of the manuscripts are not always given in full.

A glance at our list will show that nearly half a dozen of the manuscripts can be ascribed to the author's own century, and that nearly a dozen are of the following century, with four manuscripts belonging either to the end of the sixth or the beginning of the seventh. Almost a score may be assigned to the seventh century, with eight manuscripts belonging to the end of the seventh (236) or beginning of the eighth. A dozen or so can be assigned to the eighth. That a manuscript of Augustine was copied in uncial characters as late as the ninth

From *Miscellanea Agostiniana*, II (Tipographia Poliglotta Vaticana, 1931), pp. 235–51. [See Pls. **39** to **42**.]

century bears testimony to the great veneration with which his works were regarded.

OLDEST MANUSCRIPTS OF ST. AUGUSTINE IN UNCIAL AND HALF-UNCIAL SCRIPT[1]

AUTUN 107. saec. VII in. Half-uncial.

Enarrationes in psalmos 141–9.
Chatelain, *Uncialis scriptura*, pl. LXXVII (fol. 70^{v}); Delisle, *Bibliothèque de l'École des Chartes*, LIX (1898), pl. 3 (fol. 60); Liebaert, *Collection of Photographs*, 69–72 (fols. 24^{v}, 30^{v}, 99, 151).
Part of this manuscript is at Paris, B.N. Nouv. acq. lat. 1629, fols. 15–16 (q.v.).

BAMBERG B. IV. 21 (see below). saec. VI. Half-uncial.

De haeresibus, De cura pro mortuis gerenda, Enchiridion de fide, spe et caritate.
See accompanying plates and Chroust, *Monumenta palaeographica*, Serie I, Lieferung XVIII, pl. I (fols. 39, 114); Ihm, *Palaeographia latina*, I, pl. IV (fol. 10^{v}); Lowe in *The Legacy of the Middle Ages*, fig. 25c; Delitsch, *Schreibschriftformen*, pl. 3.

BERN A. 91. fragm. 8 (France). saec. VII–VIII. Uncial.

De genesi ad litteram (fragmenta).

BOULOGNE-SUR-MER 27 (32). saec. VII. Uncial.

Enarrationes in psalmos (fragmentum).
Wilmart, *Restes d'un très ancien manuscrit de la bibliothèque de Saint-Bertin* in *Bulletin historique de la Société des Antiquaires de la Morinie* (no. 268, 1924), with facsimiles.
Eight scraps of the same manuscript are bound into St. Omer 150 (q.v.). Knowledge of these fragments I owe to the kindness of Dom A. Wilmart.

CAMBRAI 300 (282). saec. VIII ex. Mixed uncial and minuscule.

De Trinitate.
Zimmermann, *Vorkarolingische Miniaturen*, pl. CLVIB (fol. 8).

CAMBRIDGE UNIV. ADDIT. 4320 (Palimpsest fragment found in Genizah at Cairo). saec. VI in. Uncial.

De sermone Domini in monte; Sermo 118 under Hebrew Masoretic text. Burkitt in *Journal of Theol. Stud.* XVII (1916), 137.

(237) ENGELBERG 59. saec. VII. Uncial.

Tractatus in evangelium Iohannis (fragmentum).

ESCORIAL, CAMARÍN DE LAS RELIQUIAS (at Spanheim saec. XV). saec. VII. Uncial.

De baptismo contra Donatistas.
Ewald–Loewe, *Exempla scripturae visigoticae*, pl. I (fol. 116^{v}).

[1] The writer is aware that a number of eighth-century manuscripts of St. Augustine of considerable textual importance exist, written in Visigothic, Insular, or pre-Caroline minuscule, but these are outside the scope of the present paper.

GENEVA MS. Lat. 16. saec. VII ex. Uncial and half-uncial on papyrus (outside of quires vellum).

Sermones; *Epistulae*.

Bordier, *Études paléographiques et historiques sur des papyrus du VIe siècle*, Geneva and Basle, 1866 (2 plates).

Formed part of the same manuscript as Leningrad F. pap. I. 1 (q.v.), and Paris B.N. lat. 11641 (q.v.).

LENINGRAD F. pap. I. 1 (one leaf). saec. VII ex. Uncial.

Sermones; *Epistulae*.

Staerk, *MSS. latins . . . de Saint-Pétersbourg*, II, pl. XIV (fol. 1v); Delisle–Traube, *Bibliothèque de l'École des Chartes*, LXIV (1903), with facsimile.

Formed part of the same manuscript as Geneva MS. Lat. 16 (q.v.), and Paris B.N. lat. 11641 (q.v.).

LENINGRAD Q. v. I. 3 (Corbie). saec. V. Uncial.

De diversis quaestionibus ad Simplicianum; *Contra epistulam Fundamenti*; *De agone christiano*; *De doctrina christiana*.

Staerk, I, pl. I (fol. 145), II, pl. II (fol. 49, colophon); Chatelain, *Uncialis*, pl. III (fol. 127, colophon); Liebaert, *Coll. of phot.*, no. 1305 (fol. 26); Thibaut, *Monuments de la notation ekphonétique et neumatique de l'Église latine*, fig. 2 (copy of Staerk, I, pl. I), fig. 3 (fol. 80); Thibaut, *Notation musicale*, pl. 2; Besson, *Saint Pierre*, fig. 85.

LENINGRAD Q. v. I. 4 (Corbie). saec. VI–VII. Half-uncial.

De civitate Dei, Lib. X.

Staerk, II, pl. XX (fol. 41, colophon).

Formed part of Paris B.N. lat. 12214 (q.v.).

LYONS 426 (352), fols. 8–185. saec. VII. Uncial and cursive half-uncial.

Enarrationes in psalmos 49–96 (abbreviated).

Recueil de fac-similés à l'usage de l'École des Chartes, pl. 151 (fol. 143); Lowe, *Codices Lugdunenses antiquissimi*, pl. XII (fol. 49), pl. XIII (fol. 2).

Part of this manuscript is now Paris B.N. Nouv. acq. lat. 1629, fols. 7–14 (q.v.).

LYONS 478 (408), fols. 1–203 (Île Barbe). saec. VI (but fols. 1–9 are in imitation uncial saec. IX). Uncial.

De consensu Evangelistarum; Sermo 110.

Recueil de fac-similés de l'École des Chartes, pl. 150 (fols. 114, 121v); Lowe, *Codd. Lugd. antiq.*, pl. VII (fol. 35), pl. VIII (fols. 4, 8).

LYONS 604 (521). saec. VII. Half-uncial. (240)

Sermones 202, 309, 348, 60, 347; De fide et symbolo; Sermones 2, 9, 170, 142, 361.

Album paléographique de l'École des Chartes, pl. 9b (fol. 92); Zimmermann, *Vorkarolingische Miniaturen*, pl. XL C, D (fols. 74v, 57v); Lowe, *Codd. Lugd. antiq.*, pls. XVI, XVII (fols. 74, 23v, 34, 86), and pl. I (initials); Gudeman-Galindo Romeo, *Literatura Latino-Cristiana*, pl. IX (fol. 92).

Paris B.N. Nouv. acq. lat. 1594 (q.v.) formed part of this manuscript.

LYONS 607 (523bis). saec. VII. Half-uncial.

De civitate Dei, libb. I–V.

Album paléogr. de l'École des Chartes, pl. 7 (fols. 53, 128): *New Palaeographical Society*, I, pl. 206 (fols. 44, 53); Lowe, *Codd. Lugd. antiq.*, pls. XXVI, XXVII (fols. 78, 34^{v}, 69^{v}, 129^{v}, 21); Gudeman–Galindo Romeo, *Literatura Latino-Cristiana*, pl. XI (fols. 53, 128).

MILAN AMBROS. G. 58 sup., fols. 74–5. saec. VI^{2}. Uncial.

De doctrina christiana (fragment).

MILAN AMBROS. M. 77 sup. fols. 1, 97. saec. VI^{2}. Half-uncial.

De doctrina christiana (fragment).

Probably from the same manuscript as G. 58 sup.

MILAN AMBROS. O. 210 sup. fols. 1–46 (Bobbio). saec. VI–VII. Half-uncial.

Epistulae 166, 172.

Chatelain, *Uncialis*, pl. LXVIII. 2 (fol. 30); Chatelain, *Notes Tironiennes*, pl. XIII (fol. 46^{v}).

MONTE CASSINO CCLXXI (348) (South Italy). saec. VII–VIII. Uncial.

(*Palimpsest under eleventh century Beneventan*).

Enarrationes in psalmos 143–50.

Part of this manuscript is in Rome, Vatic. Ottobon. 319 (q.v.) and part in Rome, Vallicell. B. 38 II (q.v.).

NAPLES VI. D. 59. saec. VII ex. Uncial.

(The manuscript was in south Italy by the tenth century. Traube connects it with Bobbio, but it is not clear on what grounds.)

Libellus de penitentia (= *Sermo 351*).

Carta–Cipolla–Frati, *Monumenta palaeographica sacra*, pl. 6 (fols. 36^{v}, 37).

NEW YORK, PIERPONT MORGAN LIBRARY M. 334. A.D. 669. Uncial.

(Written at Luxeuil, later at Beauvais and Château de Troussures.)

Tractatus decem in epistulam Iohannis.

Delisle, *Notices et Extraits*, XXXI. 2 (1886), pls. I–III (fols. 72^{v}, 73, 133^{v}); Thompson, *Introduction to Greek and Latin Palaeography*, no. 92.

(*241*) ORLÉANS 154 (131) (Fleury). saec. VIII. Uncial.

Sermones.

Delisle, *Notices et Extraits*, XXXI. 1, with two plates (fols. 56, 89 or pp. 126, 288), also reproduced in *Recueil de fac-similés de l'École des Chartes*, pl. 250.

Parts of this manuscript are in Paris B.N. Nouv. acq. lat. 1598 and 1599 (q.v.).

ORLÉANS 192 (169), fol. 31 (Fleury). saec. VII. Uncial.

Epistula 187, ad Dardanum.

Chatelain, *Uncialis*, pl. XXIX. 2 (fol. 31^{v}).

ORLÉANS 192 (169), fols. 32–3 (Fleury). saec. V. Half-uncial.

Contra duas epistulas Pelagianorum (fragmentum).

Delisle, *Mémoires de l'Académie des Inscriptions*, XXXII. 1 (1885), pl. V (fol. 33); Chatelain, *Uncialis*, LXIV. 2 (fol. 33v); Reusens, *Éléments de Paléographie*, pl. IV. 1 (fol. 33).
Parts of this manuscript are in Paris B.N. lat. 13368 (q.v.), and B.N. Nouv. acq. lat. 2199 (q.v.).

ORLÉANS 192 (169), fols. 34–7 (Fleury). saec. VII ex. Uncial.

Epistula 54, ad Ianuarium.
Chatelain, *Uncialis*, XLIX. 4 (fol. 35).

ORLÉANS 192 (169), fol. 38 (Fleury). saec. VI. Uncial.

Enarrationes in psalm. 5.
Chatelain, *Uncialis*, V. 2 (fol. 38v).

OXFORD BODL. LAUD. MISC. 126 (Würzburg). saec. VIII med. Uncial, half-uncial.

De Trinitate.

Chatelain, *Uncialis*, LII (fol. 2), XCVI (fol. 96v); *New Pal. Soc.* II, pls. 83–5 (fols. 3, 55v, 100, 87v and ten lines of library list in text); Zimmermann, pls. CXXXVIII–CXLI (fols. 5, 2, 87v, 3, 6v, 7, 42, 96v); Lowe in *Speculum*, III (1928), pl. I (fol. 260), the added Anglo-Saxon Library list.

PARIS B.N. lat. 2706 (St. Denis). saec. VII ex. Half-uncial.

De genesi ad litteram.

Bastard, *Peintures et ornements*, pl. XV; Chatelain, *Uncialis*, pl. LXXXIX (fol. 102); Zimmermann, pls. CXXIX, CXXX, CXXXIII (fols. 16, 157, 304, 233).

PARIS B.N. lat. 2769, fol. 22 (Italy). saec. VI. Uncial.

Sermo 110 (fragmentum).
Cf. De Bruyne in *Revue Bénédictine*, XXXVI (1924), 126.

PARIS B.N. lat. 9533. saec. VII. Half-uncial.

The manuscript has Visigothic symptoms.
Enarrationes in psalmos 29–36.
Chatelain, *Uncialis*, pl. LXIX. 2 (fol. 227, colophon, signature).

PARIS B.N. lat. 11641 (Luxeuil-Lyons). saec. VII ex. Uncial. *(242)*

Sermones, Epistulae.

Bastard, *Peintures et ornements*, pls. XXI–XXII; Silvestre, *Paléographie universelle*, pl. 74 = CVII = 270; Champollion-Figeac, *Chartes et Mss. sur papyrus*, XV and XVbis; *Pal. Soc.*, I, pls. XLII–XLIII; Delisle, *Cabinet*, pl. VII. 2 (fol. 8v); Chatelain, *Uncialis*, pl. XC (fol. 8); *Bibliothèque Nationale. Reproductions réduites. MSS. exposés*, pl. XII (fol. 42); Zimmermann, pls. XLIV–XLV (fols. 34, 10, 3v, 19); Lowe, *Codd. Lugd. antiq.*, pls. XXXIII–XXXIV (fols. 7v, 9, 26v). Parts of this manuscript are at Geneva MS. Lat. 16 (q.v.), and Leningrad F. pap. I. 1 (q.v.).

PARIS B.N. lat. 12190 (Corbie). saec. VIII in. Uncial, half-uncial.

De consensu Evangelistarum.

Bastard, *Peintures et ornements*, pl. XXVI; Delisle, *Cabinet*, pl. I. 5, 7, 8 (fols 181v, 45, 97); Chatelain, *Uncialis*, pl. XCIX (fol. 35v); Zimmermann, pls. CXII–CXIII (fols. 1, Av).

PARIS B.N. lat. 12205 (Corbie). saec. VII. Uncial.

Epistula ad Valentinum, De correptione et gratia.

Delisle, *Cabinet*, pl. I. 6 (fol. 65v); Chatelain, *Uncialis*, pl. XXXVIII (fol. 29); Besson, *Saint Pierre*, fig. 80 (fol. 157v).

PARIS B.N. lat. 12214 (Corbie). saec. VI–VII. Half-uncial.

De civitate Dei, libb. I–IX.

Bastard, *Peintures et ornements*, pl. V; Chatelain, *Uncialis*, pl. LXXXII (fol. 74v); Delisle, *Cabinet*, pl. VI. 1, 4–16.

Leningrad Q. v. I. 4 (q.v.) formed part of the same manuscript. See p. 305.

PARIS B.N. lat. 12634 (Corbie). saec. VII. Uncial.

Regula.

Delisle, *Cabinet*, pl. VIII. 4 (fol. 50); Casamassa in *Rendiconti della pontificia accademia romana di archeologia*, 1 (1923), pls. III–IV (fols. 10v, 20, 9).

Leningrad Q. v. I. 5 (q.v.) formed part of this manuscript.

PARIS B.N. lat. 13367 (Corbie). saec. VI. Half-uncial.

De opere monachorum, De fide et operibus, Ad Donatistas post collationem, etc.

Delisle, *Cabinet*, pl. IX. 1, 4 (fols. 240v, 39v); Chatelain, *Uncialis*, pl. LXVII. 2 (fol. 184v); *New Pal. Soc.* I, pl. LXXX (fol. 208v); Thompson, *Introduction to Greek and Latin Palaeography*, no. 99 (copy of *New Pal. Soc.*); Millares Carlo, *Paleografía española*, fig. 9 (copy of Thompson).

(243) PARIS B.N. lat. 13368, fly-leaf, fol. 256 (Fleury). saec. V. Half-uncial.

Contra duas epistulas Pelagianorum (fragmentum).

Delisle, *Cabinet*, pl. IV. 4, 5 (fol. 256, 256v).

Part of Orléans 192 (169) (q.v.); another fragment is in Paris B.N. Nouv. acq. lat. 2199 (q.v.).

PARIS B.N. Nouv. acq. lat. 1594 (Lyons). saec. VII. Half-uncial.

Sermones.

Delisle, *Catalogue ... Libri et Barrois*, pl. I. 6–7 (fols. 35, 15v); Chatelain, *Uncialis*, pl. LXIX. 1 (fol. 18v).

Part of Lyons 604 (521) (q.v.).

PARIS B.N. Nouv. acq. lat. 1598 and 1599 (Fleury). saec. VIII. Uncial.

Sermones.

Delisle, *Catalogue ... Libri et Barrois*, pl. III. 1 (Nouv. acq. 1598, fol. 4), 5 (Nouv. acq. 1599, fol. 20v); Zimmermann, pls. LXXVI–LXXVIII (Nouv. acq. 1598, fols. 1, 15, 20v, 13, 4, and Nouv. acq. 1599, fol. 20v).

Part of Orléans 154 (131), (q.v.).

PARIS B.N. Nouv. acq. lat. 1629, fols. 7–14 (Lyons). saec. VII. Uncial.

Enarrationes in psalmos.

Chatelain, *Uncialis*, pl. XVI (fol. 13).

Formed part of Lyons 426 (352) (q.v.).

Paris B.N. Nouv. acq. lat. 1629, fols. 15–16. saec. vii in. Half-uncial.

Enarrationes in psalmos.
Pal. Soc. ii, pl. 9 (fol. 15).
Formed part of Autun 107 (q.v.).

Paris B.N. Nouv. acq. lat. 2199 (fol. 1) (Fleury). saec. v. Half-uncial.

Contra duas epistulas Pelagianorum (fragmentum).
Orléans 192 (169), fols. 32–3 (q.v.), and Paris B.N. lat. 13368, fol. 256 (q.v.) formed part of the same manuscript.

Rome Vallicelliana A. 14 (Rome). saec. ix. Uncial.

Tractatus in evangelium Iohannis.

Rome Vallicelliana B. 38^{II} (South Italy). saec. vii–viii. Uncial, with two pages in half-uncial.

Enarrationes in psalmos 66–70, 82–84, 87–90.
Part of Rome Vatic. Ottobon. lat. 319 (q.v.), and Monte Cassino cclxxi (348) (q.v.).

Rome Vatic. lat. 3835–6 (Rome). saec. viii. Uncial.

Sermones varii (contained in the Homiliary of Agimund).
Silvestre, pls. ccxxxv and cliii = 81 and 83 = cxiv and cxvi (3836, p. 9, and 3835, fol. 219); M. Besson, *Saint Pierre*, fig. 92 (fol. 260^{v}).

Rome Vatic. lat. 4938 (Italy). saec. viii med. Uncial. *(244)*

Enarrationes in psalmos 61–70.

Rome Vatic. lat. 5757 (Bobbio). saec. vii–viii. Uncial.

Palimpsest over Cicero *De republica* (saec. v).
Enarrationes in psalmos 119–40.
Silvestre, pls. xxix–xxx = 64 = xcvii (p. 75); *Pal. Soc.* i, pl. clx (p. 122); Zangemeister-Wattenbach, pl. xvii (p. 6); Chatelain, *Paléographie des classiques latins*, pl. xxxix (p. 122); Reusens, pl. lx (copy of *Pal. Soc.*); Steffens, *Lateinische Paläographie*[1], pl. xiii (p. 8) and Supplement, pl. v (p. 86) = second edition pl. xv; Thompson, *Introduction*, no. 87; Ehrle-Liebaert, *Specimina codicum latinorum Vaticanorum*, pl. iv (p. 222); Johnston, *Latin Manuscripts*, pl. ii, fig. 13.

Rome Vatic. lat. 5758 (Bobbio). saec. vii in. Uncial.

Sermones 8 (Denis); *1, 7* (Frangipane); *12, 13, 14, 15, 16, 17, 19, 20, 22, 25, 26* (Mai).
Zangemeister-Wattenbach, pl. xxxiii (p. 15); Ehrle-Liebaert, pl. viii (p. 287, semicursive script).

Rome Vatic. Barb. lat. 671 (XIV. 44) (Italy). saec. viii ex. Uncial.

Sermones.

Rome Vatic. Ottobon. lat. 319 (South Italy). saec. vii–viii. Uncial.

Enarrationes in psalmos 84–86.
Chatelain, *Uncialis*, pl. xxii (fol. 40).

Part of this manuscript is Vallicellianus B. 38[II] (q.v.) and part Monte Cassino CCLXXI (348) (q.v.).

ROME VATIC. PAL. lat. 210 (Lorsch). saec. VI–VII. Uncial, half-uncial.

De bono coniugali, De sancta virginitate, De bono viduitatis, De opere monachorum, De agone christiano, Epist. 130, 36, 127, Sermones 355, 356, 65, 53, 277, 150, 5, 6, 45, 137, 351, 352.

ROME Vittorio Emanuele 2094 (Sessor. 13) (Nonantola). saec. VI. Uncial.

De genesi ad litteram.
Archivio paleografico italiano, vol. II, pls. XIII, XIV (fols. 30v, 134v); Zimmermann, pl. XX (fols. 149, 134v).

ROME Vitt. Em. 2099 (Sessor. 55) (Nonantola). saec. VI ex. Half-uncial.

(Palimpsest, upper script, over Pliny, *Historia Naturalis* in uncial).
Confessiones, Serm. 230, 247, Versus S. Augustini (*Epitaphium Diaconi Naboris*).
Pertz-Bethmann, *Bericht über die zur Bekanntmachung geeigneten Verhandlungen der Kgl. Preuss. Akad. d. Wiss. zu Berlin aus dem Jahre 1853*, with plate; Chatelain, *Uncialis*, pl. LXXXVIII (fol. 37).

(245) ST. GALL 1395, pp. 412–15. saec. VIII. Uncial.

Sermones 140, 213 (fragmenta).

ST. OMER 150. saec. VII. Uncial.

Enarrationes in psalmos (fragmenta).
Eight scraps used to repair fols. 3, 6, 7, 10, 11, 14, 15, 18. See Wilmart's article cited above under Boulogne-sur-Mer 27 (32), which has a fragment of the same manuscript.

ST. PETERSBURG, *see* LENINGRAD.

TROUSSURES, Château de, *see* NEW YORK.

TURIN, B.N. UNIV. A. II. 2* (Bobbio). saec. VII–VIII. Half-uncial.

Palimpsest, over Livy (saec. V) and Cicero (saec. IV). Destroyed by fire in 1904.
Collatio cum Maximino, Contra Maximinum libri duo.
Carta-Cipolla-Frati, *Monumenta palaeographica sacra*, pl. XI; Chatelain, *Pal. des Class.*, pl. XXIX. 2 (p. 34) and XXXVI A. 2 (Irish); Cipolla, *Codici Bobbiesi*, pls. III, IV, V. 2 and II. 2 (Irish).

TURIN B.N. UNIV. F. IV. 1, fragm. 2 (Bobbio). saec. VII–VIII. Uncial.

Enarrationes in psalmum 93 (fragmenta).
Cipolla, *Codici Bobbiesi*, pl. XXXIII (fol. 2v).

TURIN B.N. UNIV. G. V. 26 (Bobbio). saec. VI². Half-uncial.

Epistulae 238, 239, 241, ad Pascentium.
Chatelain, *Uncialis*, pl. LXX. 1–2 (fols. 27, 129); Cipolla, *Codd. Bobb.*, pl. XXI (fols. 5v, 60v), pl. XXII. 1 (fol. 41); Lindsay in Lawlor's, 'The Cathach of St. Columba' in *Proceed. R. Irish Acad.* XXXIII. C. 11, pp. 400–3 and pl. XXXIV (fol. 129).

[VERCELLI CAPITOL. 183 is given by Traube, *Vorlesungen und Abhandlungen*, I. 248, as uncial, but this must be an error; the script of St. Augustine's *Retractationes* is North Italian cursive minuscule, saec. VIII. The uncial folios at the end contain Homilies of Gregory.]

VERONA CAPITOL. X (8). saec. VIII in. Uncial and mixed half-uncial.

Enarrationes in psalmos (fragmenta).
Sickel, *Monumenta graphica medii aevi*, VIII, pl. 5; Chatelain, *Uncialis*, pl. XCVIII. 3 (fol. 39^v).

VERONA CAPITOL. XXVIII (26). saec. V. Uncial.

De civitate Dei, libb. XI–XVI.
Chatelain, *Uncialis*, pl. VI (fol. 80).

VERONA CAPITOL. XXXIII (31). saec. VIII in. Veronese half-uncial, almost (*246*)
minuscule.

De agone Christiano, *De fide et symbolo*, *Epist. 73* (fragmenta), etc.
Sickel, III, *Monumenta*, pl. I; Schiaparelli in *Studi e Testi*, 47, pls. 3^a, 3^b (fols. I, 2^v).

VERONA CAPITOL. LIX (57). saec. VII in. Half-uncial.

Sermo 341 (excerpta).
Chatelain, *Uncialis*, pl. LXXXVII. I (fol. 157); Carusi-Lindsay, *Monumenta Palaeographica Veronensia*, pls. 19–21 (fols. 9^v, 91^v, 120, 162^v, 170, 215); cf. G. Morin in *Miscellanea Agostiniana*, I (1930), 666.

EUGIPPI EXCERPTA EX S. AUGUSTINI OPERIBUS

MILAN AMBROS. C. 73 inf. (Bobbio). saec. VIII. Uncial.

Palimpsest, over Luke (saec. V) and *Parva genesis*, etc. (saec. VII).
Eugippi excerpta ex operibus sancti Augustini.

PARIS B.N. 2110 (St. Denis?). saec. VIII in. Half-uncial.

Eugippi excerpta ex operibus sancti Augustini.
Bastard, *Peintures et ornements*, pls. XVI–XVIII; Delisle, *Cabinet*, pl. XII. 3 (fol. 145); Chatelain, *Uncialis*, pl. XCV (fol. 154); Zimmermann, pls. CXXXI–CXXXII, CXXXIII *c*, *d*, CXXXIV (fols. 116^v, 154, 121, 57^v, 2^v, 136^v, 389, 120^v, 251^v, 151^v, 252^v, 153^v, 328^v).

PARIS B.N. Nouv. acq. lat. 1575 (Tours). saec. VIII^2. Uncial and half-uncial in part, but mostly minuscule.

Eugippi excerpta ex operibus sancti Augustini.
Delisle, *Notice sur un MS. Mérovingien contenant des fragments d'Eugippius* . . . Paris, 1875, pls. I–VI (fols. 85, 1, 4, 59^v, 13, 48^v); Delisle, *Catalogue* . . . *Libri et Barrois*, pl. III. 2–4 (fols. 136, 50, 65^v); Monaci, *Facsimili di antichi manoscritti*, pl. LXXXV; Lauer, *Mémoires de l'Académie des Inscriptions*, XIII (1924), pl. VII (fol. 93); Rand, *Survey of the MSS. of Tours*, pls. IV–VI (fols. 136^v, 114, 39).

Rome Vatic. lat. 3375 (South Italy). saec. vi ex. Half-uncial.

Eugippi excerpta ex operibus sancti Augustini.

See accompanying plate and Chatelain, *Uncialis*, pl. lxxxi (fol. 35^{v}); Lowe, *Scriptura Beneventana*, pl. iii (fol. 143).

(247) WORKS ATTRIBUTED TO SAINT AUGUSTINE

Carlsruhe, Fragm. 100 (Reichenau). saec. vii–viii. Half-uncial (1 leaf).

De divinis scripturis (*Speculum*).

Cologne, Dombibliothek CLXVI. saec. viii. Uncial.

De rhetorica, De principiis dialecticae.

Leningrad Q. v. I. 5 (Corbie). saec. vii–viii. Uncial.

Sermones de latrone, de penitentia = Maxim. Taurin. *Serm.* 51, 52, 53.
Staerk, ii, pl. xv (fol. 8).

Paris B.N. Nouv. acq. lat. 1596 (Fleury). saec. vii. Uncial.

De divinis scripturis (*Speculum*) (fragmentum).
Pal. Soc. ii, pl. xxxiv; Delisle, *Catalogue . . . Libri et Barrois*, pl. vii. 5 (fol. 1).

Rome B.N. Vitt. Em. 2106 (Sessor. 58) (Nonantola). saec. viii. Uncial.

De divinis scripturis (*Speculum*).
Chatelain, *Uncialis*, pl. liii (fol. 67^{v}).

Verona Capitol. II (2) fol. 1^{r}. saec. viii. Uncial.

Sermo 251 app. de die iudicii (an addition).

THE CODEX BAMBERGENSIS

The Codex Bambergensis is one of the oldest and noblest specimens of the half-uncial script, and although patristic scholars had made use of its text of Jerome and Augustine, its palaeographical importance was quite ignored until Traube and Fischer[1] won for it its proper place. In his *Vollständige Beschreibung* H. J. Jaeck had unfortunately misdated the manuscript by three centuries, and both E. C. Richardson, in his edition of the *De viris illustribus*, p. xvii, and Zycha, in the Vienna *Corpus scriptorum ecclesiasticorum latinorum*, vol. 41, p. xxxi, followed him in giving the ninth century as its date, and this probably explains why it remained so long in relative obscurity. To students of palaeography in general, the manuscript became known through the
(248) facsimiles in Chroust (*Monumenta palaeographica*, i, Lief. xviii, pl. i) and

[1] H. Fischer, *Katalog der Handschriften der Königlichen Bibliothek zu Bamberg*, Band i, i, fasc. 3, pp. 463 ff., no. 87 (Bamberg, 1903).

Ihm (*Palaeographia Latina*, I, pl. IV). Ihm correctly ascribes the manuscript to the sixth century; Chroust, however, considers it of the seventh century. Herein he was misled by Chatelain, who assigns to the seventh century the Vatican Eugippius (Lat. 3375), to which, as Chroust correctly observed, the Bambergensis has very close similarity. My own reasons for regarding the Vatican Eugippius as a manuscript of the late sixth century I have given elsewhere (*Scriptura Beneventana*, pl. III). To put it briefly, the Eugippius manuscript has a certain resemblance to Monte Cassino CL, and the latter is a half-uncial manuscript of the year A.D. 570. From this it may reasonably be argued that the Bambergensis, being extraordinarily like the Vaticanus, is also approximately of the same age. With respect to the home of the Bambergensis, scholars have expressed hesitant views. To Chroust, either Gaul or Italy seemed possible. To Traube, north Italy seemed most probable. His (249)
reason for locating it in the north of Italy he found in the character of a cursive entry at the end of St. Augustine's work, *De haeresibus* (fol. 79^{v}), a facsimile of which accompanies this article. This view Traube expressed in *Paläographische Forschungen*, IV. 8. Later, as Ihm tells us, he was inclined to (250)
associate the manuscript with Bobbio, because of certain Insular notes inserted in the margin, one of which is here reproduced. It reads: 'nihil cautius quam quod habet in corde proferre' (see Pl. **41** (*facs. III*)).

No one can examine the Vatican Eugippius and the Bambergensis without discerning very close resemblance in the half-uncial alphabet of the two manuscripts. Furthermore, there is the closest similarity between the sloping **bd**-uncial marginalia found in the two manuscripts. They are so much alike as to seem the work of one hand, as the reader may judge from the accompanying facsimiles. Besides these points of resemblance in the main script and marginalia, the two manuscripts have the same type of abbreviation and the same style for marking omitted **m**, and they are both written in long lines.

Now the Vatican Eugippius was certainly in south Italy during part of the Middle Ages, as the Beneventan insertions, corrections and added punctuation amply attest. The natural presumption is that the Eugippius Codex is a south Italian product. If this be true, the Bambergensis must be regarded as hailing from the same region, for there cannot be the slightest doubt that the two manuscripts originated in the same centre. But the Bambergensis did not long remain in south Italy. By the eighth century, apparently, it must have been in Rome or its neighbourhood, as may be gathered from the very note on fol. 79^{v} which to Traube was an argument for connecting it with the north.

It reads: 'nestoriana et eutychiana hic scriptas (*sic*) non s[unt]' (see Pl. **42** (*facs. IV*)). The peculiar characters in this note are, I believe, unmistakably in the script used by the Curia Romana and by other Roman notaries in the eighth century.[1] I am aware that a century earlier there was a resemblance between the Chancery of Ravenna and that of Rome. But we have no examples of this type of writing in Ravenna as late as the eighth century, so Ravenna must, I think,
(*251*) be excluded.[2] The Bambergensis did not long abide in Rome or its vicinity. Towards the end of the eighth century or beginning of the ninth it must have been read in a centre where the Insular script was in vogue. Unless I err, the Insular marginalia of the Bambergensis are Anglo-Saxon and not Irish. My own reconstruction of the history of the manuscript would therefore be that it was written in southern Italy, then migrated to Rome, and probably left Italy before the ninth century, along with other books collected by missionaries for Transalpine monasteries. It may easily be a book that came either to England and was then transported to some place like Fulda where Anglo-Saxon script was current at the end of the eighth and beginning of the ninth century and from Fulda or region it migrated to Bamberg, or it may have gone direct from Italy to some German centre.

[1] Cf. Steffens, *Lateinische Paläographie*², pls. 58 and 62.

[2] Cf. L. Schiaparelli in *Archivio storico italiano*, VI (1926), 165. It is also a fact that a certain resemblance is to be noted between the script of the Curia Romana and that of the chancery at Naples, but the note in the Bambergensis is manifestly more akin to that of the Curia Romana. Facsimiles in Curialesca Napolitana may be seen in M. Russi, *Paleografia e Diplomatica de' Documenti delle province Napolitane*, Naples, 1883, Saggi 6–7, and pp. 18–25, and better in *Archivio paleografico italiano*, VII, pl. 55. I may add that Professors N. Barone, L. Schiaparelli, and B. Katterbach, whom I was privileged to consult, agreed with me that the note in the Bambergensis had far greater resemblance to the script of the Curia Romana than to any other.

Nugae Palaeographicae (55)

THERE is a famous Roman proverb 'De minimis non curat praetor'. The very opposite may well be taken as the palaeographer's motto. In the following paragraphs I propose to give some instances showing how palaeographical trifles may possess larger significance than appears at first sight. The instances I shall give are taken haphazard from work I have been engaged upon from time to time.

The influence exerted by southern Italy over the rest of Christian Europe in the early Middle Ages can be gauged roughly by the spread of the Benedictine Rule. What is not so easy to gauge is the extent to which the rest of Europe affected southern Italy. The few facts gleaned from south Italian chronicles are meagre enough. In the eighth century a much-travelled Anglo-Saxon monk, Willibald, had sojourned at Monte Cassino; a Spanish priest named Diapertus had lived there at the same time; and a little later a Bavarian monk named Sturmius, destined to become the first abbot of Fulda, had been sent by the great Boniface to Monte Cassino to imbibe monastic discipline at its source. Ambrosius Autpertus, a Gaul by birth, ended his days in the abbey of St. Vincent on the Volturno, and at the close of the same century Monte Cassino was visited by Adalhard of Corbie.[1] These historic visits would gain in significance if it could be shown that the above-mentioned
monks had left some mark behind them, or if traces of Anglo-Saxon, Spanish, (56)
or Gaulish[2] methods were discoverable in south Italian work of the late eighth and early ninth centuries. Actually such traces do exist. But they can be established as fact only by the interpretation of certain palaeographical minutiae. I give a few examples.

In the abbacy of Theodemar (778–97) monks of Monte Cassino copied a very interesting compilation of grammatical treatises, now preserved in the

From *Persecution and Liberty, Essays in honor of George Lincoln Burr* (New York, Century Co.. 1931), pp. 55–69. [See Pls. **43** to **46**.]

[1] Cf. 'Leonis Marsicani et Petri Diaconi chronica monasterii Casinensis', ed. Wattenbach in *Mon. Germ. Hist., Scriptores*, VII. 551 ff.; 'Vita Willibaldi' in *Mon. Germ. Hist., Scriptores*, XV, pt. I, p. 102; L. Tosti, *Storia della Badia di Monte Cassino* (Naples, 1842–3); E. A. Loew, *The Beneventan Script* (Oxford, 1914), pp. 4–5, 107.

[2] Ambrosius Autpertus' commentary on the Apocalypse exists in an early ninth-century Beneventan manuscript (Benevento III. 9). Certain peculiarities suggest that the south Italian scribe copied from a Gaulish original. See my *Scriptura Beneventana* (Oxford, 1929), pl. XII.

Bibliothèque Nationale under the press-mark MS. lat. 7530. The compilation includes parts of Varro's *De Lingua Latina*, the scholium to Varius' *Thyestes*, and Servius' *De Metris Horatianis*. The manuscript, written in the south Italian or Beneventan minuscule, also contains Paschal tables and a calendar with the 'depositiones' of Monte Cassino abbots, which fix its home and date.[1] The exemplar, however, from which this manuscript was copied, must have been in part at least Insular, that is, Anglo-Saxon or Irish; for, in the portion containing Bede, we find a few Insular forms like $\overline{\text{at}}$ = autem, ħ = haec, 7 = et, which must have crept into the text through inadvertence.[2] In the same part of the manuscript, as Lindsay has pointed out, there occurs the gloss 'forbotan'.[3] It seems reasonable to explain the presence of this gloss and of the Anglo-Saxon abbreviations in a Monte Cassino manuscript by the
(57) connection between Monte Cassino and Fulda dating from the time of Sturmius' visit. Palaeography would thus seem to lend significance to the visit.

In the Laurentian Library there is a ninth-century Beneventan MS. (LXVI. 40) celebrated for its text—the oldest in the Latin language—of the story of Apollonius, king of Tyre.[4] It also contains the unique text of the *Exordia Scythica* and of the verses of Cellanus (d. 706), the Irish abbot of Péronne in Picardy.[5] The script shows that the manuscript was written in south Italy during the ninth century. Circumstantial evidence goes to prove that the precise centre must have been Monte Cassino, for nearly all the other Beneventan manuscripts in the Laurentian are, oddly enough, manuscripts of the classics—Varro, Caesar, Cicero, Tacitus, Apuleius, Justin—and the manuscript of Justin still has, on its opening page, the Monte Cassino ex-libris, while the rest have other unmistakable, if less obvious, signs connecting them with Monte Cassino, the most interesting being the unique manuscript of Tacitus' *Histories* and *Annals* (bks. XI–XVI).[6] There can be little doubt that

[1] On this manuscript see the writer's *Die ältesten Kalendarien aus Monte Cassino* (Munich, 1908), p. 4 and pl. 2 (*Quellen und Untersuchungen zur lateinischen Philologie des Mittelalters*, III. 3) and *Scriptura Beneventana*, pl. IX; Chatelain, *Paléographie des classiques latins* (2 vols., Paris, 1884–1900), I, pl. XIII; Steffens, *Lateinische Paläographie* (2nd ed., Trier, 1909), pl. 42A (= 1st ed., Suppl., pl. 15B).

[2] C. H. Beeson has found several other Insular forms. He says: 'I think it may be confidently asserted that these abbreviations did come from the archetype and that this archetype was a Fulda MS.' See his recent article, 'Paris Lat. 7530. A study in Insular Symptoms', published in *Raccolta di scritti in onore di Felice Ramorino* (Milan), pp. 199 ff. (*Pubblicazioni dell' università cattolica del Sacro Cuore*, ser. IV, vol. VII).

[3] W. M. Lindsay, *Notae Latinae* (Cambridge, 1915), p. xv.

[4] Cf. *Script. Benev.*, pl. XXV.

[5] Cf. L. Traube, 'Perrona Scottorum' in *Sitzungsberichte der philos.-philol. und der histor. Klasse der Königl. Bayer. Akademie d. Wiss.* (Munich, 1900, Heft IV), pp. 484 ff., reprinted in *Vorlesungen und Abhandlungen* (3 vols., Munich, 1909–20), III. 105 ff.

[6] On these manuscripts see *Benev. Script*, pp. 16 ff. [this volume, pp. 86 ff.], 70 f., and my article, 'The Unique Manuscript of Tacitus'

these manuscripts form a group and presumably have a common history, their removal from Monte Cassino being somehow connected with the visits of Boccaccio when, as his pupil Benvenuto da Imola tells us, he found the state of the library so shocking that he left it in tears. It would seem that the manuscripts were literally begging to be saved. A humanist came to the rescue and transported the works of the old Roman authors to the then safest place for classics—Florence. The verses of Cellanus mentioned above must, of course, go back to an exemplar written in an Insular centre; in fact the Insular character of the immediate exemplar from which the south Italian scribe copied (58)
is clearly suggested by certain considerations. When he wrote 'prae' for 'per', the meaningless 'scrux' for 'sed crux', and 'quatiares' for 'quatiare sed', he committed errors which betrayed his ignorance of Insular methods of abbreviating 'per' and 'sed'. When he wrote 'genubus' for 'gentibus', it was due to his unfamiliarity with Insular script in which **ti** often resembles **u.** A colophon on fol. 20 reads

EXPΛICIT IωHANNES SUBDIAC SCRIPSIT

in which the display of learning in the use of Greek letters *Λ* and *ω* and the preference for the angular forms of **S** and **C** are all strongly redolent of Insular methods. An Insular exemplar of this sort could have reached Monte Cassino through such visits as Willibald's and Sturmius's. But however it got there, the Laurentian manuscript bears testimony to Insular influence in south Italy.

The south Italian ninth-century glossary Vatic. Lat. 3320 has a text akin to that found in Monte Cassino 401, and it quite probably came into the library of Fulvio Orsini directly or indirectly from Monte Cassino.[1] The glossary itself contains numerous passages from the Fathers, including Isidore, Bishop of Seville. To make the excerpts from Isidore, the Beneventan scribe must have used a manuscript of Spanish origin or at least one written in Visigothic script, for it is only in passages taken from Isidore that we get the unmistakably Visigothic abbreviation-symbols **aūm** for 'autem', **srhl** for 'israhel', **pplrm** for 'populorum', and the typical abbreviation-mark consisting of a dot over a horizontal stroke (∸). Tangible proof of relations between south Italy and Spain is furnished by the two ninth-century Visigothic manuscripts still preserved at Monte Cassino (no. 4 containing Ambrose[2] and

Histories' in *Casinensia* (Monte Cassino, 1929), pp. 257 ff. [this volume, pp. 289 ff.] with 2 plates. Other facsimiles are to be found in Chatelain, *Pal. des class. lat.*, pl. XII (Varro), XVII. 1 (Cicero), XLIX (Caesar), CXLVI (Tacitus); in Ihm, *Palaeographia Latina* (Leipzig, 1909), pl. IX (Caesar); and in R. Helm's Teubner text of Apuleius (2nd ed., Leipzig, 1913).

[1] Cf. *Script. Benev.*, pl. XVIII.

[2] Facsimiles in *Bibliotheca Casinensis*, I, pl. 3 (i); E. A. Loew, 'Studia Palaeographica', *SBer. der philos. philol. u. histor. Klasse d. K. Bayer.*

(59) no. 19 containing Augustine,[1] which were there as early as the eleventh century, since they have Beneventan marginalia of that century), and by the beautiful Danila Bible, written in faultless ninth-century Visigothic script, now preserved in the abbey at Cava dei Tirreni near Salerno.[2] But there is no way of determining when these three Visigothic manuscripts reached southern Italy. The Spanish traces found in the Beneventan glossary, however, show that Visigothic manuscripts existed in that part of Italy as early as the ninth century. The explanation of the presence of so early a Visigothic manuscript at Monte Cassino is to be found in visits by Spanish monks, the visit of Diapertus being a case in point.

In the memorable preface to the facsimile edition of the fifth-century fragments of Jerome's translation of Eusebius' *Chronicles*, Traube remarks, 'Ego cum aetatem codicis sciscitor, statim me ad compendia verto'.[3] The trained palaeographer knows that abbreviations may not only help to date a manuscript, but will also often give him important clues as to its origin and archetype. A single symbol occasionally suffices to establish, if not the precise home, at least the region whence a given manuscript hails. Thus the Phillipps MS. 1676, now in the Staatsbibliothek in Berlin, would naturally be assigned to Verona because of its connection with Egino (fl. 796) and Ratherius (932–68), both bishops of Verona.[4] But the telltale contraction $\overline{\text{ma}}$ for 'misericordia', of which Lindsay found one example, clinches the matter; for the symbol $\overline{\text{ma}}$ is peculiar to Verona and its neighbourhood.[5]

(60) Much has been written on the origin of the world's greatest manuscript of the Latin Bible, the Codex Amiatinus, now at the Laurentian Library, formerly in the Benedictine (later Cistercian) house of San Salvatore of Monte Amiata near Siena.[6] We know that it came into the Laurentian soon after the monastery was suppressed; but how it got to Tuscany will perhaps for ever

Akad. d. Wiss. (1910, 12 Abh.), pl. 3; C. U. Clark, *Collectanea Hispanica*, pl. 12 (*Transactions of the Connecticut Academy of Arts and Sciences*, Sept. 1920, vol. 24, published in Paris); A. Millares Carlo, *Paleografía española* (2 vols., Barcelona, 1929), I, p. 291, fig. 28.

[1] Facsimiles in *Bibl. Casin.* I, pl. 10 (i).

[2] Facsimiles in Silvestre, *Paléographie universelle*, pl. 106; C. U. Clark, *Coll. Hisp.*, pls. 13–14; H. Quentin, *Mémoire sur l'établissement du texte de la Vulgate* (Rome and Paris, 1922), 1ère partie, figs. 28–9 (*Collectanea Biblica Latina*, VI).

[3] Traube, *Hieronymi chronicorum codicis Floriacensis fragmenta*, etc. (Leyden, 1902), p. vii (*Codices Graeci et Latini photographice depicti*, Suppl. vol. I).

[4] See V. Rose, *Die lateinischen Meermann-Handschriften des Sir Thomas Phillipps in der königl. Bibliothek zu Berlin* (Berlin, 1892), pp. 77 ff. For facsimiles see A. Boinet, *La Miniature carolingienne* (Paris, 1913), pl. 147; *Die Phillipps-Handschriften*, ed. J. Kirchner (Leipzig, 1926), pp. 6 ff., pl. 1 and figs. 9–11 (*Beschreibende Verzeichnisse der Miniaturen-Handschriften der preussischen Staatsbibliothek zu Berlin*, I).

[5] W. M. Lindsay, *Notae Lat.*, pp. 126 ff.

[6] A useful description of the manuscript will be found in Steffens, *Lat. Pal.*^{2}, pl. 21B (= 1st ed., pl. 28), but an exhaustive account is given by Dom Quentin in his *Mémoire sur . . . la Vul-*

remain a mystery. Its earlier history, however, has been cleared up once for all by the brilliant work of G. B. de Rossi, who proved that this manuscript was the very one which Ceolfrid, Abbot of Jarrow, was taking to Rome as a gift to St. Peter's when he died at Langres, 25 September 716.[1] His companions finished the journey and carried out his plans. The supreme interest of this complete manuscript of the Bible is its text, which biblical criticism has brought into relation with Cassiodorus. The scriptorium that produced this grand book of over a thousand folios all beautifully and carefully written in even, stately uncial characters, truly deserves well of posterity. But scholars have long been at variance over the date and nationality of this manuscript. The nineteenth-century palaeographers Zangemeister and Wattenbach, who were among the first to publish facsimiles of uncial manuscripts, were evidently of the opinion that the Codex Amiatinus was an Italian product of the sixth century.[2] They were misled by the inscription on fol. 86^{v} which reads:

Ο ΚΥΡΙϹ ϹΕΡΒΑΝΔΟϹ ΑΙΠΟΙΗϹΕΝ[3]

The Servandus here mentioned they identified with the abbot of that name, (61)
who was a contemporary of St. Benedict (d. *c.* 550?). The late Sir Edward Maunde Thompson had no hesitation in dating the manuscript between 690 and 716 (i.e. in Ceolfrid's abbacy), but the script, which is uncial, he regarded as foreign, and said: 'It is probable that the manuscript was written by Italian scribes brought over to this country.'[4] Dr. M. R. James, in his very interesting booklet entitled *The Wanderings and Homes of Manuscripts*,[5] calls attention to Sir Henry Howorth's theory, that the first quire of the Codex Amiatinus, 'which contains pictures and lists of Biblical books, is actually a portion of a Bible written for Cassiodorus'. In fact, 'Sir Henry would go farther, and

gate, pp. 438 ff., frontispiece and figs. 74–80. Of the numerous published facsimiles I mention only Silvestre, *Pal. univ.*, pl. 81 (= cxiv); Zangemeister–Wattenbach, *Exempla codicum latinorum litteris majusculis scriptorum* (Heidelberg, 1876, 1879), pl. xxxv; *The Palaeographical Society*, ii, pls. 65–6; H. Zimmermann, *Vorkarolingische Miniaturen* (4 vols. plates in-fol., 1 vol. text in-8vo, Berlin, 1916), iii, pls. 222*, 222**, and fig. 24 in text; E. M. Thompson, *Introduction to Greek and Latin Palaeography* (Oxford, 1912), facs. 93. Fuller literature in Traube, *Vorles. u. Abh.*, i. 183–4.

[1] G. B. de Rossi, 'La Bibbia offerta da Ceolfrido abbate al sepolcro di S. Pietro, codice antichissimo tra i superstiti delle biblioteche della Sede apostolica', *Al Sommo Pontefice Leone XIII. omaggio giubilare della biblioteca Vaticana* (Rome, 1888).

[2] Zangemeister–Wattenbach, *Exempla*, p. 8.

[3] It is reproduced in *Exempla*, pl. xxxv.

[4] Thompson, *Introduction*, p. 289.

[5] No. 17 in the *Helps for Students of History* series published by the Society for Promoting Christian Knowledge (London, 1919).

claim the whole book as Cassiodorian'. To which Dr. James adds, 'I do not know that expert opinion is prepared to endorse this'.[1] What is the verdict of experts? A biblical authority like Dom Quentin expresses his view in no faltering terms. He says our manuscript was written 'à la fin du viie ou tout au début du viiie siècle, en Angleterre, dans le monastère de Yarrow, par ordre de Ceolfrid, abbé de cette maison'.[2] Nor does the foremost living palaeographical authority, W. M. Lindsay, entertain any doubts. His terse description runs: 'Written at Jarrow or Wearmouth in the abbacy of Ceolfrid, 690–716, uncial—foll. 1029.' He goes on to make an observation of capital importance, since it contains objective evidence proving that the Codex Amiatinus was not the work of Italian scribes imported to England but of English scribes writing the traditional Italian hand. Lindsay's words are: 'Insular abbreviation is used, a fact which has been ignored or even mis-stated by many critics.'[3] One instance of **ꝑ** for 'per' or **ħ** for 'autem' would suffice to convince anyone conversant with the history of abbreviations that we are moving in an Insular
(62) scriptorium. And Lindsay's view can be supported by other details. Who that is familiar with Insular methods of ornamentation can fail to recognize the Insular features of the face drawn in the initial **Q** at the opening of Luke? And do not the lozenge-shaped **O** in the word ANATOL (fol. ii^{v}) and the right-angled **C** in the word ARCTOS (fol. iii^{r})[4] recall Insular title-pages? Moreover, the uncial characters of the Codex Amiatinus are, to one who has examined many uncial manuscripts, unlike those used in genuine Italian products, and practically identical with the uncials of the Stonyhurst Gospel of St. John—the little volume which according to tradition was found in St. Cuthbert's tomb (d. 687).[5] The verdict of palaeography, then, founded on a few small yet significant observations, is unequivocal: it is not likely to be shaken, since it is based on objective criteria.

C. H. Beeson's recent publication, *Lupus of Ferrières as Scribe and Text Critic*,[6] which gives us not only a complete facsimile reproduction of Cicero's *De Oratore*, written by Lupus himself, but also some insight into the methods pursued by one of the foremost humanists of his day—the pupil of Hrabanus Maurus and correspondent of Einhard—was made possible by Traube's clair-

[1] No. 17 in *Helps for Students of History* (S.P.C.K., London, 1919), p. 30.

[2] Quentin, *Mémoire*, pp. 438 ff.

[3] Lindsay, *Notae Lat.*, p. 457.

[4] The two pages are reproduced in Dom Quentin's *Mémoire*, p. 447, fig. 77.

[5] *Pal. Soc.* I, pl. 17; Westwood, *Palaeographia Sacra Pictoria* (London, 1843–5), pl. 11; E. Johnston, *Writing and Illuminating and Lettering* (London, 1906), p. 442, pl. v.

[6] *The Mediaeval Academy of America, Publication No. 4*, published by the Medieval Academy of America (Cambridge, Massachusetts, 1930).

voyant surmise that the annotator of the Berne manuscript of Valerius Maximus was no other than Lupus,[1] a surmise later confirmed by demonstration.[2] The palaeographer on the alert for peculiarities in his manuscripts cannot fail to be arrested by the critical marks he finds in the books annotated by Lupus. The capital **A** (standing for 'alter', 'aliter', or 'alibi') with dots on either side, to be found in the margins, the two or three dots which mark the *(63)*
marginal variant and the word in the text to which it refers, are easily recognizable. But the simplest way of detecting a possible Lupus manuscript is to see if there are corrections in word-division. Most scribes divided Latin words naturally as they pronounced. Lupus, however, insisted on the artificial syllabification taught by the grammarians, according to whom a syllable should begin with as many consonants as are capable of being pronounced. So that words like 'scrip-si', 'om-nis', 'dig-nus', etc., normally divided by scribes as here indicated, would be corrected by Lupus to 'scri-psi', 'o-mnis', 'di-gnus'. The visible result on the manuscript-page is that the **p** or **m** or **g** at the end of the line is struck out or expunged, and the next line begins with an inserted **p**, **m**, or **g**. The added letters by projecting outside the regular alignment easily catch the eye and call attention to the correction.[3] It is by dint of paying heed to these minutiae that Traube, Beeson, and others have been enabled to put together the manuscripts which were either written or revised by Lupus. For the benefit of the student who may be interested to see at first hand how a ninth-century scholar read, revised, and annotated his classics I here give a list of books known to have been corrected by Lupus:[4]

Berne 366	Valerius Maximus[5]	
Leyden, Voss. lat. F. 12β	Cicero, Macrobius[6]	
London, Brit. Mus. Harley 2736	Cicero de oratore[7]	
Paris, B.N. lat. 5726	Livy, 1st Decade. See Plate **43** (*pl. 1*)	*(64)*
" " 5763	Caesar (doubtful)[8]	

[1] Traube, 'Untersuchungen zur Überlieferungsgeschichte römischer Schriftsteller. I. Zu Valerius Maximus, etc.', in *S-Ber. d.philos.-philol. u. histor. Klasse d. K. Bayer. Akad. d. Wiss.* (1891), pp. 387 ff.; reprinted in *Vorles. u. Abh.* III. 3 ff.

[2] J. Schnetz, *Ein Kritiker des Valerius Maximus im 9. Jahrhundert* (Neuburg a. D., 1901), Program.

[3] A good example of Lupus' corrections is seen in Steffens, *Lat. Pal.*², pl. 60 (= 1st ed., Suppl., pl. 28).

[4] On Lupus manuscripts see Traube, *Textgeschichte der Regula S. Benedicti* (2nd ed., Munich, 1910), p. 123 (*Abhandlungen d. K. Bayer. Akad. der Wiss.* XXV. 2) and *Vorles. u. Abh.* III. 15, and Beeson's preface, pp. vii f.

[5] Facs. in Chatelain, *Pal. des class. lat.* pl. CLXXXI; Steffens, loc. cit.

[6] Chatelain, op. cit., pl. XLA.

[7] *Catalogue of Ancient MSS. in the British Museum* (2 parts, London, 1881, 1884), II, pl. 58; Chatelain, op. cit., pl. XIXA (1); and C. H. Beeson's complete facsimile edition cited above.

[8] Traube regarded this manuscript as coming from the school of Lupus (*Textgeschichte*, p. 123). I myself see no Lupus ear-marks. Facs. in Chatelain, op. cit., pl. XLVI; Steffens, op. cit.²,

Paris, B.N. lat. 6332	Cicero[1]
„ „ 7496	Priscian
„ „ 7774A	Cicero de inventione[2]
„ „ 8623	Symmachus, Epist. See Plate **44** (*pl. 2*)
Paris, N.a. lat. 1626	Lucan[3]
Vatic. lat. 474	Augustinus, Sermones[4]
Vatic. Regin. lat. 597	Aulus Gellius
„ „ 1484	Donatus in Vergilium[5]

What Traube, Schnetz, and Beeson have done for Lupus, the late S. Tafel, following similar methods, tried to do for Florus Diaconus, the theologian and poet who flourished at Lyons during the first half of the ninth century (d. 859–60). Tafel's main results were posthumously edited and published by Lindsay.[6] They received confirmation from the conclusions reached by the present writer when he was engaged in gathering material for a collection of facsimiles of the oldest Lyons manuscripts.[7] Annotations found in a number of manuscripts still preserved at Lyons clearly pointed to an erudite ecclesiastic interested in Biblical, patristic, and legal works, and particularly familiar
(*65*) with the works of St. Augustine. Tafel's view that this scholar was Florus—whether he was first led to the belief by a remark of Mommsen or of Delisle is immaterial—seems highly probable, and the more one studies the critical marks and observations made in the margin the more convincing the identification with Florus becomes. To reconstruct the library of a great scholar of the Middle Ages is not altogether without historical importance; and to know that one may any day open a manuscript which will add an item to the books heretofore known to have been in Florus' library is one of the prospects which brighten the palaeographer's day. Recently it was my privilege to find such a manuscript. In turning the leaves of the Paris MS., B.N. lat. 11709, containing a collection of Canons (the 'Hispana'),[8] it did not seem surprising,

pl. 51B (= 1st ed., Suppl., pl. 26B); H. W. Johnston, *Latin Manuscripts* (Chicago, 1897), pl. IV.

[1] Chatelain, op. cit., pl. XLIV. 1.

[2] Chatelain, op. cit., pl. XXXI; E. K. Rand, *A Survey of the Manuscripts of Tours* (2 vols., Cambridge, Massachusetts, 1929), II, pl. 105 (*Studies in the script of Tours*, I. *The Medieval Academy of America, Publication No. 3*).

[3] Chatelain, op. cit., pl. CLIV. 1, and C. M. Francken's edition of Lucan (Leyden, 1896).

[4] H. M. Bannister, *Monumenti Vaticani di paleografia musicale latina* (Leipzig, 1913), pl. 12 (*Codices e Vaticanis selecti phototypice expressi*, XII), which reproduces the important note on fol. 95: 'Hucusque ab abbate et praeceptore lupo requisitum et distinctum est.'

[5] E. K. Rand, op. cit., pls. 110–11.

[6] S. Tafel, 'The Lyons Scriptorium' in Lindsay's *Palaeographia Latina* (Oxford, 1925), IV. 40 ff. (*St. Andrews University Publications*, XX).

[7] E. A. Lowe, *Codices Lugdunenses Antiquissimi. Le Scriptorium de Lyon* (Lyons, 1924), pp. 14 f. (*Extraits des documents paléographiques, typographiques, iconographiques de la bibliothèque de Lyon*, III, IV).

[8] A study of this and other manuscripts of Canons is to be expected from the Catalan scholar Jean Tarré.

considering the nature of the text, to find numerous Spanish symptoms, e.g. the Visigothic forms **nsr, nsa, nsi,**[1] instead of the normal **nr, nra, nri,** for 'noster', '-ra', '-ri', which occurred *passim*. But the use of the unmistakably Visigothic signs for marking an omission (**dh** in the text and **SR** after the insertion in the margin) suggested a corrector familiar with Spanish methods.[2] The manuscript manifestly came from Lyons, for the first page bears the inscription in fanciful capitals: LEYDRAT LICET INDIGNUS TAMEN EPS.[3] Leidrad was Bishop of Lyons between 798 and 814. As one continues to turn the (*66*)
leaves one actually encounters additions in pure Visigothic script, e.g. on fols. 198ᵛ, 199 (seen on Plate **45** (*pl. 3*)), 201ᵛ, 209, 240ᵛ. There is no doubt that Spanish scholars were active at that time in Lyons, as we already know from the Lyons MS. 443 (372) of Origen on the Heptateuch, written partly in local half-uncial, partly in uncial, with the missing portions supplied in Visigothic minuscule.[4] Who wrote these Visigothic pages we cannot say, but it must be recalled that Agobard, who succeeded Leidrad as Bishop of Lyons, was a native of Spain; and the MS. E. 26 in the Vallicelliana in Rome in ordinary Caroline minuscule has autograph entries by Agobard which are in Visigothic.[5] Our manuscript of the canons may or may not have been a book corrected by Agobard; it certainly passed through the hands of Florus. For it has all his characteristic critical marks in the margin: the **K'** ('kaput') to mark the beginning of a chapter; the ∏·, ⌐, and ¬· to mark the beginning and end of paragraphs, with the curious dot accompanying these signs; the name of the Biblical book, placed in the margin in abbreviated form, to call attention to a citation in the text, the name appearing under a characteristic

[1] Cf. Traube, *Perrona Scottorum*, pp. 513 f., and *Nomina Sacra* (Munich, 1907), pp. 220 ff. (*Quellen u. Untersuchungen*, etc., II); and Lindsay, *Notae Lat.*, pp. 153 f.

[2] See Lindsay, 'The Laon **az**-type', *Revue des bibliothèques*, XXIV (1914), 19.

[3] Similar inscriptions are found in Lyons 599 (515) Gregor. Nazian., transl. by Rufinus, Lyons 610 (526) Augustinus, Lyons 608 (524) Augustinus (facs. in *École des Chartes. Album paléographique avec des notices explicatives*, ed. L. Delisle (Paris, 1887), pl. 19), Lyons, Bibliothèque des Pères Maristes de Sainte-Foi 128, a collection of logical treatises and creeds, and in Paris, B.N. lat. 152, fols. 21–5 Hieronym. in Isaiam. The Leidrad entry in the last three manuscripts is reproduced by Delisle in 'Notice sur un manuscrit de l'église de Lyon du temps de Charlemagne', *Notices et extraits des MSS.*, XXXV, 2ᵉ partie (Paris, 1897). They are all mentioned by Tafel, op. cit., pp. 51 f. M. Ph. Lauer calls attention to another Leidrad manuscript, Paris, B.N. lat. 12236 Eucherius, written half in uncial, half in minuscule (cf. *Bibliothèque de l'École des Chartes*, LXXXVI (1925), 386).

[4] Facs. in *Album paléographique ou recueil des documents importants relatifs à l'histoire et la littérature nationales* (Paris, 1887), pl. 6B; V. Leroquais, *Bibliothèque de la ville de Lyon, Exposition de manuscrits à peintures*, etc. (Lyons, 1920), pl. II; Lowe, *Codices Lugd. Antiq.*, pls. XVIII–XXII (of which pl. XXI shows the Visigothic script).

[5] See I. Giorgi, 'Di due codici della Biblioteca Vallicelliana recentemente ricuperati', in *Rendiconti Accad. Lincei* (1917), fasc. 6, from which Lindsay quotes fully in *Pal. Lat.* IV. 55.

bracket; the peculiar question-mark, shaped like arabic figure 3; in short, all the signs used by Florus.[1] Those who wish to become familiar with the methods followed by Florus Magister will find traces of him in the following manuscripts. The list is drawn up partly from Tafel's study referred to above, partly from data kindly supplied me by my friend Dom Wilmart, partly also from my own notes. The source is indicated by the bracketed initial.

(67) Berlin 83 (Phillipps 1745)[2] Canones. The first part is in Leningrad F. v. II. 3.
" 159 (Phillipps 1761)[3] Breviarium Alarici.
Cambridge, Univ. Libr. Nn. II. 41[4] Codex Bezae (Evang., Act.). The added pages in ninth-century uncial are probably by Florus.
Cambridge, Univ. Libr. Add. MS. 3479, probably a direct copy of Paris lat. 11641 (see below) while still complete.
Geneva MS. Lat. 16 (see Paris lat. 11641).
Leningrad F. pap. I. 1 (see Paris lat. 11641).
" F. v. II. 3 (see Berlin 83).
Lyons 431 (357)[5] Evangeliarium.
" 443 (372)[6] Origen in Heptateuchum. Part of this manuscript in Paris N.a. lat. 1591.
" 448 (377) Hieronym. in Ieremiam (doubtful).
" 466 (395) Hieronym. in Isaiam (doubtful).
" 473 (403) Beda in Evang. (T).
" 475 (405) Homiliae.
" 478 (408)[7] August. de consensu evang. (T).
" 484 (414)[8] Florus in Epist. Pauli.
" 599 (515) Gregor. Nazian. (Rufinus).
" 600 (517)[9] Hieron. Epist. Part in Paris n.a. lat. 446.
" 603 (520) August. de baptismo.
(68) " 604 (521)[10] August., Sermones. (T). Part in Paris n.a. lat. 1594.
" 605 (522) August. contra Cresconium.
" 606 (523) August. de civ. Dei.
" 607 (523 bis)[11] August. de civ. Dei. Supposed to be the exemplar of Lyons 606.

[1] Annotations by Florus may be studied in *Codd. Lugd. Antiq.*, pls. ii, viii, ix, xvi, xvii, xxxiii, xxxiv, and in xiv, xxiii, xxxv, and xxxvii*b*.

[2] Lowe, *Codd. Lugd. Antiq.*, pls. xxx–xxxii. References to other facsimiles will be found in this work and are therefore omitted here and in the subsequent notes.

[3] Ibid., pl. xxv.

[4] Complete facsimile edition (Cambridge, 1899); Lowe, op. cit., pl. xxxvii.

[5] Leroquais, *Exposition*, etc.; Ph. Lauer, *Bibliothèque de la ville de Lyon: Documents '1928'*, 17 pls.; E. A. Lowe, 'The Codex Bezae and Lyons', *Journal of Theological Studies*, xxv (1924), 274 [this volume, p. 186].

[6] Lowe, op. cit., pls. xviii–xxii.

[7] Ibid., pls. vii–viii.

[8] L. Delisle suggests that this may be Florus' autograph: 'Notice sur plusieurs anciens MSS. de la bibliothèque de Lyon', *Notices et extraits des MSS.* xxix, 2e partie (Paris, 1880), p. 402.

[9] Lowe, op. cit., pl. xxxv.

[10] Ibid., pls. xvi–xvii.

[11] Ibid., pls. xxvi–xxvii.

Lyons 608 (524)[1] August., Opuscula.
„ 610 (526)[2] August. contra Faustum.
„ 788 (706) August. de pastoribus. (T). Part of this is in Paris, B.N. Baluze 270 (fols. 107–8, 135–58). (W).
Paris, B.N. lat. 152 (fols. 9–16)[3] Hilarius in Psalmos.
„ 1622 Tertullian. Belonged to Agobard. (T) (W).
„ 2832[4] Carmina varia, including verses by Agobard and Florus. (W).
„ 2859 Florus, Varia. (T) (W).
„ 6601[5] Cicero and Augustinus. (W).
„ 8913[6] Avitus.
„ 9550[7] Eucherius, Formulae Spirituales.
„ 11641[8] August., Epist. et Serm. Parts of this manuscript in Geneva and Leningrad, q.v.
„ 11709 Canones. Agobard's manuscript. See Plate **46** (*pl. 4*).
„ N.a. lat. 446 (see Lyons 600). *(69)*
„ 1443 August., Epist., etc. (W).
„ 1591 (see Lyons 443).
„ 1594 (see Lyons 604).
Rome, Vatic. Regin. lat. 331 Augustinus and Pacianus. Part of this manuscript has Florus' notes.

[1] *New Palaeographical Society* (London, 1903–30), I, pl. 209; *École des Chartes. Album paléographique*, pl. 19; E. H. J. Reusens, *Éléments de paléographie* (Louvain, 1897–9), pl. 17 (copy of preceding).

[2] *New Pal. Soc.* I, pl. 58; Thompson, *Introduction*, facs. 152.

[3] Lowe, op. cit., pl. II.

[4] E. de Coussemaker, *Histoire de l'harmonie au moyen âge* (Paris, 1852), pl. 6; L. Delisle, *Le Cabinet des manuscrits* (3 vols. text, 1 vol. plates, Paris, 1868–81), pl. XXXVIII. 2, 3.

[5] Chatelain, *Pal. des class. lat.*, pl. XLV. 2.

[6] Steffens, *Lat. Pal.*[2], pl. 24 (= 1st ed., Suppl., pl. 9); *Pal. Soc.* I, pl. 68; Silvestre, *Pal. univ.*, pl. 128 (= 169) = CXLIV, to give only the principal works.

[7] Lowe, op. cit., pl. IX.

[8] Lowe, op. cit., pls. XXXIII–XXXIV.

Virgil in South Italy

FACSIMILES OF EIGHT MANUSCRIPTS OF VIRGIL IN BENEVENTAN SCRIPT

(43) IT is the modest object of this article to do no more than put before Virgilian scholars specimens of extant manuscripts of Virgil of assured south-Italian origin. Of the forty-odd classical manuscripts in Beneventan writing known to us[1] nearly one-fifth contain Virgil,—this is exclusive of manuscripts containing commentaries[2] on the poet—and they are all, curiously enough, very close to each other in date, belonging either to the eleventh or to the early twelfth century, with the exception of one manuscript, which belongs to the tenth. To the six Virgil manuscripts mentioned in *The Beneventan Script* Mgr. G. Mercati added a seventh: the palimpsest Vatic. Gr. 2324. It was my good fortune to come upon the eighth in the course of a summary examination of the Latin manuscripts in the Regina collection. I refer to Vatican, Regin. Lat. 2090. What value, if any, its text may have for editors of Virgil
(44) remains to be seen. It is of palaeographical interest to note that this manuscript of Virgil is not written in the familiar script of Monte Cassino, Benevento, Capua, Naples, or Cava, but in the peculiar type which we connect with Bari, south-eastern Italy, and Dalmatia. In fact three out of the eight manuscripts described in this paper are in the Bari type.[3]

From *Studi Medievali*, nuova serie, v (1932), 43–51. [See Pls. **47** to **54**.]

[1] See E. A. Lowe, *The Beneventan Script* (Oxford, 1914), pp. 16 ff. The list there given may now be augmented by at least these six items:

1. Jesi, Library of Conte Balleani—Cicero, *De Inventione*, saec. XI–XII (with *Ad Herennium* in contemporary ordinary minuscule).
2. Leyden, Voss. Lat. 4° 1—Dioscorides Latinus, saec. X–XI, partly in contemporary ordinary minuscule.
3. Paris Lat. 7536—Donatus, saec. X ex. ut vid. (Professor C. H. Beeson kindly called my attention to this manuscript).
4. Vatican, Vatic. Gr. 2324—Virgil palimpsest. See no. 5 of the manuscripts described below.
5. Vatican, Regin. Lat. 2090—Virgil. See no. 8 of the manuscripts described below.
6. Vatican, Urbin. Lat. 341—Ovid, *Metamorphoses*, saec. XII. Facsimiles in D. Slater, *Towards a Text of the Metamorphoses, of Ovid* (Oxford, 1927).

[2] I refer to Paris Lat. 7530, Naples Lat. 5 (olim Vienna 27), and Vatican, Vatic. Lat. 3317.

[3] The list of classical manuscripts in the Bari script is by no means a small one and is of sufficient interest to be set down here:

1. Eton College Library Bl. 6. 5—Ovid, *Heroides*, etc., saec. XI.
2. Jesi, Libr. of Conte Balleani—Cicero, *De Inventione*, saec. XI–XII.
3. Monte Cassino, Compactiones XV—Virgil.

It is a commonplace that Virgil was read and studied in antiquity and throughout the Middle Ages, even in the darkest period. And yet there are curious gaps. While we possess copies of very ancient manuscripts—copies in square and rustic capitals which must go back to the fourth and fifth centuries—I am thinking of the Schedae Vaticano-Berolinenses, Sangallenses, the Verona palimpsest, the Codex Romanus, the Codex Vaticanus, the Codex Mediceus, the Codex Palatinus[1]—there are no manuscripts of Virgil which are assignable to the sixth, seventh, and eighth centuries. Is this merely an accident, or does it have some significance? When one recalls that, out of the 160-odd manuscripts in half-uncial script written between the fifth and eighth centuries, apart from papyri, only three manuscripts contain classical authors (the Ambrosian fragments of Juvenal and the palimpsest leaves of Symmachus and Pliny[2]—all from Bobbio), one is tempted to interpret the centuries-wide gap in our transmission of Virgil as a reflection of a lack of interest in classical learning. Likewise, we should perhaps be not far wrong if we interpreted the survival of the Beneventan manuscripts of Virgil as marking a revival of interest in secular learning. The majority of the manuscripts belong to the century which witnessed a great artistic and literary awakening in southern Italy—the century of Abbot Desiderius. Their philological value may be, and probably is, negligible, but the student of history will appreciate their worth as witnesses of intellectual activity.

THE EIGHT MANUSCRIPTS OF VIRGIL (45)

1. Naples Lat. 6 (Cavalc. 81) olim Vienna 58. saec. x

The manuscript, imperfect at the beginning and end, contains the *Bucolics*, *Georgics*, and *Aeneid* with marginal and interlinear scholia. The books of the *Aeneid* are preceded by the *Decasticha Argumenta*, attributed to Ovid, and the whole book opens with anonymous verses on the poet and his tomb. An epigram of Martial (ix. 98) was inserted on fol. 76 by a later hand.

The manuscript has 177 fols. measuring 328×220 mm., the written space

See no. 7 of this article.

4. Naples IV. F. 3—Ovid, *Metamorphoses*, saec. xii.
5. Oxford, Bodleian Canon. Class. Lat. 50—Virgil. See no. 6 of this article.
6. Vatican, Vatic. Lat. 3327—Sallust. saec. xii–xiii.
7. Vatican, Regin. Lat. 2090—Virgil. See no. 8 of this article.
8. Vatican, Urbin. Lat. 341—Ovid, *Metamorphoses*, saec. xii.

[1] For literature on these manuscripts see Traube, *Vorlesungen und Abhandlungen* (Munich, 1909), i. 161 ff. Complete facsimile reproductions now exist of the Augusteus, Mediceus, Palatinus, and Vaticanus, and a partial reproduction of the Romanus.

[2] In Vatic. Lat. 5750+Ambros. E. 147 sup.

being 255 × 115 mm., with 36 lines on a page. Ruling is on the hair side, which is the outside of quires, four sheets being ruled at a time. Quires are normally of eight, signed originally by Roman numerals in the middle of the lower margin of the last page. Two pairs of bounding-lines enclose the text. The script is neat and careful, not having yet reached the strict regularity which it achieved in the eleventh century. Colophons are in red uncial. There are numerous coloured initials which display a not very skilful use of the interlaced pattern, dragon head, and the human figure. The Virgilian text is decorated with about a dozen miniatures which are hardly works of art. Our facsimile (Pl. **47** (*pl. 1*)) gives a fair idea of the artist's skill. The main illustrations are on folios:

1^{v}: Opening of *Eclogues*—Tityrus and Meliboeus
44^{v}: Opening of *Aeneid*—the Poet unrolling his scroll
45^{r}: *Aen.* I—ship
55^{v}: *Aen.* II—Aeneas and Dido
76^{v}: *Aen.* III—Dido and Aeneas
99^{r}: *Aen.* VI—the Poet
111^{r}: *Aen.* VII—a standing human figure
143^{v}: *Aen.* X—the Poet unrolling his scroll
156^{r}: *Aen.* XI—A human figure in a circle
168^{v}: *Aen.* XII—Turnus battling with Aeneas

The original home of this manuscript was probably Naples. It was in the library of the Augustinians of S. Giovanni a Carbonara in 1698, when Montfaucon visited the monastery (*Diarium Italicum* (Paris, 1702), p. 313). In 1718 it was removed to Vienna with many other manuscripts, among them the Beneventan Servius (MS. Vienna 27). All of these are once more in Naples, having been returned after the armistice of 1918, and are preserved in the Biblioteca Nazionale.

Facsimiles are given by Th. von Sickel, *Monumenta Graphica Medii Aevi* (Vienna, 1858), IV, pl. 7, and by E. A. Lowe, *Scriptura Beneventana* (Oxford, 1929), pl. XLV, where the following earlier literature is given: S. Endlicher, *Catalogus Codicum Manuscriptorum Bibliothecae Palatinae Vindobonensis: Pars I, Codices Philologici Latini* (Vienna, 1836), pp. 55 f., no. CXIII; *Tabulae Codicum Manuscriptorum praeter Graecos et Orientales in Bibliotheca Palatina Vindobonensi asservatorum* (Vienna, 1864), I. 8; B. Capasso, 'Sulla
(*46*) spogliazione delle biblioteche napolitane nel 1718', in *Archivio Storico per le Province Napoletane*, III (1878), 589; F. Menčik, 'Die neapolitaner Handschriften der Hofbibliothek', in *Mitteilungen des Oesterreich. Vereins für Bibliothekswesen*, VIII (1904), 133–48, 170–7, and IX (1905), 31–7; and H.

Tietze, *Die Entführung von Wiener Kunstwerken nach Italien* (Wien, 1919), p. 48; E. Martini, *Sui codici Napoletani restituiti dall'Austria* (Napoli, 1924).

Our facsimile (Pl. **47** (*pl. 1*)) reproduces the first thirty-seven lines of *Aeneid* II.

2. PARIS LAT. 10308. saec. XI²

The manuscript contains the *Bucolics*, *Georgics*, and *Aeneid*, with some contemporary glosses and more extensive scholia by a fourteenth-century hand. The fullest scholia are found in the *Georgics*. On fol. 1ᵛ is entered the *Carmen Ouidii* 'Quales bucolicis quantus', etc., followed on fol. 2 by the *Carmen Octauiani Caesaris Augusti* 'Ergone suppremis [*sic*] potuit uox improba uerbis'. The books of the *Aeneid* are preceded by the *Decasticha Argumenta*, erroneously attributed to Ovid.

The manuscript is composed of 172 leaves, measuring 330 × 220 mm., with a written space of 272 × 125 mm., containing 40 lines to a page. Quires are signed by Roman numerals on the left-hand side of the lower margin of the last page, instead of on the right which is customary. The script is the developed Beneventan of the eleventh century, and might have been written in Benevento proper or in Naples. Colophons are in red in the script of the text. The initials, in red, yellow, and green, are rather crude and betray an unskilled hand. A few pen drawings unrelated to the text of Virgil are found here and there; e.g. on fol. 2 is a drawing of a seated Christ holding a book in his left hand and blessing with his right. There are other drawings of Christ, also some of the Evangelists Luke and John, and of various animals.

How the manuscript got to Paris is unknown. It belonged formerly to the Florentine Cardinal, Giovanni Salviati (1490–1553). An excellent facsimile exists in E. Chatelain's *Paléographie des classiques latins*, pl. LXXIV, described on p. 21, and a specimen of the alphabet in N. de Wailly, *Éléments de Paléographie* (Paris, 1838), II, pl. 1, col. 4, and p. 243.

Our facsimile (Pl. **48** (*pl. 2*)) reproduces the so-called *Versus Ouidii* and the first seven lines of book I.

3. VATICAN LAT. 1573. saec. XI ex. (Pl. **49** (*pl. 3*))

The manuscript contains the *Bucolics*, *Georgics*, and *Aeneid*. Here and there Beneventan glosses occur, but most of the scholia are much later additions. The books of the *Aeneid* were preceded by the *Decasticha Argumenta* or so-called *Versus Ouidii*. The manuscript begins with the first *Eclogue* and the Beneventan portion ends on fol. 95ᵛ with the line 'Et Turno si prima domus repetatur origo' (*Aen.* VII. 371).

The portion between fols. 96 and 111 is in a Gothic hand, saec. XIII–XIV, and that between fols. 112 and 149 is in a fourteenth-century hand, written on paper.

(47) The entire manuscript is composed of 149 leaves, measuring 292 × 117 mm., with a written space of 230 × 90 mm., containing 43 lines to a page, enclosed by double bounding-lines. The ruling was done two leaves at a time. Quire-marks are reclamantes and are by the first hand. The script is not the work of an expert and the initials, rather crude in form, are not the typical Beneventan kind. A number of them were added later in the Gothic style.

There are no published facsimiles. The manuscript has been described by B. Nogara in *Codices Vaticani Latini* (Rome, 1912), III. 72. An earlier reference to it is in Bottari, *Antiquissimi Virgiliani Codicis fragmenta et picturae*, p. viii.

4. VATICAN LAT. 3253. saec. XI ex.

This manuscript contains only the *Georgics* and the *Aeneid* and those not complete. It begins with the verse 'Nunc alios alios dum nubila uentus agebat' (*Georg.* I. 421) and ends with the line 'ipsa subit manibusque undantis flectit habenas' (*Aen.* XII. 471).

The manuscript contains eighty-two leaves, measuring 340 × 190 mm., with a written space of 290 × 100 mm., containing 50 lines to a page. Ruling is on the flesh side, apparently two leaves at a time. Quires were originally marked by Roman numerals in the middle of the lower margin of the first page—an unusual position. A later hand added reclamantes. Colophons are in red in the script of the text. Otherwise there is no decoration. The script is the pure Monte Cassino type of the developed period.

The manuscript is probably the work of a Monte Cassino scribe. Before it came into the Vatican Library it formed part of the famous collection of manuscripts owned by Fulvio Orsini. The paper fly-leaf still has the entry 'Virgilio in lettera longobarda. Ful. Urs.' Cf. P. de Nolhac, *La Bibliothèque de Fulvio Orsini* (Paris, 1887), pp. 240, n. 1, and 274.

Our facsimile (Pl. **50** (*pl. 4*)) reproduces *Georgics* IV. 562; *Aeneid* I. 1–22.

5. VATICAN GR. 2324. saec. XI ex.

It is the palimpsest portion of this manuscript which interests us here.[1] The primary script contains parts of Virgil in eleventh-century Beneventan

[1] Our chief source of information on this manuscript is the excellent article by Mgr. G. Mercati, 'Un palinsesto di Virgilio in scrittura beneventana', in *Miscellanea Amelli* (Monte Cassino, 1920), pp. 99–103. Most of the details given by me are drawn from this article.

minuscule. Over the Virgil a thirteenth-century hand wrote a Euchologion in Greek minuscule of the Italian type. There are in all sixteen palimpsest leaves, now measuring 234 × 145 mm., with 43 verses to the original page, of which the written space measured *c.* 212 × 70 mm. The palimpsest leaves are fols. 7–10, 15–18, 23–26, 32–35, which are both cut down and out of
order as far as the text of Virgil is concerned.[1] One thousand one hundred and (*48*)
seventeen lines survive, of which 149 lines are of the *Bucolics*, 350 of the *Georgics*, and 618 of the *Aeneid*.

The script is of the developed Beneventan type which was practised at Monte Cassino and in the vicinity. It is very small, but expert. Here and there glosses occur.

Our facsimile (Pl. **51** (*pl.* 5)) reproduces *Aeneid* XI. 469–508.

6. OXFORD BODLEIAN CANONICI CLASS. LAT. 50. saec. XI

The manuscript contains the *Bucolics*, *Georgics*, and *Aeneid*, with the commentary of Servius. Of the forty-five manuscripts of Virgil in the Bodleian the Canonicianus ranks among the best, coming only after Auct. F. 1. 16 and Auct. F. 2. 8.[2] But its standing outside of Oxford is not high.[3] Its text was first collated by G. Butler.[4] In the fourth edition of Heyne's text of Virgil,[5] Ph. Wagner assigns our manuscript to the ninth century, and F. Blume went so far as to put it back to the seventh century.[6] But Bandini, the celebrated author of the Laurentian catalogue, correctly ascribes this manuscript to the eleventh century, as may be seen from the autograph letter of 30 January 1784,

[1] The state of the confusion may be seen from the following:

fol. 7^r = *Aen.* I. 401–36.	fol. 7^v = *Aen.* I. 445–82
fol. 8^r = *Aen.* I. 310–52.	fol. 8^v = *Aen.* I. 353–93 (?)
fol. 9^r = *Georg.* IV. 451–92 (?)	fol. 9^v = *Georg.* IV. 493–534
fol. 10^r = *Georg.* IV. 368–405 (or 406)	fol. 10^v = *Georg.* IV. 413–50
fol. 15^r = *Georg.* IV. 105–42 (?)	fol. 15^v = *Georg.* IV. 149–83 (?)
fol. 16^r = *Georg.* III. 234–271	fol. 16^v = *Georg.* III. 278–315
fol. 17^r = *Georg.* IV. 281–317	fol. 17^v = *Georg.* IV. 324–62
fol. 18^r = *Georg.* III. 411–48 (?)	fol. 18^v = *Georg.* III. 455–92
fol. 23^r = *Aen.* X. 907–8, Decastichon Argum. *Aen.* XI, *Aen.* XI. 1–24	fol. 23^v = *Aen.* XI. 31–68
fol. 24^r = *Ecl.* VII. 23–61	fol. 24^v = *Ecl.* VII. 67–VIII. 34
fol. 25^r = *Ecl.* II. 11–48	fol. 25^v = *Ecl.* II. 55–III. 18
fol. 26^r = *Aen.* XI. 251–88	fol. 26^v = *Aen.* XI. 294–332
fol. 32^r = *Aen.* X. 729–68	fol. 32^v = *Aen.* X. 773–812
fol. 33^r = *Aen.* II. 172–212	fol. 33^v = *Aen.* II. 216–56
fol. 34^r = *Aen.* I. 663–703	fol. 34^v = *Aen.* I. 707(?)–747
fol. 35^r = *Aen.* XI. 423–64	fol. 35^v = *Aen.* XI. 469–508

[2] Cf. F. Madan, 'Note on the Bodleian MSS. of Virgil', in *P. Vergilii Maronis opera* (London, 1881), I (4th ed.), p. CXIII, by Conington and Nettleship.

[3] O. Ribbeck in his *Prolegomena critica ad P. Vergili Maronis opera maiora* (Leipzig, 1866), p. 348, says of it: 'Nullius ad emendandum Vergilii textum pretii visus est codex Bodleianus', etc.

[4] *Codex Virgilianus qui nuper ex bibliotheca Canonici Abbatis Venetiani Bodleianae accessit cum Wagneri textu collatus* (Oxford, 1854).

[5] Vol. IV, p. 771 (Leipzig, 1841).

[6] F. Blume, *Iter Italicum* (Halle, 1824), I. 234.

which is bound into the front of the manuscript. The letter is addressed to 'Pione' Col.',' whose identity baffles investigation. From another fly-leaf we learn that the manuscript once belonged to a Verona notary, N. Beccaria, who lived in the early fifteenth century, and who claimed to have acquired it from the Alighieri family. The original home of the manuscript is unknown. To judge from the writing, it should be Bari or some neighbouring centre. It came into the Bodleian Library from the famous collection of the Venetian scholar, Matteo Luigi Canonici (1727–1805).

The manuscript is composed of 161 (misnumbered 151) folios, measuring 400 × 290 mm., with a written space, exclusive of commentary, measuring *c.* 280 × 130 mm., and containing from 30–44 lines to a page, between double bounding-lines. The hair side of the parchment comes on the outside of the
(49) quire; the ruling was done on this outside leaf, four leaves at a time before folding. Quires are usually signed by a letter and numeral in the lower margin of the last page, but in quires F. VI, O. XV and Q. XVII the quire-marks are in the lower left corner of the first page. Fols. 128^{r}–143^{v} have been supplied by a later non-Beneventan hand to replace two missing quires. The parchment is coarse and often imperfect. The initials are fairly well drawn, but the colouring is mediocre. The script, however, deserves special attention. It has a distinct character of its own, which we have learnt to associate with products of Bari and its neighbourhood. Nearly all the salient features of the Bari type enumerated in *The Beneventan Script*[1] will be found in this manuscript, namely (1) the frequent use of the broken **c** (ε) shaped like Greek *epsilon*; (2) the ligature **fi**, with the stem of **f** usually resting on the line and **i** forming a broad curve also resting on the base-line, and the curious roundness of **i** in other **i**-ligatures; (3) the use of a line surmounted by a dot for the abbreviation stroke; (4) the use of thin-bodied initials with large-sized 'pearls' between the spaces of the interlaced pattern.

The manuscript is described in H. O. Coxe's *Catalogi Codicum Manuscriptorum Bibliothecae Bodleianae* (Oxford, 1854), III, col. 130 ff., cf. F. Madan's *Summary Catalogue of Western MSS. in the Bodleian Library at Oxford* (Oxford, 1897), IV. 318 (no. 18631). Earlier mention is made of it in *Cartas Familiares del Abate D. Juan Andres* (Madrid, 1790), III. 177. A photolithographic facsimile is given by R. Ellis in *XII Facsimiles from Latin MSS. in the Bodleian Library* (Oxford, 1885), pl. 4.

Our facsimile (Pl. **52** (*pl. 6*)) reproduces the first sixteen lines of the fifth Eclogue.

[1] E. A. Lowe, *The Beneventan Script*, pp. 150 f.

7. Monte Cassino Compactiones xv. saec. xi–xii

Only the remains of twenty-three leaves survive. They contain portions of the *Aeneid*, books ii–vi, ix–xii, and marginal scholia of Servius's Commentary.[1] The books are preceded by the *Decasticha Argumenta*. Fols. 4 and 14 (*50*)
are out of order and properly belong between fols. 9 and 10, and 12 and 13 respectively. The leaves are of unequal size; the present measurement of the largest is 340 × 250 mm. The estimated written space, exclusive of scholia, is *c.* 290 × 130 mm. A full page contained 37 lines between single bounding-lines. Ruling apparently was on the hair side before folding. Colophons were in red, in the script of the text. The writing is not very expert. Initials as well as the script show the characteristics of the Bari type which have been described above.[2]

Our facsimile (Pl. **53** (*pl.* 7)) reproduces *Aeneid* xii. 2–35.

8. Vatican, Regin. Lat. 2090. saec. xi–xii

The manuscript contains the *Bucolics*, *Georgics*, and *Aeneid*, with some glosses, partly by a Beneventan hand, partly by a twelfth-century ordinary minuscule hand, and finally by a fifteenth-century humanist who also annotated the humanistic addition at the end; they seem puerile in matter. The Beneventan text or original manuscript begins on fol. 8 with the verse 'Phyllis amat corylos; illas dum Phyllis amabit' (*Ecl.* vii. 63), ends on fol. 151^{v} with 'Respicit ignaros rerum ingratusque salutis' (*Aen.* x. 666), and is continued

[1] A very careful and thorough study of these fragments will be found in G. Funaioli's article, 'Il Virgilio di Montecassino', in *Casinensia* (Monte Cassino, 1929), pp. 385–407, to which I am indebted for the following summary; the more precise details will be found in the article:

fol. 1^{r} = *Aen.* ii. 763–94
fol. 2^{r} = *Aen.* iii. 328–49
fol. 3^{r} = *Aen.* iii. 392–423
fol. 4^{r} = *Aen.* v. 870–vi. 19
fol. 5^{r} = *Aen.* iii. 462–88
fol. 6^{r} = *Aen.* iv. 179–205
fol. 7^{r} = *Aen.* v. 549–80
fol. 8^{r} = *Aen.* v. 680–92
fol. 9^{r} = *Aen.* v. 695–707
fol. 10^{r} = *Aen.* ix. 206–33
fol. 11^{r} = *Aen.* ix. 266–96
fol. 12^{r} = *Aen.* ix. 458–88
fol. 13^{r} = *Aen.* ix. 650–80
fol. 14^{r} = *Aen.* ix. 526–53
fol. 15^{r} = *Aen.* ix. 714–45
fol. 16^{r} = *Aen.* x. 207–38
fol. 17^{r} = *Aen.* x. 271–301
fol. 18^{r} = *Aen.* xi. 592–625
fol. 19^{r} = *Aen.* xi. 666–702
fol. 20^{r} = *Aen.* xi. 815–47
fol. 21^{r} = *Aen.* xi. 889–915
fol. 22^{r} = *Aen.* xii. 110–46
fol. 23^{r} = *Aen.* xii. 184–217
fol. 1^{v} = *Aen.* ii. 795–iii. 7
fol. 2^{v} = *Aen.* iii. 360–81
fol. 3^{v} = *Aen.* iii. 424–56
fol. 4^{v} = *Aen.* vi. 20–51
fol. 5^{v} = *Aen.* iii. 494–520
fol. 6^{v} = *Aen.* iv. 210–37
fol. 7^{v} = *Aen.* v. 581–612
fol. 8^{v} = *Aen.* v. 712–24
fol. 9^{v} = *Aen.* v. 727–39
fol. 10^{v} = *Aen.* ix. 238–65
fol. 11^{v} = *Aen.* ix. 298–329
fol. 12^{v} = *Aen.* ix. 490–520
fol. 13^{v} = *Aen.* ix. 682–712
fol. 14^{v} = *Aen.* ix. 558–85
fol. 15^{v} = *Aen.* ix. 746–77
fol. 16^{v} = *Aen.* x. 239–70
fol. 17^{v} = *Aen.* x. 303–33
fol. 18^{v} = *Aen.* xi. 629–62
fol. 19^{v} = *Aen.* xi. 703–39
fol. 20^{v} = *Aen.* xi. 852–86
fol. 21^{v} = *Aen.* xii. 2–35
fol. 22^{v} = *Aen.* xii. 147–83
fol. 23^{v} = *Aen.* xii. 222–55

[2] See also *The Beneventan Script*, pp. 150 ff. Facsimiles of the Bari type of Beneventan are also found in *Scriptura Beneventana*, pls. lxv, lxxiv, lxxv, lxxxv.

by a humanistic hand of the fifteenth century to the end, on very fine parchment. The entire fol. 14, comprising lines 148–219 of the first Georgic ('Instituit cum iam glandes atque arbuta sacrae. . . . At si triticeam in messem robustaque farra'), is also an addition, but in an Italian Gothic hand of saec. xiv. The books of the *Aeneid* are preceded by the *Decasticha Argumenta*; these were omitted by the original scribe from before books iii and vii, but supplied in the latter case by the fifteenth-century hand. Beneventan neums occur on fol. 57^{v} in the lament over Hector (ll. 274–6).

The manuscript is composed of 183 leaves, measuring 326 × 190 mm., with a written space of 240 × 110 mm., containing 36 long lines to a page, between double bounding-lines. Ruling is on the hair-side, which is outside, four leaves at a time before folding. There are no contemporary quire-signatures; the reclamantes are later additions. The pagination of quire 1, a saec. xv addition, is in confusion. The script, while not of the pure Bari type, closely resembles it. Small black capitals, sometimes washed in with yellow, chiefly edged with red, begin each verse. Initials at the beginnings of books show the slender outlines characteristic of the Bari type, with the big pearl-decoration in the interstices and the familiar dogs' and fanciful beasts' heads. The design
(*51*) is crude and the execution too mediocre for an artist coming from one of the great centres. A few sketches occur: one on fol. 34^{v}, opposite line 550 of the third Georgic; on fol. 79^{v} one of Dido looking mournful, opposite the verse 'Quae tandem Ausonia . . .' (*Aen.* iv. 349); those on fols. 29^{v} and 147 seem scarcely related to the text: the latter is of a bearded man wearing a helmet or cowl, the former two are of the Madonna type (opposite line 190 of the third Georgic).

Nothing is known of the history of the manuscript. On fol. 140 there is a scratching 'Nicholaus'; considering the type of script, one naturally thinks of St. Nicholas of Bari, but it may have no significance whatever.

Our facsimile (Pl. 54 (*pl. 8*)) reproduces the Argumentum to *Aeneid* i, and the first twenty-one lines.

The Codex Cavensis

NEW LIGHT ON ITS LATER HISTORY

AMONG the oldest Latin manuscripts of the Bible the Codex Cavensis holds (325)
a place of its own. It is by common consent one of the two most important representatives of the peculiar type of text which was current in Spain for many centuries. The Spanish manuscript closest to the Cavensis is the Toletanus;[1] editors usually cite the variant readings of both.[2] Of the two the Cavensis is by far the more accurate, as it is also the more ancient. It also happens to be a superb specimen of calligraphy, perhaps the finest manuscript ever penned by a Spanish scribe. He left us his name—DANILA SCRIPTOR—in beautiful *capitalis rustica*, entered after the colophon to the Lamentations of Jeremiah on fol. 166ᵛ. It is a Spanish name. But Danila does not tell us where he wrote or when.

The present note is not concerned with the text of the Cavensis but with its palaeography, the main object being to call attention to a scrap of fresh evidence which goes to show that the Codex must have been in south Italy ever since the twelfth century. At the same time it may be useful to state briefly what is knowable regarding its date and origin and to give as detailed a description of the manuscript as possible on the lines followed in *Codices Latini Antiquiores*,[3] in the hope that the hard and dry facts may some day prove helpful in discovering the precise locality which produced so remarkable a book.

The Codex Cavensis gets its name from its present home near La Cava in
the province of Salerno. The Benedictine Abbey situated at Corpo di Cava (326)
near the top of the hill and dedicated to the Holy Trinity was only founded in 1011. It is therefore not one of the early monastic houses. Its library,

From *Quantulacumque: Studies Presented to Kirsopp Lake* (London, Christophers, 1937), pp. 325–31. [See Pls. 55 to 57.]

[1] On the much debated question of its date see now Agustín Millares Carlo, *Contribución al 'Corpus' de Codices Visigóticos*, pp. 99–130 (Madrid, 1931). The arguments in favour of the tenth century seem thoroughly convincing.

[2] Cf. Wordsworth's and White's preface and epilogue to their edition of the N.T.: *Novum Testamentum Domini nostri Iesu Christi*, etc. Pars prior, pp. xi, xiii f., and 717 ff. (Oxford, 1889–98).

[3] Part I, The Vatican City (Oxford, 1934); Part II, Great Britain and Ireland (Oxford, 1935). Parts III and IV are devoted to Italy.

though particularly rich in charters, is not without important ancient manuscripts. Of both charters and manuscripts the oldest are written in the peculiar script of south Italy which modern palaeographers call 'Beneventan', but which formerly bore the unfortunate name 'Lombardic'—a term still used by palaeographical die-hards. The unhistoric designation 'Lombardic' has been responsible for much confusion.[1] It has manifestly played its part in obscuring the true character of the Cavensis.

For all its importance, both textually and palaeographically, the Cavensis remained practically unknown to scholars until the early decades of the last century. When the great Benedictine, Jean Mabillon, the father of Latin palaeography, visited the abbey in November 1685 he was shown a number of manuscripts, but the Cavensis apparently was not among them. Had he seen it, he could hardly have failed to have devoted some space to it in his 'Iter Italicum'.[2] One wonders whether the monks of Holy Trinity had some reason for keeping quiet about their ancient Bible. Or had the manuscript not yet migrated to that part of southern Italy? It had certainly left Spain centuries before Mabillon's time, since, as will be shown presently, it had reached some south Italian centre at latest by the beginning of the twelfth century. And it is arguable that that centre was the abbey near La Cava.

Although the Cavensis is a typically Spanish manuscript whose script, abbreviation, orthography, and ornamentation all proclaim it as such, and even the beginner in palaeography would nowadays promptly recognize its nationality, it is nevertheless a fact that the scholars who first dealt with our manuscript, like De Rozan[3] and Angelo Mai,[4] never suspected its origin, and Champollion (in Silvestre),[5] D'Aragona[6] and Ziegler[7] describe it as 'Lom-
(*327*) bardic'. This error in classification found a place, for a short time, even in a well-known textbook on palaeography, as anyone may see who examines the first edition of Wattenbach's *Anleitung*.[8] It was not until the great Florentine palaeographer Cesare Paoli attacked the mistaken ascription that the error was banished for good and all. His article published in 1879[9] convinced

[1] Cf. *The Beneventan Script*, p. 28, n. 1 (Oxford, 1914).

[2] *Museum Italicum*, tom. I. 118 (Paris, 1687).

[3] *Lettre de l'abbé Rozan sur des livres et des manuscrits précieux de la bibliothèque de la Cava* (Naples, 1822); Italian translation by Dom G. Morcaldi.

[4] *Scriptorum Veterum*, etc., III, pars 2, pp. 165 f. (Rome, 1828); *Spicilegium Romanum*, IX, p. xxiii (Rome, 1843); *Nova Patrum Bibliotheca*, I, pars 2, p. 7 (Rome, 1852).

[5] *Paléographie Universelle*, III, pl. CXLI=106 (Paris, 1839–41).

[6] *Codex Diplomaticus Cavensis*, vol. I, Appendix (Naples, 1873).

[7] In *Sitzungsberichte der Bayerisch. Akademie* (1876), pp. 607–60.

[8] *Anleitung zur lateinischen Palaeographie*, 8 (Leipzig, 1869).

[9] In *Archivio storico italiano*, serie 4, vol. III (1879), p. 256.

Wattenbach completely, and subsequent editions of the *Anleitung* correctly describe the Cava Bible as Spanish, as do all later writers who deal with its text,[1] and all palaeographers by profession.[2]

While palaeography has progressed far enough to be able to distinguish a Visigothic manuscript from a so-called 'Lombardic', it is still groping in the dark when it comes to fixing the precise home of a Visigothic manuscript. Some day perhaps, as a result of careful and exhaustive study, we may be in a position to say of a manuscript that it hails from Toledo rather than Seville, from León rather than Barcelona. But we are not there yet. And the origin of the manuscript which has been described as 'by far the finest product of Spanish penmanship and book decoration' eludes us still. What we are certain of, however, is that this manuscript could have originated only in a centre of great palaeographic traditions. There is ground for believing that this great centre was probably in the north rather than in the south, since in the north more frequent opportunity existed for coming in contact with the masterpieces of Caroline calligraphy. For according to some art critics traces of French influence are discernible in the ornamentation of the Cavensis;[3] and the palaeographer is tempted to account for the systematic use by the scribe of the Cavensis of various ancient types (*capitalis rustica*, uncial, half-uncial, and even **bd**-uncial, all seen in the accompanying plates) by his acquaintance *(328)*
with the exquisite Biblical manuscripts of the school of St. Martin's at Tours, in which one encounters the same delight in the display of nearly all ancient types of script.[4] While the Tours scribes make use of *capitalis quadrata*, not found in the Cavensis, the scribe of the Cavensis on the other hand, employs **bd**-uncial, not found in the manuscripts of Tours. I may say in passing that if one needed further proof that **bd**-uncial was considered a distinct type (the entire Codex Bezae and the Codex Claromontanus of the Epistles are in this type), its presence in the Cavensis would supply it. It also throws some light

[1] See P. Corssen, *Epistula ad Galatas*, pp. 12–14 (Berlin, 1885); G. Schepps in *Corpus Scriptorum Eccles. Lat.* XVIII (1889), xxx ff.; S. Berger, *Histoire de la Vulgate*, pp. 14 f. (Paris, 1893); Wordsworth and White, cited p. 335 n. 2; A. Amelli, *De libri Baruch vetustissima Latina versione*, etc., pp. 6 ff. (Monte Cassino, 1902); F. Stabile in *Rivista di Filologia*, XXXIX (1911), 361–84; De Bruyne in *Revue Bénédictine*, XXXI (1914–19), 373–401; H. Quentin, *Mémoire sur l'établissement du texte de la Vulgate*, pp. 299, 310 ff. (Rome and Paris, 1922).

[2] Their works are cited in the bibliographical paragraph following the description of the manuscript and pp. 336, n. 9; 338, notes 2 and 3.

[3] Marquis De Lozoya, *Historia de l'arte Hispánico*, p. 322, and fig. 397 (Barcelona, 1931–4).

[4] See the facsimiles in Delisle's *Mémoire sur l'école calligraphique de Tours*, etc., in *Mémoires de l'Académie*, XXXII. 1 (Paris, 1885) and especially the rich material offered in E. K. Rand's *Studies in the Script of Tours*, vols. I and II (Cambridge, Mass., 1929 and 1934).

on what I call the hierarchy of scripts: the **bd**-uncial in our manuscript is confined to the Capitulationes, just as in the fifth-century uncial manuscript of Jerome's Chronicle in the Bodleian the **bd**-uncial is only used for the marginal summaries.[1] The type is subordinate and ancillary in both manuscripts, and the letters are sloping in both (see Pl. **55** (*pl. 1*)). In the Cavensis there is one curious feature: letter **a** is almost *capitalis rustica.* Perhaps some clue as to the place of origin may be contained in the orthography of the Cavensis. In any case its misspellings are so extraordinary as to deserve a special study. But many manuscripts will have to be gone over with a fine-tooth comb and exhaustive data collected before it will be possible to draw any conclusions from orthographic peculiarities as regards locality.

And now a word on the date of the Cavensis. Its precise age we shall never know, but there can be little doubt that it was written in the ninth century, probably in the middle or even past it. This judgement is based mainly on palaeographic grounds, on the script. If the broad lines of the development of Visigothic script as sketched in my *Studia Palaeographica*[2] are valid guides—they were accepted by C. U. Clark in his *Collectanea Hispanica*[3]—then the Cavensis is more ancient than our extant dated manuscripts of the tenth century. On the other hand, if low broad letters with coarse strokes and
(*329*) frequent ligatures are characteristic of the eighth and early ninth century, then the Cavensis has manifestly passed that stage. The date thus derived from a study of the script is confirmed by internal evidence furnished by a few curious marginal entries which seem to refer to the theological disputes then raging on the question of predestination, in connection with which church councils were held in 848, 849, and 855. These dates fit in well with the verdict suggested by the script.

The later history of the Cavensis, like its origin, seems shrouded in mystery. We do not know when it left Spain, nor under what circumstances.

And this brings me to what I consider the scrap of evidence which is the only justification for the present note. There exist in the Cavensis at least three marginal notes recording variant readings entered by a reader whose natural script must have been, I am convinced, Beneventan, i.e. south Italian. On fol. 100 (seen in our Pl. **56** (*pl. 2*)), opposite the word 'uerbi', in Iob XL. 27, a manifestly Beneventan hand of the first half of the twelfth century wrote:

[1] Cf. Steffens, *Lateinische Paläographie*,[2] pl. 17 (Trier, 1909).

[2] Pp. 80 f. [this volume, pp. 60 f.] (Munich, 1910), published in *Sitzungsber. der Bayer. Akademie.*

[3] Pp. 106 f. (Paris, 1920), published in the *Transactions of the Conn. Acad. of Arts and Sciences*, vol. 24.

'belli'. In the upper half of fol. 254^{v} (reproduced in our Pl. **57** (*pl. 3*)), in the prologue to the Epistle to the Romans, the word 'dicentes' is entered in the margin, with a sign showing that it is to be inserted after the sentence 'gentes hetiam he contrario respondebant'. In the same column, nine lines below, the same hand inserted in the margin the words 'simulacra intuebamini' which were omitted after the words 'in nube uel igni conspicere solebatis'. Both these entries are followed by the group of two dots over a comma, which is the normal Beneventan full stop. This same full stop, as well as the point surmounted by an oblique line for lesser pauses—also a Beneventan feature —is found *passim* in this prologue. While the word 'belli' is unmistakably Beneventan, the words 'dicentes' and 'simulacra intuebamini' have elements which are foreign to the south Italian minuscule, for neither the **d** nor the **t** nor the **a** has the Beneventan form. And yet I think it can justly be claimed that the scribe who permitted himself the non-Beneventan forms of these letters was trained in the Beneventan school; the pen he used was one adapted to Beneventan calligraphy. What is more—the hand which wrote 'dicentes' also wrote 'intuebamini'. Now, while the **t** in the former is non-Beneventan, the **t** in the latter is pure Beneventan. What we have here, then, is doubtless a case which illustrates the tendency of the time to graft Caroline forms upon
the Beneventan calligraphy. And it is precisely among the manuscripts of La (*330*)
Cava that an excellent parallel is found: the early twelfth-century manuscript of Gregory's *Moralia*, which bears the number 7, is written partly in Beneventan and partly in ordinary minuscule. On fol. 34 both scripts are seen, the Beneventan continuing the non-Beneventan. What is curious and interesting is that the hand which writes the non-Beneventan is manifestly accustomed to Beneventan script and uses a pen adapted for that script. The Beneventan punctuation is used in both parts. Now the hand which entered the readings on fol. 254^{v} of the Cavensis has, to my mind, considerable resemblance to the non-Beneventan hand of the Cava Gregory MS. 7. That the variant readings just mentioned were made by a south Italian will be admitted by everyone familiar with the Beneventan style of writing. Is it not reasonable to suppose that they were made in the very abbey where the Cavensis is still preserved?

If the above account of the variant readings is not incongruous with the facts of the case, then the surmise made by the late Abbot Amelli as to how the Codex came to Italy seems attractive and even plausible.[1] He suggests that the precious and beautiful Bible once belonged to the Benedictine Mauritius Bordinho, later known as anti-Pope Gregory VIII, who had been

[1] See Dom Mattei-Cerasoli, *Codices Cavenses*, pars 1, p. 10 (Cava, 1935).

Bishop of Coimbra and Archbishop of Braga and a welcome visitor at the abbey in La Cava in the first decades of the twelfth century. This is no more than a conjecture; yet a hypothesis which connects this important Spanish manuscript with an Iberian Benedictine of high station who had relations with the Benedictine house in which the manuscript is now preserved has something at least in its favour.

La Cava, Archivio della Badia della SS^{ma} Trinità, MS. I

BIBLIA SACRA. VISIGOTHIC MINUSCULE. SAEC. IX^{2}

Fols. 303; 320×268 mm. < 265–75×215 mm. > normally in three columns of 54–6 lines (the lists of names on fols. 80^{v} ff. are in six columns). Ruling on hair-side, each leaf singly before folding. Double bounding lines enclose each column. Prickings in the outer margin guided ruling. Gatherings normally of eights, signed by a Roman numeral often followed by $\overline{\textbf{QT}}$ (quaternio) and enclosed in an artfully decorated and coloured border. Hair side outside quires. Colophons and headings mostly in elongated capitals in alternating red and black or red and blue, or in hollow capitals filled with colours, the
(331) whole usually enclosed in coloured ornamental frames of graceful lines; red is used for the first words of chapters. Punctuation: the low or medial point marks the various pauses; other points are later additions; the interrogation point is not used; Iob, the Psalms, and other metrical parts of the Bible are written *per cola et commata*. Abbreviations (apart from Nomina Sacra) include: **autm** = autem; **b** with the prolonged curve of the bow sweeping boldly below the line = bis (fol. 18, etc.); **b**^{s}, **I**^{s}, **m**^{s} = bus, ius, mus; **Ihrslm** = Ierusalem; **Srhl** = Israel; **krsmi** = karissimi; **mm** = meum; **msrcdae** = misericordiae; **nmn, nmne** = nomen, -ine, **nn** = non; **nsam** = nostram; **oma** = omnia; **p** and **ꝑ** = per; **pplm** = populum; **q̄** = que; **qnm** = quoniam; **t** with cross-bar transected vertically = tum; **usi** = uestri; the horizontal abbreviation stroke is surmounted by a dot except when placed over **q̄** (que), or when transecting the shafts of **h** or **l**. Omitted **m** at word- or line-end is marked by a flourish, usually with a dot above. Spelling: the most conspicuous feature is the perverse misuse of **h** (hadam, ha, homnia, het). Ornamental pages decorated with coloured crosses are seen on fols. I^{v} and 143; on some pages containing prefatory matter the written space is cruciform and various colours are used in the text (fols. 143^{v}, 194, 194^{v}, 220, 220^{v}, 224^{v}, 225); horseshoe formed arches enclose the canon tables (fols. 221–222^{v}); initials show the rope pattern or the leaf or bird or fish motif; the colours used are red, pink, blue, green, yellow; gold is also used (fols. I^{v}, 143, 143^{v}). Parchment good; fol. 221 is stained blue, fols. 194, 224, and 253 are stained purple. Ink grey or greyish brown; on the ornamental pages red, pink, blue, green, yellow, and white inks are used for the text. Script of the Biblical text is a finely penned, very regular Visigothic minuscule with a general inclination towards the left; uncial **d** is more common than minuscule; **i**-longa is used initially and medially for the intervocalic sound; it is occasionally forked at the top **(Yn, aYt)** and is not to be confused with letter

Y; there are frequent ligatures: **ern, rtem,** etc.; the same type of script, exceptionally tiny, is used for exegetic marginalia on fols. 186^{v} f. Uncial is used for prefaces and for the opening sentences of books; sloping **bd**-uncial is used often for *capitula* (fols. 57^{v}, 58, 64, 64^{v}, etc.); half-uncial is used for the argumenta of the Pauline Epistles (fols. 255^{v}, etc.) and where two prologues occur one is in uncial, the other in half-uncial (fols. 181^{v} and 239); rustic capital is used for some opening verses and for the scribe's signature: DANILA SCRIPTOR, on fol. 166^{v}. Some marginalia are in sloping uncial (fol. 14^{v}) or in ordinary minuscule. Beneventan variant readings saec. XII in. occur on fols. 100, 254^{v} (see facs.). Here and there are Arabic notes (fols. 32, 33), once a Hebrew note (fol. 98). The whole manuscript is in excellent condition.

Catalogues and facsimiles: Dom B. Gaetani D'Aragona, *I Manoscritti membranacei della biblioteca della SS. Trinità di Cava*, published as Appendix to vol. I of *Codex Diplomaticus Cavensis;* two plates (Naples, 1873). D. Leo Mattei-Cerasoli, *Codices Cavenses*, pars I, pp. 1 ff. (Cava, 1935). Silvestre (*Pal. Univ.*, cited above, p. 336 n. 5); the plate is composite. C. U. Clark, *Coll. Hisp.* (cited above, p. 338, n. 3), pls. 13–14 (reduced). Dom H. Quentin, *Mémoire* etc. (see above, p. 337, n. 1), fig. 28 (fol. 24). De Lozoya, *Hist. de l'arte Hisp.* (cited above, p. 337, n. 3), fig. 397.

For other works, see pp. 336, n. 9; 337, n. 1; 338, notes 3 and 4; L. Traube, *Nomina Sacra* (Munich, 1907); Z. García Villada, *Paleografía Española* (Madrid, 1923), and A. Millares Carlo, *Tratado de Paleografía Española* (Madrid, 1932).

(*191*) # *A Manuscript of Alcuin in the Script of Tours*

OF the scores of manuscripts that have come down to us in the beautiful script of Tours, few contain the works of Alcuin—few, that is, considering the popularity of his writings and his eminence in the very centre which produced these masterpieces of calligraphy. In his monumental publication on the script of Tours,[1] Professor Rand describes four Alcuin manuscripts as written in the Tours minuscule. They are, in the order of Rand's series, as follows:

No. 38. *Liber de Virtutibus et de Vitiis* (MS. Troyes 1742) written, according to Köhler, in Alcuin's time.

No. 42. *Expositio in VII Psalmos Paenitentiae et alia* (MS. Cologne CVI). Regarding the Turonian origin of this manuscript Rand entertained doubts: probably it originated at Cologne.[2]

No. 48. *Expositio in Iohannem* (MS. Cologne CVII), reproduced on pl. XLI. 3 of vol. II.[3]

No. 62. *Martinellus*, including Alcuin's sermon on St. Martin (Vatican Regin. 495), written, according to Rand,[4] 'under Alcuin or not long after his death'.

Eight other Alcuin manuscripts had reached the stage of being considered candidates for Tours membership, but on careful examination Rand rejected them: these Ishmaelites are listed under no. 232.[5]

It is therefore of some interest to publish another Alcuin manuscript whose graceful lineaments proclaim it at once a true product of Tours, copied only a few years after Alcuin's death, hardly more than a score or so. The manuscript in question contains Alcuin's *Commentary on Ecclesiastes*[6] and is pre-
(*192*) served in the Cathedral Library of Salisbury under the press-mark 133.[7] It

From *Classical and Mediaeval Studies in honor of Edward Kennard Rand* (New York, L. W. Jones 1938), pp. 191–3. [See Pl. 58].

[1] E. K. Rand, *Studies in the Script of Tours*, I, *A Survey of the Manuscripts of Tours* (Cambridge, Mass.: The Mediaeval Academy of America, 1929).

[2] Ibid., p. 115. See L. W. Jones, *The Script of Cologne from Hildebald to Hermann* (Cambridge, Mass.: The Mediaeval Academy of America, 1932), pp. 40–3.

[3] E. K. Rand and L. W. Jones, *Studies in the Script of Tours*, II, *The Earliest Book of Tours, with Supplementary Descriptions of Other Manuscripts of Tours* (Cambridge, Mass.: The Mediaeval Academy of America, 1934); for the description of the manuscript see p. 95.

[4] Vol. I, p. 126.

[5] Ibid., pp. 203–6.

[6] K. Schenkl, *Bibliotheca patrum latinorum britannica*, no. 3725.

[7] Thanks are due to Mr. N. R. Ker for calling my attention to this manuscript, and to Canon Christopher Wordsworth and the Chapter of Salisbury for their kindness in sending the manuscript to Oxford.

was in very bad condition till it was restored last year. Both the beginning and the end are lost and there are other lacunae, the precise contents being: cap. II. 14–IV. 9; IV. 12–IX. 10; X. 2–9 (fragments), and two scraps from X. 10.

What follows is a purely palaeographic description in the manner employed in *Codices Latini Antiquiores*:

Fols. 47+2 scraps (five folios are missing, one between fols. 14^v and 15, four between 45^v and 46); 245×180 mm. ⟨168×110 mm.⟩ in 19 long lines. Ruling on the hair side, two bifolia at a time; the centre opening and fols. 2^v and 7 of each quire show the direct impression. Double bounding lines. Gatherings probably of eights, with hair side outside, signed by Roman numerals in the centre of the lower margin (fol. 22^v has the quire-mark IIII). Punctuation: the medial (occasionally the high) point is used for all pauses; the question-mark and some accents over monosyllables are original; many commas, points, and accents were added. Citations are marked by an **s**-like flourish in the margin opposite each line cited. Abbreviations include **b;**, **q;** = bus, que; the Nomina Sacra **ds̄**, **dī**, **dō**, **dnō**, **xp̄s**, etc. = deus, dominus and cases, Christus, etc.; **iſr̄l** = Israel; **nr̄o**, **nr̄is** = nostro, nostris; **ur̄t**, **ur̄a** = vester, vestra; **·ē·**, **·ēē·** (between two dots) = est, esse; the usual 'per', 'prae', and 'pro' symbols; **t̄** = ter at line-ends; 'tur' is not abbreviated. Omitted **m** is indicated by a horizontal stroke over the vowel. Spelling: 'a**d**flictionem', 'a**d**quirendi', 'i**n**precatur', yet 'a**mm**oneo'. Simple initials alternately red and black project into the margin; on fols. 27^v, 28, 36^v, 37 are black initials crudely filled with red, doubtless by a later illuminator. Parchment is smooth, well prepared, and generally thin. Ink brown. Script is a beautiful Caroline minuscule of the Tours type which flourished under Alcuin's successor Fridugisus and which Rand calls the Perfected Style. Half-uncial of the unmistakably Tours type is used for the Biblical passages commented upon. The shafts of tall letters have sinuous horizontal serifs, which, according to Rand, are a survival of an earlier stage. Here and there the uncial form of **N** occurs. Ligature of **rt** is frequent in the minuscule; ligatures with **e** are very frequent in the half-uncial. Many marginalia in ordinary minuscule (see Plate **58** (*pl. I*)).

Written doubtless at Tours, to judge by the script, probably at the same time as Bamberg H J. IV. 12, containing Boethius, *Arithmetica*,[1] with which our manuscript agrees in the size of the written space and the number of lines.

Our manuscript supplies a not very accurate text of Alcuin's *Commentary on Ecclesiastes*, but it is in all probability the oldest. Such as it is, this copy survived not in its place of origin, but in England. Precisely when or how it reached Alcuin's native land it is hard to say. There are no ancient Anglo-
Saxon annotations in the manuscript to prove that it had been read in Eng- (*193*)
land; but not even that evidence would be conclusive, since Anglo-Saxon

[1] Rand, op. cit., no. 71, pls. LXXXVII, LXXXVIII.

was actually written in Alcuin's monastery at Tours—how could it be different, with Alcuin living and writing there?—as may be seen from the Laurentian copy of Donatus on Virgil (MS. XLV. 15),[1] and the British Museum manuscript of Jerome on Isaiah (Egerton 2831),[2] manuscripts which prove that Northumbrian and Tours scribes worked side by side at least in Alcuin's time.

[1] Rand, op. cit., pl. xiv.

[2] Ibid., pl. xiii; and E. A. Lowe, *Codices Latini Antiquiores*, ii (Oxford, 1935), no. 196.

A New Fragment of Arator in the Bodleian

BY NEIL R. KER, E. A. LOWE, AND A. P. McKINLAY

I. NOTE ON THE FIND (*by* Neil R. Ker)

THE inner sides of the wooden boards of Bodleian MS. e Mus. 66 (SC 3655)[1] *(351)*
show offset writing from four pages of a manuscript of Arator, *De Actibus Apostolorum*. Parts of bk. 1, lines 32–63, 85–122, 647–81, 684–724 are legible, when looked at through a mirror. The pieces of manuscript which have left traces on the boards consisted of two sheets laid sideways. That at the beginning had its upper margin and that at the end its lower margin towards the spine. I call the upper half of the offset on the front board p. 1 and the lower half p. 2, and the upper half of the offset on the back board p. 3 and the lower half p. 4, and use inverted commas when referring to the pages of the manuscript from which the offsets are derived. P. 1 contains lines 85–122, p. 2 lines 647–81, p. 3 lines 684–724, and p. 4 lines 32–63. This sequence shows that the two sheets were adjacent, the one on the back board lying outside the one on the front board, and that 'p. 1' followed immediately on 'p. 4', and 'p. 3' immediately on 'p. 2', i.e. 'p. 4' was a verso, 'p. 1' a recto, 'p. 2' a verso, and 'p. 3' a recto. In other words, the offsets are of two double openings: the first consisting of 'pp. 4+1' and the second of 'pp. 2+3'. Twenty-nine lines appear on pp. 1, 2, 30 lines on p. 3, and 25 lines on p. 4 where the writing is more widely spaced. From the number of lines missing between p. 1 and p. 2 it is probable that the quire to which the two sheets belonged was of at least five sheets (ten leaves) and that the three inner sheets (six leaves) are missing.[2]

The offsets are of the central portion of each sheet, so that line-ends are preserved on pp. 2, 4, and line-beginnings on pp. 1, 3. About three-quarters

From *Speculum*, XIX (1944), 351–2. [See Pls. **59** and **60**. McKinlay's contribution, ibid. 352–9, has not been reprinted. Ed.]

[1] The manuscript contains Beda, *In Cantica Canticorum*, well written in an English hand of the first half of saec. XII, followed by Franco, *De Gratia Dei* in a rougher and rather later hand. It was given to the Bodleian by Alexander Fetherston, vicar of Wolverton, Bucks., in 1680. The binding is of white leather over boards, saec. XV.

[2] The text on pp. 2, 3 is nearly continuous, but the text on p. 4 is separated from that on p. 1 by 22 lines of verse. I am unable to explain the discrepancy.

of the full width remains on p. 4, about two-thirds on pp. 1, 3, and rather less than half on p. 2. Some lines at the foot of pp. 1, 2 and some lines at the head of pp. 3, 4 are covered by the overfold of the skin binding, which was raised for the purposes of transcription and photography. The offset writing covered by the skin is clearer than elsewhere. Extreme measurements are 176 × 100 mm. on p. 1, 180 × 85 mm. on p. 2, 160 × 100 mm. on p. 3, and 160 × 120 mm. on p. 4. The space separating p. 1 from p. 2 and p. 3 from p. 4 is about 40 mm. wide.

2. NOTE ON THE SCRIPT

It is difficult to be precise and definite about the script of the Arator fragment discovered by Mr. Neil Ker in the Bodleian. A photograph taken of an
(352) offset which must be reversed in order to be read may distort the script to some extent. Yet, even so, this much may be said without hesitation. The script is palaeographically very interesting because it is a borderline type. It may be described as half-uncial becoming minuscule, or as minuscule emerging from half-uncial. It makes calligraphic use of the same material as we find in the marginalia of some of our oldest Latin manuscripts, e.g. the Codex Bembinus of Terence in *capitalis rustica*,[1] and the Fulda-Weingarten Fragments of the Prophets in uncial of the fifth century[2] with marginalia in tiny half-uncial which may be regarded as the very precursors of the script of the Bodleian Arator. But if we ask what texts, as opposed to marginalia, are written in similar script we find the closest resemblance in the script of the palimpsest leaves of the Bobbio Missal.[3] These leaves may go back to the fifth century; they are certainly not more recent than the sixth. The type we are discussing, therefore, has its roots in antiquity; it goes back to the fifth century and even further. The Bodleian fragment is definitely not so old as the Bobbio leaves; it can, however, safely be ascribed to the seventh century. It has the characteristic ancient ligatures of **li**, **ri**, and the numerous ligatures with **e**. Letter **n** has mostly the minuscule form, which is also true of the script in the Bobbio Missal and the Terence marginalia; **a** and **o** are fre-

[1] MS. Vatic. Lat. 3226. Facsimiles in Zangemeister–Wattenbach, *Exempla Codicum Latinorum Litteris Majusculis Scriptorum* (1876), pl. 8; Ehrle–Liebaert, *Specimina Codicum Latinorum Vaticanorum* (1912), pl. 2c; E. A. Lowe, *Codices Latini Antiquiores*, I (1934), pl. 12.

[2] The *membra disiecta* are in four different libraries: Darmstadt, Fulda, St. Paul and Stuttgart. Cf. L. Traube, *Vorlesungen und Abhandlungen*, I (1909), 240. Facsimile in Zangemeister–Wattenbach, op. cit., pl. XXI.

[3] MS. Paris Lat. 13246, fols. 296–300. Complete facsimile edition in Henry Bradshaw Society, vol. LIII (1917).

quently smaller than the neighbouring letters; the tall stems are club-shaped. The abbreviations are confined to the Nomina Sacra, and the veteran suspensions **b.** and **q.** for 'bus' and 'que'. In spelling there is confusion of **e** and **i**, **o** and **u**, **b** and **u**; but these are faults common to manuscripts of this period.

Where exactly our fragment originated it is impossible to say. I am inclined to regard north Italy as most probable, but France is not to be excluded. It is greatly to be hoped that a few actual leaves of this manuscript will some day be recovered. They would help to fill a distinct gap in our palaeographical material.

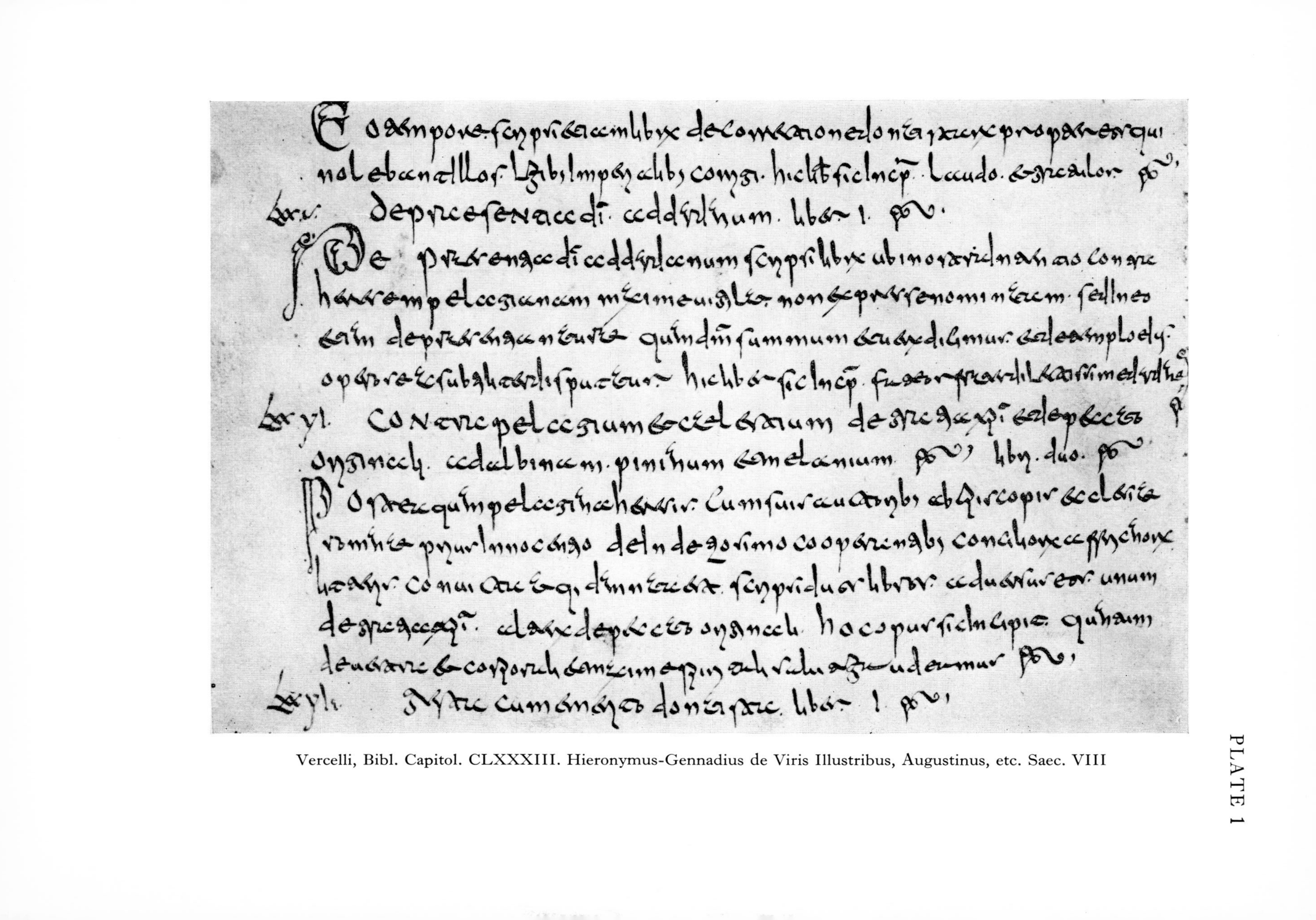

Vercelli, Bibl. Capitol. CLXXXIII. Hieronymus-Gennadius de Viris Illustribus, Augustinus, etc. Saec. VIII

PLATE 2

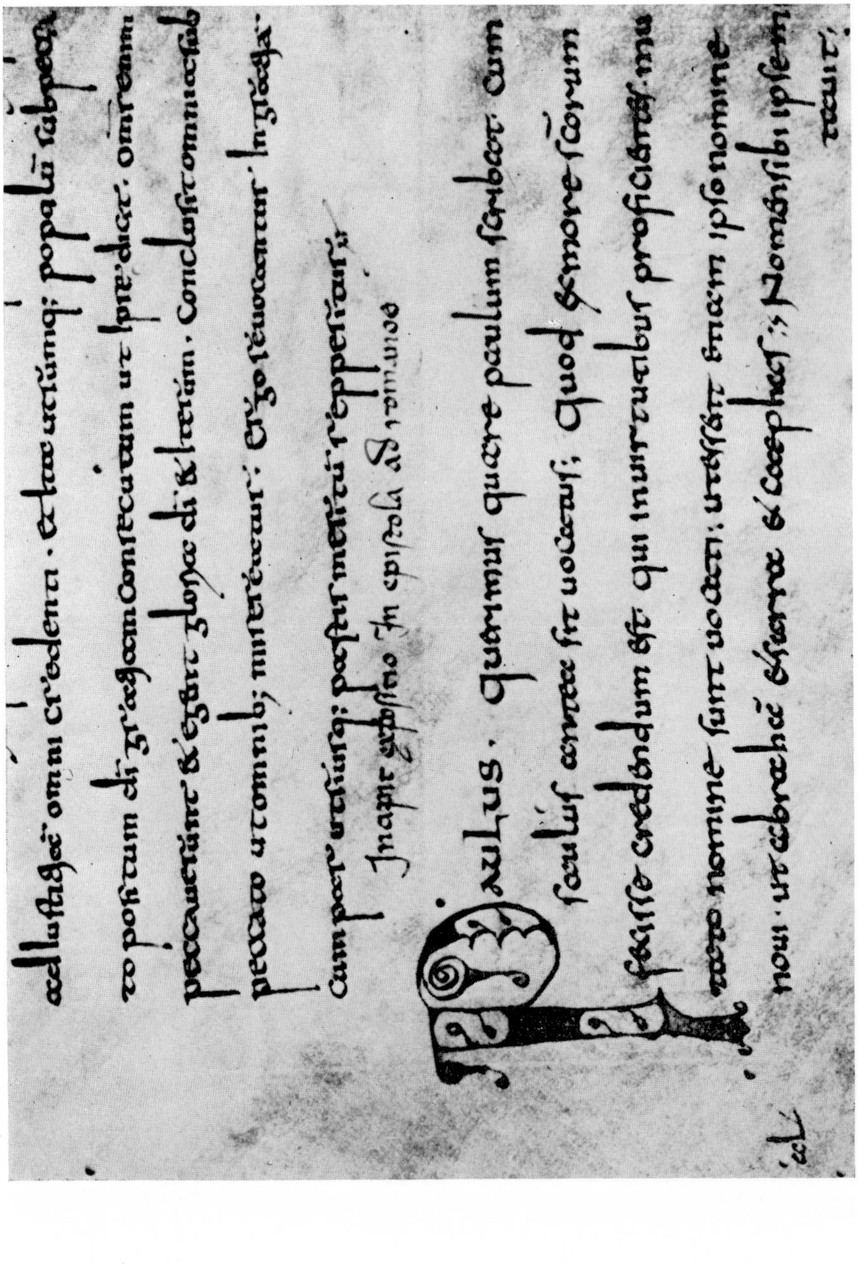

Paris, Bibl. Nat. lat. 653. Pelagius in Epist. Pauli. Saec. VIII-IX

Monte Cassino, Archivio della Badia 4. Ambrosius de Fide, de Spiritu Sancto, etc. Saec. IX in.

PLATE 4

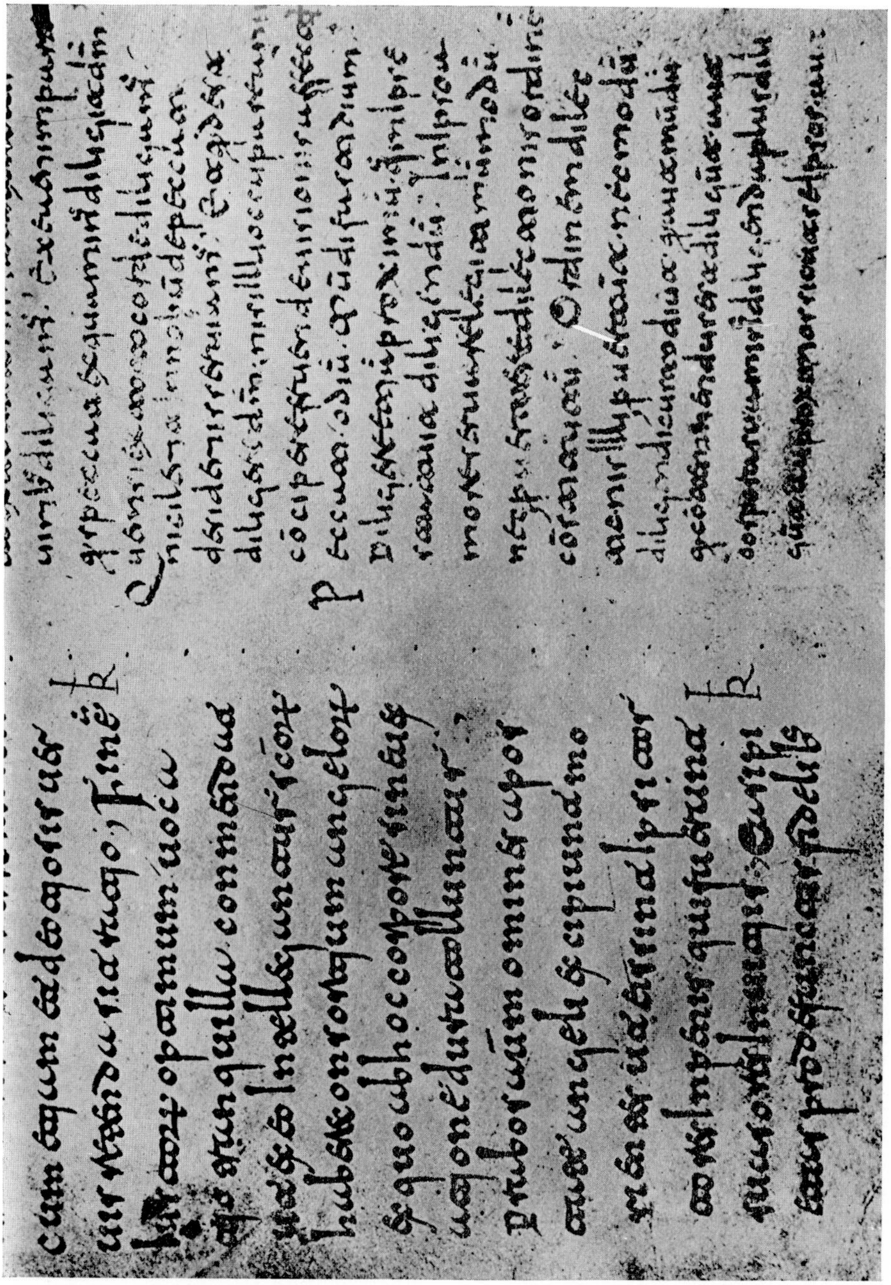

Madrid, Bibl. Nac. 10067 (Tolet. 15, 12). Isidorus de Summo Bono. A.D. 915

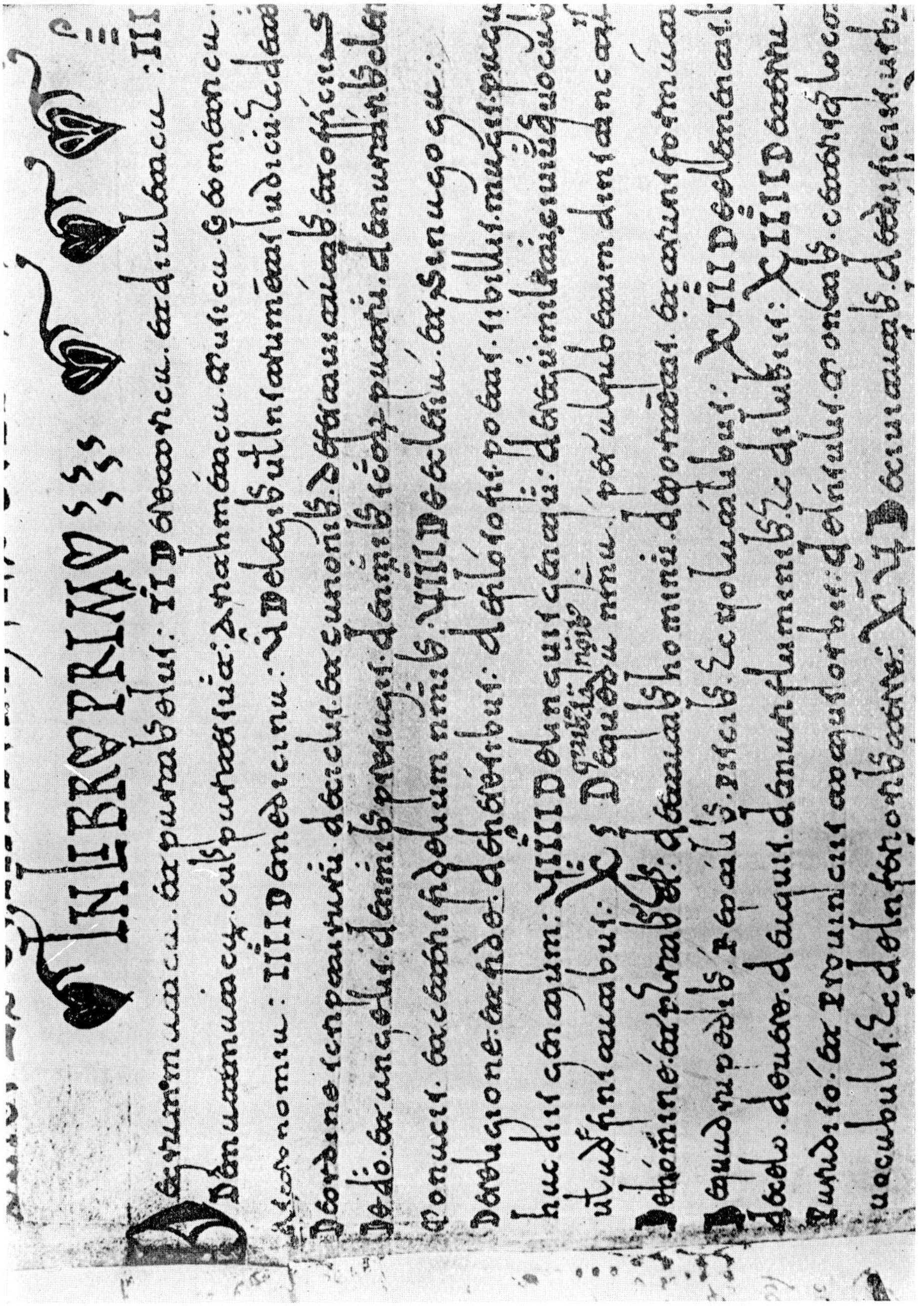

PLATE 5

Escorial, T. II. 24 (formerly Q. II. 24). Isidorus, Etymologiae. Saec. X

PLATE 6

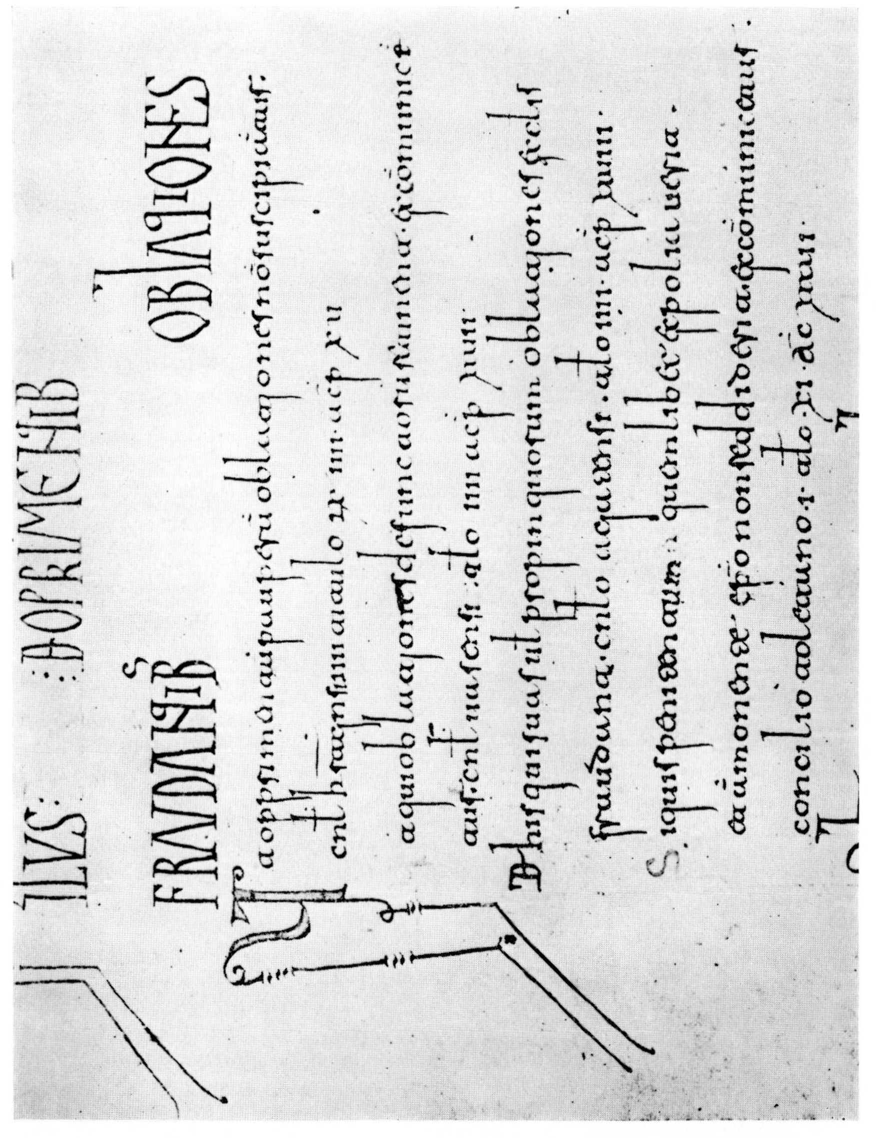

Escorial, d. I. 1. Conciliorum Collectio. A.D. 992

Rome, Bibl. Corsiniana 369. Beatus in Apocalypsin. Saec. XII

New York, Pierpont Morgan Libr. M. 462, fol. 48. Plinius Iun., Epist. *ca.* A.D. 500

AD CALUISIUM RUFUM
NESCIO AN NULLUM
AD UIBIUM · MAXIMUM
QUOD · IPSE AMICIS TUIS
AD CAERELLIAE HISPULLAE
CUM PATREM TUUM
AD CAELIUM MACRINUM
QUAMUIS ET AMICI
AD BAEBIUM MACRUM
[illegible] EST MIHI
[illegible] SEUERUM
[illegible] QUAE
AD CANINIUM RUFUM
MODO NUNTIATUS EST
AD SUETON TRANQUE
FACIS AD [illegible] CETERA
AD CORNELIUM MINICIANUM
POSSUM IAM PERSCRIB
AD UESTRIC SPURINN·
COMPOSUISSE ME QUAE[illegible]

Idem, fol. 48v

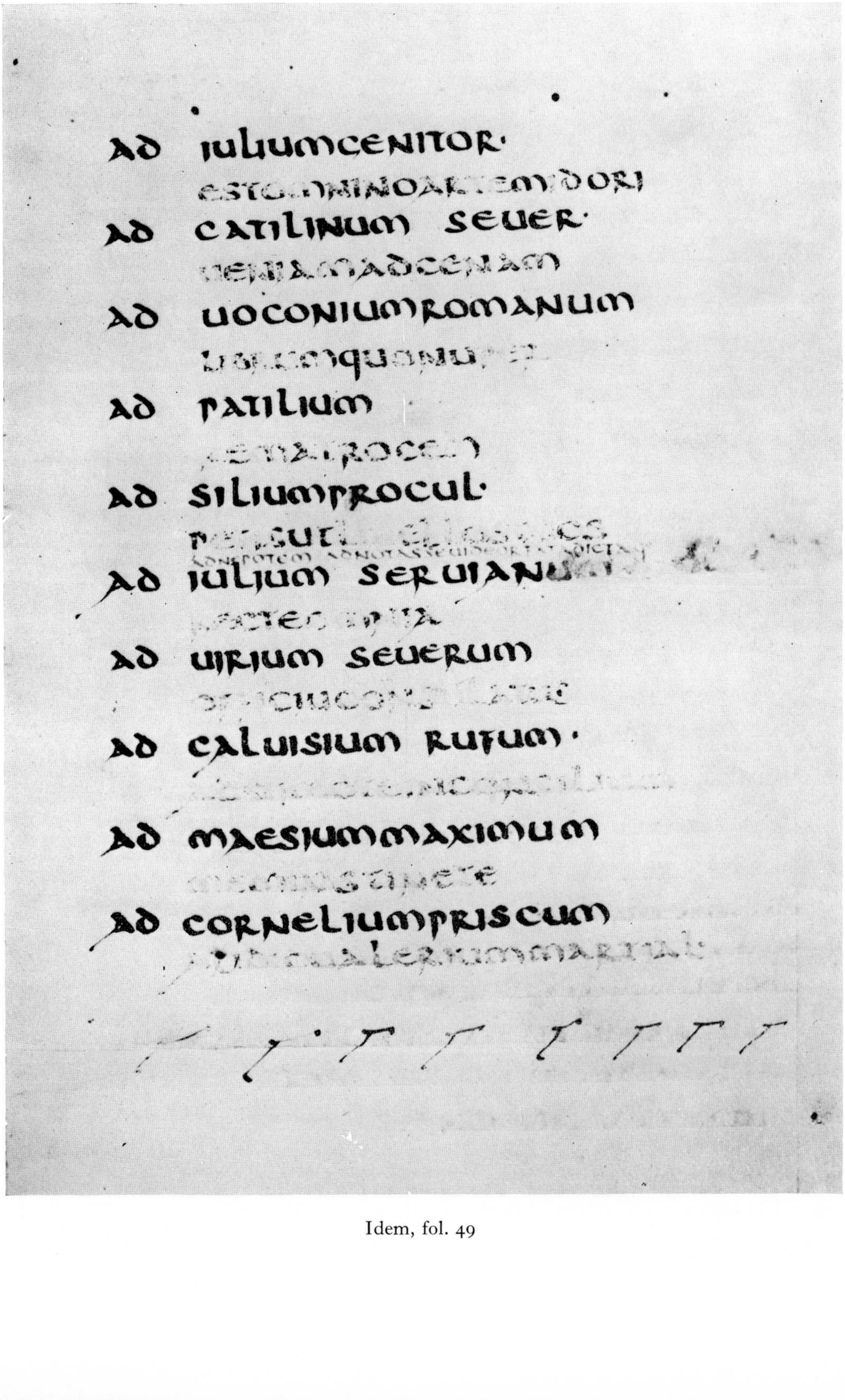

PLATE 10

AD IULIUM GENITOR.

AD CATILINUM SEUER.

AD UOCONIUM ROMANUM

AD PATILIUM

AD SILIUM PROCUL.

AD IULIUM SERUIANU[M]

AD UIRIUM SEUERUM

AD CALUISIUM RUFUM.

AD MAESIUM MAXIMUM

AD CORNELIUM PRISCUM

Idem, fol. 49

C. PLINIUS· CALUISIO SUO SALUTEM
NESCIOANULLUMIUCUNDIUSTEMPUS
EXEGERIMQUAMQUONUPERAPUDSPU
RINNAMFUIADEOQUIDEMUTNEMINEM
MAGISINSENECTUTESIMODOSENESCE
REDATUMESTAEMULARIUELIMNIHIL
ESTENIMILLOUITAEGENEREDISTIN
CTIUSMEAUTEMUTCERTUSSIDERUM
CURSUSITAUITAHOMINUMDISPOSITA
DELECTATSENUMPRAESERTIMNAM
IUUENESADHUCCONFUSAQUAEDAM
ETQUASITURBATANONINDECENTSE
NIB·PLACIDAOMNIAETORDINATACON
UENIUNTQUIB·INDUSTRIASERATURPIS
AMBITIOESTHANCREGULAMSPURIN
NACONSTANTISSIMESERUAT·QUINETIAM
PARUAHAECPARUA·SINONCOTIDIEFIANT
ORDINEQUODAMETUELUTORBECIRCUM
AGITMANELECTULOCONTINETURHORA
SECUNDACALCEOSPOSCITAMBULATMI
LIAPASSUUMTRIANECMINUSANIMUM
QUAMCORPUSEXERCETSIADSUNTAMICI
HONESTISSIMISERMONESEXPLICANTUR
SINONLIBERLEGITURINTERDUMETIAMPRAE
SENTIB·AMICISSITAMENILLINONGRAUAN
TURDEINDECONSIDITETLIBERRURSUS
AUTSERMOLIBROPOTIOR·MOXUEHICUL

Idem, fol. 49v

ASCENDITADSUMITUXOREMSINGU
LARISEXEMPLIUELALIQUEMAMICORUM
UTMEPROXIMEQUAMPULCHRUMILLUD
QUAMDULCESECRETUMQUANTUMIBIAN
TIQUITATISQUAEFACTAQUOSUIROSAU
DIASQUIB·PRAECEPTISIMBUAREQUAMUIS
ILLEHOCTEMPERAMENTUMMODESTIAE
SUAEINDIXERITNEPRAECIPEREUIDEATUR
PERACTISSEPTEMMILIB·PASSUUMITE
RUMAMBULATMILLEITERUMRESIDIT
UELSECUBICULOACSTILOREDDITSCRI
BITENIMETQUIDEMUTRAQ·LINGUALY
RICADOCTISSIMAMIRAILLISDULCEDO
MIRASUAUITASMIRAHILARITATISCUIUS
GRATIAMCUMULATSANCTITATISSCRI
BENTISUBIHORABALNEINUNTIATAEST
ESTAUTEMHIEMENONA·AESTATEOCTA
UAINSOLESICARETUENTOAMBULAT
NUDUSDEINDEMOUETURPILAUEHE
MENTERETDIUNAMHOCQUOQ·EXER
CITATIONISGENEREPUGNATCUMSE
NECTUTELOTUSACCUBATETPAULIS
PERCIBUMDIFFERTINTERIMAUDITLE
GENTEMREMISSIUSALIQUIDETDULCIUS
PERHOCOMNETEMPUSLIBERUMEST
AMICISUELEADEMFACEREUELALIA
SIMALINTADPONITURCENANONMINUS

Idem, fol. 50

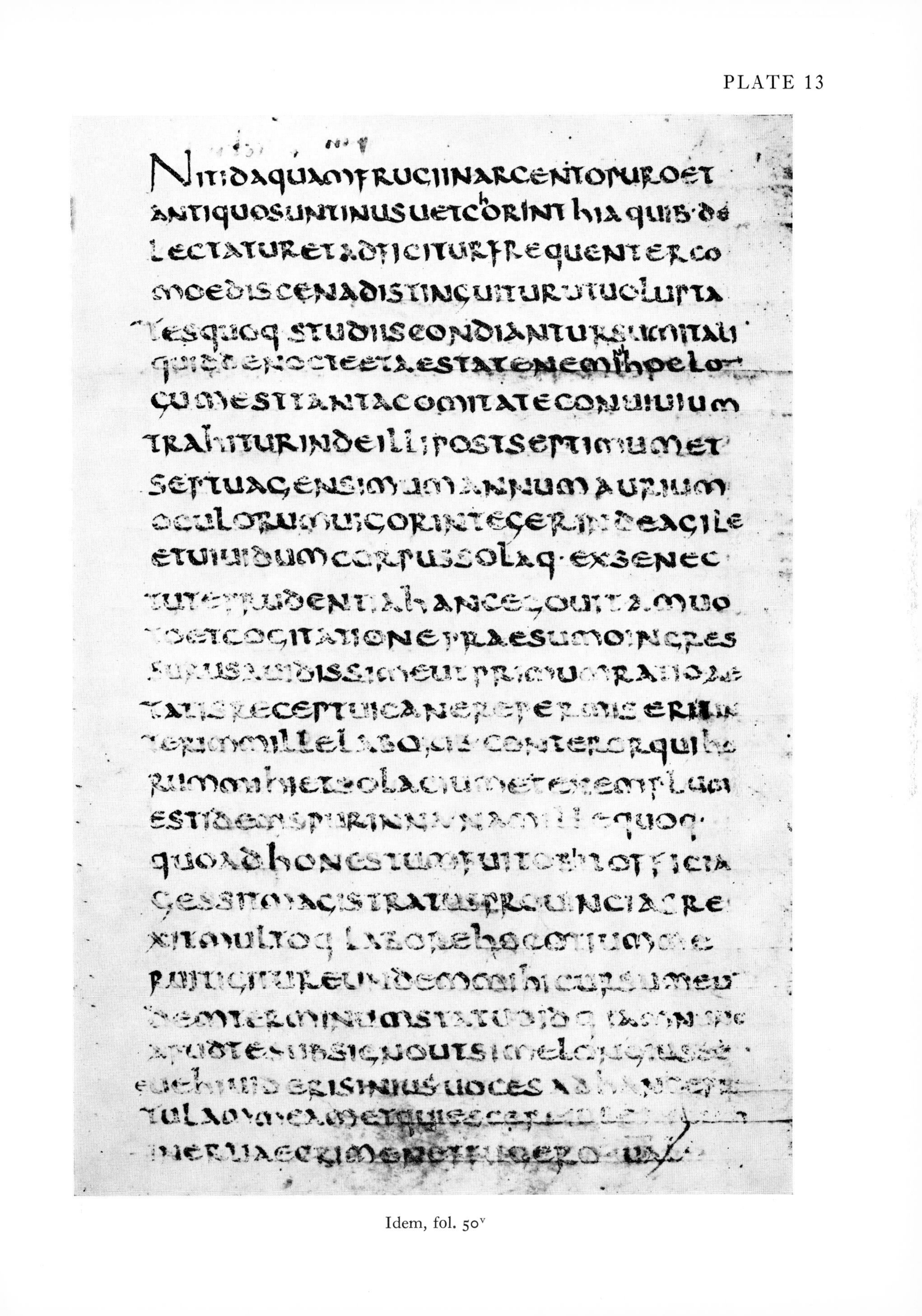

Idem, fol. 50v

C. PLINIUS · MAXIMO SUO SALUTEM

Idem, fol. 51

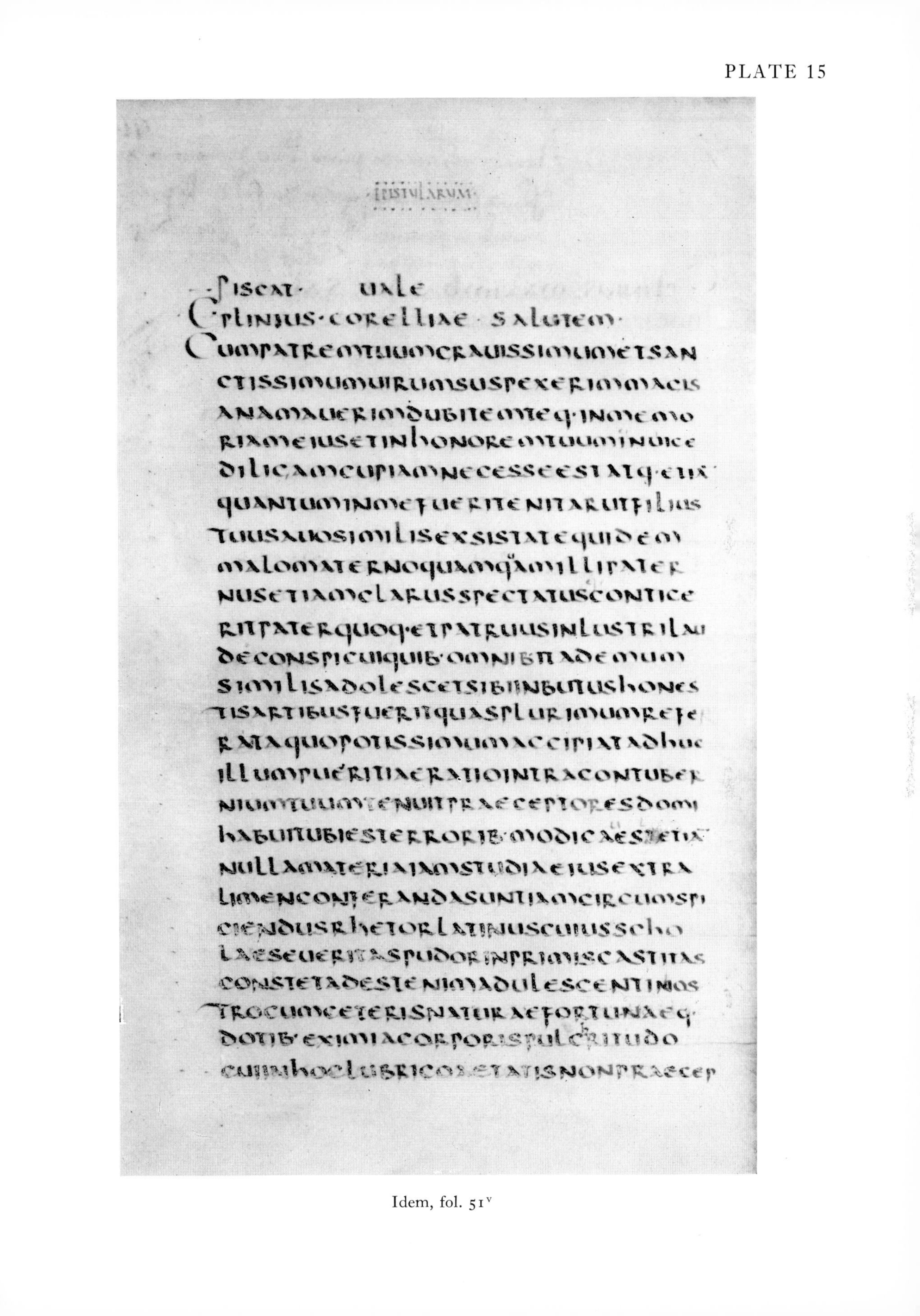

Idem, fol. 51[v]

·61·

·LIB· ·III·

TORMODOSEDCUSTOSETIAMRECTORQ·
QUAERENDUSESTUIDEORERGODEMON
STRARETIBIPOSSEIULIUMGENITOREM
AMATURAMEIUDICIOTAMENMEONON
OBSTATKARITASHOMINISQUAEEXIUDI
CIONATAESTUIRESTEMENDATUSETGRA
UISPAULOETIAMHORRIDIORETDURIOR
UTINHACLICENTIATEMPORUMQUAN
TUMELOQUENTIAUALEATPLURIB·CRE
DEREPOTESNAMDICENDIFACULTAS
APERTAETEXPOSITA·STATIMCERNITUR
UITAHOMINUMALTOSRECESSUSMAG
NASQ·LATEBRASHABETCUIUSPROGE
NITOREMESPONSOREMACCIPENIHIL
EXHOCUIROFILIUSTUUSAUDIETNISI
PROFUTURUMNIHILDISCETQUODNESCIS
SERECTIUSFUERITNECMINUSSAEPEAB
ILLOQUAMATEMEQUEADMONEBITUR
QUIB·IMAGINIB·ONERETURQUAENOMI
NAETQUANTASUSTINEATPROINDEFAUE
TIBUSDIISTRADEUMPRAECEPTORIA
QUOMORESPRIMUMMOXELOQUENTIAM
DISCATQUAEMALESINEMORIBUSDIS
CITUR UALE
C PLINIUS MACRINO SALUTEM
QUAMUISETAMICIQUOSPRAESENTES
HABESAMETSERMONESHOMINUM

Idem, fol. 52

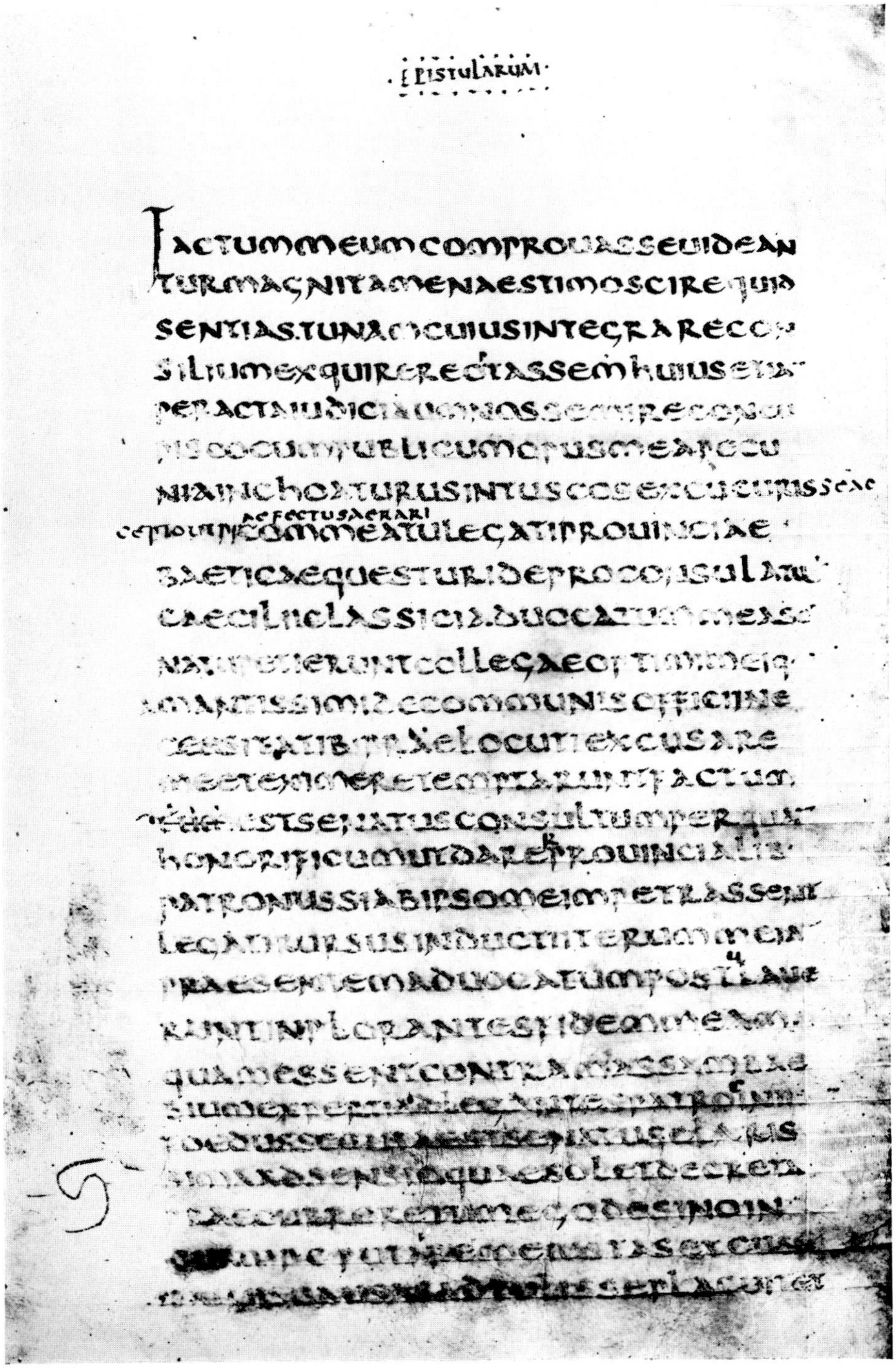

Idem, fol. 52v

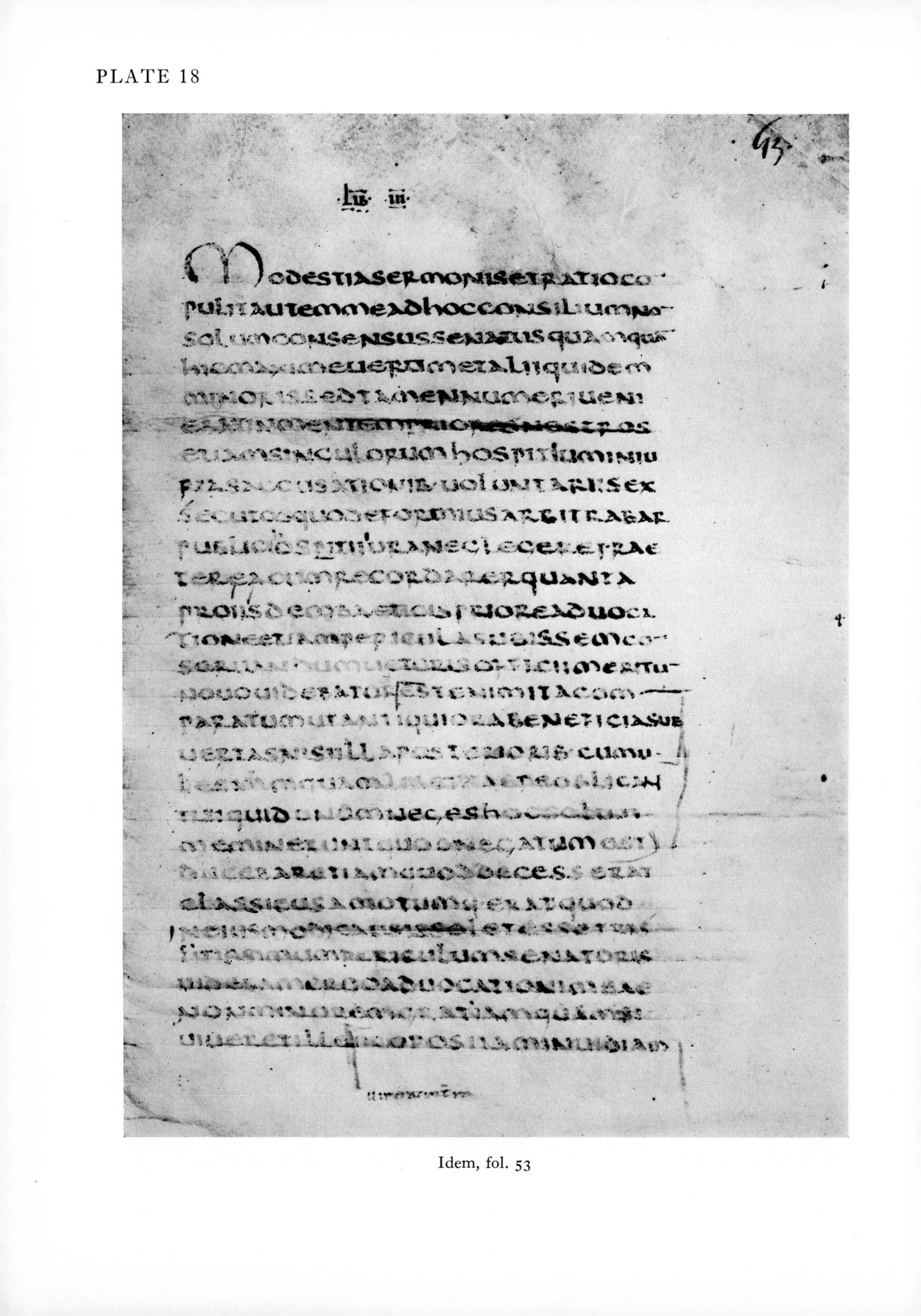

Idem, fol. 53

·EPISTULARUM·

NULLAMINUSUMMAMCOMPUTABAM
SIMUNEREHOCTERTIOFUNGERERETFACILI
OREMIHIEXCUSATIONEMFORESI
QUISINCIDISSETQUEMNONDEBEREM
ACCUSARENAMCUMESTOMNIUMOFFI
CIORUMFINISALIQUISTUMOPTIME
LIBERTATIUENIAOBSEQUIOPRAEPARA
TURAUDISTICONSILIIMEIMOTUSSUPER
ESTALTERUTRAEXPARTEIUDICIUMTUU·
INQUOMIHIAEQ·IUCUNDAERITSIM
PLICITASDISSENTIENTISQUAMCOMPRO
BANTISAUCTORITAS UALE
·C·PLINIUSMACRO·SUO·SALUTEM
PERGRATUMESTMIHIQUODTAMDILIGE
TERLIBROSAUONCULIMEILECTITASUT
HABEREOMNESUELISQUAERASQ·QUI
SINTOMNESDEFUNGARINDICISPARTIB·
ATQUEETIAMQUOSINTORDINESCRIPTI
NOTUMTIBIFACIAMESTENIMHAEC
QUOQ·STUDIOSISNONINIUCUNDACOG
NITIODEIACULATIONEEQUESTRIUNUS·
HUNCCUMPRAEFECTUSALAEMILITA
RETPARINGENIOCURAQ·COMPOSUIT·
DEUITAPOMPONISECUNDIDUOAQUO
SINGULARITERAMATUSHOCMEMORIAE
AMICIQUASIDEBITUMMUNUSEXSOL
UITBELLORUMGERMANIAEUIGINTIQUIB·

Idem, fol. 53v

PLATE 20

Berlin ms. lat. 4° 298, fol. 1, *ca.* A.D. 447. Liber Paschalis Conscriptus A.D. CCCCXLVII

A. New York, Pierpont Morgan Libr. M. 462, fol. 48, *ca.* A.D. 500. Plinius Iun., Epist.

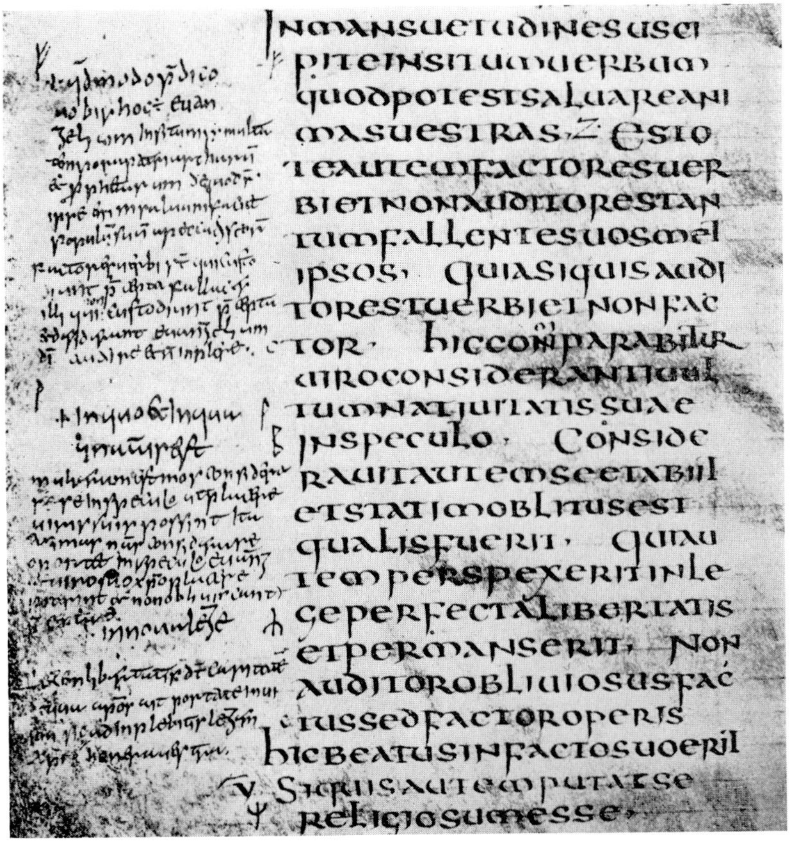

B. Fulda, Landesbibl. Bonifat. 1, fol. 436v, ante A.D. 547. Nov. Testam. (reduced size)

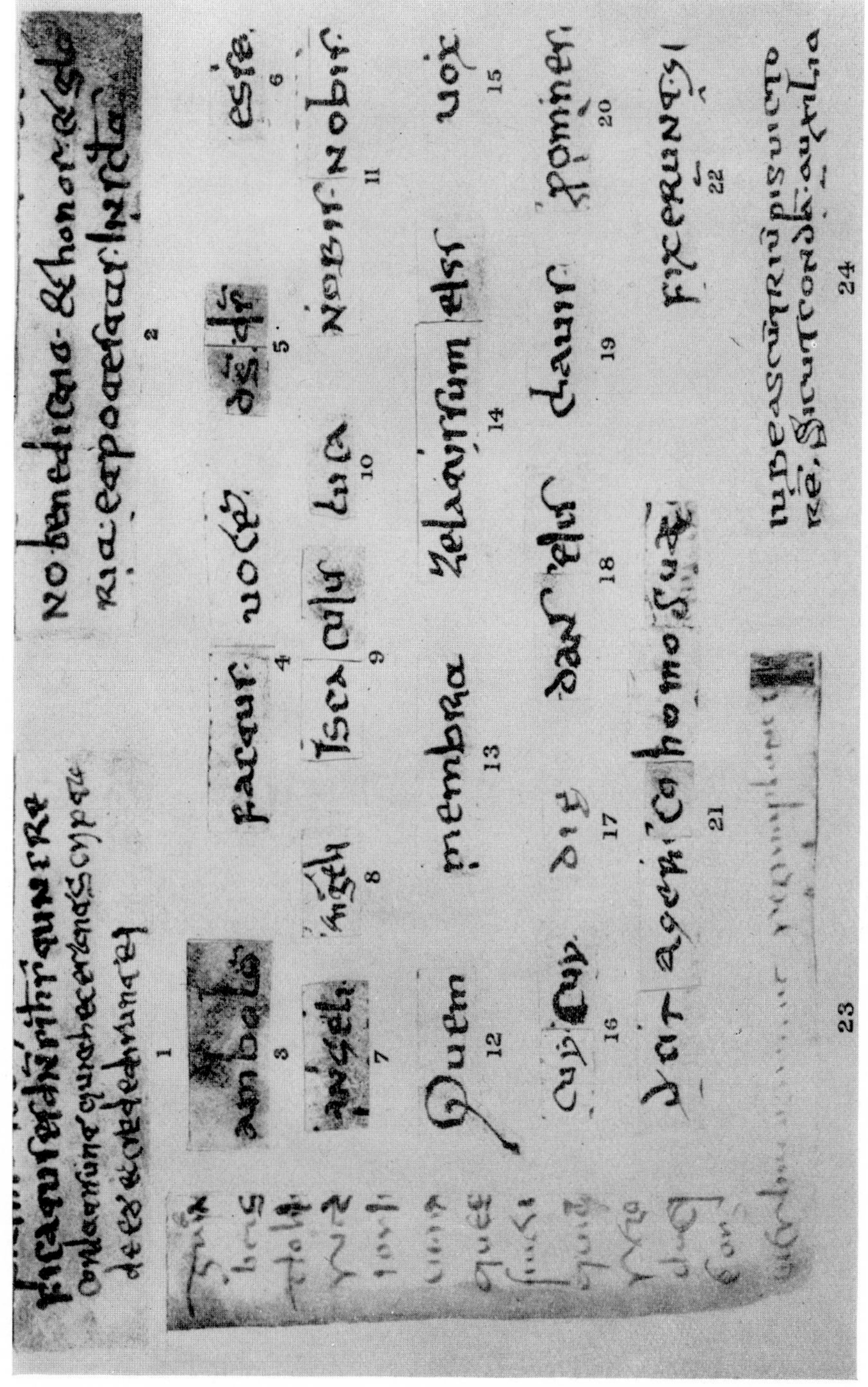

Paris, Bibl. Nat. lat. 13246. The Bobbio Missal. Illustrations of script

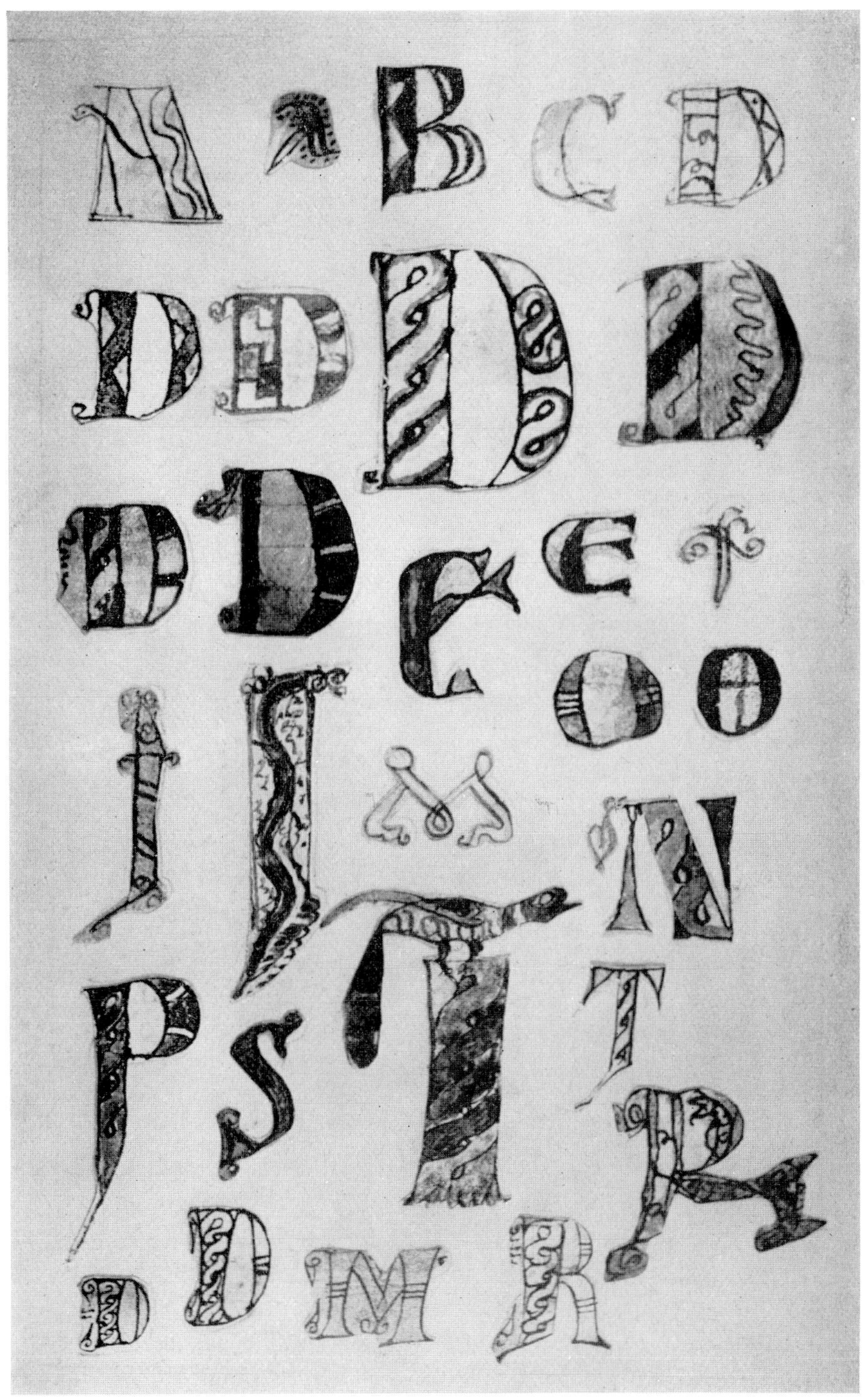

Idem. Selected initials

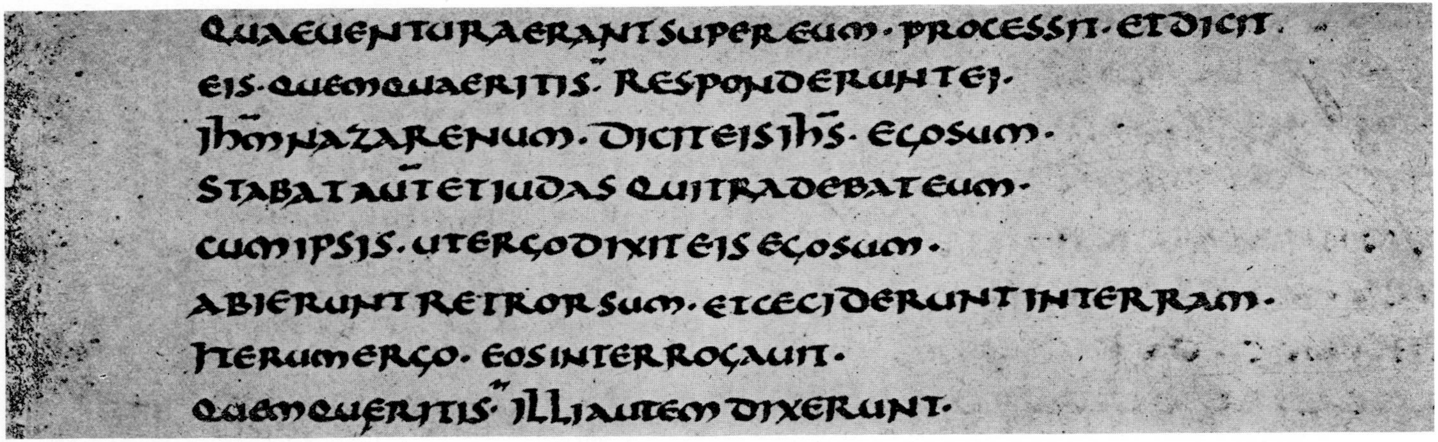
QUAE VENTURA ERANT SUPER EUM. PROCESSIT. ET DICIT
EIS. QUEM QUAERITIS. RESPONDERUNT EI.
IHM NAZARENUM. DICIT EIS IHS. EGO SUM.
STABAT AUTEM ET IUDAS QUI TRADEBAT EUM.
CUM IPSIS. UT ERGO DIXIT EIS EGO SUM.
ABIERUNT RETRORSUM. ET CECIDERUNT IN TERRAM.
ITERUM ERGO. EOS INTERROGAVIT.
QUEM QUERITIS. ILLI AUTEM DIXERUNT.

A. Cambridge, Univ. Libr. Nn. II. 41, fol. 169*. Evang., Act. Apost. Versionis Antehieronym.—'Codex Bezae' (*Dd*). Addition saec. IX

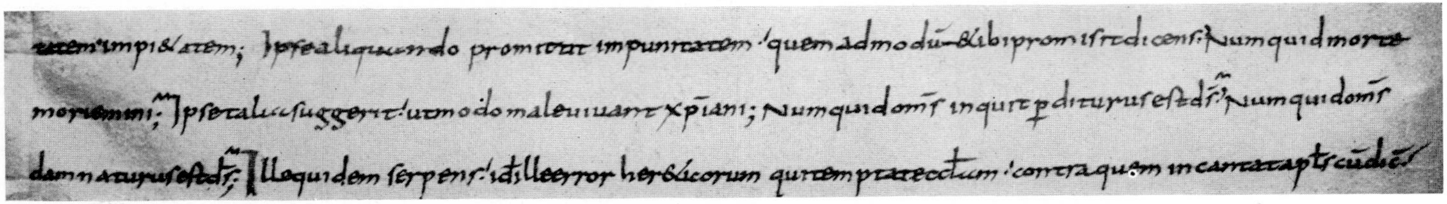

B. Lyons, Bibl. de la Ville 484 (414), fol. 28v. Florus's Excerpta ex Augustino

Lyons, Bibl. de la Ville 604 (521), fol. 74. Augustinus. Corrector saec. IX

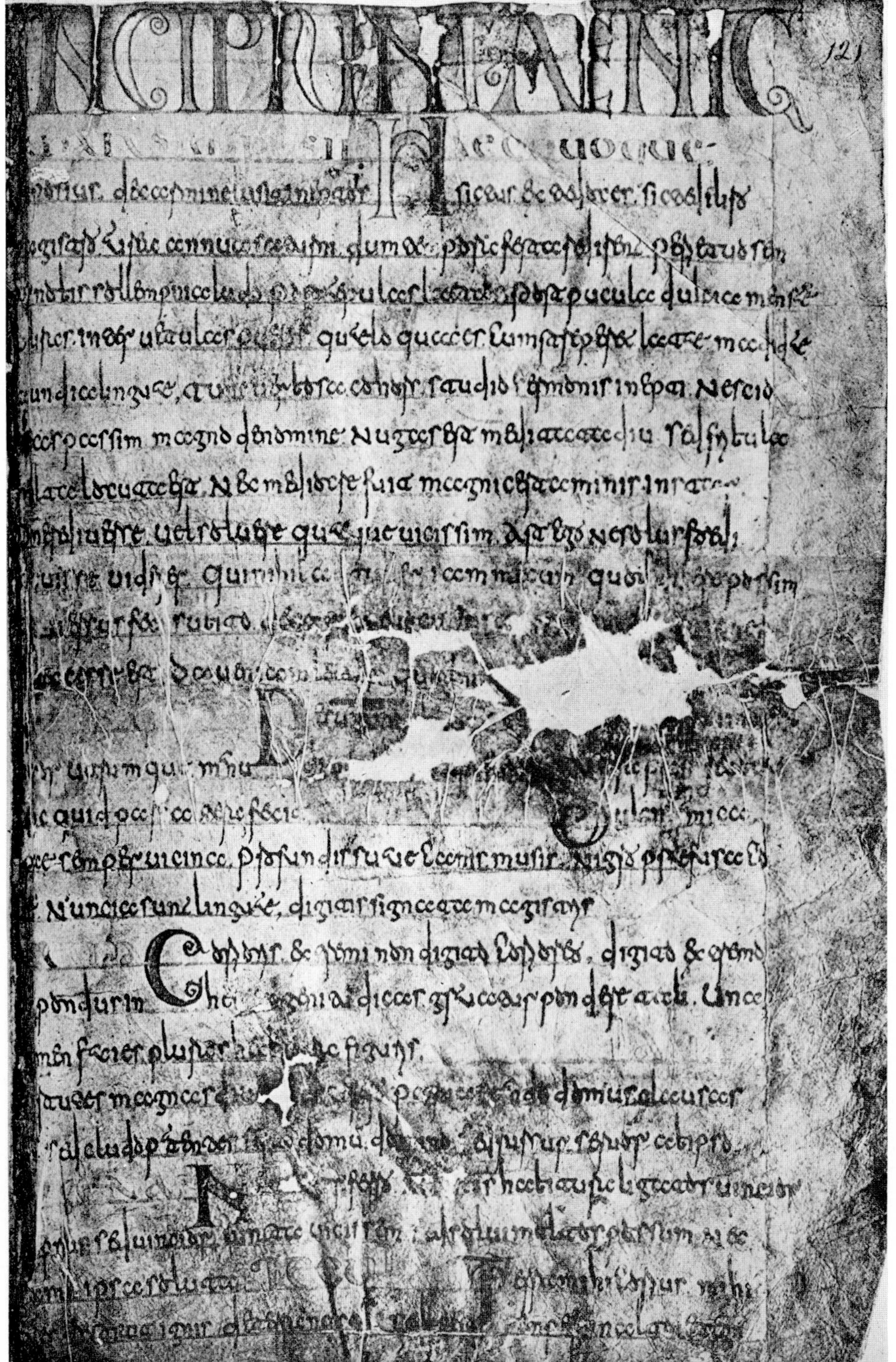

Paris, Bibl. Nat. lat. 4808, fol. 121. Symphosius

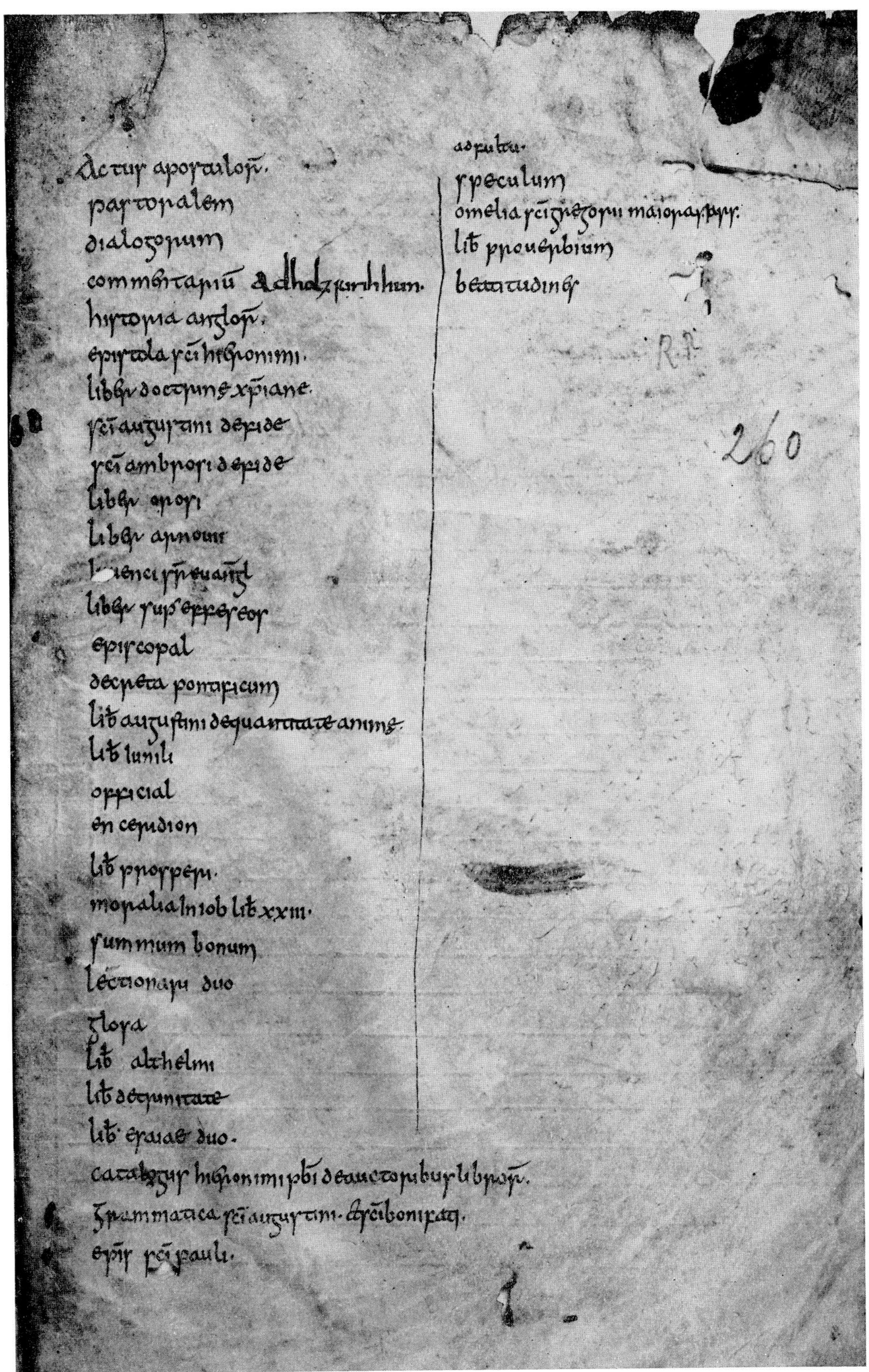
actus apostolorum.
pastoralem
dialogorum
commentarium Adhal. [illegible]
historia anglorum.
epistola sci hieronimi.
liber doctrine xpiane.
sci augustini de fide
sci ambrosi de fide
liber orosi
liber arnobii
iuuenci super euang.
liber sup epistolas
episcopal
decreta pontificum
lib augustini de quantitate anime.
lib iunili
official
en cepudion
lib prosperi.
moralia in iob lib xxiii.
summum bonum
lectionari duo
glosa
lib althelmi
lib de trinitate
lib esaiae duo.
catalogus hieronimi pbi de auctoribus librorum.
grammatica sci augustini. et sci bonifatii.
epist sci pauli.

speculum
omelia sci gregorii maioras [illegible]
lib prouerbium
beatitudines

Oxford, Bodl. Libr. Laud. Misc. 126, fol. 260. List of books saec. VIII ex.

Oxford, Bodl. Libr. Laud. Gr. 35. Act. Apost. Versionis Antehieronym. 'Codex Laudianus' (*Ee*).
A. Fol. I. The ex-libris entered in Laud's MSS. by some librarian

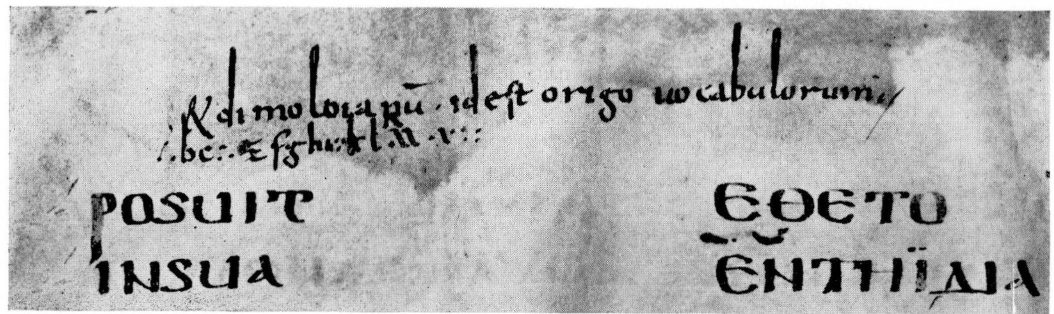

B. Idem, fol. 2^{v}. Probatio pennae

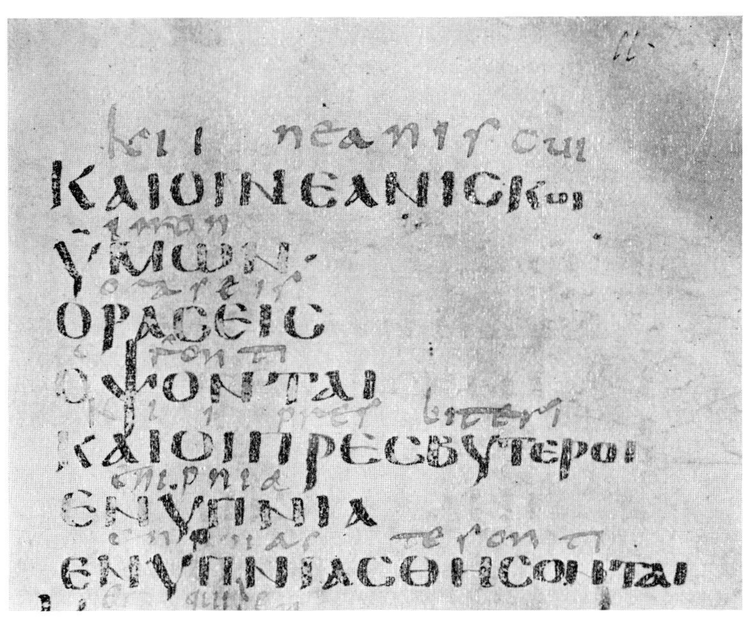

A. Idem, fol. 11. Latin transliterations of the Greek

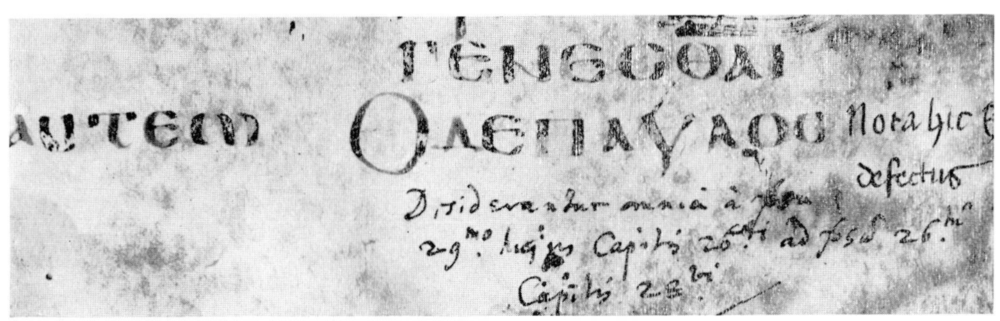

B. Idem, fol. 224v. Note by a 14th-century reader

Idem, fol. 226^v

Regula S^ti Benedicti

MS. Hatton 93

93.

AUSCUL
TA O FILI
PRAECEPTA MAGI
STRI ET INCLINA AU
REM CORDIS TUI ET
ADMONITIONEM
PII PATRIS LIBENTER
EXCIPE ET EFFICA
CITER CONPLE UT
AD EUM PER OBOE
DIENTIAE LABORĒ
REDEAS A QUO PER
INOBOEDIENTIAE
DESIDIAM RECES
SERAS · AD TE ERGO
NUNC MIHI SERMO
DIRIGETUR QUIS
QUIS ABRENUNTI
ANS PROPRIIS UO

LUNTATIBUS DNO XPO
UERO REGI MILITATU
RUS FORTISSIMA
ATQUE PRAECLARA
ARMA ADSUMIS · IN
PRIMIS UT QUIDQUID
AGENDUM INCHO
AS BONUM AB EO PER
FICI INSTANTISSI
MA ORATIONE DE
POSCAS · UT QUI NOS
IAM IN FILIORUM
DIGNATUS EST NU
MERO CONPUTARE
NON DEBET ALIQUAN
DO DE MALIS ACTIB;
NOSTRIS CON
TRISTARI · ITA ENIM
EI OMNI TEMPORE
DE BONIS SUIS IN NO
BIS PARENDUM EST
UT NON SOLUM IRA

Oxford, Bodl. Library, Hatton 48 (SC 3684). Regula S. Benedicti. Fol. 1. Saec. VII–VIII

VIII H o cofficiis diuinis
innoctibus
iemis tē
pore idr
est a kl s
nouimbris us
que in pasca iux
ta considera
tionem ratio
tionis octaua
hora noctis
surgendum
est ut modi
ce amplius de
media nocte
pausetur et
iam degestis
surgant quod
uero restat post
uigiliis a fra
tribus qui
psaltyrii uel

lectionum ali
quid indigen
meditatione
inseruiatur
a pasca autem
usque ad su
pradictas kl
nouembris
sic temperetur
tur hora uigi
liarum agen
da paruissimo
interuallo quo
fratres ad ne naturae
cessaria exe
ant mox ma
tutini qui in
cipiente lu
ce agendi sunt
subsequantur
VIIII quanti psalmi
dicendi sint

Idem, fol. 24ᵛ

XVIIII DE DISCIPLINA PSALLENDI
UBIQUECRE
DIMUSDI
UINAMES
SEPRAESENTIĀ
ETOCULOSDĪ
SPECULARIBO
NOSETMALOS·
MAXIMETAMEN
HOCSINEDUBI aliqua
TATIONECREDA
MUSCUMADO
PUSDIUINUM
ADSISTIMUS·
IDEOSEMPER
MEMORESSI
MUSQUODAIT
PROFETA·SER
UITEDÑOINTI
MORE·ETITE
RUMPSALLITE
SAPIENTERET
INCONSPECTU
ANGELORUM psallam tibi
ERGOCONSIDE
REMUSQUALI
TEROPORTEAT
INCONSPECTU
DIUINITATISET
ANGELORUME
IUSESSE·ETSIC
STEMUSADPSAL
LENDUMUT
MENSNOSTRA
CO NCORDET
UOCINOSTRAE·
XX DE REUERENTIA ORATIONIS
SICUMHOMI
NIBUSPO
TENTIBUS
UOLUMUSALI
QUASUGGERERE

Idem, fol. 33

MENSAFRA
TRUME
DENTIŪ
LECTIODEESSE
NONDEBET·NEC
FORTUITOCASU
QUISARRIPUE
RITCODICEMLE
GEREIBISEDLEC
TURUSTOTAEB
DOMADADOMI
NICAINGREDIATUR·
QUIINGREDIENS
POSTMISASET
COMMUNIONĒ
PETATABOMNI
BUSPROSEORA
RI·UTAUERTAT
ABIPSODSSPM
ELATIONIS·ET
DICATHUNCUER
SUMINORATO

RIOTERTIOCŪ
OMNIBUS·IPSO
TAMENINCIPI
ENTE·DNELABI
AMEAAPERIES
ETOSMEUMAD
NUNTIABITLAU
DEMTUAM·ET
SICACCEPTABE
NEDICTIONEIN
GREDIATURAD
LEGENDUM·ET
SUMMUMFIAT
SILENTIUMAD
MENSAM·UT
NULLIUSMUSSI
TATIOUELUOX
NISI SOLIUS
GENTI SIBIAU
DIATUR·QUAE
NECESSARIASUNT
COMEDENTIB;

Idem, fol. 44v

OCCUPANTUR·
CETERISIBISUB
CARITATEINUICE~
SERUIANT·EGRE
SURUSDESEPTI
MANASABBATO
MUNDITIASFA
CIAT·LINTEACU~
QUIBUSSIBIFRA
TRESMANUS
AUTPEDESTER
GENTLAUENT·
PEDESUEROTA~

A. Idem, fol. 42v

SECUNDAMUI
CEMPROIOCOR
RIPIATUR·SIDE
NUONONEMEN
DAUERITNONP
MITTATURAD
MENSAECOM
MUNISPARTICI
PATIONEM·SED
SEQUESTRATUS
ACONSORTIO
OMNIUMREFI
CIATSOLUSSUB

B. Idem, fol. 49v

PLATE 36

A. Idem, fol. 77v (end fly-leaf): Augustinus, Enchiridion

B. Canterbury Cathedral Library. Chartae antiquae c. 115. Episcopal profession of Ralph Bp. of Chichester, A.D. 1091

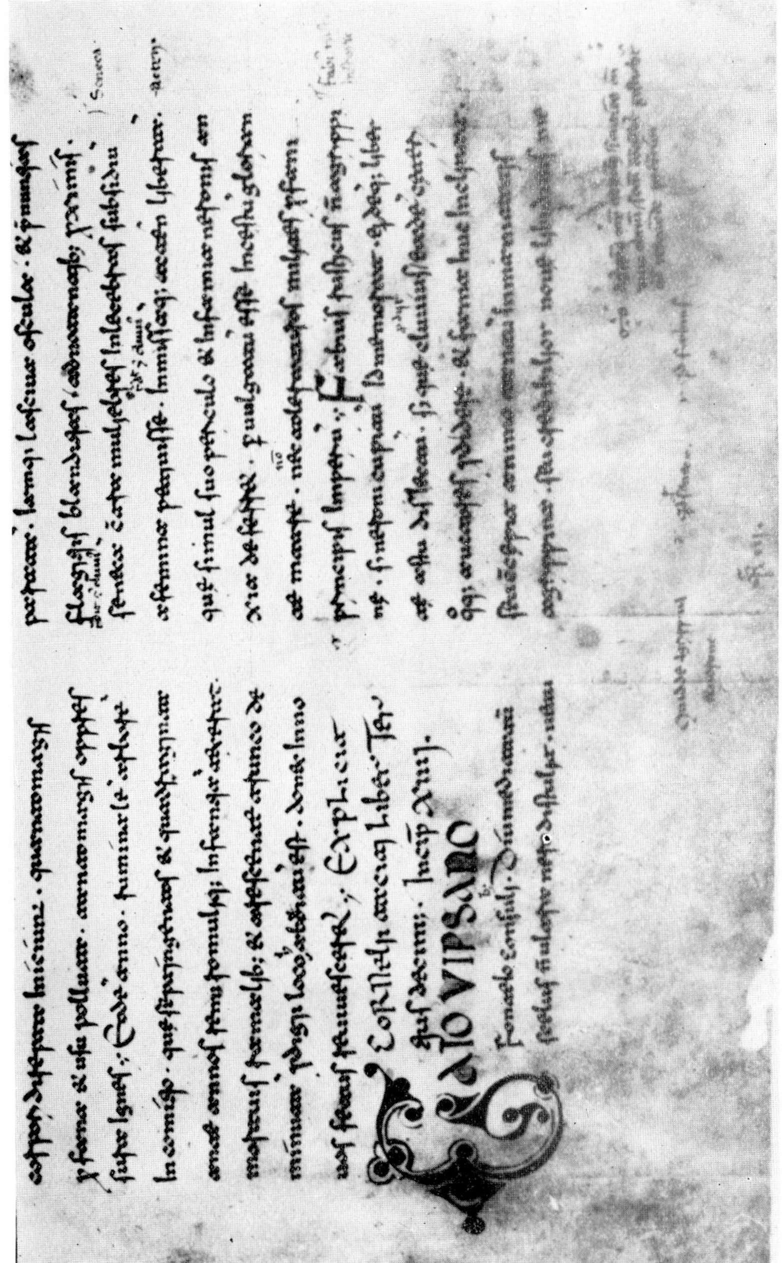

Florence, Bibl. Medic. Laurenz. 68.2, fol. 23v. Tacitus. Saec. XI med.

Idem. A. Fol. 103. Portion re-written in the 13th century

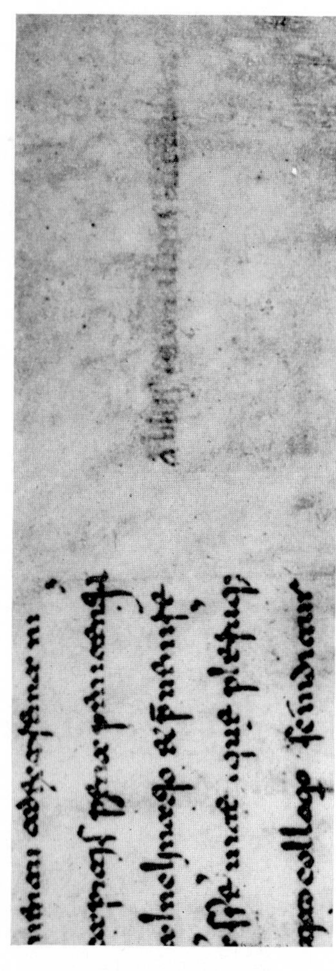

B. Fol. 103ᵛ. The added entry: *abbas raynaldus*

Bamberg, Staatl. Bibl. Patr. 87 (B. IV. 21), fol. 114. Hieronymus, Augustinus. Half-uncial text and contemporary marginalia in sloping uncial. Saec. VI

Vatican, Vatic. lat. 3375, fol. 33. Eugippius, Excerpta ex operibus Augustini. Half-uncial text and contemporary marginalia in sloping uncial. Saec. VI ex.

Bamberg, Staatl. Bibl. Patr. 87 (B. IV. 21), fol. 105ᵛ. Hieronymus, Augustinus. Half-uncial text and Anglo-Saxon marginalia. Saec. VI (text), saec. VIII–IX (marginalia)

Idem, fol. 79[v]. Half-uncial text and colophon in square capitals and cursive note in the script of the Roman Curia. Saec. VI (main text and colophon), saec. VIII (cursive note)

Paris, Bibl. Nat. lat. 5726, fol. 161 (upper half). Livy, with notes by Lupus

Paris, Bibl. Nat. lat. 8623, fol. 13. Symmachus, with notes by Lupus

Paris, Bibl. Nat. lat. 11709, fol. 199. Liber Canonum. Col. 2, last line in Visigothic minuscule

Idem, fol. 39 (lower half). Liber Canonum, with notes by Florus

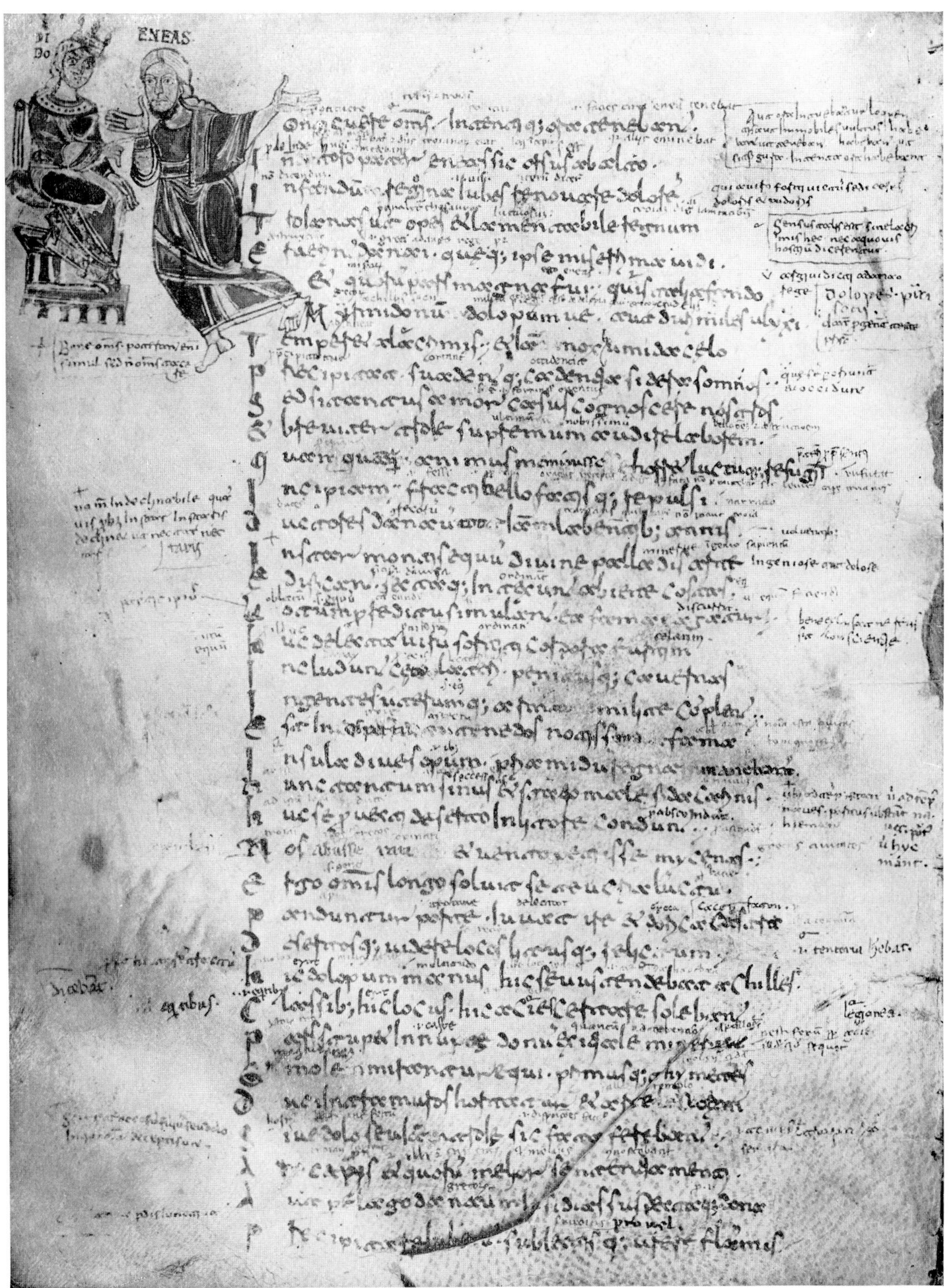

Naples, Bibl. Naz. lat. 6 (olim Vienna 58), fol. 55v. Vergilius, Aen. II, 1–37. Saec. X

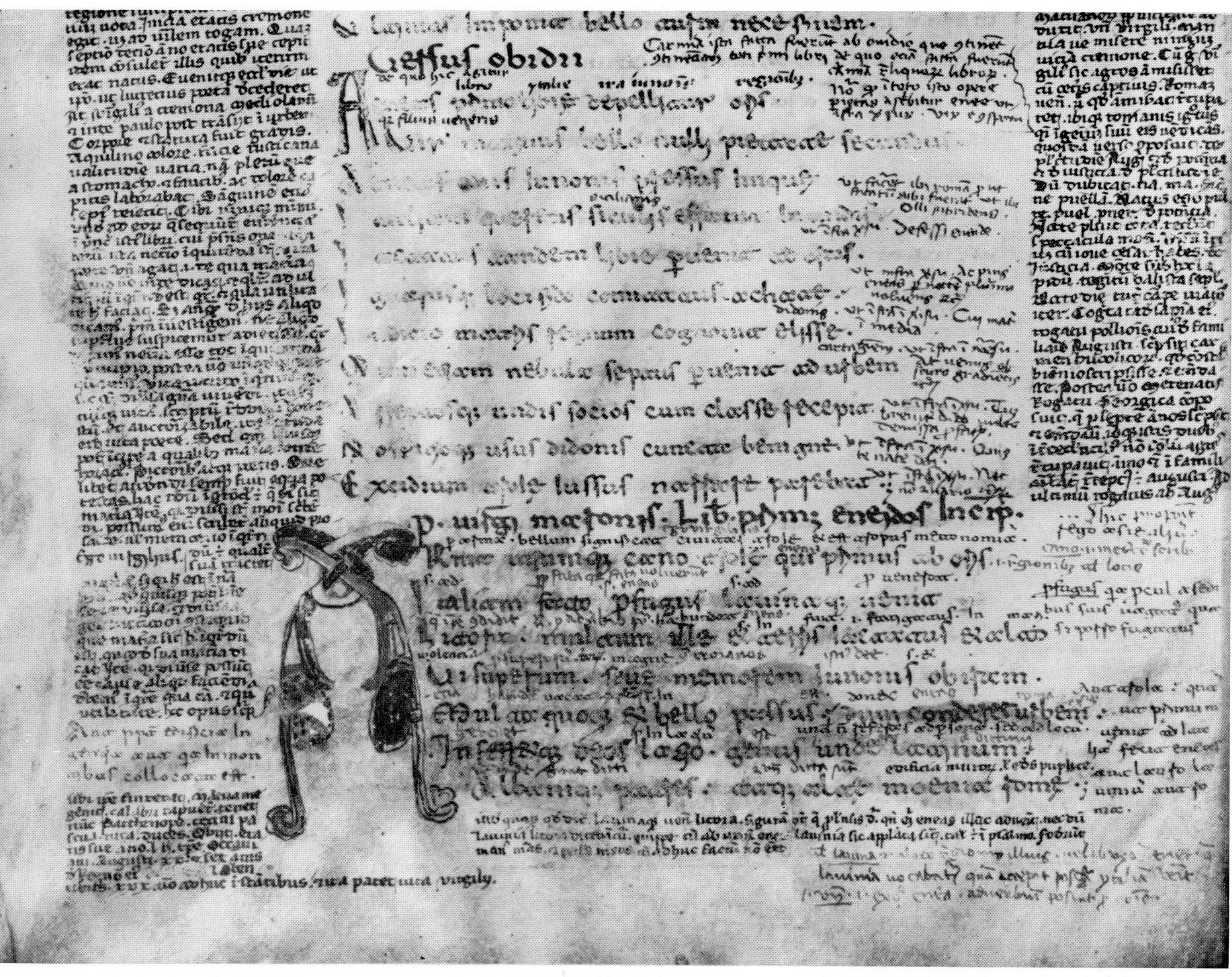

Paris, Bibl. Nat. lat. 10308, fol. 41^{v}. Vergilius, Aen. I, 1–7, preceded by the *Argumentum*. Saec. XI^{2}

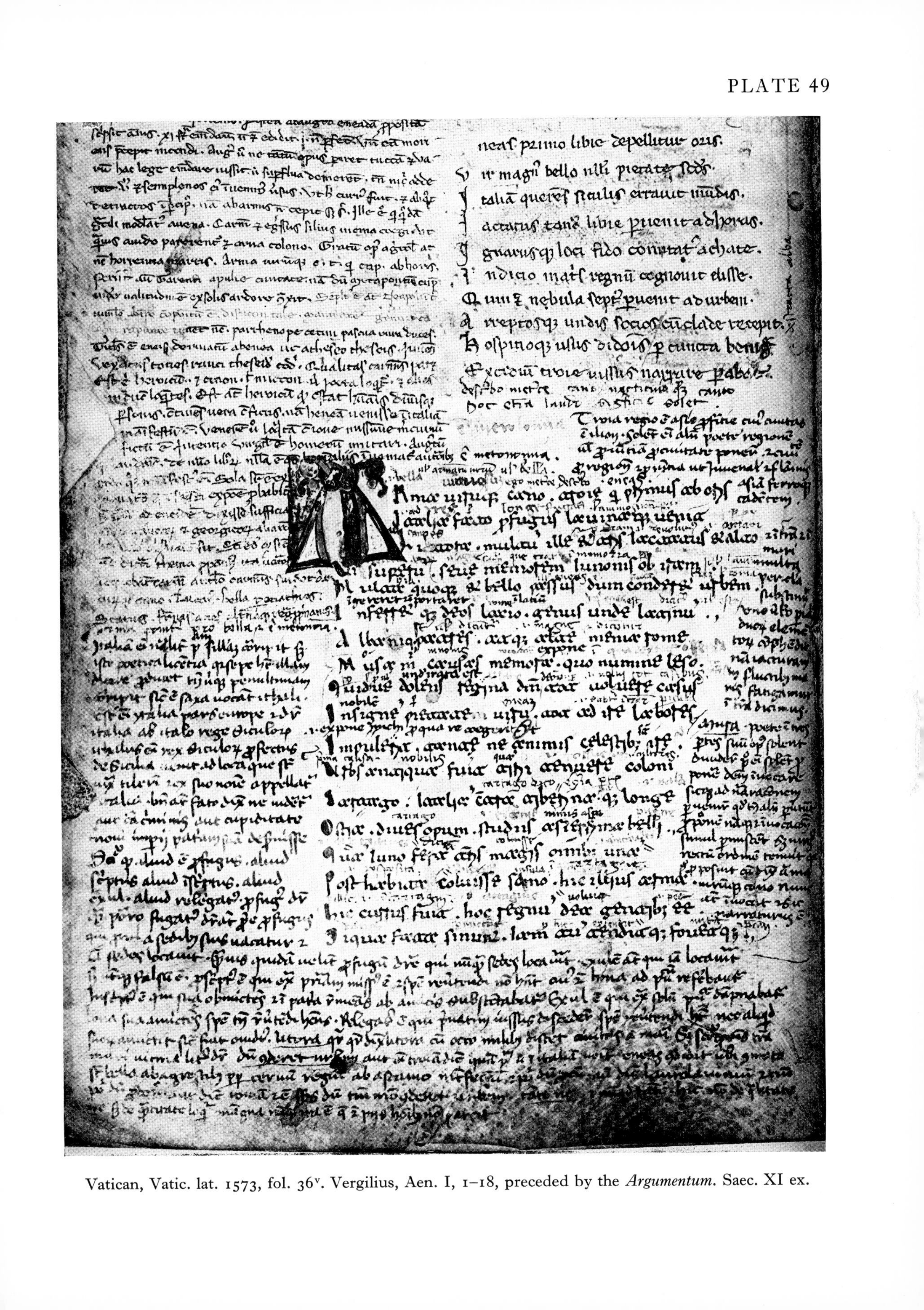

Vatican, Vatic. lat. 1573, fol. 36[v]. Vergilius, Aen. I, 1–18, preceded by the *Argumentum*. Saec. XI ex.

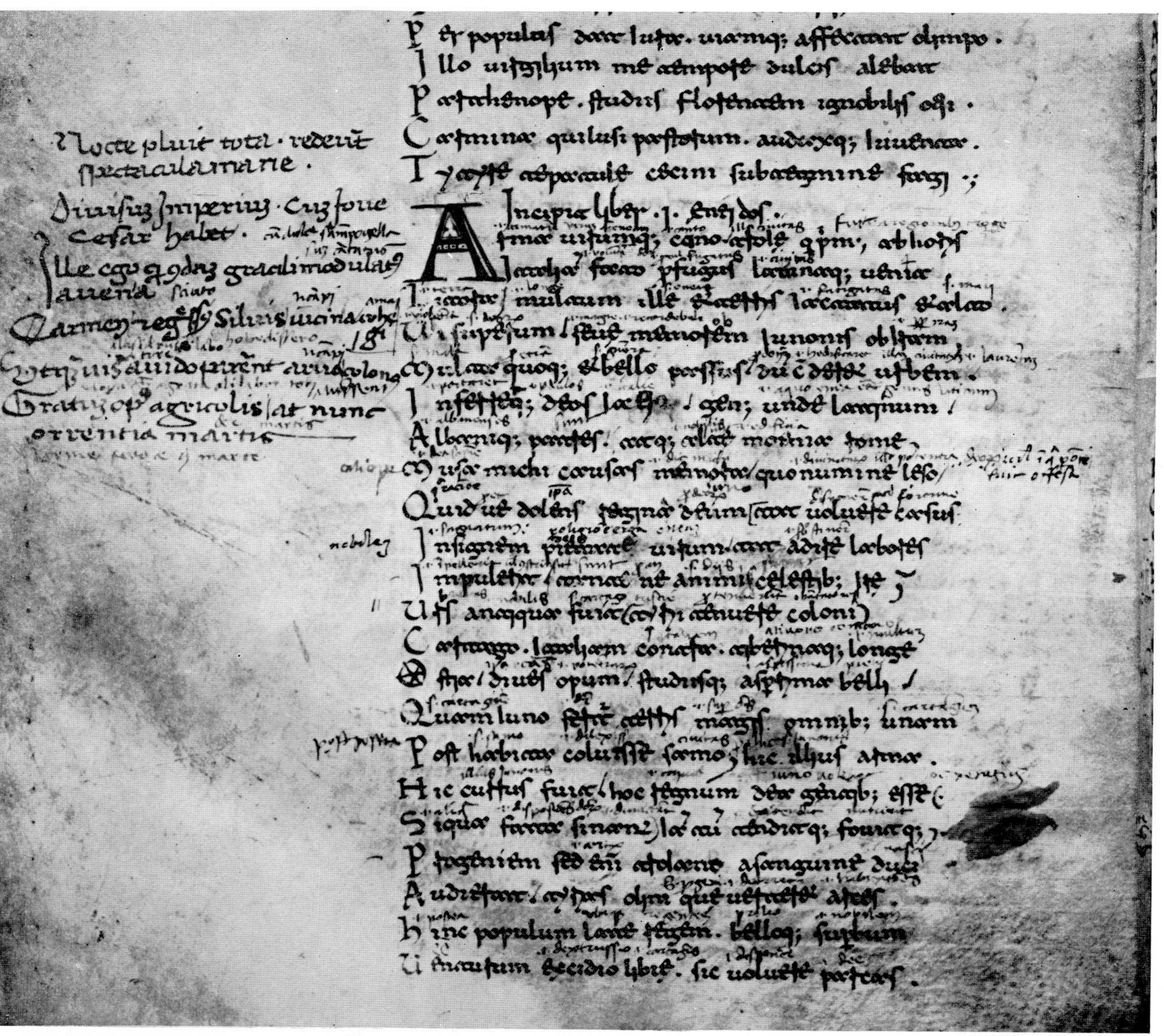

Vatican, Vatic. lat. 3253, fol. 18ᵛ. Vergilius, Georg. IV, 562–6; Aen. I, 1–22. Saec. XI ex.

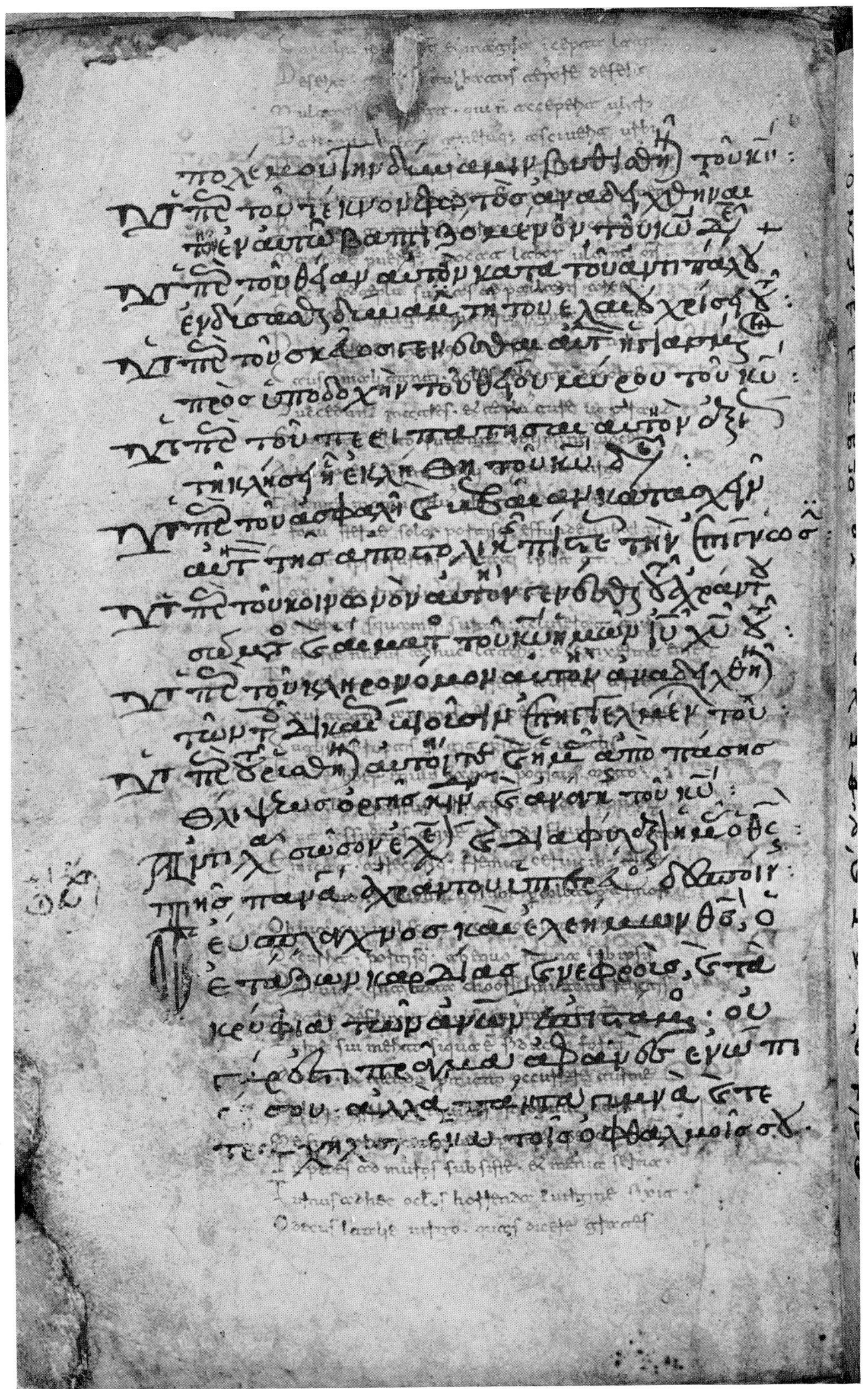

Vatican, Vatic. gr. 2324, fol. 35[v]. Vergilius, Aen. XI, 469–508. Saec. XI ex.

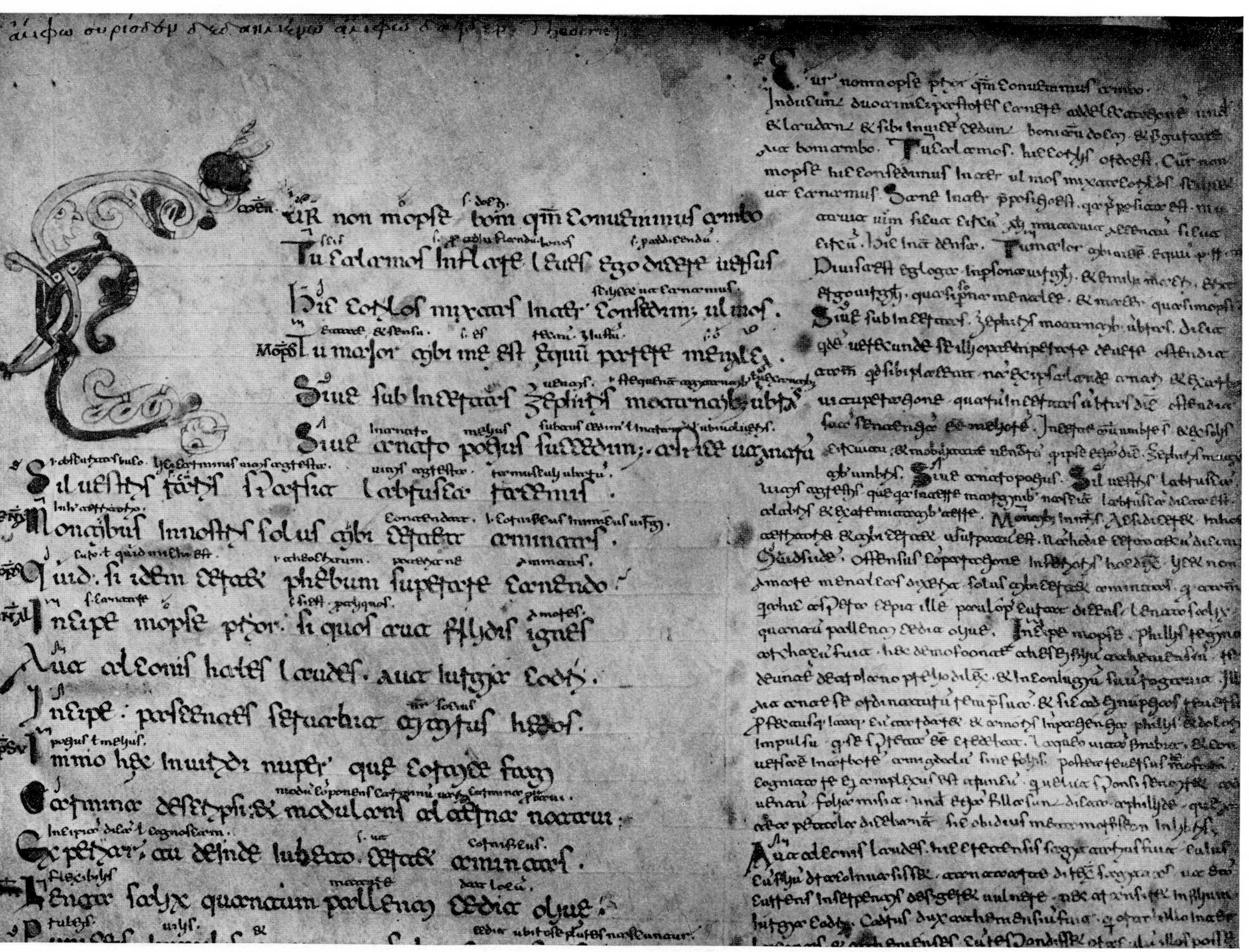

Oxford, Bodl. Libr. Canon. Class. lat. 50, fol. 7. Vergilius, Ecloga V, 1–16. Saec. XI

Monte Cassino, Archivio della Badia Compactiones XV, fol. 21ᵛ. Vergilius, Aen. XII, 2–35. Saec. XI-XII

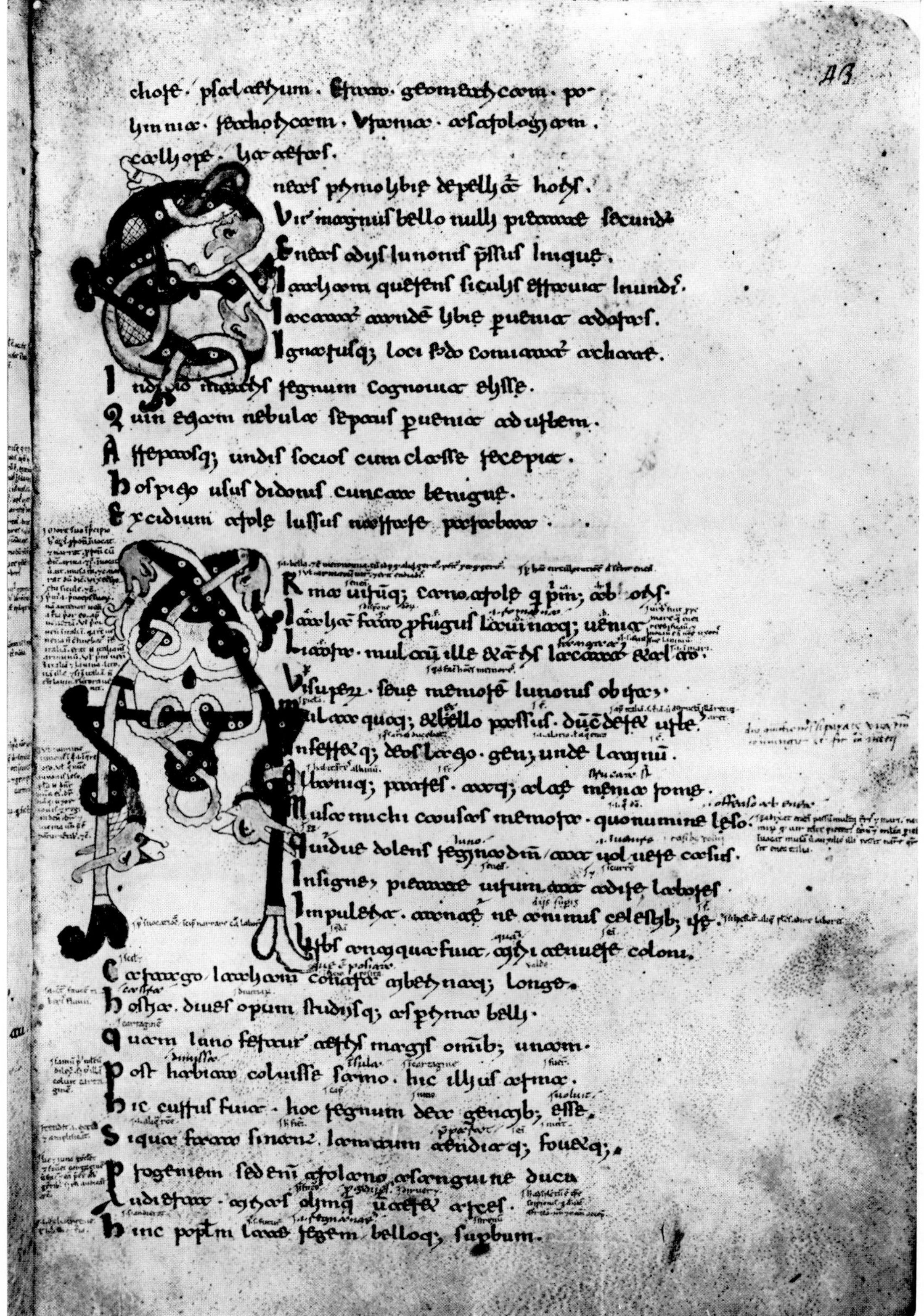

Vatican, Vatic. Regin. lat. 2090, fol. 43. Vergilius, Aen. I, 1–21, preceded by the *Argumentum*. Saec. XI-XII

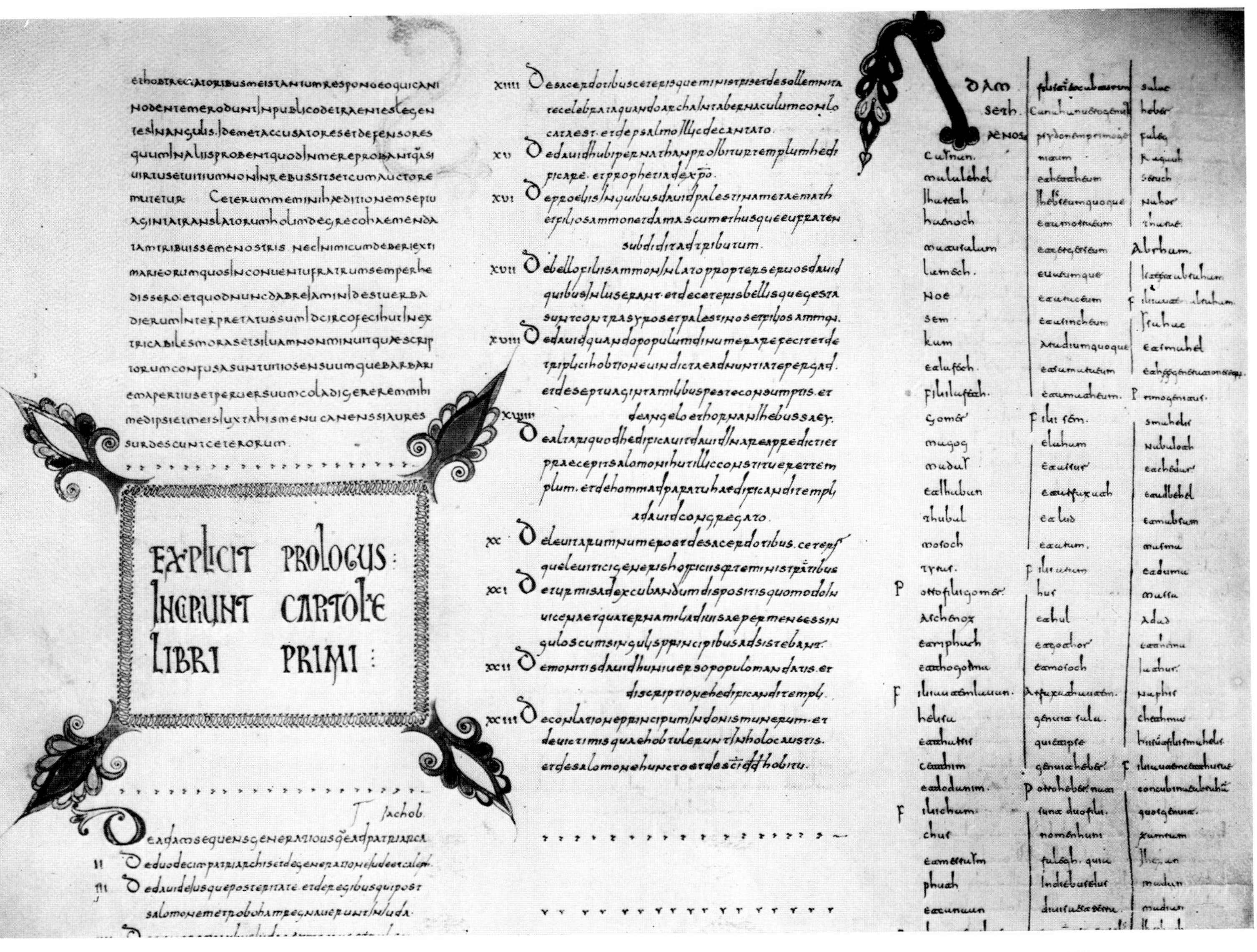

Cava, Archivio della Badia 1, fol. 80ᵛ. Biblia Sacra 'Codex Cavensis'. Paralip. I, Prolog. et cap. 1. Saec. IX

Iob xxxix, 29—xl, 14; xl, 22—xli, 14; xli, 22—xlii, 11

Idem. Epist. ad Rom., Prolog. et cap. 1

Salisbury, Chapter Libr. 133, fol. 31^{v}. Alcuin in Ecclesiasten. Saec. IX^{1}

Oxford, Bodl. Libr. E Museo 66 (SC 3655), front board, inside. Mirror view. Arator de Act. Apost. I, 85–122 (Ker's p. 1, upper half); 647–81 (Ker's p. 2, lower half). Saec. VII